MUNICIPALITIES IN DISTRESS?

How States and Investors Deal with Local Government Financial Emergencies

A 50-State Survey of: (1) Rights and Remedies Provided by States to Investors, (2) State Supervision and Oversight Mechanisms of Financially Distressed Local Governments and (3) State Authorization of Municipalities to File Chapter 9 Bankruptcy

Second Edition, 2016.

James E. Spiotto
Ann E. Acker
Laura E. Appleby

Second Edition, 2016.

ISBN: 978-0-692-62477-7

Table of Contents

Preface to Second Edition

The truism that, during an economic downturn, state and local governments across the globe experience difficulty in meeting their financial obligations is not surprising. However, in the United States, state and local governments have gone to great lengths to pay their public debt creditors. The annals of state and local government finance are filled with stories of states and local governments who left no stone unturned in attempting to make good on their promises to the investing public. Whether it is the apocryphal story of states and municipalities sending couriers through the enemy lines during the Civil War in order to ensure a bond payment was made or more recent accounts of a municipality using general obligation bonds to pay off a failed revenue bond issue so that no default would be connected with the municipality's name, there is a common theme. The great tradition of timely paying their debt obligations has given state and local governments access to the capital markets at a low borrowing cost. This tradition provides state and local governments funding to pay for necessary infrastructure improvements and essential services to their citizens. State and local governments recognize that their ability to obtain financing at a low cost allows them to make decisions on a local basis based on their needs without approval or intervention of others. Further, this dedication, nearly rising to the level of a sacred duty, to payment of debt obligations has been rewarded by the financial markets. State and local debts typically enjoy a high credit rating and, accordingly, receive some of the lowest interest rates on their debt issuances, thereby reducing the borrowing costs that are borne by their taxpayers. This symbiotic relationship between honoring the obligation to pay and rewarding those who do pay with access and low borrowing costs is a tradition that no state or local government would want to lose.

In the history of state and local government financing in the United States, there have been shocks to the system. The first recorded municipal default in U.S. history was by the city of Mobile in 1839, which had observers trying to explain and rationalize what happened. Since then, in almost every decade, there has been an event which has led to the reexamination of the status and the treatment of state and local government debt. Back in the 1800s, after the Civil War, eight states repudiated their indebtedness, and the market demanded modifications to the practices of debt issuance. That resulted in changing what had been basically a moral obligation to debt having defined rights under state constitutions or statutes and the use of bond counsel to opine that the debt was valid and binding. Rating agencies were developed to provide the investing public with some assessment of creditworthiness and from that foundation came government finance as we know it today in the United States. More recently, although over 30 years ago, the Washington Public Power Supply System, through some of its participants, repudiated its obligations. A state court affirmed that repudiation which led to another cycle of examination of the basic underpinnings of state and local government financing. From that crisis came Rule 15c2-12 under the Securities Exchange Act of 1934 and more mandated disclosure of facts by municipal issuers.

We now live in a unique time when the viability of state and local government debt financing is being questioned. There was a significant increase shortly after 2008 in Chapter 9 bankruptcies for cities and counties over 100,000 in population beginning with Vallejo, California in 2008, Jefferson County, Alabama in 2011, Stockton and San Bernardino, California in 2012, and Detroit, Michigan in 2013. This raised the question of whether the increase represented a trend or an aberration. In the fifty-five years prior to 2008, there was only one Chapter 9 filing by a city or county of size, namely Orange County, California in 1994. There is frequent discussion, precipitated by events in other countries, of whether or not there will be a wave of unprecedented municipal defaults in the United States and whether or not state and local governments can meet the significant challenges they face. Problems of underfunding of pension obligations, the need for significant infrastructure improvements, and the cost of education and public safety are leading concerns. At the same time, when one looks back over the proud municipal tradition of meeting debt obligations, it is reasonable to expect that states and municipalities will utilize the tools available to avert a financial meltdown.

The following material is directed to those who are involved in the state and local government financial market, be they municipal credit analysts, credit enhancers, investors or state or local legislators or administrators. This volume includes a compilation of the various state statutes and constitutional provisions that allow states to assist local governments by providing supervision, assistance, refinancing and hopefully a bridge to a resolution that works. Also, this compilation summarizes, on a state-by-state and comparison basis, the types of rights and remedies available to investors.

This summary of remedies includes a survey of state authorization of municipalities to file for bankruptcy. There has been a growing fear that more local governments may resort to the use of Chapter 9 municipal bankruptcy. Historically, Chapter 9 bankruptcies not only have been rare but have actually been used, with a few exceptions, only by small special tax districts. Further, the process of a Chapter 9 is time consuming, expensive, complicated and uncertain, and the results are not necessarily as advertised. Over a quarter of all Chapter 9s that have been filed since 1937 have been dismissed without a plan of debt adjustment having been confirmed. As of July 31, 2016, there have only been 666 Chapter 9 cases filed. While Chapter 9 has always been thought of as the last resort and one that should be avoided, if at all possible, it exists as the final safety net to help our municipalities deal with extreme financial distress.

The purpose of this compilation of state laws and provisions is to aid analysts, investors and legislators in their consideration of what the states provide and the alternatives. The goal is to encourage discussion and continued development of best practices and procedures for state and local governments. This is by no means a definitive study. The second edition is significantly expanded from the first edition based on additional events and requests for new topics to be examined. As this second edition since 2012 demonstrates, we intend, on a regular basis, to update it. We are aware that various state legislatures and local government officials presently are considering new and better ways of providing assurances to the market that their obligations will be paid in good times and bad. One size does not fit all. Nevertheless, we hope this study will be of some assistance in developing best practices.

I am indebted to many people who have helped in collecting and synthesizing this information. I would like to thank my former colleagues at Chapman and Cutler LLP who have encouraged and supported this effort and those at the Firm who have assisted in the actual preparation of the volume, especially Laura Appleby, as well as Ann Acker, Hannah Wendling, Mia D'Andrea, Bryan Jacobson, the Summer Associate Classes of 2010, 2011, 2013, and 2014 and Nancy Linder, Isabella Bankowski and Rebekah Alm whose administrative skills made this all possible. Further, I would like to acknowledge the excellent suggestions of Lisa Washburn, formerly of Moody's Investors Service and now Municipal Market Advisors, and of Sarah McLaughlin Emmons, formerly Manager of Research and Information, Pew Center on States, as well as encouragement from Arturo Perez, Fiscal Affairs Program Director for the National Conference of State Legislatures, Jeffrey Esser of the Government Finance Officers Association, the late John Petersen, Professor, School of Public Policy, George Mason University, Sylvan G. Feldstein of Guardian Life Insurance Company of America, Michael Pagano, Dean of the College of Urban Planning and Public Affairs, University of Illinois at Chicago, and Lois Scott, President Epoch Advisors, formerly CFO for the City of Chicago and well-respected financial advisor to state and local governments. Special thanks also are due to Richard Ciccarone of Merritt Research Services and MuniNet Guide for his thoughtful reading of the material and helpful suggestions. Over the years, the comments and critical analysis of issues by fellow members of the Society of Municipal Analysts and The Civic Federation, especially Laurence Msall, President and Sarah Wetmore, Vice President and Director of Research, and the programs of the National Federation of Municipal Analysts have educated all of us as to market and governmental needs and realities. It goes without saying that we all owe a debt of gratitude to Frank Shafroth, formerly of the National League of Cities, the National Governors Association and the MSRB, now a Professor at George Mason University, and his continuing published insights on current events in government finance, and to Cathy Spain, formerly of the Government Finance Officers Association and the National League of Cities and now with The Spain Group LLC, both of whom I worked with in advocating for the 1988 Amendments to the Bankruptcy Code for the benefit of units of local government. Among the foundations for this presentation are chapters by this author in THE HANDBOOK OF MUNICIPAL BONDS published by John Wiley & Son, Sylvan G. Feldstein, Frank Fabozzi, editors, and THE OXFORD HANDBOOK OF STATE AND LOCAL GOVERNMENT DEBT, published by Oxford University Press, John Petersen and Robert Ebel, editors and a number of articles written for *The Municipal Finance Journal* and muninetguide.com, the online website dedicated to state and local government research.

James E. Spiotto
Chapman Strategic Advisors LLC
Chicago, Illinois
July 2016

I. Introduction

Discussion of Effective Means of Addressing Financial Distress of State and Local Governments. Whether State Legislation to Provide Technical and Financial Assistance Oversight Has Been Effective. Whether Access to Chapter 9 by Municipalities Is Better Than Other Alternatives. Whether the Rights and Remedies for Investors in Public Debt of State and Local Government Are Sufficient to Allow Continued Access and the Ability to Borrow at a Low Cost.

A. Economic Cycles and Financial Distress

Financial distress is not a new phenomenon to governments, whether they are large or small, sovereign countries or sub-sovereigns. The financial cycles of the economy, both global and local, have produced challenges to the long-term survival of governments that require attention and effective action to be taken by all those concerned. The history of the payment of financial obligations of governments provides ample examples of success and notable lessons from the consequences of the failure to promptly and successfully address financial problems. The first part of our discussion will be a review of past cycles of sovereign debt default and their consequences and the degree to which past history influenced or motivated payment of federal, state and local government debt obligations in the United States.

It is not surprising that concerns arising from the most recent economic downturn continue to exist about the effects of lower state and local government revenues and the threat of higher state and local government expenses, especially costs of pensions, infrastructure, education, health care and public safety. Since the founding and early beginnings of our country in 1793, there have been six panics, thirty-eight recessions and four depressions, the most recent being the Great Depression of the 1930s and the Great Recession of 2008. Since 1949, there have been eleven economic downturns in the United States of America, and the states and their local governments have not only weathered those financial storms but have provided substantial support to the eventual economic recovery via expenditures for infrastructure and other purposes that have increased employment and GDP growth.[1] In addition, various states have developed targeted legislation to provide oversight, supervision, direction and relief to financially distressed local governments to refinance, restructure or resolve their financial problems. While the extent and nature of such legislation may vary, its goal is the same: to help that state's local government continue to provide essential governmental services to its citizens as efficiently and at the lowest cost possible. Part of that effort is to help ensure that those troubled local governments continue to have access to the financial markets so that they can continue to obtain necessary funding at the lowest cost of financing possible.

1 *See* chart on Economic Downturn and Recoveries Compared to State and Local Government Spending, at Appendix A.

B. Market Responses to Financial Distress

Past economic downturns during the 1800s, such as the Panics of 1819, 1837 and 1857 and the repudiation of debt by eight states after the Civil War,[2] were motivating factors in having the market demand, and state and local governments provide, statutory and constitutional provisions to ensure the ability to enforce payment and provide protections and remedies to bondholders if the state or local government experiencing financial difficulty fails to pay timely and subsequently defaults. The statutes and constitutional provisions of the states have continued to evolve and mature as additional threats and concerns arise in the marketplace. In fact, as will be described, there are various remedies, provisions, protections and significant market motivations and practical realities that have historically demonstrated that state and local governments will do almost anything they can to pay their debts so that they may have access to the markets to build infrastructure and capital improvements, as well as fund essential governmental services, as may be required and determined by the state or local government. In fact, the Panic of 1837 and resulting defaults thereafter showed that, while states may sometimes default, in order to gain access to the market, they typically resume payment.[3]

---

2 After the Civil War, eight Southern States (Alabama, Arkansas, Florida, Georgia, Louisiana, Mississippi, North Carolina and South Carolina) repudiated indebtedness and still do. The reasons vary but generally are attributable to debt involuntarily incurred during the "carpetbag" governments. The Fourteenth Amendment was enacted in part to assure payment of public debt of the United States and its states but not in aid of the insurrection which shall be illegal and void (U.S. Const. amend. XIV, § 4). The Civil War debt of the Confederate government was approximately $1.4 billion and the Confederate states had individual Civil War debt of about $67 million. Franklin Noll, *Repudiation! The Crisis of United States Civil War Debt, 1865-1870* (Dec. 14, 2012), Government Debt Crises: Politics, Economics and History Conference, Graduate Institute of International and Development Studies, Geneva, Dec. 14-15, 2012, http://ssrn.com/abstract=2196409 ("Noll").

3 Seven of eight states and one territory that repudiated payments of their debt between 1841 and 1843 later resumed payment of their debt between 1843 and 1848. John Joseph Wallis, Richard E. Sylla and Arthur Grinath III, *Sovereign Debt and Repudiation: The Emerging-Market Debt Crisis in the United States, 1839-1843,* NBER Working Paper 10753 (Sept. 2004), http://www.nber.org/papers/W10753 ("Wallis"). While some attribute the repudiation to the aftermath of the Panic of 1837, the real reason lies in developing states in the north borrowing money to pay for needed transportation improvements given the success of the Erie Canal or for needed banking services in the states in the south. By 1844, nineteen states and two territories had borrowed money for needed economic growth. The inflationary boon of 1834-39, with the accompanying Panic of 1837, came to an end by 1841 and there was a tightening of credit that put pressure on incomplete construction projects for transportation improvements in the North (Pennsylvania, Maryland, Indiana, Illinois and Michigan) and lack of credit for banks in the South (Arkansas, Louisiana, Mississippi and Florida Territory). All but the Florida Territory and Mississippi resumed payment by 1848. The reason was the cost of default's denial of access and/or increase in cost of borrowing. Those that repudiated but resumed payment experienced borrowing yields to complete projects of 32 percent until they resumed payment and then paid 4 percent above market to borrow. Mississippi and the Florida Territory who refused to reverse their repudiation lacked access to the public market for almost two decades. William B. English, *Understanding the Costs of Sovereign Default: American State Debt in the 1840s*, 86 THE AMERICAN ECONOMIC REVIEW, 259, 275 (1996), www.jstor.org/stable/2118266 ("English"); Frederico Sturzenegger & Jeromin Zettelmeyer, DEBT DEFAULTS AND LESSONS FROM A DECADE OF CRISIS (MIT Press 2007) ("Sturzenegger").

Likewise, studies by the various rating agencies have indicated that not only is the rate of default drastically lower for rated municipal bonds compared to rated corporate bonds, but the percentage of recovery is significantly higher.[4] Part and parcel of that is the historical precedent of refinancing and refunding troubled situations in order to maintain the credibility in the market necessary for local governments to be able to make their own decisions as to what their infrastructure, improvements and services will be.

C. Purpose and Structure of the Book

The purpose of this book is to provide a compilation of various state laws and constitutional provisions relating to rights, remedies, refinancing, refunding and restructuring mechanisms provided by the 50 states, the District of Columbia and Puerto Rico. This compilation is an example of the individual creativity of various states to develop for themselves, given their unique situation and issues, methods of addressing state and local government financial distress. It is not intended to be exhaustive, given the dynamics of our legislative process, and the rights, remedies and restructuring mechanisms discussed herein are ever evolving and changing. It is our hope that this book will be beneficial not only to bond investors and municipal credit analysts, but also to states and local governments in considering what they and others have provided and whether or not they should revisit some of these issues so that they have the most effective rights, remedies and mechanisms to address periods of financial distress they may suffer in the future. It also is intended to help bondholders, rating agencies, institutional investors, credit enhancers and funds assess more effectively the issues relating to state and local government debt financing and the proud history these governments have in doing as much as they can to pay their debts in full and generally on time. It is not a historical accident that no state has defaulted on its general obligation debt since the late 1800s, with the exception of Arkansas in 1933,[5] which then refinanced its debt. It is likewise no accident that,

---

4 *See, e.g.,* Moody's Investors Service, *U.S. Municipal Bond Defaults and Recoveries, 1970-2014* (citing 95 municipal defaults from 1970-2014 for a municipal bond default rate of .01 percent based on the average one-year default rate compared to a corporate default rate of 1.66 percent based on the average one-year default rate). Indeed, according to Moody's, on average, the municipal bond ultimate recovery rate was about 64 percent for the period from 1970-2014, whereas the recovery rate for corporate senior unsecured bonds was 53 percent for the period 1987-2014. *Id.* Standard & Poor's has noted that since 1986, the average annual number of defaults of all U.S. public finance issuances has been five, in a universe of over 21,000 S&P ratings, compared to approximately 80 defaults per year for the same time period with respect to corporate securities. Standard & Poor's, *2014 Annual U.S. Public Finance Default Study and Rating Transitions;* Standard & Poor's, *Default, Transition, and Recovery: 2014 Annual Global Corporate Default Study and Rating Transitions.*

5 There was an initial debt exchange to refund the defaulted issue but that is not the end of the story. The defaulted debt was refunded by extending some of the maturities. It was feared that the state could not pay the refunded debt as extended and the State of Arkansas tried to refund the debt ($140 million) in 1937 and 1938 only to be rebuffed by the market. In 1941, $90.8 million of outstanding highway bonds were callable on April 1, 1941 and another $45 million callable in July of 1941. The Reconstruction Finance Corporation, a federal program, purchased the refunding bonds and worked with a number of banks on the refunding purchase. But for the federal program, there would not have been funding available for the purchase of the refunding bonds. *See* Joe Mysak, *Bond Default Is About Too Much Debt, Too Little Time,* BLOOMBERG (July 20, 2010, 8:00 PM), http://www.bloomberg.com/news/articles/2010-07-21/bond-default-means-too-much-debt-too-little-time-commentary-by-joe-mysak ("Mysak"). *See also* Robert Slavin, *Is Puerto*

after the Panic of 1837 and the resulting economic downturn, state defaults were followed more likely by resumption of payment rather than a permanent repudiation.

Today, due to concerns about pension obligations, large municipal bankruptcies and stories of potential defaults by cities and states, much uncertainty exists in the municipal markets. This uncertainty relates not only to whether municipalities will be able to pay the principal and interest owed on long-term obligations, but also to a lack of clarity as to the rights of bondholders and accompanying remedies available should it become clear that a municipal default will occur. While investors may express great concern that a municipality will unilaterally file a municipal bankruptcy petition under Chapter 9 of the United States Bankruptcy Code (the "Bankruptcy Code") without any attempts to work with investors in restructuring debt, in reality the states have enacted a plethora of laws to help rehabilitate municipalities before they reach such an untenable position. As a last resort, should such restructurings fail, a municipality could pursue a municipal restructuring under the Bankruptcy Code assuming, of course, that the state in which the municipality is located permits such a filing. Rarely have municipalities filed for Chapter 9.[6]

At the most basic level, bondholders should rest assured that they receive significant protection against default from the fact that as our municipalities have grown and prospered, so has their need for continued financing. The confidence of the municipal bond market is essential, and municipalities traditionally have made every effort to honor their public debt obligations. For instance, states have enacted statutory provisions waiving sovereign rights in connection with financings to assure bondholders that if they purchase the revenue bonds of municipalities within these states, the pledge of revenue to the bondholders cannot be diverted or terminated.[7] These statutory provisions were not only for the bondholders but also for the citizens of the state so that, by providing assurance to bond investors of adequate remedies, all municipalities could make use of municipal bond financing when necessary.

Rico on a Similar Path to 1930s Arkansas?, THE BOND BUYER (Nov. 4, 2015, 11:00 AM), http://www.bondbuyer.com/news/regionalnews/is-puerto-rico-on-a-similar-path-to-1930s-arkansas-1088656-1.html.

6 Since 1937 only 666 filings have occurred, and since 1980, only 297 Chapter 9 petitions have been filed as of July 31, 2016. For the most part, these 297 Chapter 9 petitions were filed by small special tax districts and municipal utilities (approximately 60 percent of all filings) and few municipalities of any size. States, to date, cannot file for Chapter 9 protection. *See Hearing on the Role of Public Employee Pensions in Contributing to State's Insolvency and the Possibility of a State Bankruptcy Chapter Before the H. Committee on the Judiciary Subcommittee on Courts, Commercial and Administrative Law*, 112th Cong. 1 (2011) (statement of James E. Spiotto).

7 As will be discussed, *infra*, most states have statutory provisions authorizing the pledge of revenues for the payment of certain bond indebtedness and disallow the revenues so pledged from being diverted or used for purposes other than first making the required payment on bond indebtedness. *See, e.g.*, CAL. EDUC. CODE § 15250.

With respect to the states, some speculate that the U.S. Supreme Court is moving closer to establishing greater limitations on the federal government's ability to interfere with the internal governance of the states — states' rights. *See, e.g., Virginia Office for Prot. & Advocacy v. Stewart*, 131 S. Ct. 1632 (2011) (Roberts, J. dissenting; Kennedy, J. concurring).

In fact, it is important that during times of financial crisis, a municipality has the support of the municipal bond market. As was recognized by one scholar in examining municipal defaults during the Great Depression:

> It must also be remembered that drastic enforcement of claims for debt service may be to the detriment of bondholders in the long run. A city that suffers a breakdown in governmental services is apt to become less attractive to prospective residents and new industries. Progress is retarded, and the growth that would eventually have restored the city to a sound financial basis becomes stunted. The bondholder's best interests lie in a going concern.[8]

The well-developed truth is that there is a symbiotic relationship between bondholders being paid and state and local governments being able to maintain infrastructure and offer services. Failure to pay bondholders equates either to increased borrowing costs or to denial of access to the capital market, which generates less substantive and affordable services. In addition to the support of the municipal bond market, a troubled municipality may need the support of its state's laws to help guide it through severe economic hardship. The survey contained in this book examines the laws of the 50 states, the District of Columbia and Puerto Rico to provide an overview of the various state laws enacted to aid troubled municipalities and to protect bondholders in a default situation.[9] These charts are meant only to provide an overview of the rights and remedies available to bondholders in each state and should not be relied upon as legal advice. For any specific issues arising from an individual situation or for any questions relating to an individual's own affairs raised by these charts and this introduction, readers should consult with and seek the advice of counsel as to the specific application of these provisions.

The first part of this book, before the actual state survey, will provide a general overview of the municipal bond climate and examine those mechanisms that states have enacted to remedy financial distress and any evolving default situation. For instance, in all but three states, certain debt or tax limitations have been enacted to limit the amount of debt that a municipality may hold at any one time. In virtually all states, there is some form of a limitation on debt, a tax limitation or a combination of both. In addition, all states recognize refunding bond provisions, which may aid municipalities in simply "refunding" or "refinancing" a default. At some point, however, issuing refunding bonds may no longer be the most effective answer to a municipality's financial situation.

---

8 Albert Miller Hillhouse, MUNICIPAL BONDS: A CENTURY OF EXPERIENCE 362 (New York: Prentice-Hall 1936) ("Hillhouse").

9 To the extent that this text generally refers to the "states," the District of Columbia and Puerto Rico are included in this analysis. In this book, they are not included in the term "states" when the definition of who may be a debtor under Chapter 9 of the United States Bankruptcy Code is referenced. At the same time, the 50 states are co-sovereigns with the federal government, with the rights and privileges related thereto, while the District of Columbia and Puerto Rico are a district and territory, respectively, subject to the federal government's supervision and governance as provided by the United States Constitution, federal legislation and, more specifically, Puerto Rico's status as a territory.

In addition to mechanisms that may help protect a municipality from entering a default situation (financial oversight, financial control boards, intergovernmental cooperation, local government cooperation and others), certain states have enacted debt resolution provisions to help aid troubled municipalities in developing a plan for paying their debts. This book will highlight those provisions, along with a discussion of how much power each state provides to its municipalities to control their own affairs, both in and outside of a potential default situation. In addition to these debt resolution provisions, many states have enacted provisions explicitly setting forth remedies for bondholders in a default situation. While many of these remedies are available for holders of revenue bonds and, to a lesser extent, general obligation debt, the availability of such remedies may be important to any municipal investor and consequently will be addressed. Examples of such remedies include actions for mandamus; suits to force the payment of debt; suits for declaratory relief; suits to appoint a receiver; and suits for injunctive relief. Although not within the scope of these materials, under certain circumstances, bondholders may also seek relief under the federal securities laws with respect to actions based in securities fraud, and they may bring state law fraud and negligent misrepresentation claims.[10] As with any potential pitfalls a bond issue may face, because the provisions across the states addressing municipal restructuring and bondholder remedies are as diverse as the states themselves, an attorney should be consulted as to any specific facts and law and any concerns a debt holder may have.

Next, the effect of Chapter 9 of the Bankruptcy Code on the payment to bondholders will be reviewed. Filing under Chapter 9 of the Bankruptcy Code can be an alternative to municipalities from which the market does not shrink, provided that the principles and practical realities of municipal financing are not disturbed. These materials will analyze the viability of Chapter 9 as the last resort for municipalities. While state authorization is required and not all states allow their municipalities to file a municipal bankruptcy petition, municipal bankruptcy could be a powerful tool for municipalities on the brink of disaster to restructure their debt. In this regard, it would be helpful to know whether the state in which the local government is located is one that authorizes its municipalities to file for bankruptcy. As will be noted herein, currently only 12 states specifically authorize a bankruptcy filing, another 12 states have conditional authorization, 3 states have limited authorization, 2 states generally prohibit a filing and the remaining 21 states presently provide no authorization for a municipal bankruptcy filing at this time.[11]

10 For a more detailed discussion of such claims and available remedies, see James E. Spiotto, *Municipal Insolvency: Bankruptcy, Receivership, Workouts and Alternative Remedies*, STATE & LOCAL GOVERNMENT DEBT FINANCING, 1-144 (2d ed.); Robert A. Fippinger, *Fraud Concepts in Public Finance*, THE SECURITIES LAW OF PUBLIC FINANCE (3d ed., PLI 2015).

11 As mentioned, without specific authorization from the state, a municipality may not file a petition under the U.S. Bankruptcy Code. The District of Columbia and Puerto Rico currently are not authorized to make use of Chapter 9 and are not "municipalities" as defined in the Bankruptcy Code. There have been recent efforts on behalf of Puerto Rico to obtain authorization for its municipalities to file and to develop a mechanism to assist the Commonwealth with its debt resolution process such as an oversight authority like the District of Columbia had in 1995. *See, e.g.*, H.R. 5278, *The Puerto Rico Oversight, Management, and Economic Stability Act; see also* H.R. 870, *The Puerto Rico Chapter 9 Uniformity Act of 2015, Hearing before the House Judiciary Committee*, 114th Cong. (2015), judiciary.house.gov/index.cfm/

Along with a general overview of the municipal bankruptcy provisions of the Bankruptcy Code, this survey will pay particular attention to provisions allowing for the continued payment of two types of bond issuances — special revenue bonds and bonds to which a statutory lien applies — even after a municipal bankruptcy filing has occurred. Further, the survey will include the use of state intercepts of funds from taxes to assure the ability of financially challenged state and local governments to receive financing when they need it the most to bridge financial distress.

As will be evident from these pages, while certain general themes emerge across state lines, the laws of the states addressing issues of municipal insolvency are a tangled web that, even internally within a state, commingle constitutional and statutory provisions. It is our hope, however, that these materials will help bring a better understanding to the municipal marketplace of the rights and remedies available to bondholders in the unlikely event that a municipality defaults on a debt issuance. In addition, the materials aim to highlight those states that have adopted monitoring and rehabilitation provisions to aid their municipalities at the first sign of trouble.

---

hearings?ID=809AB2A9-78F5-4fCE-8E6D-955F5B6039DE; Joint Statement by Treasury Secretary Jacob Lew, National Economic CouncilDirector Jeff Zients, and Health and Human Service Secretary Sylvia Matthews Burwell on the Obama Administration's Legislative Proposal to Address Puerto Rico's Urgent Fiscal Situation (Oct. 21, 2015), released by the Department of Treasury Public Affairs, https://www.treasury.gov/press-center/press-releases/Pages/jl0228.aspx. *See also* Written Testimony of James E. Spiotto before the United States Senate Committee on the Judiciary Hearing on Puerto Rico's Fiscal Problems: Examining the Source and Exploring the Solution (Dec. 1, 2015), http://muninetguide.com/?p=134470, Written Testimony of James E. Spiotto before the House of Representatives Subcommittee on Indian, Insular and Alaska Native Affairs Regarding the Need for the Establishment of a Puerto Rico Financial Stability and Economic Growth Authority, Feb. 2, 2016, and James Spiotto, *Congress's Role in Saving Puerto Rico from Financial Meltdown and Imminent Bankruptcy*, MUNINET GUIDE, (Dec. 12, 2015), http://muninetguide.com/?p=61069, discussing Chapter 9 authorization as a last resort and creation of an oversight authority in conjunction with a recovery plan as a preferable approach. On June 30, 2016, President Obama signed into law The Puerto Rico Oversight, Management, and Economic Stability Act, or PROMESA, creating a financial control board to help restructure Puerto Rico's debt and oversee the island's finances. Public Law 114-187, 114th Cong., 2d Sess. (June 30, 2016). The bill provides for a court proceeding instituted by the control board to confirm an adjustment of the debts of a territory. It is the control board that would represent the territory in such proceeding. PROMESA is technically a financial oversight and economic stabilization legislation enacted under the territorial clause (art. IV, § 3) and bankruptcy clause (art. I, § 8, cl. 4) of the U.S. Constitution for specified territories (Puerto Rico, Guam, American Samoa, the Commonwealth of Northern Mariana Islands or the United States Virgin Islands). PROMESA will be discussed in more detail in section V.

II. Historical Background on Sovereign Debt Repudiation/Defaults and Their Consequences as Well as Theories as to Why Sovereign Debt Should Be Paid

A. History of Sovereign Defaults and Repudiation

1. Origin in Ancient Greece

Despite recent media coverage, sovereign financial distress is not new. It can be traced back to the origin of our democratic form of federal, state and local government in the United States and ultimately has its origin in ancient Greece and, thereafter, in the economic cycles of European countries. One of the first recorded defaults of European origins was in the 4th century B.C. when ten (two completely and eight partially) out of thirteen Greek municipalities in the Attic Maritime Association defaulted on loans from the Delos Temple.[12] Thus, the need arose for oversight and the development of effective means of providing payment while also supplying required services to local residents. One of the first attempts to address this was to have a representative of the creditor supervise collections and operations until payment was made. The use of "receivers" and "emergency managers" can be traced back to Assos in Ionia in the 5th century B.C. where an influential banker named Eubulus loaned money to a Persian official secured by the revenues of Assos and the neighboring town Atarneus. The banker in a debt collection effort took over the administration of Atarneus and collected taxes to satisfy the debt that became due.[13]

2. More Recent Sovereign Defaults and Their Causes (1824-2010)

In more recent history, there are a number of examples of sovereign default of central or federal governments following wars, revolutions, occupations, economic busts after economic booms and state disintegration. Some commentators have broken them down into eight periods with a number of large sovereign defaults:

- Period 1 — 1824-1834 with 17 sovereign defaults including Greece, Portugal, Spain, Argentina, Brazil, Mexico, Chile, Egypt and Liberia;
- Period 2 — 1867-1882 with 19 sovereign defaults including Austria, Spain, Turkey, Bolivia, Columbia, Mexico and Liberia;

12 Max Winkler, FOREIGN BONDS, AN AUTOPSY 22 (Roland Swain 1933); Hillhouse at 37.

13 George M. Calhoun, THE BUSINESS LIFE OF ANCIENT ATHENS 125-126 (U. of Chicago Press 1926).

- Period 3 — 1890-1900 with 14 sovereign defaults including Greece, Portugal, Serbia/Yugoslavia, Argentina and Colombia;

- Period 4 — 1911-1921 with 16 sovereign defaults including Austria, Bulgaria, Romania, Russia, Turkey, Argentina, Brazil, Ecuador and Liberia;

- Period 5 — 1931-1940 with 26 sovereign defaults including Austria, Bulgaria, Germany, Hungary, Italy, Poland, Romania, Serbia/Yugoslavia, Turkey, Argentina, Brazil, Chile, Cuba, Romania and Uruguay;

- Period 6 — 1976-1989 with 44 sovereign defaults including Poland, Romania, Serbia/Yugoslavia, Turkey, Argentina, Bolivia, Brazil, Chile, Cuba, Mexico, Panama, Egypt, Angola, Congo, Cameroon, Liberia, Morocco, Nigeria, South Africa, Zaire and Zambia;

- Period 7 — 1998-2004 with 14 sovereign defaults including Moldova, Russia, Argentina, Grenada, Gabon, Uruguay and Paraguay;

- Period 8 — 2008-2010 with 7 sovereign defaults including Afghanistan, Bermuda, Congo, Greece, Seychelles, Ecuador, Jamaica, Belize and Grenada.[14]

The causes of these sovereign debt defaults vary, from: (i) economic cycles, (ii) wars, revolutions and changes in government, (iii) disintegration of government, and (iv) poor economic development, misuse of government borrowings and resulting distrust of economic, political and social institutions. Past examples of these causes are:

- The economic cyclical result of boom to bust (see the eight economic periods noted above).

- Wars, occupations, revolutions and changes of government (WWI — Turkey, Bulgaria, Austria and Hungary; WWII — Italy, Turkey and Japan; Civil War in the United States; Soviet government in 1917).

- State disintegration (*see, e.g.*, Cuba (1960), Mexico (1914), Russia (1917) and China (1949)).

- Massive increase of public debt for a specific sovereign accompanied by a decline of employment, resulting in lower tax revenues with popular unrest and distrust of the financial market (*see, e.g.*, during the past 186 years, Brazil has defaulted seven times, Venezuela nine times and Turkey six times due to these factors).

---

14 Peter H. Lindert and Peter J. Morton, *How Sovereign Debt Has Worked*, in DEVELOPING COUNTRY DEBT AND ECONOMIC PERFORMANCE 39-106 (Jeffrey D. Sachs ed., 1989); David O. Beim and Charles W. Calomiris, EMERGING FINANCIAL MARKETS (McGraw-Hill 2001); Standard & Poor's Study: Sovereign Defaults and Rating Transition Data, 2012 Update, http://www.standardandpoors.com/en_US/web/guest/article/-/view/sourceId/7843296.

B. Sovereign Debt Restructuring Mechanisms and Vehicles Have Been Developed in Recent History as an Effective Means of Addressing and Resolving the Default

Over the last century, mechanisms have been developed to bring the defaulting sovereign and any affected creditors together in a constructive procedure to permit a reasonable and prompt resolution of the dispute. Unfortunately, sovereign debt defaults and resolutions generally can be measured by years, if not decades. It has been clear that prompt and consensual (to the extent possible) resolution has yielded the most beneficial results. Historically, sovereign debt resolution mechanisms have developed based on the kinds of creditors who held the debt, namely a London Club convention that has been developed for commercial banks holding defaulted sovereign debt, the Paris Club convention development for other governments holding the defaulted debt, and *ad hoc* methods (such as *ad hoc* creditors committee) for mixed creditor constituencies. The International Monetary Fund ("IMF") has over the years proposed the use of a tribunal established by treaty or consensual agreement to determine and resolve disputes on the extent and method of debt restructuring if consensual resolution is not possible.[15] In 2014, a number of members of the United Nations ("UN") supported a resolution for the UN to create a "multilateral legal framework for sovereign debt restructuring."[16] Some have gone so far as to suggest a modified version of Chapter 9 for sovereigns. The most common sovereign debt resolution mechanisms will be discussed below.

1. London Club (Creditor Committees)

Commercial bank loans to sovereigns have their roots in the London Stock Exchange dating back to the 1800s, which could delist from the Exchange defaulted foreign government bonds. The London Club is not statutorily created or established by treaty. It is an association of major western commercial banks that started in the 1970s on an *ad hoc* basis to deal with developing countries' financial problems. It is based on agreements in principle on debt restructurings generally held by the major western commercial banks through the Bank Advisory Committee ("BAC") or a creditors committee made up of the larger bank creditors who negotiated with the defaulting government.

2. Paris Club

The Paris Club is composed of governments who have lent money to defaulting governments (bilateral external debt). Like the London Club, it has no legal, statutory or treaty status or rules of

---

15 Anna J. Schwartz, THE IMF'S DUBIOUS PROPOSAL FOR A UNIVERSAL BANKRUPTCY LAW FOR SOVEREIGN DEBTORS, Cato Institute Foreign Policy Briefing, No. 75 (Mar. 5, 2003) ("Schwartz"); Sovereign Debt Task Force, Initiative for Policy Dialogue and United Nations Department of Economic and Social Affairs, Report of the Meeting of Authors, Columbia University (Oct. 15-16, 2004), http://www.un.org/esa/ffd/msc/sovereigndebt/09_multi_stakeholder_Report%20of%20Columbia%20Task%20Force%20meeting%20October%2015_16%202004.pdf.

16 United Nations General Assembly Resolution 63/304, adopted Sep. 9, 2014, Toward the establishment of a multilateral legal framework for sovereign debt restructuring process, http://www.un.org/en/ga/search/view_doc.asp?symbol=A/RES/68/304.

procedure. The members are nineteen governments of the largest economies who have lent mainly to developing countries. Its origins go back to 1956 when Argentina met its creditors in Paris to prevent an imminent default. Like the London Club, the government lenders of size negotiate with the defaulting or financially troubled government after it demonstrates its interest in restructuring its debt by agreeing to a structural adjustment program with the IMF. Generally, 80 percent agreement is required. Since 1989, there have been seventeen restructurings done with "Brady Bonds," which collateralize the new sovereign debt that is exchanged for the old defaulted debt.

3. Exchange Offers and Other Mechanisms

Exchange offers may be extended to institutional investors who are not major banks or governments where new debt securities or cash is offered in exchange for the old security that has or will default. Exchange offers generally are premised on new terms for the new debt securities or a discount of face value of the old securities. IMF restructuring and adjustment with the World Bank for multilateral transactions may be possible for the poorest countries. Further, there are compositions of creditors and *ad hoc* creditor settlement agreements.

4. Development of Sovereign Debt Adjustment Mechanisms

A tribunal established by treaty to approve a proposed restructuring has been discussed by the IMF and others, whereby use of a treaty signed by all participating countries (lenders and borrowers) would create an international cross-border law permitting a process that results in a binding restructuring. The dispute would be presented to a tribunal with established rules of procedure and a recovery plan would be developed for debt adjustment, proposed to creditors and presented to the tribunal for approval and creditors' vote. This has similar aspects of Chapter 9 under the U.S. Bankruptcy Code but would be international for sovereigns who participate by treaty. A similar mechanism could be established by consensual agreement of the affected creditors to the jurisdiction of the tribunal over the debt restructuring.

5. Proposals for Various Mechanisms for Resolution of Sovereign Debt Controversies

<u>The IMF's Development of Sovereign Debt Adjustment Mechanisms ("SDAM")</u>. (Tribunal by Treaty.) A tribunal established by treaty to approve a proposed restructuring has been discussed by the IMF and others, whereby use of a treaty signed by all participating countries (lenders and borrowers) would create international cross-border law permitting a process that results in a binding restructuring. The dispute would be presented to a tribunal with established rules of procedure and a recovery plan is developed for debt adjustment, proposed to creditors and presented to the tribunal for approval and creditors' vote. This has similar aspects of Chapter 9 but would be international for those sovereigns who participate by treaty.[17]

---

17 Aitor Erce, *Sovereign Debt Restructurings and the IMF: Implications for Future Official Interventions,* Globalization and Monetary Policy Institute, Working Paper No. 143, Apr. 2013, http://www.dallasfed.org/assets/documents/

<u>European Crisis Resolution Mechanism ("ECRM")</u>. This is a proposed European Union statutory legally binding mechanism. There would be three parts: (1) a financing body to provide for interim financing, especially during economic distress, (2) an economic entity to assess debt sustainability and oversee economic adjustment of the debtor country (*e.g.*, European Central Bank or European Commission), and (3) a legal body to resolve disputes between the debtor country and creditors like SDAM.

<u>Amendment to ESM (European Stability Mechanism) Treaty</u>. Under this proposal, the ESM Treaty signed in 2012 to provide a permanent source of financial assistance (bailouts) for member states would be amended to protect debtor country assets from attachment by litigious holdout creditors in response to the litigation brought against Peru and Argentina in recent years by hedge funds who held out against proposed restructurings.

<u>Sovereign Debt Tribunal ("SDT") and Fair and Transparent Arbitration Process</u>. This is a proposal for institutionalized or *ad hoc* mechanisms for an arbitration framework applicable to sovereign external debt restructuring. The proponents of SDT would take some of the processes and procedures of Chapter 9 as a starting point. Arbitration procedures could be enacted by a special arbitration clause in the debt instrument or an optional arbitration process implemented by agreement of creditors or treaty. Debtors and creditors would each propose one or two arbitrators who would choose one or two "neutral arbitrators."

<u>International Debt Restructuring Court ("IDRC")</u>. This is a proposal of UN experts envisioning the establishment of a deteriorated debt restructuring court. The court would have agreed upon principles concerning priority of claims, the size of necessary writedowns, and the sharing of pain and writedown. There could be government guarantees of recovery with assurance that the restructured entity is sustainable. The IDRC would allow interim liquidity financing. National courts of all countries must recognize the IDRC's legitimacy and be stayed from interfering. The authorization of the court through the UN or by international treaty is to be developed.

<u>Sovereign Debt Forum ("SDF")</u>. This would be a non-statutory and non-institutional neutral body created by informal consensus and would bring debtors, governments, creditors and international institutions together for constructive dialogue and negotiations. The SDF would be expected to enable early, discrete consultation and information sharing between a distressed government and its creditors to develop a recovery plan.[18]

---

institute/wpapers/2013/0143.pdf ("Erce"); IMF, *Sovereign Debt Restructuring — Recent Developments and Implications for the Fund's Legal and Policy Framework*, (Apr. 26, 2013); https://www.imf.org/external/np/pp/eng/2013/042613.pdf.

18 Francois Gianviti, Anne O. Krueger, Jean Pisani-Ferry, Andre Sapir and Jurgen Von Hagen, *A European Mechanism for Sovereign Debt Crisis Resolution: A Proposal*, Bruegel Blueprint Series, 2010; Udaibir S. Das, Michael G. Papaioannou and Christoph Trebesch, *Sovereign Debt Restructuring, 1950-2010 Literature Survey, Data and Stylized Facts* (IMF Working

C. Efforts to Provide Greater Predictability and Efficiency in Resolution Mechanisms by Provisions in the Documentation of Sovereign Debt

It certainly is helpful to have an effective process to reach resolution of a default at the time a sovereign is in financial distress. Nevertheless, there is no substitute to having the applicable sovereign debt document provide for the ability to adjust debt or an acceptable mechanism to resolve disputes between the sovereign and the holders of the debt when payment is delayed or not made. The specific law governing the debt issuance can be critical to the ability to obtain a prompt and binding resolution. Likewise, a clause in the relevant documentation that permits less than unanimous consent to effectuate a restructuring has been helpful to certain sovereign debt situations. The ability to amend or obtain effective amendment relief to documents where it would otherwise be impossible to cure a default may help prevent meltdown. States and local governments in the United States historically do not allow super-majority consent to a restructuring of the principal amount, interest rate, extent of security and maturity. Instead, they tend to require unanimous consent of all holders, which may be difficult to obtain. However, other countries have provided in their debt documentation greater flexibility for sovereigns to address financial distress. The question is raised whether a super-majority right to consent to changes in the basic terms of the debt with drag-along rights for non-consenting holders will be acceptable in the municipal market of the United States and not lead to increased borrowing costs as a result of increased risk.

1. Choice of Law

There is a movement to have agreed-upon provisions of a non-debtor forum and governing law in sovereign debt documentation. The most popular choices are New York, London and the U.K., Germany and Japan.

2. Collective Action Clauses

Collective action clauses ("CAC") provide that a super-majority, generally 75 percent of the creditors represented at a creditors meeting (bondholders meeting), can vote in favor of the terms of a debt restructuring and that vote will be binding on all creditors of the affected debt. Some provisions take the form of limiting the rights of individual holders to accelerate or litigate if a majority of holders does not support the action. Collective action clauses are generally restricted to debt issued under a trust indenture. To date, collective action clauses have not been acceptable to the municipal market in the United States for state and local government debt. (The one exception is the Puerto Rico Oversight, Management and Economic Stability Act, PROMESA, enacted in June 2016, which includes a collective action clause and provision enjoining litigation on the existing debt, as further described in section V).

Paper, 2012) ("Das"); Molly Ryan, *Sovereign Bankruptcy: Why Now and Why Not in the IMF*, 82 FORDHAM L. REV. 2473, (2014).

As a result, the consent of all creditors to a material amendment of the documentation (such as changes to maturity, interest rate, security, etc.) is generally required for debt issued by a state.

3. Amendment Clauses/Exit Consents

These provisions generally allow a majority or super-majority of consenting bondholders in an exchange to consent to an amendment stripping covenants, limiting ability to accelerate or rescinding acceleration or cross defaults, or modifying terms in an unattractive way to coerce holders to agree to a restructuring. In U.S. corporate bonds, these provisions are aggressively litigated. Further, these provisions can only affect holders of the specific debt issuance and no other separate and distinct debt issues.[19]

4. The Nature of Sovereign Debt Restructurings in the Past 60 Years

Between 1950-2010, there have been over 600 sovereign debt restructurings in 95 countries. Of the 600 restructurings, 186 were debt exchanges with private creditors (foreign bonds and bondholders) while 447 have been bilateral debt restructurings with the Paris Club for debt held by governments or government-related agencies. Of the 186 debt exchanges:[20]

- 18 were sovereign bond exchange restructurings;
- 168 affected bank loans;
- 57 involved a cut in face value (debt reduction), while 129 used a lengthening of maturity (debt maturity extension);
- 109 occurred post default, while 77 were preemptive; and
- Only 26 involved cash buyback as an exchange of old debt instruments for cash at a discount to face value.

A study of recent sovereign restructurings indicated a relationship between the duration of the resolution process, the degree of debt reduction or forgiveness, the percentage of participation and the ability to access the alternative bond market to issue debt.[21] It appears the longer the duration of the resolution process, the more likely the debt reduction or forgiveness will be larger. The smaller the debt reduction, the greater the participation, and the shorter the debt resolution process and lower the debt

19 Das, *supra* n. 18, at 5-6.

20 *Id.*

21 Erce, *supra* n. 17.

reduction, the quicker the access to the capital markets and acceptance of debt issuance in the international markets. The following chart is an example of those observations:

Analysis of Recent Sovereign Restructurings
1998-2010

Country	Default Date	Time to Completion (quarters)	Haircut (%)	First Issuance to International Bond Market (quarters after completion)	Participation (%)
Russia	08/1998	8	(40.75)	10	(75-99)
Pakistan	05/1999	11	(29-32)	18	99
Ukraine	08/1998	12	(5-59.2)	16	(82-100)
Ecuador	09/1999	5	(9-47)	24	98
Argentina	06/2001	12	(25-82)	19	(50-76)
Dominican Republic	12/2004	3	(1-2)	4	97
Serbia	12/2000	20	62	Not Yet	-
Dominica	12/2003	2	50	-	78.5
Belize	12/2006	2	(1-28)	Not Yet	98
Grenada	01/2004	3	(40-45)	Not Yet	91
Jamaica	02/2010	-	20	4	99

(Federal Reserve Bank of Dallas, Global and Monetary Policy Institute Working Paper No. 143, Aitor Erce, Apr. 2013)

D. What Motivates Sovereigns to Pay Their Debts Timely? Traditional and Developing Theories

The simple answer as to why those who borrow pay their debts is because they need to borrow again, and failure to pay has consequences. The consequences of default historically have been identified as currency debasement, loss of capital market access, restrictions on trade and economic sanctions. Certainly for sovereigns that are not countries, such as states and local governments in the United States, the consequences of sovereign defaults are applied with more difficulty to isolated parts of a country such as states and local governments (city, town, village, etc.). The traditional and developing consequences of government failure to pay can be described as follows:

1. "Currency Debasement"

Currency debasement can result from a repudiation or default by a sovereign, "inflation" or "devaluation" of that sovereign's currency as less acceptable or less valued than prior to the default. This was demonstrated in a study of the sovereign defaults experienced between 1557 and 1882. Spain defaulted 13 times and France defaulted 8 times. Germany, Portugal and Austria defaulted 5 times during the 19th century, and Greece defaulted 4 times in the 19th century, as compared to the current global market where the EU has its own currency for members and countries can use another country's currency or back their own currency by another country's currency.[22]

2. "Loss of Access to Capital Markets"

Loss of access to the financial markets due to repudiation and default that are a clear demonstration of the lack of creditworthiness and willingness to pay translates into higher interest rates to reflect risk or an all-out denial of access to borrow.[23]

3. "Use of Direct Sanctions"

A sovereign contemplating defaulting on its debt is influenced not to do so because direct sanctions would be imposed, such as trade embargos, tariffs or refusal to trade, that increase the costs of needed goods, which would stifle economic growth.[24]

4. "Demands for Ability to Fund Needed Infrastructure and Essential Governmental Services at an Acceptable Level"

The basic reason for the existence of a sovereign, and especially states and local governments in the United States, is to provide essential services and infrastructure at a level sufficient to assure the continued economic activities necessary to provide for the health, safety and welfare of citizens. This means access to funding necessary to encourage economic activity, to create and supply jobs (especially for the younger generations), fostering an environment where citizens desire to live that is safe, with educational systems that provide good training so that employers want to hire graduating students, and economic development opportunities so that businesses want to locate or expand there. Fulfilling this mandate provides the predicate for the creation of new good jobs, especially for recent graduates and other future taxpayers, which helps create increased tax revenues for the needed reinvestment in the government and the community.

---

22 Carmen M. Reinhart, Kenneth S. Rogoff and Miguel A. Savastano, *Debt Intolerance*, BROOKINGS PAPERS ON ECONOMIC ACTIVITY, 1-77 (2003).

23 Jeremy Bulow and Kenneth Rogoff, *Sovereign Debt: Is to Forgive to Forget?*, 79 AMERICAN ECONOMIC REVIEW 1, 43-50 (Mar. 1989) ("Bulow and Rogoff").

24 English, *supra* n. 3.

This theory of a deterrent to default is premised on the proposition that the perceived benefit of restructuring a defaulted sovereign debt is insufficient to compensate the sovereign for the long-term adverse effect on its ability to obtain capital to fund necessary infrastructure improvements and essential governmental services at acceptable levels.

This is a further refinement of the restriction of access to capital markets or increased borrowing costs following default or restructuring. This new mandate for payment of debt should be determinative of the question "Why pay?" Failure to pay leads to a death spiral, limited access to the capital markets, increased costs of borrowing and demand for more tax revenues at the same time services are lowered and taxes increased (corporate and individual), all causing residents and businesses to leave and thus reducing net tax collections despite the increase in taxes. If repeated, the situation will only continue to get worse, as amply demonstrated by the downward spirals of Detroit, Michigan (1960-2013) and Bridgeport, Connecticut (1988-1991).

The perceived short-term benefit of default or debt adjustment frustrates the mandate of government (to provide essential governmental services). Default or repudiation is accompanied by a stigma that causes (a) creditors to be more reluctant to extend credit and more likely to increase the costs of borrowing, and (b) businesses to decide to relocate or avoid the locale that likely reduces or eliminates business development. Also, citizens are faced with increasing taxes and decreasing essential services due to the sovereign's limited resources and lack of ability to fund, causing both corporate and individual citizens to leave, which begins a "death spiral." This is the reason why virtually every government finance official will do everything he or she can to pay government debt on time.

E. How Does This Historical Background Relate to States and Local Governments in the United States?

Sovereigns as countries are different from states and local governments because states and local governments have the benefit of a common currency and trade with the other state and local governments of that country. While countries print currency, provide for a national defense, conduct diplomatic relations and have the responsibility of border protection, those are not the concerns of state and local governments. Accordingly, the lessons of sovereign defaults need to be adjusted to be applicable to state and local governments.

1. No Real Threat of "Currency Debasement" or "Trade Sanctions"

In the United States, since the states do not print their own currency and have, through interstate commerce, the free movement of goods and services, there is no real fear of debasement of currency or trade embargo against a defaulted state or municipality because such punishment misses its mark, and there is no benefit to harming all states and local governments simply because one of them has defaulted.

2. There Is Continuing Debate as to Whether Loss of Access to the Capital Market Is an Effective Threat

Given recent entrants into the municipal finance market and their appetite for risk, the "market discipline" argument for paying governmental debt may be more historical than prospective. However, as markets tighten and especially if defaults were to increase, the effectiveness of market discipline may drastically demonstrate restricted access and increased costs of borrowing. There are consequences to default, including access and costs of borrowing. This is demonstrated by Detroit and the claim that Detroit's Chapter 9 filing and treatment of public debt raised the cost of borrowing for Michigan local governments by 50-100 basis points, and the specter of a default by Puerto Rico raised the yield on Puerto Rico's debt in October 2015 to over 12 percent.[25]

3. Needed Ability to Fund Improved Infrastructure and Essential Governmental Services May Be Major Motivation for Future Payments by State and Local Governments

Given the aging infrastructure and need for significant reinvestment in state and local governments' infrastructure, and the needed ability to fund essential services at an acceptable level, state and local governments should have little incentive to default and every reason to pay their debts on time. Prompt payment of debt maintains access to the capital market and the historical low financing cost. Even if defaults cause only a 200 to 300 basis point rise in annual interest expense, that is about 60 percent to 90 percent more payment of principal over a 30-year period. The spread between AAA and BBB (high yield) can average 200-275 basis points.[26] That additional cost could have been used to reduce taxes, pay for needed infrastructure or services or pay unfunded pension obligations. This appears to be the developing motivation for not defaulting and not filing for Chapter 9.

4. State and Local Government Defaults Have Followed the Economic Cycle Since the 1840s

As will be noted in the next section, state and local government defaults often have been the function of economic cycles and legacy costs that must be addressed. While the Civil War caused the repudiation of debt related to the southern states' involvement with the Civil War, the northern states were required to pay their lawful debts. Most states and their local governments have debt and tax limitations by statute or constitution that are aimed at protecting against massive increases of public debt and public dissatisfaction with such increases.

---

25 *See* Brian Chappatta, *Puerto Rico Bond Yields Reach Record High as Default Risk Mounts,* BLOOMBERG (Oct. 30, 2015, 10:08 AM) http://www.bloomberg.com/news/articles/2015-10-30/puerto-rico-bond-yields-reach-record-high-as-default-risks-mount.

26 Baird Fixed Income Strategy, 4/7/14, p.8.

F. The History of Payment of State and Local Government Debt in the United States

Q. Why is it important to pay state and local government debt?

A. "No pecuniary consideration is more urgent than the regular redemption and discharge of public debt. On none can delay be more injurious or economy of time more valuable."

These words were spoken over 220 years ago by George Washington in his State of the Union address of December 3, 1793 referencing the debts of the Revolutionary War incurred by former colonies, now states. Such debts were assumed by the federal government to insure continued market credibility for the newborn nation and its states. Washington and Alexander Hamilton were instrumental in having the federal government assume the states' debt since some states were balking at paying it, in the belief that to do so was a financial game, while some of the states feared their taxes would go to pay northern speculators of debt or the large war debts of other states like Massachusetts and South Carolina. Washington and Hamilton knew the progress of a new nation could be no swifter than its financial credibility. For this reason, the assured payment of the Revolutionary War debt through assumption by the federal government began the long, proud history of payment of state and local government debt to insure market credibility. Hamilton at the same time announced his principle of the "immortality of public debt,"[27] namely a government, federal, state or local, should not incur debt unless at the same time it dedicates a revenue source sufficient to pay the debt, thereby assuring payment without fear of change of circumstances, means or payment of the debt. Unfortunately, this principle has not been as clearly followed as Hamilton and Washington desired. The occurrence of defaults and the repudiation price of failing to pay debts timely by states and local governments are worthy of consideration by all market participants.

1. Panics, Recessions and Depressions

The principle of assured payment of state and local government debt has been tested many times since 1793. Since that year, the United States has had 6 panics, 38 recessions and 4 depressions — the last depression being the Great Depression of the 1930, and the last recession the Great Recession of 2008. As will be discussed in further detail, despite occasional defaults due to inability to pay rather than an unwillingness to pay, the tradition of payment of the debt obligations of state and local government has been well established. Lessons learned from past default and repudiation and the consequences suffered were part of the motivation for following the principles espoused by Washington and Hamilton. During the 1850s and 1860s, a number of municipalities failed to pay debt obligations, including San Francisco, Philadelphia, Detroit and Chicago. One of the causes of such defaults was the excessive cost of municipal financing. Another reason was speculation by municipalities in real estate and non-essential services.[28]

---

27 *See* THE PAPERS OF ALEXANDER HAMILTON (Columbia University Press ed. 1979).

28 James E. Spiotto, *Municipal Bonds: Defaults and Remedies,* RESOURCES AND REVIEW (GFOA Mar. 1983).

2. Selected Defaults (1839-1848)

Between 1839 and 1969, there were 6,195 recorded defaults of municipal issues. The first recorded default was the city of Mobile, Alabama in 1839. The Mobile default was a default on the city's issuance of $513,000. The commentators were quite apologetic for the city, citing two major fires in 1839, the Panic of 1837 and the resulting Yellow Fever epidemic as some of the leading causes for default. As with most tragic situations, the first default was more easily forgiven. When Mobile defaulted again in 1870 because of speculation in financing to support railroads, there was less sympathy. The railroad aid financing was understandable given the need for railroad connections to remain important in commerce and to increase business activity. Unfortunately, some railroads failed or chose a different route, thereby reducing or eliminating any benefit to the financing. The city had used public financing beyond its ability to pay, and commentators pronounced that the cause of non-payment was an inability to pay. Mobile ultimately had its city charter repealed in 1879 and was placed in a receivership. The railroad aid bonds and other indebtedness of the city had risen to over $4.36 million, one fifth of the entire taxable property of the city, and beyond the state constitution's limit to tax in order to pay current obligations. Between 1875 and 1878, the city attempted to refund and refinance certain of its debt obligations and was able to obtain concessions from some bondholders. By 1878, all but $570,000 had been compromised. Default on this amount continued and led to the 1879 revocation of the city charter and to receivership. These actions were condemned by the then New York City-based *ad hoc* bondholder group, which eventually accepted a compromise in 1880.[29] In 1879, by another act, a new city of Mobile was formed, incorporating the territory of the Port of Mobile as the new government. Accordingly, default and repudiation led to shortening the future of the local government, the revocation of its charter and the alternate resolution by agreement with the bondholders as restructured debt payment.[30]

Between 1841 and 1843, eight states and one territory (now a state) repudiated their debt, and seven states between 1843 and 1848 resumed payment. While some attribute the repudiation to the aftermath of the Panic of 1837, the real reason, with respect to the northern states, was that those states borrowed money to pay for needed transportation improvements beyond their current ability to pay, motivated by the success of the Erie Canal; with respect to the southern states, those states needed banking services to provide liquidity to a commodity economy based upon agriculture rather than on manufacturing and commerce. By 1844, nineteen states and two territories had borrowed money for needed economic growth. The inflationary boom of 1834-39 with the accompanying Panic of 1837 came to an end by 1841, and there was a tightening of credit that put pressure on incomplete construction projects for transportation improvements in the North (Pennsylvania, Maryland, Indiana, Illinois and

---

29 Hillhouse, *supra* n. 8, at 51-52. Most of the bonds bore a coupon of 8 percent, significantly higher than the then current market of 4.6 percent. *See also* following discussion of railroad aid bond defaults and U.S. Supreme Court decision *infra*.

30 Like Mobile, the cities of Pensacola, Fayetteville and Memphis committed "municipal suicide" by dissolution of the municipality in order to evade their debts (Hillhouse, *supra* n. 8, at 167).

Michigan) and lack of credit for banks in the South (Arkansas, Louisiana, Mississippi and the Florida Territory). All but the Florida Territory and Mississippi resumed payment by 1848. The reason for resuming payment and denouncing repudiation or default on the debt was the cost of default, specifically denial of access or increase in cost of borrowing. Those that repudiated but resumed payment experienced borrowing yields to complete the projects of 32 percent until they resumed payment on defaulted debt and then paid 4 percent above market to borrow. Mississippi and the Florida Territory lacked access to the public market for almost two decades given their continuing repudiation.[31]

3. The Cost of Default

From the earliest times of state and local government financing, the price of default appeared to be certain doom, dissolving the municipal government, as with Mobile, Alabama, and leading to the impossibility of borrowing more, a default resulting from increased borrowing costs or denial of access to the market. This was demonstrated by those states in the 1840s that defaulted and suffered high interest rates (32 percent + yield) on their borrowing until they cured the default and resumed payment. Those states continued to incur increased borrowing costs with an increased interest rate (4 percent or more above market rates) after resuming payment on repudiated debt. Those who never cured default were denied access to the market for decades (while financial memories lasted).

4. The Lessons Learned as to the Price of Default Continued after the Civil War

The Repayment Battle of Civil War Debt. In 1860, before the start of the Civil War, public debt was about $65 million and after the Civil War it was about $2.7 billion (after deducting cash in the Treasury). Public debt after the Civil War was 41 times larger than at the start of the war. The per capita cost of public debt rose from $2.06 in 1860 to $75.01 in 1865.[32] The debt incurred in the North during the Civil War created a battle over whether to repay the debt in gold or in greenbacks. The United States had gone off the gold standard, and greenbacks were a devalued currency. It clearly was more favorable to pay the cheap (discounted) value of greenbacks as opposed to the full value of gold, which raised the question of whether the easier means of discounted payment would threaten the financial credibility that Washington and Hamilton has worked so hard to establish. Democrats favored paying in greenbacks. Republicans favored paying in gold. In March 1869, President Grant, a Republican, took office and, in his inauguration speech, following the spirit of Washington and Hamilton, said, "[t]o protect the national honor every dollar of government indebtedness should be paid in gold."[33] No

---

31 English, *supra* n. 24; Wallis, *supra* n. 3; Sturzenegger, *supra* n. 3.

32 In May 2014, $75.01 in 1865 equaled $14,000.00 in May 2014 using nominal GDP per capita. *See* Samuel H. Williamson, SEVEN WAYS TO COMPUTE THE RELATIVE VALUE OF A U.S. DOLLAR AMOUNT — *1774 TO PRESENT* (MeasuringWorth 2016), https://www.measuringworth.com/uscompare/.

33 Noll, *supra* n. 2, at 20.

shortcuts, no gimmicks, but rather there was to be full payment with full value to continue the financial credibility of state and local governments.

However, eight southern states (Alabama, Arkansas, Florida, Georgia, Louisiana, Mississippi, North Carolina and South Carolina) after the Civil War repudiated their outstanding indebtedness and have never rescinded that repudiation. The reasons vary but generally are attributable to debt involuntarily incurred during the "carpetbag" governments. The southern states believed these debts were not legitimately incurred by the states for the benefit of the people due to the profiteering of the transition government staffed with northern appointees. In addition, the Fourteenth Amendment was enacted in 1868 in part to assure payment of public debt of the United States and its states but not the debt in aid of an insurrection which was declared illegal and void.[34]

The Fourteenth Amendment, Section 4 of the United States Constitution provided:

> The validity of the public debt of the United States, authorized by law, including debts incurred for payment of pensions and bounties for services in suppressing insurrection or rebellion, shall not be questioned. But neither the United States nor any State shall assume or pay any debt or obligation incurred in aid of insurrection or rebellion against the United States, or any claim for the loss or emancipation of any slave; but all such debts, obligations and claims shall be held illegal and void.

The Civil War debt of the Confederate government was approximately $1.4 billion and the Confederate states had individual Civil War debt of about $67 million.[35]

5. Railroad Aid Bonds and the U.S. Supreme Court's Support of Payment

Some of the best examples of the mandate for payment of state and local government debt were the railroad aid bonds issued by state and local governments to attract railroads to their communities. There is no doubt canals, roads and railroads during the first half of the 1800s contributed to the economic progress of many cities and states and aided the industrialization of those areas. For that reason, there was almost a universal desire of all sections of the United States, in virtually every community, to gain the advantage and benefits of their own railroad station. Local subsidies of land and donations were funded by public debt financing.[36] Unfortunately, not every railroad was successful and many municipalities found the railroad they helped support never came to their

34 U.S. Const. amend. XIV, § 4.

35 Noll, *supra* n. 2, at 11 (citing John C. Schwab, THE CONFEDERATE STATES OF AMERICA, 1861-1865, 76 (New York: Charles Scribner's Sons 1901)).

36 Frederick A. Cleveland and Fred W. Powell, RAILROAD FINANCE 31 (Appleton 1942).

community or the railroad was a failure.[37] By 1870, various states took actions to prohibit or restrict municipal investments in railroad bonds, such as the 1870 Illinois Constitution Amendment prohibiting municipal aid to railroads.[38] Also, in reaction, a number of municipalities sought to disavow or repudiate the municipal aid debt for railroads, especially where the railroad did not come or the investment was a bust. Bondholders took these repudiating municipalities to court.

Railroad Cases. While a number of lower and supreme courts of the states initially affirmed the bondholders' right to payment, as public opinion turned against payment by the municipalities, state court decisions changed to permit the repudiation of the bonds as unauthorized obligations. That resulted in appeals to the U.S. Supreme Court and initiation of cases in federal court. The U.S. Supreme Court ruled in over 300 cases between 1860 and 1896 that efforts by state and local governments to repudiate and invalidate bonds issued to subsidize railroad facilities violated the U.S. Constitution and thus the rights of bond investors. The Supreme Court took a consistent and clear stance, upholding the validity of the bonds and sometimes overruling state supreme courts.[39] These experiences of the 1800s resulted in use of state statutory and constitutional provisions to assure payment and legal safeguard for bondholders.

The Consequences of the 1860-1870 Defaults. As a reaction to these defaults, "moral obligation" bonds evolved into more definitive legal protections to assure payment by legislation, recognizing the validity of the debt and giving bondholders rights and protections to discourage any repudiation or default on public debt.

Safeguards to Protect Bondholders. As a further reaction to the events described above, in the late 1800s and early part of the 1900s, states enacted legislation to provide statutory authorization for the issuance of bonds, give bondholders even greater rights and protection and prevent unnecessary defaults on municipal obligations. The municipal bond market in effect mandated necessary changes in the documentation, legal authorization and structure of municipal financing, which included:

- debt limitations on municipal issuers to prevent excessive borrowing;
- clearly defined bondholder rights in the event of default supported by statutory and case law;
- use of bond counsel to determine the legality of the bond issue before the sale to avoid technical legal defects that could allow an issuer to repudiate the debt;

---

37 Hillhouse, *supra* n. 8, at 143-155.

38 ILLINOIS CONSTITUTION 1870, Separate Section 2; 2 DEBATES AND PROCEEDINGS OF THE CONSTITUTIONAL CONVENTION OF THE STATE OF ILLINOIS, 1869-70, at 1894-95 (Springfield 1870).

39 *Gelpcke v. Dubuque*, 68 U.S. 175 (1863); *Havemeyer v. Iowa County*, 70 U.S. 294 (1865).

- development of credit rating agencies as well as thorough credit review by investment firms and many institutional investors;
- statutory restrictions against municipal issuers borrowing for chronic deficiencies; and
- the use of indenture trustees, paying agents and others who have certain duties in order to protect the rights and interests of bondholders.

Default Rate for State and Local Government Debt Has Been Relatively Low Especially When Compared to Corporate Debt Default. Any discussion of the history of payment of state and local government debt would not be complete without review of the low default rate and documented credit performance by timely payment of these public debt obligations. Historically, while political risk of nonpayment was a possibility, it was a rare occurrence (*i.e.*, eight states and one territory repudiated their debt between 1841 to 1843, with seven of the nine resuming payment by 1849; repudiation of Civil War-related debt by eight states in the late 1860s; railroad bond and real estate defaults of the 1870s to 1890s; Washington Public Power Supply System, 1983; Jefferson County, Alabama bankruptcy in 2011; and Detroit in 2013). There are current situations that may test the long-term viability of this historical premise. However, so far the bankruptcies of Detroit, Stockton, California, San Bernardino, California and Jefferson County, Alabama are viewed as aberrations rather than being indicative of a growing trend.

G. Default Rate of State and Local Debt

1. Historic Default Rates

Historically, there is a low default rate for bonds issued by municipalities and states. The late Dr. John Petersen of George Mason University noted in his paper on "Municipal Defaults: Eighty Years Made a Big Difference"[40] that, between the 1970s and the 2000s, the municipal default rate for municipalities averaged per decade .10 percent to .24 percent (adjusted for Washington Public Power Supply System and Jefferson County, Alabama), not including the fact that over 80 percent of the defaults were for conduit financing and not for essential public financings. This is a far cry from the corporate bond default rate on average for investment grade and non-investment grade of approximately 10 percent.[41]

Since the late 1800s, states have not defaulted on general obligation bonds, with the exception of Arkansas in 1933, which debt was thereafter refinanced.[42] The default by Arkansas was due not to

40 John E. Petersen, *Municipal Defaults: Eighty Years Makes a Difference*, 33-34 MUNICIPAL FINANCE JOURNAL, Winter/Spring Parts 1 and 2 (2013) ("Petersen").

41 *Id.* at 38. *See* n. 45 for corporate bond default rate studies of 4.5 percent for 1920-2007 and default rate for corporate high yield bonds of 9.8 percent in 2001.

42 Mysak, *supra* n. 5 at 5.

overspending or excess borrowing, but because of a flood that occurred in 1927 and affected about a third of the municipalities in Arkansas. In order to protect the financial credit of its municipalities, Arkansas assumed $53 million of municipal liabilities to prevent a possible default. The economic collapse of the Great Depression in the early 1930s made this burden unsustainable.[43]

Based on the historic default rate, there is little support for the willingness to pay as a real problem. Essential service debt financing has historically enjoyed a significantly lower default rate than health care, housing and conduit state and local governmental financing.[44] Unfunded pension obligations and deferred infrastructure costs are a more recent phenomenon. Prior to the 1960s, most pension obligations were treated as gratuities and a significant number of big-ticket infrastructure costs are only now starting to age, such as the interstate highway system, electric grid, wastewater treatment facilities, etc. The states and their local governments may be closer to a tipping point and departure from the historic assurances than they have ever been. The difference may be whether there will be adherence to the Washington-Hamilton principle of honoring obligations and providing a dedicated source for the payment of public debt. Between 1839 and 1969, there were fewer than 6,200 recorded municipal defaults for over 80,000 governmental bodies. For instance, from 1839 to 1969, the average default rate for state and local governments was .058 percent compared to the rated corporate bond default rate of about 4.5 percent for the period of 1920-2007.[45]

---

43 *City Financial Emergencies: The Intergovernmental Dimension*, ACIR, COMMISSION REPORT 11 (1973) ("ACIR"); George H. Hempel, *The Post-War Quality of State and Local Debt*, NATIONAL BUREAU OF ECONOMIC RESEARCH 18 (1971).

44 *See, e.g.*, Moody's Investors Service, *U.S. Municipal Bond Defaults and Recoveries, 1970-2014* at 11 (noting, for instance, that the one-year default rate for housing is .088 percent and for hospitals and health service providers is .090 percent, compared to .017 percent for cities).

45 *See Corporate Default and Recovery Rates 1920-2007*, MOODY'S GLOBAL CORPORATE FINANCE (Feb. 2008).

2. Recorded Defaults (1839-1969)

Recorded Defaults, by Type of Local Government Unit
1839-1969

	1839-49	1850-59	1860-69	1870-79	1880-89	1890-99	1900-09	1910-19	1920-29	1930-39	1940-49	1950-59	1960-69	Total Defaults	Number of Local Governments in 1967[a]	% of Annual Default Rate over 130 Yrs.[b]
By type of Units																
Counties and parishes		7	15	57	30	94	43	7	15	417	6	12	24	727	3,049	.183%
Incorp. munics.	4	4	13	50	30	93	51	17	39	1,434	31	31	114	1911	18,048	.081%
Unincorp. munics.		4	9	46	31	50	33	5	10	88	7	4	26	313	17,105	.014%
School districts				4	5	0	11		14	1241	5	23	60	1,272	21,782	.048%
Other districts	—	—	—	2	1	12	11	7	107	1,590	30	42	70	1,872	21,264	.067%
Totals	4	15	37	159	97	258	149	36	185	4,770	79	112	294	6,195	81,248	.058%

a The number of local government units has changed rapidly. For example in 1932 there were 127,108 school districts, 8,580 other districts and 175,369 state and local government units.

b The percent of annual defaults in total defaults by type divided by number of governments divided by 130 (years).

Sources: Default information in THE DAILY BOND BUYER, THE COMMERCIAL AND FINANCIAL CHRONICLE and THE INVESTMENT BANKERS' ASSOCIATIONS BULLETIN; default lists from Federal Deposit Insurance Corporation, Life Insurance Commission and U.S. courts; and Albert M. Hillhouse, DEFAULTED MUNICIPAL BONDS (Chicago: Municipal Financial Officers Association 1935). Number of local government units from: U.S. Department of Commerce, Bureau of Census. *Governmental Organization*, I Census of Governments, 1967 (Gov't Printing Office 1969) and Advisory Commission on Intergovernmental Relations, *Report on Bankruptcy, Defaults and Other Local Government Financial Emergencies U.S. Government* (U.S. Government 1973).

3. Rated Bond Default Rate (Corporation vs. Municipal)

Historical rating agencies' default studies support the credit strength and low default rate for rated municipal bonds compared to corporations. For investment grade rated credits, the default rate for municipal credits ranges from 1/50 to 1/100 of the corporate rate.

Rated Municipal vs. Corporate Default Rates by Ratings Service

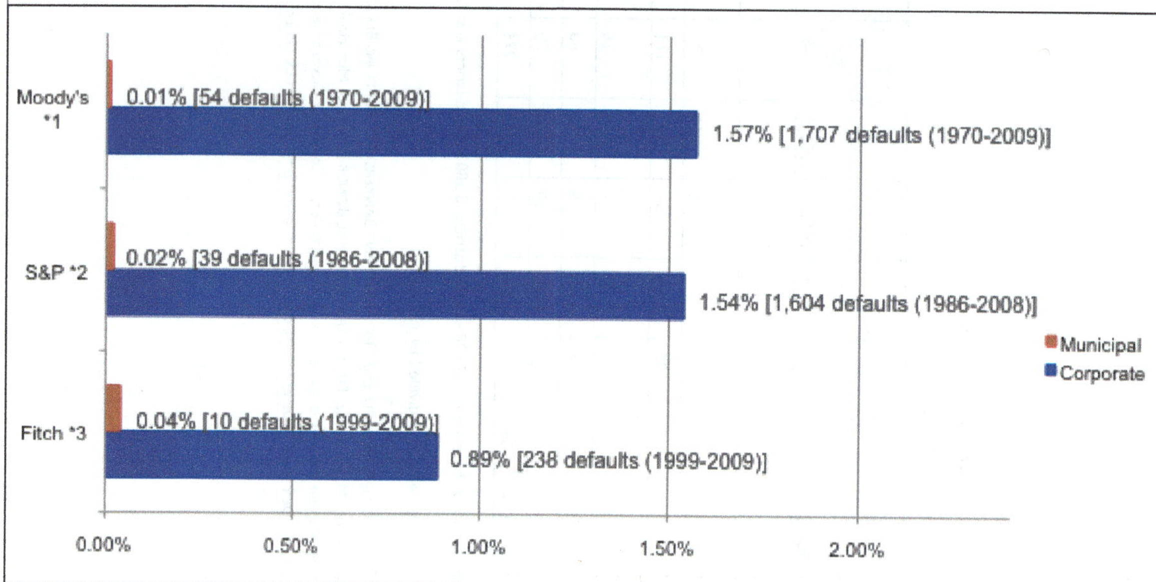

1 Moody's Investors Services, U.S. MUNICIPAL BOND DEFAULTS AND RECOVERIES, 1970-2009 (Feb. 2010); Moody's Investors Services, CORPORATE DEFAULT AND RECOVERY RATES, 1920-2009 (Feb. 2010). Percentages based on average one-year default rate.

2 Standard & Poor's, 2009 GLOBAL CORPORATE DEFAULT STUDY AND RATINGS TRANSITIONS (Mar. 17, 2010); Standard & Poor's, U.S. MUNICIPAL RATINGS TRANSITIONS AND DEFAULTS, 1986-2009 (Mar. 11, 2009). Percentages based on average default rate.

3 Fitch Ratings Inc., U.S. PUBLIC FINANCE TRANSITION AND DEFAULT STUDY (1999-2009) (Mar. 25, 2010; Fitch Ratings, Inc., GLOBAL CORPORATE FINANCE 2009 TRANSITION AND DEFAULT STUDY.

Recent rating agency default studies have continued to confirm the low default rate for municipal bonds. For example, in Moody's *U.S. Municipal Defaults and Recovery 1970-2014*, the municipal bond defaults for rated bonds remain extremely low, namely 1.3 defaults per year on average in the 1970-2007 period (0.01 percent) and 5 defaults per year in the 2008-2014 period (0 in 2014, 7 in 2013 and 5 in 2012, with an average of 5 defaults) or 0.03 percent. The Moody's report also notes that the ultimate recovery rate remains higher than corporate defaults with at least 64 percent recovery for the 1970-2014 period for municipal rated bonds versus 53 percent recovery for corporate senior unsecured rated bonds. The recovery rate ranges vary by case, including Jefferson County, Alabama, with at least 80 percent of principal and interest for sewer warrants and 100 percent of principal for G.O. warrants, Vallejo, California, Sierra Kings Healthcare District, California (health care G.O.). Detroit (water and sewer) had a 100 percent recovery for special revenue debt. The Detroit Unlimited Tax General Obligation had a 100 percent recovery for bondholders (74 percent from Detroit and 26 percent from settlement with bond insurers).

4. Defaults by Type of Financing

Moody's concentration by sector of municipal defaults from 1970-2014 demonstrates cities, counties, most traditional governmental services and general obligations are a low percent of defaults, the exceptions being financing for housing and health care:

Defaults by Sector, 1970-2014

Purpose	Number of Defaults	Percentage	One-Year Default Rate
Housing	44	46.3%	0.088%
Hospitals & Health Service Providers	23	24.2%	0.090%
Infrastructure	9	9.5%	0.010%
Fducation	4	4.2%	0.010%
Cities	4	4.2%	0.017%
Counties	3	3.2%	0.025%
Special Districts	0	0.0%	0.000%
State Governments	0	0.0%	0.000%
Pool Financings	0	0.0%	0.000%
Other	0	0.0%	0.000%
Non General Obligation	87	91.6%	0.034%
General Obligation	8	8.4%	0.002%
Total	**95**	**100%**	**0.015%**

Source: Moody's

The median rating one year before default for all municipal issuers is Ba3, while the modal rating one-year before default is B3. Moreover, 90% of all defaulted issuers were rated speculative-grade one year before default (Exhibit 10). The median (as well as the modal) rating for defaulted issuers five years before default was Baa3, one notch above speculative-grade.

5. Recent Default Statistics

Recently, monetary defaults on state and local government public debt ranged from 108 issuers for $1.95 billion in default in 2012 to 68 issuers for $8.57 billion in default in 2013 to 58 issuers for

$9.02 billion in default in 2014.[46] While there was a decline in the number of issuers in default over this two-year period by almost 50 percent, there was, however, the rise in dollar value of defaults in 2013 and 2014. This was due to Detroit's filing of its bankruptcy petition and a large energy company bankruptcy. For example, $5.4 billion of the $9.02 billion in default in 2014 were the Detroit water and sewer bonds that were listed in default due to the Detroit bankruptcy filing even though principal and interest were paid timely and ultimately unimpaired in the plan of debt adjustment. In addition, TXU, a subsidiary of Energy Future Holdings Company, declared bankruptcy in April 2014, which filing caused the default on $1.16 billion of industrial development bonds.

H. Conclusion

A review of historical background on sovereign debt repudiation and defaults, as well as the common theories as to why sovereign debt should be paid, is helpful to understanding the general causes of municipal default, as well as why various forms of government have and may in the future default on their debt. The remainder of this book focuses on the causes of municipal defaults, as well as those actions that have been taken by states and their local governments, as well as the U.S. Congress, to address financially challenged municipalities.

46 Robert Slavin, *Default Reached Record in 2014*, THE BOND BUYER (Jan. 13, 2015), http://www.bondbuyer.com/news/markets-buy side/defaults-reached-record-in-2014-1069491-1.html; Romy Varghese, *Municipal Defaulters Decline Amid Improving Economy: Muni Credit*, BLOOMBERG (Dec. 30, 2014, 7:00 PM; updated Dec. 31, 2014 9:30 AM), http://www.bloomberg.com/news/articles/2014-12-31/municipal-defaulters-decline-amid-improving-economy-muni-credit; Joe Mysak, *The Muni-Meltdown That Wasn't*, BLOOMBERG BRIEFS (Nov. 2014), http://www.bloombergbriefs.com/content/uploads/sites/2/2014/11/ MuniMeltdown_112514_ finaldoc.pdf.

III. Causes of Defaults

The United States contains the most extensive and sophisticated public works system in the world, comprised of 4,092,730 miles of roadways, 607,708 bridges, 1,100 local bus systems, 19,453 airports (of which 5,155 are for public use), 25,320 miles of inland and intercoastal waterways, at least 87,000 dams, more than 2 million miles of pipe in water supply systems and over 15,000 wastewater treatment plants provided mostly by municipalities and political subdivisions of a state.[47] Not only our local but also our national welfare and economic growth depend upon the efficient operation of municipal facilities, the majority of which are financed by bonds purchased by the municipal bond market.

In fact, our ability to supply jobs and encourage business growth in metropolitan areas will require the construction of new public work systems and the continued maintenance and operation of our present infrastructure. Significant increases in infrastructure spending at both the federal and local levels are not only necessary, but inevitable.[48] The demand for the municipal bond market to finance infrastructure improvements over the next 20 years will increase. According to the American Society of Civil Engineers, by 2020 it is estimated that $3.6 trillion in debt financing will be needed to bring our infrastructure to acceptable levels.[49] Research on the economic impact of public investment in infrastructure improvement has revealed that, in general, for every dollar of hard-cost infrastructure improvement, $3.21 of economic activity is generated over the course of 20 years.[50] In addition, for every new job created due to infrastructure improvement or economic development, there is a job

---

47 *Table 1-1: System Mileage Within the United States (Statute miles)*, http://www.rita.dot.gov/bts/sites/rita.dot.gov.bts/files/publications/national_transportation_statistics/html/table_01_01.html (last visited Feb. 9, 2016); *National Inventory of Dams*, U.S. ARMY CORPS OF ENGINEERS, http://www.agc.army.mil/Portals/75/docs/pdf/NIDentire.pdf (last visited Feb. 10, 2016); *2006 Community Water System Survey Report*, U.S. ENVIRONMENTAL PROTECTION AGENCY, http://nepis.epa.gov/Exe/ZyPDF.cgi?Dockey=P1009JJI.txt (last visited Feb. 9, 2016).

48 During economic downturns, the increased issuance of state and local bonds is followed by increases in employment and GDP growth. For charts presenting this correlation, *see* James E. Spiotto, *Historical and Legal Strength of State and Local Government Debt Financing* 8-9, CHAPMAN AND CUTLER LLP (Feb. 2011), http://www.ncsl.org/documents/fiscal/glm11spiotto.pdf (last visited Feb. 10, 2016).

49 *2013 Report Card for American's Infrastructure*, AMERICAN SOCIETY OF CIVIL ENGINEERS, http://www.infrastructurereportcard.org.

50 Isabelle Cohen, Thomas Freiling and Eric Robinson, *The Economic Impact and Financing of Infrastructure Spending*, THE COLLEGE OF WILLIAM AND MARY, THOMAS JEFFERSON PROGRAM IN PUBLIC POLICY 2 (2012), https://www.wm.edu/as/publicpolicy/documents/prs/aed.pdf. If the federal, state and local governments spent $3.6 trillion on the need for infrastructure improvements between 2015-2020 this would result in an economic impact of over $11.5 trillion to the U.S. economy over 20 years, or an increase of about 64 percent of the 2015 GDP of $17.947 trillion.

multiplier for direct, indirect and induced benefits that create additional economic value and additional jobs.[51]

Economic development and needed infrastructure expenses can aid state and local government in creating jobs and economic activities that in turn create additional tax revenues that can avoid defaults. The ability of state and local governments to borrow for such economic stimulus is essential to assist governments in avoiding financial distress. Obviously, access to the market will be enhanced by workable state laws with respect to municipalities and a workable federal statute governing municipal debt adjustment.

An understanding of applicable state and federal provisions is particularly important given a number of issues that have emerged in recent years with respect to municipal finance, including the ever-increasing underfunding of pension obligations that some states and municipalities are experiencing. If not addressed now, unfunded pension obligations will one day come to haunt both municipalities and the states in which they are located. Given the perceived increase in municipal bond defaults and the percentage of municipalities having budget deficits in recent years, it is increasingly apparent that effective and efficient debt resolution mechanisms are needed. Many state legislatures appear to understand this need and have responded with laws aimed at protecting both taxpayers and bondholders from the devastating effect a municipal default could have.

A. Analysis of Defaults of Local Government Debt in the United States of America

1. Historical Causes of Default

In order to properly structure and evaluate the creditworthiness of local government debt in the United States, it is helpful to review the underlying causes and nature of past defaults. While each default by a local governmental body (municipality) involves unique factors (particular economic,

---

51 Enrico Moretti, *Local Multipliers*, AMERICAN ECONOMIC REVIEW AND PROCEEDINGS 100 (May 2010), http://eml.berkeley.edu//~moretti/multipliers.pdf; Elizabeth Scott and Howard Wial, *Multiplying Jobs: How Manufacturing Contributes to Employment Growth in Chicago and the Nation*, UIC CENTER FOR URBAN ECONOMIC DEVELOPMENT COLLEGE OF URBAN PLANNING & PUBLIC AFFAIRS, MANUFACTURING CHICAGO'S FUTURE SERIES (May 2013), http://cuppa.uic.edu/data/CUED_Manufacturing_Jobs_May2013.pdf. This study notes the economic impact in increased employment by adding more manufacturing jobs — specifically the direct job, the indirect job in supplier industries and the induced job in local servicing industry, totaling the employment multiplier:

> For example, petroleum and coal products manufacturing has an employment multiplier of 8.3 in the Chicago region. This multiplier is composed of a direct effect of 1.0, an indirect effect of 4.7, and an induced effect of 2.6. This means that when one new job in petroleum and coal products is created in the region, 4.7 jobs are created in industries that produce intermediate inputs for petroleum and coal products manufacturing and 2.6 local-serving jobs are created. All of these together make up the multiplier:
>
> 1 "direct" petroleum and coal products job
> + 4.7 "indirect" jobs in supplier industries
> + 2.6 "induced" jobs in local-serving industries
> = 8.3 employment multiplier

industrial or tax revenue problems specific unique to the time and place), there are also notable overarching themes that can guide the future. The usual causes of defaults by municipalities in the United States are:

a. Economic Conditions

Defaults may be caused by economic conditions such as depressions, recessions and high interest rates. Such conditions may shake the most stable businesses and this will, in turn, threaten the tax base for a municipality. Historically, there is a direct link between economic depression in the United States and municipal default. Examples abound. The depression of 1837 led to the default of the city of Mobile in 1839, which was the first recorded municipal default in the United States. The depression of 1857 led to problems in, among other places, the cities of Chicago and Philadelphia. The panic and depression of 1893 brought with it a large number of municipal defaults. Of course, the Great Depression of the 1930s led to the highest municipal default statistics ever recorded in the United States. As noted, since 1949 there have been eleven economic downturns in the United States, the most significant occurring in 2008. As discussed in section II of this book, so far states and local governments not only have survived but, for the most part, have successfully navigated the downturns and have grown their economies, enhanced their infrastructure and improved the services they provide their citizens through 6 economic panics, 38 recessions and 4 depressions since 1793.

b. Non-Essential Services

In the municipal arena, financings developed to pay for services for which there is no long-term need or demand are often the subject of future defaults. Such problems are not exclusively the product of recent times. Railroad stations constructed throughout the southern part of the United States during the 1800s, where railroads were never built, were funded by municipal bonds. Real estate ventures in California in the mid 1800s were ahead of their time and led to a troubled financial situation. It is not difficult to find other recent examples of "bad ideas," such as large housing developments not supported by population or demand and refuse-burning facilities that do not work. These non-essential services are directly related to lack of or insufficient feasibility studies.

c. Feasibility of Projects and Industries

As one nameless person has remarked, "I never saw a feasibility study that showed the project would not make it." However, there are some industries, businesses and structures of financing that are simply not feasible. When financing is based on a flawed concept, disaster is inevitable. Moreover, there is a life cycle to products and businesses, and the life cycle of some of these is very short indeed. Ranger, Texas grew from an oil discovery in the early part of the 1900s and blossomed to a population of over 16,000. Ten years later, Ranger became a town of a few thousand when the oil ran out. The large infrastructure funded by municipal financing had to be paid off over decades by a population of less than 1/8 the town's previous size.

Feasibility problems do not always stem from a "crazy idea." Sometimes, for example, the developers of the financing simply misread the future. In the Washington Public Power Supply System ("WPPSS") situation, the elasticity of demand for power was not anticipated. Demand unexpectedly dropped and the projects were unsuccessful. A failed incinerator facility financing led Harrisburg, Pennsylvania to financial difficulties. Small special tax and levy districts have run into problems when they are superseded by larger utilities (sometimes private or investor-owned) or become obsolete. That is why over 60 percent of Chapter 9 filings since 1937 have been municipal utilities or special tax districts. Sometimes the feasibility of projects and governments is affected by actions of others, including other government agencies. Fort Lee, New Jersey was a borough of 8,759 people in 1930. The Port Authority of New York decided in 1928 to commence construction of the now famous George Washington Bridge across the Hudson. Many thought this development would make Fort Lee the next Brooklyn. In the late 1920s, Fort Lee borrowed $3 million to finance street and sidewalk paving and the installation of utilities in anticipation of a housing development, all to be paid off by levying improvement assessments against the new property owners. However, the building of the new bridge that was to bring with it an increased population and economic activity had a different effect. First, to build the bridge some of the highest tax-yielding property was taken. Second, the New Jersey Highway Authority condensed and purchased an even larger portion of high tax-yielding land for entrances, exits and service roads. Third, valuable land at the top of the Palisades was removed from the tax rolls after being purchased for park land by the Palisade Interstate Park Commission. Collectively, these actions eliminated more than 40 percent of the assessed valuation. Fort Lee was unable to meet its debt obligation due to this loss of a significant percentage of tax revenues and the economic downturn of the Great Depression. During the 1930s, under the New Jersey Finance Commission, Fort Lee attempted, but was unable, to reach a restructuring agreement with its creditors. Fort Lee ultimately had to file for protection under Chapter IX in 1939 and confirm a plan of adjustment.[52]

d. Fraud

When greed exceeds fear, the parties involved in the transaction may fail to comply with the terms of the relevant documents and, in essence, convert funds and benefits to the detriment of creditors. This has been rare in local government financing, but it does occur. Examples include the "baby bonds" issued by the Treasurer of Louisiana in the 1880s, $420,000 of which were double-issued for his benefit. A more recent example involves swaps entered into by Jefferson County, Alabama, which led to the imprisonment of certain individuals involved in that transaction.[53]

52 Advisory Commission on Intergovernmental Relations, *City Financial Emergencies: The Intergovernmental Dimension* 22-23 (July 1973), http://www.library.unt.edu/gpo/acir/Reports/policy/a-42.pdf.

53 *Federal Judge Sentences Investment Banker Bill Blount and Lobbyist Al LaPierre for Bribing Former Birmingham Mayor While He was Jefferson County Commission President*, FEDERAL BUREAU OF INVESTIGATION, BIRMINGHAM DIVISION (Feb. 26, 2010), https://www.fbi.gov/birmingham/press-releases/2010/bh022610.htm.

So far examples of fraud are an aberration and the municipal market has the tradition and reputation of being one of the safest and most trustworthy financial markets, and it is to the benefit of all to continue in that vein.[54]

e. Mismanagement

A municipal operation cannot succeed without proper management. Management's ability to react to the constant changes of economic cycles can make or break a default situation. Part of Orange County, California's problem in 1994 was attributable to investment strategies and borrowings to fund derivative investment schemes that were too good to be believed. Similarly, many of the problems leading to Jefferson County, Alabama's 2011 municipal bankruptcy filing were the result of both fraud and the mismanagement of a massive sewer system project and the adoption of sophisticated swap agreements by the county, with which the county had very little experience.[55] The use of oversight, refinance and financial control authorities such as MAC for New York City in 1975, PICA for Philadelphia in 1991, Act 47 for various Pennsylvania municipalities including Pittsburgh, and the Financial Control Board in New York (including for Buffalo in 2003 and Nassau County in 2011) are examples of state-imposed processes that provide effective financial management in times of distress to help local governments re-establish best practices and create financial plans that are sustainable and affordable.[56]

f. Unwillingness to Pay

Defaults can be caused by an unwillingness to pay, which leads to repudiation. Following the Civil War, in the mid 1800s, at least eight states repudiated their indebtedness. This historical event clarified the difference between default and repudiation. Default occurs when a municipality lacks the ability to pay due to economic problems: sufficient revenues to pay are not received, given a general economic depression or recession occurs, or other outside reasons, judgments or claims that prevent payments occur. However, although repudiation may be affected by economic factors, repudiation is a decision not to pay when the government has the ability to pay or makes the false claim that a legal obligation is not valid. Repudiation has always been met with a strong negative response from the municipal bond market.

---

54 Aaron Kuriloff, *U.S. Municipal Bond Market on a Tear*, THE WALL STREET JOURNAL (Dec. 28, 2014), http://www.wsj.com/articles/u-s-muni-bond-market-is-on-a-tear-1419802340; *General Safety of Municipal Bonds*, BNY MELLON WEALTH MANAGEMENT (June 13, 2013), http://www.bnymellonwealthmanagement.com/our-views/perspectives/safety-muni-bonds.html; Jason Appelson, Eric Parson and Andrew Haughwort, *The Untold Story of Municipal Bond Defaults*, LIBERTY STREET ECONOMICS (Aug. 15, 2012), http://libertystreeteconomics.newyorkfed.org/2012/08/the-untold-story-of-municipal-bond-defaults.html#.VrJeLHjnIT4.

55 For a detailed discussion of the problems leading up to Jefferson County, Alabama's municipal bankruptcy filing, *see generally In re Jefferson Cnty., Ala.*, 474 B.R. 228, 236-41 (Bankr. N.D. Ala. 2012).

56 See discussion in section V.

After the eight southern states repudiated their indebtedness after the Civil War,[57] there was a general recognition of the importance of willingness to pay. As previously discussed, the market eventually demanded numerous protections, including rating agencies, clear disclosure of bondholder remedies, statutory and constitutional provisions with respect to the obligation of municipalities to pay their debts, and the use of bond counsel as an independent professional examining the legal issues. Yet, over a hundred years later, WPPSS and Orange County, California chose not to pay in part due to a breakdown of these necessary protections.

g. Natural and Man-Made Disasters

Natural disasters can ravage a local government by causing an increase in cost and expense to repair damages that deplete revenues. For example, Galveston, Texas was hit by a hurricane in 1900 that was so devastating that default on the city's bonds was inevitable. Likewise, the attacks of September 11, 2001 on New York City and, additionally, a major hurricane in 2013 stressed that city's financings, but state and federal aid and American willpower have prevented serious consequences to New York City's operations and obligations.

h. The Evolution of New Causes for Default

State and local governments have recently experienced ever-increasing concerns about the costs of labor, including underfunded pensions,[58] and aging infrastructure that may present new challenges and a need for financial attention. The recent defaults and Chapter 9 filings involving local governments and the financial challenges states are facing in balancing their budgets have pointed to the evolution of new causes of default if these current issues are not promptly and adequately addressed. The new causes of default are:

1. Unaffordable and unsustainable personnel costs.

2. Deferred costs of capital improvements and infrastructure costs.

3. The decline of urban areas and resulting loss of tax revenues.

4. Proposition Thirteen mentality — the popularity of tax caps and limitations that restrict access to needed revenues in time of financial distress.

5. Off-balance-sheet liabilities — unforeseen judgments and derivatives, including interest rate swaps, which are problems that become too large to manage with current revenues.

---

57 *See* section II at 21.

58 *See* James E. Spiotto, *How Municipalities in Financial Distress Should Deal with Underfunded Pension Obligations and Appropriate Funding of Essential Services,* 50 WILLAMETTE L. REV. 515 (2014), http://www.chapmanstrategicadvisors.com/media/publication/13_Chapman_Municipalities_in_Distress_and_Unfunded_Pension_Obligations_WLR_CSA_2014.pdf.

These evolving causes of default can be seen as major factors in recent Chapter 9 filings that should be dealt with to assure continued ability to meet all financial obligations.

1. The problem of unaffordable and unsustainable personnel costs as evidenced by the Chapter 9 filings of Vallejo (2008) and San Bernardino, California (2012) and Detroit, Michigan (2013).

2. The harmful results of deferred costs of capital improvements and infrastructure costs as demonstrated by Detroit and Central Falls, Rhode Island (2011).

3. A decline of urban areas and resulting loss of tax revenues required for funding necessary services and infrastructure as noted in the Detroit and Central Falls cases.

4. The restriction of Proposition Thirteen mentality and the adverse effect of the popularity of tax caps and limitations as demonstrated in the limited tax revenue vehicles in Stockton (2012) and San Bernardino, California (2012).

5. Lingering legal issues and unexpected court decisions such as adverse developer litigation judgments and the resulting bankruptcy of the town of Mammoth Lakes (2012), Boise County, Idaho (2011) and Hillview, Kentucky (2015), where all three cases were ultimately dismissed and a settlement was reached with the developers.

6. Off-balance-sheet liabilities. (Underfunded pension obligations — Stockton, San Bernardino, Detroit).[59]

7. An untraditional trend toward unwillingness to pay, which could create an increasing problem (Detroit, Jefferson County, Orange County, etc.).

While an inability to pay is unfortunate and disappointing to creditors, the result is normally refinancing at a lower rate or a voluntary restructuring, which is perceived as the best result for all. The stigma of default is somewhat rehabilitated by a refinancing or voluntary restructuring that assures that everything that can be paid will be paid. The "willingness to pay" issue is a different and unprecedented one, especially if there is a financial ability to pay but not the desire to undergo the discipline and sacrifice of making the payment. It is a far more difficult task to attempt to rehabilitate the financial credibility of a default triggered by an unwillingness to pay than by an inability to pay.

2. Frequency of Municipal Defaults in the USA

Since 1839, there have been less than 11,000 municipal (local government) defaults. Almost half of these occurred between 1929-1937, during the Great Depression. The number of defaults is quite

---

59 Significantly, it has been held that pension benefits can be altered or reduced in a Chapter 9 case. *See In re City of Detroit, Mich.*, 504 B.R. 97 (Bankr. E.D. Mich. 2013).

small given that there are currently over 89,000 local governments (municipal and state entities) in the United States of America.[60]

Between 1839 and 1969, there were 6,195 recorded municipal defaults. Defaults between 1839 and 1969 involved 727 counties and parishes, 1,911 incorporated municipalities, 313 unincorporated municipalities, 1,372 school districts and 1,872 special purpose districts. Between 1929 and 1937, there were 4,770 defaults by governmental bodies.[61]

During the 1930s, local governmental bodies defaulted on the payment of interest and principal on 17.7 percent of the principal amount of $15 billion of municipal bonds outstanding. In comparison, between 1945 and 1970, municipal bonds in the principal amount of $450 million went into default, which accounted for approximately 0.4 percent of the principal amount of bonds outstanding in 1970.

Defaults by Governmental Bodies
During the Period of 1929-1937

Type of Government Unit	Number in Default	Percentage of Total Number in Default	Indebtedness of Defaulting Unit (in millions)	Percentage of Debt in Default
Counties	417	13.7	$ 360	15.1
Incorporated Municipalities	1,434	8.3	1,760	19.9
Towns, Organized Townships	88	.4	10	2.9
School Districts	1,241	.9	160	7.8
Reclamation, Levee Irrigation and Drainage Districts	944	28.2		
Other Special Districts	644	12.4	400	25.0
Total	4,770	2.7	$2,690	17.7

Source: Advisory Commission on Intergovernmental Relations, *A Commission Report "City Financial Emergencies: The Intergovernmental Dimension"* (Washington, D.C. July 1973).

Historically, municipal debt has a default rate of .1 percent compared to the 4.5 to 9.8 percent default rate for corporate bonds.[62] Financing of traditional essential services for state and local

60 *See Lists & Structure of Governments*, UNITED STATES CENSUS BUREAU (May 14, 2015), www.census.gov/govs/go/index.html (placing number of local governments in 2012 at 90,107).

61 Advisory Commission on Intergovernmental Relations, *City Financial Emergencies: The Intergovernmental Dimension* 12 (July 1973), http://www.library.unt.edu/gpo/acir/Reports/policy/a-42.pdf.

62 According to Dr. Edward Altman in his study *Defaults and Returns in the High Yield Bond Market* (2002), the corporate debt default rate for high yield bonds in 2001 was 9.8 percent, or over $63 billion. *See also* the late Professor John E. Peterson's study, referenced in footnote 40, concluding that the municipal default rate from 1970-2009 averaged per decade 0.10 percent to 0.24 percent. Of those defaults, 80 percent were conduit financings not for essential public

government (as compared to health care and housing-related debt supported by state and local government) has resulted in less than 35 percent of municipal security defaults.[63] Thus, for debt associated with essential government purposes, the effective default rate is far less than the default rate of .1 percent cited by Moody's.[64] Additionally, municipalities' use of bankruptcy has been limited, for the most part, to small special tax districts.

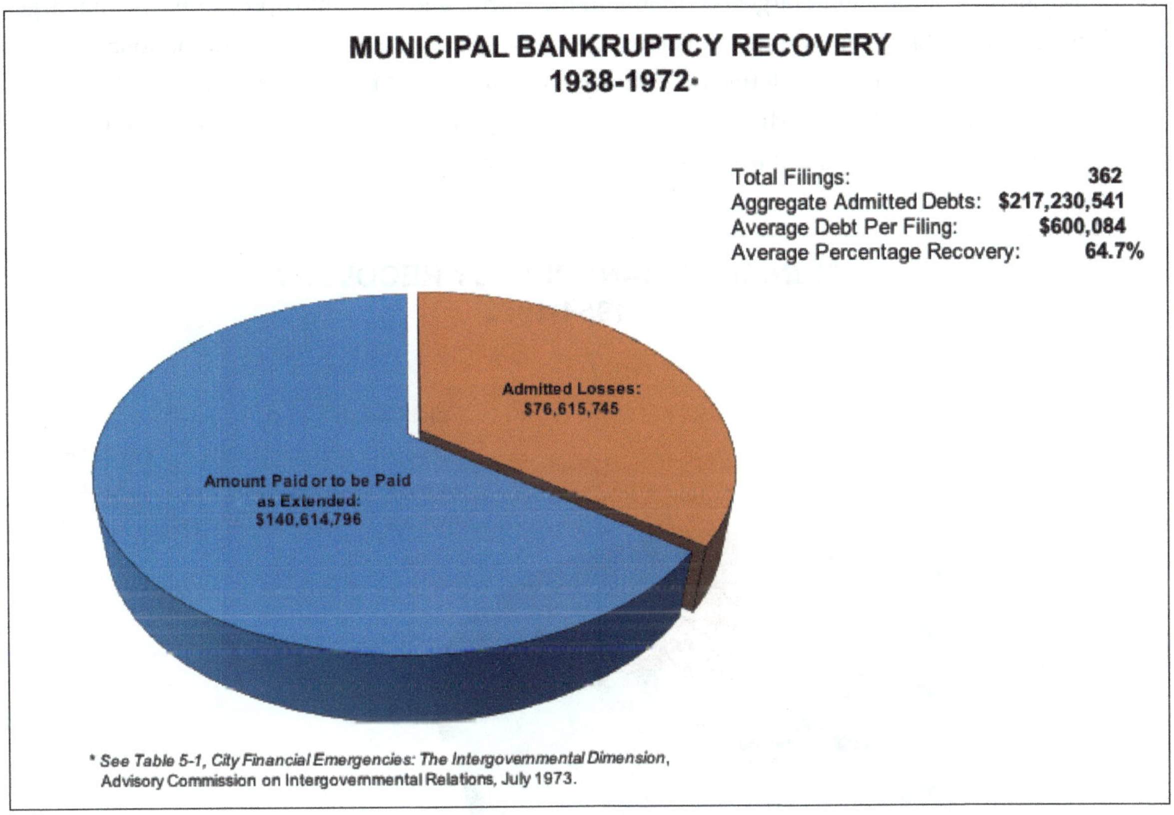

As previously mentioned, since 1937 when the Municipal Bankruptcy Act was passed, there have been at least 666 cases (as of July 31, 2016) filed involving municipal bodies. Between 1937 and 1972, there were 362 cases filed. These 362 cases involved admitted indebtedness of $217 million. In

---

services. This compares to a default rate of about 10 percent for high yield corporate bonds of about 10 percent (see footnote 41) and for investment grade and non-investment grade corporate bonds of 4.5 percent. *See* the previous discussion in section II on pages 25-30.

63 *U.S. Municipal Bond Defaults and Recoveries, 1970-2014,* MOODY'S INVESTORS SERVICE (July 24, 2015), http://www.naic.org/documents/committees_e_capad_investment_rbc_related_defaults.pdf.

64 *Id.*

these Chapter IX (Chapter 9's predecessor) cases, the amount paid on such debt exceeded $140 million, while the approximate loss was $77 million.[65]

Prior to the Detroit, Michigan filing in 2013 and the Jefferson County, Alabama filing in 2011, the largest and most significant Chapter 9 filing occurred in December 1994 when Orange County, California, the fifth largest county in the United States, filed a municipal bankruptcy petition. The State of California is itself the eighth largest economy in the world, and the bankruptcy of its second largest and one of its wealthiest communities caused shock waves in the domestic and international markets. Likewise, the recent filings by Jefferson County, Alabama (2011), Stockton and San Bernardino, California (2012) and Detroit, Michigan (2013) for Chapter 9 protection has stimulated a recent reexamination of the safety, credit basis and support for local government debt.

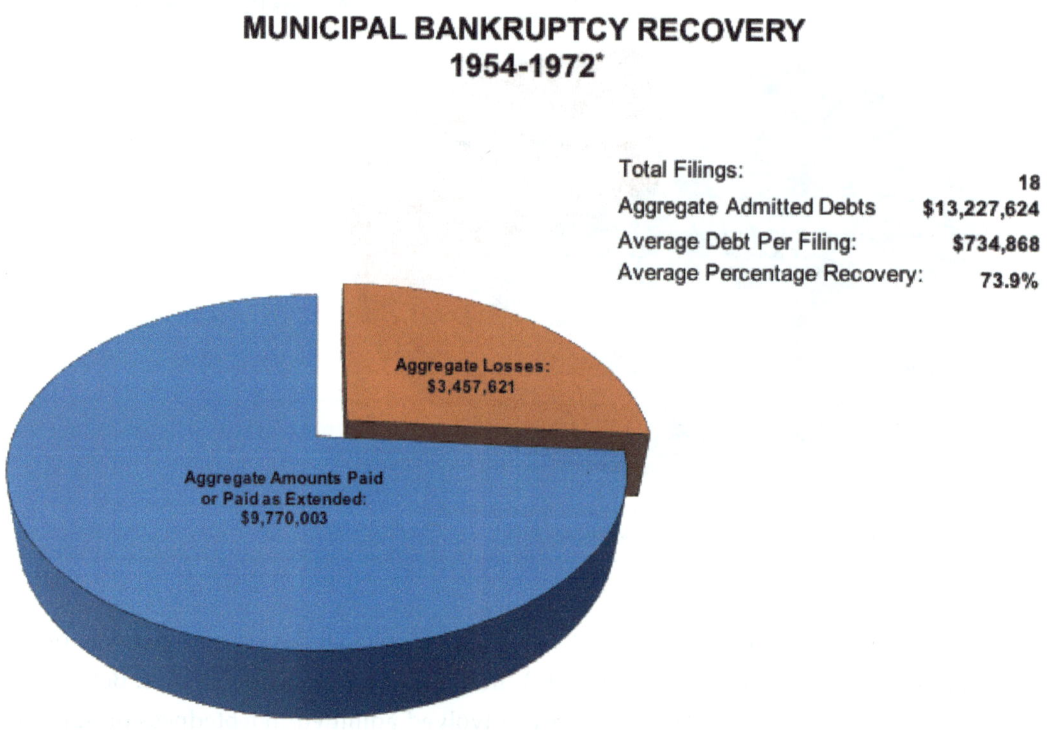

* *See Table 5-1, City Financial Emergencies: The Intergovernmental Dimension*, Advisory Commission on Intergovernmental Relations, July 1973.

65 Advisory Commission on Intergovernmental Relations, *City Financial Emergencies: The Intergovernmental Dimension* 82 (July 1973), http://www.library.unt.edu/gpo/acir/Reports/policy/a-42.pdf.

3. Selected Case Studies

a. The New York and Cleveland Experiences: Problems of Financial Controls and State and Federal Bailouts

In the spring of 1975, New York City was unable to market its debt because the bond market had discovered that the city had, for more than 10 years, been using questionable accounting and borrowing practices to eliminate its annual budget deficits. The city and its subdivisions had $14 billion of debt outstanding, of which over $5 billion was short term. The city claimed an operating budget deficit of $600 million, but others using a more refined accounting analysis asserted that the budget deficit was closer to $2.2 billion.[66] The banks refused to renew the short-term loans that were maturing or lend additional cash to the city. As a result, only state cash advances were keeping the city afloat. The city's spending for operating purposes had exceeded operating revenues for several years, and the accumulated fund deficit could only be resolved by increasing amounts of short-term borrowing. New York City itself had no funds to meet its short-term obligations. According to several commentators, the causes of this revenue shortfall included a changing population and economic characteristics, national economic difficulties, state and federal government action and inaction, and weaknesses in the political system itself. However, New York City was able to avoid a default on the payment of its notes in October 1975.

New York City's financial crisis was not an overnight disaster but rather had been brewing for over 10 years of economic meltdown. Real estate tax collection as a percentage of local revenues dropped from 61 percent of revenues in 1966 to 50 percent in 1975, with more than $500 million in property tax arrearages in 1975. More than 500,000 jobs were lost between 1969-1975, thereby diminishing local tax receipts for income and sales tax. Each city-based job was estimated to generate $820 in tax revenue for the city.

On October 29, 1975, President Ford gave a speech denying federal assistance to spare New York City from bankruptcy. The front page of the *New York Daily News* the next day read: "FORD TO CITY: DROP DEAD."[67] New York City's then-existing financial crisis was averted through use of a *deus ex machina* in the form of the state Municipal Assistance Corporation ("MAC"), which issued its own long-term securities to refinance short-term city securities, coupled with a federal loan. Two months after delivering the speech, President Ford signed legislation to provide to the city a federal loan, which was repaid with interest.[68]

---

66 *See* Roger Dunstan, *Overview of New York City's Fiscal Crisis,* 3 CALIFORNIA RESEARCH BUREAU 1 (CBR Note, Mar. 1, 1995), https://www.library.ca.gov/crb/95/notes/v3n1.pdf.

67 Sam Roberts, *Infamous "Drop Dead" Was Never Said by Ford,* N.Y. TIMES, Dec. 28, 2006, http://www.nytimes.com/2006/12/28/nyregion/28veto.html?_r=0.

68 *Id.*

In November 1975, the New York state legislature passed the New York City Emergency Moratorium Act.[69] The act imposed a three-year moratorium on action to enforce remedies on short-term outstanding debt obligations. The moratorium was only effective against debt holders who had been offered an exchange for the equal principal amount of long-term debt issued by MAC who had declined to accept the exchange. Approximately $5 billion in city notes were outstanding and scheduled to mature. After two MAC exchange offers, about $1 billion in notes remained outstanding with the public. Flushing National Bank was a short-term debt holder who declined the exchange offer and filed a lawsuit seeking to have the Moratorium Act declared unconstitutional. The Court of Appeals in New York (the highest court) held that the Moratorium Act was unconstitutional, citing New York constitutional provisions relating to full faith and credit and the city's power to levy taxes on real estate for the payment of previously contracted indebtedness. According to the court, when read together these provisions express the constitutional imperative that debt obligations must be paid, even if tax limitations are exceeded.[70] One of New York City's principal problems then as well as now is shared by most major metropolitan cities: increasing labor costs during a period of decreasing revenues. It is not unusual for 60 to 75 percent of municipal budgets to be attributed to labor costs.

In December 1978, Cleveland defaulted on $15.5 million in bond anticipation notes. When a financial emergency was declared by the state auditor in 1980, Cleveland had overdue accounts in excess of $36 million and a large general fund deficit. Again, as in the case of New York City, general fund expenditures exceeded revenues. Further, it appeared that restricted funds had been used to meet general obligations. Cleveland was able to solve its financial problems, at least for a time, by borrowing $15 million from the State of Ohio to pay overdue debts and by the issuance and sale of $36.2 million in bonds to Cleveland banks. Although the federal bankruptcy provisions relating to municipal debt adjustment had been amended following the New York City crisis to make the remedy more acceptable to the bond market, a resort to municipal bankruptcy was not seriously considered an option for Cleveland.

b. The San Jose School District and Medley, Florida Cases: Excessive Labor Costs or Judgments

The San Jose School District instituted a Chapter 9 bankruptcy proceeding on June 30, 1983.[71] Labor problems, coupled with restrictions on real estate taxes, were apparently the primary cause of this municipal insolvency. The vast majority of creditors appeared to be individual teachers. At the

---

69 New York State Emergency Moratorium Act for the City of New York, N.Y. UNCONSOL. LAWS ch. 874 (McKinney Supp. 1975), *as amended*, N.Y. UNCONSOL. LAWS ch. 875 (McKinney Supp. 1975).

70 *See* N.Y. Const. art. VIII, § 2; *Flushing Nat. Bank et al. v. Mun. Assistance Corp. for City of New York*, 40 N.Y.2d 731, 737-738 (N.Y. 1976).

71 *In re San Jose Unified School Dist.*, No. 583-02387-A-9 (Bk. N.D. Cal. 1983).

time of the filing, the average teacher in the school district made approximately $29,000 a year.[72] The average salary for teachers in the United States was approximately $21,935 a year.[73]

Bonded debt was not listed by the school district as part of its obligations to be restructured. Prior to 1978, the school district had issued general obligation bonds pursuant to the California Education Code. Section 15250 of the California Education Code provided that it was the duty of the board of supervisors of the county to levy taxes sufficient to pay the principal, interest and an annual reserve to insure the required payments of bonds issued by such school districts, and such levy was not to be used for any other purpose.

The San Jose School District made it clear that it did not in any way intend to impair the rights of its bondholders by its bankruptcy. Accordingly, the school district stated that the bonds were secured by a property tax assessed by the county treasurer's office on property within the school district at rates sufficient to make principal and interest payments. Because it had neither the authority to levy taxes nor access to bond reserve funds held by the county treasurer's office, the school district argued that the bondholders were not proper parties to the bankruptcy proceeding. The San Jose School District filed its bankruptcy petition on the same day that an interest payment was due to its bondholders. To make that payment, the school district used the tax funds that had already been collected and made the payment after it filed its municipal bankruptcy petition. This was a clear recognition by the county treasurer and school district of the continuing duty of municipalities to pay the statutorily mandated obligations they had incurred despite a general prohibition in the Federal Bankruptcy Code on paying interest during a bankruptcy proceeding where a debtor is insolvent. In the spring of 1984, the school district resolved its differences with its employees. The settlement gave the employees approximately 60 percent of the increases promised in prior years. Therefore, on June 8, 1984, the Chapter 9 proceeding was dismissed.[74] Any conflict between California-mandated payments and the Federal Bankruptcy Code was clarified in the 1988 Amendments to the Bankruptcy Code with the addition of provisions dealing with "special revenues."

The conclusion reached by the San Jose School District is not unprecedented. In 1968, the city of Medley, Florida, a small city of approximately 350 people, instituted a Chapter IX proceeding. The city was then the subject of numerous judgments and writs of mandamus issued in favor of creditors. The city stated that it did not seek in the Chapter IX proceeding to adjust the $850,000 bonded

---

72 *San Jose Schools Can Cut Pay, U.S. Bankruptcy Court Rules,* N.Y. TIMES, Aug. 30, 1983, http://www.nytimes.com/1983/08/30/us/san-jose-schools-can-cut-pay-us-bankruptcy-court-rules.html.

73 *Estimated average annual salary of teachers in public elementary and secondary schools,* NATIONAL CENTER FOR EDUCATION STATISTICS, https://nces.ed.gov/programs/digest/d07/tables/dt07_075.asp (last visited Feb. 11, 2016).

74 See section VII *infra,* discussing statutory liens, special revenues and state legislative mandates on the levying, imposition, collection and payment for bond debt that is separate from tax levies for general public purposes and can only be used for the dedicated payment of bond debt. This state law mandate must not be impaired or interfered with in a Chapter 9 proceeding. *See also* section VIII, subsection E, regarding recently enacted California S.B. 222 reaffirming a statutory lien.

indebtedness, but only the $700,000 of non-bonded indebtedness. The city proceeded to propose a plan not altering or impairing bonded indebtedness but merely extending the repayment of its non-bonded indebtedness up to 10 years.

c. Washington Public Power Supply System: Projects Fail When Expected Demand Evaporates

In 1976, WPPSS entered into agreements with 88 public utilities in the northwest part of the United States under which each participant utility purchased a percentage of the project capability of two nuclear power projects, Projects 4 and 5. Each participant agreed to pay its percentage share of costs incurred by the supply system to finance, construct and operate those projects. During the next five years, WPPSS issued $2.5 billion in bonds to finance Projects 4 and 5. Because of a perceived lack of demand for the power, construction of the projects was terminated prior to the completion of Projects 4 and 5. The terms of the participants' agreements would have obligated the participants to commence payments to WPPSS one year later, given the take-or-pay contractual arrangement. Within months of the termination of construction, however, various lawsuits were filed by ratepayers, certain utilities and the trustee for the bonds. In 1983, the Washington supreme court decided that certain of the municipal utilities who were participants had lacked authority under state law to enter into the participants' agreements. On remand to the state superior court, the participant agreements, which had unconditionally obligated the participating utilities to make payments to cover the costs of the projects whether or not they were completed, operable or operating, were invalidated and rendered unenforceable. A second decision of the Washington supreme court released the remaining utilities from the participants' agreements. The numerous class action lawsuits that were filed alleged securities law violations in connection with the sale of the bonds. Among the alleged misstatements were the region's need for power, the estimated costs of construction, the dates of operation for the projects, and the participants' willingness and authority to pay. It was alleged that the region's need for power did not meet the projected expectations, and the estimated costs of construction and dates of operation were significantly understated. There were additional issues of material information not disclosed that should have been set forth in the disclosure documents for the bonds, such as bond counsel's opinion, which positively stated that 77 participants were authorized to enter into the take-or-pay contracts without going further and noting that there were in all 88 participants. It was alleged that the failure to specifically state that not all participants were authorized meant holders could claim they were not fully informed of the risks and consequences thereto. The federal investigation into WPPSS led to the Securities and Exchange Commission adopting Rule 15c2-12 and its requirements of continuing disclosure.

d. The Colorado Special Districts: Failed Special Project

The real estate boom and bust in Colorado during the 1980s had ramifications for municipal finance. The infrastructure for residential real estate development — streets, sewers, utilities and the like — was financed with bonds issued by "special districts" created under Title 32 of the Colorado Revised Statutes.

Briefly stated, Colorado Special District Bonds are a type of special assessment bond where the land benefiting from the capital improvements is charged for the cost of improvements and their related financing costs through annual real estate taxes. In some incarnations, the bonds outstanding are general obligations of a district payable from unlimited ad valorem taxes on the public property (e.g., the Dawson Ridge Metropolitan District). In other forms, a group of districts is set up to do staged construction over time, and a "lead" district issues revenue bonds pursuant to intergovernmental agreements with the underlying districts. The underlying districts, in turn, promise to make payments to the lead district from taxes levied in and by the underlying districts.

With the bust in the Colorado real estate market in the 1980s, the funded interest was largely paid out to bondholders, and most of the real estate developers either were in some form of bankruptcy themselves or were otherwise unable to pay the taxes necessary to cover the bonds. Unlike a "real city," these partially completed special districts generally were not mature enough to tap the municipal credit markets for their day-to-day expenditures, which were generally minimal. Given their circumstances, they were also unlikely to be future borrowers in the long-term credit markets. Thus, a liquidation or bankruptcy became the only resolution for most of these projects.

e. City of Bridgeport, Connecticut: City Troubled by Flight of Population and Business and the Use of Intercept

In 1991, the city of Bridgeport, Connecticut created a stir in the municipal finance community by filing a petition under Chapter 9 of the Bankruptcy Code. Bridgeport, the largest city in Connecticut, was the first city of major proportions to so file. Unlike the special purpose district bankruptcies that had become common in recent years, Bridgeport was a "real" city, with multiple creditors possessing competing interests. Bridgeport had over $200 million in long-term bonded debt. At the same time, some 4,000 people were employed by the city pursuant to union contracts to deliver services to approximately 150,000 citizens.

The financial problems of the city did not arise overnight. Previously, the State of Connecticut had enacted special legislation known as the "Special Act" to recognize the otherwise illegal deficits of the city, to provide a financial oversight review board to supervise and discipline city finances, and to provide certain financial assistance to the city. The Special Act authorized the financing of the deficit and provided for the state to make certain payments to bondholders of the city in order to enhance its creditworthiness. This intercept mechanism, which functioned in connection with the review by the oversight board, was not an uncommon mechanism but could be subject to challenge in the Chapter 9 proceeding.

After the city of Bridgeport filed for bankruptcy, Connecticut moved to dismiss the bankruptcy petition on a number of grounds. Following an extensive hearing, the court concluded that Bridgeport was not "insolvent" at the time it filed its petition; and, therefore, the petition should be dismissed. As will be discussed, the test for an insolvent municipality is that the municipality is generally not paying its debts as they become due or is unable to pay debts as they become due. It was undisputed that, on the date of filing, Bridgeport was paying its debts as they became due. The issue was whether, on the date of filing, Bridgeport was *unable* to pay its debts as they became due. The court concluded that the city had not presented persuasive evidence that it would be unable to pay its debts anytime in the future. While the court rejected the state's argument that the analysis of insolvency could not be prospective in nature, the court found that the evidence established that Bridgeport would not run out of cash during the fiscal year 1991-1992. The court disagreed with a cash flow analysis that demonstrated that Bridgeport would run out of cash early in the next fiscal year. According to the court, financial difficulties short of insolvency are not a basis for Chapter 9 relief. The court concluded that Bridgeport was not insolvent when the petition was filed, that the petition must be dismissed and that Bridgeport must continue with the budget and collective bargaining process.

In summary, while the court agreed with Bridgeport that a city should not have to wait until it runs out of money to qualify for Chapter 9 protection, it ruled that the city must demonstrate as a condition precedent to filing that, in the near future, it will run out of money and be unable to pay its debts as they become due. Because of the election of a new mayor in Bridgeport, an appeal of these rulings was not pursued. Therefore, there was no review of the bankruptcy court's rulings. The Bridgeport filing and its dispute with the state served as a motivating factor for the 1994 legislation requiring a municipality to be "specifically authorized" by a state before it can file a Chapter 9 proceeding, as opposed to the prior test of "generally authorized to sue and be sued."

f. City of Philadelphia: Successful Legislation and State and Local Cooperation Avoid Disaster

In 1991, the city of Philadelphia also encountered a financial crisis that nearly denied it access to the short-term municipal bond market. The city was required to have a balanced budget. It had accumulated a long-term operating deficit of approximately $200 million and had another $200 million in short-term tax and revenue anticipation notes maturing that the city expected to "rollover" with a refinancing. Inquiries to the market from the city and its investment bankers indicated that a refinancing would not be possible, and default loomed on the horizon.

As a result, the Pennsylvania legislature enacted the Pennsylvania Intergovernmental Cooperation Authority Act for Cities of the First Class (the "Act"),[75] the effect of which was to avoid default. The Act created an "authority that will enable cities of the first class to access capital markets for deficit elimination and seasonal borrowings to avoid default on existing obligations and chronic cash shortages that will disrupt the delivery of municipal services." The Authority is known as PICA. A review of the Act's provisions is instructive:

75 53 PA. STAT. ANN. § 12720.209.

- Authority Created. The Pennsylvania Intergovernmental Cooperation Authority was created as a public authority and instrumentality of the Commonwealth, exercising public powers of the Commonwealth, as an agency and instrumentality thereof.

- Governing Body. The Authority's governing body had five members: one appointed by the governor, one by the president pro tempore of the Senate, one by the minority leader of the Senate, one by the Speaker of the House and one by the minority leader of the House. The Secretary of the Budget and the Director of Finance of the Commonwealth were ex officio members without a vote and not counted for quorum purposes. Actual expenses incurred by the members were reimbursable.

- Avoidance of Particular State Constitutional Problems. Because its members were not elected, the Authority had constitutional impediments to levying any tax under the Pennsylvania Constitution, and care was needed so that the non-elected board was not the entity that caused any taxes to be levied or increased.

- Use of Intergovernmental Agreements. The Authority was given the authorization to enter into intergovernmental cooperation agreements with cities, and such agreements were preconditions to the issuance of any obligations by the Authority.

- The Authority Could Issue Bonds and Refund City Obligations. The Authority had the legal ability under the Act to issue bonds and other evidences of obligations for borrowed money, but only at the request of the assisted city. As was true for the New York Municipal Assistance Corporation, the Authority was specifically authorized to issue its bonds to refund the obligations of the city.

- City and Authority Develop Five-Year Recovery Financial Plans. Assisted cities (Philadelphia) were required to develop, implement and periodically revise financial plans that projected revenues and expenses over five-year periods. The objectives of the plans were to eliminate deficits, restore special fund account moneys that had been misused, create balanced budgets, provide procedures to avoid future fiscal emergencies and enhance the ability of the city to regain access to the short-term and long-term credit markets. The Act required the city and the Authority to maintain an ongoing dialogue regarding the budget, the plan and actual expenditures.

- Budget Approval. The Authority was given approval power over the city budget.

- Collective Bargaining Agreements. Collective bargaining agreements that were in existence were to be honored until they expired by their terms. New collective bargaining agreements were required to comply with the financial plan which itself required the consent of the Authority.

- Limited Availability of Federal Bankruptcy. The Act imposed limits or denied the ability of assisted cities to file for protection under the Federal Bankruptcy Code.

- New Tax Revenue Created; Receipts to State for Distribution to Authority. Certain new sales and use taxes, a tax on real estate transfers and a sort of city income tax were created, with the taxes to be initially collected by the Department of Revenue of the Commonwealth of Pennsylvania, paid to the State Treasurer and deposited in the Intergovernmental Cooperation Authority Tax Fund. The taxes were to have a duration so long as bonds issued by the Authority remained outstanding.

- Original Jurisdiction to State Supreme Court. The Act gave original jurisdiction to the supreme court of the Commonwealth to hear any cases or controversies arising out of the statute and to render declaratory judgment concerning the constitutionality of the Act.

The Act was successful in one of its purposes — preventing a potentially catastrophic municipal bankruptcy filing by Philadelphia.

The structure of oversight and assistance of the New York MAC and the Pennsylvania PICA was the basis for the U.S. Congress passing the District of Columbia Responsibility and Management Assistance Act of 1995.[76] The District of Columbia Financial Control Board was to oversee the finances and approve the budget and financial operation of Washington, D.C. This board superseded and had the power to override any decision of the District of Columbia's mayor and city council. The board continued in existence until September 30, 2001 when, as set forth in the legislation, the District of Columbia achieved its fourth consecutive balanced budget. While the board's operation and power were similar in structure to those of MAC and PICA, the use of an executive director provided an additional degree of oversight and control.

g. Orange County, California: Creative Financing to Solve Tax Revenue Shortfalls

In 1994, Orange County, California was the fifth largest county in the United States with an annual budget of approximately $4 billion. An unwise leveraged investment policy, including investment in derivatives, which in periods of falling interest rates had produced as much as 20-30 percent of the revenues for the county, created a liquidity crisis in the late fall of 1994 as a consequence of rising interest rates. The county filed a petition for relief under Chapter 9 of the Federal Bankruptcy Code on December 6, 1994.

---

76 District of Columbia Financial Responsibility and Management Assistance Act of 1995, Pub. L. No. 104-8, 109 Stat. 97 (1995). This legislation, signed by the President on April 17, 1995, created an oversight authority known as the District of Columbia Financial Control Board, a five-member body appointed by the President in consultation with the respective chairs of the Appropriations and Oversight Committees of the House of Representatives, the chairs of the Appropriations and Governmental Affairs Committees of the Senate, and Delegate to the House of Representatives of the District of Columbia.

While the real impact of the Orange County Chapter 9 filing took years to determine, a number of observations were readily apparent. The bankruptcy was shocking in the first instance because the county originally exhibited a posture of unwillingness to pay and made no attempts to raise taxes or otherwise address the financial problem. There had been no market perception that Orange County had any real inability to pay as opposed to unwillingness to pay. Unlike New York City, Philadelphia and Cleveland, which clearly demonstrated an inability to pay and took extraordinary measures (including raising taxes) to avoid default, the wealthy county of Orange County, California made the surprising and speedy decision to file for bankruptcy after it had suffered a dramatic loss because of investments in derivative securities. A proposal to raise the sales tax by half a cent to help the county out of its financial crisis was defeated in June 1995 during the course of the bankruptcy proceedings. Such action is consistent with the anti-tax sentiment in California that led to legislative measures such as Proposition Thirteen.

Approximately $2 billion of Orange County short-term obligations (due in one year or less) came due in July and August 1995, while the bankruptcy was still pending. Principal was not paid when due. As part of the plan of adjustment, the holders of these obligations voluntarily agreed to have the maturity date extended for an additional year (at an increased interest rate). The county's ability to pay these obligations when they matured depended on the refinancing of the debt in the public markets.

The long-term and short-term debt of Orange County held by the public was paid from the proceeds of two financings: the issuance of tax-exempt certificates of participation and taxable refunding pension obligation bonds. These securities were sold but at a cost to Orange County. The county paid a penalty of 10 to 23 basis points and, including underwriting fees and costs of bond insurance, approximately $60 million more because of the county's status as a bankrupt issuer.

h. City of Vallejo, California: The Consequences of Too Rich Benefit Programs

The city of Vallejo filed for Chapter 9 in 2008. The principal causes of the filing were unsustainable public employee compensation and pension packages. In terms of Chapter 9 jurisprudence, the case produced an important ruling on Chapter 9 eligibility. Specifically, insolvency is to be determined by a cash flow analysis. In the Vallejo case, the debtor filed a motion to reject collective bargaining agreements, which was met by protracted litigation and ultimately with the unions agreeing to certain modifications of benefits given the court's ruling that the contracts could be rejected. However, Vallejo chose not to adjust the pension payments for current retirees because of the penalties CalPERS would impose in the event of failure to make the originally scheduled payments. This policy prohibited altering benefits of those already in the system even though benefit reduction was a part of the rationale for the bankruptcy filing. Current employees were asked to pay an increasing cost of their medical coverage. Further, for current employees, it was able to do away with such contractual obligations as binding arbitration and minimum manning for the fire department. The city also eliminated a contract clause that required the city to pay firefighters an average of what their peers made in ten area cities, including major cities like Sacramento, the state capital. Unfortunately, there were dramatic cuts in public safety with the budgets of the police and fire departments slashed by almost 50 percent. Interest payments to bondholders were to be suspended for three and half years. At least $9.5 million in legal fees were spent by the city in the process.[77] Unfortunately, the austerity required by the plan of adjustment did not lead to prompt economic recovery or even a balanced budget. By 2014, Vallejo had a budget deficit, and there were claims that municipal services were less than during the crisis.[78]

i. Central Falls, Rhode Island: Bondholders Come First

In 2010, Central Falls, Rhode Island, a financially troubled town, sought a court-appointed receiver under then-existing state law. A judge appointed an outside lawyer as temporary receiver and gave him oversight over the town's finances, including vendor contracts. State officials and others worried that the move could have a ripple effect beyond Central Falls, disrupting the municipal bond market and alarming rating agencies. As a result, a new bill was enacted that prohibited cities and towns in Rhode Island from entering into judicial receiverships and called on the state to intervene with financially troubled communities at an earlier stage. The law introduced new levels of state oversight for struggling municipalities.

The first level allows the state director of revenue to appoint a fiscal overseer for communities in financial distress. The overseer has the authority to review all proposed contracts, approve the annual budget and supervise expenditures. If a town is still unable to produce a balanced budget, the law authorizes the creation of a budget commission. Thereafter, if problems still persist, the state can appoint a receiver, who aside from having oversight of the city or town has authority to file for federal bankruptcy protection. This bill was written to apply retroactively in order to cover Central Falls. In addition, a statute has since been enacted that requires municipalities in Rhode Island to guarantee lenders and holders of bonds and notes a first lien right to property taxes and general revenues in the event of a bankruptcy or financial distress, in an effort to improve the ability of Rhode Island municipalities to borrow money in challenging financial markets.[79]

---

77 Alison Vekshin and Martin Z. Braun, *Vallejo's Bankruptcy 'Failure' Scares Cities Into Cutting Costs*, BLOOMBERG (Dec. 13, 2010, 11:01 PM), http://www.bloomberg.com/news/articles/2010-12-14/vallejo-s-california-bankruptcy-failure-scares-cities-into-cost-cutting. Others report a higher number, $13 million, for legal costs. *See* Hannah Dreier, *Vallejo Bankruptcy: California City Emerges From Financial Disaster*, HUFFINGTON POST (July 23, 2012), http://www.huffingtonpost.com/2012/07/23/vallejo-bankruptcy_n_1693863.html.

78 Mike Shedlock, *Vallejo Faces 2nd Bankruptcy Because They Didn't Restructure Pensions*, UNION WATCH (Oct. 2, 2013), http://unionwatch.org/vallejo-faces-2nd-bankruptcy-because-they-didnt-restructure-pensions. Vallejo had a budget deficit for 2014 and a projected budget deficit of $9 million for 2015. Adan Shapiro, *Back to the (Bankruptcy) Drawing Board for California Towns?*, FOX BUSINESS NEWS (Feb. 21, 2014), http://www.foxbusiness.com/politics/2014/02/21/back-to-bankruptcy-drawing-board-for-california-towns.html.

79 *See* section VIII, 50 State Survey, Rhode Island.

In August 2011, Central Falls filed for Chapter 9 bankruptcy. The Central Falls receiver had indicated that everything had been done to avoid filing and that taxes had been raised to the maximum level allowable, but the receiver had tried in vain to persuade retirees to accept voluntary reductions in their benefits and was unsuccessful in obtaining voluntary concessions from retired police and firefighters. In the bankruptcy proceeding, the receiver reduced pension benefits to Central Falls police and firefighters by as much as 55 percent.[80] Due to the state law provision, general obligation bondholders received payments throughout the proceeding. In addition, the confirmed plan of adjustment provided full payment to general obligation bondholders.

j. Harrisburg, Pennsylvania: Eligibility

In September 2010, Harrisburg, Pennsylvania announced it would miss a payment on general obligation bonds that had been insured by Assured Guaranty Municipal Corp. This followed Harrisburg's earlier default on conduit bonds for a failed incinerator project. The governor of Pennsylvania responded with an advance on state aid to meet the $3.3 million in bond payments. In December 2010, Harrisburg entered into Pennsylvania's Act 47 Municipal Recovery Program, the commonwealth's program for a distressed city to prepare a fiscal recovery plan. A fiscal recovery plan was prepared proposing the sale of city assets, freezing wages and changing workers' contracts to help pay debt related to the troubled incinerator project, the debt from which was five times the size of the city's general fund. In July 2011, the Harrisburg City Council rejected the Act 47 fiscal recovery plan and voted to file Chapter 9 without the consent and approval of the mayor. The commonwealth objected to the Chapter 9 filing on the grounds that Harrisburg was not specifically authorized to file and in fact was forbidden to do so since the fiscal code section for financially distressed municipalities at the time prohibited any filing prior to July 1, 2012. This prohibition was extended once, to November 30, 2012, but the commonwealth permitted the provision to expire. The objection of the commonwealth to the Chapter 9 petition was sustained and the bankruptcy court dismissed the petition, ruling that Harrisburg was not authorized by state law to file. This dismissal was affirmed by the district court.

In response to the city council's rejection of the Act 47 fiscal recovery plan, the Commonwealth of Pennsylvania enacted amendments to Act 47, which provided for a declaration of fiscal emergency when a financially distressed city of the third class has failed to adopt a recovery plan. These amended provisions permitted the appointment and confirmation of a receiver when a city of the third class has failed to adopt a consent agreement or a recovery plan. As a result of this new provision and

---

80 *See* Cate Long, *The Real History of Public Pension in Bankruptcy,* REUTERS (Aug. 8, 2013) http://blogs.reuter.com/muniland/2013/08/08/the-real-history-of-public-pensions-in-bankruptcy/. The article discusses pension treatment in bankruptcy in the following cases: Central Falls, Rhode Island; Prichard, Alabama; Jefferson County, Alabama; Stockton, California; and Vallejo, California.

Harrisburg's failure to act, in October 2011 the Pennsylvania governor declared a fiscal emergency in Harrisburg. In December 2011, a receiver was appointed over Harrisburg by a state court.[81]

During the receivership, in March 2012, Harrisburg first defaulted on its general obligation debt totaling $425.5 million. In April 2012, after the initial receiver resigned, the Pennsylvania court overseeing Harrisburg's receivership appointed a new receiver. The newly appointed receiver issued a recovery plan — titled "Harrisburg Strong" — which was approved by the Pennsylvania state court in September 2013. In December 2013, as a part of its recovery plan, Harrisburg entered into a negotiated settlement with its general obligation bond creditors, in which Moody's calculated that those creditors would receive an overall initial recovery rate of 75 percent.[82] Harrisburg emerged from its receivership on March 1, 2014. In December 2011, after the ill-fated bankruptcy filing, the governor appointed a receiver under state law for Harrisburg. The receiver, working with creditors, developed a recovery plan that involved concessions from creditors, including workers represented by unions. The recovery plan provided for the sale to the Lancaster County Solid Waste Authority of the incinerator facility, which had a related financing that was in default and subject to litigation; proceeds of the sale were to be paid to the bondholders. Also, the plan provided for a long-term lease of the Harrisburg parking facility, with the parking revenues primarily used to repay creditors. A $430 million bond issuance was used to fund the sale of the incinerator and the forty-year lease of the parking facility. Some of those bonds were backed by Dauphin County and Assured Guaranty Municipal Corp., the city's two largest creditors. By March 2014, the receivership was terminated and Harrisburg was no longer in a financial crisis, even though it continued under Act 47 supervision for implementation of the "Harrisburg Strong" plan.

k. Jefferson County, Alabama: The Scope of Special Revenues

Jefferson County, Alabama, burdened by millions of dollars in sewer bonds, filed a Chapter 9 petition in 2011. Previously, the state court in Alabama had appointed a receiver for the county's sewer system. Like Central Falls, Jefferson County exemplifies the result when parties are unable to reach a consensual resolution and ensuing litigation renders a Chapter 9 filing almost inevitable. Even though the county, its sewer warrant holders and the trustee were drafting settlement documents for a consensual refinancing on the eve of the Chapter 9 filing, the purported delay by the state in calling for a special session of the state legislature to pass legislation to aid the county in refinancing its sewer debt, along with difficulties in communications among the parties and an unfavorable political climate for a consensual resolution, resulted in the Chapter 9 filing. In the Jefferson County Chapter 9 proceeding, the bankruptcy court recognized that the warrant holders' bonds were secured by special revenues that were not subject to the automatic stay, which, if applicable, would have prevented

81 *See About the Office of Receiver*, PENNSYLVANIA DEPARTMENT OF COMMUNITY & ECONOMIC DEVELOPMENT, http://community.newpa.com/local-government/act-47-financial-distress/office-receiver (last visited Feb. 12, 2016).

82 *Harrisburg's GO Creditors Get Wide-Ranging Recovery Rates Averaging 75%*, MOODY'S INVESTOR SERVICES (Feb. 24, 2014), http://media.navigatored.com/documents/Harrisburg+GO+Recovery+Rates.pdf.

payment to warrant holders. Similarly, the bankruptcy court also ruled that the county could only withhold operating expenses contracted for between the trustee and the county specifically defined in the underlying bond indentures from sewer revenues before making payment to warrant holders. Thus, the bankruptcy court prevented Jefferson County from withholding from payment to warrant holders amounts that were never contemplated to be withheld in the indentures, including amounts for a reserve for depreciation, amortization or future expenditures in relation to the sewer system or an estimate for professional fees and expenses in relation to the bankruptcy case.[83] However, the court did allow actual legal fees in the bankruptcy attributable to the sewer system to be included as a deduction from gross revenues.[84]

Jefferson County emerged from bankruptcy in December 2013 after reaching a settlement with its sewer debt holders. Pursuant to the settlement with respect to its sewer debt, the county's sewer-related indebtedness was reduced from approximately $3.2 billion to approximately $1.738 billion. In return, the county agreed to increase its sewer rates to ensure that its sewer system would generate adequate funds to service the system's indebtedness, maintain operations, meet capital needs and preserve and improve services.[85] Certain ratepayers of the county objected to the bankruptcy court's confirmation of the Jefferson County claim and have since appealed the bankruptcy court's rejection of their objection to the U.S. Court of Appeals for the Eleventh Circuit. The Eleventh Circuit is also currently entertaining an appeal by the county from an order denying their motion to dismiss the ratepayers' appeal by the U.S. District Court for the Northern District of Alabama. Because the county's bankruptcy plan has been substantially consummated, and the county has already sold $1.8 billion of new sewer warrants to retire its old sewer warrants valued at approximately $3.2 billion (as required by the settlement), the county has argued that the ratepayers' appeal is moot.[86]

One of the major predicates for Jefferson County's Chapter 9 filing was the controversy surrounding its sewer debt, as well as the declaration from the Alabama supreme court in March 2011 that the county's occupation tax was unconstitutional.[87] The occupation tax provided around $70 million, or one third of the county's operating revenues. Under Alabama law, any new tax to replace the financial hole left by the elimination of the occupation tax would have to be approved by the Alabama legislature. That approval was not forthcoming and despite claims of a virtual settlement of the sewer debt with the county, the trustee and major holders, the county chose to file Chapter 9 in

83 *See In re Jefferson Cnty., Ala.*, 482 B.R. 404 (Bankr. N.D. Ala. 2012).

84 *See In re Jefferson Cnty., Ala.*, 503 B.R. 849 (Bankr. N.D. Ala. 2013).

85 *See* Motion for Approval Pursuant to the Confirmation Order of Compromises and Settlements and Related Relief with respect to the Chapter 9 Plan of Adjustment for Jefferson County, Alabama, *In re Jefferson Cnty., Ala.*, Case No. 11-5736-CRJ9, 7 (Bankr. N.D. Ala. Nov. 6, 2013), ECF No. 2183.

86 *See Bennett v. Jefferson Cnty., Ala.*, No. 2:14-cv-0213-SLB, *appeal docketed*, No. 15-11690 (11th Cir. Apr. 22, 2015).

87 *Alabama Supreme Court Rules County Tax Unconstitutional*, REUTERS (Mar. 16, 2011), http://www.reuters.com/article/us-usa-alabama-jeffersoncounty-idUSTRE72F74A20110316.

November 2011. When the county emerged from Chapter 9 in December 2013, there was still no replacement for the lost occupation tax revenues. The county was forced to implement an austerity program, closing certain public health care facilities and reducing hours and availability for access to public services. While a plan of debt adjustment was approved, the county's significant problem of reduction in government services was not appropriately addressed.[88]

I. Stockton, California: Generous Pay and Employee Benefits

In June 2012, the city of Stockton, California filed a Chapter 9 petition, seeking to restructure more than $700 million in debt. At the time Stockton filed its Chapter 9 petition, and until the city of Detroit, Michigan filed its Chapter 9 petition a little over a year later, Stockton, a city of approximately 300,000 residents, was the largest city in the United States in the prior sixty years to seek protection under the Bankruptcy Code. Stockton was hit especially hard by the plummeting housing market during the Great Recession. The combination of significantly lower housing prices and increased unemployment created significant budget deficits for the city. Indeed, the median home price in Stockton in 2006 was $397,000, and just six years later, in 2012, the median home price in the city was $109,000 — a 72 percent decrease.[89] During this same period, the city's property tax revenues decreased by $17.5 million, from $61.1 million in fiscal year 2007-08 to $43.6 million in fiscal year 2012-13.[90]

Previous to its bankruptcy filing, the city was strapped with expenses that it had accumulated during more robust financial times, including labor costs, retiree health care benefits and public debt. For instance, the city had guaranteed all firefighters full healthcare benefits in retirement, which led to the same treatment for the city's police and other public safety workers. In addressing Stockton's significant pension obligations, the bankruptcy court ruled that such obligations could be restructured as a part of a Chapter 9 bankruptcy proceeding. The court in the Stockton case examined the issue of the impairment of the retirees' contract on a preliminary basis and noted that, while the "Contracts [sic] Clause is a key navigational star in the firmament of our constitution and economic universe, it is subject to being eclipsed by the Bankruptcy Clause: 'The Congress shall have power to … establish … uniform Laws on the subject of Bankruptcies throughout the United States.' U.S. Const., article 1, § 8, clause 4."[91] Rather than analyzing the Supreme Court precedent that supports a state's impairment of a contract for the public good, the *Stockton* court focused on the nature of bankruptcy as a land of broken promises and impaired contracts. Significantly, the court noted, "the Contract Clause bans a *state* from making a law impairing the obligations of a contract; it does not ban *Congress* from making

88 *See* Disclosure Statement Regarding Chapter 9 Plan of Adjustment for Jefferson County, Alabama at 21-22, *In re Jefferson Cnty., Ala.*, Case No. 11-05736 (Bankr. N.D. Ala. June 30, 2013), ECF No. 1977.

89 Disclosure Statement with respect to First Amended Plan for the Adjustment of Debts of City of Stockton, California, *In re City of Stockton, Ca.*, Case No. 12-32118 (Bankr. E.D. Cal. Nov. 15, 2013), ECF No. 1205.

90 *Id.*

91 *In re City of Stockton, Cal.*, 478 B.R. 8, 15 (Bankr. E.D. Cal. 2012).

a law impairing the obligation of a contract."[92] According to the *Stockton* judge, "[t]his asymmetry is no accident. The Bankruptcy Clause necessarily authorizes Congress to make laws that would impair contracts. *Sturges v. Crowninshield*, 17 U.S. (4 Wheat.) 122, 191 (1819)."[93] According to the *Stockton* court, that authorization even extended to retired city employees' health benefits. The judge ruled that "[t]he federal bankruptcy power also, by operation of the Supremacy Clause, trumps the similar contracts clause in the California state constitution."[94]

In the end, the bankruptcy court approved a plan of adjustment for the city that permitted full payment to the city's pensioners but drastically cut returns to the city's general obligation bondholders. The pensioners, however, agreed to accept a $5.1 million payment from the city, in lieu of the lifetime health care benefits that had been promised them by the city.[95] The plan became effective in February 2015. The holder of lease debt objected to the plan, complaining that $35,080,000 Stockton Public Finance Authority Lease Revenue Bonds ("Lease Revenue Bonds") were not appropriately treated.[96] The holder claimed that in discussions during the neutral evaluator phase (required by California law) before being able to file for Chapter 9, the Lease Revenue Bonds were subject to the city's offer of full payment over 40 years or a net present value recovery of 54.5 percent. The city claimed that if the bondholder were to gain possession of the money, losing a golf course and parks and suffering other losses, it would receive less than a 1 percent recovery. The bondholder contended that the public facility fees were sufficient to permit payment in full or a higher recovery. Stockton's plan offered to pay less than a 1 percent recovery or about $94,000 based on the alleged collateral coverage and non-recourse nature of the claim. The bondholder argued it should receive the true value of the collateral or dedicated source of payment as noted above and argued that the unsecured claim recovery should

---

92 *Id.* at 15.

93 *Id.*

94 *Id.* at 16. The bankruptcy court in *Stockton* stated in open court that even if Stockton entered into a consensual plan with all its creditors, the court might rule that pension debts are subject to reduction in a Chapter 9. Dale Kasler, *Judge Suggests Stockton Worker Pensions Could Be Reduced in City's Bankruptcy Case*, THE SACRAMENTO BEE (July 8, 2014), http://www.sacbee.com/news/business/article2603243.html. *See also Moran v. City of Cent. Falls*, 475 B.R. 323 (Bankr. D.R.I. 2012) (affirming rejection of employment agreement between the city and a police officer in Chapter 9 proceeding). The Chapter 9 plan in *Central Falls* provided for the restructuring and reduction of pension claims. *See In re City of Central Falls, Rhode Island*, Case No. 1:11-bk-13105 (Bankr. D.R.I. 2012), ECF No. 479. Rhode Island officials and a federal mediation agency reached an agreement to settle lawsuits by public sector unions challenging Rhode Island's 2011 law that overhauled state pension benefits. The settlement tweaked the formula for COLA adjustments and permitted employees with more than 20 years of service to shift back into a defined benefit plan. *See* Paul Burton, *Rhode Island Strikes Pension Settlement*, THE BOND BUYER (Feb. 14, 2014), http://www.bondbuyer.com/issues/123_32/rhode-island-strikes-pension-settlement-1059911-1.html.

95 *In re City of Stockton, Cal.*, 526 B.R. 35 (Bankr. E.D. Ca. 2012).

96 Summary Objection of Franklin High Yield Tax-Free Income Fund and Franklin California High Yield Municipal Fund to Confirmation of First Amended Plan of Adjustment of Debts of City of Stockton, California, *In re City of Stockton, Cal.*, Case No. 12-32118 (Bankr. E.D. Ca. Feb. 26, 2014), ECF No. 1273.

equal that of the retiree health benefits and similar claims.[97] In responding to the claims of CalPERS, the bankruptcy court repeated that the pension obligation could be adjusted in order to make the plan feasible. However, the city of Stockton did not choose to modify pension obligations and the court ultimately confirmed the plan over the objection of the bondholder of the Lease Revenue Bonds.[98] Purportedly, the city feared that the penalties that reduced payments to CalPERS would have generated, including increased annual payments and the significant discount of the value of assets attributable to the city's pension, would be unacceptable to the city. It was less detrimental, in the city's estimate, to permit the pension obligation to continue unimpaired. The bondholder appealed from the confirmation order, arguing that the plan was unfairly discriminatory in favor of pension benefits and not proposed in good faith. The Bankruptcy Appellate Panel of the Ninth Circuit dismissed the appeal of the confirmation order generally as equitably moot and otherwise affirmed the bankruptcy court's decision with respect to the treatment of the bondholder's unsecured claim.[99]

m. Detroit, Michigan: Systemic Neglect and a Plan of Negotiation and Settlement

The events leading up to the Chapter 9 bankruptcy proceeding of the city of Detroit, Michigan were long in the making. Detroit's history reflects the unfortunate reality that as essential governmental services and infrastructure deteriorate, business and residents leave. The exodus of business and residents then erodes the tax base, creating a situation in which no matter how high a municipality raises its taxes, those tax revenues are insufficient to fund the necessary investment by the municipality in essential governmental services and the infrastructure needed to attract new residents and businesses. By example, in 1950, almost 2 million people lived in Detroit, whereas by December 2012, the city was home to approximately 585,000 people.[100] In early March 2013, the governor of Michigan declared a financial emergency within the city of Detroit and later that month appointed Kevyn D. Orr as Detroit's emergency financial manager.

In an attempt to force creditors into negotiations, in June 2013 the emergency manager sent a 128-page proposal to creditors of the city, which proposed drastic cuts across the board to Detroit's finances, regardless of the relative security of particular bond issuances by the city. The emergency manager's proposal, while common in attempts to restructure a corporation's debts, was relatively unheard of in municipal restructuring and ultimately proved unsuccessful. In July 2013, following approval by Michigan's governor as required under Michigan law, the city of Detroit filed a petition under Chapter 9 of the Bankruptcy Code. In support of the Chapter 9 filing, the emergency manager

---

97 *Id.* at 21.

98 *In re City of Stockton, Cal.*, 526 B.R. 35 (Bankr. E.D. Ca. 2012).

99 *In re City of Stockton (Franklin High Yield Tax-Free Income Fund v. City of Stockton)*, Case No. EC-14-1550 (B.A.P. 9th Cir. dismissed Dec. 11, 2015), ECF No. 50.

100 *See* Fourth Amended Disclosure Statement with Respect to Fourth Amended Plan for the Adjustment of Debts of the City of Detroit, *In re City of Detroit, Mich.*, Case No. 13-53846 (Bankr. E.D. Mich. May 5, 2014), ECF No. 4391.

cited decades of fiscal mismanagement, a plummeting population, deficient employment and revenues, decaying infrastructure, deteriorating services and excessive borrowing that provided short-term Band-Aids at the cost of deepening insolvency.[101]

The Detroit bankruptcy proceedings were contentious and ultimately resulted in settlements among the various constituencies, providing little in guidance for future Chapter 9 proceedings by similar-sized municipalities, should such filings occur. Indeed, legal fees of over $170 million were paid by the city or by the state of Michigan in connection with the Detroit bankruptcy.[102] This figure should provide pause to both municipalities and creditors and evidence that if they can, the various constituencies with respect to a municipal restructuring should attempt to reach a consensus outside of the Chapter 9 process.

In an order dated December 5, 2013 relating to the city of Detroit's eligibility for bankruptcy protection, the bankruptcy court ruled that the Tenth Amendment to the United States Constitution does not prohibit the impairment of contract rights that are otherwise protected by the state constitution, since such provisions impose no constraint on the bankruptcy process.[103] Importantly, the court ruled that "nothing distinguishes pension debt in a municipal bankruptcy case from any other debt."[104] According to the court, "[i]f the Tenth Amendment prohibit[ed] the impairment of pension benefits in [the Detroit] case, then it would also prohibit the adjustment of any other debt ...."[105] The court held that, because under the Michigan Constitution pension rights are contractual rights, they are subject to impairment in a federal bankruptcy proceeding.[106] Nevertheless, the bankruptcy court emphasized that "no one should interpret this holding ... to mean the [c]ourt [would] necessarily confirm any plan of adjustment that impairs pensions."[107] The court emphasized "that it [would] not lightly or casually exercise the power under federal bankruptcy law to impair pensions."[108] The court stated that "before the [c]ourt confirms any plan that the city submits, the [c]ourt must find that the plan fully meets the requirements of 11 U.S.C. §943(b) and the other applicable provisions of the

101 *See* Declaration of Kevyn D. Orr in Support of City of Detroit, Michigan's Statement of Qualifications Pursuant to Section 109(c) of the Bankruptcy Code, *In re City of Detroit, Mich.*, Case No. 13-53846 (Bankr. E.D. Mich. July 18, 2013), ECF No. 11.

102 *See* Amended Opinion and Order Regarding the Reasonableness of Fees Under 11 U.S.C. Sec. 943(b)(3), *In re City of Detroit, Mich.*, Case No. 13-53846 (Bankr. E.D. Mich. Feb. 12, 2015), ECF No. 9257.

103 Opinion Regarding Eligibility, *In re City of Detroit, Mich.*, Case No. 13-53846 (Bankr. E.D. Mich. Dec. 5, 2013), ECF No. 1945.

104 *Id* at 74.

105 *Id.*

106 *Id.* at 80.

107 *Id.*

108 *Id.*

Bankruptcy Code."[109] "Together these provisions of law demand the [c]ourt's judicious legal and equitable consideration of the interests of the [c]ity and all of its creditors as well as laws of the State of Michigan."[110]

The Saga of Special Revenue Water and Sewer Bonds and Unlimited Tax General Obligation Bonds in Detroit. The Detroit bankruptcy is notable due to the challenges it posed to the traditional understanding of the municipal market. The emergency manager continued during the bankruptcy to propose modified treatment reflecting an adjustment and concession of the water and sewer bonds, which had debt service and operational costs fully covered by rates. This demand for impairment was made even though the pledge of revenues to the water and sewer bondholders met the test of special revenues which, given the 1988 amendments to the Bankruptcy Code, should be unimpaired and unmolested in a Chapter 9 by a municipality. Ultimately, Detroit made a tender offer to cash out those holders who wanted to exit promptly and treated the remaining holders as unimpaired in its confirmed plan of debt adjustment. Debt service as originally scheduled continued to be paid to the water and sewer bondholders throughout the case and continues pursuant to the plan of debt adjustment.

The unlimited tax general obligation bonds ("UTGOs") likewise were subject to an unconventional approach by the city of Detroit, which was a departure from the assumed tradition of honoring the voter-approved levy (intended for and dedicated to paying the UTGOs), by not paying the bondholders but using the tax revenues for other purposes.

This raised questions about the ability of a municipality and the bankruptcy court to act contrary to state statutes or authorize the voter-approved tax revenues to be used for purposes other than what state statutes and voter mandates direct.[111] As will be discussed in section VII of this book, Section 903 and Section 904 of the Bankruptcy Code and the early case law of Chapter 9 make it clear that the bankruptcy court and the municipality cannot propose treatment in a plan or authorize action contrary to state law and constitutional mandates. While vigorous litigation in Detroit would have helped clarify the issues in favor of the bondholders, the litigation of this matter was settled with the

---

109 *Id.*

110 *Id.* Detroit subsequently filed an Eighth Amended Chapter 9 Plan for the Adjustment of Debts of the City of Detroit. Eighth Amended Chapter 9 Plan for the Adjustment of Debts, *In re City of Detroit, Mich.*, Case No. 13-53846 (Bankr. E.D. Mich. Oct. 22, 2014), ECF No. 8045. The Eighth Amended Chapter 9 Plan reflected a settlement with the city's retired police and firefighters in which they agreed to take a 55 percent reduction in annual cost of living adjustments. Pensions for general retirees were reduced by 4.5 percent with a freeze of cost of living increases.

111 What does it mean to have a tax revenue pledge approved by the voters and dedicated to pay the general obligation bonds? What does Article IX, Section 25 of the Michigan Constitution mean when it states that "The repayment of voter approved bonded indebtedness is guaranteed"? What consequences are there to the municipal bond market if UTGOs are ultimately treated as unsecured debt? Can the plan of debt adjustment be confirmed if it is not in compliance with state law? See also Article IX, Section 6 of the Michigan Constitution regarding voter-approved bonds without limitations to be paid.

bondholders receiving 100 percent recovery — 74 percent paid under the Detroit plan and 26 percent paid by the bond insurers to the bondholders under their insurance policy.

Further, the emergency manager and the city of Detroit also claimed that the $1.1 billion certificates of participation for the pension bonds were illegally issued and thus invalid obligations.[112] That controversy was also settled with the bond insurers and the liquidity providers, rather than fully litigated to what could have been an instructive conclusion for the municipal bond market.[113]

Ultimately, the Detroit plan included a "Grand Bargain" that traded corporate and not-for-profit contributions for the separate status and operation of the municipal art museum, an asset for the city of Detroit, along with state aid aggregating over $800 million devoted to public employees' pensions. This "Grand Bargain" raised the question of why the consideration paid for transferring the asset to a new entity for the continuing benefit and use of an art museum by the public should be dedicated solely to pension creditors rather than all creditors and interested parties in the bankruptcy. Again, the fully litigated answer will never be known because this was part and parcel of all the major creditor settlements requiring agreement with the "Grand Bargain." The plan was confirmed on November 12, 2014, with a supplemental opinion regarding the plan confirmation, approving settlements and approving exit financing providing for the treatment of various bondholders' claims based for the most part on settlements rather than fully litigated determinations.[114]

The ruling of the bankruptcy court in Detroit and the settlement contained and approved therein resulted in the following recovery for various public debt claims:

---

112 Caitlin Devitt, *Detroit Revenue Bond, COP Holders Object to Bankruptcy Exit*, THE BOND BUYER (May 13, 2014), http://www.bondbuyer.com/issues/123_92/detroit-revenue-bond-cop-holders-object-to-bankruptcy-exit-plan-1062409-1.html.

113 James Spiotto, *Detroit's Bankruptcy Repudiation of COPs Defies History*, MUNINET GUIDE (July 22, 2014), http://muninetguide.com/detroits-bankruptcy-repudiation-of-cops-defies-history-2/.

114 Supplemental Opinion Regarding Plan Confirmation, Approving Settlements, and Approving Exit Financing, *In re City of Detroit, Mich.*, Case No. 13-53846 (Bankr. E.D. Mich. December 31, 2014), ECF No. 8993.

Detroit Bankruptcy Estimated Recovery of Certain Classes of Creditors Based on Supplemental Opinion			
Type of Claim	Claim Amount	Plan Treatment	Estimated Recovery
Water and Sewer Bond (Classes 1A, 1B, 1C) Unimpaired/Nonvoting Class			100%
Secured GO Series 2010, 2010(A), 2012(A)(2), 2012 (A2-B), 2012(B), 2012(B2) (Classes 2A, 2B, 2C, 2D, 2E, 2F)			100%
Limited Tax General Obligation Bonds ("LTGO") (Class 7)	$163.5 million	$55 million (cash in lieu of new LTGO bonds)	41%
Unlimited Tax General Obligation Bonds (Class 8)	$388 million		
	Bond Insurer	$288 million	74%
	Bondholders	$388 million (26% of recovery from bond insurer)	100%
Syncora Settlement on Certificates of Participation for 24.05% of Pension Bonds (COPS) (Class 9)	$354 million	$23.5 million New B Notes $21.3 million New C Notes	13%
FGIC Settlement Certificates of Participation for 75.94% of Pension Bonds (COPS) (Class 9)	$1.119 million	$74.2 million New B Notes $67.2 million New C Notes	13%

n. Lessons Learned from the Detroit and Other Recent Chapter 9 Bankruptcies

In July 2013, Detroit was the largest city in Michigan and largest municipality in the country to seek protection under Chapter 9 of the Bankruptcy Code for municipal debt adjustment. Previously, Chapter 9 had been a remedy used rarely by any city, town, village or county, especially those of any size with significant public debt. As noted earlier, historically, financially challenged large cities obtained help from their states and refinanced without resort to Chapter 9. For example, as the largest city in the state, each of New York City in 1975, Cleveland in 1978 and Philadelphia in 1991 received assistance from their respective states in the forms of loans, grants or the transfer of services to other governmental entities and financial supervision. Such state assistance made Chapter 9 unnecessary by increasing cash liquidity, reducing expenses and providing financial oversight, support and guidance to help those cities to refinance debt, address systemic problems and solve financial difficulties.

Chapter 9 is simply a process of debt restructuring that can provide a municipality with the breathing room it needs to implement a recovery plan that will allow it to reinvest in the municipality, stimulate its economy, generate new jobs, attract new businesses and residents, add to its tax base and increase revenues to create an economic recovery.

The fact that Detroit has confirmed a plan of debt adjustment is one important step in a longer process of recovery. At this stage, it is not absolutely certain that Detroit, having confirmed a plan of debt adjustment, will make a full recovery. Hopefully, that will be the case through the hard work of its mayor and city council, its citizens and taxpayers to attract new business and new residents and to return the city to where it was in its past economic greatness. We are able at this time to note that the Detroit experience has been constructive in offering a number of important lessons that should be considered.

Lesson One:
Do not defer funding of essential services and infrastructure

Detroit offers a warning to others to the effect that there is never a good reason to defer funding of essential services and infrastructure at an acceptable level. If a municipality does defer such funding, Detroit's fate will be its fate. Detroit's history reflects the unfortunate situation that as essential services and infrastructure erode, business and residents leave, reducing the tax base such that any increase in the tax rate is insufficient to cover the requisite investment in essential services and infrastructure.

One of the most beneficial outcomes of the Detroit filing has been the wake-up call to other municipalities suffering financial distress as to the realities of the Chapter 9 process, namely, that Chapter 9 in many situations can be time consuming, expensive and uncertain, and it can lead to political and social unrest. In other words, the process does not achieve the desired result. Further, every city must make sure that essential services are at a level that attracts business and new residents, and that infrastructure supports an economic base so that goods, services and employees can move in that system with appropriate efficiency. It is also important that the work force is sufficiently educated to suit the needs of the business community, and that all have a well-deserved feeling of safety and protection.

It is interesting to note that since Detroit filed in July 2013, only one city, town, village or county has filed for Chapter 9.[115] Significantly, that Chapter 9 case was dismissed in the spring of 2016 without a plan of debt adjustment being confirmed. A contract dispute over the purchase of land resulting in a judgment against the city that the city could not pay ultimately was settled, and an "affordable payment" schedule was agreed to, thus resolving the reason for the Chapter 9 filing. Many cities have attempted to address their problems in order to find solutions that will not result in Chapter 9 municipal debt adjustment. The prophecy that, after Detroit, others would quickly follow in filing Chapter 9 bankruptcies has apparently proven false. In fact, Detroit taught other municipalities that they must promptly and efficiently deal with and effectively support essential services, infrastructure and reinvestment in the municipality to prevent any economic downturn.

Lesson Two:
Labor and pension contracts under state constitutional and statutory provisions should not be interpreted as a suicide pact

It appears that one of the reasons why resolution of pension and labor costs was not achieved in Detroit prior to filing Chapter 9 was the belief of the workers and retirees that, under the Michigan constitution, those contractual rights could not be impaired or diminished to any degree. This position failed to take into consideration the reality that a municipality can only pay that which it has revenues to pay and, in a declining financial situation, there cannot be sufficient funds to pay all obligations, especially those that may be unaffordable and unsustainable. So far, recent bankruptcy court decisions have been unanimous, be it in Detroit, Stockton or San Bernardino, that in a Chapter 9 proceeding, unaffordable and unsustainable labor costs and pension benefits can be impaired and adjusted to what is sustainable and affordable.

The *Stockton* court ruled that it wasn't going to substitute its judgment for the city as to whether or not the city will be capable of making those payments, but reaffirmed that such contractual obligations can be adjusted in a Chapter 9 filing to provide for the survival of a municipality. The real issue is whether or not the myth that unaffordable and unsustainable costs cannot be impaired will continue to prevent the rational consensual adjustment outside a Chapter 9. It is clear that an interpretation of state law and constitutional provisions to the effect that the municipality has no choice but to pay that which is unsustainable and unaffordable is illogical and unworkable. Necessary adjustments must be made. This should never be an excuse not to pay as much as can be paid for worker and retiree benefits but, at the same time, worker and retiree benefits cannot be the reason for the municipality's financial erosion. Continued loss of taxpayers and overall revenues will only further frustrate the underfunding of benefits and ultimately provide even less to workers and retirees.

---

115 On August 20, 2015, the City of Hillview, Kentucky filed a Chapter 9 petition. *In re Hillview, Kentucky*, Case No. 15-32679 (Bankr. W.D. Ky.). *See* also Shelly Sigo, *Hillview Ky. Returns to Investment Grade on Chapter 9 Settlement*, SOURCE MEDIA (Apr. 20, 2016), https://fixedincome.fidelity.com/ftgw/ti/fnewsarticle?id=201604201904SM_BNDBUYER_0001101776_110.1.

Lesson Three:
Don't question that which should be beyond questioning and is needed for the long-term financial survival of the municipality

Detroit sought to significantly reduce its payments to the UTGOs and to obtain concessions from its water and sewer bondholders, both of which claimed a sufficient tax revenue base and a certainty that their payments were assured by a dedicated source of funds pursuant to various statutory and constitutional provisions under Michigan law. There was no legitimate dispute that the water and sewer bonds had sufficient revenue flow to pay those bonds during the bankruptcy. The 1988 Amendments to Chapter 9 of the Bankruptcy Code and their legislative history mandated that such revenue bond financing be unimpaired. If there are sufficient revenues to pay operation, maintenance, debt service and all other expenses, there is no basis for failing to comply with contractual obligations. Sections 922(d) and 928(a) of the Bankruptcy Code require. Pursuant to language contained in the relevant state statute and the intent of the voters' referendum in authorizing the UTGOs to have taxes levied above the tax cap to pay these bonds, it appeared clear that there should have been a levy of tax sufficient to pay the UTGOs and, if not, a continuing unlimited levy to meet that obligation.

The problem with Detroit's efforts to contest and question certain types of financing is the contagion effect that this could have on other municipalities in Michigan in terms of their ability to use such financing to meet their municipal needs. The questioning and the cloud placed on the financing causes the cost of financing to increase, which means taxpayers will pay more. A 1 percent to 2 percent increase in annual interest costs for bond financing with a bullet maturity due to the uncertainty and cloud of Chapter 9 over the life of a thirty-year bond means that 30 percent to 60 percent more of the principal amount will be paid as additional interest expense with additional taxpayer dollars.[116] These dollars could have been utilized for other necessary municipal expenses.

In the end, the issues in Detroit were settled and it was recognized by the settlement that there was no underlying legal basis to question the right to payment. It is important to reaffirm for all municipalities in Michigan, and for that matter elsewhere, the basic principle that, if there is a dedicated source of payment sufficient to pay the obligations, those promises to pay must not be broken or rewritten in a municipal bankruptcy. A dedicated source of payment, statutory lien or special revenues established under state law must be honored and should not be contested. Capital markets work more effectively when credibility and predictability of outcome are clear and unquestioned.

---

116 Further, an additional interest cost per year of 2 percent on future borrowing because of the stigma and cloud of Chapter 9 bankruptcy on $1 billion of principal financing with a 20-year bullet maturity results in $250 million more present value cost of financing at a 5 percent discount. To a struggling municipality, this can make all the difference.

Lesson Four:
Debt adjustment is a process, but a recovery plan is a solution

As noted above, while a debt adjustment can provide the additional leeway required for recovery, such a plan is not the cure for systemic problems. Rather, the debt adjustment provides additional breathing room so the municipality, through its mayor and its elected officials, may proceed with a recovery plan, reinvest in Detroit, stimulate the economy, create new jobs, clear and develop blighted areas and raise the level of services and infrastructure to that which is acceptable and attracts new business and new citizens. That is not simply a short-term effort but typically a five- to ten-year (or longer) process. While Chapter 9 may be necessary to provide the breathing room, the recovery plan is what will provide the resolution. If the recovery plan is not accomplished and the systemic problem is not addressed, the confirmation of a plan of debt adjustment will not prevent the reoccurrence of an uncured systemic problem.

Lesson Five:
Successful plans of debt adjustment have one common feature: virtually all significant issues have been settled and resolved with major creditors

While the Detroit plan started with sound and fury between the emergency manager and creditors over what they would receive, in the end, similar to what occurred in Vallejo, Jefferson County and even in Stockton (with one exception), the major creditors reached agreement and supported a plan of debt adjustment that allowed the municipality to begin its journey to recovery. "Buy-in" on a local level with citizens and taxpayers, public workers and retirees, as well as with supplier-creditors and the capital markets, is important to ensure a successful recovery and continuing cooperation to resolve the municipality's financial difficulties.

Lesson Six:
One size does not fit all

There are many ways to draft a plan of debt adjustment and sometimes, the more creative, the better. As noted above, traditionally major cities with significant debt did not file Chapter 9. They refinanced their debt with the backing of the state, which reduced their future borrowing costs and allowed them to recover by having the liquidity and the lower borrowing costs necessary to deal with their financial difficulties.

Detroit chose a different path, and one of the primary considerations in a Chapter 9 filing is how a plan of debt adjustment should be structured. As indicated by the Grand Bargain, third-party foundations and contributors along with the state provided $816 million to save the municipal art museum and to address the pension issues. This was a creative and constructive mechanism to provide funds that were otherwise unavailable to the municipality. While some noted, with some basis, that it appeared the unsecured creditors were treated dissimilarly from retirees, ultimately the municipality created a plan that virtually all of the creditors approved, thereby ameliorating any argument of dissimilar treatment. More likely than not, it would have been a greater problem if the major creditors had not come together with virtually unanimous support for the plan of debt adjustment. In addition, the resolutions with some major creditors including the bond insurers Syncora and FGIC were creative. There should be no doubt that Syncora and FGIC could have been significant obstacles in confirmation and in appeals relating to issues that were not necessarily guaranteed to turn in Detroit's favor. Syncora and FGIC's acceptance of interests in real estate and leases meant in essence that they would reinvest in Detroit and therefore improve their recovery — a purported win-win. The insurers resolved their issues, recognizing the significant cost and expense of litigation with no guaranty of victory. Settlement offered these creditors certainty, and an opportunity to improve their recoveries by leveraging their skills and abilities in investing in and management of real estate opportunities. Such creativity should be encouraged, to the extent it is consistent with applicable bankruptcy and state law.

Lesson Seven:
A recovery plan must provide for essential services and infrastructure

The "best interests of creditors" and "feasibility" tests can only mean an appropriate reinvestment in the municipality through a recovery plan where there is adequate funding of essential services and infrastructure at an acceptable level to stimulate the municipality's economy and attract new employers and taxpayers to increase tax revenues and address the systemic problem. It is important to recognize that Chapter 9 is a process, not a solution.

While no plan of debt adjustment is perfect or assured, there should be, as the bankruptcy court in Detroit throughout the case pointed out, a plan to demonstrate the survivability and future success of the city. This is in essence a recovery plan where the reinvestment provides a cure to the systemic problem that led to the Chapter 9 — namely, investing in infrastructure and essential services that had been lacking in the past in order to stimulate and enhance the economy, to create opportunities for jobs, and to increase the tax revenues necessary for the recovery. Failure to address these issues, even after confirming a plan of debt adjustment, will lead to the same systemic problems and economic downturns that led to the Chapter 9 filing. The "best interests of creditors" and "feasibility" tests cannot be interpreted as requiring paying creditors more and sacrificing necessary funding of infrastructure and essential services. This would not be in the best interests of creditors and would eventually lead to the downturn of the economy and less ability for payment to all.

Lesson Eight:
Confirmation of a plan of debt adjustment is only the beginning of the journey to financial recovery — not the end

It is important to recognize, as noted above, that Chapter 9 is a process, not a solution. A recovery plan, which takes dedication and immense effort by the elected officials of the city, along with residents, public workers and other creditors, to successfully implement, is the only way to achieve success. Recovery is measured not by months but by years, and it requires constant vigilance to ensure that systemic problems are effectively and permanently addressed.

Obviously, as Detroit proceeds to implement its recovery plan, additional lessons may be learned. However, the eight lessons identified above should assist every municipality facing financial difficulties deal more effectively with their problems and motivate them to identify and address economic financial distress earlier, encourage help from the state and others, and avoid that which should be the last and least desired result, namely the filing of a Chapter 9 bankruptcy.

B. Conclusion

As discussed, knowledge of the causes and case studies of some of the major municipal defaults is helpful in considering the extent and development of provisions of state law intended to deal with the financial distress of municipalities. The following discussion of state law provisions further develops this overview of established state law addressing financially challenged municipalities. Section VIII, the 50-State Survey, provides a more general overview of how states have either responded to or attempted to prevent such defaults. The next section of this book will provide a general overview of the techniques employed by the states to attempt to prevent municipal defaults.

IV. State Provisions Regarding Government Debt Default Prevention

At the front line of protecting the municipal marketplace are debt limitations imposed by state constitutions and statutory law to restrict the amount of debt that a municipality may issue at any one time. In addition to debt limitation provisions, all states include provisions in their statutory law for the issuance of refunding bonds. This next section will discuss protective measures taken by the various states.

A. Dillon's Rule and the Demise of the Cooley Doctrine [117]

The tension between municipal and state governments has a long and storied history. Evidence of conflict concerning the rights and privileges of municipal government dates back to the mid-19th century. While state and local officials debated this topic in all regions of the country, the tension was exemplified through the treatises and opinions of two midwestern state supreme court justices.

In 1850, John F. Dillon, a medical doctor at the age of 20, left his hometown of Davenport, Iowa, to practice his profession. However, a painful medical condition of his own left him unable to ride horseback — a requirement of being a country doctor at the time — so he changed his career path and became a lawyer. He taught himself the law while he was running a family drugstore in Davenport. By 1862 he was serving on the Iowa Supreme Court. In 1872, based on his unprecedented research on the topic, Dillon published the first edition of his *Commentaries on the Law of Municipal Corporations*, a treatise that would lay the groundwork for settling future debates as to the powers of local government relative to the state.

Dillon's findings, as set forth in the seminal case on the topic, *City of Clinton v. Cedar Rapids & Mo. River R.R.*, decided by the Iowa Supreme Court in 1868, are known to this day as "Dillon's Rule." Dillon's Rule stands for the premise that cities and villages owe their origin to, and derive their powers wholly from, their state legislatures. The holding in *Cedar Rapids* states that the legislature creates the powers of local government, and consequently it may rescind them. The court further noted that while the chance is quite remote, a state legislature could, by a single piece of legislation, sweep from existence all of the cities and villages in its state.

In 1868, the same year as Dillon's eloquent opinion on the matter, Thomas M. Cooley, a former professor of law at the University of Michigan and a Michigan Supreme Court Justice, published his own treatise concerning the powers of municipalities. The book, *A Treatise on the Constitutional*

---

117 Subsection A is excerpted with permission from author, Lawrence E. White, *Home Rule in Illinois: A Modern Controversy Reignites an Old Debate,* Illinois Government Finance Officers Association Dispatch, Late Winter 2014.

Limitations Which Rest upon the Legislative Power of the States of the American Union, went through six editions by 1890 and has been referenced as the best-known legal treatise in the late 19th century. Cooley argued that local government (in the form of towns and counties) should have and does have greater autonomy than other state-created municipal corporations because such municipalities represent a collective of people who are united by location and community ties, a bond not found in state-created municipal corporations.

In 1871, soon after the first edition of his treatise was published, Cooley and the Michigan Supreme Court staked out a position opposite that of Dillon and the Iowa Supreme Court with respect to local government rights. In *Leroy v. Hurlbut,* the Michigan court found that each city operated under the protection of certain fundamental principles that no power in the state could override or disregard. The court added that local government is a matter of absolute right and the state cannot take such right away. Further, the court stated that it would be "the boldest mockery" to say a system of government meets the requirements of constitutional freedom where it is equally permitted to give people full control of their local affairs, or no control at all.

By the mid-1800s, most state courts had heard cases concerning the extent to which state legislatures could control municipal government, with differing results. Some state courts outside of Michigan adopted Cooley's idea of the inherent right of local governments to self-government, while others adhered to some form of Dillon's Rule. The uncertainty regarding local government powers as they related to those of the state was firmly settled by the U.S. Supreme Court in favor of Dillon's position. In 1891, the Supreme Court in *Merrill v. Monticello* reversed an Indiana decision on the subject of powers of local government. The court, quoting Dillon, stated:

> It is a general and undisputed proposition of law that a municipal corporation possesses and can exercise the following powers and no others: First, those granted in express words; second, those necessarily or fairly implied in or incident to the powers expressly granted; third, those essential to the declared objects and purposes of the corporation — not simply convenient but indispensable. Any fair, reasonable doubt concerning the existence of power is resolved by the courts against the corporation, and the power is denied.

The court's opinion and the temporary resolution of the state-city conflict had a chilling effect on local authorities. As a result, state governments were able to provide a substantial, although not always successful, check on local governments. Accordingly, given the Tenth Amendment to the Constitution, the states and the federal government are co-sovereigns, and local governments are sub-sovereigns of their respective states subject to the statutory and constitutional limitations set forth by the state.

B. Debt and Tax Limitations

Among the most important protections for bondholders are the limitations that the various states have imposed on the amount of debt a municipality may issue and hold at any one time. In fact, all states with the exception of Alaska, Florida and Tennessee impose some sort of debt limit.[118] Municipalities in 27 states and Puerto Rico are restricted by debt or tax limits imposed by their respective constitutions. The District of Columbia and the other 20 states that impose debt or tax limitations on their municipalities do so via statutory provisions.

These municipal debt limits range from a percentage of a valuation of assessed property in the local unit of government to a set monetary amount.[119] In addition, states handle debt for certain "essential" services differently. For instance, in Arizona, the constitutional debt limit with voter consent is 15 percent of the taxable property in the local unit of government if bonds are issued for certain other purposes, such as for supplying water or for law enforcement.[120] In Kansas, bonds issued by cities with respect to sewer systems or to acquire or enlarge a municipality utility, and certain street improvement bonds, are not counted toward the issuing city's bond indebtedness calculation.[121] Revenue bonds issued in Kansas are also not included in this calculation.[122] In Arkansas, industrial development bonds do not count toward the state's debt limit.[123]

In Idaho, two-thirds of voters must approve bond issuances in which a local government would incur debt exceeding the income and revenue the local government would receive in a year.[124] Should voters approve a bond issuance, the state constitution requires that the local government collect an annual tax sufficient to pay the bond interest as it comes due and to establish a sinking fund for payment of the principal within 30 years.[125] A few states, such as Louisiana, have set debt limits based on the type of project rather than a blanket limit into which all debt issued by a particular local government falls.[126] The Puerto Rico constitution directs the Puerto Rico legislature to fix municipal

118 *See* section VIII, 50 State Survey. Even Alaska and Florida have some indirect control on debt. Alaska has a limitation on taxes and a municipality may not levy ad valorem taxes for any purpose in excess of 3 percent of the assessed value of the property in the municipality. Florida has a limitation on ad valorem taxes to finance or refund capital projects only if approved by the voters.

119 *Compare* Alabama (ALA. CONST. art. XII, § 225 and amend. § 342 (debt may not exceed a particular percentage of valuation)) *with* Washington, D.C. (D.C. CODE § 47-102 (setting debt limit at 1878 levels)).

120 ARIZ. CONST. art. IX, § 8. *See also* section VIII.

121 KAN. STAT. § 10-309. *See also* section VIII.

122 *Id.* at § 10-311.

123 ARK. CONST. amend. § 62. *See also* section VIII.

124 IDAHO CONST. art. VIII, § 3. *See also* section VIII.

125 *Id.*

126 LA. CONST. art. VI, § 34; LA. REV. STAT. § 39:562. *See also* section VIII.

debt limits, but these limits may not be less than 5 percent or more than 10 percent of the aggregate tax valuation of the property within the municipality.[127] In other states, such as Rhode Island, a debt limit has been set for cities and towns, but the debt measurement is net of any tax anticipation bonds and the amount in any sinking fund.[128]

There have been recent attempts in some states to tighten local debt limits. For instance, in November 2010, Colorado voters considered a state constitutional amendment that would have greatly limited the ability of local governments to borrow funds. This amendment, which was overwhelmingly defeated by 73 percent of voters, would have prohibited a local government borrowing after 2010 unless the voters approved the borrowing. Specifically, the amendment would have required voter approval for all borrowing, limited local government borrowing to bond debt and established a debt limit for local governments to 10 percent of the assessed value of the real property therein. The length of borrowing would also have been reduced from the typical term of 20 to 30 years to a constitutional limit of ten years. Currently, Colorado imposes a debt limit on school districts of 20 percent of the last valuation on taxable property, or 6 percent of the most recent determination of actual value of the property.[129] In July 2011, Rhode Island enacted legislation that created a statutory lien for the payment of bond debt with a first priority lien on revenues of a municipality as proceeds of ad valorem taxes upon all the taxable property within the municipality and general fund revenues of the municipality in order to assure the municipal market of the dedication to payment.[130] Other states have passed similar legislation creating a statutory lien to assure the financial markets of a dedicated source of payment that would survive Chapter 9 and provide greater access to the market and lower borrowing costs to its municipalities.[131]

Although states attempt to limit the amount of debt that their municipalities may incur, local governments sometimes take certain actions to avoid these debt limitations. For instance, revenue bonds financed by particular rents, tolls or charges generated from a project are exempt from debt

---

127 P.R. CONST. art. VI, § 2. *See also* section VIII.

128 R.I. GEN. LAWS § 45-12-2. *See also* section VIII.

129 COLO. REV. STAT. § 22-42-104. *See also* section VIII.

130 R.I. GEN LAWS §§ 45-12-1, 45-12-22.4. These provisions were successfully tested in the bankruptcy proceeding involving the City of Central Falls, Rhode Island. *See In re City of Central Falls, Rhode Island*, Case No. 11-13105 (filed Sept. 22, 2011).

131 *See* CAL. EDUC. CODE § 15251(b) and CAL. GOV'T. CODE § 53515(a) (effective Jan. 1, 2016), confirming a statutory lien for unlimited ad valorem tax general obligation bonds of cities, counties, school districts and special districts), and James Spiotto, *Reducing Risk to Payment of State and Local Government Debt Obligations, Statutory Liens from Rhode Island to California SB 222*, MUNINETGUIDE (July 28, 2015), http:www.muninetguide.com/articles/reducing-risk-to-payment-of-state-and-local-government-debt-7401. *See also* Rhode Island (R.I. GEN. LAWS § 45-12), Colorado (COLO. REV. STAT. § 11-57-208), Idaho (IDAHO CODE § 57-234). *See also* Michigan H.B. 4495 that passed the House in 2015 and is now pending before the Michigan Senate, http://www.legislature.mi.gov/(S(jkpurq2bb1oxovquxrx1sm34))/mileg.aspx?page=GetObject&objectname=2015-HB-4495.

limitation calculations in many states. Similarly, many local governments issue tax increment financing ("TIF"), which is generally not counted in the debt limitation valuation. In fact, the Supreme Court of Iowa has held that a TIF district's issuance of bonds does not count toward a city's constitutional debt limit because the bonds are not a legally enforceable obligation to the city.[132] In other situations, a local government may attempt to use "nonappropriation" financing, in which a local government agrees to make rental payments on a facility built by either a private company or a public entity. The payment of the rent is contingent on the local governing board appropriating money for the rental payment. Courts have had a mixed reaction as to whether so-called nonappropriation funding should be counted in a local government's debt limit.[133] In California, there are three major exceptions to the state constitution's debt limit, including the "Offner-Dean" lease exception allowing for certain long-term lease obligations, if they meet certain criteria, to be exempt from the state's debt limit; the "Special Fund Doctrine," which is a judicially created debt limit exception applicable to long-term indebtedness financed through a special fund, such as enterprise revenues; and the "Obligation Imposed by Law" exception applicable to involuntary indebtedness such as a money judgment.[134] Also in California, municipalities sometimes issue "certificates of participation," a strategy generally exempt from state constitutional debt limits, whereby local governments market lease obligations through the retail securities market by means of certificates of participation that pay tax-exempt interest and are liquid.[135] These are just a few examples of strategies that a municipality might utilize to circumvent a constitutionally or statutorily imposed debt limit. For specific questions, an attorney familiar with the laws and processes of a particular state should be consulted.

C. Refunding Bonds

Perhaps the most common way that municipalities restructure their debt is through the issuance of refunding bonds. Refunding bonds, as the name implies, are bonds that are issued to redeem the principal of outstanding bonds. Every state provides some sort of refunding bond provision for its municipalities.[136] By issuing refunding bonds, a municipality may be able to refinance its debt at a rate more favorable to itself or to let its debt mature at a time when the municipality believes it will be more flush with money. Refunding bonds also may help a municipality push off its debt troubles

---

132 *Fults v. City of Coralville*, 666 N.W.2d 548, 556 (Iowa 2003).

133 *Compare Shulz v. State*, 639 N.E.2d 1140 (N.Y. 1994) (upholding "nonappropriation" financing as exempt from debt limit) *with Brown v. City of Stuttgart*, 847 S.W.2d 710 (Ark. 1993) (rejecting notion that "nonappropriation" financing is exempt from debt limit).

134 For a more detailed discussion of California debt limitations and the issuance of public bonds in California in general, *see* California Debt and Investment Advisory Commission, *California Debt Issuance Primer* (2005), http://www.treasurer.ca.gov/cdiac/debtpubs/primer.pdf.

135 For a general overview of lease financing and certificates of participation in California, *see* California Debt Advisory Commission, *Guidelines for Leases and Certificates of Participation* (1993), http://www.treasurer.ca.gov/cdiac/reports/Guidelines93-8.pdf.

136 *See* section VIII *infra*.

for another day. Generally, the issuance of refunding bonds does not constitute indebtedness for the purposes of debt limitations imposed by almost all of the states. This is because the purpose of refunding bonds is to refinance already existing bonds.

Refunding bonds generally may be issued at any time before the final maturity of the debt to be refinanced. Although municipalities generally have flexibility in refunding their current obligations, many states impose provisions limiting the use of refunding bonds in an attempt to protect the financial solvency of a particular municipality. For instance, in Pennsylvania, refunding bonds may only be issued to (1) reduce total debt service over the life of the bond issuance; (2) reduce annual debt service; (3) eliminate unduly burdensome or restrictive covenants or restrictions; (4) refund any maturity or maturities to a later date; (5) substitute bonds for notes or bond anticipation notes, or substitute notes for bonds; or (6) adjust lease rentals.[137] Pennsylvania law further limits municipalities in their issuance of refunding bonds by disallowing local governments from extending the term of the outstanding debt through refunding to a maturity date that could not have been included in the original issue unless "in the case of an emergency refunding of stated maturity date to avoid a default occasioned by an unforeseen shortage in total revenues."[138] This provision, however, would only apply if the municipality in question were to first petition the state government and the petition received state approval.[139] As outlined in section VIII, the 50-State Survey, other states have similar provisions with respect to circumstances under which a municipality may issue refunding bonds.[140]

D. Conclusion

By setting debt limits and taxing limits and allowing for the issuance of refunding bonds, the states have attempted to curb the number of municipal financial crises and defaults. Section VIII, the 50-State Survey, provides a more general overview of these provisions for each state. In addition to these provisions, and as will be discussed next, some states have gone a step further to help beleaguered municipalities resolve their financial issues at the initial signs of a problem.

---

137 53 PA. STATS. §§ 8241 - 8251. *See* the Pennsylvania chart in section VIII.

138 *Id.* at § 8243.

139 *Id.*

140 *See* section VIII *infra*.

V. Debt Resolution Mechanisms: State Oversight, Supervision and Assistance for Fiscal Emergencies of Local Governments

A. Introduction and List of State Intervention Provisions

In addition to debt limitations and allowing for the issuance of refunding bonds, over 20 states have implemented municipal debt monitoring, supervision, financial assistance or restructuring mechanisms to aid municipalities. These programs, many of which are identified in the chart immediately following this paragraph, take a number of approaches. For example, in Georgia Government Monitoring, municipalities and subdivisions submit annual audits. If any violation of state law is disclosed by the auditors, the local government must submit a plan of corrective action. Other states also structure their programs in various ways, such as the California Debt and Investment Advisory Commission and the Florida Local Government Financial Technical Assistance Program, which provide guidance for and keep records of the issuance of municipal bonds in those states. This differs from the layered approach of Rhode Island to aid municipalities depending on their level of financial instability, or the procedure in other states, such as Michigan and Indiana, for the appointment of an emergency manager to take over supervision, operation and financial oversight of the local government. States with these provisions have effectively used these mechanisms to control the restructuring of their municipalities. States that contain provisions allowing for state intervention into a municipality's finances include:[141]

141 A more detailed analysis of each state's restructuring regime is provided in section VIII. While most of the states that have some form of intervention provide for a financial monitoring system, the list of states that allow for state intervention does not include Colorado, Iowa, Maryland, South Dakota and Washington, which have some form of auditing or financial monitoring of local governments but do not provide for intervention or further action. *See, e.g.* IOWA CODE § 11.6 (Examination of Governmental Subdivisions — Consultative Services — Association of Counties) and COLO. REV. STAT. § 29-1-601 *et seq.* (Local Government Audit Law). For a detailed analysis of state auditing and monitoring systems, *see* The Pew Charitable Trusts, State Strategies to Detect Local Financial Distress: How States Assess and Monitor Financial Health of Local Government, www.pewtrusts.org/en/research-and-analysis/fact-sheets/2016/07-state_strategies-for-detecting-fiscal-distress-in-local-governments.html (last visited July 19, 2016), and the Pew Charitable Trust, The State Role in Local Government Financial Distress, www.pewtrusts.org/en/research-and-analysis/reports/2013/07/23/the-state-role-in-local-government-financial-distress.html (last visited July 19, 2016).

	State	Intervention Provision
1.	Arizona	School District Receivership
2.	California	Debt and Investment Advisory Commission
3.	Connecticut	Ad Hoc State Intervention
4.	District of Columbia	Financial Responsibility and Management Assistance Authority
5.	Florida	Bond Financial Emergencies Act; Division of Bond Finance and Local Government Financial Technical Assistance Program
6.	Georgia	Government Monitoring
7.	Idaho	Debt Readjustment Plans
8.	Illinois	Financially Distressed City Law; Financial Planning and Supervision
9.	Indiana	Distressed Political Subdivision Protections and Township Assistance
10.	Kentucky	County Restructuring Provisions
11.	Louisiana	Appointment of a Fiscal Administrator
12.	Maine	Board of Emergency Municipal Finance
13.	Massachusetts	Ad Hoc State Intervention and State Bond Payment Intervention
14.	Michigan	Local Financial Stability and Choice Act
15.	Minnesota	Back-up Payment Procedures for Municipalities and School Districts
16.	Nevada	Local Government Financial Assistance and Audit Enforcement Act
17.	New Hampshire	Emergency Financial Assistance
18.	New Jersey	Local Government Supervision Act; Municipal Rehabilitation and Economic Recovery Act of 2002; Special Municipal Aid Act
19.	New York	Emergency Financial Control Board; Municipal Assistance Corporation; New York Financial Control Board; State Comptroller's Fiscal Stress Monitoring System
20.	New Mexico	Financial Auditing and Emergency Loans
21.	North Carolina	Local Government Finance Act

	State	Intervention Provision
22.	Ohio	State Auditor's Fiscal Caution and Fiscal Watch; Fiscal Emergencies and Financial Planning and Supervision Commission
23.	Oregon	County Technical Assistance Program; Municipal Debt Advisory Commission
24.	Pennsylvania	Financially Distressed Municipalities Act; Intergovernmental Cooperation Act; Municipal Receiver
25.	Puerto Rico	Puerto Rico Oversight, Management and Economic Stability Act
26.	Rhode Island	Fiscal Overseer; Municipal Receiver; Budget Commission
27.	Tennessee	Emergency Financial Aid to Local Governments; Financially Distressed Municipality Procedures
28.	Texas	Municipal Receivership
29.	Virginia	Bond Payment Guarantee Provisions
30.	Wisconsin	Deficiency Protection for Public Improvement Bonds

The idea of state remedial measures to aid troubled municipalities is not a recent phenomenon. The earliest instances in the United States of remedial mechanisms occurred in January 1879 in Memphis, Tennessee, and Mobile, Alabama.[142] In Memphis, the city was placed into a temporary administrative receivership when the Tennessee legislature disincorporated the city and placed it into the "Taxing District of Shelby County." The governor was authorized to appoint two individuals to compromise the existing indebtedness of the former city. In Mobile, the Alabama legislature repealed the city's charter and the governor appointed a three-member commission vested with the assets of the former city and authorized to compromise the existing indebtedness.[143]

B. States Recognizing Municipal Receivers — Louisiana, Pennsylvania, Rhode Island and Texas

Similar situations occur even today and at least four states — Louisiana, Pennsylvania, Rhode Island and Texas — permit the appointment of a municipal receiver or similar officer by a court in the event of a municipal financial emergency. For instance, in Rhode Island, the city of Central Falls

---

142 Hillhouse, *supra* n. 8, at 324-25.

143 This is not unusual and follows historical precedent going back to the 5th century B.C. and the Greek town of Atarneus, where a Greek banker took over administration due to a defaulted loan. See the more detailed discussion of City of Mobile, Alabama defaults in 1839 and 1879 in section II at 21.

petitioned a state court and was placed into judicial receivership for its financial woes in May 2010. The city of 18,000 had over $20 million of general obligation debt.[144] In response to the city's filing for judicial receivership, in June 2010 the Rhode Island legislature passed and the governor signed into law a process of progressive state intervention for municipalities in financial distress. The new law created a three-step process for distressed governments, in what was possibly an attempt by Rhode Island to prevent *ad hoc* efforts by municipalities to restructure with tactics that could be unfriendly to the municipal markets.[145] The law applied retroactively to prevent the Central Falls judicial receivership from continuing.

After the legislation became law, Central Falls was placed into municipal receivership when a state commission found that the municipality had insufficient power to restore fiscal responsibility. The city council of Central Falls attempted to challenge the new state law, but a state court judge in October 2010 upheld the constitutionality of the state-appointed receiver. Shortly thereafter, in November 2010, the receiver exercised his significant power to disband the Central Falls City Council and replace it with a three-member advisory council. Additionally, Rhode Island has enacted legislation to give the municipal debt holders a guarantee of first rights to property taxes and general revenues in the event of default or bankruptcy. This was in an apparent effort to demonstrate the creditworthiness and improve the market access of Rhode Island's municipal debt issuers that is vital to ensure financing for essential infrastructure improvement and recoveries.[146] On August 1, 2011, Central Falls' state-appointed receiver filed a Chapter 9 petition for municipal bankruptcy on behalf of the city. General obligation bondholders received payment on their bonds during the bankruptcy proceeding and as a part of Central Falls' bankruptcy plan of adjustment, general obligation bondholders were unimpaired, meaning that they would continue receiving the payments that were contractually promised to them when they had purchased the general obligation bonds before Central Falls filed its bankruptcy petition.

In May 2014 the governor of Rhode Island expanded the state's financial receivership law to apply to fire districts. This permitted the state to step in and appoint a receiver to manage the Central Coventry Fire District. When negotiations by the receiver to restructure the fire district's debts proved unsuccessful, in December 2014 that receiver filed a Chapter 9 bankruptcy petition on behalf of the fire district.[147] A miscalculated budget and increased labor and other costs led to the fire district's insolvency.

---

144 Patrick McGee & Taylor Riggs, *Central Falls Aims to Protect GOs*, THE BOND BUYER (Aug. 1, 2011), http://www.bondbuyer.com/news/central-falls-bankruptcy-1029523-1.html (last visited Jan. 25, 2016).

145 *See* R.I. GEN. LAWS §§ 45-9-1-45-9-23.

146 R.I. GEN. LAWS §§ 45-12-1, 45-12-22.4. For a more detailed discussion of the *Central Falls* bankruptcy proceeding see section III at 50-51.

147 *In re Central Coventry Fire District, Rhode Island*, Case No. 14-12785 (Bankr. D. R.I., Dec. 23, 2014).

Similarly, as a result of the tumultuous insolvency of Harrisburg, Pennsylvania, that led to a deadlock by city officials in 2010-11 as a result of a failed waste incinerator project, Pennsylvania has enacted its own municipal receiver regime.[148] In Harrisburg, the state recommended and a state court appointed a municipal receiver, who reached a settlement with the debt holders of the municipality to restructure its debt. As a result of Harrisburg's successful restructuring, Pennsylvania incorporated the concept of a municipal receiver into its Financially Distressed Municipalities Act. Pennsylvania's municipal receivership provisions are available to any distressed municipality, as defined under Pennsylvania law, for which the Pennsylvania governor has declared a fiscal emergency.[149] A state court controls the process and the court-appointed receiver is required to present a recovery plan to the court for approval within 30 days of his or her appointment.

In addition to the Rhode Island law, Pennsylvania law, Louisiana law and a law in Texas allowing for a judicially appointed municipal receiver, other states have chosen to allow for financial control boards, emergency managers, coordinators, overseers or financial commissions to aid troubled municipalities. As background, the concept of a financial control board first made its appearance with the creation of a financial commission to oversee Manchester, New Hampshire in 1921.[150] Although the Manchester financial commission was appointed by the governor, it was the mayor and aldermen of Manchester who fixed the commission's compensation. The commission was allowed to control and regulate appropriations, expenditures and bond issuances but could not control the collection of taxes.

C. Financial Control Boards and Active Supervision Examples

Today, the laws of Florida, Illinois, Indiana, Michigan, Nevada, New Jersey, New York, North Carolina, Ohio, Oregon, Pennsylvania and Rhode Island include a variation on a provision allowing for the appointment of a financial control board or commission, emergency manager, coordinator or overseer over a troubled unit of local government.[151] The intent of many of these provisions is to identify early signs of financial distress for a city or municipality so the state may intervene before the city or municipality reaches the level of a municipal crisis. Importantly, such provisions are not just a web of buried state laws never to be used but, rather, are applied when situations call for intervention. An outgrowth of these efforts has been the development of the concept of a neutral evaluator by the California legislature and other attempts to create a municipal protection commission.

---

148 53 PA. STAT. ANN. § 11701.701-712. For a more detailed discussion of the Harrisburg, Pennsylvania financial saga section III at 51-52.

149 *Id.*

150 Hillhouse, *supra* n. 8, at 326.

151 *See* section VIII.

I. The New York Experience

Perhaps the most well-known appointment of a financial commission was the implementation of the New York City Financial Control Board. In the spring of 1975, New York City was unable to market its debt because the bond market had discovered that New York had, for more than ten years, been using questionable accounting and borrowing practices to eliminate its annual budget deficits.[152] Banks refused to renew short-term loans that were maturing or to loan additional cash to the city, and only state cash advances were keeping the city afloat. The city's spending for operating purposes exceeded operating revenues over several years, and the accumulated fund deficit could only be resolved by increasing amounts of short-term borrowing. New York City itself had no funds to meet its short-term obligations. New York nearly defaulted on the payment of its notes in October 1975, and it was predicted that a default would be likely in December 1975 absent federal aid.[153] In response, the State Municipal Assistance Corporation, or MAC, issued a series of securities on behalf of the city and a financial control board was appointed.

The New York City Financial Control Board was given the power and responsibility to review and provide oversight with respect to the financial management of New York City's government. Among other things, the act establishing the board required the city to prepare and submit a "rolling" four-year financial plan to the Financial Control Board prior to the beginning of each city fiscal year. The Financial Control Board, today, although essentially dormant since the mid-1980s, can be reactivated if certain conditions are triggered, including the inability of the city to meet its debt service payments.[154]

In addition to the New York City Financial Control Board, the New York legislature may implement Emergency Financial Control Boards for any municipality outside of New York City. This provision was used in November 1975 to take control of the City of Yonkers (the board was terminated on December 31, 1978) and most recently with regard to Nassau County in January 2011.[155] Additional financial control boards in New York include: (a) the Buffalo Fiscal Stability Authority, (b) the Erie County Fiscal Stability Authority, (c) the Nassau County Interim Finance Authority, (d) the New York City Financial Control Board, and (e) the Municipal Assistance Corporation for the City of Troy. In

---

152 For a detailed study of the New York City fiscal crisis see Shalala & Bellamy, *A State Saves a City: The New York Case*, 1976 DUKE L.J. 1119 (1976); United States Congress, House of Representatives Committee on Banking, Finance and Urban Affairs, Subcommittee on Economic Stabilization, SECURITIES AND EXCHANGE COMMISSION STAFF REPORT ON TRANSACTIONS IN SECURITIES OF THE CITY OF NEW YORK (95th Cong. 1st Sess., Aug. 1977).

153 Martin Tolchin, *Top Bankers Say Default Can Hurt World's Markets*, N.Y. TIMES, Oct. 19, 1975, at 1. For a more detailed discussion of the City of New York, New York's financial struggle see section III at 41-42 *supra*.

154 *See* THE BOND BUYER (Nov. 30, 1990) at 1, 45.

155 David M. Halbfinger, *New York State Seizes Finances of Nassau County*, N.Y. TIMES, Jan. 26, 2011, at A1.

addition, today the comptroller of the State of New York has implemented a fiscal stress-monitoring program to monitor the fiscal health of New York's municipalities.[156]

2. The Pennsylvania Experience and District of Columbia Control Board

Similar to the New York experience, Pennsylvania has implemented a series of provisions to aid ailing cities. Pennsylvania law contains the Financially Distressed Municipalities Act, commonly known as Act 47, which applies to any county, borough, incorporated town, township or home-rule municipality.[157] Under the provisions of Act 47, if the state Department of Community & Economic Development determines that a municipality is financially distressed based on certain triggering events, the department may appoint a coordinator to guide the municipality in getting its financial affairs in order. There have been 29 filings under these provisions since 1987 and 11 rescissions of such filings.[158] Examples of municipalities that were determined by the department to be financially distressed include Pittsburgh in 2003, the Borough of Wilkinsburg in 1988 and Harrisburg in October 2010.[159] Recently, in the wake of extreme dysfunction in the restructuring of Harrisburg's debts, Act 47 was expanded to include a municipal receivership option.[160]

In October 2014, amendments to Act 47 were enacted to expand the provision in addition to adding a receivership option. Those amendments provided: (a) a time limit of five years with the ability to request a onetime three-year extension in order to encourage an exit in five years with an approved recovery plan, (b) a program of early intervention with increased assistance and financial support to address problems earlier, (c) expanded use of a receiver if the municipality fails to develop or approve a recovery plan acceptable to the secretary of the Department of Community & Economic Development, under which option the secretary can adopt an emergency action plan and the governor can take emergency action for the continuation of vital and needed services as well as ultimately have a receiver appointed (as was done in Harrisburg) that would exercise the power of elected officials if they fail to act, (d) enhancement of revenues through earned income tax on residents and commuters but only for the period Act 47 is in effect and (e) use of disincorporation for non-viable municipalities.[161]

In addition to the Financially Distressed Municipalities Act, Pennsylvania law contains the Intergovernmental Cooperation Authority Act, or PICA, which was created in 1991 to deal with fiscal

---

156 *See* FISCAL MONITORING, www.osc.state.ny.us/localgov/index.htm (last visited Jan. 26, 2016).

157 53 PA. STAT. §§ 11701.101-11701.501. For a more detailed discussion of Philadelphia, Pennsylvania see section III at 46-48.

158 For a full list of municipalities, *see* community.newpa.com/local-government/act-47-Financial-distress.

159 For a detailed list of cities determined by the department to be financially distressed, *see* section VIII, Pennsylvania chart.

160 53 PA. STAT. ANN. §§ 11701.701-715.

161 *See* Pennsylvania Act of Oct. 31, 2014, P.L. 2983, No. 199 and section VIII, Pennsylvania.

distress issues faced by Philadelphia. The act created a five-member authority with authorization to enter into intergovernmental cooperation agreements with cities, which agreements were preconditions to the issuance of any obligations by the authority. Among other things, the authority could issue bonds and the city and the authority were required to work together to develop a five-year financial recovery plan.

Another example of a "control board" established by special legislation similar to MAC for New York City and PICA for Philadelphia was the response of the U.S. Congress to the financial distress of the District of Columbia in the 1990s. In 1995, Congress passed the District of Columbia Responsibility and Management Assistance Act creating the District of Columbia Financial Control Board.[162] Like PICA, the Financial Control Board had five members who were appointed by the president with input from Congress and the district. An executive director coordinated the supervision and oversight of the Financial Control Board, including review of budgets and operational issues. The Financial Control Board could override any decision of the mayor and the council for the District of Columbia. If the board did not approve a budget or action, it could provide recommendations for action which the district could implement, or it could allow the district to make its own changes and re-submit the proposal. The Financial Control Board could withhold funds if budgets or actions were not approved.

3. The Michigan Experience

Likewise, the State of Michigan, under its former Local Government Fiscal Responsibility Act, has taken over the Detroit Public Schools, the city of Pontiac, the city of Escorse, the village of Three Oaks, the city of Hamtramck,[163] the city of Highland Park and the city of Flint.[164] Showing the controversy that can exist with respect to municipal restructuring laws, in 2011 and the Michigan legislature replaced the Local Government Fiscal Responsibility Act with the Local Government and School District Fiscal Accountability Act. Then, in a November 2012 voter referendum, Michigan voters repealed portions of the Local Government and School District Fiscal Accountability Act that they found distasteful. Following this development, in December 2012 the Michigan legislature passed and the Michigan governor signed the Local Financial Stability and Choice Act.[165] Under the Local Financial Stability and Choice Act, if a local emergency financial assistance board determines that a

---

162 Pub. L. No. 104-8, 109 Stat 97. *See also supra* n. 75 at 46-48, Philadelphia.

163 Under a previous version of Michigan's municipal restructuring laws, in November 2010 the Emergency Financial Assistance Loan Board for the city of Hamtramck rejected a request by the city to file a municipal bankruptcy petition. This request was denied by the state that same month.

164 Former MICH. COMP. LAWS. § 141.2802 (this provision has been replaced by the Local Government and School District Fiscal Accountability Act). *See also* Eric Scorsone, *Local Government Financial Emergencies and Municipal Bankruptcy, Michigan Senate Fiscal Agency Issue Paper*, http://www.senate.michigan.gov/sfa/publications/issues/localgovfin/localgovfin.pdf (last visited Jan. 26, 2016).

165 MICH. COMP. LAWS ANN. § 141.1541 *et seq.*

local government is experiencing financial stress, and it is then determined that a local government is experiencing a financial emergency, the local government must choose to (a) enter into a consent decree with the state, (b) agree to the appointment of an emergency manager, (c) enter into a neutral evaluation process or (d) file a Chapter 9 bankruptcy petition if so approved by the governor. If it does not choose an option, the local government must proceed under a neutral evaluation process to reach a resolution to its financial emergency.

With respect to the City of Detroit, Kevyn Orr was appointed by the governor of Michigan as the city's emergency financial manager on March 14, 2013, pursuant to the Local Financial Stability and Choice Act, with control over the city's financial matters and the authority to recommend to the governor that a Chapter 9 bankruptcy be filed. With the consent of the governor, Detroit filed its Chapter 9 petition on July 18, 2013.[166] Additionally, in July 2015 the governor of Michigan declared a financial emergency pursuant to the Local Financial Stability and Choice Act with respect to Wayne County, Michigan, the county in which the city of Detroit is located. As a result, in August 2015 the county entered into a Consent Agreement with the State of Michigan, by means of which Wayne County has agreed to implement a recovery plan to eliminate the $52 million structural deficit that existed in the county.[167]

4. The Massachusetts and Connecticut *Ad Hoc* Experiences

Analogous to the laws of states establishing specific authority for financial control boards or similar commissions, Massachusetts has typically employed a system of implementing legislation on an *ad hoc* basis to create a financial control board or overseers for municipalities in severe financial distress. For instance, in the 1990s the city of Chelsea was placed into a state receivership. The receiver cut city payroll by 25 percent and cut non-pecuniary employment benefits. In one year, the receiver was able to cut city expenses by 10 percent of the city's budget (by $5 million).[168] In March 2010, the governor of Massachusetts signed into law provisions allowing the city of Lawrence to borrow $35 million from the market and establishing a fiscal overseer for the municipality.[169] In a July 2010 report the financial overseer stated that Lawrence's fiscal emergency was the result of years of mismanagement and fiscal challenges. The fiscal overseer has aided the city in producing a balanced budget.[170] In another instance, in 2004 Massachusetts made a $52 million state loan to the city of

---

166 For a more detailed discussion of the Detroit, Michigan bankruptcy case and lessons learned, see section III at 56-66.

167 *See* Consent Agreement between Wayne County, a Michigan body corporate, and State Treasurer N.A. Khouri, a Michigan state officer, http://www.michigan.gov/documents/treasury/Wayne_County_Consent_Agreement_2015_498140_7.pdf. The implementation of the plan will require concessions from the county's numerous stakeholders.

168 *See* Omer Kimhi, *Reviving Cities: Legal Remedies to Municipal Financial Crises*, 88 B.U. L. REV. 633, 671 - 672 (2008).

169 *See* 2010 MASS. ACTS ch. 58.

170 Letter from Robert G. Nunes, Fiscal Overseer to Secretary Jay Gonzalez of the Office for Administration and Finance; the Massachusetts Senate Committee on Ways and Means and the Massachusetts House Committee on Ways and Means, dated July 22, 2010.

Springfield and established a financial control board to oversee the city.[171] Section VIII of this book, the 50-State Survey, provides a general overview of these Massachusetts provisions and the provisions of other states.

Likewise, Connecticut typically has employed a system of implementing legislation on an *ad hoc* basis to create financial assistance designed to turn around a municipality in severe financial distress. Such *ad hoc* legislation was enacted to provide for financial oversight boards for the city of Bridgeport in 1988 and the city of Waterbury in 2001 and for a receiver for the city of Jewitt in 1993.[172]

5. The California Experience — Neutral Evaluator

California also has experimented with the concept of introducing a third party to assist in the resolution of municipal financial difficulties. In 2011 California enacted a provision restricting the ability of its municipalities to file petitions to institute Chapter 9 proceedings before a Chapter 9 proceeding is filed in an effort to provide a period of objective and dedicated negotiation and resolution of issues affecting major creditors or financial problems.[173] The legislation provides for a neutral evaluation process, otherwise known as mediation, for major creditors and parties to the financial problems. A professional, independent, neutral advisor to serve as the supervising adult is the essence of a neutral evaluator. The neutral evaluator can foster negotiations among the municipality and representatives of major creditor constituencies, including workers and union representatives, vendors, contract suppliers, holders of major claims including bondholders, judgment creditors or others whose interests could affect the financial fate of the municipality. The neutral evaluator process may not last more than 60 days from the date the evaluator is chosen unless the municipality or a majority of participating interested parties elects to extend the process up to an additional 30 days. The procedure is intended to be expedited and cannot last more than 90 days from the date of the selection of the neutral evaluator.

The process for selecting the neutral evaluator is set out by law and participation of major creditors is permitted. The goal of the selection process is to establish "buy-in" by the major constituencies, including the municipality, its elected officials, major creditors, taxpayers and the public at large as to the credibility, objectivity and professionalism of the neutral evaluator. The municipality is required to pay 50 percent of the costs of the neutral evaluator, and creditors are required to pay the balance unless the parties otherwise agree.

---

171 *See* 2004 MASS. ACTS ch. 169. The Springfield Financial Control Board ended five years of direct management on June 30, 2009. Springfield emerged from a $41 million deficit in fiscal year 2005 to a reserve fund balance of nearly $40 million at the close of fiscal year 2009.

172 *See* 2001 CONN. SPEC. ACTS 01-1 (City of Waterbury) and section VIII, Connecticut.

173 CAL. GOV'T CODE §§ 53760, 53760.1, 53760.3, 53760.5 and 53760.7.

The neutral evaluator must meet with the municipality's representatives and with representatives of each of the major creditors' constituencies and must apply basic mediation techniques, including having each side state its position, identifying areas of concessions or agreement, pointing out to each the weaknesses and strengths of the respective positions and explaining the consequences of going forward without a resolution, such as in terms of costs, risks, uncertainties and adverse results.

Following the truism that you do not have to continue to touch the stove to know it is hot, the goal of the California law is to avoid the costs, deterioration of services, loss of tax revenues, delay and uncertainty in the resolution that Chapter 9 or other litigation avenues present. Nevertheless, as a safety valve, the California law permits a municipality to immediately file a Chapter 9 petition if it declares that a "fiscal emergency" exists and it provides a finding that its financial status jeopardizes the health, safety or well-being of its residents and that it is or will be unable to pay its obligations within the next 60 days.

The use of a neutral evaluator is recent and is in a developmental stage. Other states have considered the adoption of similar legislation.[174] Interestingly, the legislation introduced in California was supported by the labor unions as a reaction to the difficulties they experienced in the city of Vallejo's Chapter 9 bankruptcy proceeding. Indeed, the legislation followed and was a reaction to the Vallejo experience in 2008. The neutral evaluator process was first used in connection with the Stockton Chapter 9 filing in 2012, and months of legal courtroom arguments ensued as to whether there was good faith participation by the debtor and creditors in that process. The bankruptcy court ultimately decided that the debtor's efforts met the good faith requirements of the Bankruptcy Code.[175] Likewise, the town of Mammoth Lakes[176] and the Mendocino Coast Health Care District,[177] both of which filed in 2012, also used the neutral evaluator process. However, San Bernardino, which also filed in 2012, used the "fiscal emergency" exception to the requirement of the neutral evaluator process.[178]

---

174 For instance, in 2012 Illinois considered similar legislation, but the Illinois legislature did not consider the bill before the 97th Illinois General Assembly adjourned on January 8, 2013 (H.B. 5669, 97th Gen. Assemb. (Illinois 2012) (introduced Feb. 16, 2012 by Rep. John E. Bradley)). The concept also was part of Illinois Governor Rauner's proposed reform legislative package in 2015. *Illinois Governor Proposes Sweeping Pension Legislation*, REUTERS (July 8, 2015), www.reuters.com/article/usa-Illinois-Governor-idUSKCN0PI2AW20150708.

175 *In re City of Stockton, Ca.*, 493 B.R. 772 (Bankr. E.D. Cal. 2013). For a more detailed discussion of the Stockton, California bankruptcy experience see section VIII at 54-56.

176 The Town's Statement of Qualifications Under Section 109(c), *In re Town of Mammoth Lakes, Ca.*, Case No. 2012-32463 (Bankr. E.D. Cal. July 3, 2012).

177 *In re Mendocino Coast Recreational & Park District*, 2012 WL 1431219 (N.D. Cal. Apr. 22, 2012).

178 Statement of Qualifications under Section 109(c), *In re City of San Bernardino, Ca.*, Case No. 12-28006 (Bankr. C.D. Cal. Aug. 13, 2012).

Given California's experience with the neutral evaluator approach, questions exist as to whether it fully accomplishes its intended goal of promoting an effective process to obtain a resolution of disputes and avoiding a Chapter 9 filing, or whether it is merely a required waiting period preceding a fated Chapter 9 filing. Questions about the neutral evaluator process linger, such as: (a) how do you ensure participation by all affected creditor representatives; (b) how do you motivate the municipality and creditors to drop public posturing, adopt realistic demands and explore realistic alternatives; (c) who determines what is sustainable and affordable; (d) where do needed additional revenues come from; (e) what rights under state laws and constitutional provisions are protected from change, if any, including recognition that statutory liens and special revenues cannot be altered by a municipality or impaired; (f) are constitutional and statutory laws against impairment of pension benefits a bar to changing labor costs and pension benefits; (g) what should be allowed to be public about the neutral evaluation process and what should be kept confidential for the sake of honest negotiation, such as whether exceptions from open meetings and freedom of information laws should apply and how confidentiality will be protected; and (h) what if more than 90 days is required to reach agreement?

6. Developments in Indiana — Appointment of an Emergency Manager

Following the successes of other states in dealing with municipalities in distress, in 2012 the Indiana legislature approved and the Indiana governor signed into law a provision under which an emergency manager may be appointed to oversee a distressed political subdivision in the state.[179] Pursuant to this provision, an eligible local government may file a petition with Indiana's Distressed Unit Appeal Board requesting that it be designated as "distressed." If certain conditions apply, such a designation may be made and the board may appoint an emergency manager to oversee the troubled municipality. The emergency manager may assume and exercise the authority of the executive and board of the political subdivision but does not have the power to impose taxes or fees in addition to the taxes and fees authorized before the political subdivision was designated as distressed. The emergency manager may also prepare the political subdivision's budget; make expenditures; approve or disapprove contracts, expenditures and loans; renegotiate existing labor contracts; reduce or suspend employee salaries; and enter into agreements with other political subdivisions regarding services. Chapter 9, however, is not an option for Indiana municipalities.

7. Attempts by Puerto Rico to Impose State-Level Bankruptcy Scheme and Enactment by Congress of PROMESA

The Commonwealth of Puerto Rico, a protectorate of the United States, and its municipalities are ineligible under the Bankruptcy Code to file a petition under Chapter 9 and have very few tools available to them, outside of a consensual agreement with all creditors, to restructure their debts. Currently, Puerto Rico is facing an unprecedented financial emergency. In August 2015, Puerto Rico's Government Development Bank defaulted on a $58 million general obligation bond payment due

---

179 IND. CODE §§ 6-1.1-20.3-1 to -15 (distressed political subdivisions).

bondholders, making a payment of merely $628,000.[180] In addition to the commonwealth's inability to pay its debts as they come due, the municipal corporations in Puerto Rico providing operation and financing for such public services as water, highways and electricity are experiencing financial distress.

Puerto Rico Public Corporations Debt Enforcement and Recovery Act

In an attempt to help its municipal corporations restructure their debt, the commonwealth, in June 2014, enacted the Puerto Rico Public Corporations Debt Enforcement and Recovery Act (the "Act"). The Act attempted to create a commonwealth-level, bankruptcy-like mechanism for restructuring the debts of many of Puerto Rico's public corporations. The Act was designed to establish a new Puerto Rico court, with the authority to issue any order and conduct any process necessary or appropriate to carry out the provisions of the Act. The court's mission was to hear cases arising under the two mechanisms for restructuring contained in the Act. Pursuant to the Act, when questions arise in interpreting the Act, the court is directed to consider case law under the U.S. Bankruptcy Code.

Almost immediately after the Act was introduced, creditors filed suit in the U.S. District Court for the District of Puerto Rico, asserting that it was unconstitutional. In February 2015 the District Court found the Act unconstitutional,[181] concluding that it was preempted by Section 903 of the Bankruptcy Code and therefore in violation of the Supremacy Clause of the U.S. Constitution. In July 2015 the U.S. Court of Appeals for the First Circuit affirmed this decision,[182] and in December 2015 the U.S. Supreme Court granted the petition for a writ of certiorari.[183] In a 5 to 2 decision, the U.S. Supreme Court affirmed the decision by the Court of Appeals.[184] The Supreme Court held that the amendment of Chapter 9 of the Bankruptcy Code providing that the term "State" under the title does not include Puerto Rico for the purpose of defining who may be a debtor under Chapter 9 did not remove Puerto Rico from the reach of Chapter 9's pre-emption provision.[185] Accordingly, Puerto Rico is barred from enacting its own municipal bankruptcy scheme.

Puerto Rico Oversight, Management and Economic Stability Act ("PROMESA")

Even as the Supreme Court considered the constitutionality of the Act, both the United States Senate and House of Representatives held hearings on possible legislative solutions to the problems of

---

180 Michelle Kaske and Elizabeth Campbell, *Puerto Rico Debt Crisis Grows as Island Defaults, Conserves Cash*, BLOOMBERG, (Aug. 3, 2015), www.bloomberg.com/news/articles/2015-08-04/puerto-rico-debt-crisis-grows-as-payments-halt-agency-defaults.

181 *Franklin California Tax-Free Trust v. Puerto Rico*, 85 F. Supp. 3d 577 (D.P.R. 2015).

182 *Federal California Tax-Free Trust v. Puerto Rico*, 2015 WL 4079422 (1st Cir. July 6, 2015).

183 *Acosta-Febo, et al. v. Franklin California Tax-Free Trust*, 2015 WL 5096465 (S. Ct. Dec. 4, 2015).

184 *Commonwealth of Puerto Rico v. Franklin California Tax Free Trust*, 136 S. Ct. 1938 (2016).

185 *Id.*

Puerto Rico.[186] The House Committee on National Resources introduced a version of PROMESA (Puerto Rico Oversight, Management, and Economic Stability Act) providing for the creation of a seven-member independent oversight board appointed by the United States president. The board would have the power to file for restructuring if a consensual solution can't be reached. PROMESA was approved by both the House and the Senate and signed into law by President Obama on June 30, 2016.[187]

PROMESA's Reason for Existence

This legislation is to a degree a result of the experience and use of the Pennsylvania Intergovernmental Cooperation Authority Act and the District of Columbia Control Board as well as the Detroit bankruptcy. Further, PROMESA is a product of Congress' efforts to aid Puerto Rico without authorizing it or its municipalities to file for Chapter 9 and without enacting bailout legislation. PROMESA creates an oversight board for Puerto Rico and for other specified territories if they should so petition. The authority for Congress' creation of PROMESA arises from the Territorial Clause (U.S. Const. Article IV, Section 3, Clause 2): "Congress shall have Power to dispose of and make all needful Rules and Regulations respecting the Territory ... belonging to the United States ..." and the Bankruptcy Clause (U.S. Const. Article I, Section 8, Clause 4): "The Congress shall have power to ... establish ... uniform Laws on the subject of Bankruptcies throughout the United States ..." PROMESA is not part of the Bankruptcy Code but, rather, is uniform legislation providing rules and regulation regarding territories concerning insolvent or financial distress situations to aid such territories in managing their public finances and developing economic stability. The legislation is applicable to Puerto Rico and, in certain instances, could be applicable to Guam, American Samoa, the Commonwealth of Northern Mariana Islands or the United States Virgin Islands. This legislation immediately creates an Oversight and Management Board for Puerto Rico.

The Role of PROMESA's Board

The board will consist of seven members appointed by the president of the United States, each of whom is independent and autonomous from Puerto Rico. This board will have control over the finances of Puerto Rico. Specifically, the board's role is not just supervisory but is an active role approving and recommending key financial decisions. The board would approve all major financial decisions, including development of a fiscal plan to achieve fiscal responsibility and access to the

186 *See* Written Testimony of James E. Spiotto before the United States Senate Committee on the Judiciary Hearing on Puerto Rico's Fiscal Problems: Examining the Source and Exploring the Solution (Dec. 1, 2015) http://muninetguide.com/?p=134470, and Written Testimony of James E. Spiotto before the House of Representatives Subcommittee on Indian, Insular and Alaska Native Affairs Regarding the Need for the Establishment of a Puerto Rico Financial Stability and Economic Growth Authority (Jan. 26, 2016). In this testimony, the author suggested that Chapter 9 was not the most desirable vehicle for assisting Puerto Rico in resolving its financial problems and that a financial control board such as that utilized in the past to aid Washington, D.C. was preferable.

187 Public Law 114-187, 114th Cong., 2d Sess. (June 30, 2016).

capital markets, approval of budgets, approval of actions related to debt issuance, and analysis of the pension system. With the establishment of the board, PROMESA imposes a short-term stay of creditor litigation against Puerto Rico. This addresses the fear of unconstructive litigation preventing a reasonable restructuring and recovery.

The Board's Powers

Upon being appointed, the board is required to consult with the governor of Puerto Rico to establish a schedule for the commonwealth to deliver the five-year fiscal plan, thereby encouraging a spirit of cooperation and coordination between the commonwealth and the board. The Board is separate, independent and autonomous from the governor and the legislature of Puerto Rico. If the board does not approve a budget, new legislation involving finance, a fiscal plan or other financial matter, it may state its reasoning by way of recommendations to aid the commonwealth and its legislature in addressing the concerns and obtaining approval. The commonwealth's failure to have expenditures be consistent with the limits of the approved budget can trigger a report to the president, the House of Representatives Committee on Natural Resources, the governor and the legislature of Puerto Rico detailing the inconsistency. In addition, the board has the power to make appropriate adjustment in non-debt expenditures to ensure consistency. The board has the power to obtain information from Puerto Rico's creditors and to enter into negotiation with creditors to resolve claims in accordance with the fiscal plan. The goal is a sustainable and affordable budget and fiscal plan that fosters a true recovery. The United States, while providing oversight and management through the board, is not to be liable for any debt or obligation of the commonwealth.

PROMESA Permits Collective Action by Creditors

PROMESA creates a creditor collective action mechanism, whereby a pool of similar debt can bind all holders of debt of such pool to a restructuring by a vote of two-thirds of outstanding principal amount of the pool voting, provided fifty percent of the outstanding principal amount of the bonds vote to approve the modification. No state or local government in the United States has the power by a super-majority vote outside of Chapter 9 to effectuate changes to adjust debt and to modify terms as part of a restructuring of its debt, which will be binding on all affected creditors. Outside of Chapter 9, 100 percent consent of the affected creditors is required. This is a significant development for Puerto Rico following the increased use of collection action clauses in debt transactions of foreign countries as opposed to the traditions of 100 percent consent for state and local governments.

PROMESA Provides a Court Procedure to Adjust Debts

If a consensual resolution cannot be reached, the board can file a petition on behalf of the commonwealth or its public corporations or instrumentalities with the U.S. District Court to adjust the debts. Certain of the provisions and procedures are similar to those of Chapter 9. PROMESA recognizes treatment of special revenues and statutory liens. There are limitations on the district court's jurisdiction, similar to Section 904 of the Bankruptcy Code, whereby the court cannot stay, order or interfere, unless the board consents, with the political or governmental power, property, revenues, use or engagement of property of the commonwealth or any applicable instrumentality. In addition, there is a prohibition from impairing or limiting the power of the commonwealth relating to legislative control over the powers of the territory or its instrumentalities, including as to expenditures, similar to Section 903 of the Bankruptcy Code. Only the board, acting as the commonwealth's representative, can institute a debt adjustment proceeding or file a plan of adjustment under PROMESA. The board can in its discretion subject the commonwealth's public corporations (*e.g.*, PREPA, PRHTA, PRASA) and its instrumentalities to the provisions of PROMESA.

8. Development of the Municipal Protection Commission

The experience of the New York Financial Control Board, the Rhode Island receiver approach and the mediator of the California statutory scheme have coalesced in the concept of a "municipal protection commission."A municipal protection commission would utilize some of the best aspects of the mediation process of the neutral evaluator and the oversight and supervision of financial control boards and a receiver.[188] Under this municipal debt resolution mechanism, the state would establish an entity that would have a quasi-judicial function and power similar to a commission or special master appointed by a state supreme court. The members of the commission would be independent, experienced experts in governmental operation or finance as well as mediation and debt resolution techniques, including bankruptcy. The commission would start with those municipalities that petition for help or that have triggered certain established criteria where the jurisdiction of the commission is mandated by state law.

Triggers for the commission's jurisdiction would be the petition by the municipality, its workers or its taxpayers that a governmental function emergency exists, certain creditor litigation or actions threatening a fair resolution of the open issues for all creditors, the municipality and its citizens. The petition must state that established criteria for the commission's jurisdiction have occurred or otherwise essential services as to health, safety and welfare of its residents are being threatened and that the forced reduction in services, given the municipality's financial condition and its revenues, impairs the health, safety and general welfare of its residents.

The structure of the commission would assure all parties a fair, impartial process designed to foster consensual resolution of issues. The procedures of the commission would require transparent financial information that is vetted and determined to be accurate and the basis of sustainable and affordable budgets and financial proposals. Consideration must be given to financial goals and triggers to ensure balanced budgets, as well as oversight and assistance to prevent further financial erosion.

188 The Civic Federation of Chicago has over the last several years proposed a Local Government Protection Authority ("LGPA"), previously referenced as the Illinois Municipal Protection Authority ("IMPA"), which proposed legislation takes into consideration the lessons from New York City, Philadelphia and the District of Columbia as well as recent Chapter 9 bankruptcies. Some of the principles and structures contained in PROMESA follow the precedent of the Civic Federation of Chicago's work.

Such oversight and assistance would address the financial and operational problems along with social programs to ensure adequate funding of essential services such as infrastructure, stimulate economic development and promote financial credibility in dealing with creditors and citizens.

As a first phase, the commission would take action to ensure that accurate financial information is available to all interested parties in order for interim and long-term budgets and any necessary financing to ensure liquidity and funding are available to the distressed municipality during the process This is to ensure that: (a) human suffering from inadequate services and infrastructure is reduced or eliminated and (b) dealing with creditors is not complicated by financial illiquidity. The more expedited the agreement of the local government and its creditors on the basic financial numbers and the extent of the financial crisis, the quicker and better the resolution is for all. Without this process, there could be obstacles of dueling financial numbers and debate over whether a particular payment can be made or not, and whether payment would lead to financial meltdown. If the creditors and the municipality could not agree on projected revenues and expenses, the commission would make a determination binding on all the parties. This process is aimed at reducing or eliminating unprofitable debate by either having all interested parties agree to the financial numbers or having the commission, through a vetting process with the input from all parties, determine what is sustainable and affordable for the distressed municipality.

Once the critical budgeting and financial transparency of the first stage are accomplished, the concurrent steps of discussion, mediation and resolution of financial issues and creditor disputes can be effectively addressed and resolved. Resolution is more probable and more constructive when everyone is on the same financial statement page. The goal of the commission is consensual agreement by the local government and its creditor constituencies. However, participation may be voluntary by acceptance by the local government and other affected constituencies or otherwise mandated by the financial emergency. Negotiation, mediation and discussion of positions are strictly confidential. Laws establishing the commission may have an exception to any open meetings and freedom of information laws to allow for open discussion of any sensitive and confidential topics and activities.

If the distressed municipality requires additional tax revenues or loans or grants from the state, recommendations to the state by the commission would take effect unless blocked by the state legislature within a specified period of time. The commission can likewise call for a referendum on a local basis for increased taxes or other actions. Specified time periods for resolution would be set forth in the authorizing legislation and, if the voluntary process is not successful, the second phase, discussed next, would be mandatory if the commission so requires.

In the second phase, if creditors and the local government do not reach agreement on a recovery plan and what can be paid on outstanding creditor claims, the commission and its designated members would become a quasi-judicial panel. The municipality would be required to set forth a resolution proposal (recovery plan) directed to its designated financial problem. Creditors, workers and taxpayers would have the ability to comment and to attempt, through negotiation, to modify the recovery plan within a set period of time. Then, the recovery plan, including any objections thereto, would be submitted to the vote of creditors by class. Then the recovery plan and any objections or agreement with creditors would be presented to the panel members of the commission for determination of the plan's feasibility and whether it is reasonably fair to creditors' interests in relationship to the requirement that, under all circumstances, essential governmental services, at least at an established level, must be maintained for the reasonable future. The commission, after hearing all sides (municipality, workers, taxpayers, affected creditors), would determine:

- what debt level of the municipality is sustainable and affordable,
- what the municipality can afford, and
- what adjustments must be made to the recovery plan to allow the municipality to continue to provide essential governmental services to its residents at mandated levels, to preserve the health, safety and welfare of its residents and to pay what is feasible to its creditors, including workers' wages and pensions.

The commission would act as an "honest broker" to review budgets, operational efficiency and the municipality's financial plan and to approve or make recommendations so that good decisions are recognized and supported and questionable ones are vetted to avoid becoming bad decisions. To the extent justified by financial analysis, the commission may recommend increases in taxes; increases in contributions or concessions by the various interested parties who agree; or reduction, delay or stretching out of payments to creditors if legally permitted. Further, if necessary to preserve the public health, safety and welfare of the municipality's residents, the commission would have the power to recommend adjustments to workers' wages, pensions or other benefits.

A municipality that underestimates in its recovery plan its ability to pay creditors and workers would have necessary increases in the payments recommended and imposed by the commission, with the benefits going to the workers and the creditors. A municipality that overestimates its ability to pay or makes promises that are not sustainable and affordable would be subject to the recommendation by the commission that specified payments be adjusted to be sustainable and affordable. The commission would specify if its findings are final and enforceable by the parties or if further negotiations or proceedings are necessary, and the commission would be charged with ensuring that the municipality and the state maintain access to the financial markets. This would be required to protect all parties, workers, vendors and creditors and the taxpayers and the municipality so they would have needed means of continued financing that can be accomplished on the local level based upon maintaining market credibility. In addition, the commission can authorize the municipality to enforce its findings. Such means of enforcement can include having the recovery plan approved or revised by the commission as the basis for a pre-negotiated or "pre-packaged" Chapter 9 plan. The commission can authorize the municipality to file a Chapter 9 proceeding based on the recovery plan as a pre-packaged Chapter 9 plan. Such a pre-packaged Chapter 9 plan could significantly reduce costs, expenses, uncertainty and the financial market risk of a freefall Chapter 9 proceeding. Pre-packaged Chapter 11 plans (corporate plans of reorganization) have been confirmed in weeks rather than months or years with reduced costs, risks and uncertainties. A pre-packaged plan of adjustment is where the municipality, through the process, meets the requirement of the Bankruptcy Code as to the disclosures to and vote of the various classes of creditors. A pre-negotiated plan is where the plan has been negotiated with various classes of creditors but the disclosure to and voting of the various classes of creditors do not comply with Bankruptcy Code requirements. The confirmation of a pre-negotiated plan of adjustment will take 60-90 days more for required disclosures, solicitation and voting, assuming the final disclosure statement is filed along with the bankruptcy petition.

This concept of a municipal protection commission is still in its formative stages and is being discussed by various parties. It could be the means of providing state and local government cooperation and oversight while allowing the municipality and its elected officials, workers and unions, creditors and bondholders to have a means of participation with a definitive end result. Further, the resolution for affected workers and creditors can be hard-wired for a payment source of dedicated taxes for assured payment of wages, benefits and creditor claims rather than the speculative hope of future payment at the willingness of future legislative actions.[189]

D. The Structure for Oversight and Emergency Financing

The chart in subsection F below portrays possible responses to troubled local government debt. The chart generally identifies some of the key issues involved in an oversight commission or authority. Local governments that have encountered financial distress have resorted to financing and oversight authorities (as was the case in both New York City and Philadelphia). This approach can involve various degrees of formal oversight and control. In the beginning, it can be as simple and benign as a "commission" that reviews the city budget and makes recommendations based on new revenue sources. The commission can develop into a refinancing authority with full power to refinance existing debt of the local government and to authorize collection of new revenue sources or withdraw use of new revenue sources if budget recommendations are not followed or met. There are two advantages to this approach: (1) the new authority can have financial credibility and, therefore, access to borrowing in the capital marketplace *if* it has an assured source of revenue to pay debt service that is isolated from the bankruptcy and other legal risks facing creditors of the local government; and (2) an independent authority can use various tools to impose fiscal discipline on the local government because it can be removed from political pressures.

The basic idea is that the independent authority is given a revenue source. It then borrows and assigns the revenue source to pay debt service on the bonds. The authority makes the bond proceeds available to the local government to refinance expensive debt, pay its expenses, retire its deficit and

---

189 Mary Williams Walsh, *Stepping Up With a Plan to Save American Cities*, N.Y. TIMES, Nov. 12, 2013, http://dealbook.nytimes.com/2013/11/11/stepping-up-with-a-plan-to-save-american-cities/?_r=0.

provide funds for necessary infrastructure enhancement to foster improved economic growth. A fundamental legislative choice is whether the local government levies the new taxes and pledges the proceeds to the authority or the authority is the taxing body authorized to levy taxes. In addition, the sub-sovereign's ability to levy new taxes may be conditioned on a balanced budget or approval of the authority.

Financing through the authority can be utilized both for a long-term amortization of the cumulative deficit and, if necessary, for an interim period, to accomplish the annual revenue anticipation note borrowings that are necessary for the sub-sovereign to operate. Different revenue sources might be utilized for each type of borrowing.

The types of disciplinary tools and ability to act that are found in oversight and emergency financing entities for distressed governments can vary, can be far-ranging and may include the authority to take such actions, request or impose such discipline as follows:

- Grants from the Federal, State or Regional Governmental Bodies. Obviously, a source of funds must exist from which to make grants. The grant becomes a tool if the federal, state or regional governmental body imposes performance requirements as a precondition to any grant. The federal, state or regional governmental body can make the process more politically palatable by freely making a grant to the authority while requiring either in the legislation or in the grant documents that the authority impose performance conditions.

- Loans from the Federal, State or Regional Governmental Bodies. Instead of a grant, the federal, state or local governmental body could make loans that require ultimate repayment. The repayment terms can be varied depending upon the local government's compliance with an approved financial plan and the achievement of goals over time. That is, interest rates could be increased or decreased as needed; in a worst-case scenario, principal payment could be accelerated for a default. In certain states there can also be the assumption of the obligations by the state.

- Intercepts and Refinancing. Part of the discussion in structuring grants and loans should consider "intercepting" the payments to the local government. Legislation can be written that permits the state or regional governmental body to withhold these payments if the local government acts inappropriately or fails to act, or the legislation can permit those revenues to be pledged (e.g., paid directly) to lenders or bondholders. Refinancing, if economically practical, can lessen the cost of debt and build market acceptance. Refinancing through an authority or oversight conduit with a dedicated source for repayment may provide bridge financing for interim liquidity or retire high interest rate debt with lower cost debt. In the implementation stage, there is an issue of whether special interest groups, such as unions, local financial institutions or pension funds, might have the ability and willingness to invest in such financing. New York City had support from unions in purchasing significant positions of its refinancing debt.

- Budget Process Involvement. Having a financial plan to work out of the deficit, following that plan and changing the plan as experience dictates are the keys to a successful workout. The first step is to identify the problems and to stop the financial bleeding to the degree possible.

- Required Financial Performance. Through legislative measures, the authority can be given powers to participate in and monitor the local government's budget process across a broad spectrum. Ultimately, the teeth in the program are that bond proceeds or new tax revenue sources are not made available to the local government until it complies with the plan, and continued compliance is required for a continuing revenue flow. The legislation itself can contain the requirements or can allow the authority to develop and establish the requirements.

- Legislative Assistance. A financially distressed local government comes as a somewhat recalcitrant beggar to the legislature. An authority that is monitoring (and actively participating in) the local government's recovery can give it credibility with the legislature or, alternatively, if the local government fails to make progress, it can assist the legislature in developing new criteria and programs.

- Moral Obligations of the State. Some states may be constitutionally able to assume debt of a local government. In such states an "extra-legal" state guarantee called a "moral obligation" is sometimes used to credit enhance bonds.

- Appointment of Authority Members. The makeup of the governing body of the authority is key to its success. Payment of its staff is important. It is conceivable that some community leaders may be willing to serve without compensation if they believe the authority and its tools are capable of success. Whether or not the local government is able to appoint or be represented on the authority is a question for the drafters of the legislation and the need for local "buy-in."

- Acceleration of Loans. If the authority makes loans to the local government, a loan could include the right to accelerate if the local government fails to comply with a financial recovery plan and projections.

- Publicity. By participating in the local government recovery process, the authority can become a mechanism for disseminating both good and bad information about the progress of the local government's recovery efforts. Such information flow and disclosure will be helpful in building credibility with the investment community. The experiences of New

York City, Cleveland and Philadelphia stress the importance of accurate and clear communication with the financial market.

- Powers. The authority can have as many or as few powers as the legislature may require, including but not limited to:

    1. authorizing filing of a judicial action for municipal debt adjustment by the local government;
    2. granting, after hearing and notice, a stay against litigation and debt enforcement;
    3. approval or withdrawal of future use of increased tax revenues;
    4. rejecting or approving budgets, financial plans and future financing;
    5. determining financial emergency or recovery;
    6. approving, expediting or withholding state aid and entitlement to taxes distributed to the local government;
    7. approving or issuing bonds for refinancing or for paying local government deficits, bridge financing or extraordinary operating expenses;
    8. reporting to the state regarding the need for further legislative or disciplinary tools; and
    9. transferring certain governmental services to other governmental bodies or consolidating governmental services on a regional basis or with other municipalities.

- Consolidation of Regional Essential Governmental Services. One interesting proposition for states is determining whether certain essential governmental services such as public safety (police and fire) or public health or education should be consolidated and combined on a regional basis and considering the benefits of the efficiencies and elimination of duplicative and overlapping services and administration.

As noted, legislation can be written so that some or all of the above-described tools are available to the authority. These tools can be designed and enacted so that they are mandatory or discretionary. The choices and options can be further delineated. A variation of the intercept and periodic financial reporting has been used in connection with troubled debt securities issued by local government as a mechanism to ensure the flow of payments from taxes or fees to the bondholders.

E. State Municipal Refinancing, Restructuring or Restructuring Assistance Authority Requirements (Could Be Pursuant to Special Legislation)

The authority should have sufficient power under law to effectively supervise a distressed government. Accordingly, any such authority should be permitted to:

1. Require balanced budgets and provide economic discipline and reporting;
2. Issue debt in the name of the state or a separate entity to obtain market credibility and access;
3. Have power to negotiate debt restructuring and quasi-judicial jurisdiction;
4. Review services or costs that can be transferred to other governmental bodies;
5. Have the right to intercept tax revenue and ensure payment for essential services and necessary operating costs;
6. Have power to authorize Chapter 9 if needed;
7. Obtain bridge financing or refinancing of troubled debt;
8. Transfer certain services to other governmental agencies to reduce expenditures;
9. Grant funds to the municipality to bridge the financial crisis;
10. Loan funds to the municipality on terms that are realistic or payable from out-of-state tax sources that can be offset;
11. Create private-public partnerships to lease or sell municipal properties to provide bridge financing and cash flow relief;
12. Develop a vendor assistance program to provide vendor payments through securitization financing of payables or through financing of the purchase of vendor claims at a discount (fixed discount) and secured by payment from dedicated tax revenues over time, or to provide current cash flow relief from current or future vendor payments;
13. Explore consolidation on a regional basis of certain governmental services or, in the more drastic cases, consider dissolving the financially troubled governmental entity; and
14. Monitor compliance with any restructuring or recovery plan to ensure compliance and prevent financial erosion.

F. Examples of Structure for Municipal Financial Oversight and State Supervision of Financially Distressed Municipality

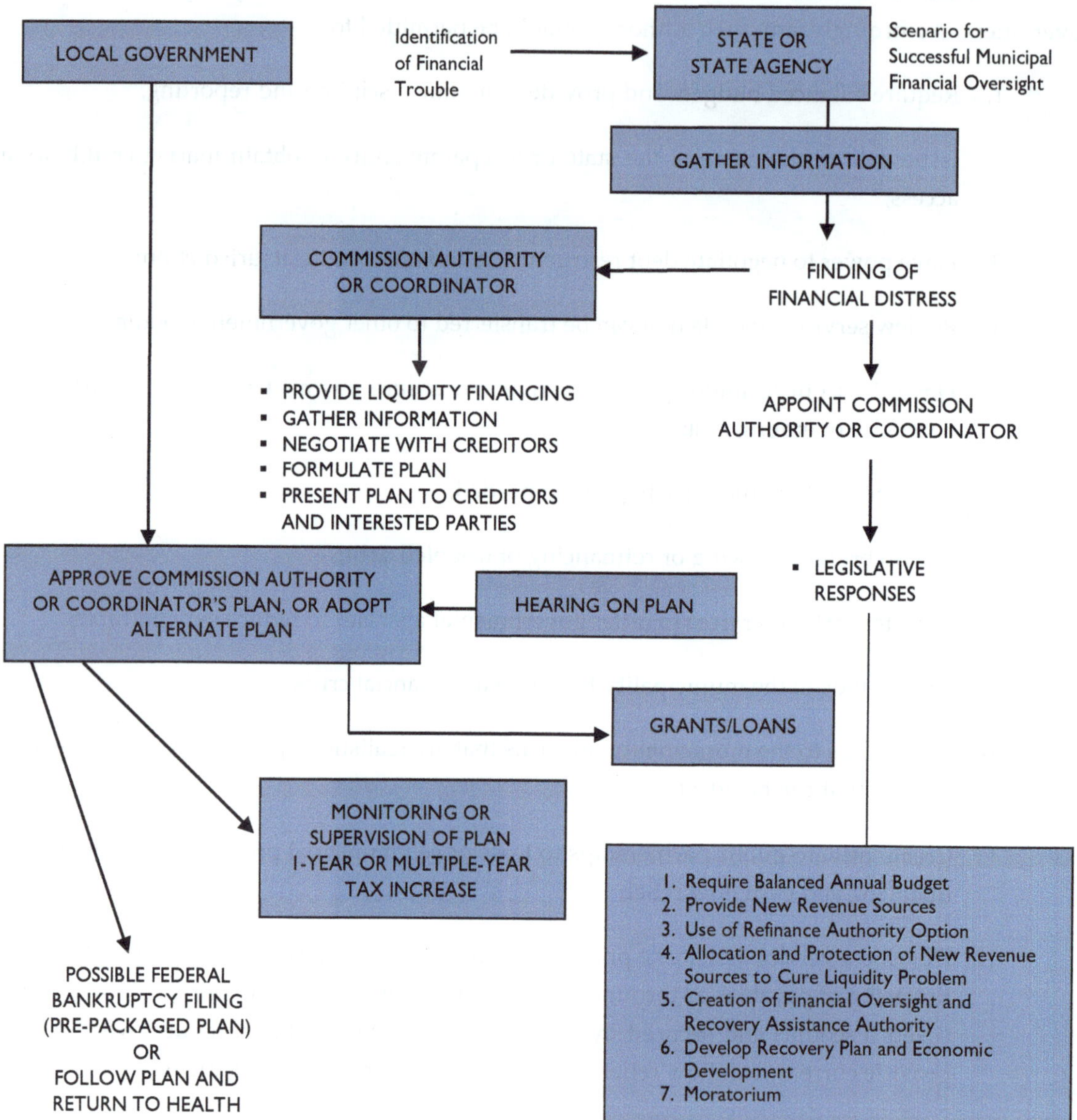

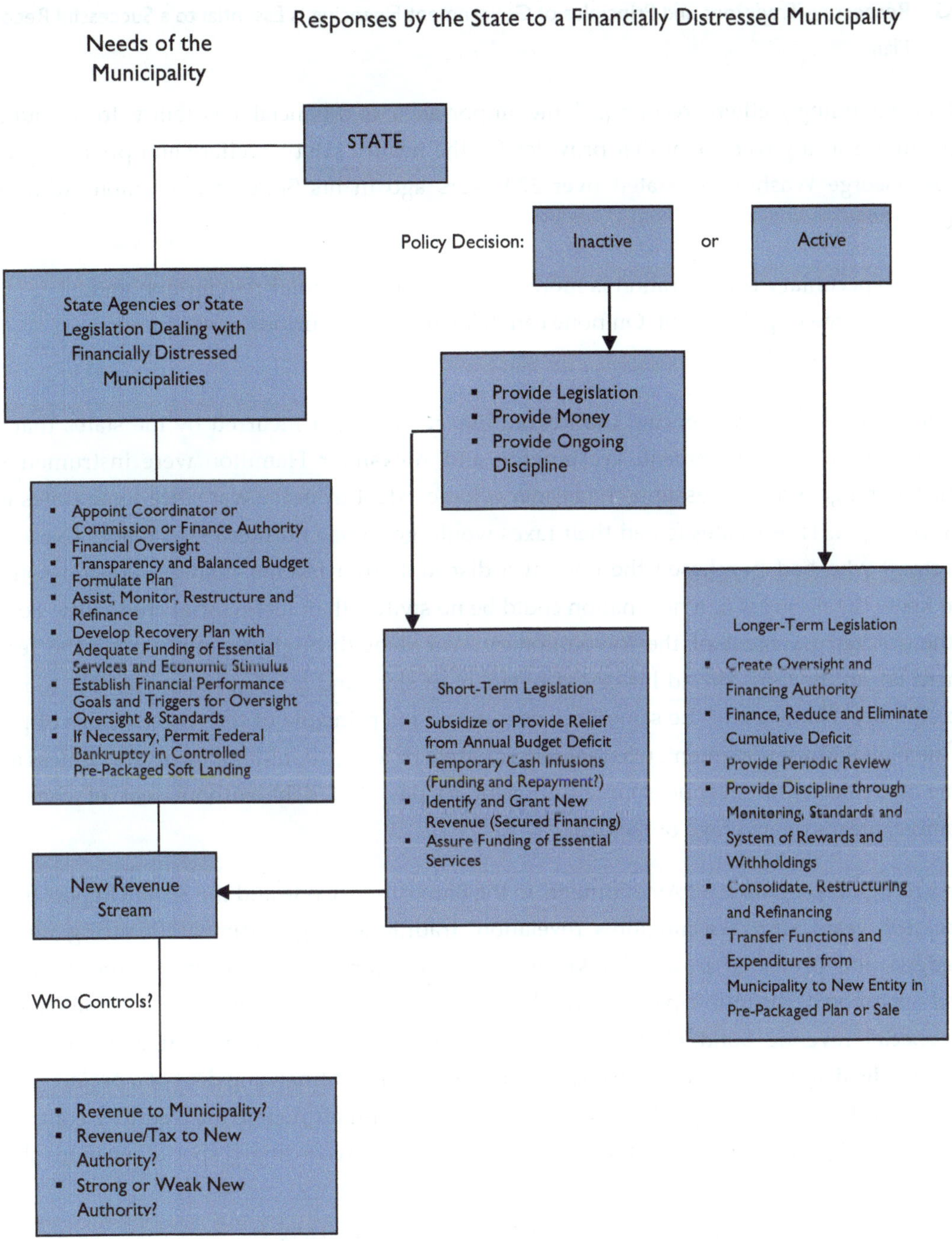
Responses by the State to a Financially Distressed Municipality
Needs of the Municipality
STATE
Policy Decision:
Inactive
or
Active
State Agencies or State Legislation Dealing with Financially Distressed Municipalities
▪ Provide Legislation
▪ Provide Money
▪ Provide Ongoing Discipline
▪ Appoint Coordinator or Commission or Finance Authority
▪ Financial Oversight
▪ Transparency and Balanced Budget
▪ Formulate Plan
▪ Assist, Monitor, Restructure and Refinance
▪ Develop Recovery Plan with Adequate Funding of Essential Services and Economic Stimulus
▪ Establish Financial Performance Goals and Triggers for Oversight
▪ Oversight & Standards
▪ If Necessary, Permit Federal Bankruptcy in Controlled Pre-Packaged Soft Landing
Short-Term Legislation
▪ Subsidize or Provide Relief from Annual Budget Deficit
▪ Temporary Cash Infusions (Funding and Repayment?)
▪ Identify and Grant New Revenue (Secured Financing)
▪ Assure Funding of Essential Services
Longer-Term Legislation
▪ Create Oversight and Financing Authority
▪ Finance, Reduce and Eliminate Cumulative Deficit
▪ Provide Periodic Review
▪ Provide Discipline through Monitoring, Standards and System of Rewards and Withholdings
▪ Consolidate, Restructuring and Refinancing
▪ Transfer Functions and Expenditures from Municipality to New Entity in Pre-Packaged Plan or Sale
New Revenue Stream
Who Controls?
▪ Revenue to Municipality?
▪ Revenue/Tax to New Authority?
▪ Strong or Weak New Authority?

G. Respecting Traditions and Principles of Government Financing Is Essential to a Successful Recovery Plan

Our Founding Fathers recognized the importance of financial credibility to a country's long-term success as a government that provides for the health, safety, welfare and prosperity of its citizens. As George Washington stated over 220 years ago in his State of the Union Address of December 3, 1793:

> No pecuniary consideration is more urgent than the regular redemption and discharge of public debt. On none can delay be more injurious or economy of time more valuable.

These words were referencing the Revolutionary War debt incurred by the states that was assumed by the federal government. Washington and Alexander Hamilton were instrumental in having the federal government assume the former colonies' debt from the war since some states were balking at paying it. Those states feared their taxes would go to pay northern speculators (New York City investors) who had purchased the debt at a discount from foreign holders. Washington and Hamilton knew the progress of a new nation could be no swifter than its financial credibility. For this reason, the assured payment of the Revolutionary War debt through assumption by the federal government began the long, proud history of payment of state and local government debt to insure market credibility. Hamilton at the same time announced his principle of the "immortality of public debt,"[190] namely that a government, whether federal, state or local, should not incur debt unless at the same time it dedicates a revenue source sufficient to pay that debt without fear of change of circumstances, means or coverage of the debt.

As recognized in the 1988 Amendments to the Bankruptcy Code and the Senate Report on that legislation, 195 years after Washington's revelation, traditions of government financing must be acknowledged and protected in any bankruptcy or restructuring law. To ensure the continued, undelayed operation of the municipal bond market, Congress incorporated heightened protections for so-called special revenue bondholders. "Special revenues" are tax revenues that a government specifically pledged and dedicated to the payment of the associated financing debt of a project, system or financing vehicle that must be paid as bargained for without impairment to the creditors' contractual rights. (See §§ 902(2), 922(d) and 928 of the Bankruptcy Code.)[191] Accordingly, special revenues should

---

190 *See* THE PAPERS OF ALEXANDER HAMILTON (Columbia University Press ed. 1979).

191 The Senate Report for the 1988 Amendments, S. REP. NO. 100-506, 100th Cong., 2d Session (1988) (the "Senate Report"), made it clear that the intention of the 1988 Amendments was to address the real worry in the marketplace that revenues dedicated to the repayment of municipal revenue obligations would be diverted to other purposes once a local government entered bankruptcy; that this worry rendered clarification of the law a necessity; and that revenue debt could not be impaired in a Chapter 9 proceeding. The same concern was reflected in the House Report for the 1988 Amendments, which noted that the bill "remedies the inconsistencies between bankruptcy law and principles of municipal finance to remove the potential for problems that now exist."

be so respected in the oversight or financial restructuring of any commission or authority. Likewise, statutory liens as well as payment priorities, set-asides and appropriations that are created and mandated by the force and effect of state statute or constitutional provisions must be honored and not impaired, delayed or interfered with. This follows from the principles that will be discussed later, articulated by the U.S. Supreme Court in the 1930s relating to municipal debt adjustment arising out of the cases of *Ashton* and *Bekins*. Namely, Congress and the federal court cannot limit, impair, stay or interfere with a state's control over a municipality's exercise of governmental powers as required by Sections 903 and 904 of the Bankruptcy Code.[192]

Examples of the "special revenues" mentioned in clause (A) include receipts derived from or received in connection with the ownership, financing, operation or disposition of a municipal water, electric or transportation system. An excise tax on hotel and motel rooms or the sale of alcoholic beverages would be a special excise tax under clause (B). "Special excise taxes" are taxes specifically identified and pledged in the bond financing documents and are not generally available to all creditors under state law. Without specific language, general state sales, general income or general property taxes would not be special excise taxes deemed levied to finance a specific project or system. In a typical tax increment financing referred to in clause (C), public improvements are financed by bonds payable solely from and secured by a lien on incremental tax receipts resulting from increased valuations in the benefited area. Although these receipts may be part of the general tax levy, they are considered attributable to the improvements so financed and are not part of the preexisting tax base of the community. Examples of revenues from particular functions under clause (D) would include regulatory fees and stamp taxes imposed for the recording of deeds or any identified function and related revenues identified in the municipality's financing documents, such as tolls or fees related to a particular service or benefit. Under clause (E), an incremental sales, income, or property tax specifically levied to pay indebtedness incurred for a capital improvement and not for the operating expenses or general purposes of the debtor would be considered special revenues. Likewise, any special tax or portion of a general tax specifically levied to pay for a municipal financing should be treated as special revenues. This concept will be discussed further in section VII, subsections E, G and H.

192 In certain situations, a bondholder may continue to receive payment in the wake of a Chapter 9 filing if the underlying statute authorizing the bond issuance contains a statutory lien, which lien comes into existence by virtue of the statute and arises by force of the statute on specific circumstances or conditions and does not require further action by the municipality. A statutory lien cannot be canceled on the filing of a bankruptcy petition or by the bankruptcy court. This approach was recognized by the district court on appeal in the Orange County bankruptcy. There, the court found that the lien securing tax and revenue anticipation notes pursuant to a California statute authorizing the county to pledge assets to secure notes was a statutory lien. Since the statute, not a security agreement, imposed the pledge, such pledge survived the filing of a Chapter 9 petition. At least 15 states and Puerto Rico recognize some form of statutory lien in relation to their bond obligations. See Appendix B.

In 2011 the State of Rhode Island was faced with issues of financial distress of its municipalities and, in particular, the City of Central Falls, an old manufacturing town of 19,000 that had lost its industrial base and fallen on hard times. The bond rating agencies had reacted to Central Falls' efforts to have a court-appointed receiver placed as new management of the city. The state adopted a new law in 2010 providing that, with state supervision, depending on the degree of distress, there could be use of a state-appointed overseer, a budget commission of state and local appointed members to approve budgets going forward or a receiver who would replace local government with the power to file under Chapter 9. The governor and others feared that the new law allowing Chapter 9 filings might cause a restriction in access to the financial market or an increase in borrowing costs by all municipalities in Rhode Island as a potential result of a municipal bankruptcy filing. Accordingly, Rhode Island passed a law granting a first statutory lien on all ad valorem taxes and general funds assessments for payment of all public debt (bonds and notes). This was well received by rating agencies and the municipal market so that, when Central Falls filed a Chapter 9 bankruptcy later in 2011, there was no real contagion to other Rhode Island municipalities as to restriction of access to or increase in the

Failure to follow these principles not only will make the restructuring process and recovery of a distressed municipality more difficult, if not impossible, but also may cause future necessary borrowing costs to be too expensive for long-term financial survival. The lesson learned from past and recent sovereign debt crises is that any adverse effect to the government's financial credibility going forward increases its future cost of borrowing and frustrates economic recovery and future governmental services. As noted above, Greece has defaulted on its sovereign debt at least five times since 1826 and prior to its recent fiscal crisis (1826, 1843, 1860, 1894 and 1932). Greece's ten-year bonds in March 2012 had an annual yield of 37.1 percent, and even after its recent bailout its annual yield is over 10.5 percent with a 52-week range of 5.5 percent and 19.5 percent. Brazil has a large economy and has defaulted at least 11 times since 1826, the last time in 1990, and still had an average ten-year bond annual yield between 2006 and 2015 of approximately 12.3 percent with an all-time high of 17.91 percent in October 2008. Puerto Rico is presently experiencing annual bond yield in excess of 10 percent if financing is available (see yield on ten-year Puerto Rico General Obligation Bonds in February 2014). At the same time, the bond yields for the United States, Germany, France and Canada are around 2 percent or less (as of September 2015). The consequences of not following the principles of government finance are clear and painful.

H. Government Operations and Creditor Protections

While in an oversight, a restructuring process or a Chapter 9 proceeding, a municipality will still have to function as a government. Depending upon the constitutional or statutory mission of the government, certain necessary and basic government services must be provided, such as public safety (police and fire), public health and welfare (education and health, transportation, building and zoning and, in certain instances, sewer, water and electrical services). History has shown that governments in financial distress need a recovery plan that stimulates economic activity in the government and encourages businesses to locate or expand there. This business expansion typically creates new, good jobs that increase tax revenues and lead to recovery and the solution of financial distress. Also, to effectuate a recovery plan, which is necessary for a turnaround, and to prevent future financial distress, there must be funding of essential government services. This will stimulate the economy and encourage growth of the municipality, which will attract new businesses and new citizens. Such economic growth will create needed jobs, especially for younger workers who will in turn become taxpayers, resulting in increased tax revenues. To accomplish the recovery plan, improved infrastructure is vital to ensure the required movement of goods, services and workers. In addition, enhanced education programs are

---

cost of borrowing. This is unlike the experience in Michigan where other municipalities claimed an increase in borrowing costs for unlimited ad valorem tax general obligation bonds ("ULTGOs") as high as 100 basis points or more (1 percent or more per annum) due to Detroit's filing in 2013 and the emergency manager's unprecedented claim that such bonds were unsecured. Even though ultimately the ULTGOs bondholders were to receive 100 percent recovery under the Detroit Plan of Debt Adjustment, the cloud on ULTGOs remains. This concept is further discussed in section VII, subsections F and H.

important to train young workers for the specific jobs created. Further, improved public safety and welfare programs will lead to a constructive environment fostering economic growth and recovery.

Defining these necessary governmental services is a question of constitutional or statutory law and local choice and may by itself be a complex issue. However, the economic benefits of reinvesting in the government are real and essential to a successful recovery. This is demonstrated by an economic study that shows that for each $1 invested in hard infrastructure expense there is an economic impact of $3.21 over 20 years.[193] For each new job created, there is a job multiplier from two to four jobs or more depending on the ancillary services necessary and the material services or goods required to be purchased for the job and the job's salary or benefits.[194]

I. Lengthy Litigation on the Competing Rights of Creditors May Not Be in Their Best Interests

Governments cannot pay that which they have no revenues to fund. Further, when obligations become so overwhelming to a government as to crowd out necessary expenses for essential governmental services and infrastructure, the consequences can be devastating and can lead to the meltdown of the government and the economy.

Without a successful recovery plan, there will not be enough funds to employ workers, provide essential services and programs, and fund necessary infrastructure improvements. In reality, the future of paying creditors, including pension funding along with workers' continued employment and a recovery plan, is dependent upon determining what costs and expenses are sustainable and affordable. This would include determining what amount of current expense can be paid that is reasonable, prudent and feasible. Such determination must take into account the necessity of sufficient funding for a recovery plan whereby essential governmental services can be raised to an acceptable level and infrastructure provided to encourage, stimulate and insure business growth and expansion with its accompanying creation of good, new jobs, especially for young citizens. This will insure not only short-term recovery, but also long-term success.

The financial oversight mechanisms recovery assistance described herein would help a state and its municipalities as well as all concerned parties in developing an effective recovery plan rather than litigating over payment issues, which would not be efficient or cost effective.

Fortunately, the answer to all of this is simple. Rather than positioning and fighting over what can be paid, what cannot be paid and what must be paid, it is in the best interests of all parties striving for the recovery and success of the government to recognize and determine what is sustainable and affordable, acknowledging that the resulting increase in the revenues or adjustments is simply a

---

193 Isabelle Cohen, Thomas Freiling & Eric Roberson, THE ECONOMIC IMPACT AND FINANCING OF INFRASTRUCTURE SPENDING 1 (2012), http://www.wm.edu/as/publicpolicy/documents/prs/aed.pdf.

194 Enrico Moretti, *Local Multipliers*, AMERICAN ECONOMIC REVIEW: PAPERS 6 PROCEEDINGS 100 (May 2010): 1-7, http://www.aeaweb.org/articles.php?doi=10.1257/acer.100.2.1.

recognition of reality. This can be accompanied through a consensual process prior to filing under Chapter 9 through the financial oversight and recovery assistance of the authority as well as in a Chapter 9 proceeding, as the last resort. In the long term, this will pay more than the best litigation strategy.

Obligations of the government can be appropriately adjusted to what is sustainable and affordable, allowing the government to invest in that which will help it recover and grow. Certain determined affordable fixed payments and contingent payments would only be paid if there are increased revenues from the success of the recovery. If the government does better, there will be more funding; obligations are not impaired or diminished because realistically all that can be paid is being paid. Creditors have improved expectations that the government operating under a realistic recovery plan in the development of which they participated will make future payments to fund their obligations based on the anticipated recovery and success of the municipality. Also, there could be periodic adjustments to the fixed and contingent payments based on actual results of the recovery and what is affordable.

There should be a periodic review of the progress in the recovery plan. If there is a need to adjust available revenues or payment obligations so that what is paid is sustainable and affordable, those adjustments should be made.

J. The Need for a Workable Government Debt Restructuring Mechanism

Past historical mechanisms appear to be inefficient in reaching a quick, effective resolution. The reasons for inefficiencies in past debt resolution mechanisms for sovereigns (countries) and for state and local governments in the United States appear to revolve around the following factors:

1. The Diversity of the Type of Debt Holders Has Increased

a. Sovereign Debt Resolutions

In past centuries, a sovereign's external debt creditors were generally a known group of governments or government agencies or were led by a known group of commercial banks and financial institutions that lent to the debtor government, including either the London Club for commercial banks or the Paris Club for government or government agency debt. These parties tended to reach an effective consensual resolution. The known lenders were usually the same grouping that had experience working together and following the lead of the largest lenders. In the latter part of the 1900s and the beginning of the 2000s, new, diverse and unknown participants evolved, namely high yield bond funds, hedge funds and special situation funds, which brought a novel challenge to the old closed groups of traditional lenders' quick resolution. This was true for sovereign country debt, as well as state and local government debt in the United States.

b. State and Local Government Debt Resolution

States cannot file Chapter 9 proceedings and must address financial distress by increasing taxes, by reducing expenditures (services) or through slow or significant delays in paying creditors until the financial distress is adjusted. No state has defaulted on its general obligation bonds since the late 1880s, with the exception of Arkansas in the 1930s. As has been noted herein, Chapter 9 filings have been rare and until recently limited, for the most part, to small utilities, special tax districts and other local governments (cities, towns, villages, hospitals, etc.). The debt holders of state and local debt, especially publicly traded bonds, have changed over the past 50 years. Banks, institutional holders (traditional bond funds and insurance companies) and retail (mom and pop) holders have transitioned in recent times of distress into more high yield funds and hedge funds that are more focused on short-term yields and less tolerant of prolonged workouts. The new entrants are more likely and sooner to resort to litigation and assertion of remedies; they have neither the long-term market relations nor the desire to slavishly go along with past resolution mechanisms.

2. There Has Been a Rise in Litigious Debt Holders Using Foreign Courts

a. Sovereign Debt

The Peru debt litigation in the 1990s and Argentina's litigation of the 2000s have proven that foreign courts and attempts to attack the foreign debtor government's assets in other jurisdictions could present a real obstacle to past resolution mechanisms. Recently, the court in the Argentina litigation held that Argentina's Central Bank's assets are not available for creditor attachment, which is consistent with similar rulings by the courts of other countries, intended to foster consensual rather than litigious resolution of sovereign debt.[195]

b. State and Local Debt

There has been a rise of more extreme litigation in connection with local government defaults in the United States. Two examples are the litigation between bond insurers, warrant holders and the trustee in *Jefferson County* that was ultimately settled in the Chapter 9 Plan of Adjustment and the litigation between banks and bond insurers and the emergency manager as to ULTGOs, SWAPs and water and sewer bonds in Detroit's Chapter 9 proceedings. The eligibility issue and lease treatment in the *Stockton* Chapter 9 filing and the Puerto Rico litigation with bond funds and hedge funds over the Puerto Rico Debt Enforcement and Recovery Act are other examples.[196]

---

195 *EM Ltd. v. Banio Central de la Republica Argentina*, 800 F.3d 78 (2d Cir. 2015).

196 *Franklin California Tax-Free Trust v. Commonwealth of Puerto Rico*, 805 F.3d 322 (1st Cir. 2015), *cert. granted*, 2015 WL 5096465 (Dec. 4, 2015), *aff'd sub nom. Commonwealth of Puerto Rico v. Franklin California Tax Free Trust*, 136 S. Ct. 1938 (2016).

3. The Number and Extent of Holdouts Who Do Not Care What Others Think Have Grown

In sovereign defaults, when the London Club or Paris Club was used, the lender participants knew in the next restructuring that they would be facing the same institutions and that being a holdout had adverse consequences, as some large institutions had developed long memories. In Chapter 9 filings and local government default situations in the United States, there had been a tradition that since the municipal market participants and the ongoing lenders to local governments were quite defined, prolonged distress hurt everyone. There was a feeling of pressure to "go along to get along" with a refinancing or restructuring the terms of which were not the absolutely desired result. The new entrants whose role in future financing is not assured feel less pressure to conform and more freedom to take a holdout path. The increase in the types of lenders and their ability through mutual or hedge fund vehicles to bring billions of dollars to the table resulted in the expansion of the small group of friendly lenders to the unknown lenders with significant capital and staying power. This is evidenced by the unsuccessful use of the collective action clause, or CAC, where a super-majority could modify principal, interest or maturity in the Greek restructuring (only 17 of 30 financings that had CACs reached agreement of a super-majority approving the bailout terms) and the dynamic of the Detroit, Jefferson County, Stockton, San Bernardino and Vallejo Chapter 9 cases and the Puerto Rico debt restructurings of its public corporations.

4. The Upsurge of Legacy Costs of Government and Crowding out of Funding for Essential Services and Infrastructure Mandate a More Complex Restructuring of Past Financial Mistakes

The civil and public pensions that lack funds dedicated to pay, with rising costs of benefits, have strained the past restructuring methods of reaching an agreement. The age and delay in infrastructure improvements and increased costs of public workers and essential government services reduce dollars available for the restructuring.

5. Tension Has Increased Between Repayment of Debt of Governments and the Governments' Right to Reserve Funds for the Public and Social Good

Recent efforts in Belgium and under English law to establish dedicated reserve funds to be used for pensions, governmental services or infrastructure that could not be attached by creditors have raised new concerns and created a new battleground. Litigation in the United States over pension reform due to unaffordable and unsustainable underfunded public pensions that crowd out funding for governmental services and needed infrastructure improvements has not been resolved in a satisfactory manner. These struggles are tied to the notions of sovereign immunity and that the provision of essential governmental services is not a commercial activity that should be involved in sharing the pain in a financial debt restructuring. Since a government cannot be sold, liquidated or capitalized, there are practical limits to the extent a restructuring can infringe on social and political issues.

6. Investment in the Government to Stimulate Economic Development May Be the Best Assurance to Creditors That They Will Be Paid

Generally sovereigns, states and local governments have fallen into financial distress due to years, if not decades, of neglecting to provide services at a level that attracts new businesses and business development and of failing to make infrastructure improvement desired by citizens and businesses.[197] The best recovery plan for a financially struggling sovereign is to reinvest in essential services and needed infrastructure to stimulate the economy, encourage business expansion and create new, good jobs, all of which create additional tax revenues to pay restructured creditors. Economic studies have shown that $1 spent on necessary infrastructure improvements yields over $3.21 in economic stimulus over 20 years,[198] most of which is front-end loaded. This is what is meant by the term "job multiplier," where the creation of one good job provides stimulus for the creation of two to three or more jobs due to the direct, indirect and induced effects of economic activity. Starving the government's economic development can directly adversely affect the ability of restructured creditors to be paid.

K. There Is a Growing Awareness of the Need for a New Mechanism for Government Debt Problems

1. The Problem of Past Practices

In sovereign defaults, the London Club and Paris Club have been less frequently used and less efficient due to the significant growth of nontraditional non-bank and non-government participants who will not necessarily play by the old rules. This has been evident in the recent debt restructurings of Peru, Argentina and Russia and, most recently, in the Greek debt crisis.[199] Likewise, less than effective pension reform and the financial distress of state and local governments in the United States have created dynamic uncertainty for bondholders, workers and taxpayers. As a result, local governments are left with less ability to proceed with the traditional refinancing and are more likely to face partisan battles over who will be paid and when. While the process of Chapter 9 provides debt adjustment, it does not necessarily assure the development of a recovery plan that is sustainable and affordable and that provides funding for necessary services and needed infrastructure.

---

197 The 2013 American Society of Civil Engineers' Report Card for American Infrastructure claims that $3.6 trillion of investment is needed by 2020 to bring the infrastructure in the United States up to an acceptable level. In 2009 the last prior report of the American Society of Civil Engineers said the cost over five years to bring the infrastructure up to an acceptable level was $2.2 trillion, as the delay over the past five years in doing so had caused an increase from $2.2 trillion in 2009 to $3.6 trillion in 2013, for a total difference of $1.4 trillion. Delay is not only painful for those living through it with less than acceptable infrastructure, it is also expensive. AMERICAN SOCIETY OF CIVIL ENGINEERS, 2013 REPORT CARD FOR AMERICAN INFRASTRUCTURE, http://www.infrastructurereportcard.org/ and http://www.cnn.com/2009/US/01/28/infrastructure.report.card/index.html.

198 Cohen, Freiling & Roberson, *supra* n.50.

199 Viktoria Dendrinou, *Eurozone Fund Weighs Greece Debt Relief Options,* WALL STREET JOURNAL (Dec. 10, 2015).

2. No Quick Fixes

In international sovereign debt restructurings, the use of contractual or statutory resolution mechanisms for *ad hoc* or nontraditional banks or government lenders has not been as effective as expected. The use of CACs, exit consents and exchange offers and forbearance or standstill agreements in countries such as Argentina, Peru and Greece has been less effective recently due to the less collegial nature of lenders. For local governments in the United States, the lack of structured support, interim financing and expertise in developing effective recovery plans acceptable to all has made Chapter 9 filings and municipal defaults time consuming, expensive and less than desirable.

3. Need for Predictability of Results

The desired predictability of results has fallen to the questions of uncertainty of method to be used, the lack of willingness and ability of the government and lenders to reach and honor the agreement, the unpredictable nature of nontraditional lenders and the questionable availability of interim or future financing and liquidity. Accordingly, a new mechanism is needed to provide more predictability, less contentious litigation and a faster and more transparent process that is fair and impartial to all and does not carry the stigma, costs, consequences or uncertainty of past mechanisms.

L. The Development of a New Mechanism Must Address the Needs of the Government and the Concerns of the Creditors and Lenders

1. The Needs of Government

Governments believe their debt restructurings are more complicated than a corporate restructuring or bankruptcy. For governments, there is a difference between mere survival and a real economic recovery. A government in financial distress cannot be liquidated or sold. The government requires the continued ability to provide essential services and necessary infrastructure to its citizens, economic stimulus for jobs and commercial activity, and national and public safety, education, health and welfare. As was apparent with the extensive local resident objections to the emergency manager appointed in Detroit, Michigan, receiverships and overbearing oversight are not socially or politically popular, especially in a democracy.

2. Lender Concerns

Lenders do not want to fund wasteful governments or unjustifiable lifestyles or to explain to their participants or stockholders why losses have been incurred without reasonable justification. Lenders want to be assured of a predictable, just and fair system that addresses all issues so there is no continuing systemic problem and no use of a Band-Aid as opposed to a permanent fix.

Sovereigns, lenders and creditors alike desire the following:

1. A formal method of announcing and beginning the process;

2. The ability to coordinate the creditors and avoid the holdouts or free-ride problem;
3. A means of building consensus and knowing there will be support or at least a definite resolution if some parties cannot agree;
4. An automatic stay of litigation for any court in any country;
5. A full, transparent means of classifying and providing a treatment of all claims that will be disclosed to all creditors, including the ability to pay and justification for treatment;
6. Recognition of the unimpaired status of fully secured creditors (like statutory liens and special revenues in Chapter 9) along with provision for priority funding of necessary services and infrastructure;
7. Interim and continuing financing to assure liquidity of the sovereign to preserve the ongoing ability to pay;
8. The ability of the government to "cram down" or reduce debt to what is sustainable and affordable without impairing the economic growth and future of the government; and
9. Assurance to the lenders that the agreed-upon restructuring is also feasible and capable of stimulating and, to the extent possible, growing the economy since that is really the essence of best interests of creditors, government and taxpayers.

M. Government Oversight, Recovery and Debt Adjustment Commission (GORDAC)

1. Creation

As a result of the concerns addressed in this section, there should be established by treaty or agreement of affected creditors and lenders for sovereigns and by U.S. congressional legislation for territories of the United States (under Article IV, Section 3 of the U.S. Constitution)[200] and by federal or state legislation for local governments in the United States, to the extent possible, a three-phase process under an independent, separate and newly established Government Oversight, Recovery and Debt Adjustment Commission, or GORDAC.

2. Phases of GORDAC Process

- Phase One. Initiate, investigate and determine sustainable and affordable governmental services, needed infrastructure and debt with transparency of all financial information, budget and liabilities ("Sustainability Determination"). Also provide for interim or bridge

200 The recently enacted Puerto Rico Oversight, Management and Economic Stability Act ("PROMESA") in June 2016 directly or indirectly follows most of the protocol and structure set forth in GORDAC. To the degree further refinement may be necessary as to PROMESA, its differences with GORDAC can be the subject of further legislation.

financing with dedicated revenue sources and good-as-gold structures to provide liquidity and essential services during oversight and recovery.

- <u>Phase Two</u>. Develop recovery plans for the government consistent with the Sustainability Determination that sets forth the recovery plan, demonstrating the governmental services to be funded and stimulus for economic development to encourage business activity, creation of jobs and increase in GDP and tax revenues so that assurances can be given to creditors as to the recovery and increasing revenues for payment of the debt owed to the lenders.

- <u>Phase Three</u>. Present the recovery plan after creditors have the opportunity to comment, negotiate and raise objections to recovery plan proposals. If through GORDAC oversight and mediation the desired agreement on a recovery plan cannot be reached by the government and the creditors, then the less preferred quasi-judicial determination and hearing stage would proceed similar to Chapter 9, with creditor voting by affected class and the approval of the recovery plan by the commission. Make any modifications or changes the commission believes are necessary to be consistent with the Sustainability Determination. The goal of the recovery plan and this process is a permanent resolution of the systemic financial issues of the government in order to avoid a recurrence of the problems of the past and to provide a fresh start.

3. Commission

The GORDAC commission shall consist of a panel of at least three commissioners and a professional staff with experience in finance, government, accounting and governmental and financial restructuring sufficient to fulfill its mission. The commission shall initially have an oversight and technical assistance function which, if not successful, would progress into a quasi-judicial and final resolver of open issues. The commission shall be funded by fees from the participating governments who are subject to the treaty and by fees imposed upon the distressed governments (state and local) who use GORDAC. The commission shall be completely independent of governments or lenders.

4. The Process.

a. Initiation

A petition is made by the participating government or designated percentage of debt outstanding that demonstrates the government has defaulted on a designated percentage of debt or cannot pay its debts as they will mature and that the government will default within a year or has a function emergency. The commission can request a response from the government if the petition was initiated by a designated percentage of creditors. Within a short period of time, the commission will decide if government financial distress exists such that GORDAC should take jurisdiction. If the commission takes jurisdiction, then it will immediately issue an order to:

1. Stay all litigation involving the government or actions to obtain a preference by one creditor over others.

2. Schedule discussions, discovery, negotiations or mediation as the commission deems necessary to determine what debt and governmental services are sustainable and affordable. The Sustainability Determination is to be made first and then the recovery plan debt adjustment determination will be made.

3. Establish the timing for determination of sustainability, government filing of the recovery plan and comments from creditors on the recovery plan.

4. Schedule dates for hearings on sustainability and, if necessary, the process of voting on the proposed recovery plan and dates for hearings on objections to the recovery plan.

5. Schedule dates when the commission will make its determination of sustainability and ruling on the recovery plan with any commission-imposed modifications thereto.

b. Commission Management of the Process

The commission is to (i) manage the collection of information necessary for transparency and for review and approval of interim and annual budgets as well as for the determination of sustainability of a recovery plan and (ii) supervise and facilitate negotiation, mediation and resolution of issues and the development of a recovery plan. The process will start more like a financial oversight authority assisting with and facilitating review and approval of budgets and negotiations and resolutions of issues in a recovery plan. If agreement is not reached, the oversight turns to judicial determination of issues binding on all parties with the power of the commission to enforce its decisions on all parties in all courts of all jurisdictions. The commission will consist of at least three commissioners, who would be designated as:

1. The *Chair*, who would preside over hearings and be the ultimate determiner of designated matters and the recovery plan;

2. The *Commissioner for Mediation*, who would be in charge of supervising and establishing the procedures and rules for mediation and appoint the special master or the associate judge to preside over mediation and settlements to be recommended to the Chair and commission; and

3. The *Commissioner for Sustainability Determination*, who would be in charge of the Sustainability Determination and budget review and approval process and the work of the professional staff of GORDAC as well as the disclosure of all necessary discovery and collection of information from the government and creditors necessary for the Sustainability Determination and the recovery plan.

GORDAC is a blend of the benefits of a financial oversight authority (such as Act 47 in Pennsylvania, the Financial Control Board in New York and the emergency manager in Michigan) and Chapter 9, with expanded powers and a limited right to appeal. This strong medicine is intended to encourage early agreement to avoid a harsher judicial result.

c. Power

The commission shall have the power to:

1. Subpoena or request from the sovereign or creditors information required to fulfill its mission.

2. Engage any professionals necessary to fulfill its mission.

3. Mediate and determine, if necessary, issues related to budget and appropriation, desired levels of governmental services, costs, taxes, pension funding and benefits to ensure sustainability during the process and ability of the sovereign to pay its adjusted debts and provide essential services to its citizens.

4. Encourage and approve settlements between the government and creditor groups or individual creditors.

5. Review, recommend and approve government interim and annual budgets, short-term and long-term financing and continued financing with, if necessary, super-priority protection to ensure liquidity and funding during the process at the lowest borrowing cost possible. If necessary, negotiate and obtain needed funding.

6. Recommend cuts in governmental spending and tax increases as necessary for continued operation of the government.

7. Recommend mediation by government and any creditor or creditor group and require attendance and participation of affected creditors.

8. Require update on mediation discussion with creditors and the government, progress reports and status of recovery plan and resolution with creditors.

9. Recommend the approval or disapproval of contracts, expenditures, loan creation or elimination of certain positions or operations.

10. Recommend staffing levels in relation to determination of sustainability and adjustment to staffing, hiring and compensation.

11. Recommend or require sale or other transfer of any asset, right or claim of the sovereign, including privatization and lease.

12. Take any other action necessary for the fulfillment of its mission.

d. GORDAC to Encourage Sovereign to Resolve Matters Before Having to Issue a Ruling Binding on All Parties

The government and creditors are encouraged to use the process to quickly and effectively resolve their issues and to develop a sustainable and affordable recovery plan that stimulates growth and development of business and provides for essential governmental services and the best return to creditors consistent with the Sustainability Determination. Only if the government fails to act in good faith or fails to reach agreement on a recovery plan shall the commission rule and be the final word binding on all without the right to appeal.

e. Recovery Plan

The recovery plan shall provide for:

1. The continued operation of government, consistent with the Sustainability Determination.
2. Payment of the debt as adjusted, if necessary.
3. Any necessary modification, rejection, termination, renegotiation or replacement of contracts, including social programs and public workers' pensions paid for by the government.
4. Justification of the reduction in services or adjustment of debt, the reinvestment in the government and projected increases in GDP, employment and tax revenues, if any.
5. Any other matters that the commission or the circumstances may require to allow the government to alleviate the financial emergency and accept the recovery plan.

f. Final Approval and Continuing Oversight

The commission may require as part of its approval that, post-approval, there be some form of continued oversight of operation, budgeting, tax collection or any other matters as a condition for approval of the recovery plan. This oversight may be by a board or overseer selected by the commission or by periodic reports to the commission.

g. Sovereign Immunity for GORDAC

GORDAC and its judges, employees, agents and professionals shall all have global sovereign immunity from any claim or damage suffered.

5. Now Is the Time to Enact GORDAC before the Next Wave of Government Debt Crisis

(a) As noted above, sovereign, state and local government debt crises follow economic downturns, war, political unrest and unforeseen events. Now is the time to prepare before the next wave of crises hits.

(b) On the sovereign level, the London Club, Paris Club, the Sovereign Debt Restructuring Mechanism proposed by the International Monetary Fund, use of CAC, exit consents and exchange offers have merit but have not been as effective as desired. On the state, territory and local government levels Chapter 9 either is not available or has been marked with experiences of stigma, high costs, significant delay and less-than-hoped-for results. With changing times and recently experienced problems, GORDAC appears to provide the promise of the best, most effective and most efficient means of resolving government debt crises in the best interests of all constituents.

N. Conclusion

The states have divergent techniques for addressing the financial woes of their municipalities. These general provisions are more fully addressed in section VIII, the 50-State Survey. As always, because each state contains unique laws for addressing municipal issues, for any specific questions, details or issues, further analysis and consultation with professional advisors is advisable. States should continue to be vigilant to the changing times and the evolution of current mechanics to better address new financial and operational issues and challenges. The traditions of the past respecting the principles of government finance and avoiding litigation meltdown by prompt use of effective mechanisms to address financial and operational problems as soon as possible should not be forgotten. In addition, should a state's assistance or oversight mechanism to a troubled municipality fail to produce the desired result, a number of alternatives for municipalities and their creditors will be discussed, such as bondholders' rights and remedies in the event of default and municipal bankruptcy.

VI. Bondholder Rights and Remedies

In addition to the more general provisions addressing municipal restructuring issues, the states have implemented a series of patchwork provisions allowing bondholders to protect their rights and granting certain remedies in the event of a default. Section VIII of this book includes a general overview of representative provisions of each state.

A. General Types of Municipal Bonds: General Obligations, Revenues, TANS, BANS, Conduit Bonds and Others

As background, state laws generally allow for the issuance of bonds within two broad categories — general obligation and revenue bonds. General obligation bonds are those bonds to which the state or local government has pledged its full faith and credit. The primary source of payment will likely be ad valorem taxes or other legally available sources rather than revenues from a given project.[201]

Revenue bonds are those bonds issued by state and local governments that are paid solely based upon the revenues to be collected by the municipal body in connection with the financed improvement. Revenue bonds normally have no other recourse to the issuing municipality — such as recourse to its general credit. State or local government revenue bond are generally non-recourse to the governmental entity issuing the bonds and project specific as to revenues from a governmental system, project or enterprise. An example of a revenue bond would be a bond payable solely from a pledge of the net revenues of a water or sewer system. As a further example, many states have separate laws, and in many other states (for instance, Arkansas) laws exist for authorizing the issuance of numerous types of revenue bonds including, but not limited to, parking meter bonds, suburban improvement district bonds, property owners' improvement district bonds, municipal property improvement district bonds, water distribution district bonds, drainage and levee improvement district bonds, public

201 However, general obligation bonds also may have revenue or tax pledges specifically pledged and dedicated to their payment. These pledges, such as on the unlimited ad valorem tax pledge to general obligation bonds of cities, counties, school and health care districts in California, provide what is intended to be bankruptcy-remote revenue sources by the language of the state statute authorizing their issuance and the legislative history of the 1988 Amendments to the Bankruptcy Code. Additionally, a specific dedicated revenue pledge in addition to a state or local government's full faith and credit pledge may have a statutory or constitutionally mandated payment, set-aside, appropriation or priority that cannot be interfered with, stayed, modified or terminated by a federal bankruptcy court under Sections 903 and 904 of the Bankruptcy Code and the Tenth Amendment to the U.S. Constitution. Similarly, a municipality must adhere to state law and cannot consent to any involuntary stay, modification or termination of a pledge that would be contrary to its state constitution or statute or authority, although if the municipality violates state law, the bankruptcy court likely would not possess jurisdiction to adjudicate such a claim (*see, e.g.*, a rate case). Further, such dedicated payments may be secured by a statutory lien or special revenues under Sections 902, 922(d) and 928 of the Bankruptcy Code.

corporations for municipal facility bonds, public utility bonds, and bridge improvement district bonds.[202] In general, each of these provisions contains different mechanisms to protect bondholder rights.

There are other commonly used municipal securities.[203] An appropriation bond is a type of moral obligation bond. The obligation to pay debt service is contingent upon the inclusion of the debt service payment in the issuer's annual budget (appropriation). A legislature cannot bind successor legislatures to appropriate funds. The issuer is not *legally* obligated to make the appropriation, the failure to make the appropriation is not an event of default, and the full faith and credit of the borrower are not implicated.

A certificate of participation (COP) shares some of the characteristics of the appropriation bond. The COP evidences an undivided fractional interest in a pledged revenue stream, often lease payments, subject to annual appropriation. The certificate holder is entitled to its proportionate share of the payments made, which typically are assigned to a trustee. The risk to the COP holder is that the lessee will lose the willingness to make lease payments.

A conduit financing involves the issuance of municipal securities by a governmental unit to be used by a third party (conduit borrower) for a general public purpose. The conduit borrower is liable for making the debt service payments on the bonds, no government funds are at risk and the bonds are without recourse to the municipality or other governmental entity issuing the bonds. Upon default the remedies are more similar to those available to holders of corporate debt; likewise, the default rate is more accurately reflected by the corporate default rate to the extent the recourse is to the corporate entity.

In addition, there are common forms of short-term debt. A tax anticipation note or TAN is a short-term debt security issued by a state or local government to finance a current project before the revenues are received. A specific tax levy is pledged to pay the notes, normally as the sole source of payment, and the notes are dependent upon collections sufficient to pay the notes.

A bond anticipation note (BAN) is a short-term interest-bearing security issued in advance of a future bond issue. The proceeds of the future bond issue are pledged to pay the notes, normally the sole source of payment, and the notes are dependent upon the bonds being issued and the proceeds being sufficient to pay the BANs in full.

When a municipality defaults on a bond issuance, bondholders may institute a lawsuit requesting that the municipality take certain actions, immediately pay all amounts due and owing to

---

202 *See*, for instance, section VIII, Arkansas endnote ix.

203 *See* MUNICIPAL SECURITIES RULEMAKING BOARD GLOSSARY OF MUNICIPAL SECURITIES TERMS, www.msrb.org.

bondholders, or otherwise cure the default.[204] Such actions may be in the form of a suit for money judgment, mandamus, specific performance or other equitable relief, such as requesting the issuance of an injunction. Where bondholders are owed principal or interest by a municipal body that has not been paid, the bondholders may bring a suit for payment of that debt. In this situation, the municipal body, absent filing a petition under Chapter 9 of the Bankruptcy Code, likely cannot take any action to obtain a moratorium of such a suit.[205] In light of these principles the next few subsections will provide an overview of the general rights and remedies available to bondholders.

B. Acceleration

One of the most powerful tools available to bondholders is the remedy of acceleration, where bondholders or their trustee declares the entire principal amount of the securities they hold outstanding and immediately due and payable. Whether or not bondholders may accelerate the payment of principal and interest depends on the terms of the underlying governing documents. It is standard for such governing documents to permit the acceleration of principal and interest upon the occurrence of an event of default. While conduit financing bonds and certain structured financings permit acceleration upon the occurrence of an event of default, general obligation bonds, revenue bonds and appropriation obligations by their nature do not. For example, acceleration for a water or sewer bond payable from periodic rate payments by customers makes little sense given the limited cash flow and the ability to appoint a receiver to address mismanagement and operational problems or actions to enforce a rate covenant. Likewise, for general obligation bonds mandamus would be a more effective remedy than acceleration because mandamus requires the levying of taxes to pay, thereby increasing available funds. The indenture trustee and a certain percentage of the holders as provided under the indenture, normally 25 percent, are empowered to accelerate. In other circumstances, the bond documents may provide for an automatic acceleration without notice, based upon the occurrence of certain specified events.

Bondholders may choose to accelerate to receive a stepped-up interest rate. The indenture may provide that, upon acceleration, all overdue principal and interest may earn an increased interest rate as permitted by law.[206] Acceleration is also necessary in order to obtain a deficiency judgment or judgment for principal and accrued interest against the obligor.

---

204 For a more detailed discussion of such remedies, *see* James E. Spiotto, *Municipal Insolvency: Bankruptcy, Receivership, Workouts and Alternative Remedies*, STATE & LOCAL GOVERNMENT DEBT FINANCING, ch. 13 (2d ed. 1993).

205 *See Flushing Nat'l Bank v. Mun. Assistance Corp. for the City of New York*, 40 N.Y.2d 731 (1976). In *Flushing National Bank*, a moratorium was issued by the city of New York against payment and institution of lawsuits by noteholders. The highest court in New York found that the moratorium violated the contractual obligation of the municipality and the constitutional rights of the noteholders to the full faith and credit of the city. The court held that the noteholders, whose principal and interest were due, had a right to bring suit and demand payment, and the municipality did not have the right to enjoin or stop such payment.

206 *Thompson v. Getz (In re Plymold Corp.)*, 178 F.2d 325 (1st Cir. 1949) (where the court utilized the statutory rate for post-maturity interest because the interest would only be owed "from the date hereof to maturity"); *Guaranty Trust*

In practicality, acceleration may have little immediate effect. An obligor who is unable to pay a principal or interest installment will probably be unable to pay the full amount of the issue outstanding. Acceleration may tie the hands of the indenture trustee and bondholders in certain workout scenarios. Normally, a much higher percentage of the holders (50 percent or more) is required to rescind the acceleration than to accelerate (25 percent or less). It may be that, depending on all factors, acceleration should not take place immediately.

C. Mandamus

The applicable law of all states likely would permit a bondholder to petition a court for a writ of mandamus to enforce the rights granted to the bondholders in a bond issuance. A writ of mandamus is a tool that bondholders, or their trustee, could use to compel the state or local government or official to perform some ministerial action that is required by law to levy taxes to pay past-due debt. Specifically, if the law requires the local government or official to take such an action and such government or official refuses, the court may order the government or official to act, regardless of whether the government or official was reasonable in not acting. For instance, if a local government or official with power to act refuses to collect taxes or fees or to levy taxes sufficient to pay the current payment of debt as it comes due, and the underlying bond authorization statute requires the collection of taxes or fees, a bondholder could petition for a writ of mandamus to compel such action. The remedy is "extraordinary" and one court has provided:

> It is not to be used to establish rights but to enforce rights that have already been established. The writ can be used to compel a tribunal to act but cannot control its discretion. If there is a plain, speedy, and adequate remedy at law, mandamus does not lie. When such a remedy is available through certiorari or appeal, mandamus should not be ordered. The other available remedy, however, must be competent to afford relief on the very subject matter in question, and be equally convenient, beneficial and effectual.[207]

The Seventh Circuit Court of Appeals, in *Connett v. City of Jerseyville*, 125 F.2d 121 (7th Cir. 1941), held that where a mortgage or a statute requires a city to adopt a schedule of rates for a waterworks sufficient to pay the indebtedness of the waterworks, a court may compel the city to adopt the schedule. The Seventh Circuit found, however, that although a court had the power to compel the city to adopt the statutory schedule, it had no power to fix the rates for the waterworks. Thus, if a local

---

Co. v. Henwood, 86 F.2d 347 (8th Cir. 1936), *cert. denied*, 300 U.S. 661 (1937); *see also* U.C.C. § 3-112 (if an instrument provides for interest but the amount of interest cannot be ascertained on its face, interest is payable to the statutory judgment rate).

207 *Hewitt v. Ryan*, 356 N.W.2d 230, 233 (Iowa 1984) (internal citations omitted).

government is provided discretion in its act, mandamus would be a difficult remedy to assert unless the local board's acts were arbitrary or capricious.[208]

Practical problems in a mandamus action may exist where an office is vacant or the municipality's officers have resigned. Such events remove the benefit of any mandamus action because the holders do not have the right to cause the court to fill such vacancies. Mandamus actions sound simple and easy, but the municipality and its taxpayers may engage in a prolonged fight before bondholders are paid. For example, in 1949, the California Supreme Court ordered a recalcitrant irrigation district to levy a tax to pay on defaulted bonds that had been issued in the late 1920s. Over 30 years after the issuance of the bonds, with exception to the payment of interest in 1927, 1928 and 1929, the bondholders had yet to receive any money and were still fighting in court.[209] Another practical issue is that, if the defaulting government is at its constitutional or statutory limit for taxation or debt, the court cannot order the governmental official to levy taxes beyond constitutional or statutory limits.[210]

In the event a local board refuses to take some action required by law, such as collecting taxes on fees to pay for a bond issuance, if a consensual restructuring fails, pursuing a writ of mandamus may be an alternative.[211]

D. Receivership

In addition to allowing bondholders or their representative to accelerate debt or to file a petition with a court for a writ of mandamus to force a local government to take a required action, many bond issuances allow for the appointment of a receiver to oversee the particular project in question and, if appropriate, raise rates or taxes sufficient to pay debt issued to finance the public improvement.[212] A modern example of such an action occurred recently in Jefferson County, Alabama. In September 2010, an Alabama state court appointed a receiver to operate and administer the county's sewer system. The county had $3.2 billion in sewer debt that it was unable to pay, related largely to a failed interest-rate swap transaction. The receiver was given the power to operate and administer the

---

208 *See, e.g., Reed v. Gaylord,* 216 N.W.2d 327, 331 (Iowa 1974).

209 *Water Users Ass'n v. Bd. of Dirs.,* 34 Cal. App. 3d 131 (Cal. Ct. App. 1973).

210 *See, e.g., Eakin v. State ex rel. Capital Improvement Bd. of Managers,* 474 N.E. 2d 62 (Ind. 1985).

211 For further discussion as to the pursuit of a writ of mandamus against a municipality with respect to a bond issuance, *see* W. Michael Garner, *Procedural Aspects of Municipal Finance Litigation,* STATE & LOCAL GOVERNMENT DEBT FINANCING § 14:50 (1986 & Supp.).

212 *See, e.g.,* section VIII, 50 State Survey, charts for Alabama, Arizona, Arkansas, California, Colorado, Connecticut, District of Columbia, Florida, Georgia, Hawaii, Idaho, Illinois, Indiana, Iowa, Kansas, Kentucky, Louisiana, Maine, Maryland, Massachusetts, Michigan, Mississippi, Missouri, Montana, Nebraska, Nevada, New Hampshire, New Jersey, New Mexico, New York, North Carolina, North Dakota, Ohio, Oklahoma, Oregon, Pennsylvania, Puerto Rico, Rhode Island, South Carolina, South Dakota, Tennessee, Texas, Utah, Vermont, Virginia, Washington, West Virginia and Wyoming.

sewer system, including, as allowed by the bond indenture, the ability to raise rates. Once the county filed under Chapter 9, the bankruptcy court held that the automatic stay would *not* be modified to permit the prepetition state receivership case to continue.[213]

Authorizing provisions for revenue bond financing in 46 states, the District of Columbia and Puerto Rico allow for the appointment of a receiver in the event of a default. These provisions are generally tied to specific revenue bond issuances. For instance, Maryland law contains certain provisions allowing for the appointment of a receiver should a municipality default on sewage facility bonds.[214] Under Maryland law, should a local unit of government default on bonds for sewage facilities, a receiver may enter, take possession of the facility to operate and maintain it, and set facility rates, fees or charges. In addition, the receiver may collect, receive and apply all revenues of the facility. Such receivership provisions are generally tailored by a state's laws to address the type of bond that is being issued.

As may be seen from section VIII, the 50-State Survey, such provisions are generally bond specific. Thus, to establish the rights and remedies, including the ability to appoint a receiver with respect to a particular bond issuance, specific review and analysis may be required to determine the particular legal authorization, and a thorough review of the authorizing language in the bond indenture is necessary.

E. Suit to Recover Judgment

A lawsuit may be initiated for past-due principal or interest on the debt. The lawsuit may be filed for a missed principal or interest payment or upon the accelerated debt if acceleration has taken place. The initiation of a lawsuit for the payment of principal and interest is certainly not identical to collecting such, and in some circumstances the indenture trustee and bondholders should be aware that the filing of such a lawsuit may push the municipal obligor to take actions opposed by bondholders. If the holders are faced with a defaulted municipal issue, additional complications may arise. While sovereign immunity is a possible defense to suits to compel the payment of money from a municipal body, courts have generally held, given statutory waivers of sovereign immunity or implied waiver by entering into the debt obligation, that debt holders' rights to commence an action for payment of their debts should not be restrained.[215] A money judgment against a municipality is additionally complicated by the fact that, generally, courts on public policy grounds do not allow

---

213 *In re Jefferson Cnty., Ala.*, 474 B.R. 228 (Bankr. N.D. Ala. 2012).

214 MD. CODE ENVIR. § 9-807.

215 *See, e.g., Flushing Nat'l Bank v. Mun. Assistance Corp. for the City of New York*, 40 N.Y.2d 731 (1976) (declaring debt moratorium unconstitutional under the state constitution); *State v. City of Lakeland*, 154 Fla. 137 (1943) (some courts have held that a contractual municipal debt obligation is a waiver of sovereign immunity); *Grant Constr. Co. v. Burns*, 92 Idaho 408 (1968).

seizure municipal property to pay debt obligations, as such seizure would disrupt local government.[216] Likewise, in the absence of specific statutes authorizing the seizure of private property to satisfy a judgment on a defaulted municipal bond, there can be no remedy directly to the property held by the residents or inhabitants of the municipal body.[217]

To ensure a bond trustee's authority to represent bondholders in such suits, a bond indenture should contain language permitting the indenture trustee in its own name, as trustee of an express trust, to institute a judicial proceeding for the collection of the sums due and unpaid, to foreclose the mortgage, to prosecute such proceeding to judgment and to enforce the same against the municipality or other obligor under the issue without the requirement of having possession of the bonds, notes or other evidence of indebtedness. The purpose of such provisions is to allow the indenture trustee to collect a deficiency judgment in a mortgage foreclosure action or to obtain a judgment on an unsecured issue. Without such provisions, a municipality or other interested parties may raise defenses as to the power of the indenture trustee to proceed to collect and enforce the judgment.[218]

F. Accounting

In addition to the provisions discussed above, some states, depending on the type of bond, may allow bondholders to seek an accounting. Specifically, at least 23 states, the District of Columbia and Puerto Rico allow for bondholders or a representative trustee to bring an action for an accounting to require the local government to explain how a bond fund has been spent, in the same manner as a trustee would be required to take such action.[219] If a municipality has diverted or has threatened to divert funds collected and reserved for a specific bond issuance, a bondholder or trustee, depending on the specific indenture, may bring an equitable action for an accounting and recovery of any amount diverted. Along with this, the bondholder could seek an injunction to enjoin any diversion. A

---

216 *See Delta County Levee Improvement Dist. No. 2 v. Leonard*, 516 S.W.2d 911 (Tex. 1974), *cert. denied*, 423 U.S. 829 (1975); *Meriwether v. Garrett*, 102 U.S. 472 (1880) (if there are funds not held for a municipal purpose such as a "rainy day" fund, then those funds may be seized or levied under certain state laws); *see also Nat'l Surety Corp. v. Friendswood Indep. Sch. Dist.*, 433 S.W. 2d 690, 694 (Tex. 1968).

217 *See Merritt-Chapman & Scott Corp. v. Pub. Util. Dist. No. 2 of Grant Cty., Wash.*, 319 F.2d 94 (2d Cir. 1963), *cert. denied*, 375 U.S. 968 (1964).

218 *See, e.g.*, 15 U.S.C. § 317(a) (Trust Indenture Act of 1939); *Cont'l Bank & Trust Co. v. First Nat'l Petroleum Trust*, 67 F. Supp. 859 (D.R.I. 1946); *Browning Debenture Holders' Comm. v. DASA Corp.*, 454 F. Supp. 88 (S.D.N.Y. 1978), *aff'd*, 605 F.2d 35 (2d Cir. 1978); *MacKay v. Randolph Macon Coal Co.*, 178 F. 881 (1910).

219 *See, e.g.*, section VIII, 50 State Survey, charts for California, Colorado, District of Columbia, Florida, Hawaii, Idaho, Indiana, Kansas, Kentucky, Maine, Mississippi, Missouri, Nevada, New Jersey, New York, North Dakota, Ohio, Oklahoma, Pennsylvania, Puerto Rico, Rhode Island, South Carolina, Tennessee, West Virginia and Wyoming. This list could be more expansive based on the facts and analysis of the individual situation and a determination of whether a bondholder could pursue an action for an accounting with respect to a particular bond issuance. A court in equity may require in a default situation that the issuer of the bond debt account for the use of the proceeds of the debt issue or the taxes collected for payment of the debt even though there may not be a specific statutory right to an accounting under the state constitution and statutory laws.

bondholder considering this option must act quickly, however, because the equitable doctrine of laches (unreasonable delay in taking action) could apply, causing the bondholder to lose its right to bring such an action if a court finds the bondholder waited too long to bring the action after learning of a diversion of funds.[220] Because bondholders may lose their rights if they don't act within a reasonable period of time, it is imperative that bondholders remain vigilant and consult legal representation should they suspect a misapplication of funds.

G. Foreclosure Action

Much like in a civil context where a mortgagee holds a mortgage on a mortgagor's home and may bring a foreclosure action if obligations are not paid, some states allow bondholders or their representative to pursue a foreclosure action against a certain project, although such an action generally is allowed only in the conduit finance context against property owned or financed by a private concern.[221] For instance, in California, state law has established an industrial development authority for each public agency. Each agency may issue industrial development revenue bonds to help private business purchase property for certain uses, such as industrial uses, energy development, research and development activities, commercial uses, processing or manufacturing of recycled or reused products, business activities, residential real property for families, airports, sewage and solid waste disposal activities, water-furnishing activities or any other activity qualifying as exempt under § 501 of the Internal Revenue Code.[222] The authorities may issue bonds for a project payable solely as special obligations out of the revenues or other sources specified in the bond proceedings.[223] In the event of default, the bond indenture may include, among other remedies, enforcement by foreclosure or sale.[224] Generally, foreclosure is not permitted for essential governmental property, as it would be against public policy.

---

220 *See, e.g., Pasco Cty. v. State Bd. of Admin*, 156 Fla. 37 (Fla. 1945) (noting action not barred by laches because complaint was brought as soon as complainant was aware of sufficient facts to bring such a suit, among other things).

221 Foreclosure is generally allowed in conduit financing. There, collateral owned or financed by the private concern is involved. *See, e.g.*, section VIII, 50 State Survey, charts for Alabama, Alaska, Arizona, California, Hawaii, Idaho, Illinois, Indiana, Kansas, Louisiana, Maine, Missouri, Mississippi, Nebraska, Nevada, New Jersey, New York, North Carolina, Ohio, Oregon, Rhode Island, South Carolina, Texas, Vermont, Washington, West Virginia, Wisconsin and Wyoming. This list could be more expansive, and further review and evaluation as well as the specific facts should be considered to determine whether a bondholder could pursue a foreclosure remedy with respect to a particular bond issuance. It should be noted that care should be exercised in foreclosing on collateral since some states, including California, Idaho, Michigan, Montana, Nevada, New York and Utah, are "one action" jurisdictions, which means if a creditor forecloses on collateral, the creditor must exhaust such security before suing on the underlying debt for any deficiency. *See, e.g.* CAL. CIV. PROC. CODE. § 726(a); *Security Pacific Nat'l Bk. V. Wozab*, 51 Cal 3d 991 (1990).

222 CAL. GOV. CODE §§ 91502 - 91574.

223 *Id.* at § 91535.

224 *Id.* at § 91537. Other allowed remedies include mandamus, appointment of a receiver, injunction, specific performance, equitable relief or any one or more of such remedies or any other remedy.

H. Suit to Obtain Specific Performance

The indenture trustee on behalf of the bondholders may initiate a lawsuit to obtain an order requiring the obligor to comply with the terms of the indenture. Such an action is called an action for specific performance. There is no need for acceleration if the performance sought does not require the payment of all principal and accrued interest. In the municipal context, a suit for specific performance may take the form of a mandamus action described above.

I. Suits by the Indenture Trustee for Instructions

When the facts facing the bondholders and indenture trustee present them with a quandary, a suit for judicial instructions may be appropriate. While a request for instructions by the indenture trustee may sometimes be brought as a declaratory judgment action,[225] some states have specific statutes permitting trustees to request instructions as to the proper interpretation of a governing trust instrument or whether a settlement affecting bondholders is fair and reasonable.[226] By giving notice to the affected parties of such a proceeding, the order is binding *in rem* upon the trust estate and upon the interests of the beneficiaries.[227]

J. Other Lawsuits

The trustee and bondholders should examine the language of the indenture and the applicable governing law as to whether, given the considerations, any other causes of action exist and should be pursued, such as breach of contract, breach of implied covenants of good faith and fair dealing, tortious interference with contractual relationships, common law fraud or negligent misrepresentations.

K. Acknowledgment of Debt and Consent to Judgment

In some situations, the most efficient remedy is to have the obligor acknowledge the debt and any defaults and consent to the judgment of a monetary amount or specific performance to become effective after an agreed-upon period of time for curing the default. This remedy saves time, money and effort. It can be used when the obligor believes it will shortly be able to cure the default and satisfy the judgment but needs time, not litigation, to accomplish this. In utilizing such a technique, preliminary legal research should be done as to the enforceability of such an agreement in the particular jurisdiction of the obligor and the jurisdiction in which enforcement will be sought.

---

225 28 U.S.C. § 2201 *et seq.*

226 *See, e.g.*, MINN. STAT. § 501C.0202; N.Y. CPLR § 7701. It has been held that a Section 77 proceeding is not removable to federal court. *Blackrock Fin. Mgmt. Inc. v. The Segregated Account of AMBAC Insurance Corp.*, 673 F.3d 169 (2d Cir. 2012).

227 *In the matter of the Trusteeship Created by Am. Home Mortg. Inv. Trust 2005-2*, 2014 WL 3858506 (S.D.N.Y. July 24, 2014).

L. Right to Appoint Consultants

Some municipal issues, especially revenue bond issues for municipal utilities, provide for certain consultants to confer with the municipal body regarding the rates or taxes to be charged and provide those consultants the power to approve decreases in rates and recommend increases in rates. Such provisions, so long as they are not an improper delegation of a municipal unit's powers, are helpful in structuring a workout or resolution of a defaulted revenue bond issue. Consideration should be given in structuring a revenue bond issue as to the use of such provisions.

M. Acceptance of Default

With respect to widely held public issues, it may be impossible to acquire the percentage threshold under an indenture of holders required to direct certain action to resolve a defaulted issue. Circumstances may be such that the remedies discussed in this section are inappropriate and it is in the best interests of the holders to accept the default. Examples of when it may be in the best interests of bondholders to accept a default may include situations in which collateral has been destroyed by a natural disaster or where the credit enhancer has become insolvent and is liquidating its assets. Court approval of acceptance of the default may be in the best interests of the obligor, the indenture trustee and the bondholders.[228]

N. Other Relief

In addition to the forms of relief discussed previously, a wide variety of provisions exist in the states to allow bondholders to protect their interests. For instance, at least 14 states specifically allow for injunctive relief in the event of a default.[229] One such example is Kentucky, where certain bondholders may petition a court for injunctive relief to enjoin any unlawful act or any act taken violating bondholders' rights.[230] Other states allow bondholders to pursue any action necessary,

---

228 *See Chase Nat'l Bank v. Manila Elec. Co.*, 40 N.Y.S.2d 385 (N.Y. Sup. Ct. 1943) (no distribution of sinking fund or foreclosure due to default since foreign troops occupied the mortgaged property); *New Jersey Nat'l Bank & Trust Co. v. Lincoln Mortg. Title Guarantee*, 148 A. 713 (N.J. Ch. 1930) (requirement that acceptable mortgages be placed as collateral was impossible given the default rate during the Depression). *See also Groseclose v. Merchants Nat'l Bank & Trust Co. of Syracuse*, 335 N.Y.S.2d 652 (N.Y. Sup. Ct. 1972) (in response to minority bondholders' lawsuit, court ordered trustee to foreclose mortgage even though the majority of bondholders consented to acceptance of default).

229 These specific statutes are in addition to the general availability of injunctive relief under the civil procedure code of most states to prevent irreparable harm when there is no adequate remedy at law. This issue is a difference as to public policy and irreparable harm with respect to municipal debt and, thus, a specific state statute may provide more expansive relief. *See, e.g.*, section VIII, 50 State Survey, charts for Alabama, California, Colorado, Connecticut, Florida, Illinois, Indiana, Kentucky, Mississippi, Nevada, Ohio, Washington, West Virginia and Wyoming. This list could be more expansive based on the specific facts and circumstances of a particular situation, and an attorney should be consulted to determine whether a bondholder could pursue injunctive relief with respect to a particular bond issuance and applicable state law and procedure.

230 *See* KY. REV. STAT. § 96.184(5)(b).

including contractual remedies, to enforce and protect their rights.[231] Section VIII provides a more general analysis of the types of relief available in each state.

O. Conclusion

In the early 1800s, the courts, issuers and bondholders viewed municipal and state debt obligations as moral obligations, and few if any statutes or constitutional provisions permitted a legal basis for such obligations. The repudiation of debt by eight states after the Civil War led to the implementation of statutory and constitutional debt limits and other provisions and remedies to provide assurance to the market that state and municipal debt was a safe and protected investment. As can be seen by the 50-State Survey in section VIII, since the late 1800s the states have implemented a wide array of provisions to protect the rights of bondholders and allow for certain remedies in the event of a default. While these rights provide bondholders with protection once a default occurs, they cannot replace the vigilant oversight of the state or of a trustee or bondholder who takes action and attempts to work with a municipality or local form of government when it becomes more likely than not that a default will occur. As will be discussed in the next section, however, if a municipality is truly in trouble and is located in a state that authorizes its municipalities to file a municipal bankruptcy petition, bondholders may have further protection depending on the type of bonds they hold. This is because the bankruptcy filing would not cut off payments of principal and interest to special revenue bondholders, although in most cases a municipality would be required to pay the operations costs of the particular project before paying bondholders. In addition, those holding bonds secured by a statutory lien are guaranteed payment of collected taxes since a bankruptcy court cannot invalidate or interfere with the rights granted by state law to debt holders.

---

231 *See, e.g.,* section VIII, 50 State Survey, charts for Arizona, California, Colorado, Connecticut, District of Columbia, Georgia, Hawaii, Illinois, Louisiana, Maine, Minnesota, Mississippi, Missouri, Montana, New Hampshire, Ohio, South Carolina, Utah and Virginia. This list could be more expansive, and an attorney should be consulted to determine the rights a bondholder may have and any remedies the bondholder could pursue with respect to a particular bond issuance.

VII. Municipal Bankruptcy

A. Introduction: Use of Chapter 9

Historically, municipal bankruptcy — known as "Chapter 9" because the municipal bankruptcy provisions of the U.S. Bankruptcy Code are contained in Chapter 9 — has been used generally by small tax districts and small municipalities to adjust their debts in the face of financial insolvency, while major issuers of municipal debt have generally refrained from proceeding with a Chapter 9 filing. In fact, the use of Chapter 9 is quite rare — since 1937, when Chapter 9 was constitutionally enacted, municipalities have only filed 666 Chapter 9 petitions as of July 31, 2016 (322 since 1954; 297 since 1980), an average of 8.5 filings per year since 1937. To place this low number is context, there are over 80,000 municipal entities that could be authorized to file. Most cases have been special tax districts and utilities (approximately 60 percent) that rarely need to issue public debt. Since 1954, less than 20 percent of all Chapter 9 filings have been by cities, towns, villages and counties (64 of 322). In comparison, corporate Chapter 11 reorganizations have numbered over 10,000 a year for most years since 1985. The following charts break down Chapter 9 filings by municipalities by frequency and by year, state, region and type since 1980.

FREQUENCY OF MUNICIPAL BANKRUPTCIES • 1937-2016
(as of 7/31/2016)

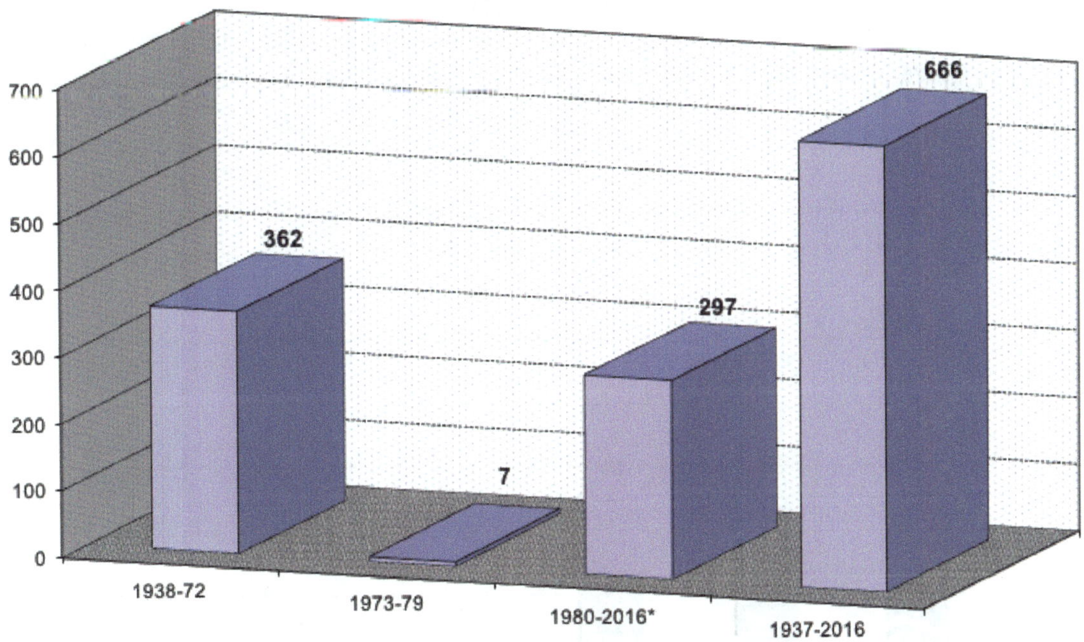

** Since passage of the Bankruptcy Code.*

CHAPTER 9 FILINGS BY STATE • 1980-2016
(as of 7/31/2016)

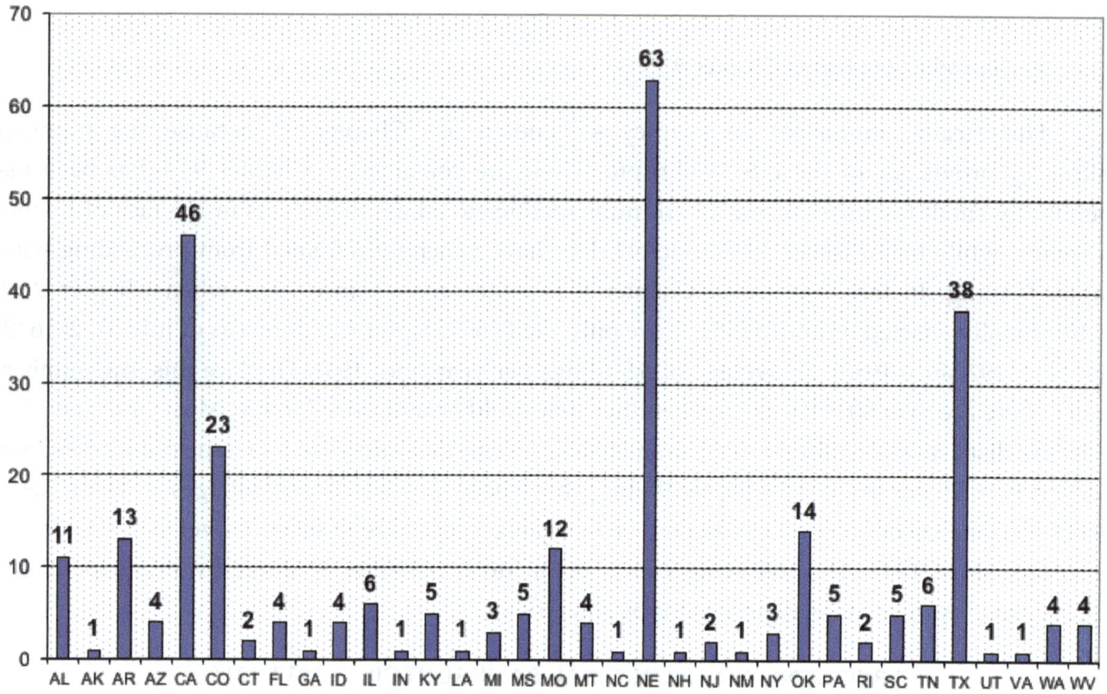

CHAPTER 9 FILINGS BY TYPE • 1980-2016
(as of 7/31/2016)

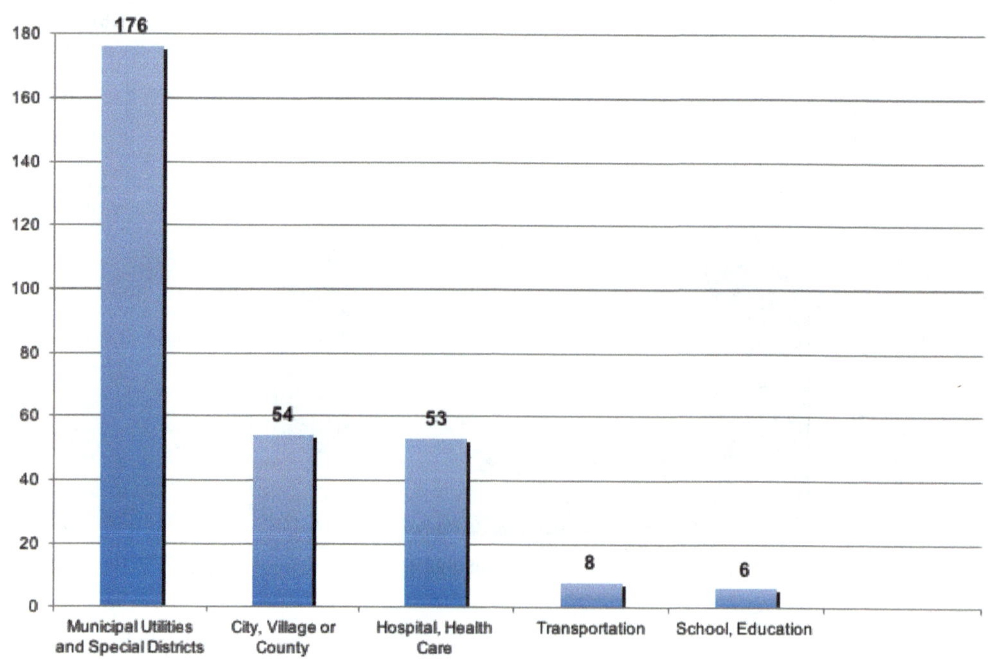

CHAPTER 9 FILINGS BY REGION • 1980-2016
(as of 7/31/2016)

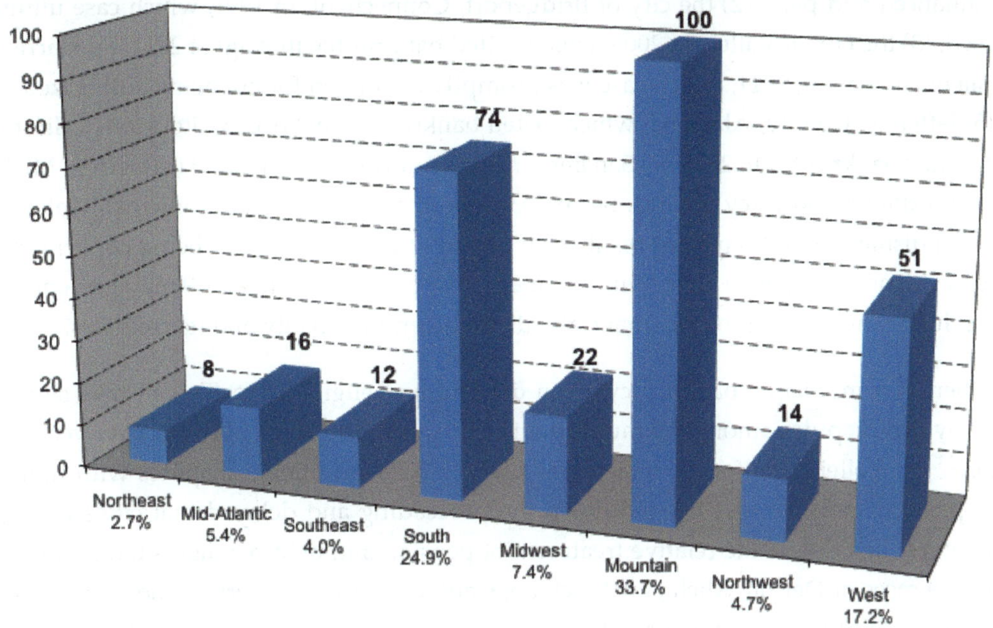

CHAPTER 9 FILINGS BY YEAR • 1980-2016
(as of 7/31/2016)

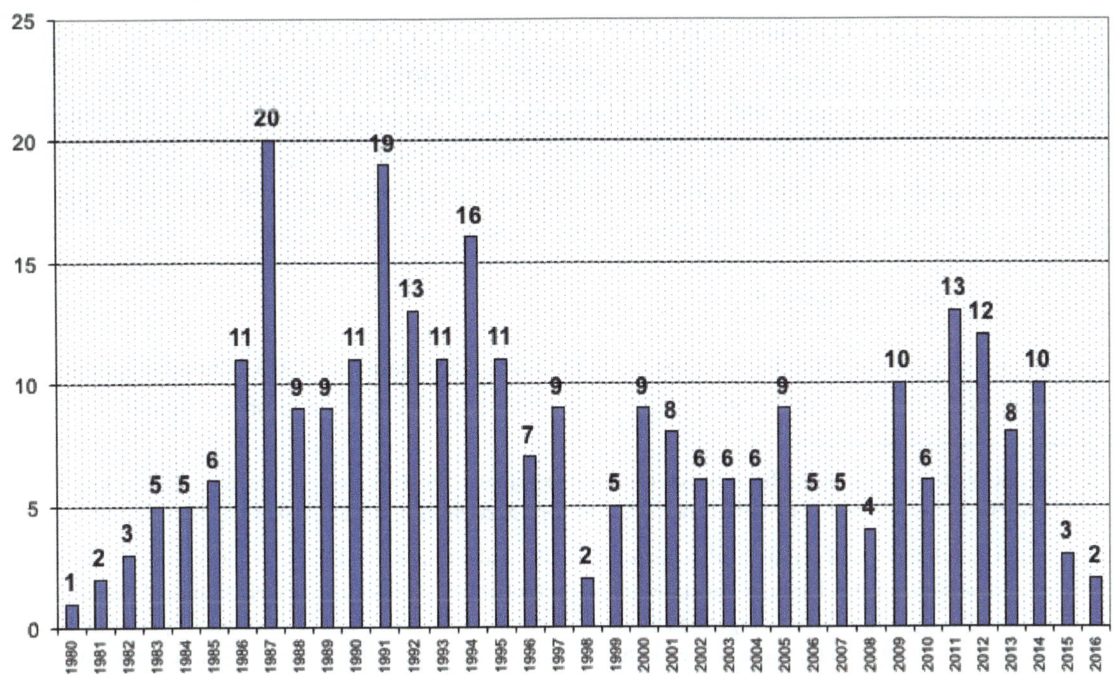

As mentioned, of the entities filing Chapter 9 petitions since 1954, only a handful have been municipal debt issuers of any significant size, namely: (1) Orange County in 1994, in which the public debt was refinanced and paid, (2) the city of Bridgeport, Connecticut, in 1991, which case ultimately was dismissed, (3) the city of Vallejo in 2008, which exited bankruptcy in August 2011, (4) Harrisburg, Pennsylvania in September, 2011, which case was promptly dismissed for not being authorized under state law, (5) Jefferson County, Alabama, which exited bankruptcy in 2013, (6) Stockton, California in 2012, which exited bankruptcy in 2015, (7) San Bernardino, California in 2012, and (8) Detroit, Michigan in 2013, which exited bankruptcy in 2014. Since 1937, about a quarter of all municipal bankruptcies filed have been dismissed and have not resulted in a plan of debt adjustment being confirmed. This phenomenon evidences that, even after filing, an alternative other than Chapter 9 may present a more attractive resolution mechanism for the financially distressed municipality and its creditors.

Further, in a municipal bankruptcy, even determining eligibility to file can take significant time, and delay and disputes among the municipality and its creditors can play out over years rather than months.[232] In Vallejo, California, which was filed in 2008, additional disputes with municipal unions over pensions and benefits bogged down the proceeding and delayed that city's emergence from bankruptcy. The issue of the relative treatment of pension and debt payments took center stage in the Chapter 9 cases of Detroit, Michigan; Stockton, California; and San Bernardino, California. The decision on the eligibility of Stockton alone took almost ten months. With respect to San Bernardino, after more than a year in bankruptcy, the issue of the eligibility was finally determined, paving the way for a battle between the competing interests. The Detroit bankruptcy was time consuming, uncertain and expensive. As a result, it is safe to say that the availability of a bankruptcy option has not proven to be a "quick or easy fix" to municipalities.[233] This is particularly true where contention exists between the major players in the case. Historically and practically, Chapter 9 debt adjustments should be the last resort after all other alternatives have been unsuccessful. As noted in section V, many states have provided assistance, refinancing, oversight and other mechanisms to help local governments avoid Chapter 9 if at all possible. The authorization of a government to file should not be interpreted as precluding efforts such as financial oversight, technical assistance and guidance.

B. The Limits of Chapter 9

It is no accident that New York City in 1975, Cleveland in 1978, Philadelphia in 1991, Washington, D.C. in 1995, Pittsburgh in 2003 and other significant issuers of municipal debt, when

232 In the Vallejo bankruptcy, the issue of eligibility consumed the first year of the case. *In re City of Vallejo*, No. 08-26813-A-9, 2008 WL 4180008 (Bankr. E.D. Cal. Sept. 5, 2008), *aff'd*, 408 B.R. 280 (B.A.P. 9th Cir. 2009).

233 In fact, not all fifty states permit their municipalities to file under Chapter 9. Only twelve states specifically authorize municipal bankruptcies. For more detail, see the analysis of which states authorize their municipalities to file under Chapter 9 (generally or based on specified conditions) and those that do not permit their municipalities to file under Chapter 9. In section VIII, there is a 50-state survey of state laws dealing with financial emergencies of local governments, rights and remedies provided by states and state authorization of municipalities to file for Chapter 9 bankruptcy.

faced with a financial crisis, chose other viable alternatives rather than filing Chapter 9.[234] Chapter 9 provides no additional revenues or tax sources to solve the problem, and it affects all creditor relationships, including successful ones, not just the few that are the problem.[235] Further, the stigma, complexity, travail and cost of Chapter 9 are more than many local governments can tolerate.

Chapter 9 is a process of debt adjustment to what is sustainable and affordable, not a vehicle for elimination of debt. However, Chapter 9 is not a solution to financial distress. It is a *process* of debt adjustment to reduce that which is not sustainable and affordable to that which is sustainable and affordable and to provide more runway or time to develop a recovery plan. A recovery plan, which is the key to a successful municipal restructuring, addresses the systemic problems that have caused the financial and operational distress. Merely reducing debt without addressing the systemic problems has proven to be a futile effort, and financial distress reappears shortly thereafter. A recovery plan should be the solution to financial distress.

A Chapter 9 proceeding is a mechanism for a debtor municipality, through a court-supervised proceeding, to attempt to settle disputes with its creditors. Since a municipality cannot liquidate its assets to satisfy creditors and continue to function as a municipality, the primary purpose of Chapter 9 of the Bankruptcy Code is to allow the municipality to continue operating while it adjusts or refinances creditor claims. Indeed, one of the stated purposes of the municipal bankruptcy provisions of the Bankruptcy Code was to provide a "workable procedure so that a municipality of any size that has encountered financial difficulties may work with its creditors to adjust its debts."[236]

As a comparison, globally, many of the 600 sovereign debt restructurings in 95 countries since 1950 have been Band-Aids and not permanent fixes. Likewise, the same has been true as to some Chapter 9 proceedings in the United States. That is because those Chapter 9 filings merely dealt with external debt issues and did not address the systemic problems that brought the financial crisis to a boil. What is needed for a successful municipal bankruptcy, or any restructuring for that matter, is a detailed recovery plan that takes a holistic approach to: (a) determine what is sustainable and affordable and what is not, (b) allow for development of accurate, transparent and mutually agreed-upon financial statements and projections, (c) provide appropriate funds for needed governmental services and infrastructure improvements, (d) permit, if necessary, debt adjustment consistent with the traditions and principles of government finance and restructuring of debt and (e) provide for economic stimulus and motivate business development in order to expand business and attract new business activities that create good new jobs to increase the percentage of those meaningfully employed.

---

234 It is of note, however, that under the Bankruptcy Code, Washington, D.C. is not permitted to file a Chapter 9 petition.

235 The complications of the Chapter 9 filing by a traditional municipality that provides essential services obviously differ from the Chapter 9 filing by a gambling operation. *See* Andrew Coan, *Suffolk OTB Reorganization Viewed as Chapter 9 Model,* Jan. 9, 2015, http://www.bondbuyer.com/news/regionalnews/suffolk-otb-reorganization-viewed-as-chapter-9-model-1069404-1.html.

236 Report of the Comm'n on the Bankr. Laws of the United States, H.R. Rep. No. 93-137, 93rd Cong., 1st Sess. (1973).

A recovery plan should foster (a) financial credibility and create increased revenues due to increased business activity and (b) new, better compensated employees and better services and infrastructure to attract and encourage business activity and a healthier, safer and more prosperous future for the citizens of the distressed municipality. This needed recovery plan can only be developed with financial credibility buy-in and participation by the municipality, elected officials, citizens and taxpayers, vendors, bondholders and other creditors, as well as the financial markets. Without such a recovery plan, a Chapter 9 proceeding will not result in long-term success.

C. Initiation of Chapter 9 Proceeding and Effect on Bondholder Rights and Remedies

Only a municipality, as defined in the Bankruptcy Code, may initiate an action and be a debtor under Chapter 9 of the Bankruptcy Code.[237] Unlike Chapters 7 and 11, an involuntary Chapter 9 proceeding instituted by creditors is not permitted. Specifically, to be a debtor in a Chapter 9 proceeding, an entity must:

- Be a municipality (political subdivision or public agency or instrumentality of the state) and not an entity created by a municipality;
- Be specifically authorized under state law to be a debtor;
- Be insolvent (generally determined on a cash flow basis as being unable to pay its debts when they mature);
- Be willing to effectuate a plan; and
- Either have obtained the agreement of creditors holding a majority amount of the claim of each class that the municipality intends to impair, attempted to negotiate in good faith but was unable to do so, or found that it was impractical to negotiate with creditors or that a creditor is attempting to obtain a preference.

In addition to the requirement that a municipality be a subdivision of an agency or a subdivision or instrumentality of the state, since the 1994 Amendments to the Bankruptcy Code, it must be specifically authorized to file a Chapter 9 proceeding by the state in which it is located. The states have adopted different approaches to this requirement. Twelve states have statutory provisions specifically authorizing the filing of a Chapter 9 petition by an in-state municipality.[238] Another 12 states authorize a filing conditioned on a further act of the state, an elected official or a state entity or

---

237 11 U.S.C. § 109(c).

238 *See* section VIII, 50 State Survey, charts for Alabama, Arizona, Arkansas, Idaho, Minnesota, Missouri, Montana, Nebraska, Oklahoma, South Carolina, Texas and Washington.

through some other required process like use of a neutral evaluator mechanism.[239] Three states grant limited authorization[240] and two states prohibit filing (Georgia and Iowa), but Iowa has an exception to the prohibition.[241] The remaining 21 states either are unclear or do not provide specific authorization with respect to filing as part of their state law. At the time of this writing, the District of Columbia and Puerto Rico, including municipalities in Puerto Rico, are not permitted to file pursuant to the terms of the Bankruptcy Code.[242]

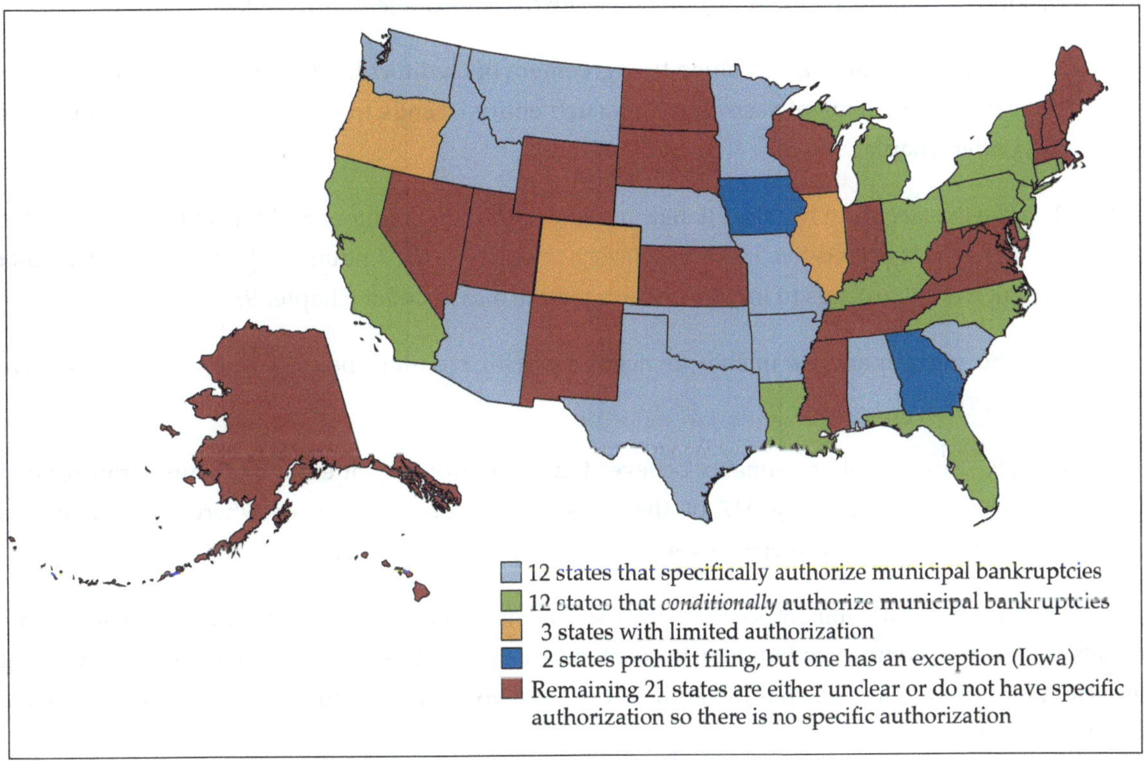

Further, a municipality must be insolvent or unable to pay or otherwise satisfy its debts as they mature and must desire to effect a plan to adjust its debts, although the determination of insolvency is not as easy as it seems.[243] In the Detroit, Michigan proceeding, the court found that the city of Detroit

239 *See* section VIII, 50 State Survey, charts for California, Connecticut, Florida, Kentucky, Louisiana, Michigan, New Jersey, New York, North Carolina, Ohio, Pennsylvania and Rhode Island.

240 *See* section VIII, 50 State Survey, charts for Colorado, Illinois and Oregon.

241 *See* section VIII, 50 State Survey, charts for Georgia and Iowa.

242 The term "State" is defined in the Bankruptcy Code as including "the District of Columbia and Puerto Rico, except for the purpose of defining who may be a debtor" under Chapter 9. 11 U.S.C. § 101(52).

243 11 U.S.C. § 109(c)(3) and (4). For a municipality, the Bankruptcy Code defines "insolvent" as a "financial condition such that the municipality is: (i) generally not paying its debts as they become due unless such debts are the subject of a bona fide dispute; or (ii) is unable to pay its debts as they become due." 11 U.S.C. § 101(32)(c).

was insolvent under both definitions of insolvency applicable to municipalities. The city had failed to make certain scheduled debt payments. Moreover, it was in a state of "service delivery insolvency," as there were many services that did not function properly because of the city's financial situation.[244] Similarly in the Stockton, California bankruptcy, the court held that long-term budget imbalances (budget insolvency) and the degrees of inability to fund essential governmental services (service delivery insolvency) would inform the court of the likely duration of cash insolvency.[245]

In addition, a municipality must demonstrate that one of the following has occurred:

1. The municipality has obtained the agreement of creditors holding at least a majority in the amount of claims of each class that such entity intends to impair under a plan in a case under Chapter 9;

2. The municipality has negotiated in good faith with creditors and has failed to obtain the agreement of creditors holding at least a majority in the amount of claims of each class that such entity intends to impair under a plan in a case under Chapter 9;

3. The municipality is unable to negotiate with creditors because such negotiations are impractical; or

4. The municipality reasonably believes that a creditor may attempt to obtain a transfer that is avoidable under § 547 of the Bankruptcy Code (a transfer where one creditor is attempting to be preferred over others as to payment of similar debt).[246]

With regard to an unincorporated tax or special assessment district that does not have its own officials, an action is commenced under Chapter 9 when a petition is filed by such district's governing authority or board or body that has the authority to levy taxes or assessments to meet the obligations of such district.[247]

The fact that a municipality has filed a petition does not necessarily ensure that its debts will be adjusted in that proceeding. Section 921(c) of the Bankruptcy Code's municipal provisions provides that, after objection to the petition, the court, after notice and a hearing, may dismiss the petition if a challenger can show to the bankruptcy court that a petition was not filed in good faith or not in accord with the requirements of Chapter 9.[248]

---

244 *In re City of Detroit, Mich.*, 504 B.R. 97, 169 (Bankr. E.D. Mich. 2013).

245 *In re City of Stockton, Cal.*, 493 B.R. 772, 789 (Bankr. E.D. Cal. 2013).

246 11 U.S.C. § 109(c)(5)(A) and (B).

247 11 U.S.C. § 921(a).

248 For further discussion and detail with respect to Chapter 9 of the U.S. Bankruptcy Code, *see* James E. Spiotto, *Primer on Municipal Debt Adjustment, Chapter 9: The Last Resort for Financially Distressed Municipalities* (on file with Chapman and Cutler LLP) and James E. Spiotto, *Chapter 9: The Last Resort for Financially Distressed Municipalities*, THE HANDBOOK

D. Unique Features of Chapter 9 and Municipal Operations

Chapter 9 contains unique features, including (a) in Section 903 of the Bankruptcy Code, a reservation of state power to control a municipality, which specifically limits the bankruptcy court so that the court may not limit or impair the power of the state to control by legislation or otherwise a municipality's exercise of its political or governmental powers, including expenditures for such exercise and (b) in Section 904 of the Bankruptcy Code, a limitation on the jurisdiction and powers of the bankruptcy court providing that such court cannot, without consent of the municipality, interfere with the governmental or political powers or the revenues, property, use or enjoyment of the property of the municipality. These provisions require that if, by state statute, certain liens or claims are established, are granted and come into existence by means of the state statute, such as will be described below regarding statutory liens, the bankruptcy court cannot impair, limit or adversely affect such liens. If the state limits the power of the municipality to take certain actions or to modify certain pledges pursuant to a statutory lien, the bankruptcy court is not authorized or empowered to modify or change that limitation. Likewise, the bankruptcy court under Section 904 may not interfere with any political, governmental power of the municipality or any property or revenue of the municipality or the municipality's use and enjoyment of any income-producing property without that municipality's consent; the municipality, consistent with Section 903, cannot act inconsistent with the provisions, requirements and limits placed on it under state law. This is a significant difference from a debtor in a Chapter 11 proceeding whereby the court can proceed to supervise any change in expansion or contraction of business out of the ordinary course and has to approve increases in borrowings or other changes in operation and business.

Thus, while in a Chapter 9 proceeding, a municipality must still function as a municipality. Depending upon the statutory mission of the municipality, there are certain necessary and basic municipal services that must be provided, such as police, fire and, under certain instances, sewer, water, transportation and electrical. In addition, these services could include education, health and economic development. Defining what these necessary municipal services are is a question of state law and may by itself be a complex issue. A bankruptcy court and creditors should not be able to successfully interfere with such services, because Section 904 of the Bankruptcy Code precludes a bankruptcy court's interference with the municipality's political and governmental powers. For instance, even municipal debt secured by "special revenues," which pledge is preserved by reason of Section 928 of the Bankruptcy Code, is subject to the payment of necessary operating expenses for the related project or system.[249]

OF MUNICIPAL BONDS, 145-80 (Sylvan G. Feldstein & Frank J. Fabozzi eds., 2008); American Bankruptcy Institute, MUNICIPALITIES IN PERIL, THE ABI GUIDE TO CHAPTER 9 (2012); and National Association of Bond Lawyers, MUNICIPAL BANKRUPTCY: A GUIDE FOR PUBLIC FINANCE ATTORNEYS (Oct. 2015), https://www.nabl.org/portals/0/documents/municipal_bankruptcy_a_guide_for_public_finance_attorneys.pdf.

249 11 U.S.C. § 928(b).

E. "Special Revenues" Pledged to Bondholders

1. What Are Special Revenues?

Many municipal bonds are revenue bonds secured by a pledge of revenues derived from a specific project or a special tax levy. In fact, as indicated in section VIII, the 50-State Survey, all states recognize some form of a revenue bond. As defined in Section 902(2) of the Bankruptcy Code, a special revenue pledge is one that promises to pay the debt from a pledge or dedication of revenues from a specific source or governmental enterprise, special excise taxes, incremental tax receipts for tax incremental financing, revenues derived from a particular governmental function or taxes levied to finance a project or system (except for general sales, property and income taxes levied for general purposes).[250] Examples of the "special revenues" mentioned in clause (A) of Section 902(2) include receipts derived from or received in connection with the ownership, financing, operation or disposition of a municipal water, electric or transportation system. An excise tax on hotel and motel rooms or the sale of alcoholic beverages would be a special excise tax under clause (B). "Special excise taxes" are taxes specifically identified and pledged in the bond financing documents and are not generally available to all creditors under state law. General state sales, general income or general property taxes levied for general governmental purposes would not be special excise taxes without specific language providing that such tax was deemed levied and dedicated to pay for the financing of a specific project, system or public purpose. In a typical tax increment financing referred to in clause (C), public improvements are financed by bonds payable solely from and secured by a lien on incremental tax receipts resulting from increased valuations in the benefited area. Although these receipts may be part of the general tax levy, they are considered to be attributable to the improvements so financed and are not part of the preexisting tax base of the community. Examples of revenues from particular functions under clause (D) would include regulatory fees and stamp taxes imposed for the recording of deeds or any identified function and related revenues identified in the municipality's financing documents, such as tolls or fees related to a particular service or benefit. Under clause (E), an incremental income, sales or property tax specifically levied to pay indebtedness incurred to finance a governmental project, system or purpose and not levied to pay for the operating expenses or general purposes of the debtor

---

250 "Special revenues" is defined in 11 U.S.C. § 902 as:

(A) receipts derived from the ownership, operation, or disposition of projects or systems of the debtor that are primarily used or intended to be used primarily to provide transportation, utility, or other services, including the proceeds of borrowings to finance the projects or systems;

(B) special excise taxes imposed on particular activities or transactions;

(C) incremental tax receipts from the benefited area in the case of tax-increment financing;

(D) other revenues or receipts derived from particular functions of the debtor, whether or not the debtor has other functions; or

(E) taxes specifically levied to finance one or more projects or systems, excluding receipts from general property, sales, or income taxes (other than tax-increment financing) levied to finance the general purpose of the debtor.

would be considered "special revenues." Likewise, any special tax or portion of a general tax specifically levied to pay for a municipal financing should be treated as "special revenues."[251] Special revenue treatment can be afforded revenue bonds issued under the law of the state or even general obligation bonds that, in addition to the general full faith and credit language, have a pledge and dedication of a specific revenue source pursuant to state constitution, state statutes, bond resolution or ordinance to be used first or solely for purposes of paying debt service on the general obligation bonds.

A special revenue pledge is to be unaltered by a Chapter 9 municipal bankruptcy, and the timely payment of the pledged revenues by the municipality is required by the Bankruptcy Code.[252] Special revenues are intended to be unimpaired in a Chapter 9 proceeding, and the debt holders are intended to receive the benefit of the bargain. This rule was respected in the Sierra Kings Health Care District Chapter 9 (Eastern District of California),[253] the Jefferson County Chapter 9 (Northern District of Alabama),[254] the Stockton Chapter 9[255] and the Detroit Chapter 9 (for those who continued to hold water and sewer revenue bonds, the case reaffirmed the unaltered status and timely payment of special revenue pledges in a Chapter 9 proceeding).[256]

2. Special Revenues: A Departure from Corporate Bankruptcy

As background, in a corporate bankruptcy context, Section 552 of the Bankruptcy Code provides that property acquired by the estate or the debtor after commencement of a case is not subject to any lien resulting from a security agreement entered into by the debtor before the commencement of the case. Thus, in a corporate bankruptcy, if a revenue pledge were to exist prepetition, such as a lien on inventory or accounts receivable, the pledge (namely, any property or revenue created postpetition, such as inventory manufactured or accounts receivable generated from sales of inventory after the filing of the case) likely would not survive the filing of a bankruptcy petition. In a municipal bankruptcy, however, this is not the case. Specifically, Section 928 of the Bankruptcy Code provides

---

251 *See In re Heffernan Mem'l Hosp. Dist.*, 202 B.R. 147, 148 (Bankr. S.D. Cal. 1996) and footnote 21.

252 11 U.S.C. § 928(a).

253 *In re Sierra Kings Health Care District*, 2010 WL 10018073 (Bankr. E.D. Cal. Sept. 13, 2010).

254 *In re Jefferson Cnty., Ala.*, 474 B.R. 228 (Bankr. N.D. Ala 2012). There was a settlement among warrant holders, bond insurers and Jefferson County incorporated into the plan of debt adjustment whereby warrant holders agreed to be paid less than 100 cents given other issues related to prevailing rates charged and to be charged, pending litigation relating to the original issuance and the sustainability and affordability of payment.

255 Order Confirming First Amended Plan for the Adjustment of Debts of City of Stockton, California, as Modified, *In re City of Stockton, California*, Case No. 12-32118 (Bankr. E.D. Ca. Feb. 4, 2015), ECF No. 1875.

256 Supplemental Opinion Regarding Plan Confirmation, Approving Settlements, and Approving Exit Financing, *In re City of Detroit, Mich.*, Case No. 13-53846 (Bankr. E.D. Mich. Dec. 31, 2014) ("Supplemental Detroit Opinion"), ECF No. 8993. *See* also Order Pursuant to (I) 11 U.S.C. Secs. 105, 364(c), 364(d)(1), 364(e), 902, 904, 921, 922 and 928 (A) Approving Postpetition Financing and (B) Granting Liens and (II) Bankruptcy Rule 9019 Approving Settlement of Confirmation Objections, *In re City of Detroit*, Case No. 13-53846 (Bankr. E.D. Mich. Aug. 25, 2014), ECF No. 7028.

that in the case of "special revenues," the security interest in "special revenues" remains valid and enforceable even though such revenues are received after a Chapter 9 filing.[257]

Section 928 was incorporated into the Bankruptcy Code by the Municipal Bankruptcy Amendments, which were adopted in 1988, as part of an Act to Amend the Bankruptcy Law to Provide for Special Revenue Bonds, and for Other Purposes, Pub. L. No. 100-597 (1988) ("1988 Amendments"). As discussed by the bankruptcy court in the Jefferson County, Alabama bankruptcy proceeding, the 1988 Amendments became necessary because, at the time, there was great concern in the municipal bond market that the application of general commercial finance concepts rendered the extension of credit to a troubled municipality fraught with risk.[258] The result of the application of the Bankruptcy Code at the time in the municipal context generally was to strip the lien of revenue bondholders as to tax revenues collected postpetition.[259] Thus, prior to the 1988 Amendments, revenue bondholders would become unsecured creditors as to a claim against the postpetition revenues that had previously served as the only security for the municipality's revenue bonds, and their non-recourse claims would become part of the general obligations of the municipality and transformed into recourse claims against the municipality. The general funds would then be used to pay all creditors including the holders of revenue bonds, which previously had been non-recourse debt of the municipality. As a result, rather than taking the risk that a specific revenue stream would be sufficient to pay debt service on their bonds, which was the original bargain, revenue bondholders would be forced to take the risk that the general fund of the municipality would not be sufficient to repay all debts of the municipality. Section 928 resolved this problem by providing that revenue bondholders continue to have a lien on special revenues generated after the bankruptcy case.

In fact, "[a] major purpose [of the 1988 Amendments] was to change from using corporate debt principles in the municipal financing context when their application would be at odds with how municipal financing has evolved. This was and remains especially apt for revenue based municipal financing transactions."[260] As is clearly set forth not only in the specific provisions added to Chapter 9 by the 1988 Amendments, but also in the legislative history for the 1988 Amendments, Congress concluded that, without the 1988 Amendments, the uncertainty of the effect of Chapter 9 as it then existed on municipal debt could have dire effects. This was especially true with respect to concerns

---

257 As noted, subsection (b) of Section 928 provides that, in the case of project or system financing, the bondholders' lien on "special revenues" is subject to necessary operating expenses of the project or system. Thus, subject to the payment of operating expenses, holders of special revenue bonds would continue to receive payment on those bonds, regardless of the bankruptcy filing. *See In re Jefferson Cnty., Ala.*, 474 B.R. 228 (Bankr. N.D. Ala. 2012); *In re Jefferson Cnty., Ala.*, 482 B.R. 404 (Bankr. N.D. Ala. 2012).

258 *In re Jefferson Cnty. Ala.,*, 474 B.R. at 267; Senate Report *supra* n. 191, at 4.

259 *See* 11 U.S.C. § 552.

260 *In re Jefferson Cnty., Ala.*, 474 B.R. at 271.

regarding the continuation of a lien on revenues in a Chapter 9 proceeding.[261] The Senate Report for the 1988 Amendments[262] made it clear that the intention of the 1988 Amendments was to address the real worry in the marketplace that revenues dedicated to the repayment of municipal revenue obligations would be diverted to other purposes once a local government entered bankruptcy; that this worry rendered clarification of the law a necessity; and that revenue debt could not be impaired in a Chapter 9 proceeding.[263]

Indeed, the 1988 Amendments were enacted, in part, to protect the municipal bond market from the uncertainty common in other commercial credit markets; provide for readily available, inexpensive financing for municipalities and municipal projects; and ensure that municipal revenue bondholders receive the benefit of their bargain without the uncertainty typical in non-government financing. In enacting the 1988 Amendments, Congress specifically recognized that "the proposed amendments reflected the principles that have long been the premise for municipal finance but have not been expressly stated in the Bankruptcy Code."[264] The Senate Report stated:

> The potential problems created by the incorporation of general commercial finance concepts into municipal bankruptcy provisions first came to light as a result of the financial crisis confronting the City of Cleveland, Ohio in 1979. Cleveland needed additional financing but lenders were unwilling to lend for a variety of reasons, including the incorporation into Chapter 9 of the general bankruptcy concepts of Section 552 of the Code. ... Thus lenders who contemplated providing financing during financial troubles of the City were discouraged given the concern that their security interest might terminate upon a Chapter 9 filing of the city ... Such uncertainty may have dire effects in the future. ...[265]

Section 928 is intended to ensure that revenue bonds do not become transformed into general obligation bonds with a call against all the assets of the municipality upon the filing of bankruptcy petition. The Bankruptcy Court in *Jefferson County* explains:

> The bigger picture of what was to be accomplished by the 1988 Amendments comes from knowing that the post-bankruptcy loss of a security interest in pledged special revenues via § 552(a) or the § 547 avoidance of a payment to a

261 *Id.*

262 Senate Report at 5.

263 For further discussion on the importance of the 1988 Amendments, *see In re Jefferson Cnty., Ala.*, 474 B.R. 228 (Bankr. N.D. Ala. 2012); *In re Jefferson Cnty., Ala.*, 482 B.R. 404 (Bankr. N.D. Ala. 2012) (analysis of necessary operating expenses).

264 *In re Jefferson Cnty., Ala.*, 474 B.R. at 268 (quoting Senate Report at 1).

265 Senate Report at 4.

> bond or warrant holder pursuant to a special revenue financing could have made the obligation or avoided transfer unsecured. As an unsecured indebtedness, it was then potentially repayable from the general revenues of the municipal entity. Under this scenario, it might have been changed by the pre-1988 version of the Bankruptcy Code from an obligation repayable solely from the revenues of the system or project or a specified tax into one repayable from the general revenues of the municipality. Essentially, it may have been turned from a non-recourse into a recourse obligation of the municipal government.[266]

In addition to providing that the lien on special revenues continues after a Chapter 9 filing, the 1988 Amendments also dealt with the problem of timely payment. In order to avoid the delay in payment caused by the automatic stay of Section 362, the 1988 Amendments added a new subsection to Section 922 of the Bankruptcy Code, making the automatic stay provision inapplicable to the payment of pledged special revenues to the holders of municipal indebtedness.[267] The Senate Report observed that the payment of the net revenues, after payment of operation and expenses of the income-producing property, should be paid to the holders of secured bonds without the application of the automatic stay, which is the derivation of Section 922(d) in the Code, as the Senate Report states:

> This provision [362] is overly broad in Chapter 9, requiring the delay and expense arising from a request for relief from automatic stay to accomplish what many state statutes mandate: the application of pledged revenues after the payment of operating expenses to the payment of secured bonds. The automatic stay should specifically be inapplicable to application of such revenues.[268]

In fact, as the Senate Report noted at page 21,

---

266 482 B.R. at 432.

267 *See generally In re Jefferson Cnty., Ala.*, 474 B.R. at 268 ("It is clear from both the House and Senate Reports accompanying the 1988 amendments that eliminating the potential loss of a creditor's lien on revenues was a critical purpose behind the enactment of § 928 and § 922(d).").

268 *Id.* at 271 (quoting Senate Report at 11). To the extent the revenues are attributable to a municipal enterprise where fees, rates or tolls are charged for the use of the municipal service such as water, sewer, electricity or transportation, it makes perfect sense that the cost of current operation and maintenance be paid to assure continued operations to generate revenues to pay the debt. Further, where a specific revenue source is dedicated and pledged to be paid first or solely for debt service on the debt obligation, the cost of operation or maintenance to be paid after satisfaction of the debt service and the federal court and municipality must follow the mandate of the state statute or constitutional provision that require that the pledged revenues are first or solely paid to the debt. Accordingly, it is important to properly understand and respect the nature of the source of revenues and the language of the state statute or constitutional provision, bond ordinance or resolution.

> Reasonable assurance of timely payment is essential to the orderly marketing of municipal bonds and notes and continued municipal finance.

The clear intent of Congress in enacting the 1988 Amendments was to provide assurances to the capital markets that special revenues essential to municipal financing remain unimpaired in the event of a Chapter 9 filing. "[T]he amendments insure that revenue bondholders receive the benefit of their bargain with the municipal issuer, namely, they will have *unimpaired rights to the project revenue pledged to them.*"[269] The then newly added Section 928 along with the definition of special revenues in Section 902(2) protect the lien on revenues.[270] In sum, Congress made clear that municipal revenue bondholders are entitled to receive the revenues pledged to them without any interference and on a timely basis.

F. Statutory Liens Protect Bondholders

1. Basic Provisions for a Statutory Lien

States in their statutes authorizing the issuance of municipal bonds may provide by the language contained in the statute or constitutional provision that the bonds will be paid by the dedicated revenues pledged or mandated by the statute to be used to pay that bond debt obligation. The statutory lien arises "solely by force of a statute on specified circumstances or conditions ..."[271] If the force and effect of the language of the state statute create a charge against or interest in specific property including revenue and rights to receive funds, then a state law creates a lien on certain assets that is a statutory lien.[272] By contrast, a statutory lien does not include a security interest that arises solely out of a contractual arrangement between the issuer and the debt holder, such as a consensual lien created by a bond indenture or bond resolution or ordinance;[273] nor does a statutory lien require any further act of the municipality beyond issuing the bond pursuant to the statute.

---

269 *Id.* at 270 (emphasis in original) (quoting Senate Report at 12).

270 Senate Report at 12. Note the Senate and House Bills varied in that 928 in the House was 927 in the Senate and the House number was used. There is a technical clarification that in Section 922(d) the reference to Section 927 should be to Section 928.

271 *See* 11 U.S.C. § 101(53); *In re Badger Mountain Irr. Dist.*, 885 F.2d 606, 608, n. 2 (9th Cir. 1989).

272 The following terms are defined in the Federal Bankruptcy Code. The term "lien" means charge against or interest in property to secure the payment of a debt or performance of an obligation. *See* 11 U.S.C. § 101(37). The term "security agreement" means an agreement that creates or provides for a security interest. *See* § 11 U.S.C. 101(50). The term "security interest" means a lien created by agreement. *See* 11 U.S.C. § 101(51).

273 Accordingly, a consensual lien created solely by agreement would not be a statutory lien. However, a consensual lien created by an agreement that is also separately created by the force of a statute upon which the governmental body chooses to issue the debt that has, by the words of the statute, a dedicated source of payment that is mandated and dedicated to the payment of the obligation by the words of the statute is a statutory lien. *See In re County of Orange*, 189 B.R. 499, 504 (C.D. Cal. 1995) (in dicta).

Some state statutes are very clear by their language and may even use the words "statutory lien." Other states in their statutory language may simply provide that the taxes, revenues and other income pledged by the municipality under the statute are immediately subject to the lien of such pledge from the time the pledge is made (*i.e.*, from the time the bonds are issued). In either case, the law establishes the lien and therefore a statutory lien is present.

Generally, the statute from which the statutory lien arises:

- Provides that the *force and effect of the statute* create the charge against interest in or the dedicated revenues or proceeds to pay the debt without need of further action by the issuing governmental entity.

- May in addition provide for the *priority of payment*, a first lien or provision that the dedicated pledged revenues can only be used to pay the debt or in the order specified in the statute or authorizing documents.

- May also provide an *intercept or segregation* of the revenues or require a governmental entity or officer to collect and pay over to a special account or to the bond trustee.

There are a number of states with statutory lien provisions. *See, e.g.*, Rhode Island, California, Idaho, New Jersey (Municipal Qualified Bond Act) and Colorado.[274] There is statutory lien legislation pending in Michigan (HB 4495) and in Nebraska (LB 67).[275] Where a statutory lien exists, even if the bondholder is holding general obligation bonds for which the contractual pledge of a municipality's taxes or revenues generally would terminate on the filing of a municipal bankruptcy petition, such bondholder may continue to receive payment in the wake of a Chapter 9 filing if the underlying statute authorizing the issuance of the bonds contains a statutory lien, which lien comes into existence by virtue of the statute and arises by force of the statute on specific circumstances or conditions and does not require further action by the municipality.[276]

---

274 *See, e.g.*, statutes in California (CAL. EDUC. CODE § 15251 and CAL. GOV'T CODE § 53515), Rhode Island (R.I. GEN. LAWS § 45-12), Colorado (COLO. REV. STAT. § 11-57-208), Idaho (IDAHO CODE § 57-2-234). Compare, *e.g.*, Louisiana (LA. REV. STAT. § 39:14301), Oregon (OR. REV. STAT. § 287A.310), Texas (TEX. GOV'T. CODE ANN. § 1202.006, 1208.002) and Utah (UTAH CODE ANN. §§ 11-14-501, 37-48-186).

275 Michigan Public Act 17 of 2015 (amending MCL 117.36a) provides for a statutory lien for financial recovery bonds issued by certain cities with a population less than 10,000.

276 *See In re County of Orange*, 189 BR. 499 (C.D. Cal. 1995). *See also* Order Pursuant to (i) 11 U.S.C. Secs. 105, 364(c), 364(d)(1), 364(e), 902, 904, 921, 922 and 928 (A) Approving Postpetition Financing and (B) Granting Liens and (II) Bankruptcy Rule 9019 Confirmation Objections, *In re City of Detroit*, Case No. 13-53846 (Bankr. E.D. Mich. Aug. 25, 2014), ECF No. 7028.

2. Treatment in Chapter 9 of Statutory Liens

A statutory lien is intended to remain unaltered in a Chapter 9 proceeding, and there is a continuing right to be timely paid after the filing of a Chapter 9. This was recognized in the Orange County Chapter 9 in 1994 (delay in payment due to appeal and reversal of bankruptcy court as to effect of a statutory lien) and Sierra Kings Health Care District Chapter 9 in 2009 (relating to general obligation bonds). At least 15 states and Puerto Rico recognize some form of a statutory lien in relation to their bond obligations.[277] In July 2015, the State of California enacted SB 222, which creates a first lien priority for certain general obligation debt issued by California's municipalities and by California's school districts.[278] Specifically, SB 222 applies to those general obligation bonds payable from ad valorem taxes levied pursuant to Article XIIIA, Section 1(b)(2) and (3) of the California Constitution and issued by California's cities, counties, cities and counties, school districts, community college districts, authorities and special districts.

In 2011, when Rhode Island was confronted with the economic difficulties of the city of Central Falls and the looming financial questions surrounding the city of Providence, its legislature, led by the governor, passed a law granting a first statutory lien to all bonds and notes and, in essence, stating that the law was confirming the intended priority of and assurance of payment for those obligations.

The Rhode Island statute provides:

---

277 *See* section VIII, 50 State Survey. The states include Alabama, California, Colorado, Florida, Idaho, Illinois, Indiana, Iowa, Kentucky, Michigan, New Jersey, New York, Pennsylvania, Rhode Island and South Carolina. The 50 State Survey and Appendix B take state statutes that arguably could be viewed as creating a statutory lien and break them into three categories. The three-category analysis consists of:

(i) SL-1: The language of the statute appears to strongly support a determination that it is a statutory lien (15 states and Puerto Rico).

(ii) SL-2: While the language of the statute may appear to create a statutory lien, further clarification would be helpful to reaffirm the intent to create a statutory lien (15 states).

(iii) SL-3: While the language of the statute may appear to create a statutory lien, it is insufficient and additional language is required to clarify the intent and to create a statutory lien. The language could be read as just providing for perfection of a pledge or lien without the intent to create a statutory lien (10 states).

It should be noted that some states may be in more than one category. The purpose of this three-part analysis is to encourage further review and analysis by government issuers, state legislatures and market participants (rating agencies, bond insurers, investors and professional advisors). The needed clarification could include a clear legal opinion, additional legislation being more explicit as to the existence or not of a statutory lien and further analysis and determination by market participants including the issuer that a statutory lien is intended and effective. The analysis contained in section VIII is not intended to be definitive or exhaustive. It is intended to continue, if not commence, a more targeted discussion, disclosure and determination by market participants.

278 S.B. 222, Chapter 78 (Cal. July 13, 2015).

> "The faith and credit ad valorem taxes, and general fund revenues of each city, town and district shall be pledged for the payment of the principal of, premium and the interest on, all general obligation bonds and notes of the city or town ... and shall constitute a first lien on such ad valorem taxes and general fund revenues."[279]

The Rhode Island legislation was intended, given the economic downturn of 2008 and the financial hardship of Central Falls and other issuers, to provide assurances to the credit market so that municipalities would continue to have access to the market at the lowest cost possible in order to fund necessary services and infrastructure. At the end of 2014, a bill was introduced into Michigan's House of Representatives providing and confirming that unlimited tax general obligation bonds ("ULTGO Bonds") would have a statutory first lien on all taxes subject to an unlimited tax pledge and that a statutory first lien would apply to any ULTGO pledge made prior to or after the date of the enactment of the law. The Michigan House recently passed the bill, HB 4495, that would confirm a statutory lien on any ULTGO Bond, and it is now pending in the Michigan Senate. Other states in 2014 introduced similar legislation for ULTGO Bonds or other bond debt, such as California's SB 222 noted above and Nebraska's LB 67 (2015) that is still pending legislative action.[280]

G. Provisions of the Bankruptcy Code and Supreme Court Decision Require Revenues Subject to a Statutory Lien or Special Revenues under State Law to Be Paid as Intended

The fact that a municipality may file for Chapter 9 does not allow the municipality to act contrary to its state law, as Section 903 of the Bankruptcy Code requires that state law be honored. Chapter 9 does not limit or impair the power of the state to control the municipality in the exercise of its political and governmental powers, including expenditures.[281] The limitation on the court's jurisdiction under Section 904 of the Bankruptcy Code with regard to political governmental powers, properties and revenues of the debtor as well as the debtor's use and enjoyment of income-producing property means the municipality cannot consent to something that is contrary to the mandate of state law.[282] Because state law provisions establishing statutory liens relate to the exercise of a state's

279 R.I. GEN. LAWS § 45-12-1(a).

280 The National Federation of Municipal Analysts has issued for comment the draft *White Paper on General Obligation Bond Payments: Statutory Liens and Related Disclosure, Draft of July 12, 2016*, www.nfma.org.

281 *See* 11 U.S.C. § 903, which provides: "Reservation of State power to control municipalities. This chapter does not limit or impair the power of a State to control, by legislation or otherwise, a municipality of or in such State in the exercise of the political or governmental powers of such municipality, including expenditures for such exercise, but — (1) a State law prescribing a method of composition of indebtedness of such municipality may not bind any creditor that does not consent to such composition; and (2) a judgment entered under such a law may not bind a creditor that does not consent to such composition".

282 *See* 11 U.S.C. § 904, which provides: "Limitation on jurisdiction and powers of court. Notwithstanding any power of the court, *unless the debtor consents or the plan so provides, the court may not, by any stay, order, or decree,* in the case or

political and governmental power, and not to the process of debt adjustment, these state laws should be honored in a Chapter 9 bankruptcy proceeding pursuant to Sections 903 and 904 of the Bankruptcy Code.

Sections 903, 904, 922(d) and 928 of the Bankruptcy Code can all be read to mandate timely payment of revenue as collected and pledged to the debt holders that hold debt secured by a statutory lien or a pledge of special revenues. The purpose of Sections 903 and 904 can only be interpreted as requiring timely payment of such revenues, as noted above, as to statutory liens and other state law mandated payments. Under Sections 922(d) and 928(a) of the Bankruptcy Code, special revenues as collected are to be paid (applied) as set forth in the relevant documents (the bond indenture or bond resolution should be clear it is the security agreement providing for the payment of pledged revenues).

The legislative history of the 1988 Amendments supports the timely and unimpaired payments of revenue subject to statutory lien and a pledge of special revenues. The Senate Report on the 1988 Amendments specifically noted that the amendments to Chapter 9 of the Bankruptcy Code providing for special revenues were consistent with the requirement that payment of the pledged revenues created by a statutory lien or other state law mandated payment even in Chapter 9 must be timely paid and not impaired.

The Senate Report for the 1988 Amendments provides:

> The application of Section 552 in a Chapter 9 bankruptcy proceeding may also defy practical reality and state law mandates. As in the case of the San Jose School District, *In re San Jose Unified School District*, No. 5-83-02387-A-9, (B.C.N.D. Cal. 1983), the continued payment of interest to bondholders not only helped ensure the debtor's continued access to credit markets but also helps fulfill the requirement of state law that such collected funds be used to pay bondholders. Cal. Educ. Code Ann. 15251.
>
> Accordingly, as a practical matter, even though Section 552 of the Bankruptcy Code provides that the pledge is terminated, given the mandate of the law and the practical reality of municipal finance, *a municipality might well attempt to ignore that provision and continue to pay the bondholders as originally promised. Municipalities, prior to and after the enactment of the Bankruptcy Code, have so acted, such as the San Jose School District* … .
>
> In the municipal context, therefore, *the simple answer to the Section 552 problem is that Section 904 and the tenth amendment should prohibit the interpretation that pledges of revenues granted pursuant to state statutory or constitutional provision to*

---

otherwise, *interfere with* — 1. any of the *political or governmental powers* of the debtor; 2. any of the *property or revenues* of the debtor; or 3. the debtor's *use or enjoyment of any income-producing* property" (emphasis added).

> *bondholders can be terminated by the filing of a chapter 9 case.* Likewise, under the contract clause of the Constitution (article I, section 10), a municipality cannot claim that a contractual pledge of revenue can be terminated by the filing of a chapter 9 proceeding.
>
> S. Rep. No. 100-506 at 6 (1988) (emphasis added).

The Supreme Court in *Ashton v. Cameron County Water Sup. District No. 1*[283] found the 1934 version of Chapter 9 unconstitutional because it interfered with the sovereign power of the states. Further, as the U.S. Supreme Court held in *United States vs. Bekins*[284] in ruling on the constitutionality of the then version of Chapter 9 (known as Chapter IX), in implementing any plan of debt adjustment, the municipality must comply with state law, and clearly the municipality cannot in its implementation of its plan or in taking action in a Chapter 9 act contrary to state law. These cases as well as the provisions of the Bankruptcy Code require that a Chapter 9 proceeding cannot violate the mandates and priorities of state law. In the case of *In the matter of Sanitary and Imp. Dist. No. 7*, the court recognized where a plan proposes action not authorized by state law or without satisfying state law requirements, the plan cannot be confirmed.[285] At issue was whether the state law priority of payment of bonds over warrants required the plan to provide for full payment of bonds as mandated by state law in order to be confirmed. While these were unsecured claims (not covered by a statutory lien or special revenues) that can be modified in a Chapter 9, the court noted payments required under state law as well as state law provisions for payment post-confirmation should be honored in order for the court to confirm a plan.[286]

H. Special Revenues and Statutory Liens in the Courts

1. Special Revenues

The significance of special revenues and statutory liens was illustrated by the case of *Sierra Kings Health Care District*, in which a court order reaffirmed the fact that a Chapter 9 proceeding and any order or plan of debt adjustment cannot interfere with notes, bonds or municipal obligations that are paid from the pledge of taxes or revenues that are special revenues or subject to a statutory lien. Of special significance is the fact that the *Sierra Kings* court confirmed, for the first time, the postpetition effectiveness of a municipality's pledge of ad valorem taxes which qualified as both a special revenue pledge and a statutory lien. The Chapter 9 proceeding, orders and plan would not affect the timely payment on these bonds according to their terms.[287]

---

283 298 U.S. 513 (1936).

284 304 U.S. 27 (1938).

285 98 B.R. 970, 974 (Bankr. D. Neb. 1989).

286 *See In re City of Colorado Springs Creek Gen. Imp. Dist.*, 177 B.R. 684 (Bankr. D. Colo. 1995).

287 *In re Sierra Kings Health Care District, supra* n. 253; 11 U.S.C. § 928(a).

The court in the Jefferson County, Alabama bankruptcy proceeding recognized special revenue treatment for sewer debt and payment consistent with the terms of the documents.[288] While the case authorized payment of special revenues to pay debtor counsel fees, it was arguable due to the language of the indenture being interpreted to allow such payment.[289] The ultimate plan treatment was a compromise or settlement. Accordingly, the Jefferson County case does not stand for any impairment or delay in payment of revenues as collected other than as purportedly authorized by the documents or to which the parties have voluntarily agreed. In the Vallejo, California and Stockton, California bankruptcy proceedings, the court recognized the mandated and the timely payment of special revenue bond issues (even though disputes existed regarding lease financing relating to the extent of the collateral and payments with one major holder). In the Detroit bankruptcy proceeding the special revenues that had been pledged to secure the water and sewer bonds issued by the city were timely paid and if the holder did not accept Detroit's tender offer in the plan, those remaining holders were unimpaired (except for those who voluntarily settled and took the tender offer). In the Heffernan Memorial Hospital District case, the court held that a special tax or a portion of a general tax specifically levied to pay for a municipal financing and not for general purposes should be treated as special revenues and timely paid as collected to the debt holders.[290]

One issue that has not been definitively determined by the courts is the application of Section 1129, the cramdown provisions of the Bankruptcy Code, to special revenue bonds. While this potential has been raised in such Chapter 9 cases as *Jefferson County* and *Detroit*, settlements and compromise have prevented a clear judicial determination. Certain debtors and commentators have taken the position that, given the applicability of Section 1129(b)(2)(A) to Chapter 9, a debtor may force holders of special revenue bonds to receive only the present value of the revenue stream securing the bond issuance as part of any plan of adjustment.[291] This would be accomplished through valuation of the secured stream of revenue and a discount to a present value. In other words, recovery would be less than the amount the special revenue bondholder should have received either under the original contract or if the revenue stream were allowed to continue to pay until the debt was paid in full. But such a result would be contrary to congressional intent in passing the municipal bankruptcy provisions in 1988. There was a clear intention in the 1988 Amendments that the rights of special revenue bondholders should not be altered,[292] even in a cramdown situation. That is due to the forced election

288 *In re Jefferson Cnty., Ala.*, 482 B.R. 404 (Bankr. N.D. Ala. 2012).

289 *In re Jefferson Cnty., Ala.*, 503 B.R. 849 (Bankr. N.D. Ala. 2013).

290 *In re Heffernan Memorial Hospital District*, 202 B.R. 147, 149 (Bankr. S.D. Cal. 1996).

291 *See* discussion in Slayton Dabney, Jr., Patrick Darby, Daniel G. Egan, Marc A. Levinson, George B. South III, Emily Tidmore, MUNICIPALITIES IN PERIL: THE ABI GUIDE TO CHAPTER 9 (2d ed. 2012).

292 *See* Senate Report at 12, providing: "To eliminate the confusion and to confirm various state laws and constitutional provisions regarding the rights of bondholders to receive the revenues pledged to them in payment of debt obligations of a municipality, a new section is provided in the amendment to ensure that revenue bondholders receive the benefit

contained in Section 927 of the Bankruptcy Code prohibiting treating the holder of a claim payable as having recourse to the municipal debtor on account of such claim pursuant to Section 1111(b) of the Bankruptcy Code. Section 927 requires the claim to be payable solely from special revenues against the debtor and instead treating the holder as having made the election to receive the stream of revenue payments without further recourse to the debtor to the full extent that such revenues may pay in the future. A court may not reduce the revenue pledge attached to the bonds absent agreement of the bondholders.

2. Statutory Lien

A statutory lien cannot be canceled on the filing of a bankruptcy petition or by the bankruptcy court. This approach was recognized by the district court on appeal in the Orange County bankruptcy. There, the court found that the lien securing tax and revenue anticipation notes pursuant to a California statute authorizing the county to pledge assets to secure notes was a statutory lien. Since the statute, not a security agreement, imposed it, the pledge survived the filing of a Chapter 9 petition.[293] Thus, if there is a statutory lien by the force and effect of the state statute that pledges taxes and revenue to pay the financial debt, then the existence of a bond resolution, indenture or similar document, including a security agreement, reiterating the grant, the pledge or dedicated revenues arising under state statute or referring to the total pledge as a lien does not adversely affect the statutory lien status and the rights of the bondholders. In the Central Falls, Rhode Island bankruptcy referenced previously, the state statute confirming a statutory lien on municipal revenues for general obligation bonds was honored, and the bondholders were not diminished by the plan of adjustment. Further, there was no noticeable contagion in Rhode Island from the Chapter 9 bankruptcy of Central Falls in 2011 or the restructuring that Providence implemented in 2012.[294]

In the Detroit bankruptcy proceeding, the city had previously issued certain (i) limited tax general obligation bonds (the "LTGO Bonds"), which did not have a separate pledge but did have a first budget obligation pledge of the General Fund and (ii) the ULTGO Bonds, which were backed by a separate voter-approved property tax levied for the sole purpose of paying the bonds. Michigan, at the time of the Detroit crisis, did not have any type of specific statement in its statutes explicitly stating the pledge was a "statutory lien" similar to the statutory lien provision in SB 222 in California, and the city's emergency manager argued that these two bond issuances constituted unsecured debt. Ultimately, after a settlement of these issues, holders of the LTGO Bonds received less than full payment on their bonds from the bankruptcy estate, and even less than other creditors (such as pension

---

of their bargain with the municipal issuer and that they will have unimpaired rights to the project revenues pledged to them."

293 *See In re County of Orange*, 189 BR. 499, 505 (C.D. Cal. 1995).

294 *See* James Spiotto, *Reducing Risk to Payment of State and Local Government Debt Obligations, Statutory Liens from Rhode Island to California SB 222*, MUNINET GUIDE (July 28, 2015), http://www.muninetguide.com/articles/reducing-the-risk-to-payment-of-state-and-local-government-debt-7401.

claimants) who were similarly situated. The ULTGO Bonds, however, received 100 percent recovery albeit 26 cents payable from the bond insurer under an insurance policy settlement with Detroit.

The ULTGO Bonds had voter approval of additional tax revenue dedicated to payment of these bonds, which raises some fundamental government finance issues as noted above as to the application of Sections 903 and 904 of the Bankruptcy Code. What does it mean to have a tax revenue pledge approved by the voters and dedicated to pay the general obligation bonds? Does Article IX, Section 25 of the Michigan Constitution mean that the repayment of voter-approved bonded indebtedness is guaranteed? What consequences are there to the municipal bond market if ULTGO Bonds are ultimately treated as unsecured debt? Can the plan of debt adjustment be confirmed if it is not in compliance with state law and if the claimant does not consent to a settlement that provides for an impairment? The answer according to *Ashton* and *Bekins* is clearly no.[295]

I. Summary of Basic Creditor Treatment in a Chapter 9 Proceeding

The following chart summarizes the intended treatment of bonds and notes, depending on how they are secured, in a Chapter 9 proceeding.

Summary of Basic Treatment of Bonds and Notes in Chapter 9		
	Type of Bonds/Notes	Bankruptcy Effects
1.	General Obligation Bonds Without a Specific Pledge	Postpetition, a court may treat general obligation bonds as unsecured debt which does not have a statutory lien or constitutionally mandated payment of dedicated revenues or a pledge of revenues that classifies as special revenues and order a restructuring of the bonds. Payment on such bonds during the bankruptcy proceeding likely will cease. Prepetition, unlimited general obligation bonds are backed by the unlimited taxing power of the municipality (its "full faith and credit") and are historically subject to conditions such as voter authorization, limitations on particular purposes, or debt limitation to a percentage of assessed valuation on the power of municipal entities to incur such debts.

295 *Ashton v. Cameron County Water Imp. Dist. No. 1*, 298 U.S. 513 (1936); *U.S. v. Bekins*, 304 U.S. 27 (1938).

Summary of Basic Treatment of Bonds and Notes in Chapter 9		
Type of Bonds/Notes		Bankruptcy Effects
2.	General Obligation Bonds Plus Pledged Revenues	Assuming that the general obligation pledge is an actual pledge of specific revenues and to the extent that it may be classified as a statutory lien or constitutionally mandated payment of dedicated revenues or special revenues, this secured issuance will be respected to the degree it is consistent and authorized under state law. A contractual pledge of revenues that is not a statutory lien or constitutionally mandated payment of dedicated revenues or special revenues may be attacked as not being a valid continuing postpetition lien under Section 552 of the Bankruptcy Code. However, state law mandated payments of revenues whereby the force and effect of language of the state statute or constitutional provision payments related to dedicated revenues, set-asides, priorities, or appropriateness are mandated to be made ("State Law Mandated Payments") should be paid post-petition as collected without delay. This would be consistent with Sections 903 and 904 of the Bankruptcy Code because the *Ashton* and *Bekins* cases prohibit the court from interfering with the power of a state to control a municipality in its exercise of political or governmental powers in the government affairs or revenues of the municipality.
3.	Special Revenue Bonds	A pledge of special revenues will survive a bankruptcy filing. Pre-petition, a special revenue bond is an obligation to repay solely and only from specific revenues of a municipal enterprise (net of operations and maintenance costs, if applicable) or dedicated funds or tax revenues that are pledged to bondholders. No stay during the Chapter 9 proceeding in applying such special revenues to pay the debt it is pledged to pursuant to the terms of the documents (§ 922(d)). The contemplated remedy for default often focuses on a covenant to charge rates sufficient to amortize the debt and, if necessary, on the appointment of a receiver. Defaulted bondholders are expected to seek mandamus in court to require the municipal borrower to raise its rates or, if necessary, request the appointment of a receiver to enforce the rate covenant and prudent operations of the municipal enterprise. To enforce such remedies after the filing of a Chapter 9 would require the lifting of the automatic stay.

Summary of Basic Treatment of Bonds and Notes in Chapter 9		
	Type of Bonds/Notes	Bankruptcy Effects
4.	Revenues Subject to Statutory Lien	Assuming the pledge is authorized under state law through a statutory lien, the bankruptcy court should respect that statutory lien. Thus, as long as the revenues are subject to a statutory lien, payments to the bondholders should be protected postpetition and, based on Sections 903 and 904 of the Bankruptcy Code and the *Ashton* and *Bekins* cases, should be paid to the bondholder as mandated by the statute.

The secured claims referenced in the chart thus should receive special treatment in a bankruptcy. As noted in *Faitoute Iron & Steel Co. et al. v. City of Asbury Park,*[296] discretion must be exercised in dealing with secured claims. In that case, while the court recognized that New Jersey's Depression-era Municipal Finance Commission Act of 1931 could impair municipal debt, there was recognition that secured claims and tax anticipation and revenue notes stand on an entirely different footing from other municipal obligations and, in relation to them, no claim was affected by the Municipal Finance Commission Act of New Jersey. The plan adopted by Asbury Park paid general obligation bondholders who did not have a specific pledge of revenues (secured property right) a compromise payment (less in amount and with a delay in payment).

296 316 U.S. 502 (1942).

The following chart summarizes the priorities of creditor payments were a municipality to file a Chapter 9 petition.

Summary of Chapter 9 Priorities		
	Type of Claim	Explanation
1.	Obligations secured by a statutory lien to the extent of the pledged revenue collected[a,b]	Debt (bonds, warranties, notes, Trans, Rans) issued pursuant to statute that itself imposes a pledge. (There should not be any delay in payments due to automatic stay since the bankruptcy court and the municipality have no authority to do otherwise due to the mandate of state law to only use or expend revenues or proceeds for the designated purpose under Section 903 of the Federal Bankruptcy Code; the municipality cannot act or consent differently since it is unable to do so under state law that controls under Section 904 of the Federal Bankruptcy Code.)

a Chapter 9 incorporates Section 506(c) of the Bankruptcy Code, which imposes a surcharge for preserving or disposing of collateral. Because a municipality cannot mortgage city hall or the police headquarters, municipal securities tend to be secured by a pledge of a revenue stream. Hence, it is rare that a surcharge would be imposed. *But see* numbers 3 and 4.

b Chapter 9 incorporates § 364(d) of the Bankruptcy Code, which permits a debtor to obtain postpetition credit secured by a senior or equal lien on property of the estate that is subject to a lien if the prior lien holder is adequately protected. However, if state law mandates the use of the pledged revenues solely or first to pay the statutory lien or special revenue debt, that mandate of state law cannot be violated and no priming lien or other use of revenues can be authorized. State Law Mandated Payments where the force and effect of the state statutory or constitutional language mandate that the municipality make the payment of dedicated revenues to the specified debt pursuant to pledged revenues, set-asides, priorities as to the use of revenues or required appropriation shall be treated similarly to a statutory lien as set forth in subsection F above and Sections 903 and 904 of the Bankruptcy Code and the U.S. Supreme Court rulings in the *Ashton* and *Bekins* cases.

Summary of Chapter 9 Priorities		
	Type of Claim	Explanation
2.	Obligations secured by special revenues (subject to necessary operating expenses of such project or system, if applicable) to the extent of the pledged revenue collected.[a,b] These obligations are often non-recourse and, in the event of default, the bondholders have no claim against non-pledged assets. (Reaffirmed in the Jefferson County court ruling and the ultimate treatment of water and sewer revenue bonds in Detroit.)	Special revenue bonds secured by any of the following: (A) receipts derived from the ownership, operation or disposition of projects or systems of the debtor that are primarily used or intended to be used to provide transportation, utility or other services, including the proceeds of borrowings to finance the projects or systems; (B) special excise taxes imposed on particular activities or transactions; (C) incremental tax receipts from the benefited area in the case of tax-increment financing; (D) other revenues or receipts derived from particular functions of the debtor, whether or not the debtor has other functions; or (E) taxes specially levied to finance one or more projects or systems, excluding receipts from general property, sales or income taxes (other than tax-increment financing) levied to finance the general purposes of the debtor.[c] There should be no delay in payment since automatic stay is lifted under Section 922(d). If the state statute also creates a statutory lien or mandate that the pledged tax revenues can be used only for payment of the debt obligations and for no other purposes before payment in full of the obligation then there is no reduction for necessary operating expenses (Sections 903, 904 and 928 of the Federal Bankruptcy Code).

c A pledge of revenues that is not a statutory lien or special revenue pledge may be attacked as not being a valid continuing postpetition lien under Section 552 of the Bankruptcy Code.

Summary of Chapter 9 Priorities		
	Type of Claim	Explanation
3.	Secured lien based on bond resolution or contractual provisions that does not meet test of statutory lien or special revenues to the extent perfected prepetition, subject to the value of prepetition property or proceeds thereof.[c]	Under the language of Sections 552 and 928, liens on such collateral would not continue postpetition. After giving value to the prepetition lien on property or proceeds, there is an unsecured claim to the extent there is recourse to the municipality or debtor. You may expect the creditor to argue that pursuant to Section 904, the court cannot interfere with the property or revenues of the debtor (without the debtor's consent, consistent with state law), and that includes the grant of security to such secured creditor.
4.	Obligations secured by a municipal facility lease financing.	Under Section 929 of the Bankruptcy Code, even if the transaction is styled as a municipal lease, a financing lease will be treated as long-term debt and secured to the extent of the value of the facility.
5.	Administrative expenses (which would include expenses incurred in connection with the Chapter 9 case itself).[d] Chapter 9 incorporates Section 507(a)(2) which, by its terms, provides a priority for administrative expenses allowed under Section 503(b). These would include the expenses of a committee or indenture trustee making a substantial contribution in a Chapter 9 case.	Pursuant to Section 943, all amounts must be disclosed and be reasonable for a plan of adjustment to be confirmed.

d These expenses strictly relate to the costs of the bankruptcy. Because the bankruptcy court cannot interfere with the government and affairs of the municipality, general operating expenses of the municipality after th filing of the Chapter 9 are not within the control of the court (unless the municipality consents and is not otherwise prohibited under state law from interfering with the payment), are not discharged and will remain liabilities of the municipality after the confirmation of a plan or dismissal of the case.

Summary of Chapter 9 Priorities		
	Type of Claim	**Explanation**
6.	Unsecured debt includes:	
A	Senior unsecured claims with benefit of subordination paid to the extent of available funds (without any obligation to raise taxes) which include any of B, C, D or E below.	
B	General Obligation Bonds.	With a general pledge of "full faith and credit" of the issuing municipality (unlimited or limited) without a dedication of special revenues or a statutory lien. Postpetition, a court may treat general obligation bonds without a statutory lien or special revenues pledge as unsecured debt and permit an adjustment or restructuring of the bonds. Payment on the bonds during the bankruptcy proceeding likely will cease.[e]
C	Trade.	Vendors, suppliers, contracting parties for goods or services. Payment will likely cease for prepetition goods or services.[f]
D	Obligations for accrued but unpaid prepetition wages and pensions and other employee benefits.	These do not enjoy any priority, unlike in a Chapter 11.[g]
E	Unsecured portion of secured indebtedness.	

e However, if state law mandates specific appropriation, set-aside or priority of payment of revenues collected, the failure to honor state law may be an obstacle to confirming a plan of debt adjustment since the plan, court and municipality cannot go forward. *See* Section 903 of the Federal Bankruptcy Code.

f Section 503(b)(9) provides for a priority claim to be paid on confirmation of a plan for the value of goods provided prepetition within 20 days of the petition date.

g Chapter 9 does not incorporate Section 1113 of the Bankruptcy Code, which imposes special provisions for the rejection of collative bargaining agreements (making the standard less restrictive, *i.e.*, "impairs ability to rehabilitate") or Sections 507(a)(4) and (5), which give a priority (before payment of unsecured claims) to wages, salaries, commissions, vacation, severance, sick leave or contribution to pension plans of $12,475 per employee currently.

Summary of Chapter 9 Priorities		
	Type of Claim	Explanation
F	Subordinated unsecured claims.	Any debt subordinated by statute or by contract to other debt would be appropriately subordinated and paid only to the extent senior claims are paid in full. Senior debt would receive combined senior and subordinate *pro rata* distribution (the distribution attributable to the aggregate senior and subordinated unsecured claim) until the senior is paid in full.

J. Payments to Bondholders Are Not Preferences

The Bankruptcy Code also provides assurance to holders of all municipal bond or note obligations that payments received within 90 days of the commencement of a municipal bankruptcy petition are not preferences that may be clawed back.[297] Specifically, Section 926(b) of the Bankruptcy Code provides that a transfer of property of the debtor to or for the benefit of any holder of a bond or note on account of such bond or note may not be avoided under Section 547. This would include interest and principal payments as well as bond defeasance payments received within the presumed preference period of 90 days before filing. While this section refers to "bonds or notes," there is nothing in the legislative history to support the view that this provision is limited only to instruments bearing such titles. The intent appears to be that Section 926(b) should be applicable to all forms of municipal debt and allow such holders to keep such payments where the Bankruptcy Code would otherwise require any payments made within 90 days of a bankruptcy filing to be returned to the estate.

K. Collective Bargaining Agreements and Pensions in Chapter 9

1. Rejection of Executory Contracts and Unexpired Leases, Including Collective Bargaining Agreements

On February 22, 1984, in *National Labor Relations Board v. Bildisco & Bildisco*, the U.S. Supreme Court held that Section 365(a) of the Bankruptcy Code provides that, with certain limitations, the debtor may unilaterally assume or reject any executory contract of the debtor, including a collective bargaining agreement.[298] The test set forth in *Bildisco* was whether the debtor could show both that the agreement burdens the estate and that the equities balance in favor of rejection. Congress responded to the *Bildisco* decision with Section 1113 of the Bankruptcy Code, which set a much more difficult test, in addition to setting a detailed procedure that must be followed for the rejection of a collective bargaining agreement. Under Section 1113(c), the court will approve an application for rejection of a collective

297 11 U.S.C. § 926.

298 465 U.S. 513 (1984).

bargaining agreement only if the court finds that (a) the debtor has, prior to the hearing, made a proposal to modify the collective bargaining agreement that is necessary to permit the debtor to reorganize, (b) the authorized representative of the employees has refused to accept such proposal without cause and (c) the balance of the equities clearly favors rejection of such agreement. This more difficult test under Section 1113 has *not* been incorporated into Chapter 9, and the *Bildisco* standard appears to be applicable to Chapter 9 debtors.

The issue of the rejection of executory contracts in Chapter 9, and in particular the rejection of collective bargaining agreements, has been dealt with in several municipal bankruptcies. In the Central Falls, Rhode Island case, the city filed a motion pursuant to Section 365 to reject several of its collective bargaining agreements. While the court granted the city's motion,[299] the city and its unions already had agreed to new terms prior to the entry of the order. The unions did agree to reduce terms while the bondholders, beneficiaries of the statutory lien legislation, were unimpaired.

The Central Falls case followed the earlier opinion of the bankruptcy court in the Eastern District of California in the *City of Vallejo*. There, the court held that the city could reject its agreement with current employees in the Chapter 9 case.[300] The issue in *Vallejo*, which involved its firefighters' and electrical workers' union, was hotly contested, and the motion to reject was opposed by a number of creditor groups. *Vallejo* demonstrated that despite the more lenient test to reject a municipal collective bargaining agreement in *Bildisco*, the nature of the litigation process and the time and expense involved in obtaining a final order with respect to such an emotional and political issue are likely to absorb the attention of a municipality and take many months to reach a conclusion.[301]

2. Treatment of Municipal Pensions, Including Accrued Benefits

The bankruptcy proceedings involving the City of Stockton, California and the City of Detroit, Michigan have brought to the forefront the treatment of municipal pensions in a Chapter 9 bankruptcy proceeding. In each of these proceedings, the bankruptcy courts determined that a municipality could alter its pension obligations in a Chapter 9 proceeding, even if a constitutional provision existed providing that such contractual obligations could not be altered.[302] These cases have shown that, absent a settlement, pension obligations of a municipality can be treated equally with other unsecured debt.

---

299 ORDER ON CITY'S MOTION TO APPROVE REJECTION OF THREE COLLECTIVE BARGAINING AGREEMENTS, *In re City of Central Falls*, No. 11-bk-13105 (Bankr. D.R.I. Jan. 10, 2012), ECF No. 339.

300 403 B.R. 72, 79 (Bankr. E.D. Cal. 2009), *aff'd* 432 B.R. 262 (E.D. Cal. 2010).

301 *In re City of Vallejo, CA*, 432 B.R. 262, 272 (E.D. Cal. 2010) (upholding bankruptcy court's decision to permit the debtor-city to reject a collective bargaining agreement under Section 365 as applied in *Bildisco*).

302 *In re City of Detroit, Mich.*, 504 B.R. 97 (Bankr. E.D. Mich. 2013); *In re City of Stockton, Cal.*, 478 B.R. 8 (Bankr. E.D. Cal. 2012).

In the Vallejo and Central Falls cases discussed previously, at issue were the collective bargaining agreements affecting current employees. The pension benefits that were the subject of *Stockton* and *Detroit* included accrued benefits. The *Stockton* initial opinion, citing Sections 903 and 904 of the Bankruptcy Code, ruled that the bankruptcy court had no power to require the debtor to keep paying for retirees' health benefits in Chapter 9.[303] In the decision confirming the plan of debt adjustment, the *Stockton* bankruptcy court held that, as a matter of law, the city's pension administration contract with CalPERS, as well as the city-sponsored pensions themselves, may be adjusted as part of a Chapter 9 plan.[304] Stockton chose to adjust health care payments but not to impair or adjust pension payments to retirees despite the court's recognition that both would be impaired. The purported reasoning of the city was that, under the terms of contractual arrangements with CalPERS, penalties imposed on any modification of pension benefits were too severe to justify impairment. Despite protests from a large debt holder, the court found that employees and retirees were sharing the pain with capital market creditors.[305] At the same time, pensions received more than certain other unsecured creditor groups.

Citing *Stockton,* the bankruptcy court in the Detroit, Michigan Chapter 9 proceeding specifically held that, in Chapter 9, the bankruptcy court had the power "to impair contracts and to impair contractual rights relating to accrued vested pension benefits. Impairing contracts is what the bankruptcy process does."[306] Nonetheless, under the negotiated compromise plan of debt adjustment in Detroit, certain unsecured creditor groups received less than pensions.

In the city of Detroit's bankruptcy, as a part of a settlement with the city, the city's pensioners recovered an initial 82 percent of the amount which they had been promised by the city before its bankruptcy proceeding.[307] With respect to the city of Stockton, although Stockton's bankruptcy plan of adjustment did not impair the city's pension obligations, as a part of a settlement with the city, the lifetime health care that had been promised to certain retirees was eliminated in exchange for a onetime payment of $5.1 million into a retirees' health care trust. As indicated above, the court in *Stockton* repeatedly noted that the obligation to CalPERS could be impaired if necessary to have a viable plan but because of the cost to Stockton in failing to make scheduled pension payments given a "penalty"

---

303 *In re City of Stockton, Cal.*, 478 B.R. at 20.

304 AMENDED OPINION REGARDING CONFIRMATION AND STATUS OF CALPERS, *In re City of Stockton, California*, No. 12-32118-69 (Bankr. E.D. Cal. Feb. 27, 2015), ECF No. 1907, *aff'd* BAP No. EC-14-1550 (9th Cir. BAP Dec. 11, 2015).

305 Accrued pension and health benefits, which are not executory contracts, would be unsecured prepetition claims that, under certain circumstances, would have to be estimated under Section 502. Indeed, the bankruptcy court held that the health benefits of the retirees were not executory contracts. 478 B.R. at 22.

306 504 B.R. at 150.

307 ORDER CONFIRMING EIGHTH AMENDED PLAN FOR THE ADJUSTMENT OF DEBTS OF THE CITY OF DETROIT, *In re City of Detroit, Mich.*, No. 13-53846 (Bankr. E.D. Mich. Nov. 12, 2014), ECF No. 8272; *see also* SUPPLEMENTAL DETROIT OPINION.

discount to the valuation of pension assets and increased future costs, Stockton chose in its plan of debt adjustment not to impair the prepetition obligation to CalPERS.[308]

L. Confirmation of Plan

The confirmation requirements of Sections 1128 and 1129 of the Bankruptcy Code are applicable to a Chapter 9,[309] and there are additional Chapter 9 requirements.[310] After notice to all interested parties, the court shall hold a hearing on the confirmation of a plan. A party in interest and a special taxpayer may object to the confirmation of a plan.[311]

The court shall confirm a plan only if it meets the specific requirements of Chapter 9, including being proposed in good faith and not by method means forbidden by law. This means that there are no hidden agreements between the parties not specifically set forth in the plan nor any acceptances of the plan obtained through such hidden agreements.

In addition, at least one class of claims that is impaired under the plan and that is not an insider claim must have accepted the plan by a vote of two-thirds of the dollar amount and fifty percent of the number of creditors voting, and the court must have determined that the plan does not discriminate unfairly and is fair and equitable with respect to each class of claims or interests that is impaired under, and has not accepted, the plan.[312] In other words, even if such claimants constituted impaired classes, the acceptance of the plan by affiliates, elected officials or relatives of elected officials would not support confirmation since such claimants are insiders.[313]

In addition to the requirements set forth above, the court shall confirm the plan if:

(A) The plan complies with the provisions of Chapter 9;[314]

---

308 Marc Lifsher and Melody Petersen, *Judge Approves Stockton Bankruptcy Plan; Worker's Pensions Safe*, LA Times (Oct. 30, 2014), http://www.latimes.com/business/la-fi-stockton-pension-court-ruling-cuts-20141029-story.html.

309 11 U.S.C. § 901. *See generally* Norton Bank, L. & PRAC. § 63.01 *et seq.* for confirmation under Chapter 11.

310 11 U.S.C. § 943.

311 11 U.S.C. §§ 1128(a) and (b); 943(a). A "special taxpayer" means record owner or holder of legal or equitable title to real property against which a special assessment or special tax has been levied, the proceeds of which are the sole source of payment of an obligation issued by the debtor to defray the cost of an improvement relating to such real property. 11 U.S.C. § 902(3). A general change in all assessments or in the tax rate would not qualify any property holder in the district as a special taxpayer affected by the plan.

312 11 U.S.C. §§ 1129(a)(2), (3), (8), (10) and (b). See pages 134-139 regarding special revenue bonds and the forced election under § 927 to receive the revenue stream payments of the special revenues that cannot be valued or subject to a cramdown.

313 An affiliate may include the municipality that leases substantially all of the property of a municipal lease authority. 11 U.S.C. § 101(2)(D).

314 Section 943(b)(2), which is similar to 11 U.S.C. § 1129(a)(1).

(B) The plan complies with the provisions of other chapters of the Bankruptcy Code made applicable to Chapter 9;

(C) All amounts to be paid by the municipality to any person for services or expenses in the case or incident to the plan have been fully disclosed and are reasonable;[315]

(D) The municipality is not prohibited by law from taking any action necessary to be taken to carry out the plan;[316]

(E) The plan provides that each holder of a claim of the kind specified in Section 507(a)(1) of the Bankruptcy Code (administrative expenses during the course of the proceeding) will receive, on account of such claim, property of a value, as of the effective date of the plan, equal to the amount of such claim, except to the extent that the holder of a particular claim of such kind has waived such payment on such claim;[317]

(F) Any regulatory or electoral approval necessary under non-bankruptcy law in order to carry out any provision of the plan has been obtained or such provision is expressly conditioned on such approval;[318] and

(G) The plan is in the best interests of the creditors and is feasible.[319]

---

315 Section 943 (b)(3), which is similar to 11 U.S.C. § 1129(a)(4).

316 11 U.S.C. §§ 1129(a)(3), 943(b)(4).

317 11 U.S.C. § 943(b)(5).

318 11 U.S.C. § 943(b)(6).

319 11 U.S.C. §§ 943(b)(7), 1129. The "best interest of creditors" test does not mean liquidation value. Rather, it means the development of a recovery plan that addresses the systemic problems that caused the financial distress so that the causes of financial distress should not reoccur in the foreseeable future. The failure to have an affordable and sustainable recovery plan means that promised payments to creditors will not be made and needed reinvestment in the local government will be missing. The "best interest of creditors" requires a sustainable and affordable plan where projected revenues are more than sufficient to pay scheduled liabilities. Overpromising revenues leads to insufficient revenues to fund necessary services and infrastructure; at the same time, creditors are better off being paid a realistic recovery that allows for economic stimulus and funding of services and infrastructure at an acceptable level so that business development and new good jobs are encouraged that increase tax revenues and bring forth a recovery and assurance of payment to creditors.

It is expected that a court would be guided by standards set forth in *Kelly v. Everglades Drainage District*, 319 U.S. (1943) and *Fano v. Newport Heights Irrigation District*, 114 F.2d 563 (9th Cir. 1940). In *Kelly*, the court found that, in approving a plan, the bankruptcy court must make adequate findings bearing on the probable future tax revenues of the district, such as the revenues received in the past from each source of taxation, the present assessed value of property subject to each tax, the tax rates currently prescribed, the probable effect on future revenues of a revision made in the tax structure, the extent of past tax delinquencies, and any general economic condition of the district which may reasonably be expected to affect the percentage of future delinquencies. Similarly, in *Fano*, which involved a Chapter IX filed by an irrigation district that had a $15,000 deficit on accrued interest on its bonds, a plan to pay 62.50 cents on the dollar was not confirmed as "equitable" or in the "best interest of creditors" where the district was debt free, except

The debtor may modify a plan at any time prior to confirmation so long as the modified plan meets the requirements of Chapter 9.[320] The court will dismiss a case under Chapter 9 if confirmation of a plan under Chapter 9 is refused.[321] If a plan is confirmed, the court may retain jurisdiction over the case for such period of time as is necessary for the successful implementation of the plan.[322]

A party in interest (creditor, special taxpayer or debtor) may request the court within 180 days after the date of confirmation to revoke such order if and only if the order was procured by fraud.[323] Such an order revoking an order of confirmation should contain provisions necessary to protect any entity acquiring rights in good faith reliance on such an order and should also revoke the discharge of the debtor.

A 1989 decision by a bankruptcy court in Nebraska reflects the interplay between the various requirements for plan confirmation imposed by Chapter 9 and state law considerations.[324] Like so many of the Chapter 9 filings, the case involves a special district. The debtor had issued unsecured bonds and warrants prepetition. Under state law, bonds had priority over warrants. That is, the law required that bonds be fully paid according to their terms prior to utilizing revenues for payments of warrants. The plan of adjustment did not pay the bondholders the full amount of their claim with interest but paid some recovery to warrant holders. Despite the state law constraints, the court held

---

for interest, with assets in good condition and in value greatly exceeding the indebtedness of the district, and there was no sufficient showing as to why the district's tax rate could not have been increased sufficiently to meet the district's obligations.

It may be helpful in evaluating whether the requirements of Chapter 9 are met to review other cases applying the more stringent "fair and equitable" test. Where a court was presented with a dismal history and bleak financial future of a drainage district, it approved a plan for payment of 20 cents for each dollar of principal amount of the bonds. *Delno v. Market St. Ry. Co.*, 124 F.2d 965 (9th Cir. 1942); *see also Mason v. Paradise Irrigation District*, 326 U.S. 536 (1946) (52.521 cents on each dollar of principal). Also interesting is the decision in *Getz v. Edinburg Consol. Independent School District*, 101 F.2d 734 (5th Cir. 1939); which approved a plan pursuant to which refunding bonds that included accrued overdue interest were issued and 51 percent of moneys held in the sinking fund were permitted to be used to fund the maintenance of schools.

Of course, a plan cannot benefit some unfairly. Where some bondholders who purchased the bonds at bargain prices acquired an appreciable quantity of taxable property in the city, a plan that would result in the unjustified lowering of tax levies would not be approved even if creditors (who also are property owners in the city) would vote to accept the plan. *Town of Belleair, Fla v. Groves*, 132 F.2d 542 (5th Cir. 1942), *cert. denied*, 318 U.S. 769 (1943).

320 11 U.S.C. § 942.

321 11 U.S.C. § 930(b).

322 11 U.S.C. § 945(a).

323 11 U.S.C. § 1144.

324 *Matter of Sanitary & Imp. Dist., No. 7*, 98 B.R. 970 (Bankr. D. Neb. 1989).

that under the Bankruptcy Code, the debt of the municipality could be adjusted; therefore, the plan was not objectionable in this respect.

However, the new bonds and warrants to be issued to the holders under the plan received different scrutiny. The zero bonds had a call provision that permitted payment at less than par and permitted payments on the new warrants even if the bonds were taken out at less than par. In other words, the bondholders, as contemplated under the plan, could receive securities under the plan that would not be paid in full. Because of the state law requiring priority of the bondholders, the court held that such treatment was in violation of state law and the plan could not be confirmed. The case stands for the proposition that a plan can modify existing prepetition debt, regardless of state law prohibitions, but the plan cannot contemplate the violation of state law going forward.

Chapter 9 is one mechanism for resolution of disputes regarding the allocation of resources of a troubled municipality. It is difficult to achieve a consensual plan after a contested confirmation hearing. As a result, a debtor should consider negotiation with trade creditors, public debt holders and employee groups to work out the terms of the plan. To be confirmed, a plan must be fair. If creditors are unreasonably "crammed down" so that the distribution to public debt holders is less than justified, the municipality may find it difficult to have any plan confirmed. Further, the market will recall such unfair treatment the next time the municipality attempts to enter the market.

M. How Does Chapter 9 Differ from Chapter 11?

Generally, a municipality filing a Chapter 9 proceeding will be subject to a number of provisions that differ from those pertaining to a corporate debtor in a Chapter 11 proceeding. The following points highlight why a Chapter 9 proceeding is unlike a Chapter 11 proceeding:

- In Chapter 9, only the debtor can file the case;
- In Chapter 9, only the debtor can file the plan of debt adjustment;
- In Chapter 9, there is no Section 1113 criteria for sharing information with employee representatives or workers or any process of information sharing prior to rejection of union or employment contracts;
- In Chapter 9, there is no limitation on damages on real estate leases held by a trustee for a municipal building authority, and lease financing obligations will be treated as debt;
- In Chapter 9, municipal bond and note payments made to defease or make current payments on prepetition debt, even within 90 days of the filing, are not capable of being voided or deemed preferential;
- In Chapter 9, there are no priorities for prepetition wages, benefits, accrued vacation and health care benefits. There is no $12,475 per-employee priority claim;

- In Chapter 9, special revenues liens and statutory liens are not and should not be limited or terminated by filing a Chapter 9 petition, are intended to continue to provide payment to the secured creditors postpetition and are unimpaired by the Chapter 9 filing[325] (this is a significant difference from secured creditors in a Chapter 11 proceeding that have a lien on accounts receivable or inventory or pledge of a revenue source impaired and terminated upon filing a Chapter 11 petition under Section 552(a) of the Bankruptcy Code);

- In Chapter 9, a bankruptcy court cannot interfere with any limitation or requirement of state law regarding a municipality's exercise of governmental power and cannot impair or limit the power of its state to control the municipality's exercise of governmental powers such as to expenditures (payment of debt); and

- In Chapter 9, a municipality can sell assets, incur debt, borrow money and engage in governmental affairs without the necessity of having to obtain the approval of the bankruptcy court.

The following chart will further illustrate the differences between Chapter 9 and Chapter 11:

In a Chapter 9	In a Chapter 11
Only the municipality can initiate a Chapter 9 if authorized by state law.	The corporation (voluntary) or its creditors (involuntary) can initiate a Chapter 11 case if the corporation is a moneyed entity (not a non-for-profit) and insolvent.
Only the municipality can file a plan of debt adjustment.	The corporate debtor (during the exclusive period) or any creditor (after the exclusive period) may file a plan of reorganization or liquidation.
The plan of debt adjustment can only adjust debt. It cannot liquidate the municipality.	A corporate plan can be for reorganization or liquidation.

325 While statutory liens do not have the benefit of Section 922(d) of the Bankruptcy Code, which specifically excludes special revenues from the automatic stay, the state law mandated payment of the pledged revenues related to a statutory lien indicates the intention of the state that these revenues are to continue to be paid even in a Chapter 9 pursuant to a proper interpretation of Sections 903 and 904 above and the *Ashton* and *Bekins* cases. While some may contend that there is a stay on payment as to statutory lien debt in Chapter 9 since there is no language like Section 922(d), Sections 903 and 904, as noted above, can be read to provide that the court and the debtor do not have the power to impair, limit or interfere with such mandated payment.

In a Chapter 9	In a Chapter 11
A labor agreement can be rejected in a Chapter 9 if the labor agreement burdens the municipality and the equities balance in favor of rejection. This is a lower standard that a Chapter 11.	Section 1113 of the Bankruptcy Code sets forth the requirements for sharing information with employee representatives and workers and the process of information sharing, and the proposal by the debtor prior to the rejection of the labor agreement. It is a higher standard than Chapter 9.
There is no limitation on damages on real estate leases held by a trustee or municipal building authority for a lease financing, and the lease financing will be treated as a debt financing.	There is a limitation of the greater of one year's rent or 15 percent of the remaining terms of the lease not to exceed three years for lease damages in a corporate Chapter 11 filing. It is not treated as secured debt of the corporate debtor if it is a true lease.
Payments to defease or pay current interest or principal on bonds or notes within the 90-day preference period before a Chapter 9 filing are not capable of being voided or deemed a preference.	Payment of principal or interest not secured by collateral could be voided or deemed a preference during the 90-day period prior to filing a Chapter 11 if the holder would receive more than what it would be entitled to in a Chapter 7 liquidation.
There are no priorities ahead of unsecured claims for prepetition claims due to employee wages, pensions, accrued vacations, health care and other employment benefits.	There is a priority ahead of unsecured claims of up to $12,475 per employee for prepetition wages, benefits, accrued vacation and health care benefits.
Both "special revenues" and "statutory liens" are not limited or terminated by a Chapter 9 filing, are intended to continue to be paid to secured creditors and are unimpaired by the Chapter 9 filing and, as noted above, as to statutory lien. The intent is for continued payment pursuant to the statute even though there is no specific Bankruptcy Code section that specifically exempts statutory liens from the automatic stay other than Sections 903 and 904 generally (there is no Chapter 11 provision comparable).	Accounts receivable and inventory created postpetition are not covered by the prepetition lien of a secured lender, and the prepetition lien is terminated except for "proceeds" of the prepetition lien.

In a Chapter 9	In a Chapter 11
A bankruptcy court cannot interfere with any restrictions or requirements of state law regarding a municipality's exercise of its governmental powers (including payment of statutory liens). The bankruptcy court cannot interfere with the property, revenue and affairs of the municipality.	The corporate debtor cannot take any action outside the ordinary course of business without bankruptcy court approval.
The municipality can sell its assets, incur debt, borrow money and engage in governmental affairs without the necessity of having to obtain the approval of the bankruptcy court.	The corporate debtor cannot borrow money, sell assets or expand or contract its business without bankruptcy court approval.

N. The Current Challenge Facing Municipalities in Distress Is Determining the Recovery for Debt and Pension Benefits and Obligations That Is Sustainable and Affordable

The current challenge in Chapter 9 is determining the appropriate level of debt adjustment, including pension benefits, that will permit a municipality to prosper. In a plan of debt adjustment, creditors' recovery, including as to pensions, is a long-term obligation that needs to be addressed. As much as can be paid should be paid to meet previously promised obligations. However, unsecured debt obligations can and must be adjusted if the payment level frustrates the fundamental purposes of government, namely providing essential services that promote the health, safety and welfare of its citizens. Reductions should be based upon the municipality's realistic ability to pay and, at the same time, assure that the ability to provide essential public services and needed infrastructure at an acceptable level is not impaired. This is for the benefit of all. Creditors, including workers and retirees, rely on the continued success and growth of the municipality for continued recovery, including continued employment and pension payments.

It is in the best interests of all parties working on the recovery and future success of the municipality to determine what is sustainable and affordable, acknowledging that the resulting adjustment is simply a recognition of reality. Reasonable adjustment is to the benefit of creditors, including workers and retirees. If the municipality does not recover and continues to erode, there will be less money available to fund pensions, to keep workers employed and to pay creditors. Fair-minded persons obviously will regret that some promises made to creditors including employees were not attainable, realistic or based on any prudent notion of government. Rushing to pay unaffordable debt or unfunded pension obligations while crowding out payments for essential public services obviously can be counterproductive. To be viable, a plan of debt adjustment must include the notion of providing adequate public services for the continued survival of the government.[326]

1. Standard for "Feasibility" under Chapter 9

While corporate bankruptcy (Chapter 11) may judge feasibility as the ability to pay pursuant to the plan over the short term,[327] the standard for Chapter 9 should also include the assurance that the municipality can provide for essential public services at an acceptable level going forward, specifically in the foreseeable future. Following this standard should provide sufficient economic stimulation to grow business opportunities and increase employment, thus fostering growth of municipal taxpayers and tax revenues so the municipality will survive and, hopefully, thrive. The solution should be a permanent fix, not a Band-Aid. A court-approved debt restructuring that does not embody a recovery plan that provides for essential public services at the required level for economic growth and increased tax revenues for the foreseeable long term will be doomed to failure. The systemic problem that caused the financial distress to the municipality should be addressed and resolved in a recovery plan. If not, the problem may well reoccur to the detriment of all. If a plan of debt adjustment does not address the systemic problems that led to the Chapter 9, it will fail.[328]

2. Same Standard for Addressing Financial Obligations in an Out-of-Court Restructuring

The same test should be applied in an out-of-court municipal debt restructuring. The solution is not really filing for Chapter 9 and a plan of debt adjustment, but rather it is identifying a viable recovery plan. Whether outside or inside a municipal bankruptcy in Chapter 9, the legal issue of what is sustainable and affordable must be addressed and important public priorities must be established. The unavoidable conclusion in an out-of-court restructuring and in Chapter 9, as has been raised by the courts in the Chapter 9 of cases of *Stockton* and *Detroit*, is that recovery to creditors, including public pensions and public pension obligations, may have to be adjusted if they are not sustainable and affordable and if such obligations prevent the municipality from obtaining a fresh start.

Municipalities, especially large ones, need to develop a viable recovery plan and, either outside a municipal bankruptcy or within it, insure that the implementation of the plan results in reinvestment in the community via essential governmental services and needed infrastructure. Obligations can be

---

326 *See* James E. Spiotto, *How Municipalities in Financial Distress Should Deal with Underfunded Pension Obligations and Appropriate Funding of Essential Services*, 50 WILLAMETTE L. REV. 515 (2014), http://www.chapmanstrategicadvisors.com/media/publication/13_Chapman_Municipalities_in_Distress_and_Unfunded_Pension_Obligations_WLR_CSA_2014.pdf.

327 *See* 11 U.S.C. § 1129(a)(11)(2012).

328 The issue of who represents the taxpayers, the public in a municipal bankruptcy, has been raised. The Chapter 9 debtor itself through its elected officials should be protecting the interests of its citizens by proposing only a plan that will provide long-term economic growth and essential public services — a feasible plan. If the plan does not succeed, then the voters can decide at the ballot box whether their elected officials should be retained.

appropriately adjusted to what is sustainable and affordable, allowing the municipalities to invest in that which will help them recover and grow. Creditor obligations including pensions are not inappropriately impaired or diminished through implementation of such a plan because, realistically, all that can be paid is being paid.[329] The plan should determine affordable fixed creditor payments including on pensions (ideally at least comparable to the Social Security level or better) that would be guaranteed by a dedicated annual payment source and additional contingent payments that would only be paid if there were increased revenues created by the success of the recovery plan. If the municipality's finances improve, there will be more funding available to pay obligations, including pensions.[330]

In no event should a contingent obligation be one that casts a dark cloud over the ability of the municipality to succeed and thrive. In determining the priority of payment from tax funds that are available, it is important to recognize (i) the higher public purpose for assuring the future of the municipality, (ii) the mandate that essential government services must be provided at an acceptable level and (iii) the fact that the municipality above all must provide for the health, welfare and safety of its citizens through services that are both essential to its function and mandated by its purpose.

From the standpoint of workers and retirees, a resolution can be achieved that is better than what can be obtained in the best-fought litigation or under any other mechanism by recognizing that, together with the municipality, they must (1) determine what is sustainable and affordable to allow recovery and growth for the municipality and (2) develop how the municipality can stimulate and attract business and new jobs to the community. Through these steps, workers and retirees can advocate for (and, hopefully, participate in) a share of the new tax revenues to be used in fulfilling their future pension funding needs. In following this approach, the solution to underfunding can be identified. Namely, the price for the adjustment to what is sustainable and affordable is the hardwiring of creditor recovery funding going forward. The municipality must identify and dedicate a sustainable and sufficient revenue source for the funding of creditor recovery obligations, including pensions. For pension obligations, this will ensure that the municipality will not repeat the unfortunate scenario of balancing budgets by forgoing pension contributions and promising future pension benefits that are not sustainable and affordable. Instead, pension obligations are funded on an agreed-upon, ongoing basis from an agreed-upon source which the municipality is obligated to fund to ensure the payment

---

329 *See Faitoute,* 316 U.S. 502 (1942).

330 The creditor recovery (including pension obligations) could be split into the sustainable and affordable piece (a fixed sum payable over the years) and a contingent piece (payable if the recovery plan is successful and more revenues are available). In any event, the recovery plan should provide for periodic review and adjustment of non-liquidated variable obligations such as pension obligations for the continued survival of the government and the pension fund. Obviously, any suggestion of increases in pension benefits going forward would be tied to a specific source of funding so that, at all times, the cost of pensions is sustainable and affordable.

of the pensions.[331] Thus, the burden of unfunded pension obligations is not put on our children and grandchildren to the detriment of the workers, especially the youngest.[332]

O. Why, Historically, School Districts Have Chosen Not to Use Chapter 9 Bankruptcy[333]

1. Use of Chapter 9 by School Districts

Experience has shown that, historically, Chapter 9 has rarely been used by school districts. Only four school districts in the last 60 years have filed Chapter 9, and half of those dismissed the case for other resolutions.[334] No school districts have filed for Chapter 9 in the last twenty years. Since 1954, only four school districts for elementary and/or high school have filed Chapter 9, namely:

a. San Jose School District, California filed Chapter 9 on July 1, 1983 and the case was dismissed on May 8, 1984 without a plan of debt adjustment ("Plan") being confirmed;

b. Copper River School District, Alaska (filed in 1986, confirmed Plan 1988);

---

331 As discussed, our Founding Fathers recognized the importance of economic credibility for the nation, its states and local governments. Alexander Hamilton, the first Secretary of the Treasury, urged the young country to pay off the Revolutionary War debt of the federal government as well as that of the states. Further, he noted that the secret to making public credit "immortal" is that whenever public debt is increased, it should be accompanied by a sufficient tax increase dedicated to its payment. 6 HAROLD C. SYRETT, THE PAPERS OF ALEXANDER HAMILTON (1962); 18 HAROLD C. SYRETT, THE PAPERS OF ALEXANDER HAMILTON (1973).

332 A possible solution is the use of an independent, quasi-judicial structure at the state level (*i.e.*, a public pension funding authority) that would assist a municipality in sorting out the facts as to what is sustainable and affordable and then help the troubled municipality restructure its debts. Such a structure has been proposed by the Civic Federation of Chicago in its Illinois Municipal Protection Authority. *See, e.g.*, James E. Spiotto, *The Role of the State in Supervising and Assisting Municipalities, Especially in Time of Financial Distress*, 34 MUN. FIN. J. 1, 22 (2013), http://www.chapmanstrategicadvisors.com/media/publication/1_Role_of_State_Supervising_Assisting_Municipalities_in_Distress_%202011_MFJ_csa.pdf; James E. Spiotto, *Less is More: Lessons Learned from Detroit: Bankruptcy's Unfunded Pension Battles*, MUNINET (Aug. 21, 2013), http://www.muninetguide.com/articles/less-is-more-lessons-learned-from-detroit-bankruptcy-unfund-603; Mary W. Walsh, *Stepping Up with a Plan to Save American Cities*, N.Y. TIMES DEALBOOK (Nov. 11, 2013), http://dealbook.nytimes.com/2013/11/11/stepping-up-with-a-plan-to-saveamerican-cities/?_php=true&_type=blogs&_r=0.

333 *See* articles by James E. Spiotto, *Is Chapter 9 the Best Resolution Mechanism for Financially Distressed Schools or Are There Better Alternatives – Part One*, MUNINET GUIDE (Apr. 7, 2016), http://www.muninetguide.com/?p=134646; and *Is Chapter 9 the Best Resolution Mechanism for Financially Distressed Schools or Are There Better Alternatives – Part Two*, MUNINET GUIDE (Apr. 25, 2016), http://muninetguide.com/?p=134799.

334 There have been two other educational-related Chapter 9 filings in the last 60 years: Lassen Community College District in California in 1986, involving a community college that confirmed a plan of debt adjustment with a further amendment in July 1991, and Elliott School Building Authority, Colorado in 1992, which was dismissed without any plan of debt adjustment being confirmed. Since one was a community college and not a school district and the only Chapter 9 college filing in 60 years, it was excluded as an aberration. The other was a building authority that had its Chapter 9 filing dismissed in March 1993 and is not applicable here *per se*, to school districts given it dealt with building construction and not education.

c. Richmond Unified School District (filed in 1991 and dismissed in 1991 without a Plan being confirmed); and

d. Chilhowee R-IV School District in Missouri (filed in 1992 and confirmed Plan 1993).

One of the reasons Chapter 9 has rarely been used for school districts with financial problems is that the problems of school districts are more technical and complex than a debt adjustment. School district problems can be financial, operational or academic. Chapter 9 is merely a debt adjustment process with a stigma and consequences on future access to and increased cost of borrowing, which school districts need on an affordable basis to make capital improvements.

The experience of the San Jose School District in 1983 was that Chapter 9 had no benefit once teachers agreed to an affordable contract. In that case, after losing a labor arbitration with teachers, the school district filed a Chapter 9 petition, paid its bond debt throughout the proceeding and used Chapter 9 to renegotiate an unaffordable arbitration award into an affordable settlement with teachers. Upon settlement with its teachers, the San Jose School District promptly dismissed the Chapter 9. There was no benefit to it in being in Chapter 9 except as leverage.

Likewise, the experience of the Richmond School District was that Chapter 9 created more issues than it solved, and there are better solutions. The Richmond School District filed for bankruptcy in 1991 and threatened to close schools. The Chapter 9 debt adjustment process gave no power to the bankruptcy court to deal with operational or educational issues. Parents filed lawsuits to prevent the closing of any school, resulting in the dismissal of the bankruptcy and a $29 million loan from the state. Richmond School District has changed its name to West Contra Costa School District and has paid off its debt while benefitting from a supervised turnaround. The Copper River and Chilhowee districts were too small and rural to be good examples of any benefits of Chapter 9. Copper River School District had only 511 students, 8 schools (6 schools at the time of filing) and 37 full-time teachers with a student-to-teacher ratio of 14 to 1. The school district covers 25,000 square miles including Wrangell-St. Elias National Park. In the Chapter 9 bankruptcy proceeding, Copper River School District filed to reject the teachers' union contract due to an inability to pay salaries. In the plan of debt adjustment, the salaries of teachers were frozen and significantly reduced. The results in a Chapter 9 may very well portray the limited resources of the school district without further increase of tax revenues. Chilhowee R-IV School District had 164 students with 2 schools, 20 full-time teachers and an 8 to 1 student-to-teacher ratio. The Chapter 9 filing was caused by a judgment of $200,000 in favor of five former teachers against the school district. The school district had an annual budget of $650,000 in 1992. The school board had been assessing the highest levy that could be levied prior to the judgment, and the bankruptcy court ruled it was a good faith filing by an insolvent school district with little ability to pay or increase the levy for the school district. These rural school districts are no comparison to larger urban school districts and their problems.

2. The Problems of Using Chapter 9 for School Districts

No school district of size in the last 60 years has to date used Chapter 9 to successfully address its school district problems. For any school district of size, bankruptcy historically has been viewed as too simplistic a financial adjustment and not suited to address the multi-year oversight experience of school reform, especially as to operational and academic issues. This has been the experience of the multi-year local or state oversight in such school districts as (1) Philadelphia schools and its School Reform Commission since 2001, (2) Los Angeles unified school districts and efforts for reform over the last two decades and issues of local control, (3) the efforts of Cleveland to reform schools, including 2012 legislation, (4) Missouri legislation, as used by St. Louis or Kansas City schools, (5) the use of three oversight districts in New Jersey, (6) the use of an emergency manager for the Detroit district schools, and Michigan Heights and Highland Park schools with emergency managers in 2012, (7) nine school districts in California that required emergency loans from the state, including Richmond, since 1990, or (8) the use of financial oversight panels or independent or finance authorities in Illinois such as for North Chicago School District 187 Independent Authority, East St. Louis School District 189 Financial Oversight Panel and Independent Authority, Proviso Township High School District 209 Financial Oversight Panel, Cairo Unit School District #1 Financial Oversight Panel, Hazel Crest School District 152-5 School Finance Authority, Venice Community School District #3 Financial Oversight Panel and Round Lake Area School District #116 School Finance Authority. These situations indicate that school districts in distress require greater oversight but, in all cases, Chapter 9 municipal bankruptcy may not be a viable option.

The stigma of a Chapter 9 municipal bankruptcy for a school district would threaten the financial status of the community by raising concern about the education level of the workforce. Education is one of the pillars of economic development. Recovery is created by increasing economic activity such as business development in the community, which creates new good jobs. If the workforce is appropriately educated to fill those jobs, businesses will expand. Chapter 9 sends the wrong message. A pending Chapter 9 proceeding could prevent new business development and the creation of new jobs for school district graduates. The financial distress of Chapter 9 for a school district translates into the community not being a place where a business wants to expand or into which new business wants to move. Further, Chapter 9 could reduce the tax base and threaten the needed funding source for schools. Anything that impedes economic development and threatens and drains the full funding of essential services in the community may contribute to the increased likelihood that taxpayers will move out (as was the case in Detroit and in Bridgeport, Connecticut and elsewhere), reducing the tax base and funding source for schools. Further, Chapter 9 could be a distraction from efforts for school district reform. Chapter 9 and the controversies it can involve are time consuming, expensive and uncertain and can have a negative effect on a school district's ability to address operational and academic issues as well as financial concerns. Further, the cloud of Chapter 9 may cause the best teachers and employees to seek employment elsewhere before the situation gets worse. Those with skill and ability are the most likely to find new employment elsewhere. Likewise, those students whose parents can do so will look for a better, more stable educational provider, most likely in another community. No one looking to relocate will want to move into an ongoing and uncertain Chapter 9 bankruptcy of a school district. One of the major factors in the decision to locate in an area is the quality of the schools for both employers and employees.

Traditionally, school districts, which are of vital importance to local government, are refinanced and restructured under local or state supervision. The most tried and effective means of addressing school district financial, operational and academic issues are outside of bankruptcy on the local and state levels. Unlike Chapter 11, where the bankruptcy court has to approve any action taken by the debtor out of the ordinary course of business, such as new financings, settlements with creditors, any significant change in business operations, creating or modifying product models and sale or transfer of assets, including fixed assets and intellectual property rights, in a Chapter 9 the bankruptcy court's jurisdiction is limited to debt adjustment and the court cannot, without consent of the debtor, interfere with the municipality's (school district's) property, revenues, exercise of governmental powers or affairs (Section 904 of the Bankruptcy Code). Further, the municipality and the bankruptcy court cannot impair or limit the state control of a municipality (school district), by state legislation or otherwise, in the exercise of governmental power, including as to expenditures (Section 903 of the Bankruptcy Code). As a result, the bankruptcy court would not have jurisdiction over operations or academics, important factors in any recovery plan for a school district. Accordingly, Chapter 9 is not designed to deal with a school district's problems in a holistic manner. Chapter 9 is the wrong tool for the delicate job of correcting the troubles of a school district. Chapter 9 lacks the ability to bring new liquidity or tax revenues to a school district, and the limitations on the bankruptcy judge's jurisdiction prevents the court from dealing with operational and academic issues. Virtually all successful school district rehabilitations to date have been outside of Chapter 9 and have been in essence locally produced with support from the state.[335]

The ability to replace administrators or the school board and to adjust budgets, operations, personnel and academic standards locally is more effective than a bankruptcy court's ability to adjust debt. A school district is not only a financial matter but, more importantly, an operational and academic one, so the power to change the administrators or board may have a more beneficial effect than rearranging the pieces of debt. Giving a local oversight board the authority to approve or modify budgets, expenditures, hiring and firing practice, curriculum, operations and standards is a proven method of addressing a failing school problem. Chapter 9, by the limitations on jurisdiction of the court, can involve none of these necessary actions.

School districts require the ability to borrow funds at a low cost for needed capital improvements and interim financing of operations that Chapter 9 adversely affects or limits. Generally,

335 *See, e.g.*, Richmond School District's final resolution above.

school districts must borrow from the capital markets to fund uneven tax collections and capital improvements necessary to maintain quality education. Chapter 9 is a financial stigma that can increase future borrowing cost by at least 1 percent to 3 percent annually. Any economic benefit of Chapter 9 is more than overcome by the increased cost of borrowing for large urban school districts. Assuming refinancing or borrowing $10 billion to be repaid in 20 years with a bullet maturity, a 2 percent per year additional interest cost means $200 million more in interest cost per year or a net present value of $2.5 billion for 20 years at a 5 percent discount rate. That cost could make all the difference to a financially troubled school district.

3. The Various State Alternatives to Chapter 9 — Monitoring, Oversight, Intervention, Refinancing and Consolidation Take Over

Generally, each state provides for a variety of monitoring, oversight, intervention, refinancing and, if necessary, takeover or dissolution provisions for a distressed school district as an alternative to Chapter 9 and as the preferred and intended means of rehabilitating and assisting a school district. While each state may by its statutes and regulation fashion its own formula to address distress, there are some common themes. Most states provide for periodic monitoring of financial, operational and academic performance. Based on the results of monitoring, some states establish a watch list or group for further oversight on the local, county or state level with review of budgets and operations, using outside advisors or assistance from local or state agencies. If the situation is not corrected, the oversight and review become more intense, with the use of loans, grants and refinancing to address liquidity issues, and with the ability to prohibit non-salary expenditures, cancel purchase orders and require interim or additional financial reports or development of a recovery plan, often with the assistance of external or state consultants or advisors, all subject to school board and superintendent approval. If those efforts are not successful, then a more hands-on approach of the state replacing the superintendent or even replacing the school board, or consolidating or dissolving the school district, may be considered.

For the most part, states have a solid track record of success dealing with troubled school districts, many times building on the interactive and collaborative review and oversight process they have developed. This is best demonstrated by a quick review of a few approaches taken by some states.

California Approach. California has a multi-tiered process[336] of proactive (a) monitoring of periodic reports and fiscal operation policy, (b) support of technical advisors on local and state levels, (c) financial management from oversight to assumption of financial management and control over the local school board with the possibility of financing additional funds as needed, and (d) state administrative control with the state assuming leadership of school duties with a state-appointed administrator where the school board is advisory and with emergency loans from the state general fund. All of this is aimed at avoiding bankruptcy and replacing ineffective management.

---

336 CAL. EDUC. CODE § 1240 *et seq.* and § 42131 *et seq.*

Ohio Approach. Ohio passed legislation in 2007 and 2015[337] that reflects increased intervention efforts of states over school districts in distress. In 2007, Ohio established an academic distress commission to be triggered when the academic performance of a school district is low. There is normally a direct correlation between financial, operational and academic distress. The academic distress commission, once it has detected poor academic performance, assists the school district. The five-member commission has three members appointed by the state superintendent and two by the president of the local school board, with the chair designated by the state superintendent. The commission must adopt a recovery plan and has some additional managerial power such as reassigning or appointing school administrators, terminating contracts and developing a budget, but these powers are permissive, not mandatory. The commission exists to assist the school district in developing a recovery plan. The local elected president and school board remain in place, so there is potential tension between the board and the commission. The 2015 legislation gave the commission more power by allowing it to appoint the district's chief executive officer ("CEO"), with this CEO having full managerial power and control. It reduced the local school board appointments to the commission to one from two. Further, the commission will be responsible for expanding higher quality schools with additional funds being available from the state.

Illinois Approach. In Illinois, the approach is more *ad hoc* and local in nature through the Illinois State Board of Education.[338] Annual financial information is required with evaluation of the categories of risk. The State Board of Education can investigate and determine if a school district is in financial difficulty.[339] For school districts in cities of 500,000 or more inhabitants (Chicago), if the State Board of Education finds the district to be in financial difficulty it sends a letter to the governor and to the mayor of the city. For school districts of fewer than 500,000 inhabitants, the State Board of Education can provide further monitoring and oversight, including requiring a financial plan and compliance as follows. Distressed school districts are given technical assistance to determine whether a deficit reduction plan is necessary. If the district does not follow its plan or is still at risk, then the state may seek a financial oversight panel ("FOP"). While the school board remains in operation, the FOP may approve or veto all financial decisions. The FOP can petition the state for emergency grants and loans if needed. If the FOP is not successful in improving the school's outlook, the state can take stronger action such as consolidating or dissolving the school district or a more direct role in the management of the school district with a school financial authority or independent authority, which would include financial, operational and academic oversight. A school district with less than 500,000 in population that has been certified by the State Board of Education to be in financial difficulty is prohibited from incurring debt unless and until the board approves the district's financial plan.

337 OHIO REV. CODE § 3302.10.

338 105 ILL. COMP. STAT. 5/1B-1 *et seq.*

339 105 ILL. COMP. STAT. 5/1A-8(b).

Accordingly, while states may vary in approach, there is almost universal recognition that schools are so important and of such a sensitive nature that state and local monitoring oversight, refinancing and recovery assistance have generally proven to be the most effective means of resolution, especially compared to the virtually never used alternative of Chapter 9.[340]

4. The Detroit Public Schools: A Case Study

a. The Detroit School Crisis

A recent example of how state legislatures and states create distress resolution mechanisms in lieu of the less-favored Chapter 9 municipal bankruptcy for school districts is the effort of the State of Michigan to find an out-of-court method of resolving the long saga of the Detroit public schools. In 1999, the Michigan legislature, responding to allegations of mismanagement and poor performance in the Detroit public schools, removed the locally elected board of education. The legislature replaced the local board with a seven-member reform board. That reform board had six members that were appointed by the mayor and one member appointed by the state superintendent of public instruction. However, once the reform board was installed and began to take action, the reform board appeared unable to address the growing problems and increased deficits of the Detroit public schools, at least in the estimation of voters. In November of 2004, the voters of Detroit chose to return to an elected school board following the phase-out of the reform board. Unfortunately, with the elected school board, the fate and performance of the Detroit public schools did not improve. By the end of fiscal year 2008, the school district's deficit was $369.5 million, down from a $100 million surplus in 2005 and $200 million deficit in the 2007 fiscal year. The school district had $1.5 billion of debt in 2008.

b. Action by the Governor

Accordingly, the then Governor of Michigan, Jennifer Granholm, appointed an Emergency Manager for the Detroit public schools in January, 2009. In 2011, the new Governor, Rick Snyder, appointed a new Emergency Manager, Roy Roberts. However, by the end of fiscal year 2014, the Detroit Public School deficit had risen to $763.7 million with long-term debt of $2.1 billion. Thereafter, a new Emergency Manager, Darnell Earley, was appointed by Governor Snyder in January, 2015. In January, 2016, there were continuing concerns. Teachers raised issues about the health and safety of the schools. There were strikes and various sick-outs caused by the closing of various schools. At that time, a report on the Detroit public schools, which traced the history of Detroit public schools between 1842 and 2015, reported that, of the 554 schools that existed in recent history, their current status was: active 91, charter

340 For individual state information, see section VIII, 50 State Survey.

41, merged 7, repurposed 31, vacant 82, reverted 16 and demolished 186.[341] It was clear that a resolution of this growing issue was needed immediately for the sake of the students and city.[342]

c. The Response of the Legislature

The state legislature responded in the first half of 2016 by passing legislation that created a new separate school district that would take over the operation of the Detroit public schools and their property and educational mission without the burden of the past accumulated debt load, leaving the old school district responsible for the debt that had accumulated. In 2016, the school district had approximately $3.4 billion of outstanding liabilities, most of which were secured by means of a tax or state aid pledge. The legislature found, consistent with virtually every state facing a troubled school district, that the school district would not benefit from a bankruptcy as it would predominantly shift liabilities on to other governmental units and involve significant cost, expense and uncertainty. It was noted that, over the past decade, the Detroit public school system had reduced expenditures by over half, closed over 150 schools (62%), but it had not been able to keep pace with the nearly 70% decline in students. The accumulated annual deficits had led to a large buildup of debt, namely the $3.4 billion in 2016 from $1.5 billion in 2008.

The alternative legislation, which actually was a combination of a number of bills addressing various issues, passed the legislature in the first half of 2016 and took effect on June 21, 2016.[343] The legislature took that action based on the conclusion that bankruptcy was expensive, possibly costing $75-$100 million for lawyers, bankers and consultants, and would disrupt the district for eight to twelve months, if not more, and the process and results were uncertain. Accordingly, using the mechanism of creating and designating (1) the new school district for ongoing educational efforts and holding educational assets for operations and (2) the old school district for past liabilities appeared reasonable and appropriate. This same mechanism had been used in other distress situations such as the "good bank", "bad bank" used by the Federal Deposit Insurance Company in the 1980's and 1990's, the "good insurance company", "bad insurance company" relied upon in insurance company rehabilitations including certain bond insurers in the 2000's, and the "old company" and "new company" utilized in corporate restructurings. The legislation provided that the state would: (i) split the Detroit public school district into the new school district, charged with the mission of educating the students of the City of Detroit, and the old school district that would pay off the debt, both separate, distinct legal

---

341 *See* John Grover and Yvette vanderVelde, A SCHOOL DISTRICT IN CRISIS – DETROIT PUBLIC SCHOOLS 1842-2015, (Loveland Technologies, 2016).

342 Detroit Public School went from a student enrollment of 300,000 in 1966 to just 147,000 in 2015. A State of Michigan report noted that between fiscal year 2005 and 2015, student enrollment went from 141,100 to 47,200, and the number of elementary schools, middle schools, high schools, alternative education schools, special education schools and career technical and vocational center went from 255 in 2006 to 96 in 2015.

343 2016 Mich. Pub. Acts 192, 193, 194, 195, 196 and 197.

entities,[344] (ii) supply additional revenue sources for the old school district to pay its debts by a $72 million annual infusion into the Detroit Education Trust Fund from the tobacco settlements and, if needed, additional state appropriations after the tobacco settlement payments expire,[345] (iii) place the new school district under the jurisdiction of the financial review commission which had jurisdiction over the City of Detroit[346] thereby providing supervision of the financial operations of the school district and review of financial matters just as Detroit was subject to after the city's Chapter 9 exit, (iv) permit the Emergency Loan Board to authorize a loan up to $150 million to Detroit public schools,[347] (v) appoint an Emergency Manager to serve as a transition manager for the old school district and appoint a superintendent for the new school district,[348] and(vi) given the concern raised as to teacher strikes, tighten the restrictions on teacher strikes.[349] Following the tradition of other states in dealing with troubled school districts, the Michigan legislature formulated a means of supervision and oversight, addressed financial concerns by providing additional revenue sources and relieved the new operating school district of the concerns of past debt. Further, the legislature aided the old school district in addressing past debt by providing that the *ad valorem* tax levy for operation of a school district along with additional revenues would be available to the old school district for the payment of that debt under the new legislation.

d. Precedent for the Detroit School Structure

There was some reaction in the municipal market that creating an old school district/new school district formulation for an entity such as the school district that had issued a significant amount of bond debt raised concerns as to the impact on bondholders. While the idea of the creation of a new governmental entity to help resolve financial distress of an old government entity may seem unique, new and cutting edge, it actually has its roots in the distant past history of municipal finance. One of the first examples of a state legislature creating a new municipal government to solve the problems of financial distress of an old municipal government goes back to the late 1800's.

i. Duluth, Minnesota

The City of Duluth, Minnesota, in the late 1870's and early 1880's, defaulted on its bonds due to real estate speculation and promotion related to the creation of an eastern terminal for the Northern Pacific Railroad. Duluth, with a population of only 3,000 in 1877, had already piled up debt of $400,000. The Duluth default and financial distress motivated the Minnesota legislature to carve the Village of

---

344 2016 Mich. Pub. Acts 195.

345 2016 Mich. Pub. Acts 192.

346 2016 Mich. Pub. Acts 195.

347 2016 Mich. Pub. Acts 197.

348 2016 Mich. Pub. Acts 196.

349 2016 Mich. Pub. Acts 194.

Duluth out of the city territory and to create a new governmental body. The Village of Duluth had the entire business section, harbor, railroad depots, tracks and nearly all the dwelling houses within its boundaries. As noted by the federal court in addressing the bondholder challenges to the legislation, 19/20th of all taxable property and all the population except for about 100 persons were transferred to the new village.[350] This attempt to defeat creditors' rights by the creation of a new municipal corporation from the ashes of the old defaulting municipal corporation was met by the bondholder challenge asserting that successor liability for the debt must be imposed on the new village. The legislature did not provide for the payment of the city's debt by the village unless the creditors agreed to a drastic reduction in their claim, about 55%. Further, in order to defeat collection of the remaining debt from property left in the city (the old municipal corporation), the legislature provided that service of all summons and process against the city should be made on the mayor and that service made on any other officer would not be valid.[351] The term of the mayor ceased on the following April of 1877, less than two months after the passage of the legislation on February 23, 1877, and there was no provision made for the election of a successor mayor or for the filling of a vacancy. Further, no taxes could be levied without the affirmative vote of all four aldermen of the old city. The legislation also provided that the levy of taxes by St. Louis County was authorized provided all collections were paid to the new Village of Duluth.[352]

Ultimately, the federal court for the District of Minnesota, hearing a bondholders' complaint against the creation of the Village of Duluth, as a means of avoiding the obligations of the City of

---

350 *Brewis vs. City of Duluth and Village of Duluth*, 9 F. 747 (C.C. D. Minn. 1881).

351 This was not the only time that state legislatures and courts attempted to frustrate efforts of bondholders to mandamus tax payments. Also, in the late 1870's, the Tennessee legislature, in an effort to prevent a writ of mandamus against taxes levied to pay defaulted bonds of the City of Memphis, passed legislation to serve as an obstacle to such bondholder collection efforts. The legislature, in a combination of coordinated public acts in January of 1879, repealed the charter for the City of Memphis. In March of 1879, the legislature authorized the governor to appoint a receiver for the city. This was after the successful application by bondholders holding defaulted bonds for a writ of mandamus to have a lower federal court appoint a receiver for the city. As a result, there was, in March of 1879, both a state appointed receiver and a federal court receiver for the city. The U.S. Supreme Court eventually resolved the competing receiverships in the case of *Meriwether v. Garrett*, 102 U.S. 472 (1880). The Supreme Court ruled that a federal court of equity through its officers could not supplant the state's power to appoint a receiver or legislate over taxes to be imposed upon a dissolved city, since the creation of a municipal corporation was reserved to state and levying of taxes was legislative and not a property right. However, the Supreme Court ruled that the state appointed receiver and other agents of the state for collection of special taxes can be compelled by a federal court or other means under the law, as officers of a municipality, to proceed with collection of taxes and sale of property and to apply the proceeds to the federal court judgment. *Id.* at 520. These are some of the earliest examples of state legislative actions and mechanisms to address defaulting municipalities: namely old city and new Village of Duluth, City of Mobile and Port of Mobile and receivership of the City of Memphis. Similar other efforts by state legislatures to develop mechanisms to deal with the defaults of municipalities include: State Commissioners for adjustment, compromise and settlement of defaulting counties enacted by Alabama in 1882 and board of liquidators in Texas to collect and pay bondholders and creditors of defaulting municipalities established by state statute in Texas in 1887. HILLHOUSE at 324 and 325.

352 Hillhouse, pp. 74 and 75.

Duluth, found that while the legislature had the right to create the Village out of the territory of the City, as between the City and the Village, apportionment of the existing indebtedness was required if there were not ample resources left in the old City to pay the debt. The court ruled "both are liable to the extent of the property setoff to each respectively".[353] The court did note that, to the degree the legislature can provide that both the new municipal corporation and the old municipal corporation will have ample means to pay the debt each is responsible for, then the creditors would be required to look to that municipal corporation that is liable for its debt since there are ample means for payment and, accordingly, no need for the court to apportion the debt between the two.[354]

ii. Supreme Court Precedent

The U.S. Supreme Court, by the late 1870's, had recognized if a municipality has been abolished and its territory divided among other municipalities, then the creditors suffering a failure to pay by the old municipality may pursue their creditor claims against the newly created municipality for their equitable proportion thereof.[355] Accordingly, the success of any splitting of a municipal corporation into an old municipal corporation and new municipal corporation and having the prior debt reside in the old municipal corporation requires, in order to avoid successful challenges by creditors, the demonstration of the ample ability of the old municipal corporation to be able to satisfy the creditors' claims. If not, an apportionment of that debt can be made by the court rather than as designated by the legislature.

As noted in Section II, a similar effort was made in 1879 by the City of Mobile to create a new Port of Mobile to avoid the debts of the old City of Mobile. The City of Mobile petitioned the Alabama legislature in February, 1879 to repeal Mobile's charter and provide for the receivership of the city affairs. In a companion act, a portion of the former territory that was the City of Mobile was incorporated as the Port of Mobile and provisions were made for a new government. As with the City of Duluth and Village of Duluth, this effort by the Alabama legislature and the City of Mobile to resolve financial distress, again partially related to railroad assistance bonds, was not favorably received by the courts.

In the United States Supreme Court case of *Port of Mobile vs. Watson*,[356] the Court found that the Port of Mobile comprised about eight square miles of the seventeen square miles of the City of Mobile, and the newly created Port of Mobile covered all of the densely populated area of the city that was the taxable property within the old city. Of the $16,255,093 of taxable property of the old City of Mobile, only $900,000 was excluded from the Port of Mobile and about 14/15 of the resident inhabitants

353 *Brewis vs. City of Duluth and Village of Duluth*, 9 F. 747 (C.C. D. Minn. 1881).

354 *Id.*

355 *See Commissioners of Laramie County vs. Commissioners of Albany County*, 92 U.S. 307 (1875); *Broughton vs. Pensacola*, 93 U.S. 266 (1876).

356 116 U.S. 289 (1886).

of the City of Mobile were incorporated in the Port of Mobile. There was no apportionment of debt to the Port of Mobile. The Court found that the bonds issued by the City of Mobile were valid obligations of that city for which the city was bound by its contract to levy and collect annual taxes to pay the debt service on the bonds and that the assets of the remaining land that made up the City of Mobile, after giving effect to the legislation, was insufficient to be able to satisfy the debt service on the obligations. Therefore, according to the Court, there were not ample means for the City of Mobile to be able to pay the past obligations of the City of Mobile and, accordingly, the legislation apportioning the liability between the city and the Port of Mobile interfered with the contract rights of creditors of the city. Accordingly, the Port of Mobile, its successor, would be liable since "the [P]ort of Mobile has the machinery and officers requisite for the assessment of property, and for the levy and collection of taxes to carry on the city government".[357] Since the law of the State of Alabama purportedly took away the local court's power to honor a writ of mandamus that would require the Port of Mobile to pay the bonds issued by the City of Mobile, and since there was not a provision that was ample and sufficient for the City of Mobile, as redefined, to pay the outstanding obligations of the City of Mobile, the Court ruled that the liabilities as well as the rights against the property of the old city should accompany the new municipal corporation, the Port of Mobile, created by the legislature. This case reaffirms the precedent that, in any legislation created by the state to alter the boundaries of an existing public corporation so that there is a new public corporation that arises from part of the old public corporation's territory, and the old debt of the old public corporation is not satisfactorily apportioned so that there are ample resources to assure payment of that debt, that the court will determine that the new municipal corporation is the successor of the old. The court will either apportion the debt for payment or have the successor new municipal corporation be liable for the debt of the old.

e. Future of the Detroit Public School Structure

It appears the Michigan legislature has attempted, in its creation of a new Detroit public schools, to provide ample means for the old Detroit public schools, as redefined, to pay prior debt. The legislation provided that the property tax levied for school operating purposes pursuant to state statute would continue to be levied by the old Detroit public schools entity and a portion of tobacco settlement funds and possibly additional state appropriation would be available if needed in order to assist in the payment of the old debt. As a result, there was purported assurance of ample and sufficient resources to meet the old obligations. It remains to be seen if the bondholders will accept that apportionment without testing in court the sufficiency of the allocation. However, as noted, U.S. Supreme Court cases with regard to the division of an existing municipal corporation in order to respond to financial distress require ample resources in the old municipality burdened with the debt to assure bondholders they will be paid. It appears the Michigan legislature had such precedent in mind in constructing the recent legislation for the new and old Detroit public schools. Time will tell whether other states will follow the lead of the Michigan legislature in creating a new municipal corporation and old corporation to

---

357 *Id.* at 305.

address financial distress. In order to be successful they will have to follow the precedent of Duluth and Mobile as the U.S. Supreme Court has so ruled.

P. Conclusion

The above is meant to provide a general overview to bondholders and other investors regarding the effects of a municipal bankruptcy on the payment of principal and interest on bonds. Because of the complexities of the Bankruptcy Code, and indeed of the Chapter 9 municipal restructuring process, an attorney should be consulted regarding any specific questions an investor may have related to his or her individual situation.[358]

---

358 *See* James E. Spiotto, *Why Financially Distressed School Districts Have Wisely Chosen Not to File Chapter 9 Bankruptcy*, MUNINETGUIDE (Apr. 17, 2016), http://www.muninetguide.com/articles/spiotto-chapter-9-school-districts-.

VIII. 50-State Survey

Introduction — How to Use the Survey

The prior sections were intended to provide an overview of the elements of the 50-State Survey, including an analysis of defaults of state and local government debt; case studies of various significant past municipal financial emergencies, indicating the various events that trigger such problems; the state statutory and constitutional laws enacted to prevent default; the various state provisions regarding local government debt oversight, supervision and resolution mechanisms; a review of bondholder rights and remedies; and a brief primer on municipal bankruptcy. With this background, an analysis of the 50 states, Puerto Rico and the District of Columbia can be better understood. In conducting any 50-state survey, the question always comes down to how best to present the information to the reader. In consulting with various municipal analysts, members of credit rating agencies, institutional investors and government officials, we learned that these industry participants desired a breakdown into simple comparative categories. Accordingly, in the pages to follow, we have set forth major categories for each state, the District of Columbia and Puerto Rico, as an analysis of their laws and constitutional provisions, including: (1) Municipal Bankruptcy Authority, (2) Home Rule and Taxing Power of Municipalities, (3) Debt Default Preventions, (4) Mechanisms for Resolution After Default, (5) Remedies on Default and (6) Other Bondholder Protections (including whether there are provisions for special revenues and statutory liens).

We have, in addition, provided under each of these major categories further detail and sub-categories such as:

(1) Municipal Bankruptcy Authority. This category includes a description of and specific reference to any existing authorizing laws in the particular state or territory to file a Chapter 9 municipal bankruptcy petition, examples of the number of filings since 1980 and some description of the nature of those filings.

(2) Home Rule and Taxing Power of Municipalities. This category includes a description of the ability of a municipality in a particular state to self-govern — that is, the amount of control that a state's laws or constitution provide to a municipality to govern its own affairs, including issuing debt. In addition, this section includes a discussion of any taxing limitations applicable to a particular state's municipalities.

(3) Debt Default Prevention. This category includes a description of debt limitations in the particular jurisdiction and addresses the ability for municipalities in the jurisdiction to refund troubled financings. Additionally, this category includes provisions, if any, establishing oversight authority, including whether the jurisdiction provides oversight before a municipality may issue debt, requires annual budgets or permits the state provision of technical assistance to a troubled municipality. This category further

includes a review of whether the particular state's laws contain any provisions establishing terms for local government fiscal accountability authorities or any bond guarantees, back-up payment procedures or deficiency protections.

(4) Mechanisms for Resolution after Default. This category provides a description of whether the laws of the state in question permit any financial supervision, aid or assistance to local governments in financial emergency. This category, further, includes an analysis of any receivership, monitoring, fiscal manager and trustee provisions exist under the state's laws with respect to a municipality's finances. Additionally, this category offers an analysis of whether the particular state's laws include any provisions for revenue set-asides or moratoriums; whether there is state oversight, financial control boards, refinancing authorities, forms of coordination or recovery plan development; and whether the state's laws permit debt adjustment outside of Chapter 9.

(5) Remedies upon Default. This category contains a description of remedies available to a particular municipality's creditors, including whether creditors may pursue remedies against a municipality, such as seeking an accounting, bringing bondholder actions, filing for foreclosure, seeking injunctive relief, pursuing mandamus, bringing suits to enforce contractual provisions and other remedies.

(6) Other Bondholder Protections. Finally, this category includes a description of whether special revenues and statutory liens are available under statutory or constitutional provisions.

Keeping in mind the market interest in pledges of revenue or property that are special revenues or statutory liens, especially given the issues raised in the Detroit and Jefferson County bankruptcies, there is an expanded analysis of statutory liens and special revenues.[359] From a review of the various statutes in the 50 states, Puerto Rico and the District of Columbia, there appear to be different categories as to the clarity and effectiveness of the language that purports to create the statutory lien. The categories range from strong language that is clear as to the legislative intent to create a statutory lien effective and enforceable both in and outside of a Chapter 9 proceeding to other language that is

---

359 S&P GLOBAL RATINGS, "Statutory Liens: Not a Game-Changer, but a Possible Boost to Distressed Creditors in Bankruptcy States," Lisa Schroeer, Horacio Aldrete-Sanchez, Matthew Reining, and Jane Ridley. March 24, 2015; MOODY'S INVESTOR SERVICES, "Sector In-Depth: Local Government GO Pledges Vary Across States," Gregory Lipitz, Alfred Medioli, Sarah Jensen, and Naomi Richman, March 19, 2015; FITCH RATINGS, "Statutory Liens Do Not Boost Debt Ratings," Thomas McCormick, Amy Laskey, Arlene Bohner, Karen Ribble, and Michael Rinaldi, July 16, 2015; MOODY'S INVESTOR SERVICES, "Sector In-Depth: Local Government GO Pledges Vary Across States," Gregory Lipitz, Alfred Medioli, Sarah Jensen, and Naomi Richman, March 19, 2015; "Special Revenues' Opinion Boosts San Diego School Bonds, THE BOND BUYER, Dec. 1, 2015; KROLL BOND RATINGS, "Not all G.O. Bonds are Created Equal," Alessandra D'Imperio and Kate Hackett, April 18, 2013; Spiotto, Reducing Risk of State and Local Government Debt Obligation, Statutory Liens from Rhode Island to California SB222, http://muninetguide.com/articles/reducing—risk-to-payment-of-state-and-local-government-debt-740.

probably best described as providing an assurance that a pledge is effective and perfected outside of Chapter 9 and is exempt from any further filing or action under the Uniform Commercial Code. It should be noted that the application of these categories to specific statutes is not free from debate. Accordingly, these categories are used to illustrate the differences in language in order to stimulate further discussion and analysis and possibly motivate further clarification or legislative exposition of the lien as a statutory lien. Accordingly, as previously noted, we have divided the various examples of attempts to create a statutory lien into three main categories. They are:

1. SL-1. The language of the statute appears to strongly support a determination that it is a statutory lien.

2. SL-2. While the language of the statute may appear to create a statutory lien, further clarification would be helpful to reaffirm the intent to create a statutory lien.

3. SL-3. While the language of the statute may appear to create a statutory lien, it is insufficient and additional language is required to clarify the intent to create a statutory lien. The language could be read as just providing for perfection of a pledge or lien without the intent and effect to create a statutory lien.

The following analysis has attempted to be as complete and thoughtful as possible. At the same time, we recognize that, in matters such as statutory liens, there is always room for differences of opinion as to whether a statutory lien is created or whether other statutes should be included. Also, while we have attempted to identify the major examples in the statutes, we recognize this breakdown may not be exhaustive. Further, the purpose of this exercise is to be helpful in developing further market discussion of this topic and, as noted, if necessary, obtain *inter alia* legislative clarification by additional legislation or opinions of counsel as to the existence of a statutory lien. This analysis is intended to aid the institutional investors, municipal credit analysts, rating agencies, bond insurers and state legislators as well as local government finance officers in identifying where further legislative clarification would be helpful as to the intended existence of a statutory lien. While a statute does not have to say it is a statutory lien to be a statutory lien, market acceptance may be greater where there is language specifically stating it is a statutory lien and the force and effect of the statute are to create a statutory lien without any action required beyond the issuance of the respective bonds thereunder. The language of the statute should be clear that the force and effect of the words are to create a statutory lien that is valid, binding, fully perfected and enforceable, and senior to any other interests; it must also be clear that the pledged revenues or property cannot be used for any other purpose than payment of the pledged bond debt until the debt is paid in full. The statute may also provide for possible intercepts or third-party set-asides. Hopefully this review will result in greater clarity and assurance to the market as to an issuer's intent regarding when, how and why payment will be made both outside Chapter 9 and in Chapter 9. Further, this effort and analysis should lead to greater clarity in the disclosures relating to statutory liens and special revenues in the bond offering for such securities.

While these categories will be repeated for each state, whether a particular state permits or requires any of the items discussed above will be described in the text and in the endnotes that will contain references to applicable constitutional or statutory provisions. The final pages of this appendix include a pull-out chart, which will provide an overview of all of the categories addressed above, and some of the sub-categories, so that the reader may quickly assess a particular state's provisions addressing municipal finance and distress, on a comparative basis. The purpose of this appendix and concluding chart is to be a reference tool and a guide. As we noted, no 50-state survey is an exhaustive study and it cannot be anything more than an overview or compilation of continuing developing legislation and constitutional provisions. It provides some direction as to what is generally provided on a state-by-state basis, including the District of Columbia and Puerto Rico. As is evident, each state has developed its own formula for handling not only debt issuance, but also local governments in distress, what role, aid and assistance the state will provide and what remedies and alternatives investors may have.

A. Alabama

Municipal Bankruptcy Authority	Alabama law grants municipalities the authority to file a municipal bankruptcy petition under Chapter 9 of the Bankruptcy Code. The Alabama Code authorizes any county, city or town with bonded debt under Section 11-81-3 of the Alabama Code, including certain municipal authorities created in relation to playgrounds and other recreational and athletic fields organized under Sections 11-47-210 to 11-47-239 of the Alabama Code, to file a Chapter 9 petition. Unless an entity is specifically identified above, it is not authorized to file a municipal bankruptcy petition. In Alabama, ten municipal entities between 1980 and July 31, 2016 (with a total of 11 municipal bankruptcies because one municipality filed two petitions) have filed petitions under Chapter 9 of the Bankruptcy Code. Of particular import, on November 9, 2011, Jefferson County, Alabama filed a Chapter 9 petition in response to, among other things, the county's default on over $3.2 billion in sewer warrant debt. Of the municipal entities filing, seven bankruptcies were by cities or counties; two were municipal utilities; and two were special municipal units.[i]
Home Rule and Taxing Power of Municipalities	**Municipalities' Ability to Self-Govern** Alabama is a Dillon's Rule state, meaning that its local governments possess only those powers that are specifically delegated to them by state law. Before an Alabama municipality or local government may levy a tax, the Alabama state legislature must first approve the tax.[ii] In certain instances, the Alabama Constitution has been amended to permit counties and municipalities to levy taxes, including property taxes, special building taxes and certain taxes related to hospitals.[iii] **Taxing Limitations** The Alabama Constitution includes provisions limiting the amount of ad valorem property tax that a local government may assess against a parcel of property.[iv]
Debt Default Prevention	**Debt Limitation** No county in Alabama may have outstanding bonds that exceed 5 percent of the assessed property in the county. Further, no city, town or other municipal corporation with a population of less than 6,000 may become indebted in an amount exceeding 20 percent of the assessed property in the entity, except for construction or purchase of waterworks, gas or electric lighting plants, or sewerage, or for improvement of streets, for which an additional indebtedness not exceeding 3 percent may be created. Towns and cities with a population of 6,000 or more, and certain other towns, may become indebted not to exceed 20 percent of the assessed value of the property in the entity.

A. Alabama

Debt Default Prevention *continued*	For towns and cities with populations over 6,000, the debt limit does not include bonds issued for schools, waterworks and sewers, or street and sidewalk improvements where the cost is to be borne by the property abutting the improvement.[v] **Refunding Bonds** The governing body of any municipality may issue refunding bonds to fund outstanding notes. The refunding bonds cannot exceed 30 years and the amount of the refunding bonds cannot exceed the sum of the outstanding principal due on the original bonds, the interest accrued and unpaid, and the amount of any redemption premium.[vi]
Mechanisms for Resolution after Default[vii]	**Receivership** Generally, the Alabama Code allows for the appointment of a receiver with respect to revenue bonds where a default situation has occurred relating to bonds issued by a public body.[viii]
Remedies on Default	**Foreclosure** In certain default situations generally involving special revenue bonds, bondholders may foreclose on any mortgage or deed of trust related to the project.[ix] **Injunctive Relief** Certain provisions of the Alabama Code allow for injunctive relief or similar proceedings to enforce the payment of principal and interest on bonds where a municipality fails to make such payment when required.[x] **Mandamus** In certain situations, bondholders or their trustee may bring a court action to compel the local governing body to perform a ministerial action that it has refused to undertake, such as collecting taxes or fees where the underlying bond authorization requires such a collection.[xi]
Other Bondholder Protections	**Special Revenue Bonds** As provided by Section 922(d) of the Bankruptcy Code, payments to bondholders holding special revenue bonds would not be stayed on the filing of a municipal bankruptcy petition, and payments to holders could continue. Whether an issuance would qualify as a special revenue bond depends on the provisions of the authorizing statute with respect to the bonds at issue.[xii]

A. Alabama

Other Bondholder Protections *continued*	**Statutory Liens** Were a municipal entity to file a petition under Chapter 9 of the Bankruptcy Code, bondholders holding bonds to which statutory liens have attached would continue to receive payment on those bonds. For a statutory lien to apply, the authorizing law of the bond issue must contain such a lien. Category SL-1.[xiii]

i See ALA. CODE §§ 11-81-3 and 11-47-9. Specifically, § 11-81-3 provides: "the governing body of any county, city or town, or municipal authority organized under Article 9, Chapter 47 of this title which shall authorize the issuance of refunding or funding bonds" has the authority to file a petition under Chapter 9 of the Bankruptcy Code. The Alabama Supreme Court has determined that this provision of the Alabama Code permits every county, city, town and municipal authority organized under Article 9, Chapter 47 of the Alabama Code to file a petition regardless of whether the municipality has outstanding bonded indebtedness. *City of Pritchard v. Balzar*, 95 So. 3d 1 (Ala. 2012).

ii The Alabama Constitution provides that the legislative power of the state is vested in the legislature. ALA. CONST. art. IV, § 44. Furthermore, the Alabama Constitution provides that the state legislature has no power to authorize any municipal corporation to pass any law inconsistent with the general laws of the state. *Id.* at § 89. As a further matter, section 104 of the Alabama Constitution prevents the Alabama legislature from approving 31 specific laws, including: "Authorizing any county, city, town, village, district, or other political subdivision of a county, to issue bonds or other securities unless the issuance of said bonds or other securities shall have been authorized before the enactment of such local or special law, by a vote of the duly qualified electors of such county, township, city, town, village, district, or other political subdivision of a county, at an election held for such purpose, in the manner that may be prescribed by law; provided, the legislature may, without such election, pass special laws to refund bonds issued before the date of the ratification of this Constitution." *Id.* at § 104.

iii *See, e.g.*, ALA. CONST. art. XI, § 215 (allowing but limiting county property taxes) and ALA. CONST. art. XI, § 216 (allowing but limiting cities, towns, villages and other municipal corporations to levy property taxes). The state code is more expansive, and the Alabama Code should be consulted in determining whether a local government in that state has been authorized to take a particular action.

iv ALA. CONST. art. XI, § 217. This provision divides property in Alabama into four classes and, based on the classification, provides ratios of assessed value to the fair and reasonable market value of such properties for taxing purposes. In addition, the Alabama Constitution includes taxing limitations such as ALA. CONST. art XI, § 216 (Limitation on property tax rates of municipal corporations); ALA. CONST. art. XI, § 215 (allowing but limiting county property taxes); and ALA. CONST. art. XI, § 216 (allowing but limiting cities, towns, villages and other municipal corporations to levy property taxes).

v ALA. CONST. art. XII, § 224 (counties); ALA CONST. art. XII, § 225 (cities, towns and municipal corporations). Section 225, however, does not apply to the towns of Sheffield and Tuscumbia.

vi An example of a refunding bond provision under Alabama law is ALA. CODE § 11-81-4.

vii In 1839, Mobile, Alabama was the first reported municipal default in the United States. George H. Hempel *The Postwar Quality of State and Local Debt*, NAT'L BUREAU OF ECON RESEARCH, 1971, at 16.

viii For instance, in Jefferson County, Alabama, a receiver was appointed on September 22, 2010, to operate and administer the county's sewer system, due to the county's default on about $3.2 billion in sewer debt. Similar examples of provisions allowing for the appointment of a receiver on default include provisions related to bonds issued by a public athletic board (ALA. CODE § 11-59-10); public parks and recreation authority (ALA. CODE § 11-22-10); counties for industrial development (ALA. CODE § 11-20-6); revenue bonds issued by municipal power districts (ALA. CODE § 37-5-8); waterworks, gas, sewer or electric systems (ALA. CODE § 11-81-180); and district electric corporations (ALA. CODE § 11-50-529).

The state code may be more expansive than the examples presented here, and the statutory authority for each individual bond issuance should be reviewed before assessing whether such a remedy is applicable. Further, the state code should be consulted to determine whether any default is sufficient to trigger the appointment of a receiver or whether a default in payment of principal and interest is required to trigger this right.

ix In certain situations, bondholders may be entitled to foreclose on a mortgage or deed of trust related to a project. Provisions allowing for foreclosure include, but may not be limited to, certain bonds issued by public park and recreation boards (ALA. CODE §§ 11-22-10 and 11-60-11) and industrial development boards (ALA. CODE § 11-54-90). The state's foreclosure provisions may be more expansive than those examples presented here, and the statutory authority for each individual bond issuance should be reviewed before assessing whether such a remedy is applicable. Further, the authorizing provisions should be consulted to determine the type of default that could trigger this right.

x In the event of default of payment of principal or interest, holders of bonds issued by public library authorities may be entitled to injunctive relief (ALA. CODE § 11-57-20); *see also* ALA. CODE § 37-5-8 (allowing holders of bonds issued by public utilities to pursue injunctive relief). The state code may be more expansive and the statutory authority for each individual bond issuance should be reviewed before assessing whether such a remedy is applicable.

xi Generally related to revenue bonds, in certain situations, the Alabama Code allows for a writ of mandamus. Examples of such Alabama Code provisions include, but are not necessarily limited to, bonds issued for the promotion of industry, trade and pollution control (ALA. CODE § 11-54-25); by an industrial development board (ALA. CODE § 11-54-90); by public building authorities (ALA. CODE §§ 11-56-13 and 11-56-15); and by public park and recreation boards (ALA. CODE § 11-60-11); and by public library authorities in default on payment of principal or interest (ALA. CODE § 11-57-20); or revenue bonds issued by municipal power districts (ALA. CODE § 37-5-8). The Alabama Code is more expansive and an attorney should be consulted to examine any specific situation involving a default. Further, it is possible that an aggrieved bondholder could pursue a writ of mandamus even absent authorizing statutory law.

In relation to sinking fund payments, the Alabama Code allows for mandamus for the levy and collection and proper applications of taxes or for the setting aside and proper application of the sinking fund payments as required by law. ALA. CODE § 11-81-26. The court may only issue a writ of mandamus on proper proof of noncompliance with the law by any taxpayer or bondholder.

xii *See, e.g.,* ALA. CODE § 11-20-38 (industrial development board revenue bonds); ALA. CODE § 11-20-5 (project bonds); ALA. CODE § 11-22-9 (public park and recreation board bonds); ALA. CODE § 11-50A-19 (Municipal Electric Authority revenue bonds); ALA. CODE § 11-54-24 (project bonds for the promotion of industry, trade and pollution control); ALA. CODE § 11-56-13 (bonds issued by public building authorities); ALA. CODE § 11-57-11 (bonds issued by public library authorities); ALA. CODE § 11-58-7 (bonds issued by medical clinic boards); ALA. CODE § 11-59-9 (bonds issued by public athletic boards); ALA. CODE § 11-28-3 (warrants issued for public construction); and ALA. CODE § 11-81-166 (bonds issued by waterworks, gas, sewer or electric systems). These are examples of special revenue bonds. The state code may be more expansive and an attorney should be consulted to examine any specific situation involving a default.

xiii Category SL-1: *See, e.g.,* ALA. CODE § 11-28-3 (warrants issued for public construction). This is an example of a statutory lien. The state code may be more expansive and an attorney should be consulted to examine any specific situation involving a default.

B. Alaska

Municipal Bankruptcy Authority	Alaska does not specifically authorize its municipalities to file petitions under Chapter 9 of the Bankruptcy Code. As of July 31, 2016, and since 1980, the Copper River School District in 1986 is the only municipal entity to file a Chapter 9 petition in Alaska. This filing occurred before Congress in 1994 set further limits on municipal bankruptcy filings, including requiring that a state specifically authorize an entity to file a petition.[i]
Home Rule and Taxing Power of Municipalities	**Municipalities' Ability to Self-Govern** Alaska is not a Dillon's Rule state.[ii] Pursuant to the Alaska Constitution, all local governmental powers are vested in the boroughs and cities. The governing body of each borough may authorize the levying of taxes, charges or assessments within its service area and municipalities may levy their own property taxes, use taxes and mobile telecommunication taxes.[iii] In fact, the Alaska Constitution provides for "maximum local self-government with a minimum of local government units" and that the powers of local governments shall be given "liberal construction."[iv] **Taxing Limitations** A municipality may not levy any ad valorem tax for any purpose in excess of 3 percent of the assessed value of property in the municipality. These limitations do not apply to taxes levied for payment of principal and interest on bonds.[v]
Debt Default Prevention	**Refunding Bonds** If a municipality has outstanding general obligation or revenue bonds and the governing body determines it financially advantageous to refund the bonds, the municipality may provide for the issuance of negotiable or nonnegotiable refunding bonds. The refunding bonds may refund all or a part of the outstanding bonds before their maturity or redemption date and may include various series and issues of bonds.[vi]
Remedies on Default	**Appointment of Trustee** If the Alaska Municipal Bond Bank Authority defaults on the payment of principal or interest on an issue of notes or bonds and the default continues for more than 30 days, fails or refuses to comply with the provisions establishing the Authority or defaults on an agreement made with bond or noteholders, the holders of 25 percent in aggregate principal amount of outstanding notes or bonds of that issue may appoint a trustee to represent them.[vii]

B. Alaska

Remedies on Default *continued*	**Foreclosure** In certain default situations generally involving revenue bonds, bondholders may foreclose on any mortgage or deed of trust related to the project.[viii] **Mandamus** In certain situations, bondholders or their trustee may bring a court action to compel the local governing body to perform a ministerial action that it has refused to undertake, such as collecting taxes or fees where the underlying bond authorization requires such a collection.[ix]
Other Bondholder Protections	**Special Revenue Bonds** As provided by Section 922(d) of the Bankruptcy Code, payments to bondholders holding special revenue bonds would not be stayed on the filing of a municipal bankruptcy petition, and payments to holders could continue. Whether an issuance would qualify as a special revenue bond depends on the provisions of the authorizing statute with respect to the bonds at issue.[x] **Statutory Liens** Were a municipal entity to file a petition under Chapter 9 of the U.S. Bankruptcy Code, bondholders holding bonds to which statutory liens have attached would continue to receive payment on those bonds. For a statutory lien to apply, the authorizing law of the bond issue must contain such a lien. Category SL-2. [xi]

i Although Alaska law does not allow Alaskan municipal entities to file petitions under Chapter 9 of the Bankruptcy Code, in 1986 the Copper River School District filed a petition. The school district's plan of adjustment was confirmed in April 1988. As mentioned, the school district filed its petition before Congress in 1994 amended the Bankruptcy Code to require specific state authorization before a municipality would be allowed to file a Chapter 9 petition.

ii *See, e.g., Liberati v. Brisol Bay Borough,* 584 P.2d 1115, 1120, 19 (Alaska 1978).

iii ALASKA CONST. art. X, § 11 ("A home rule borough or city may exercise all legislative powers not prohibited by law or by charter."). The Alaska Supreme Court has held that the test derived from this provision is one of express or implicit prohibition, rather than traditional tests such as statewide versus local concern. *Jefferson v. State,* 527 P.2d 37, 43 (Alaska 1974). *See also* ALASKA CONST. art. X, § 2 (vesting local government power in boroughs and cities); ALASKA CONST. art. X, § 9 (allowing adoption or repeal of charter by any borough of the first class or city of the first class); ALASKA CONST. art. X, § 10 (allowing legislature to extend home rule to other boroughs and cities); ALASKA STAT. § 29.45.010 (allowing unified municipalities, boroughs and home rule or first-class cities to levy a property tax); ALASKA STAT. § 29.45.550 (allowing home rule and first-class cities outside boroughs to assess, levy and collect property tax); ALASKA STAT. § 29.45.650 (allowing a borough to levy and collect a sales tax on sales, rents and services provided in the borough); ALASKA STAT. § 29.45.700 (allowing a city in a borough to levy and collect areawide sales and use taxes); ALASKA STAT. § 29.45.750.

iv ALASKA CONST. art. X, § 1.

v ALASKA STAT. § 29.45.090. In addition, a municipality or combination of municipalities occupying the same geographic area may not levy taxes resulting in revenues that exceed either $1,500 per year for each person residing within the municipal boundaries or a value that, when combined with the taxable property in the municipality, equals the product of 225 percent of the average per capita assessed value of property in the state multiplied by the number of residents of the taxing municipality. ALASKA STAT. § 29.45.090. ALASKA STAT. § 29.45.100 provides that there is no limitation on taxes to pay bonds regardless of whether or not the bonds are in default or in danger of default.

vi An example of a refunding bond provision in Alaska is ALASKA STAT. §§ 29.47.300-29.47.340.

vii ALASKA STAT. § 44.85.310.

viii In certain situations, bondholders may be entitled to foreclose on a mortgage or deed of trust related to a project. Provisions allowing for foreclosure include, but may not be limited to, any default in payment due on a special assessment bond (ALASKA STAT. § 29.46.140), defaults on port authority bonds (ALASKA STAT. § 29.35.625) and defaults on bonds by the regional solid waste management authority (ALASKA STAT. § 29.35.825). The state code may be more expansive, and the statutory authority for each individual bond issuance should be reviewed before assessing whether such a remedy is applicable. Further, the authorizing provisions should be consulted to determine the type of default that could trigger this right.

ix *See Douglas v. Glacier State Telephone Co.*, 615 P.2d 580 (Alaska 1980) (recognizing that a taxpaying citizen may bring a writ of mandamus to force uniform collection of taxes). It is possible that an aggrieved bondholder could pursue a writ of mandamus even absent authorizing statutory law.

x *See, e.g.*, ALASKA STAT. § 29.47.240 (providing for the issuance of revenue bonds for a public enterprise or public corporation where the revenue of the project is the only security for the bonds). These are examples of special revenue bonds. The state code may be more expansive and an attorney should be consulted to examine any specific situation involving a default.

xi Category SL-2: While certain statutes contain language that may appear to create a statutory lien, further clarification would be helpful to determine or reaffirm the intent to create a statutory lien. As noted, some statutory language may provide for an effective and perfected pledge but not necessarily a statutory lien. *See, e.g.*, ALASKA STAT. § 29.35.635 and bonds issued by a Regional Solid Waste Management Authority (ALASKA STAT. § 29.35.835). The state code may be more expansive and an attorney should be consulted to examine any specific situation involving a default.

C. Arizona

Municipal Bankruptcy Authority	Pursuant to Arizona state law, any taxing district, as defined in the U.S. Bankruptcy Act of 1898, as amended, may file a Chapter 9 petition, but before filing, the taxing district must adopt an authorizing resolution. In its plan of adjustment, the taxing district is authorized by the state to (1) cancel in whole or in part, or remit or reduce, moneys payable under any bonds, warrants or evidences of indebtedness or other obligations of or issued by the plan of adjustment and (2) issue refunding bonds subject to certain constraints. The 1898 Bankruptcy Act defined "taxing districts" to include: any "municipality or other political subdivision of any State, including (but not limiting the generality of the foregoing) any county, city, borough, village, parish, town, or township, unincorporated tax or special assessment district, and any school, drainage, irrigation, reclamation, levee, sewer, paving, sanitary, port, improvement or other district." Section 80 of the U.S. Bankruptcy Act of 1898, which contained the definition of "taxing district," however, was found unconstitutional in the U.S. Supreme Court opinion *Ashton v. Cameron County Water Imp. Dist. No. 1*, 298 U.S. 513 (1936). Unless an entity is specifically identified above, it is not authorized to file a municipal bankruptcy petition. As of July 31, 2016, and since 1980, only four municipal entities in Arizona have filed a Chapter 9 petition, the most recent of which occurred in 1997.[i]
Home Rule and Taxing Power of Municipalities	**Municipalities' Ability to Self-Govern** Arizona is a Dillon's Rule state.[ii] The Arizona Constitution, however, allows the legislature to vest incorporated cities, towns and villages with the power to make local improvements by special assessment or special tax on the property benefited. The legislature may vest municipal corporations with the authority to assess and collect taxes.[iii] In addition, any city with a population greater than 3,500 people and any county may adopt a charter, as long as the charter conforms with the constitution and laws of the state.[iv] **Taxing Limitations** The state constitution generally limits the maximum amount of ad valorem residential property taxes to 1 percent of a property's full cash value, but this amount does not apply to taxes or special assessments levied to pay amounts due on bonded indebtedness.[v]

C. Arizona

Debt Default Prevention	**Debt Limitation** The Arizona Constitution sets a local debt limit for counties, cities, towns, school districts or other municipal corporations to 6 percent of the taxable property in the entity's area, without the consent of voters. With voter consent, for incorporated cities and towns, the debt may not exceed 15 percent, unless incurred for supplying the town or city with water, artificial light or sewers or for purchasing and developing land or interest for open space preserves, parks, playgrounds and recreational facilities, public safety, law enforcement, fire and emergency services facilities and streets and transportation facilities, for which the debt limit may not exceed 20 percent. A unified school district may incur indebtedness not to exceed 30 percent of taxable property.[vi] **Refunding Bonds** A county, city, town, similar municipal corporation or school district may issue refunding bonds when expedient to do so. Refunding bonds may not be issued to call or redeem outstanding, unmatured bonds unless the holder or holders of all or any portion of the bonds first consent in writing. Bonds refunded in advance of maturity, however, may be issued in certain circumstances.[vii]
Mechanisms for Resolution after Default	**Receivership** In certain situations, Arizona law allows for the appointment of a receiver with respect to revenue bonds where a default has occurred.[viii] **School District Receivership** The state board of education may review allegations that a school district is insolvent or has been grossly mismanaged. If the state board of education determines that a school district is insolvent or has grossly mismanaged its finances, the state board may appoint a receiver for that school district.[ix]
Remedies on Default	**Any Action Necessary** Holders of certain bonds may take any action necessary to compel performance on the bonds.[x] **Foreclosure** In certain default situations generally involving special revenue bonds, bondholders may foreclose on any mortgage or deed of trust related to the project.[xi]

C. Arizona

Remedies on Default *continued*	**Mandamus** In certain situations, bondholders or their trustee may bring a court action to compel the local governing body to perform a ministerial action that it has refused to undertake, such as collecting taxes or fees where the underlying bond authorization requires such a collection.[xii]
Other Bondholder Protections	**Special Revenue Bonds** As provided by Section 922(d) of the Bankruptcy Code, payments to bondholders holding special revenue bonds would not be stayed on the filing of a municipal bankruptcy petition, and payments to holders could continue. Whether an issuance would qualify as a special revenue bond depends on the provisions of the authorizing statute with respect to the bonds at issue.[xiii] **Statutory Liens** Were a municipal entity to file a petition under Chapter 9 of the Bankruptcy Code, bondholders holding bonds to which statutory liens have attached would continue to receive payment on those bonds. For a statutory lien to apply, the authorizing law of the bond issue must contain such a lien. No statutes covered by the categories were identified.

---

i ARIZ. REV. STAT. §§ 35-601, 35-603, 35-604 and 35-607. Of the four municipalities filing municipal bankruptcy petitions in Arizona since 1980, three petitions were filed by special municipal districts and one petition was filed by a city. *See also* Bankruptcy Act of 1989, Ch. 9, sec. 80(a), 48 Stat. 798 (1934) (definition of "taxing district").

It is important to note that the current version of the Bankruptcy Code does not contain a definition of the term "taxing district," and this definition was included in provisions found unconstitutional by the U.S. Supreme Court in *Ashton v. Cameron County Water Imp. Dist. No. 1*, 298 U.S. 513 (1936). As was stated by one court in Idaho, whose statutes also incorporate the definition of "taxing district" into the provisions authorizing municipal bankruptcy petitions: "The current Bankruptcy Code lacks a definition of 'taxing district.' Instead…it uses the term 'municipality' to describe those entities that may seek relief under chapter 9, provided that they are authorized to do so under state law. This raises questions regarding the interpretation and effect of [the Idaho Code]. For example, does [the Idaho Code] continue to incorporate by reference the description of 'taxing district' contained in the now-repealed Bankruptcy Act of 1898, does it somehow embrace the definition of 'municipality' in the current version of the Code, or is the definition of 'taxing district' for purposes of [Idaho law] left open-ended or untethered due to the repeal of the Bankruptcy Act?" *In re Boise County, Idaho*, 465 Br. 156, 167 (Bankr. D. Id. 2011) (presenting questions, but finding court need not answer because the county was ineligible to file a Chapter 9 petition on other grounds). With respect to the Arizona statute, the same questions could be presented in any challenge. It should be noted, however, that Arizona provisions were adopted by the Arizona legislature in 1935, before the provision containing the definition of "taxing district" in the Bankruptcy Act was declared unconstitutional.

ii *See Bonito Partners LLC v. City of Flagstaff*, 229 Ariz. 75, 82-83 (Ariz. 2012) ("A municipal corporation has 'no inherent power. Instead, '[a] city can exercise only such powers as are delegated to it by the Constitution and the laws of the state and its charter'" (internal citations omitted)). The Arizona court in *Bonito Partners* further noted, "the powers derived by a municipality from its charter are three-fold: those granted in express words, those fairly implied in the powers expressly granted, and those essential to the accomplishment of the declared objects and purposes of the corporation — not simply convenient, but indispensable." *Id.* at 83.

iii ARIZ. CONST. art. IX, § 6.

iv ARIZ. CONST. art. XIII, § 2 (cities); ARIZ. CONST. art. XII, § 7 (counties).

v ARIZ. CONST. art. IX, § 18.

vi ARIZ. CONST. art. IX, §§ 8 and 8.1.

vii An example of a refunding bond provision in Arizona law is ARIZ. REV. STAT. §§ 35-471 to 35-475 (refunding county and other municipal indebtedness). The Arizona Code, further, contains provisions for refunding certain special revenue bond issuances, such as improvement bonds. ARIZ. REV. STAT. §§ 48-651 to 48-662.

viii *See, e.g.,* ARIZ. REV. STAT. § 35-724 (industrial development bonds), ARIZ. REV. STAT. § 35-822 (pollution control bonds) and ARIZ. REV. STAT. § 3-1010 (Arizona coliseum and exposition center, if bond resolution so provides). These are examples of situations in which the Arizona Code allows for the appointment of a receiver. The Arizona Code may be more expansive and an attorney should be consulted to examine any specific situation involving a default.

ix *See* ARIZ. REV. STAT. § 15-103. This provision contains seven factors that a state board of education may use to determine if a school district is insolvent, including the school district defaulting in payment of its bonds or interest on bonds. The provision also includes a detailed list of duties that a receiver may perform and requires the receiver to begin a full review and investigation of the school district's financial affairs and submit to the state board of education a detailed report of findings and a financial improvement plan and budget detailing how the school district will eliminate any continuing gross financial mismanagement and achieve financial solvency. The report must be submitted within 120 days after the receiver's appointment.

x Holders of tax anticipation notes (ARIZ. REV. STAT. § 35-465.07), grant anticipation notes (ARIZ. REV. STAT. § 35-466.07) and revenue anticipation notes (ARIZ. REV. STAT. § 35-467.07) may take any action necessary to compel performance of any duty under the provisions governing those notes. The state code may be more expansive than those examples presented here, and the statutory authority for each individual bond issuance should be reviewed before assessing available remedies. Further, the authorizing provisions should be consulted to determine the type of default that could trigger this right.

xi *See, e.g.,* ARIZ. REV. STAT. § 35-724 (industrial development bonds) and ARIZ. REV. STAT. § 35-822 (pollution control bonds). These are examples of situations in which the Arizona Code allows for foreclosure. The Arizona Code may be more expansive and an attorney should be consulted to examine any specific situation involving a default.

xii *See, e.g.,* ARIZ. REV. STAT. § 35-724 (industrial development bonds) and ARIZ. REV. STAT. § 35-822 (pollution control bonds). These are examples of situations where the Arizona Code allows for a writ of mandamus. The Arizona Code may be more expansive and an attorney should be consulted to examine any specific situation involving a default. Further, it is possible that an aggrieved bondholder could pursue a writ of mandamus even absent authorizing statutory law.

xiii Examples of special revenue bonds under Arizona law include industrial development board bonds (ARIZ. REV. STAT. § 35-724) and pollution control bonds (ARIZ. REV. STAT. § 35-822). These are examples of special revenue bonds. The state code may be more expansive and an attorney should be consulted to examine any specific situation involving a default.

D. Arkansas

Municipal Bankruptcy Authority	Any and all taxing agencies and instrumentalities acting through their governing boards may file a petition under Chapter 9 of the Bankruptcy Code. Such taxing agencies and instrumentalities include drainage, drainage and levee, levee, reclamation, water, irrigation or similar districts; local improvement districts such as road, highway or similar districts; public school districts or authorities; local improvement districts such as port, navigation or other similar districts; and any city, town, village, borough, township or other municipality. Unless an entity is specifically identified above, it is not authorized to file a municipal bankruptcy petition. Between 1980 and July 31, 2016, 13 municipal entities in Arkansas have filed municipal bankruptcy petitions under the Bankruptcy Code.[i]
Home Rule and Taxing Power of Municipalities	**Municipalities' Ability to Self-Govern** Arkansas is a Dillon's Rule state, but Dillon's Rule does not apply to the municipal affairs of cities of the first class. A municipality may perform any function and exercise full legislative power in any and all matters pertaining to its municipal affairs, including the power to tax.[ii] **Taxing Limitations** No county in Arkansas may levy a tax exceeding 1/2 of 1 percent for all purposes. Municipal corporations may not levy any tax on real or personal property in one year greater than 5 mills on the dollar.[iii]
Debt Default Prevention	**Debt Limitation** A county may not incur debt secured by a tax on real or personal property exceeding 10 percent of the total assessed value for tax purposes of real and personal property in the county, and a municipality may not issue debt exceeding 20 percent of the same. Industrial development bonds are not included in the calculation.[iv] **Refunding Bonds** Any county may refund its outstanding bonded indebtedness on terms it deems best for the county. A county judge may also exchange refunding bonds for the outstanding bonds of the county. The refunding bonds may not be issued in a greater amount or at a higher interest rate than the bonds being refunded and must mature over a period of not more than 40 years from the date issued. In addition, any municipality owning and operating a waterworks facility may issue bonds to refinance existing debt and any city of the first or second class may issue refunding bonds.[v]

D. Arkansas

Mechanisms for Resolution after Default	**Appointment of an Assessor** In certain situations, Arkansas law allows for the appointment of an assessor to reassess the benefits of a bond issuance. Such provisions are triggered after a payment default lasting longer than 60 days.[vi] **Receivership** In certain situations, Arkansas law allows for the appointment of a receiver with respect to revenue bonds where a default has occurred.[vii]
Remedies on Default	**Mandamus** In certain situations, bondholders or their trustee may bring a court action to compel the local governing body to perform a ministerial action that it has refused to undertake, such as collecting taxes or fees where the underlying bond authorization so requires.[viii]
Other Bondholder Protections	**Special Revenue Bonds** As provided by Section 922(d) of the Bankruptcy Code, payments to bondholders holding special revenue bonds would not be stayed on the filing of a municipal bankruptcy petition, and payments to holders could continue. Whether an issuance would qualify as a special revenue bond depends on the provisions of the authorizing statute with respect to the bonds at issue.[ix] **Statutory Liens** Were a municipal entity to file a petition under Chapter 9 of the Bankruptcy Code, bondholders holding bonds to which statutory liens have attached would continue to receive payment on those bonds. For a statutory lien to apply, the authorizing law of the bond issue must contain such a lien. Category SL-2.[x]

---

i ARK. CODE ANN. §§ 14-74-102 and 14-74-103.

ii ARK. CODE ANN. § 14-43-602 (inapplicability of Dillon's Rule to Cities of the First Class). Cities of the First Class include all cities with a population exceeding 2,500 as of the last federal census. ARK. CODE ANN. § 14-37-104. Although Dillon's Rule appears to be a viable concept in Arkansas, the Arkansas Supreme Court has chosen not to address the validity of the rule for cities outside of Cities of the First Class. *See Paragould Cablevisions Inc. v. City of Paragould*, 305 Ark. 476, 484 (Ark. 1991).

iii ARK. CONST. art. 16, § 9 (counties); ARK. CONST. art. 12, § 4 (municipal corporations). The Arkansas Constitution contains other similar measures, for instance: ARK. CONST. am. 32, § 1 (a tax for a county or city public hospital may not exceed one mill on the dollar of the assessed value of real and personal property in the county); ARK. CONST. am. 38, § 1 (county library tax may not exceed 5 mills on the dollar); ARK. CONST. 38, § 5 (tax for capital improvements or construction may not exceed 3 mills on the dollar); ARK. CONST. am. 61 (county road tax may not exceed 3 mills on the dollar); ARK. CONST. am. 62, § 1 (local capital improvement bonds may not exceed 5 mills on the dollar of taxable real and personal property in the district); and ARK. CONST. am. 31, § 1 (tax levy may not exceed 2 mills on the dollar for police and firefighters' retirement salaries and pensions).

iv ARK. CONST. am. 62, § 1.

v An example of a refunding bond provision in Arkansas law is ARK. CODE ANN. §§ 14-72-201 through 14-72-205. In addition, any municipality owning and operating a waterworks facility may issue bonds to refinance or retire existing debt related to the waterworks system. ARK. CODE ANN. § 14-234-104. Further, ARK. CODE ANN. §§ 14-72-503 through 14-72-504 allow for the issuance of refunding bonds, but the bonds may not be in a greater amount or bear a higher interest rate than the bonds being refunded. *See also* ARK. CODE ANN. § 14-74-104 (allowing taxing authorities to refund debt).

vi *See* ARK. CODE ANN. § 14-89-302 (municipal improvement districts, allowing for the appointment of an assessor to reassess benefits if the bonds have not been paid within 60 days after maturity); ARK. CODE ANN. § 14-92-235 (suburban improvement district bonds); ARK. CODE ANN. § 14-93-126 (property owners' improvement district); and ARK. CODE ANN. § 14-94-125 (municipal property owners' improvement district).

vii Examples of statutes allowing for the appointment of a receiver on default include: ARK. CODE ANN. § 14-57-609 (parking meter revenues, allowing for a receiver to charge and collect rates sufficient to pay bonds and operating expenses); ARK. CODE ANN. § 14-92-235 (suburban improvement district bonds, allowing for appointment of a receiver to collect taxes); ARK. CODE ANN. § 14-93-126 (property owners' improvement district); ARK. CODE ANN. § 14-94-125 (municipal property owners' improvement district); ARK. CODE ANN. § 14-116-704 (regional water distribution district act); ARK. CODE ANN. § 14-117-418 (irrigation, drainage and watershed improvement district); ARK. CODE ANN. § 14-120-243 (drainage and levee improvement districts); ARK. CODE ANN. § 14-121-442 (drainage improvement districts); ARK. CODE ANN. § 14-125-806 (conservation districts); ARK. CODE ANN. § 14-137-122 (public facilities boards); ARK. CODE ANN. § 14-138-117 (public corporations for municipal facilities); ARK. CODE ANN. § 14-138-122 (public corporations and municipal facilities); ARK. CODE ANN. § 14-139-110 (municipal exhibition grounds and buildings); ARK. CODE ANN. § 14-140-209 (public marketplaces in cities and towns); ARK. CODE ANN. § 14-269-110 (acquisition, construction and maintenance of recreational facilities); ARK. CODE ANN. § 14-143-118 (regional intermodal facilities); ARK. CODE ANN. § 14-144-309 (research park authority); ARK. CODE ANN. § 14-164-221 (municipalities' and counties' industrial development revenue bonds); ARK. CODE ANN. § 14-164-521 (economic industrial development revenue bonds); ARK. CODE ANN. § 14-164-217 (energy conservation and renewable energy resource financing); ARK. CODE ANN. § 14-169-233 (housing authorities); ARK. CODE ANN. § 14-169-1007 (surplus federal housing facilities); ARK. CODE ANN. § 14-170-211 (tourism revenue bonds); ARK. CODE ANN. § 14-185-137 (metropolitan port authority facilities); ARK. CODE ANN. § 14-186-311 (metropolitan port authority facilities); ARK. CODE ANN. § 14-186-413 (joint operation of ports by municipalities and counties); ARK. CODE ANN. § 14-188-115 (rural development authorities); ARK. CODE ANN. § 14-201-120 (municipal boards and commissions); ARK. CODE ANN. § 14-202-115 (joint municipal electric power generation); ARK. CODE ANN. § 14-203-114 (municipal electric system financing); ARK. CODE ANN. § 14-204-109 (municipal and county hydroelectric development); ARK. CODE ANN. § 14-217-112 (general consolidated public utility system improvement districts); ARK. CODE ANN. § 14-232-108 (refuse disposal); ARK. CODE ANN. § 14-233-111 (joint county and municipal solid waste disposal); ARK. CODE ANN. § 14-234-208 (waterworks and water supply); ARK. CODE ANN. § 14-234-515 (waterworks and water supply joint systems); ARK. CODE ANN. § 14-235-220 (municipal sewage systems); ARK. CODE ANN. § 14-238-118 (rural waterworks facilities boards); ARK. CODE ANN. § 14-265-109 (health care facilities); ARK. CODE ANN. § 14-267-111 (pollution control facilities); ARK. CODE ANN. § 14-269-110 (acquisition, construction and maintenance of recreational facilities); ARK. CODE ANN. § 14-303-508 (tollway revenue bonds); ARK. CODE ANN. § 14-317-114 (rural road improvement districts); ARK. CODE ANN. § 14-319-102 (county bridge improvement districts); ARK. CODE ANN. § 14-320-115 (Interstate Bridge Districts); ARK. CODE ANN. § 14-360-309 (municipal airport improvements); and ARK. CODE ANN. § 14-362-118 (regional airports). The state code may be more expansive and the statutory authority for each individual bond issuance should be reviewed before assessing whether a receiver may be appointed.

viii *See, e.g.*, ARK. CODE ANN. § 14-92-235 (suburban improvement district bonds); ARK. CODE ANN. § 14-93-126 (property owners' improvement districts); ARK. CODE ANN. § 14-94-125 (municipal property owners' improvement districts); ARK. CODE ANN. § 14-121-442 (drainage improvement districts); ARK. CODE ANN. § 14-138-117 (public corporations for municipal facilities); ARK. CODE ANN. § 14-138-122 (public corporations and municipal facilities); ARK. CODE ANN. § 14-303-507 (tollway revenue bonds); and ARK. CODE ANN. § 14-320-115 (interstate bridge districts). It is possible that an aggrieved bondholder could pursue a writ of mandamus even absent authorizing statutory law.

ix Examples of special revenue bonds include: ARK. CODE ANN. § 14-92-235 (suburban improvement district bonds); ARK. CODE ANN. § 14-93-126 (property owners' improvement districts); ARK. CODE ANN. § 14-94-125 (municipal property owners' improvement districts); ARK. CODE ANN. § 14-116-704 (regional water distribution districts); ARK. CODE ANN. § 14-121-442 (drainage improvement districts); ARK. CODE ANN. § 14-122-208 (municipal drainage improvement districts); ARK. CODE ANN. § 14-125-806 (conservation districts); ARK. CODE ANN. § 14-139-110 (municipal exhibition grounds and buildings); ARK. CODE ANN. § 14-140-209 (public marketplaces in cities and towns); ARK. CODE ANN. § 14-169-1007 (surplus federal housing facilities); ARK. CODE ANN. § 14-170-211 (tourism revenue bonds); ARK. CODE ANN. § 14-186-311 (municipal port authority facilities); ARK. CODE ANN. §14-186-413 (joint operation of ports by municipalities and counties); ARK. CODE ANN. § 14-204-109 (municipal and county hydroelectric power development); ARK. CODE ANN. § 14-234-208 (waterworks and water supply systems); ARK. CODE ANN. § 14-234-515 (waterworks and water supply joint systems); ARK. CODE ANN. § 14-238-118 (rural waterworks facilities boards); ARK. CODE ANN. § 14-265-109 (health care facilities); and ARK. CODE ANN. § 14-320-115 (interstate bridge districts). These are examples of special revenue bonds and the state code may be more expansive. An attorney should be consulted to examine any specific situation.

x Category SL-2: *See, e.g.*, ARK. CODE ANN. § 14-92-235 (suburban improvement district bonds secured by lien on all benefited real property); ARK. CODE ANN. § 14-93-126 (property owners' improvement district bonds secured by lien on real property located in district); ARK. CODE ANN. § 14-116-704 (regional water distribution district bonds secured by lien on benefited land); ARK. CODE ANN. § 14-121-442 (drainage improvement district bonds secured by lien on all lands, railroad and tramroads in the district); ARK. CODE ANN. § 14-122-208 (municipal drainage improvement district bonds secured by lien on assessments levied against the real property in district); ARK. CODE ANN. § 14-125-806 (conservation district bonds secured by lien on all benefited lands of project area); ARK. CODE ANN. § 14-139-110 (municipal exhibition grounds and building bonds secured with statutory mortgage lien on exhibition grounds and buildings); ARK. CODE ANN. § 14-140-209 (public marketplaces in cities and towns bonds secured with statutory mortgage lien); ARK. CODE ANN. § 14-169-1007 (statutory mortgage lien securing bonds issued in relation to surplus federal housing facilities); and ARK. CODE ANN. § 14-186-413 (statutory mortgage lien on ports constructed from proceeds of bonds issued under the provisions of the joint operation of ports by municipalities and counties provisions). While the language of these statutes may appear to create a statutory lien, further clarification would be helpful by reaffirming legislation or opinion of counsel to determine or reaffirm the statutory lien created. These are examples of possible statutory liens bonds and the state code may be more expansive. An attorney should be consulted to examine any specific situation.

E. California

Municipal Bankruptcy Authority	Any county, city, district, public authority, public agency or other entity, without limitation, other than a school district, that is a "municipality" as defined under the Bankruptcy Code or that qualifies as a debtor under any other federal bankruptcy law applicable to local public entities may file a petition under Chapter 9 of the Bankruptcy Code. Unless an entity is specifically identified above, it is not authorized to file a municipal bankruptcy petition.[i] A municipality, as identified in the previous paragraph, may file a petition only if it meets one of two conditional options. The first option is that the municipality participate in a "neutral evaluation process," otherwise known as mandatory mediation, with interested parties. If the process does not resolve all pending disputes with creditors, the municipality may file a Chapter 9 petition. A neutral evaluation process may not last more than 60 days from the date a neutral evaluator is chosen, unless the municipality or a majority of participating interested parties elect to extend the process for up to an additional 30 days. The neutral evaluation process shall not last for more than 90 days following the date the evaluator is selected unless the local public entity and majority of interested parties agree to an extension. Further, the local public entity will be required to pay 50 percent of the costs of the neutral evaluation, and the creditors will be required to pay the balance, unless otherwise agreed to by the parties. The second option is for the municipality to declare a "fiscal emergency" and adopt a resolution at a noticed public hearing that includes findings that the financial state of the local government jeopardizes the health, safety or well-being of its residents absent bankruptcy protections before filing a petition. The resolution must declare that the municipality is or will be unable to pay its obligations within the next 60 days.[ii] Additionally, any school district in California may file a municipal bankruptcy petition if the state has assumed control of the school district and the state's appointed administrator files the municipal bankruptcy petition on behalf of the school district.[iii] Between 1980 and July 31, 2016, 46 entities in California have filed petitions under the municipal bankruptcy provisions of the Bankruptcy Code.

E. California

Home Rule and Taxing Power of Municipalities	**Municipalities' Ability to Self-Govern** California is a Dillon's Rule state.[iv] A county or city, however, may adopt a charter, which has the force and effect of a state legislative enactment.[v] Because charters adopted by charter cities and counties are considered the law of the state, Dillon's Rule does not apply to these charter counties and cities.[vi] Cities, counties and special districts may impose special taxes on such district, except ad valorem taxes on real property or a transaction tax or sales tax on the sale of real property by a two-thirds vote of the qualified electors of that district.[vii] **Taxing Limitations** The California Constitution limits ad valorem tax rates. Specifically, the maximum amount of any ad valorem tax on real property in California may not exceed 1 percent of the full cash value of the property. Further, the value of the property is set at the 1975-76 market value, unless the property is sold or significantly modified. The limitation does not apply to ad valorem or special assessments to pay interest and redemption charges on indebtedness arising before July 1, 1978 and for any bonded indebtedness incurred for the acquisition or improvement of real property approved after July 1, 1978, so long as two-thirds of voters approve the proposition.[viii]
Debt Default Prevention	**California Debt and Investment Advisory Commission** The California Debt and Investment Advisory Commission provides technical assistance on debt issuance and public fund investments to local public agencies and professionals in the public finance field. The commission serves as a clearinghouse for public debt issuance information and to assist state and local agencies with monitoring, issuing and managing debt. Further, all public debt issuers in California are required to submit information to the commission 30 days before the proposed sale date of the debt. No later than 45 days from the actual date of sale, issuers must submit to the commission a report on the final sale, which includes, but is not limited to, the issuer's name, type of sale, principal amount, type of debt instrument, sources of repayment, purpose of the financing, the issuance's rating and the members of the finance team.[ix] **Debt Limitation** No county, city, town, township, board of education or school district may incur debt exceeding in any year the income and revenue of that year, without a two-thirds vote. Debt may be incurred for public school purposes by majority vote.

E. California

Debt Default Prevention *continued*	The California Code contains further limitations. For instance, for a school district or community college district, the total amount of bonds issued for certain purposes as defined in the statute may not exceed 1.25 percent of the taxable property in the school district or community college district, or school facilities improvement district. For a county, the total amount of bonded indebtedness may not at any time exceed 5 percent of the taxable property in the county. If a water conservation, flood control, irrigation, reclamation or drainage works, improvements, or the construction of select county roads is included in a proposition, the total indebtedness may exceed 5 percent but cannot exceed 15 percent of the taxable property of the county.[x] **Negotiations** At least one provision of the California Code provides that if a district is in debt, it has no power to impair or destroy any of its indebtedness without bondholder consent. The district may make arrangements with creditors to surrender the indebtedness at less than par and may levy an assessment for bondholder payment.[xi] **Refunding Bonds** The governing body of certain municipal entities may issue refunding bonds to refund outstanding notes.[xii] **School District Budget Requirements** Certain California school districts are required to submit a budget to the county superintendent, which may disapprove the budget in certain situations. Should a disapproval occur, the county superintendent may call for the formation of a budget review committee. The budget review committee will then work with the school district to create an approvable budget. After the appointment of a budget review committee, if the school district still fails to create an allowable budget, the county superintendent may take over certain functions of the school district. In addition, there is state department of education and superintendent of public education to provide assistance to school districts.[xiii]
Mechanisms for Resolution after Default	**Receivership** In certain situations, California law allows for the appointment of a receiver with respect to revenue bonds where a default has occurred.[xiv]
Remedies on Default	**Accounting** In certain default situations, bondholders may bring a proceeding in any court of competent jurisdiction to require the authority in question to account as if it were a trustee of an express trust.[xv]

E. California

Remedies on Default *continued*	**Bondholder Action** In certain situations, bondholders may bring any appropriate suit on default.[xvi] **Foreclosure** In certain default situations generally involving special revenue bonds, bondholders may foreclose on a project when a default has occurred.[xvii] **Injunctive Relief** In certain situations, California law authorizes bondholders to bring any action or suit in equity to enjoin any act that may be unlawful or that may violate the rights of bondholders.[xviii] **Mandamus** In certain situations, bondholders or their trustee may bring a court action to compel the local governing body to perform a ministerial action that it has refused to undertake, such as collecting taxes or fees where the underlying bond authorization requires such a collection.[xix] **Any Other Remedies** Certain provisions of California law allow for a bond resolution to set forth the rights and remedies of holders of the bonds.[xx]
Other Bondholder Protections	**Special Revenue Bonds** As provided by Section 922(d) of the Bankruptcy Code, payments to bondholders holding special revenue bonds would not be stayed on the filing of a municipal bankruptcy petition, and payments to holders could continue. Whether an issuance would qualify as a special revenue bond depends on the provisions of the authorizing statute with respect to the bonds at issue.[xxi] **Special Tax Bonds** In certain situations, on approval of two-thirds of eligible voters voting, in the case of community facilities districts, the district may incur bonded indebtedness and establish or change appropriations limits. The proceeds of the bonds issued are pledged and committed to pay or repay the principal and interest on the bonds. Category SL-1.[xxii]

E. California

Other Bondholder Protections *continued*	**Statutory Liens** Were a municipal entity to file a petition under Chapter 9 of the Bankruptcy Code, bondholders holding bonds to which statutory liens have attached would continue to receive payment on those bonds. For a statutory lien to apply, the authorizing law of the bond issue must contain such a lien.[xxiii] On January 1, 2016, a new law became effective in California that specifically created a first lien priority for general obligation debt issued by certain local agencies (*e.g.*, cities, counties, school districts and special districts) in California, so long as the debt was secured by a levy of ad valorem taxes pursuant to certain provisions of the California Constitution. Category SL-1.[xxiv]

---

i CAL. GOV'T CODE § 53760. California courts have determined that the term "municipality" should not be narrowly construed, although an entity under government control is not necessarily a municipality. *In re County of Orange*, 183 B.R. 595 (Bankr. C.D. Cal. 1995) (finding Orange County Investment Pool not a municipality eligible to file a Chapter 9 proceeding). The court described a "public subdivision" as "any county or parish or any city, town, village, borough, township, or other municipality," the common thread of which is "their ability to exercise various sovereign powers such as the power to tax, the power of eminent domain or the police power." *Id.* at 602. Public agencies are "incorporated authorities, commissions, or similar public agencies organized for the purpose of constructing, maintaining and operating revenue producing enterprises." *Id.* The Bankruptcy Code defines "municipality" as any political subdivision or political agency or instrumentality of a state.

ii CAL. GOV'T CODE §§ 53760, 53760.1, 53760.3, 53760.5 and 53760.7 (as amended and added by CAL. A.B. 506 (signed into law on October 9, 2011)). Whether or not a municipality has taken the steps necessary to file a bankruptcy petition has been subject to challenge in municipal bankruptcies filed in California. *See, e.g., In re City of Stockton*, 475 BR. 720 (Bankr. E.D. Cal. 2012); *In re City of San Bernardino*, Case No. 12-28006, Dkt. No. 797 (Bankr. C.D. Cal. Sept. 17, 2013) (finding City of San Bernardino eligible to file Chapter 9 petition).

iii *See* CAL. EDUC. CODE § 41326(b)(10)(A).

iv *See Irwin v. Manhattan Beach*, 415 P.2d 769, 773 (Cal. 1966), in which the California Supreme Court found: "A general law city has only those powers expressly conferred upon it by the Legislature, together with such powers as are 'necessarily incident to those expressly granted or essential to the declared object and purposes of the municipal corporation.' The powers of such a city are strictly construed so that 'any fair, reasonable doubt concerning the exercise of a power is resolved against the corporation.'" (internal citations omitted). *See also G.L. Mezzetta v. City of Am. Canyon*, 93 Cal. Rptr. 2d 292, 295 (Cal. Ct. App. 2000) (same).

v CAL. CONST. art XI, § 3.

vi *See, e.g., First Street Plaza Partners v. City of Los Angeles*, 65 Cal. App. 4th 650, 659-60 (Cal. Ct. App. 1998) (differentiating "charter cities" and "general law cities").

vii CAL. CONST. art. XIIIA, § 4.

viii CAL. CONST. art XIIIA, §§ 1-2.

ix CAL. GOV'T CODE §§ 8855, 8856, 8857 and 8859 (establishing California Debt and Investment Advisory Commission); CAL. GOV'T CODE § 6586.7 (requiring reporting to the commission by issuers under the Marks-Roos Local Bond Pooling Act of 1985); and CAL. GOV'T CODE § 53359.5 (reporting requirements).

x CAL. CONST. art. XVI, § 18; CAL. EDUC. CODE § 15102 (school district); and CAL. GOV'T CODE § 29909 (counties).

xi *See* CAL. WAT. CODE § 50901 (reclamation districts).

xii An example of a refunding bond provision in California law is CAL. GOV'T CODE §§ 43720-43747. This provision applies to any city, except a city and a county, if the city has outstanding bonded indebtedness or a judgment against it, or if any department, board or special fund of the city has any outstanding bonds and the bonds were created for a purpose for which the city could have authorized and issued the bonds. The interest on the bonds cannot exceed 8 percent per year. Until the legislative body has sufficient amounts set aside to pay all principal and interest on the bonds as they become due, the legislative body must levy and collect a tax sufficient to make such payments. Another provision allows for local agencies, including any city, county, city and county, or municipal or public corporation or district authorized to acquire, construct, own or operate an enterprise, to issue refunding bonds. CAL. GOV'T CODE §§ 54660-54662 (Refunding Bonds for Revenue Bond Law of 1941). *See also* CAL. HARB. AND NAV. CODE § 3917 (Harbor Development Bond Law of 1958).

xiii CAL. EDUC. CODE §§ 42122-42129 (budget requirements). The county superintendent may: (1) develop and adopt, in consultation with the school district's superintendent and governing board, a fiscal plan allowing the district to meet its financial obligations; (2) cancel purchase orders, prohibit the issuance of nonsalary warrants, and otherwise stay or rescind any action that is inconsistent with the budget adopted; (3) monitor and review the operation of the school district; (4) determine the need for additional staff; (5) require the school district to encumber all contracts and other obligations; (6) determine any financial problem areas; and (7) withhold compensation of the members of the governing board and the district superintendent for failure to provide requested financial information. CAL. EDUC. CODE § 42127.3.

xiv *See, e.g.,* CAL. GOV'T CODE § 15842 (state building construction revenue bonds); CAL. GOV'T CODE § 91537 (industrial development authorities); CAL. WAT. CODE § 36361 (California water districts); and CAL. WAT. CODE § 36361 (California water districts action to secure payment of revenue bonds). The state code may be more expansive, and the statutory authority for each individual bond issuance should be reviewed before assessing whether a receiver may be appointed.

xv *See, e.g.,* CAL. GOV'T CODE § 15842 (state building construction revenue bonds); CAL. GOV'T CODE § 54643 (Revenue Bond Law of 1941); and CAL. GOV'T CODE § 67620 (San Francisco Bay Area Transportation Terminal Authority). The state code may be more expansive and the statutory authority for each individual bond issuance should be reviewed before assessing whether an accounting may be pursued.

xvi *See, e.g.,* CAL. GOV'T CODE § 91537 (industrial development authorities); CAL. GOV'T CODE § 66540.48 (San Francisco Bay Area Water Emergency Transportation Response and Disaster Recovery Act); CAL. EDUC. CODE § 81960 (Community College Revenue Bond Act of 1961); CAL EDUC. CODE § 90072 (The State University Revenue Bond Act of 1947); CAL. EDUC. CODE § 92491 (The State University Revenue Bond Act of 1947); CAL. GOV'T CODE § 6569 (joint exercise of powers: power to issue revenue bonds); CAL. GOV'T CODE § 15843 (state building construction revenue bonds); CAL. GOV'T CODE § 26370 (revenue bonds for county improvements); CAL. GOV'T CODE § 26470 (revenue bonds for county incinerators); CAL. GOV'T CODE § 50770 (revenue bonds for public improvements); CAL. GOV'T CODE § 54702.8 (cities, counties and other agencies: employee rental housing); CAL. GOV'T CODE § 64118 (California Transportation Financing Authority); CAL. PUB. RES. CODE § 26034 (California Alternative Energy and Advanced Transportation Financing Authority); CAL. PUB. RES. CODE § 32205 (California Urban Waterfront Restoration Financing Authority Act); CAL. PUB. UTIL. CODE § 13106 (Municipal Utility District Act electric system improvements); CAL. PUB. UTIL. CODE § 30981 (Southern California Rapid Transit District); CAL. PUB. UTIL. CODE § 100492 (Santa Clara Valley Transportation Authority); CAL. PUB. UTIL. CODE § 102602 (Sacramento Transit District); CAL. PUB. UTIL. CODE § 103602

(San Mateo County Transit District); CAL. PUB. UTIL. CODE § 105262 (Sonoma-Marin Area RAIL Transit District); CAL. PUB. UTIL. CODE § 120702 (transit development boards); CAL. PUB. UTIL. CODE § 125716 (North County Transit District); CAL. PUB. UTIL. CODE § 132370.10 (transportation consolidation for San Diego); CAL. PUB. UTIL. CODE § 170082 (San Diego County Regional Airport Authority); CAL. STS. & HIGH. CODE § 31171 (El Dorado County Toll Tunnel Authority Act); CAL. STS. & HIGH. CODE § 35417 (Parking District Law of 1951); and CAL. UNCOD. WATER DEER, Act 400 § 33 (Kings River Conservation District Act). The state code may be more expansive and the statutory authority for each individual bond issuance should be reviewed before assessing whether a bondholder action may be brought.

xvii *See, e.g.*, CAL. GOV'T CODE § 91537 (industrial development authorities). The state code may be more expansive and the statutory authority for each individual bond issuance should be reviewed before assessing whether bondholders may foreclose on a project.

xviii *See, e.g.*, CAL. GOV'T CODE § 15842 (state building construction revenue bonds); CAL. GOV'T CODE § 91537 (industrial development authorities); CAL. GOV'T CODE § 6569 (joint exercise of powers: power to issue revenue bonds); CAL. GOV'T CODE § 54644 (Revenue Bond Law of 1941); and CAL. GOV'T CODE § 67620 (San Francisco Bay Area Transportation Terminal Authority). The state code may be more expansive and the statutory authority for each individual bond issuance should be reviewed before assessing whether injunctive relief may be pursued.

xix *See, e.g.*, CAL. GOV'T CODE § 15841 (state building construction revenue bonds, allowing bondholders to appoint a trustee to enforce rights of bondholders, including requiring board to collect moneys adequate to carry out the agreement); CAL. GOV'T CODE § 91537 (industrial development authorities); CAL. GOV'T CODE § 66540.48 (San Francisco Bay Area Water Emergency Transportation Response and Disaster Recovery Act); CAL. PUB. UTIL. CODE APPX 2, § 10.1 (West Bay Rapid Transit Authority Act); CAL. EDUC. CODE § 17186 (California School Finance Authority); CAL. EDUC. CODE § 81960 (Community College Revenue Bond Act of 1961); CAL. EDUC. CODE § 90072 (The State University Revenue Bond Act of 1947); CAL. EDUC. CODE § 92491 (The State University Revenue Bond Act of 1947); CAL. EDUC. CODE § 94148 (California Educational Facilities Authority Act); CAL. GOV'T CODE § 6569 (joint exercise of powers: power to issue revenue bonds); CAL GOV'T CODE § 15444 (Health Facilities Financing Authority Act); CAL. GOV'T CODE § 26370 (revenue bonds for county improvements); CAL. GOV'T CODE § 26470 (revenue bonds for county incinerators); CAL. GOV'T CODE § 50770 (revenue bonds for public improvements); CAL. GOV'T CODE § 54642 (Revenue Bond Law of 1941); CAL. GOV'T CODE § 54702.8 (cities, counties and other agencies: employee rental housing); CAL. GOV'T CODE § 64118 (California Transportation Financing Authority); CAL. GOV'T CODE § 66540.48 (San Francisco Bay Area Water Emergency Transportation Response and Disaster Recovery Act); CAL. GOV'T CODE § 67620 (San Francisco Bay Area Transportation Terminal Authority); CAL. GOV'T CODE § 92308 (California Passenger RAIL Financing Commission Act); CAL. HARB. & NAV. CODE APPX. § 66 (San Diego Unified Port District and Humboldt Bay Harbor, Recreation and Conservation District); CAL. PUB. RES. CODE § 26034 (California Alternative Energy and Advanced Transportation Financing Authority); CAL. PUB. RES. CODE § 32205 (California Urban Waterfront Restoration Financing Authority Act); CAL. PUB. UTIL. CODE § 13106 (Municipal Utility District Act electric system improvements); CAL. PUB. UTIL. CODE § 30981 (Southern California Rapid Transit District); CAL. PUB. UTIL. CODE § 100492 (Santa Clara Valley Transportation Authority); CAL. PUB. UTIL. CODE § 102602 (Sacramento Transit District); CAL. PUB. UTIL. CODE § 103602 (San Mateo County Transit District); CAL. PUB. UTIL. CODE § 105262 (Sonoma-Marin Area Rail Transit District); CAL. PUB. UTIL. CODE § 120702 (transit development boards); CAL. PUB. UTIL. CODE § 125716 (North County Transit District); CAL. PUB. UTIL. CODE § 132370.10 (transportation consolidation for San Diego); CAL. PUB. UTIL. CODE § 170082 (San Diego County Regional Airport Authority); CAL. STS. & HIGH. CODE § 31171 (El Dorado County Toll Tunnel Authority Act); CAL. STS. & HIGH. CODE § 35417 (Parking District Law of 1951); CAL. WAT. CODE § 11708 (conservation, development and utilization of state water resources); CAL. WAT. CODE § 36360 (California water districts, bondholders holding at least 25 percent in outstanding unpaid bonds may bring an action to compel the district to fix and collect sufficient charges to pay the principal and interest due on bonds); and CAL. UNCOD. WATER DEER, Act 400 § 33 (Kings River Conservation District Act). It is possible that an aggrieved bondholder could pursue a writ of mandamus even absent authorizing statutory law.

xx *See, e.g.*, CAL. EDUC. CODE § 90032 (State University Revenue Bond Act) and CAL. EDUC. CODE § 17184 (California School Finance Authority). The state code may be more expansive than the examples cited here, and the statutory authority for each individual bond issuance should be reviewed before assessing whether other remedies may be available to bondholders.

xxi *See, e.g.*, CAL. GOV'T CODE §§ 6540-6579.5 (joint exercise of powers: power to issue revenue bonds); CAL. GOV'T CODE §§ 54300-54700 (Revenue Bond Law of 1941). These are examples of revenue bonds. The California state code is more expansive and an attorney should be consulted to examine any specific situation involving a default.

xxii CAL. GOV'T CODE §§ 53345-53365.7.

xxiii For example, *see In re Sierra Kings Health Care Dist.*, Case No. 09-19728-8-9 (Bankr. E.D. Cal. Sep. 13, 2010) (confirming the postpetition effectiveness of a municipality's pledge of ad valorem taxes which qualifies as both a special revenue pledge and a statutory lien). The bond issuance in *Sierra Kings* was subject to a statutory lien pursuant to CAL. HEALTH & SAFETY CODE § 32300. Also, in 1983, the San Jose School District payment of bonds to bondholders was unaffected by a Chapter 9 filing on July 1, 1983 due to CAL. EDUC. CODE § 15250, which provided a tax pledge to bondholders collected by the county or tax collector to pay bondholders first.

xxiv Category SL-1: CAL. GOV'T CODE § 53515. "Local Agencies" include cities, counties, cities and counties, school districts, community college districts, authorities and special districts. The levy securing the general obligation debt must have arisen pursuant to paragraphs 2 and 3 of subdivision (b) of Section 1 of Article XIIIA of the California Constitution. A similar corresponding provisions was also enacted by the California legislature and went into effect on January 1, 2015 with respect to certain general obligation debt issued by school districts. CAL. EDUC. CODE § 15251(b). *See also* CAL. HEALTH & SAFETY CODE § 32312. This provision permits a statutory lien bond issue by a hospital district where the county board of supervisors pursuant to the statute shall levy and collect annually, as part of the annual assessment, a sum sufficient to pay interest and principal on such bonds as they become due as well as for a sinking fund if so provided. The taxes so collected shall be held separate and apart from other tax revenue, and the tax so levied to pay these bonds shall be in addition to all other taxes and shall be used for no purpose other than the payment of the bonds and accruing interest. While this provision for hospital district bonds was not specifically part of S.B. 222, which reaffirmed a statutory lien as to unlimited tax general obligations bonds for school districts, cities, counties, etc., the force and effect of the statutory language are clear to be a statutory lien without specifically using the words. This was the conclusion of the bankruptcy court in ruling to approve a reaffirmation that hospital district bonds had the benefit of both special revenues and a statutory lien. *See In re Sierra Kings Health Care District*, Case No. 09.19728-B-9 pending in the United States Bankruptcy Court, Eastern District of California, Fresno Division in its ruling on September 13, 2010.

F. Colorado

Municipal Bankruptcy Authority	Colorado allows for any insolvent taxing district, irrigation or drainage district organized under certain acts of the Colorado Revised Statutes to file a petition under Chapter 9 of the Bankruptcy Code. The parameters of entities authorized to file a municipal bankruptcy petition are more fully discussed in the endnotes. Unless an entity is specifically identified, it is not authorized to file a municipal bankruptcy petition. An "insolvent taxing district" means a taxing district able to show that it has been unsuccessful with other existing alternatives to bankruptcy and which would be unable to discharge its obligations as they become due by means of a mill levy of not less than 100 mills to be imposed by: (a) the taxing district; or (b) any other taxing district pursuant to a contract that pledges the revenues of such contract to the payment of such obligations. "Taxing district" means a special district organized in Colorado. Special districts include any quasi-municipal corporation and political subdivision identified as a "special district" under Title 32 of Colorado law but do not include local improvement districts established for the underground conversion of utilities; solid waste disposal sites and facilities; urban renewal authorities; or conservation and irrigation districts (although irrigation and drainage districts are authorized to file a petition under Title 37 of the Colorado Statutes). As mentioned, any irrigation or drainage district organized under the laws of the State of Colorado is authorized to file. Between 1980 and July 31, 2016, 23 municipal bankruptcy petitions have been filed in Colorado.[i]
Home Rule and Taxing Power of Municipalities	**Municipalities' Ability to Self-Govern** Colorado is a Dillon's Rule state, but counties may choose to adopt a home-rule charter and exercise greater power to preserve public health and safety. The general assembly cannot impose taxes on behalf of any county, city, town or other municipal corporation but may vest in corporate authorities the power to assess and collect taxes for all purposes of such corporation.[ii] In addition, the people of each city or town with a population exceeding 2,000 hold the power to make, amend, add to or replace its charter, which, once enacted, becomes the organic law to all local and municipal matters.[iii] **Taxing Limitations** For taxation purposes, residential real property shall be valued for assessment at 21 percent of its actual value and all other taxable property is valued for assessment at 29 percent of its actual value.[iv]

F. Colorado

Debt Default Prevention	**Debt Limitation** The Colorado Code includes certain limitations for school districts. Specifically, a school district's bonded indebtedness is limited to the greater of 20 percent of the last valuation of taxable property in the district or 6 percent of the most recent determination of the actual value of the taxable property in the district.[v] As a further matter, the Colorado Constitution includes a provision under which no political subdivision may contract a general obligation debt except by adopting an irrepealable legislative measure pledging an amount sufficient to pay the interest and principal on the debt. Unless the political subdivision is a home-rule entity whose charter provides otherwise, the debt may not be incurred unless approved by a majority of qualified taxpaying electors.[vi] **Refunding Bonds** Certain public bodies may issue refunding bonds for the purpose of refunding any or all bonded indebtedness of the entity.[vii]
Mechanisms for Resolution after Default	**Receivership** In certain situations, Colorado law allows for the appointment of a receiver with respect to revenue bonds where a default has occurred.[viii]
Remedies on Default	**Accounting** In certain situations of default, any obligee holding or representing a specified amount in bonds as designated in the trust indenture may bring a suit, action or proceeding in any court of competent jurisdiction to require the authority in question to account as if it were a trustee of an express trust.[ix] **Bondholder Action** In certain situations, bondholders may bring suit on default.[x] **Injunctive Relief** In certain situations, Colorado law authorizes bondholders to bring any action or suit in equity to enjoin any act that may be unlawful or that may violate the rights of bondholders.[xi] **Mandamus** In certain situations, bondholders or their trustee may bring a court action to compel the local governing body to perform a ministerial action that it has refused to undertake, such as collecting taxes or fees where the underlying bond authorization requires such a collection.[xii]

F. Colorado

Other Bondholder Protections	**Special Revenue Bonds** As provided by Section 922(d) of the Bankruptcy Code, payments to bondholders holding special revenue bonds would not be stayed on the filing of a municipal bankruptcy petition, and payments to holders could continue. Whether an issuance would qualify as a special revenue bond depends on the provisions of the authorizing statute with respect to the bonds at issue.[xiii] **Statutory Liens** Were a municipal entity to file a petition under Chapter 9 of the Bankruptcy Code, bondholders holding bonds to which statutory liens have attached would continue to receive payment on those bonds. For a statutory lien to apply, the authorizing law of the bond issue must contain such a lien. Category SL-1.[xiv]

i COLO. REV. STAT. §§ 32-1-1402, 32-1-1403, 32-1-1403.5 and 37-32-102. Examples of "special districts" include, but may not be limited to, water and sanitation districts; regional service authorities; the Moffat Tunnel Improvement District; regional transportation districts; mass transportation districts; the Three Lakes Water and Sanitation District; urban drainage and flood control districts; the Fountain Creek Watershed, Flood Control and Greenway District; rail districts; scientific and cultural facility districts; the Denver Metropolitan Major League Baseball Stadium District; metropolitan football stadium districts; mental health care service districts; forest improvement districts; health assurance and health service districts; and the Colorado New Energy Improvement District.

A bankruptcy court sitting in Colorado has determined that a not-for-profit corporation that issued bonds for the construction of a city hall, which did not require a public vote, where the city did not have control over the authority and where bonds issued did not create public debt, was not a "municipality" within the meaning of the Bankruptcy Code and, thus, was ineligible to proceed as a Chapter 9 debtor. *In re Ellicot Sch. Bldg. Auth.*, 150 B.R. 261, 264 (Bankr. D. Colo. 1992).

Of the municipal entities filing for bankruptcy protection, 20 such petitions were filed by special municipal districts, one was filed by an education-related entity, and one was filed by a municipal utility.

ii COLO. CONST. art. X, § 7.

iii COLO. CONST. art. XX, § 6. *See also City and County of Denver v. Colorado*, 788 P.2d 764, 766-67 (Colo. 1990) (noting that article XX, section 6 of the Colorado Constitution abrogated Dillon's Rule) and *Fraternal Order of Police, Colorado Lodge No. 27 v. City and County of Denver*, 926 P.2d 582, 586 (Colo. 1996) (same).

iv COLO. CONST. art. X, § 3.

v COLO. REV. STAT. § 22-42-104. Certain exceptions, as outlined in the statute establishing debt limits for school districts, apply. In 2010, Colorado voters considered Amendment 61, which would have greatly tightened state and local debt limits. This amendment was defeated by an overwhelming majority of voters, with 73.0 percent of voters voting "no" on the initiative. *See* http://data.denverpost.com/election/results/amendment/2010 (last visited Sep. 23, 2013).

vi COLO. CONST. art. XI, § 6.

vii Examples of refunding bond provisions in Colorado law include COLO. REV. STAT. §§ 23-71-601 to 23-71-610 (allowing junior college districts to refund any bonded indebtedness); COLO. REV. STAT. § 31-35-412 (allowing refunding of sewer and water district refunding bonds for the purpose of reducing interest costs); COLO. REV. STAT. § 32-1-1302 (allowing for refunding of any lawful general obligation bond of a special district); COLO. REV. STAT. § 30-20-410 (county public improvements for sewers and water systems); COLO. REV. STAT. § 32-11-564 (urban drainage and flood control indebtedness); COLO. REV. STAT. § 22-43-102 (school district refunding bonds); COLO. REV. STAT. § 37-50-141 (republican river water conservation districts); COLO. REV. STAT. § 29-3-116 (county and municipality development revenue bond act); COLO. REV. STAT. § 30-35-701 (home-rule counties refunding bonds); COLO. REV. STAT. § 32-12-120 (Rail District Act authorization of refunding bonds); COLO. REV. STAT. § 25-29-117 (Denver Health and Hospital Authority); COLO. REV. STAT. § 37-43-144 (irrigation districts of 1905 and 1921 refunding bonds); COLO. REV. STAT. § 37-26-101 (drainage and drainage districts refunding bonds); COLO. REV. STAT. § 31-21-202 (municipal refunding bonded indebtedness, allowing governing body of any municipality to issue refunding bonds); COLO. REV. STAT. § 32-4-533 (metropolitan sewage disposal district); COLO. REV. STAT. § 30-26-401 (county bonds: refunding); COLO. REV. STAT. § 37-48-194 (Rio Grande Water Conservation District); COLO. REV. STAT. § 25-8.5-113 (Cherry Creek Basin Water Quality Authority); COLO. REV. STAT. § 37-26-111 (drainage district refunding bonds); COLO. REV. STAT. § 35-75-111 (Colorado Agricultural Development Authority refunding bonds); COLO. REV. STAT. § 23-3.1-208 (student obligations and institutional loans); COLO. REV. STAT. § 23-15-110 (Colorado Educational and Cultural Facilities Authority Act); COLO. REV. STAT. § 25-25-110 (Colorado Health Facilities Authority); COLO. REV. STAT. § 25-29-117 (Denver Health and Hospital Authority); and COLO. REV. STAT. § 43-3-210 (special highway construction: turnpikes).

viii *See* COLO. REV. STAT. § 32-4-530 (metropolitan sewage disposal districts; a bond resolution may allow for the appointment of a receiver to take possession of the system); COLO. REV. STAT. § 32-11-557 (urban drainage and flood control districts; a bond resolution may allow for the appointment of a receiver to take possession of the system); COLO. REV. STAT. § 29-4-117 (city housing law relating to a housing project); COLO. REV. STAT. § 29-4-219 (city housing authorities relating to a housing project); COLO. REV. STAT. § 29-4-718 (housing and business development and financing); COLO. REV. STAT. §§ 32-4-529 and 32-4-530 (metropolitan sewage disposal districts); COLO. REV. STAT. § 32-11-556 (indebtedness and financial provisions for urban drainage and flood control); COLO. REV. STAT. § 32-9-144 (regional transportation districts); COLO. REV. STAT. § 32-11-556 (Urban Drainage and Flood Control Act); COLO. REV. STAT. § 32-11-631 (urban drainage and flood control assessment bonds); COLO. REV. STAT. § 37-47-145 (Southwestern Water Conservation District); COLO. REV. STAT. § 37-46-145 (Colorado River Water Conservation District); COLO. REV. STAT. § 37-48-187 (Rio Grande River Water Conservation District); COLO. REV. STAT. § 37-50-136 (Republican River Water Conservation District); and COLO. REV. STAT. § 29-3-112 (County and Municipality Development Revenue Bond Act). The state code may be more expansive and the statutory authority for each individual bond issuance should be reviewed before assessing whether a receiver may be appointed.

ix *See* COLO. REV. STAT. § 29-4-117 (city housing law relating to a housing project); COLO. REV. STAT. § 29-4-219 (city housing authorities relating to a housing project); COLO. REV. STAT. § 32-4-530 (metropolitan sewage disposal districts); COLO. REV. STAT. § 41-5-106 (county airport revenue bonds); COLO. REV. STAT. § 30-20-409 (sewer and water system bonds); COLO. REV. STAT. § 31-25-814 (Downtown Development Authority bonds); COLO. REV. STAT. § 32-9-144 (regional transportation districts); COLO. REV. STAT. § 32-11-556 (Urban Drainage and Flood Control Act); COLO. REV. STAT. § 32-11-631 (urban drainage and flood control assessment bonds); COLO. REV. STAT. § 37-47-145 (Southwestern Water Conservation District); COLO. REV. STAT. § 37-46-145 (Colorado River Water Conservation District); COLO. REV. STAT. § 37-48-187 (Rio Grande River Water Conservation District); and COLO. REV. STAT. § 37-50-136 (Republican River Water Conservation District). The state code may be more expansive and the statutory authority for each bond issuance should be reviewed before assessing whether such a remedy is applicable.

x *See, e.g.*, COLO. REV. STAT. § 30-20-409 (sewer and water system bonds) and COLO. REV. STAT. § 31-25-814 (Downtown Development Authority bonds).

xi *See, e.g.*, COLO. REV. STAT. § 32-4-530 (metropolitan sewage disposal districts); COLO. REV. STAT. § 30-20-409 (sewer and water system bonds); COLO. REV. STAT. § 31-25-814 (Downtown Development Authority bonds); COLO. REV. STAT. § 32-9-144 (regional transportation districts); COLO. REV. STAT. § 32-11-556 (Urban Drainage and Flood Control Act); COLO. REV. STAT. § 32-11-631 (urban drainage and flood control assessment bonds); COLO. REV. STAT. § 37-47-145 (Southwestern Water Conservation District); COLO. REV. STAT. § 37-46-145 (Colorado River Water Conservation

District); COLO. REV. STAT. § 37-48-187 (Rio Grande River Water Conservation District); and COLO. REV. STAT. § 37-50-136 (Republican River Water Conservation District). The state code may be more expansive and the statutory authority for each bond issuance should be reviewed before assessing whether injunctive relief under the statute is a viable option.

xii *See, e.g.,* COLO. REV. STAT. § 32-4-530 (metropolitan sewage disposal districts); COLO. REV. STAT. § 32-11-556 (indebtedness and financial provisions for urban drainage and flood control); COLO. REV. STAT. § 41-5-106 (county airport revenue bonds); COLO. REV. STAT. § 30-20-409 (sewer and water system bonds); COLO. REV. STAT. § 31-25-814 (Downtown Development Authority bonds); COLO. REV. STAT. § 32-9-144 (regional transportation districts); COLO. REV. STAT. § 32-11-556 (Urban Drainage and Flood Control Act); COLO. REV. STAT. § 32-11-631 (urban drainage and flood control assessment bonds); COLO. REV. STAT. § 37-47-145 (Southwestern Water Conservation District); COLO. REV. STAT. § 37-46-145 (Colorado River Water Conservation District); COLO. REV. STAT. § 37-48-187 (Rio Grande River Water Conservation District); COLO. REV. STAT. § 37-50-136 (Republican River Water Conservation District); COLO. REV. STAT. § 43-3-211 (special highway construction turnpikes); and COLO. REV. STAT. § 29-3-112 (County and Municipality Development Revenue Bond Act). It is possible that an aggrieved bondholder could pursue a writ of mandamus even absent authorizing statutory law.

xiii *See, e.g.,* COLO. REV. STAT. § 43-4-509 (Public Highway Authority Law); COLO. REV. STAT. § 40-9.7-107 (Colorado Clean Energy Development Authority); COLO. REV. STAT. § 37-95-111 (Colorado Water Resources and Power Development Authority); COLO. REV. STAT. § 37-50-135 (Republican River Water Conservation Districts); COLO. REV. STAT. § 37-48-186 (Rio Grande Water Conservation District); COLO. REV. STAT. § 37-46-144 (Colorado River Water Conservation District); COLO. REV. STAT. § 37-47-144; COLO. REV. STAT. § 32-15-114 (Metropolitan Football Stadium District); COLO. REV. STAT. § 32-14-118 (Denver Metropolitan Major League Baseball Stadium District); COLO. REV. STAT. § 32-11.5-402 (Fountaincreek Watershed, Flood Control, and Greenway District Bonds); COLO. REV. STAT. § 32-11-555 (Urban Drainage and Flood Control Act); COLO. REV. STAT. § 32-9-131 (regional transportation districts); COLO. REV. STAT. § 30-26-506 (county capital improvement trust funds); COLO. REV. STAT. § 29-23-110 (Pueblo Depot Activity Development Authority Bonds); and COLO. REV. STAT. § 31-25-534 (special improvement districts in municipalities). These are examples of special revenue bonds. The state code may be more expansive and an attorney should be consulted to examine any specific situation involving a default.

xiv Category SL-1: *See, e.g.,* Colo. Rev. Stat. § 11-57-208, which deals with creation, perfection, enforcement and priorities of pledged revenues (including ad valorem taxes) to secure or pay bonds issued by state and local government. This statute authorizes any public entity to pledge revenues for the payment of bonds, the lien to be immediate upon being received by the public entity with no further act being required, the pledge and lien being valid, binding and enforceable against all persons with priority over other obligations. Further, under the taxpayer bill of rights in 1992, there were restrictions placed on taxes and spending under article X of the Colorado Constitution. Colorado's Constitution article XI, section 6 requires dedicated tax revenues to the payment of debt incurred by local government after the question of incurring the debt is presented to the electorate and approved by the majority. The legislation pledging and incurring the debt is irrepealable until the debt is paid in full. This statutory language with the constitutional mandate for taxes to be levied and paid to the bondholder appears to be strong support for the creation of a statutory lien as well as mandated payment by statute and constitution that should not be inferred with or adversely affected under §§ 903 and 904 of the Bankruptcy Code as well as the rulings of *Ashton* and *Bekins, supra* at 144. COLO. REV. STAT. § 37-46-144 (Colorado River Water Conservation District bonds secured by statutory lien); COLO. REV. STAT. § 37-48-186 (Rio Grande Water Conservation District bonds secured by statutory lien); and COLO. REV. STAT. § 37-50-135 (Republican River Water Conservation District bonds secured by statutory lien). These are examples of statutory liens. The state code may be more expansive, and an attorney should be consulted to examine any specific situation involving a default.

G. Connecticut

Municipal Bankruptcy Authority	A "municipality" may only file a municipal bankruptcy petition with the express prior written consent of the governor. If the governor consents, he or she shall submit a report to the treasurer and general assembly committee on matters relating to finance, revenue and bonding, setting for the reasons for consent. "Municipality" includes any town; city; borough; consolidated town and borough; metropolitan district; fire district; sewer district; fire and sewer district; lighting district; village; beach or improvement association; other district or association, except a school district, wholly within a town and having the power to make appropriations or to levy taxes; and other state subdivisions with power to levy taxes or issue debt. Unless specifically identified, an entity is not authorized to file a municipal bankruptcy petition. Two entities in Connecticut have filed petitions between 1980 and July 31, 2016, including the City of Bridgeport in 1991, dismissed in August, 1991, and the Westport Transit District in 1992, dismissed in April 1994. The court dismissed the Westport Transit District bankruptcy petition, finding that Connecticut law did not specifically authorize the district to file.[i]
Home Rule and Taxing Power of Municipalities	**Municipalities' Ability to Self-Govern** Connecticut is a Dillon's Rule state but has adopted home-rule provisions to provide its local governments some autonomy from the state legislature. All towns, cities or boroughs adopting a home-rule charter are granted the power to "manage, regulate and control the finances and property, real and personal, of the town, city or borough and to regulate and provide for the sale, conveyance, transfer and release of … property to provide for the execution of contracts and evidences of indebtedness…"[ii] **Taxing Limitations** Connecticut law does not contain any provisions limiting the amount of taxes that may be assessed by local government taxing authorities in the state.
Debt Default Prevention	**Debt Limitation** Connecticut law contains statutory debt limits based on type of debt. The provisions apply to towns, consolidated towns and cities, consolidated towns and boroughs, and other independent and dependent political and territorial divisions and subdivisions.[iii] **Refunding Bonds** Certain public bodies may issue refunding bonds for the purpose of refunding any or all bonded indebtedness of the entity.[iv]

G. Connecticut

Mechanisms for Resolution after Default	***Ad Hoc* State Intervention** Connecticut has typically employed a system of implementing legislation on an *ad hoc* basis to create financial assistance boards to turn around a municipality in severe financial distress.[v] **Appointment of Trustee** In certain situations, should a default continue for 30 days or should the municipality refuse to comply with law or default on an agreement, holders of at least 25 percent of the aggregate principal amount of the bonds may appoint a trustee to represent them.[vi] **Receivership** In certain situations, state law allows for a receiver with respect to revenue bonds where a default has occurred.[vii] **Revenue Set-Aside** In certain default situations, the chief fiscal officer of the defaulting municipal entity must set aside from the first revenues received by the entity from whatever source, except revenues pledged as security for other bonds and federal or state grants or loans, an amount sufficient to pay the principal and interest due and owing on the bonds and immediately apply that amount to the default.[viii]
Remedies on Default	**Bondholder Action** In certain situations, bondholders may bring suit on default.[ix] **Contractual Remedies** Certain provisions of Connecticut law allow for provisions in any bond resolution or resolutions setting forth acts constituting default and the rights and remedies of holders of the bonds.[x] **Injunctive Relief** In certain situations, Connecticut law authorizes bondholders to bring any action or suit in equity to enjoin any act that may be unlawful or that may violate their rights.[xi] **Mandamus** In certain situations, bondholders may bring an action to compel the local governing body to perform a ministerial action that it has refused to undertake, such as collecting taxes or fees where the underlying bond authorization requires such a collection.[xii]

G. Connecticut

Other Bondholder Protections	**Special Revenue Bonds** As provided by Section 922(d) of the Bankruptcy Code, payments to bondholders holding special revenue bonds would not be stayed on the filing of a municipal bankruptcy petition, and payments to holders could continue. Whether an issuance would qualify as a special revenue bond depends on the provisions of the authorizing statute with respect to the bonds at issue.[xiii] **Statutory Liens** Were a municipal entity to file a petition under Chapter 9 of the Bankruptcy Code, bondholders holding bonds to which statutory liens have attached would continue to receive payment on those bonds. For a statutory lien to apply, the authorizing law of the bond issue must contain such a lien. Category SL-2. [xiv]

i CONN. GEN. STAT. § 7-566.

ii CONN. GEN STAT. §§ 7-187 to 7-194.

iii CONN. GEN. STAT. § 7-374. Pursuant to the provision, no town or municipality may issue debt exceeding a multiple applicable to the project type times its aggregate annual receipts, including: (1) all debt other than debt for urban renewal projects, water pollution control projects, certain school building projects and the funding of an unfunded past benefit obligation, two and one-quarter; (2) urban renewal projects, three and one-quarter; (3) water pollution control projects, three and three-quarters; (4) certain school building projects, four and one half; (5) an unfunded past benefit obligation, three; and (6) total debt, seven. Certain exclusions apply as set forth in the statute.

iv Examples of provisions in Connecticut allowing for the issuance of refunding bonds include CONN. GEN. STAT. § 7-370c (allows a municipality — any town, city, borough, consolidated town and city, consolidated town and borough, metropolitan district, district, and other municipal corporation having the power to levy taxes and to issue bonds — with appropriations or incurred debts exceeding $10,000 to issue refunding bonds); CONN. GEN. STAT. § 7-242 (municipal waterworks systems); and CONN. GEN. STAT. § 7-273cc (municipal resource recovery authorities).

v *See, e.g.*, 2001 CONN. SPEC. ACTS 01-1 (enacted to address the fiscal crisis of the City of Waterbury). For a discussion of the creation of the Waterbury Financial Planning and Assistance Board, *see School Administrators of Waterbury v. Waterbury Financial Planning and Assistance Board*, 276 Conn. 355 (2005). The Waterbury Financial Planning and Assistance Board dissolved itself in January 2007. *See Walker v. City of Waterbury*, 253 Fed. Appx. 58, 62 (2d Cir. 2007). A Financial Review Board was also appointed for the City of Bridgeport in 1988, which was dissolved in 1995 (1988 CONN. SPEC. ACTS 88-80); and in 1992 a Financial Planning and Assistance Board was appointed over the City of West Haven. *See* Kirk Johnson, *West Haven Bailout Plan Calls for Hartford to Take the Rudder*, N.Y. TIMES, Apr. 2, 1992, http://www.nytimes.com/1992/04/02/nyregion/west-haven-bailout-plan-calls-for-hartford-to-take-the-rudder.html (last visited Sep. 23, 2013). Likewise, a receiver was appointed over Jewett City in 1993. *See also Labor Provisions of Three Financial Oversight Acts, OLR Research Report*, http://www.cga.ct.gov/2000/rpt/2000-R-1112.html (discussing labor provisions with respect to the Bridgeport, West Haven and Jewett City financial oversight acts) (last visited Sep. 23, 2013).

vi *See, e.g.*, CONN. GEN. STAT. § 7-495 (Connecticut City and Town Development Act) and CONN. GEN. STAT. § 7-564 (municipal debt financing).

vii *See, e.g.*, CONN. GEN. STAT. § 7-233f (municipal electric energy cooperatives) and CONN. GEN. STAT. § 7-243 (municipal waterworks systems). The state code may be more expansive and the statutory authority for each individual bond issuance should be reviewed before assessing whether a receiver may be appointed.

In *Save Our Police Force Committee v. Driscoll*, 1994 Conn. Super. LEXIS 1622 (Conn. Super. Ct. June 27, 1994), a receiver was appointed by the governor under An Act Concerning Certain Obligations of Jewitt City to review and conduct the financial affairs of the city, and community members filed suit to prevent a plan established by the receiver from going into effect. The court denied the committee's request for a temporary injunction, finding that by law the receiver could disband the police department and replace it with resident state troopers.

viii *See, e.g.*, CONN. GEN. STAT. § 7-273g (transit districts). The state code may be more expansive and the statutory authority for each individual bond issuance should be reviewed before assessing whether a set-aside is a viable alternative for injured bondholders.

ix *See* CONN. GEN. STAT. § 7-564 (municipal debt financing). The state code may be more expansive and the statutory authority for each individual bond issuance should be reviewed before assessing what actions a bondholder may bring.

x *See, e.g.*, CONN. GEN. STAT. § 7-233e (municipal electric energy cooperatives); CONN. GEN. STAT. § 7-130g (public recreational facilities authorities); CONN. GEN. STAT. § 7-136n (joint issuance of bonds by multiple municipalities); CONN. GEN. STAT. § 7-266 (municipal sewage systems); CONN. GEN. STAT. §§ 7-273cc and 7-273jj (Municipal Resource Recovery Authority); CONN. GEN. STAT. § 7-329g (fire, sewer and other districts); CONN. GEN. STAT. § 7-406o (Municipal Pension Solvency Loan Program); CONN. GEN. STAT. § 7-491 (Connecticut City and Town Development Act); and CONN. GEN. STAT. § 7-620b (federally designated empowerment zones). The state code may be more expansive and the statutory authority for each individual bond issuance should be reviewed before assessing what actions a bondholder may bring.

xi *See* CONN. GEN. STAT. § 7-564 (municipal debt financing). The state code may be more expansive and the statutory authority for each individual bond issuance should be reviewed before assessing the appropriateness of contractual remedies.

xii *See* CONN. GEN. STAT. § 7-564 (municipal debt financing). It is possible that an aggrieved bondholder could pursue a writ of mandamus even absent authorizing statutory law.

xiii *See, e.g.*, CONN. GEN. STAT. § 7-273pp (Municipal Resource Recovery Authority bonds may include provisions for a pledge and lien on revenues) and CONN. GEN. STAT. § 7-491 (Connecticut City and Town Development Act). These are examples of special revenue bonds. The state code may be more expansive and an attorney should be consulted to examine any specific situation involving a default.

xiv Category SL-2: *See, e.g.*, CONN. GEN. STAT. § 7-233f (municipal electric energy cooperatives); CONN. GEN. STAT. § 7-130i (public recreational facilities authorities); CONN. GEN. STAT. § 7-329i (fire, sewer and other districts); CONN. GEN. STAT. § 7-491 (Connecticut City and Town Development Act); and CONN. GEN. STAT. § 7-620b (federally designated empowerment zones). These are examples of language of statutes that appear to create a statutory lien. Further legislative clarification or opinion of counsel would be helpful to determine with possibly additional language or to reaffirm whether the legislative intent was to create a statutory lien. The state code may be more expansive and an attorney should be consulted to examine any specific situation involving a default.

H. Delaware

Municipal Bankruptcy Authority	Delaware does not specifically authorize its municipalities to file a petition under Chapter 9 of the Bankruptcy Code. Since 1980 and as of July 31, 2016, no entity in Delaware has filed such a petition.
Home Rule and Taxing Power of Municipalities	**Municipalities' Ability to Self-Govern** Delaware is a Dillon's Rule state.[i] Any city, town or village, however, with a population of at least 1,000 people may amend its municipal charter to become a home-rule entity, entitling the municipality to assume all powers that would otherwise need to be granted by the state legislature. As a further matter, every municipality in Delaware with a population over 50,000 may levy, assess and collect a tax for general revenue purposes on the general income of residents or money earned by nonresidents within the municipality's borders.[ii] **Taxing Limitations** Delaware law permits municipalities to collect an income tax on municipal residents and income earned in the municipality, but limits the tax to not exceed 1.25 percent of residents' income and 1.25 percent of the amount earned by nonresidents within the municipality per year.[iii] In addition, the Delaware Code limits the ad valorem tax assessment amount for one Delaware county.[iv]
Debt Default Prevention	**Debt Limitation** Cities with populations in excess of 50,000 with the power to borrow money and issue bonds may issue bonds up to an amount not in excess of 16 percent of the assessed valuation of real estate taxable by the city, but there are exceptions to this debt limit.[v] **Refunding Bonds** Municipalities may issue refunding bonds.[vi]
Remedies on Default	**Mandamus** In certain situations, bondholders or their trustee may bring a court action to compel the local governing body to perform a ministerial action that it has refused to undertake, such as collecting taxes or fees where the underlying bond authorization requires such a collection.[vii]

H. Delaware

Other Bondholder Protections	**Special Revenue Bonds** As provided by Section 922(d) of the Bankruptcy Code, payments to bondholders holding special revenue bonds would not be stayed on the filing of a municipal bankruptcy petition, and payments to holders could continue. Whether an issuance would qualify as a special revenue bond depends on the provisions of the authorizing statute with respect to the bonds at issue.[viii] **Statutory Liens** Were a municipal entity to file a petition under Chapter 9 of the Bankruptcy Code, bondholders holding bonds to which statutory liens have attached would continue to receive payment on those bonds. For a statutory lien to apply, the authorizing law of the bond issue must contain such a lien. No statutes covered by the categories were identified.

i *See Harvey v. City of Newark,* 2010 WL 4240625 (Del. Ch. Oct. 20, 2010) (discussing application of Dillon's Rule in Delaware).

ii DEL. CODE ANN. tit. 22, § 802 (granting of home rule); DEL. CODE ANN. tit. 22, § 901 (authorizing cities, towns and villages with a population over 50,000 to tax for general revenue purposes).

iii DEL. CODE ANN. tit. 22, §§ 901-02 (municipal users tax).

iv DEL. CODE ANN. tit. 9, § 8103. A similar provision exists eliminating the state's ability to levy, assess or collect a tax on personal property. In addition, the Delaware Code contains a provision limiting the tax rate for Kent County, Delaware to not exceeding the sum of 50 cents on each $100 of assessed valuation. DEL. CODE ANN. tit. 9, § 8002(b).

v This percentage does not include bonds issued to supply water to the city; bonds issued for sewer purposes for which the city collects rates, rents or fees; bonds for school purposes, but not to exceed 3 percent of the assessed value of the real estate unless the city has not met its debt limit, in which case it may issue school-related bonds above 3 percent as long as the 16 percent limit is not met; other bonds issued for which an exclusion may be authorized by law; guaranties or other obligations excluded by law; and bonds issued to fund outstanding notes not otherwise excluded, until such notes are retired. DEL. CODE ANN. tit. 22, § 106.

vi An example of a refunding bond provision in Delaware is DEL. CODE ANN. tit. 16, § 1417 (revenue refunding bonds).

vii *See Mayor and Council of Wilmington v. State ex rel Du Pont,* 57 A.2d 70 (Del. 1947) (considering mandamus action to compel city council to appropriate certain moneys to the board of education for the operation of public schools). It is possible that an aggrieved bondholder could pursue a writ of mandamus even absent authorizing statutory law.

viii *See, e.g.,* DEL. CODE ANN. tit. 16, § 1409 (revenue bonds issued for water and/or sewer authorities payable solely from rates, fees and charges on project) and DEL. CODE ANN. tit. 22, § 1310 (bonds issued by electric company secured by pledge of revenues). These are examples of special revenue bonds. The state code may be more expansive and an attorney should be consulted to examine any specific situation involving a default.

I. District of Columbia

Municipal Bankruptcy Authority	The District of Columbia is not authorized to file a petition under Chapter 9 of the Bankruptcy Code.[i]
Home Rule and Taxing Power of Municipalities	**Self-Governance** The U.S. Congress oversees the governance of Washington, D.C. In 1973, the U.S. Congress passed and the president signed the District of Columbia Self-Government and Governmental Reorganization Act delegating certain governing powers to a mayor and city council and in 1974, the citizens of Washington, D.C. approved a city charter.[ii] The Washington D.C. Code contains provisions allowing for local taxation.[iii] **Budget Requirements** The Washington, D.C. Code provides that each annual budget must include sufficient funds to pay all principal and interest on general obligation bonds becoming due and payable during the applicable fiscal year. The mayor is required to insure such payments, and if the budgeted funds are insufficient, the mayor must pay the principal and interest coming due from funds that are otherwise legally committed.[iv] **Taxing Limitations** The laws of Washington, D.C. do not contain any provisions limiting the amount of taxes that the taxing authority may assess.
Debt Default Prevention	**Debt Limitation** The District of Columbia may not increase its total amount of indebtedness above that existing on June 11, 1878.[v] **District of Columbia Financial Responsibility and Management Assistance Authority (commonly referred to as "District of Columbia Financial Control Board")** The authority is vested with the power to make recommendations and issue orders, rules or regulations "to ensure compliance by the District government with a financial plan and budget" and to promote the financial stability, management responsibility and service delivery efficiency of the District government.[vi] Further, if the District of Columbia enters into a "control period" where it fails to provide sufficient revenue to a debt service fund or a default occurs, it may not borrow money unless the authority provides prior authorization.[vii] **Refunding Bonds** In certain situations, a municipal entity may issue refunding bonds to refund and refinance outstanding debt.[viii]

I. District of Columbia

Mechanisms for Resolution after Default	**Receivership** In certain situations, courts may allow for a receiver with respect to revenue bonds where a default has occurred.[ix]
Remedies on Default	**Remedial Action** In certain situations, should a payment default occur, bondholders may (a) enforce all of their rights; (b) require the district to account as if it were a trustee; (c) petition to enjoin any acts in violation of the rights of holders; and/or (d) declare all bonds due and payable.[x] **Mandamus** In certain situations, bondholders or their trustee may bring a court action to compel the local governing body to perform a ministerial action that it has refused to undertake, such as collecting taxes or fees where the underlying bond authorization requires such a collection.[xi]
Other Bondholder Protections	**Special Revenue Bonds** Washington, D.C. is not authorized to file a petition under Chapter 9 of the Bankruptcy Code. Despite a lack of authorization, Washington, D.C. does recognize certain special revenue bonds.[xii] **Statutory Liens** Were a municipal entity to file a petition under Chapter 9 of the Bankruptcy Code, bondholders holding bonds to which statutory liens have attached would continue to receive payment on those bonds. For a statutory lien to apply, the authorizing law of the bond issue must contain such a lien. No statutes covered by the categories were identified.

---

i The term "municipality," as defined by the Bankruptcy Code, does not include the District of Columbia. H.R. Rep. No. 595, 95th Cong., 1st Sess. 312-13 (1977); H.R. Rep. No. 989, 95th Cong., 2d Sess. 25 (1978). Further, the term "State" is defined in the Bankruptcy Code as including "the District of Columbia ... except for the purpose of defining who may be a debtor under chapter 9 of this title." 11 U.S.C. § 101(52).

ii D.C. CODE § 1-201, *et seq.*

iii *See generally* Title 47 of the D.C. Code.

iv D.C. CODE § 1-204.83.

v D.C. CODE § 47-102. Should the district increase its indebtedness above the 1878 amount, any officer or person aiding and abetting the officer in increasing the total indebtedness "shall be punished by imprisonment not exceeding 10 years" and by a fine not exceeding $10,000.

vi D.C. CODE §§ 47-392.07 and 47-392.22.

vii D.C. CODE §§ 47-392.04 through 47-392.21.

viii Examples of refunding bond provisions in Washington, D.C. include D.C. CODE §1-204.63 (recognizing existence of general obligation refunding bonds); D.C. CODE § 9-911 (District of Columbia Regional Airports Authority revenue refunding bonds); D.C. CODE § 50-2512 (Public Parking Authority revenue bonds refunding provisions); and D.C. CODE § 10-1202.10 (allowing Washington Convention Center Authority to issue refunding bonds).

ix *See District of Columbia v. Jerry M.*, 738 A.2d 1206, 1213 (D.C. 1999) (noting that a court can appoint a receiver in equity even without a statute).

x D.C. CODE § 1-308.08; *see also* D.C. CODE § 9-920 (District of Columbia Regional Airports Authority; allowing for multiple remedies for bondholders on default); D.C. CODE § 9-1115.03 (Woodrow Wilson Bridge and Tunnel Compact); and D.C. CODE § 9-1107.01 (Washington Metropolitan Area Transit Authority Compact). The D.C. Code may be more expansive and an attorney should be consulted to examine any specific situation involving a default.

xi *See Debevoise v. Back*, 359 A.2d 279 (D.C. 1976) (dismissing mandamus claim because claim failed to base allegations on a statute setting forth specific procedures requested by plaintiff). It is possible that an aggrieved bondholder could pursue a writ of mandamus even absent authorizing statutory law.

xii *See, e.g.*, D.C. CODE § 9-910 (revenue bonds for District of Columbia Regional Airports Authority). This is an example of a special revenue bond. The D.C. Code may be more expansive and an attorney should be consulted to examine any specific situation involving a default.

J. Florida

Municipal Bankruptcy Authority	A municipality, taxing district or political subdivision may file a municipal bankruptcy petition. A local government entity or district school board otherwise eligible to file under Florida law must first receive prior approval from the governor for local governmental entities and from the commissioner of education for school districts. "Local government entity" includes a county, municipality or special district. Between 1980 and July 31, 2016, four entities in Florida have filed municipal bankruptcy petitions — two utility districts and two transportation districts.[i]
Home Rule and Taxing Power of Municipalities	**Municipalities' Ability to Self-Govern** The Florida Constitution provides that municipal governments shall have the "governmental, corporate and proprietary powers" to operate, except as otherwise provided by law, thus indicating that Florida is not a Dillon's Rule jurisdiction.[ii] Florida grants municipalities governmental, corporate and proprietary powers to enable them to conduct municipal government, perform municipal functions and render municipal services; however, there is no fiscal home rule. The state reserves all taxing authority. Specifically, the Florida Constitution states that counties, school districts and municipalities must be authorized by law to levy ad valorem taxes and may be authorized by law to levy other taxes.[iii] **Taxing Limitations** Municipalities have the power to levy ad valorem taxes on real and tangible personal property in an amount not to exceed 10 mills, exclusive of taxes levied for the payment of bonds and taxes levied for periods of not longer than two years and approved by a vote of the electors.[iv]
Debt Default Prevention	**Debt Limitation** Florida law does not appear to include any debt limits on its local units of government with respect to the issuance of bonds. Counties, school districts, municipalities, special districts and local government bodies with taxing powers may issue bonds payable from ad valorem taxes to finance or refinance capital projects only when approved by voters holding non-exempt property.[v]

J. Florida

Debt Default Prevention *continued*	**Division of Bond Finance and Local Government Financial Technical Assistance Program** Florida law contains provisions establishing the Division of Bond Finance of the State Board of Administration to provide information to local governments on the preliminary planning of new bond issuances and to recommend changes in law and local practices to improve the sale and servicing of bonds. Further, Florida law provides for a Local Government Financial Technical Assistance Program to advise local governments on debt issues.[vi] **Alteration of Labor Contracts If Financial Urgency Exists** Florida law allows municipalities to modify labor contracts if a "financial urgency" exists.[vii] **Receivership** In certain default situations, a receiver may be appointed to take possession of and operate the project.[viii] **Refunding Bonds** In certain situations, a municipal entity may issue refunding bonds to refund and refinance outstanding debt.[ix]
Mechanisms for Resolution after Default	**Bond Financial Emergencies Act** Should a state agency determine a triggering event has occurred in a municipality, the agency must notify the governor and the governor must determine whether state assistance to resolve the financial condition is needed. If the condition is considered an emergency, the governor may require the municipality to submit a budget for state approval; inspect and review the municipality's records; prohibit the local government from issuing debt; and authorize a loan to the municipality. In addition, a financial control board may be created that has advisory authority. When a triggering event has occurred or will occur, the entity must notify the appropriate governing body (such as the governor and Legislative Auditing Committee in the case of a local government entity). Should a state agency determine that one or more of the conditions applies and the local unit does not take any action, the agency must within 30 days after a determination report it to the appropriate supervising body and the Legislative Auditing Committee. If the governor or the commissioner of education, as appropriate, determines that state assistance will resolve or prevent the condition from occurring, the local unit is considered to be in a state of financial emergency and the governor or commissioner of education may take certain actions as defined by statute to assist the local unit in resolving the financial emergency.[x]

J. Florida

Remedies on Default	**Accounting** In certain default situations, bondholders may bring a proceeding to require the authority in question to account as if it were a trustee of an express trust.[xi] **Injunctive Relief** In certain situations, an interested person may bring an action against a board to enjoin or mandate the board to act.[xii] **Mandamus** In certain situations, bondholders may bring an action to compel the local governing body to perform a ministerial action that it has refused to undertake, such as refusing to collect taxes or fees where the underlying bond authorization requires such a collection.[xiii]
Other Bondholder Protections	**Special Revenue Bonds** As provided by Section 922(d) of the Bankruptcy Code, payments to bondholders holding special revenue bonds would not be stayed on the filing of a municipal bankruptcy petition, and payments to holders could continue. Whether an issuance would qualify as a special revenue bond depends on the provisions of the authorizing statute with respect to the bonds at issue.[xiv] **Statutory Liens** Were a municipal entity to file a petition under Chapter 9 of the Bankruptcy Code, bondholders holding bonds to which statutory liens have attached would continue to receive payment on those bonds. For a statutory lien to apply, the authorizing law of the bond issue must contain such a lien. Category SL-1.[xv]

---

i FLA. STAT. §§ 218.01 and 218.503.

ii FLA. CONST. art. VIII, § 2(b); *see also City of Boca Raton v. Florida*, 595 So. 2d 25, 28 (Fla. 1992) (discussing status of Dillon's Rule in Florida and noting that municipalities may "exercise any governmental, corporate, or proprietary power for a municipal purpose except when expressly prohibited by law, and a municipality may legislate on any subject matter on which the legislature may act, except [certain subjects prohibited by law by FLA. STAT. ANN. § 166.021(3)]").

iii FLA. CONST. art. VIII, § 2 (authorizing home rule); FLA. CONST. art. VII, § 9 (authorizing counties, school districts and municipalities to levy taxes); FLA. STAT. ANN. § 166.201 (authorizing municipalities power to tax).

iv FLA. CONST. art. VII, § 9. Pursuant to this provision of the Florida Constitution, ad valorem taxes, exclusive of taxes levied to pay bonds and taxes levied for periods not longer than two years when authorized by certain voters, may not be assessed at a rate greater than 10 mills for each of county purposes, municipal purposes or school purposes. This provision contains additional limitations and should be reviewed before determining the applicable tax limitation for a given project/local government. In addition, pursuant to FLA. STAT. ANN. § 166.211, municipalities may levy ad valorem taxes on real and tangible personal property in an amount not to exceed 10 mills, exclusive of taxes levied to pay principal and interest on bonds.

v FLA. CONST. art VII, § 12.

vi *See* FLA. STAT. §§ 218.37 and 163.055 (Local Government Financial Technical Assistance Program). Florida law also includes a technical assistance program for counties with a population of less than 75,000. FLA. STAT. § 163.05.

vii FLA. STAT. § 447.4095. This provision allows a municipality to impair collective bargaining rights in the event of a "financial urgency." "Financial urgency" is not defined in the Florida law, but one court has concluded that it is a "dire financial condition requiring immediate attention and demanding prompt and decisive action, but not necessarily a financial emergency or bankruptcy." *Headley v. City of Miami*, 118 So. 3d 885, 892 (Fla. Dist. Ct. App. 1st Dist. 2013). Another Florida appellate court, however, after agreeing with the definition of "financial urgency" cited in *Headley*, disagreed with the constitutional standard applied by the court in *Headley* with respect to when a municipality may impair collective bargaining rights. *Hollywood Fire Fighters, Local 1375, IAFF, Inc. v. City of Hollywood*, 133 So. 3d 1042 (Fla. Dist. Ct. App. 4th Dist. 2014).

viii Examples of refunding bond provisions in Florida include FLA. STAT. § 190.016 (bond resolution may allow for appointment of a receiver with respect to revenue bonds issued by community development districts); FLA. STAT. § 153.66 (bond resolution with respect to water and sewer systems may allow for appointment of receiver on default of principal or interest on a bond or other obligation or the breach of any covenant or condition of such authorizing proceedings or the provisions and requirements of Florida law controlling water and sewer systems); and FLA. STAT. § 159.618 (housing finance authority has power to confer on bondholders the right to obtain the appointment of a receiver). The state code may be more expansive and an attorney should be consulted to examine any specific situation involving a default.

ix Examples of refunding bond provisions in Florida include FLA. STAT. §§ 132.01 to 132.47 (general refunding law applicable to counties, municipalities, school districts or other taxing districts of the state); FLA. STAT. § 191.012 (refunding bonds regarding independent special fire control districts); FLA. STAT. § 298.52 (drainage and water control districts); FLA. STAT. § 190.016 (community development districts); FLA. STAT. § 331.333 (Space Florida); FLA. STAT. § 418.306 (mobile home park recreation district); FLA. STAT. § 349.04 (Jacksonville Transportation Authority); FLA. STAT. § 315.10 (port facilities financing); and FLA. STAT. § 159.13 (Revenue Bond Act of 1953; revenue refunding bonds). *See also* FLA. CONST. art. VII, § 12 (allowing counties, school districts, municipalities, special districts and local government bodies with taxing authorities to issue bonds payable from ad valorem taxation and maturing more than 12 months after issuances only to finance and refinance capital projects or to refund outstanding bonds and interest and redemption premium thereon at a lower average interest cost rate).

x FLA. STAT. §§ 218.50 to 218.504 (The Local Governmental Entity, Charter School, Charter Technical Career Center, and District School Board Financial Emergencies Act). Triggering events include: (a) failure within the same fiscal year in which due to pay short-term loans or failure to make bond debt service or other long-term debt payments when due, as a result of a lack of funds; (b) failure to pay uncontested claims from creditors within 90 days after a claim is presented, as a result of a lack of funds; (c) failure to transfer at the appropriate time, due to lack of funds: (1) taxes withheld on the income of employees; or (2) employer and employee contributions for: (i) federal social security; or (ii) any pension, retirement or benefit plan of an employee; (d) failure to pay, due to lack of funds: (1) wages and salaries owed to employees; or (2) retirement benefits owed to former employees; or (e) an unreserved or total fund balance or retained earnings deficit, or unrestricted or total net assets deficit, as reported on the balance sheet or statement of net assets on the general purpose or fund financial statements, for which sufficient resources of the local governmental entity, charter school, charter technical career center or district school board, as reported on the balance sheet or statement of net assets on the general purpose or fund financial statements, are not available to cover the deficit.

In 1996, the State of Florida intervened in the affairs of Miami when the city manager of Miami informed the governor of the city's fiscal crisis and requested intervention based on the fiscal emergency.

xi *See, e.g.*, FLA. STAT. § 159.618 (if a resolution, trust indenture or other contract so provides, a bondholder may require a housing finance authority and its members to account as if they were the trustees of an express trust). The state code may be more expansive and an attorney should be consulted to examine any specific situation involving a default.

xii *See, e.g.*, FLA. STAT. § 159.617 (allowing a bondholder of a housing finance authority to seek injunctive relief). The state code may be more expansive and an attorney should be consulted to examine any specific situation involving a default.

xiii *See, e.g.*, FLA. STAT. § 159.38 (applicable to certain revenue bonds); FLA. STAT. § 159.12 (Revenue Bond Acts of 1953); FLA. STAT. § 159.617 (housing finance authorities); FLA. STAT. § 243.69 (higher education facilities bonds); and FLA. STAT. § 243.32 (County Higher Educational Facility Authorities Law). It is possible that an aggrieved bondholder could pursue a writ of mandamus even absent authorizing statutory law.

xiv *See, e.g.*, FLA. STAT. § 159.33 (Florida Industrial Development Financing Act bonds payable solely from revenues of underlying project) and FLA. STAT. § 159.08 (Revenue Bond Act). These are examples of special revenue bonds. The state code may be more expansive and an attorney should be consulted to examine any specific situation involving a default.

xv Category SL-1: *See, e.g.*, FLA. STAT. § 132.43 (providing that liens become valid and binding on issuance of general obligation refunding bonds and investments held by escrow agent shall be immediately subject to lien). Note that this is an example of language that appears to strongly support that it is a statutory lien for use of proceeds of refunding bonds to pay the intended refunded bonds. The state code may be more expansive and an attorney should be consulted to examine any specific situation involving a default.

K. Georgia

Municipal Bankruptcy Authority	Georgia specifically prohibits its municipal entities from filing petitions under Chapter 9 of the Bankruptcy Code.[i]
Home Rule and Taxing Power of Municipalities	**Municipalities' Ability to Self-Govern** Although Georgia is a Dillon's Rule state, the Georgia Constitution specifically grants municipalities and counties home-rule authority, and state statute grants the same to cities. Georgia grants counties and municipalities authority to "adopt clearly reasonable ordinances, resolutions, or regulations relating to [their] property, affairs, and local government for which no provision has been made by general law," but explicitly withholds from municipalities the power to take any "action adopting any form of taxation beyond that authorized by law or by [the] Constitution."[ii] **Taxing Limitations** At the local level, Georgia state law includes only a taxing limitation for school districts, which are limited to 20 mills per dollar.[iii]
Debt Default Prevention	**Debt Compromise** In certain situations, an authority of a municipal corporation may compromise the municipal corporation's bonded debt.[iv] **Debt Limitation** A county, municipality or other political subdivision, including a special district, may not incur debt above 10 percent of the assessed value of the taxable property within the municipal entity.[v] **Governmental Monitoring Provisions** Local governments with a population exceeding 1,500 or expenditures of $300,000 or more must submit an annual audit to the state auditor. All other local governments act on a two-year audit cycle. If the auditor performing the audit includes in the audit any apparent material violations of state or local law, the local government must submit a plan of corrective action to the state government.[vi]
Mechanisms for Resolution after Default	**Receivership** In certain situations, a receiver may be appointed to take possession of and operate the project.[vii] **Refunding Bonds** In certain situations, a municipal entity may issue refunding bonds to refund and refinance outstanding debt.[viii]

K. Georgia

Remedies on Default	**Court Action** When bonds become due, bondholders, if necessary, may enforce their collection by action in the proper court.[ix] **Mandamus** In certain situations, bondholders or their trustee may bring a court action to compel the local governing body to perform a ministerial action that it has refused to undertake, such as collecting taxes or fees where the underlying bond authorization requires such a collection.[x]
Other Bondholder Protections	**Special Revenue Bonds** In the event Georgia law changes to allow for municipal bankruptcy filings, as provided by Section 922(d) of the Bankruptcy Code, payments to bondholders holding special revenue bonds would not be stayed on the filing of a petition, and payments to holders could continue. Whether an issuance would qualify as a special revenue bond depends on the provisions of the authorizing statute with respect to the bonds at issue.[xi] **Statutory Liens** In the event Georgia law changes to allow for municipal bankruptcy filings, were a municipal entity to file a petition under Chapter 9 of the Bankruptcy Code, bondholders holding bonds to which statutory liens have attached would continue to receive payment on those bonds. For a statutory lien to apply, the authorizing law of the bond issue must contain such a lien. No statutes covered by the categories were identified.

---

i GA. CODE ANN. § 36-80-5. The statute specifically prohibits any county, municipality, school district, authority, division, instrumentality, political subdivision or public body corporate created under the Georgia Constitution or laws of the state from filing a petition under the federal bankruptcy laws. Despite the fact that Georgia law specifically prohibits the filing of municipal bankruptcy petitions, in 2012 the Hospital Authority of Charlton County, Georgia filed a Chapter 9 petition. The Hospital Authority's petition was dismissed on July 3, 2012 for lack of state authorization. See *In re Hosp. Auth. of Charleston Cnty.*, No. 12-50305, 2012 WL 2905796 (Bankr. S.D. Ga. July 3, 2012).

ii GA. CONST art. IX, § II (granting legislature authority to set home-rule provisions); and GA. CODE ANN. § 36-35-6 (withholding taxing power from municipalities).

iii GA. CONST. art. VIII, § VI, ¶ 1.

iv GA. CODE ANN. §§ 36-38-20 to 36-38-23 (applies to municipal corporations including cities, towns, municipalities and villages). An authority in any municipal corporation may compromise the bonded debt, provided that the rights of creditors who refuse to assent to the compromise are not prejudiced. The authority, where outstanding bonds exist, may issue new bonds to be exchanged and stand in the place of the old bonds, which shall not exceed the amount of the previously existing total bonded debt, with interest.

v GA. CONST. art. IX, § V, ¶ I ("Debt limitations of counties, municipalities, and other political subdivisions"). Further, if a school district was authorized by law to incur debt in excess of 10 percent as of June 30, 1983, it may continue to be authorized to incur such debt. *Id.* In addition, pursuant to paragraph VI of section V, any county, municipality or other political subdivision intending to incur debt must first assess and collect an annual tax sufficient to pay the principal and interest on the debt within 30 years. GA. CONST. art. IX, § V, ¶ VI.

vi GA. CODE ANN. § 36-81-7.

vii *See, e.g.,* GA. CODE ANN. § 36-82-67 (holders of 25 percent in principal amount of revenue bonds outstanding or trustee may apply for receivership on default of payment continuing for more than 30 days with respect to bonds issued by counties, municipal corporations and other governmental entities); GA. CODE ANN. § 12-3-210 (Stone Mountain Memorial Association bonds); and GA. CODE ANN. § 46-3-147 (holders of 25 percent in principal amount of Municipal Electric Authority bonds outstanding or trustee may apply for receivership on default of payment continuing for more than 30 days with respect to bonds). The state code may be more expansive and the statutory authority for each individual bond issuance should be reviewed before assessing whether a receiver may be appointed.

viii The Georgia state constitution authorizes the issuance of refunding bonds by the state's municipalities. GA. CONST. art. IX, § V, ¶ III (the governing authority of any county, municipality or other political subdivision may issue refunding bonds).

ix *See, e.g.,* GA. CODE ANN. § 36-82-4. The state code may be more expansive and the statutory authority for each individual bond issuance should be reviewed before assessing remedies that may be available to bondholders.

x *See, e.g.,* GA. CODE ANN. § 32-10-43 (Georgia Highway Authority revenue bonds). It is possible that an aggrieved bondholder could pursue a writ of mandamus even absent authorizing statutory law.

xi *See, e.g.,* GA. CODE ANN. § 32-10-43 (Georgia Highway Authority revenue bonds); GA. CODE ANN. § 6-4-8 (Georgia Airport Development Authority revenue bonds); and GA. CODE ANN. § 10-9-40 (Georgia World Congress Center revenue bonds). The state code is more expansive with respect to provisions authorizing the issuance of revenue bonds, and an attorney should be consulted to examine any specific situation involving a default.

L. Hawaii

Municipal Bankruptcy Authority	Hawaii does not specifically authorize its entities to file for municipal bankruptcy under Chapter 9 of the Bankruptcy Code. Between 1980 and July 31, 2016, no Hawaiian municipal entity has attempted to file such a petition.
Home Rule and Taxing Power of Municipalities	**Municipalities' Ability to Self-Govern** Hawaii is a Dillon's Rule jurisdiction.[i] The power to levy property taxes is specifically reserved for the counties, except for the county of Kalawao. The state legislature, however, may delegate other taxing powers to the state's political subdivisions. Further, the state's political subdivisions may provide for home-rule charters without legislative approval. Counties may enact ordinances deemed necessary to protect life, health and property, so long as those ordinances do not conflict with state law. The state, however, reserves the right to reallocate that power.[ii] **Taxing Limitations** Hawaii state law does not include any ad valorem taxing limitations.
Debt Default Prevention Mechanisms	**Debt Limitation** No political subdivision may hold outstanding and unpaid debt above a sum equal to 15 percent of the total of the assessed value for tax rate purposes of real property in the political subdivision.[iii] **Refunding Bonds** In certain situations, a municipal entity may issue refunding bonds to refund and refinance outstanding debt.[iv]
Mechanisms for Resolution after Default	**Receivership** In certain situations, a receiver may be appointed to take possession of and operate a project.[v]
Remedies on Default	**Accounting** In certain default situations, bondholders may bring a proceeding to require the authority in question to account as if it were a trustee of an express trust.[vi] **Foreclosure** In certain default situations, bondholders may seek possession of a project on the occurrence of an event of default with respect to the bonds financing the project.[vii]

L. Hawaii

Remedies on Default *continued*	**Mandamus** In certain situations, bondholders may bring an action to compel the local governing body to perform a ministerial action that it has refused to undertake, such as collecting taxes or fees where the underlying bond authorization requires such a collection.[viii] **Bondholder Action** On default of payment of principal at maturity or interest when it comes due, a bondholder may bring an action at law against a defaulting county for the amount due. The holders may also request that state payments to the county be garnished to pay the defaulted bonds.[ix]
Other Bondholder Protections	**Special Revenue Bonds** As provided by Section 922(d) of the Bankruptcy Code, payments to bondholders holding special revenue bonds would not be stayed on the filing of a municipal bankruptcy petition, and payments to holders could continue. Whether an issuance would qualify as a special revenue bond depends on the provisions of the authorizing statute with respect to the bonds at issue.[x] **Statutory Liens** Were a municipal entity to file a petition under Chapter 9 of the Bankruptcy Code, bondholders holding bonds to which statutory liens have attached would continue to receive payment on those bonds. For a statutory lien to apply, the authorizing law of the bond issue must contain such a lien. No statutes covered by the categories were identified.

---

i *See, e.g., In the Matter of the Application of Pacific Oil Transp. Co.*, 17 Haw. 575 (1906).

ii HAW. CONST. art. VIII, § 1 (granting state legislature authority to create counties and other political subdivisions, but noting "[e]ach political subdivision shall have and exercise such powers as shall be conferred under general laws"); § 2 (granting each political subdivision the power to frame and adopt a home-rule charter without state legislative approval); § 3 (allowing state legislature to delegate taxing powers to the political subdivisions, but specifically reserving property tax power for the counties).

iii HAW. CONST. art. VII, § 13. In determining the funded debt power of a political subdivision, certain exceptions apply, as more fully described in art. VII, § 13(1)-(9) of the Hawaii Constitution.

iv Examples of refunding bonds include HAW. REV. STAT. § 47.17 (allowing for issuance of general obligation refunding bonds by counties of Hawaii, Kauai and Maui and by the city and county of Honolulu); HAW. REV. STAT. § 356D-21 (refunding bonds for Hawaii Public Housing Authority); HAW. REV. STAT. § 266-55 (revenue refunding bonds for special facility revenue bonds for harbors); HAW. REV. STAT. § 227D (refunding bonds for special purpose bonds issued under Natural Energy Laboratory of Hawaii Authority); HAW. REV. STAT. § 206M-9 (refunding bonds for High Technology Development Corporation); HAW. REV. STAT. § 206-27 (refunding bonds for Oahu Land Development);

HAW. REV. STAT. § 206J-12 (Aloha Tower Development Corporation refunding bonds); HAW. REV. STAT. § 304A-2685 (University of Hawaii System refunding bonds); HAW. REV. STAT. § 53-16 (Urban Renewal Law refunding bonds); and HAW. REV. STAT. § 201H-71 (Hawaii Housing Finance and Development Corporation refunding bonds).

v *See, e.g.*, HAW. REV. STAT. § 206-31 (allowing appointment of receiver for Oahu Land Development bond projects) and HAW. REV. STAT. § 53-16 (bonds of redevelopment agency). The state code may be more expansive and the statutory authority for each individual bond issuance should be reviewed before assessing whether a receiver may be appointed.

vi *See, e.g.*, HAW. REV. STAT. § 53-16 (bonds of redevelopment agency). The state code may be more expansive and the statutory authority for each individual bond issuance should be reviewed before assessing whether an accounting may be sought.

vii *See, e.g.*, HAW. REV. STAT. § 53-16 (bonds of redevelopment agency). The state code may be more expansive and the statutory authority for each individual bond issuance should be reviewed before assessing whether bondholders may seek possession of a project.

viii An aggrieved bondholder likely could pursue a writ of mandamus even absent authorizing statutory law.

ix *See, e.g.*, HAW. REV. STAT. § 47-18 (recognizing actions of defaults of general obligation bonds issued by county).

x *See, e.g.*, HAW. REV. STAT. § 39-64 (recognizing that revenue bonds are payable solely from revenue of project or program for which the bonds were issued). This is an example of a special revenue bond. The state code may be more expansive, and an attorney should be consulted to examine any specific situation involving a default.

M. Idaho

Municipal Bankruptcy Authority	In Idaho, any "taxing district," as defined by the 1898 Bankruptcy Act, as amended, may file a petition under Chapter 9 of the Bankruptcy Code. The 1898 Bankruptcy Act defined "taxing districts" to include any "municipality or other political subdivision of any State, including (but not limiting the generality of the foregoing) any county, city, borough, village, parish, town, or township, unincorporated tax or special assessment district, and any school, drainage, irrigation, reclamation, levee, sewer, paving, sanitary, port, improvement or other district." Section 80 of the U.S. Bankruptcy Act of 1898, which contained the definition of "taxing district," however, was found unconstitutional in the U.S. Supreme Court opinion *Ashton v. Cameron County Water Imp. Dist. No. 1*, 298 U.S. 513 (1936). Between 1980 and July 31, 2016, four municipal entities in Idaho have filed municipal bankruptcy petitions, three of which were hospital districts. In March 2011, Boise County, Idaho filed a Chapter 9 petition. Boise County had no bond debt but filed likely due to a significant judgment against the county that it could not pay. This case was later dismissed due to the court finding that sufficient funds were available, and so the County was not insolvent.[i]
Home Rule and Taxing Power of Municipalities	**Municipalities' Ability to Self-Govern** Idaho is a Dillon's Rule state, but its state constitution includes provisions allowing local governments to adopt home-rule charters. The Idaho Constitution also allows the state legislature to approve provisions allowing the state's counties, cities, towns or other municipal corporations to assess and collect taxes for all municipal purposes.[ii] **Taxing Limitations** Property taxes in Idaho are capped at 1 percent of a property's market value. Debt service and special assessments are excluded from this cap.[iii]
Debt Default Prevention	**Bond Guaranty Act** In certain situations, the state may guarantee payment of bonds.[iv] Although in certain situations the state may guarantee bonds, the Idaho Constitution specifically prevents the state from assuming the debts of any county, town or other municipal corporation unless those debts were created to "repel invasion, suppress insurrection or defend the state in war."[v]

M. Idaho

Debt Default Prevention *continued*	**Debt Limitation** Under the Idaho Constitution no county, city, board of education, school district or other state subdivision may incur debt exceeding in that year the income and revenue provided for it in that year, without the assent of two-thirds of the voters. The Idaho Constitution also includes provisions to ensure the collection of an annual tax sufficient to pay the bond interest as it comes due and for the creation of a sinking fund for payment of the principal within 30 years.[vi] **Refunding Bonds** In certain situations, a municipal entity may issue refunding bonds to refund and refinance outstanding debt.[vii]
Mechanisms for Resolution after Default	**Accounting** In certain default situations, bondholders may bring a proceeding to require the authority in question to account as if it were a trustee of an express trust.[viii] **Debt Readjustment Plans** If an irrigation, drainage or highway district defaults on a bond payment or believes it is impossible for the district to pay its outstanding bonds, the board must prepare a statement of financial condition and prepare a plan for rehabilitating its finances. The plan may be irrevocably approved by a majority in amount of each class of creditors directly affected, and a court may approve a plan. Dissenting creditors are not bound.[ix] **Foreclosure** In certain default situations, bondholders may seek possession of a project on the happening of an event of default with respect to the bonds financing the project.[x] **Receivership** Idaho has traditionally allowed for the appointment of a receiver to levy and collect taxes with respect to defaulted revenue bond issuances.[xi]
Remedies on Default	**Mandamus** In certain situations, bondholders or their trustee may bring a court action to compel the local governing body to perform a ministerial action that it has refused to undertake, such as collecting taxes or fees where the underlying bond authorization requires such a collection.[xii]

M. Idaho

Other Bondholder Protections	**Special Revenue Bonds** As provided by Section 922(d) of the Bankruptcy Code, payments to bondholders holding special revenue bonds would not be stayed on the filing of a municipal bankruptcy petition, and payments to holders could continue. Whether an issuance would qualify as a special revenue bond depends on the provisions of the authorizing statute with respect to the bonds at issue.[xiii] **Statutory Liens** Were a municipal entity to file a petition under Chapter 9 of the Bankruptcy Code, bondholders holding bonds to which statutory liens have attached would continue to receive payment on those bonds. For a statutory lien to apply, the authorizing law of the bond issue must contain such a lien. Category SL-1.[xiv]

---

i IDAHO CODE ANN. § 67-3903. *In re Boise County*, 465 B.R. 156 (Bankr. D. Id. 2011). It is important to note that the current version of the Bankruptcy Code does not contain a definition of the term "taxing district," and this definition was included in provisions found unconstitutional by the U.S. Supreme Court in *Ashton v. Cameron County Water Imp. Dist. No. 1*, 298 U.S. 513 (1936). As one bankruptcy court in Idaho has stated: "The current Bankruptcy Code lacks a definition of 'taxing district.' Instead ... it uses the term 'municipality' to describe those entities that may seek relief under chapter 9, provided that they are authorized to do so under state law. This raises questions regarding the interpretation and effect of [the Idaho Code]. For example, does [the Idaho Code] continue to incorporate by reference the description of 'taxing district' contained in the now-repealed Bankruptcy Act of 1898, does it somehow embrace the definition of 'municipality' in the current version of the Code, or is the definition of 'taxing district' for purposes of [Idaho law] left open-ended or untethered due to the repeal of the Bankruptcy Act?" *In re Boise County, Idaho*, 465 Br. 156, 167 (Bankr. D. Id. 2011) (presenting questions, but finding court need not answer because the county was ineligible to file a Chapter 9 petition on other grounds). Interestingly, the Idaho statute was adopted in 1939, after the Supreme Court issued its decision in *Ashton*, finding the provisions that included the definition of "taxing districts" to be unconstitutional. Courts in Idaho at that time, however, appear to have accepted the use of the term "taxing districts" in determining who may be a debtor under Chapter 9. *See In re Drainage Dist. No. 2 of Ada Cy.*, 28 F. Supp. 84 (D. Id. 1939) (noting that Idaho provided drainage district with consent to file a municipal bankruptcy petition under the 1939 Idaho act).

ii IDAHO CONST. art. VII, § 6; *Caesar v. State*, 101 Idaho 158, 160 (1980) (noting that Idaho is a Dillon's Rule state).

iii IDAHO CODE ANN. § 63-1313.

iv IDAHO CODE ANN. § 33-5307 (state financial assistance intercept mechanism). Under this provision, if the state treasurer makes one or more payments of bonds payable by a school district, the treasurer shall: (1) immediately intercept any payments from any source of operating moneys provided by the state to the school district; and (2) apply the intercepted payments to reimburse the state for payments made pursuant to the state's guaranty until all obligations of the school district to the state arising from those payments, including interest and penalties, are paid in full. Via the statutory scheme, the state treasurer may impose a penalty of not more than 5 percent of the amount paid by the state. *See also* IDAHO CODE ANN. § 67-8725(d) (if a municipality does not make payment to paying agent within 10 days before scheduled payment date, the Bond Bank Authority or the state treasurer shall cause sufficient funds to be transferred from the reserve fund to the paying agent).

v IDAHO CONST. art. XII, § 3.

vi IDAHO CONST. art. VIII, § 3.

vii Examples of refunding bonds in Idaho include IDAHO CODE ANN. § 31-1901 (allowing any county in the state to issue refunding bonds to refund outstanding indebtedness); IDAHO CODE ANN. §§ 57-501 to 57-504 (allows counties, cities, villages, school districts, highway districts, good roads districts, irrigation districts and drainage districts to issue refunding bonds); IDAHO CODE ANN. § 43-610 (irrigation district refunding bonds); IDAHO CODE ANN. § 63-3106 (anticipation of revenue by taxing districts); IDAHO CODE ANN. § 33-1121 (school bonds, advance refunding bonds); IDAHO CODE ANN. § 50-1030(i) (municipal corporation refunding bonds); IDAHO CODE ANN. § 33-3804(i) (State Institutions of Higher Education Bond Act); IDAHO CODE ANN. § 40-414 (Idaho Turnpike Authority) and IDAHO CODE ANN. § 42-4104(g) (water and sewer district revenue bonds); and IDAHO CODE ANN. § 67-8916 (Idaho Energy Resources Authority Act).

viii IDAHO CODE ANN. § 50-1925 (allowing for housing authority to include in trust indenture ability of bondholder to seek an accounting). The state code may be more expansive and the statutory authority for each individual bond issuance should be reviewed before assessing whether an accounting may be sought.

ix IDAHO CODE ANN. § 43-2101 *et seq*. The plan may include (a) scaling down of classes of indebtedness, (b) extending payment time, (c) reducing interest, (d) determining whether the plan may be accomplished by cash or refunding bonds, and (e) the time in which a majority of creditors must approve the plan.

x IDAHO CODE ANN. § 50-1925 (allowing for housing authority to include in trust indenture ability of bondholder to seek possession of a project for so long as the housing authority remains in default); IDAHO CODE ANN. § 50-2717 (Municipal Industrial Development Program). The state code may be more expansive and the statutory authority for each individual bond issuance should be reviewed before assessing whether the remedy may be sought.

xi A.M. Hillhouse, 310-11; 344 MUNICIPAL BONDS: A CENTURY OF EXPERIENCE (New York: Prentice-Hall 1936) (noting that in 1932, Idaho allowed for receivers and further provided for receivership of special districts). *See also* IDAHO CODE ANN. § 31-4506 (pollution control financing under counties and county law); IDAHO CODE ANN. § 70-2108 (Idaho Port District Economic Development Financing Act); IDAHO CODE ANN. § 50-1925 (housing authorities); IDAHO CODE ANN. § 50-1037 (municipal corporation revenue bonds); and IDAHO CODE ANN. § 50-2717 (Municipal Industrial Development Program). The state code may be more expansive and the statutory authority for each individual bond issuance should be reviewed before assessing whether a receiver may be appointed.

xii *See, e.g.*, IDAHO CODE ANN. § 31-4506 (pollution control financing under counties and county law); IDAHO CODE ANN. § 70-2108 (Idaho Port District Economic Development Financing Act); IDAHO CODE ANN. § 67-6214 (Idaho Housing and Finance Association); and IDAHO CODE ANN. § 50-2717 (Municipal Industrial Development Program). It is possible that an aggrieved bondholder could pursue a writ of mandamus even absent authorizing statutory law.

xiii *See, e.g.*, IDAHO CODE ANN. § 70-2108 (Idaho Port District Economic Development Financing Act, allowing for revenue bonds to be secured by pledge on revenues and that lien is valid and binding from time pledge became binding on port district) and IDAHO CODE ANN. § 31-4506 (pollution control financing revenue bonds secured by pledge of revenues on project). These are examples of special revenue bonds. The state code may be more expansive, and an attorney should be consulted to examine any specific situation involving a default.

Along with provisions in the state code, the Idaho Constitution contains provisions related to special revenue bonds, including IDAHO CONST. art. VIII, § 3A (authorizing counties to issue environmental pollution control revenue bonds if approved by voters) and IDAHO CONST. art. VIII, § 3B (authorizing port districts to issue revenue bonds).

xiv Category SL-1: *See, e.g.*, IDAHO CODE ANN. § 57-234 (providing that a governmental unit securing its bonds by revenues, fees, rent, charges, taxes or other property shall be subject immediately to a lien of that pledge which shall be valid, binding and fully perfected having a priority over all other parties and shall continue until those bonds are paid in full). *See also* IDAHO CODE ANN. § 67-8717 (Bond Bank Authority may pledge sales tax revenues as security and revenues immediately subject to lien of pledge without physical delivery) and IDAHO CODE ANN. § 70-2108 (Idaho Port District Economic Development Financing Act, allowing for revenue bonds to be secured by pledge on revenues and that lien is valid and binding from time pledge became binding on port district). Note that these are examples of language in statutes that appear to support the existence of a statutory lien. The state code may be more expansive, and an attorney should be consulted to examine any specific situation involving a default.

N. Illinois

Municipal Bankruptcy Authority	Specific state authority to file a municipal bankruptcy petition only exists with respect to the Illinois Power Agency. With the exception of the Illinois Power Agency, no other municipal entity in Illinois is authorized to file a municipal bankruptcy petition without further state authorization. Courts in Illinois have entertained municipal bankruptcy petitions, including *In re Village of Brooklyn*, Case No. 03-34272 (Bankr. S.D. Ill. Nov. 23, 2004) (confirmation of plan); *In re Village of Alorton*, Case No. 05-30055 (Bankr. S.D. Ill. Dec. 11, 2006) (confirmation of plan); *but see In re Slocum Lake Drainage Dist. of Lake County*, 336 B.R. 387 (Bankr. N.D. Ill. 2006) (finding no specific authority and dismissing); *In re Washington Park*, Case No. 09-31744 (dismissed Dec. 21, 2010 due to lack of authorization). The cases in which plans were confirmed likely were not dismissed because the municipal filings were not challenged.[i]
Home Rule and Taxing Power of Municipalities	**Municipalities' Ability to Self-Govern** Illinois operates under Dillon's Rule by default. However, counties in Illinois with a chief executive officer elected by the electors of the county or any municipality with a population of more than 25,000 are automatically deemed home-rule units. Any other municipality can become home rule by referendum. Similarly, those units that are automatically home-rule units may elect not to be a home-rule unit through referendum. The state legislature may not deny or limit the power of home-rule units to levy or impose taxes upon areas within their boundaries. Additionally, municipalities that are not home-rule units are still granted the authority to levy taxes upon areas within their boundaries in order to provide special services to that area.[ii] **Taxing Limitations** In certain taxing districts, property taxes may not be increased by more than the lesser of 5 percent or the increase in the national Consumer Price Index for the year preceding the levy year, but this rate may be increased by a majority of voters voting in a taxing district.[iii]
Debt Default Prevention	**Debt Limitation** Various debt issuance provisions in the Illinois Code contain limitations on how much debt a particular municipal entity may issue. For instance, municipalities with fewer than 500,000 people may issue debt up to 8.625 percent of the total equalized assessed valuation of taxable property in the municipality. A school district for either kindergarten through eighth grade or ninth grade through twelfth grade may only issue bonds up to 6.9 percent of the taxable property in the district. Should a school district contain kindergarten through twelfth grade, the district may issue bonds up to 13.8 percent of the taxable property in the district.

N. Illinois

Debt Default Prevention *continued*	Other debt limitations include (a) 2.875 percent of taxable property in counties with populations less than 500,000 and townships, schools or municipal corporations with populations less than 300,000, or park districts, but this 2.875 percent limit does not apply to schools for acquiring or improving a site; constructing, extending, improving and equipping school buildings; or establishing a working cash fund; and (b) 5.75 percent of the value of taxable property for fire protection districts.[iv] **Financially Distressed City Law** Under this provision, a financially distressed city may receive assistance from the Illinois Finance Authority, which may provide financial aid to the city so that it can provide basic municipal services, while permitting the distressed city to meet its obligations with creditors and bondholders.[v] **Refunding Bonds** In certain situations, a municipal entity may issue refunding bonds to refund and refinance outstanding debt.[vi]
Mechanisms for Resolution after Default	**Financial Planning and Supervision** Under the *Local Government Financial Planning and Supervision Act*, a local government with a population less than 25,000 and suffering a "fiscal emergency" in certain instances may upon two-thirds vote of the members of its governing body petition the governor for the establishment of a financial planning and supervision commission in order to remove the "fiscal emergency." A unit of local government may contract out of the provisions of the *Local Government Financial Planning and Supervision Act*.[vii] **Receivership** In certain revenue bond default situations, a receiver may be appointed to take possession of and operate the project for which the bonds were issued.[viii]
Remedies on Default	**Appropriate Relief** In certain situations, a bondholder may obtain relief from an "appropriate civil action in the appropriate circuit court."[ix] **Foreclosure** In certain default situations, bondholders may foreclosure on a mortgage and seize and sell the underlying asset.[x] **Injunctive Relief** In certain situations, bondholders may obtain injunctive relief to enjoin an action with respect to a bond issuance.[xi]

N. Illinois

Remedies on Default *continued*	**Mandamus** In certain situations, bondholders or their trustee may bring a court action to compel the local governing body to perform a ministerial action that it has refused to undertake, such as collecting taxes or fees where the underlying bond authorization requires such a collection.[xii]
Other Bondholder Protections	**Special Revenue Bonds** As provided by Section 922(d) of the Bankruptcy Code, payments to bondholders holding special revenue bonds would not be stayed on the filing of a municipal bankruptcy petition, and payments to holders could continue. Whether an issuance would qualify as a special revenue bond depends on the provisions of the authorizing statute with respect to the bonds at issue.[xiii] **Statutory Liens** Were a municipal entity to file a petition under Chapter 9 of the Bankruptcy Code, bondholders holding bonds to which statutory liens have attached would continue to receive payment on those bonds. For a statutory lien to apply, the authorizing law of the bond issue must contain such a lien. Categories SL-1 and SL-2.[xiv]

i 20 ILL. COMP. STAT. 3855/1-20(4)(b)(15) (specific authorization for Illinois Power Agency).

Under the *Local Government Financial Planning and Supervision Act*, the financial planning and supervision commission has the power to recommend that a "local governmental unit," as defined in 50 ILL. COMP. STAT. 320/3(d), file a petition under Chapter 9 and to submit this recommendation to the state. 50 ILL. COMP. STAT. 320/9(b)(4). The Illinois Code, however, does not include any provisions specifically authorizing a public entity, with the exception of the Illinois Power Agency, to file a petition.

ii ILL. CONST. art. VII, § 6 (setting power of home-rule units) and ILL. CONST. art. VII, § 7 (discussing powers delegated to counties and municipalities other than home-rule units); *see also Tri-Power Resources, Inc. v. City of Carlyle*, 967 N.E. 2d 811, 813 (Ill. Ct. App. 2012).

iii 35 ILL. COMP. STAT. ANN. 200/18-185 *et seq.* (Property Tax Extension Limitation Law).

iv 65 ILL. COMP. STAT. 5/8-5-1 (municipalities less than 500,000). Certain exceptions to this provision exist, such as debt incurred for constructing a wastewater facility to comply with the Clean Water Act. This provision, further, does not apply to home-rule municipalities. 105 ILL. COMP. STAT. 5/19-1 (school district for either kindergarten through eighth grade or ninth grade through twelfth grade); 105 ILL. COMP. STAT. 5/19-1 (school district containing kindergarten and grades one through twelve); 50 ILL. COMP. STAT. 405/1 (local governments including counties with populations less than 500,000 and townships, schools or municipal corporations with populations less than 300,000); 50 ILL. COMP. STAT. 405/1.2 (providing exception for working cash fund); 70 ILL. COMP. STAT. 705/12 (fire protection districts); and 70 ILL. COMP. STAT. 1205/6-2 (park districts).

These statutes have been provided as examples of statutory debt limitations under the Illinois Code. The state code may be more expansive, and an attorney should be consulted to examine any specific situation.

v 65 ILL. COMP. STAT. 5/8-12-1 *et seq.* "Financially distressed City" means any municipality which is a home-rule unit and which (i) is certified by the Department of Revenue as being in the highest 5 percent of all home-rule municipalities in terms of the aggregate of the rate percent of all taxes levied pursuant to statute or ordinance upon all taxable property of the municipality and as being in the lowest 5 percent of all home-rule municipalities in terms of per capita tax yield, and (ii) is designated by joint resolution of the General Assembly as a financially distressed city. 65 ILL. COMP. STAT. 5/8-12-3.

A designation as "financially distressed city" shall last for 10 years until the city submits a balanced budget and proves its responsibility.

vi Examples of refunding bond provisions in Illinois include 65 ILL. COMP. STAT. 5/8-4-14 (allowing for refunding revenue bonds issued by municipalities with a population less than 500,000) and 65 ILL. COMP. STAT. 5/11-130-12 (allowing for water supply and sewerage system refunding bonds). The state code may be more expansive and the statutory authority for each bond issuance should be reviewed with respect to each proposed refunding bond issuance.

vii 50 ILL. COMP. STAT. 320/1 *et seq.* "Local governments" include counties, cities, villages, incorporated towns, townships, special districts and units of local government that exercise limited governmental powers, but do not include school districts. "Fiscal emergency" includes the existence of any one or more of the following conditions: (1) the existence of a continuing default in the payment of principal and interest on any debt obligation for more than 180 days; (2) the failure to make payment of over 20 percent of all payroll to employees of the unit of local government in the amounts and at the times required by law, where the failure has continued for more than 30 days after such time for payment, unless two-thirds of such employees agree in writing to such extension; (3) the insolvency of the unit of local government, being a financial condition that the unit is (A) generally not paying its debt as it becomes due unless it is the subject of a bona fide dispute or (B) unable to pay its debts as they become due. 50 ILL. COMP. STAT. 320/3.

In 1980 the Chicago Board of Education was placed under supervision of the state, and in 1989 East St Louis was placed under state supervision.

viii *See, e.g.,* 50 ILL. COMP. STAT. 445/6 (Industrial Building Revenue Bond Act); 50 ILL. COMP. STAT. 455/6 (Medical Services Facilities Revenue Act); 50 ILL. COMP. STAT. 465/20 (Local Government Housing Finance Act); 65 ILL. COMP. STAT. 5/11-103-15 (airports for municipalities of less than 500,000); 65 ILL. COMP. STAT. 5/11-119.1-6 (Joint Municipal Electric Power Agencies' bond documents may contain provisions allowing for appointment of receiver); 65 ILL. COMP. STAT. 5/11-119.2-6 (Joint Municipal Natural Gas Agencies' bond documents may contain provisions allowing for appointment of receiver); and 65 ILL. COMP. STAT. 5/11-130-7 and 5/11-130-12 (water supply and sewerage system bonds). The state code may be more expansive and the statutory authority for each bond issuance should be reviewed before assessing whether a receiver may be appointed.

ix *See, e.g.,* 50 ILL. COMP. STAT. 445/6 (Industrial Building Revenue Bond Act) and 50 ILL. COMP. STAT. 465/20 (Local Government Housing Finance Act). The state code may be more expansive and the statutory authority for each bond issuance should be reviewed before assessing whether such a remedy is applicable.

x *See, e.g.,* 50 ILL. COMP. STAT. 445/6 (Industrial Building Revenue Bond Act); 50 ILL. COMP. STAT. 455/6 (Medical Service Facility Revenue Bond Act); and 50 ILL. COMP. STAT. 465/20 (Local Government Housing Finance Act). The state code may be more expansive and the statutory authority for each bond issuance should be reviewed before assessing whether bondholders may pursue a foreclosure action.

xi *See, e.g.,* 50 ILL. COMP. STAT. 445/6 (Industrial Building Revenue Bond Act). The state code may be more expansive and the statutory authority for each individual bond issuance should be reviewed before assessing the availability of injunctive relief under the particular statute.

xii *See, e.g.,* 70 ILL. COMP. STAT. 200/2-51 (Civic Center Code); 65 ILL. COMP. STAT. 5/11-48.3-11 (municipal zoo authorities); 50 ILL. COMP. STAT. 445/6 (Industrial Building Revenue Bond Act); 50 ILL. COMP. STAT. 455/6 (Medical Service Facility Revenue Bond Act); 50 ILL. COMP. STAT. 465/20 (Local Government Housing Finance Act); and 65 ILL. COMP. STAT.

5/11-103-15 (airports for municipalities of less than 500,000). It is possible that an aggrieved bondholder could pursue a writ of mandamus even absent authorizing statutory law.

xiii *See, e.g.*, 65 ILL. COMP. STAT. 5/8-4.1-11 (revenue bonds issued by municipalities paid by revenues from operation of utility system or revenue-producing enterprise) and 65 ILL. COMP. STAT. 5/11-130-7 (water supply and sewage system bonds). These are examples of special revenue bonds. The state code may be more expansive, and an attorney should be consulted to examine any specific situation involving a default.

xiv Category SL-1: *See, e.g.*, a statutory lien (105 ILCS 5/34A-511) provided for the debt issued by the Chicago School Finance Authority created in 1970 (105 ILCS 5/34A-102) which was discharged on June 1, 2009. *See also, e.g.*, 105 ILL. COMP. STAT. 5/1E-110 (creating statutory lien for Downstate School Finance Authority) and 65 ILL. COMP. STAT. 5/11-103-15 (airports for municipalities of less than 500,000 establishing statutory mortgage lien). These are examples of statutory liens. The state code may be more expansive, and an attorney should be consulted to examine any specific situation involving a default.

Category SL-2: *See also* 30 ILL. COMP. STAT. 350/13 of the Local Government Debt Reform Act dealing with certain pledges of specified revenues providing such pledge is valid, binding, immediately subject to the lien without further action, binding on other parties and capable of being escrowed. While the language appears to create a statutory lien on such pledged revenues, further clarification or opinion of counsel would be helpful to determine or reaffirm the legislative intent that a statutory lien was created. Further, there is provision for double-barrel bonds contained in 30 ILL. COMP. STAT. 350/15 where, in addition to a pledge of revenue, there is an ad valorem tax levied to pay the bonds if the revenue pledged is insufficient and the levy is abated if the payment is made from the pledged revenues. In addition, the state can issue general obligation bonds which have a set-aside mandated by statute where tax revenues are deposited into a general obligation bond retirement and interest fund where 1/12 of the next 12-month principal amortization and 1/6 of the next six months of interest are deposited. Again, while the language of these statutes is helpful to bondholders as statutory mandates for payment, further clarification would be appropriate before any analysis of a statutory lien could determine whether the intent was to create anything similar to a statutory lien. State Representative Sandack in 2015 sponsored a bankruptcy bill (H.B. 4214, 99th Gen. Assemb., Reg. Sess. (Ill. 2015)) which would provide the clarification and reaffirmation that the pledges of revenues to secure payment of bonds, notes and other obligations of state and local government are covered by a statutory lien. When and whether that legislation will pass the Illinois house and senate are yet to be determined.

O. Indiana

Municipal Bankruptcy Authority	Indiana does not specifically authorize municipalities to file for municipal bankruptcy under Chapter 9 of the Bankruptcy Code. Between 1980 and July 31, 2016, only one municipal entity in Indiana has filed a bankruptcy petition. This case occurred in 1989 before Congress greatly limited the ability of municipalities to file by requiring specific state authorization.
Home Rule and Taxing Power of Municipalities	**Municipalities' Ability to Self-Govern** In Indiana, Dillon's Rule applies only to townships.[i] Under the state's Home Rule Act, municipalities and local governments may exert such powers that are (1) not expressly denied by the Indiana Constitution and (2) not expressly granted to another entity. A township may not exercise any powers already exercised by another unit in which the township is located. Local governments, however, may not impose a tax unless expressly granted by state statute.[ii] **Taxing Limitations** Indiana state law sets aggregate tax rates for tangible property within a political subdivision depending on the location of the political subdivision. These taxation limits do not apply to funds needed to pay principal and interest on bonds.[iii]
Debt Default Prevention	**Debt Limitation** A political subdivision may not become indebted in an amount in the aggregate that exceeds 2 percent of the latest adjusted value of taxable property determined for the political subdivision immediately preceding the incurring of the indebtedness.[iv] **Distressed Political Subdivision Protections (Appointment of Emergency Manager)** Municipal corporations and special taxing districts in Indiana may file a petition with the state's Distressed Unit Appeal Board requesting that the entity be designated as a distressed political subdivision. If one or more of eight conditions apply to the political subdivision, the board may designate it as a distressed political subdivision and appoint an emergency manager. Separate conditions are delineated for school corporations.

O. Indiana

Debt Default Prevention *continued*	Should a public entity in Indiana be designated as a distressed political subdivision, and such public entity is not a school corporation, the Distressed Unit Appeal Board must appoint an emergency manager over the public entity. The emergency manager has the power, among other things, to assume and exercise the authority of the executive and board of the political subdivision but does not have the power to impose taxes or fees in addition to the taxes and fees authorized before the political subdivision was designated as distressed. The emergency manager may also prepare the political subdivision's budget; make expenditures; approve or disapprove contracts, expenditures and loans; renegotiate existing labor contracts; reduce or suspend employee salaries; and enter into agreements with other political subdivisions regarding services. Although the law contains provisions addressing distressed school districts, it expressly provides that an emergency manager may not be appointed over a school district.[v] **Refunding Bonds** In certain situations, a municipal entity may issue refunding bonds to refund and refinance outstanding debt.[vi] **Township Assistance** A township may be placed in control of a management committee and control board by the governor if it is determined that the township is a distressed township. The management committee shall take actions, as provided in the authorizing statute, to assess and audit the financial operations of the township. The management committee shall take claims for the payment of township assistance, such as claims for food and shelter, and pay the unpaid claims of these township assistance creditors in accordance with the waterfall provided in the authorizing statute. The control board supervises the township trustee in the administration of township assistance.[vii]
Mechanisms for Resolution after Default	**Receivership** Scholars have indicated that receiverships could be created to manage projects when payment on bonds is refused. In addition, Indiana law includes receivership provisions.[viii] **Redemption Bonds** If a bond fund of a county or township is insufficient to pay bonds as of the date of maturity together with interest, the board may enter into a contract with the owners of bonds for the issuance of redemption bonds.[ix]

O. Indiana

Remedies on Default	**Accounting** In certain default situations, bondholders may bring a proceeding to require the authority in question to account as if it were a trustee of an express trust.[x] **Foreclosure** In certain default situations, bondholders may foreclosure on a mortgage and seize and sell the underlying asset.[xi] **Injunctive Relief** In certain situations, an interested person may bring an action against a board to enjoin or mandate the board to act.[xii] **Mandamus** In certain situations, bondholders or their trustee may bring a court action to compel the local governing body to perform a ministerial action that it has refused to undertake, such as collecting taxes or fees where the underlying bond authorization requires such a collection.[xiii]
Other Bondholder Protections	**Special Revenue Bonds** As provided by Section 922(d) of the Bankruptcy Code, payments to bondholders holding special revenue bonds would not be stayed on the filing of a municipal bankruptcy petition, and payments to holders could continue. Whether an issuance would qualify as a special revenue bond depends on the provisions of the authorizing statute with respect to the bonds at issue.[xiv] **Statutory Liens** Were a municipal entity to file a petition under Chapter 9 of the Bankruptcy Code, bondholders holding bonds to which statutory liens have attached would continue to receive payment on those bonds. For a statutory lien to apply, the authorizing law of the bond issue must contain such a lien. Categories SL-1 or SL-2.[xv]

---

i IND. CODE. ANN. § 36-1-3-5 (township exception to inapplicability of Dillon's Rule).

ii IND. CODE. ANN. § 36-1-3 (Home Rule Act); IND. CODE. ANN. § 36-1-3-8 (power of taxation withheld). The Indiana Code grants local government units "all the powers that they need for the effective operation of government as to local affairs." IND. CODE. ANN. § 36-1-3-2. As a further matter, § 36-1-3-4 abrogates Dillon's Rule.

In fact, the Indiana Supreme Court has noted with respect to the general manner of local elections, "we will not adopt a 'Dillonist' mindset in trying to answer that question. Indeed, as the long march away from the Dillon Rule makes plain, it is far less burdensome on both the courts and the Legislature for the law to presume the existence of local authority to act absent some express prohibition, than it is to require legislation spelling out every detail of every permissible action a municipality may take." *Kole v. Faultless*, 963 N.E.2d 493-498 (Ind. 2012).

iii IND. CODE. ANN. § 6-1.1-18-3. The maximum aggregate tax rate is set at $0.4167 per $100 assessed valuation in areas outside of the corporate limits of a city or town and $0.677 per $100 assessed valuation in territory inside the corporate limits of a city or town.

iv IND. CODE § 36-1-15-6. A "permitted excess of debt limitation" authorizes a political subdivision to incur debt that exceeds the maximum amount allowed "for the public protection and defense only": (1) "in time of war, foreign invasion, or other great public calamity"; and (2) "upon petition of a majority of the property owners in number and value within the limits of the political subdivision." IND. CODE § 36-1-15-7.

In *Lake County Council v. Allen*, the county claimed that all debt incurred by the township in excess of 2 percent of its assessed valuation, Indiana's debt limitation provision, was in violation of article XIII, § 1, of the Indiana Constitution. 524 N.E.2d 771 (Ind. 1988). Upon declaring the township "distressed" on March 25, 1986, the trustees thus sought protection under the Distressed Township Act of 1986. Despite funding from the state of $7 million, the county refused to continue any plan, claiming that poor relief was the obligation of the township and not the county. *Id.* The issue on appeal was whether poor relief was ultimately the responsibility of the county and thus governed by its constitutional debt limit, rather than the responsibility of the township. *Id.* at 771-72. Affirming, the court held that the county indeed has an affirmative obligation to fund the township poor relief, therefore upholding the validity of the liabilities resulting from the distress of the township. The court stated that "clearly, the Lake County Council had an affirmative duty" to fund the township, "whether it was to be reimbursed by the township or not." Both poor relief and the Distressed Township Act which set up a four-person team to manage the finances of the "distressed" township were constitutional exercises of state authority.

v IND. CODE § 6-1.1-20.3 *et seq.* (distressed political subdivisions). These provisions apply to municipal corporations and special taxing districts. A municipal corporation under Indiana law is a unit, school corporation, library district, local housing authority, fire protection district, public transportation corporation, local building authority, local hospital authority or corporation, local airport authority, special service district or other separate local governmental entity that may sue and be sued. IND. CODE § 36-1-2-10. A special taxing district is any geographic area where an ad valorem tax may be assessed for a local public improvement. IND. CODE § 36-1-2-20.

Pursuant to the provision, a five-person Distressed Unit Appeal Board may designate a political subdivision as distressed upon the petition of the political subdivision and a finding of any one of the following: (a) a default on payment of principal or interest on bonds; (b) failure to make required payments to payroll employees for 30 days or two consecutive payrolls; (c) failure to make required payments to judgment creditors for 60 days beyond when the judgment was recorded; (d) failure for at least 30 days to forward required employee taxes, transfer FICA contributions or deposit minimum pension fund payments; (e) accumulation of a deficit equaling or exceeding 8 percent of the political subdivision's revenues; (f) negotiation of a resolution of an adjustment of a claim in the aggregate exceeding 30 percent of the political subdivision's anticipated annual revenues, if claim is 90 days or more past due; (g) carrying over interfund loans for the benefit of the same fund at the end of two successive years; and (h) a showing of severe distress from certain property tax credits provided under Indiana law. In the case of a school corporation, the Distressed Unit Appeal Board may designate a school corporation as distressed if the school corporation (a) issues refunding bonds under § 5-1-5-2.5 under Indiana law or adopts a resolution under Indiana Code § 5-1-5-2.5(g) with respect to issuing refunding bonds; (b) has a debt ratio among the ten highest of all school corporations in the state with respect to the 2011 ADM rankings; (c) has a debt ratio among the ten highest of all school corporations in the state based on total calendar year 2011 assessed valuation; or (d) the amount of homestead valuation in the school corporation in calendar year 2011 was at least 60 percent of the total amount of assessed valuation in the school corporation for calendar year 2011.

As discussed in the chart, the Distressed Unit Appeal Board has the power to appoint an emergency manager, except with respect to a school corporation. With respect to a school corporation, the board may make recommendations to the state board of finance as to whether the school corporation is entitled to a loan from the countercyclical revenue and economic stabilization fund established under § 6-1.1021.4-3(b) of the Indiana Code.

With respect to other political subdivisions, an appointed emergency manager possesses the powers to: (1) assume and exercise the authority and responsibilities of both the executive and fiscal bodies of the political subdivision relating to fiscal stability, but the emergency manager does not have the power to impose additional taxes or fees other than those already existing; (2) review the political subdivision's budget; (3) review employee salaries; (4) develop a written financial plan within six months after appointment; (5) develop a plan for paying all outstanding obligations; (6) review existing labor contracts; (7) adopt a budget for each year in which the political subdivision remains a distressed political subdivision; (8) review payroll and other claims for payment against the political subdivision; (9) make, approve or disapprove any contract, expenditure, loan, creation of any new position or the filling of any new position; (10) submit a report to the Distressed Unit Appeal Board every three months; and (11) petition the Distressed Unit Appeal Board when the political subdivision is no longer distressed. As a part of his or her duties, an emergency manager may renegotiate any existing labor contract; reduce and suspend employee salaries; and enter into agreements with other political subdivision for services. *See* IND. CODE § 6-1.1-20.3-8.5.

In 2012, three political subdivisions in Indiana filed petitions under these provisions: the Mt. Vernon Community School Corporation, Franklin Township Community School Corporation and the MSD Wayne Township. *See* Distressed Unit Appeals Board, Department of Local Government Finance, http://www.in.gov/dlgf/9083.htm (last visited June 22, 2015).

Additionally, in 2013 two political subdivisions in Indiana filed petitions under these provisions: the Beech Grove School Corporation and the Mount Vernon Community School Corporation. *See* http://www.in.gov/dlgf/9368.htm (last visited June 22, 2015). In 2014 one political subdivision in Indiana, the MSD Boone Township, filed a petition under these provisions. *See* http://www.in.gov/dlgf/7175.htm (last visited June 22, 2015).

vi An example of a refunding bond provision in Indiana is IND. CODE § 5-1-6 (revenue bond refinancing).

vii IND. CODE §§ 12-20-25-0.3 to 12-20-25-55. A "distressed township" is defined as a township that (A) has a valid township assistance claim that the county auditor cannot pay within 30 days after the claim is approved; (B) has township assistance expenditures during a year that exceed the year's township assistance revenues; (C) has imposed and dedicated to township assistance of at least 90 percent of the maximum permissible ad valorem property tax levy permitted for all of the township's money; and (D) has outstanding indebtedness that exceeds 1.8 percent of the township's adjusted value of taxable property; or (A) has been a controlled township during any part of the preceding 5 years; (B) has a valid township assistance claim that the county auditor cannot pay within 30 days after the claim is approved; and (C) uses advances from the county from proceeds of certain bonds.

viii A.M. Hillhouse, 508 MUNICIPAL BONDS: A CENTURY OF EXPERIENCE (New York: Prentice-Hall 1936) (discussing possible receivership to manage auditorium and recreation works of Indiana municipalities under 1933 statute).

See, e.g., IND. CODE § 36-9-11.1-16 (allowing for appointment of receiver to enforce revenue bonds issued by Marion County); IND. CODE § 5-1-4-20 (hospital bonding authorities); *see also* IND. CODE § 36-9-30-20 (solid waste collection and disposal revenue bonds); and IND. CODE § 36-9-23-23 (revenue bonds issued for municipal sewage works). The state code may be more expansive and the statutory authority for each bond issuance should be reviewed before assessing whether a receiver may be appointed.

ix *See, e.g.*, IND. CODE § 5-1-7-1 (redemption bonds of counties and townships).

x IND. CODE § 8-22-3-18.1(q) (local airport authorities); IND. CODE § 5-1-6-15 (revenue bond refinancing); and IND. CODE § 14-33-20-36 (water supply systems). The state code may be more expansive and the statutory authority for each bond issuance should be reviewed before assessing whether an accounting may be sought.

xi *See, e.g.*, IND. CODE § 36-9-36-47 (allowing for foreclosure of bonds issued in anticipation of collection of assessments with respect to lots or parcels of land) and IND. CODE § 5-20-2-9(c) (housing facilities). The state code may be more expansive and the statutory authority for each bond issuance should be reviewed before assessing whether foreclosure is an option for bondholders.

xii For instance, although not specifically contained in a particular provision authorizing the issuance of a bond, IND. CODE § 14-33-5-24 allows for a party adversely affected by an action committed or omitted by a board of a conversancy district to petition a court with jurisdiction to enjoin or mandate the board to act. *See also* IND. CODE § 14-33-20-36 (water supply systems).

xiii *See, e.g.*, IND. CODE § 5-1-4-20 (hospital bonding authorities); IND. CODE § 14-33-20-36 (water supply systems); IND. CODE § 8-5-15-14 (Commuter Transportation Districts); IND. CODE § 5-1-16-31 (Indiana Finance Authority financing of health facilities); IND. CODE § 8-22-3-18.1(q) (local airport authorities); IND. CODE § 5-20-2-9(c) (housing facilities); IND. CODE § 8-15-2-16 (operation financing of toll roads); IND. CODE § 8-10-1-19 (Indiana ports); IND. CODE § 5-1-6-15 (revenue bond refinancing); IND. CODE § 14-14-1-41 (Recreational Development Commission); IND. CODE § 14-33-5-24 (applicable to actions of Conservancy District boards). It is possible that an aggrieved bondholder could pursue a writ of mandamus even absent authorizing statutory law.

xiv *See, e.g.*, IND. CODE § 8-1.5-2-24 (bonds issued to establish municipally owned utilities shall be payable from revenue of the utility). This is an example of a special revenue bond. The state code may be more expansive, and an attorney should be consulted to examine any specific situation involving a default.

xv Category SL-1 or SL-2: *See, e.g.*, IND. CODE § 36-9-11.1-16 (establishing statutory lien on property acquired or improved from proceeds of bonds issued by Marion County for parking facilities). While the language of this statute appears to create a statutory lien and specifically refers to the lien as a statutory lien, further clarification as a reaffirmation or additional legislative language may help to confirm that it is legislatively intended to be a statutory lien; hence the designation SL-1 or SL-2. The state code may be more expansive, and an attorney should be consulted to examine any specific situation involving a default.

P. Iowa

Municipal Bankruptcy Authority	Iowa has no specific municipal bankruptcy authorization and prohibits municipalities from being a debtor in a Chapter 9 bankruptcy, except that a city, county or other political subdivision may file a petition under Chapter 9 of the Bankruptcy Code if it is rendered insolvent as a result of a debt involuntarily incurred which is not pursuant to a valid and binding collective bargaining agreement or a previously authorized bond issue. Between 1980 and July 31, 2016, no entity in Iowa has filed such a petition.[i]
Home Rule and Taxing Power of Municipalities	**Municipalities' Ability to Self-Govern** Iowa is not a Dillon's Rule state and, in fact, the Iowa Constitution specifically provides that "[t]he rule or proposition of law that a municipal corporation [county or joint county-municipal corporation government] possesses and can exercise only those powers granted in express words is not a part of the law of this state."[ii] Although with respect to its municipal corporations Iowa is not a Dillon's Rule jurisdiction, Iowa case law indicates that Dillon's Rule *does apply* to Iowa school corporations.[iii] The state constitution also provides for municipal and county home rule, but municipalities do not have the power to tax unless expressly authorized by the state legislature.[iv] **Taxing Limitations** The Iowa Code limits levies of property tax in counties and cities.[v]
Debt Default Prevention	**Debt Limitation** No county or other political or municipal corporation may incur debt in the aggregate exceeding 5 percent of the value of the taxable property within it, as ascertained by the last state and county tax lists previous to incurring the indebtedness.[vi] **Refunding Bonds** In certain situations, a municipal entity may issue refunding bonds to refund and refinance outstanding debt.[vii]
Mechanisms for Resolution after Default	**Receivership** In most default situations, a receiver may be appointed to take possession of and operate the project.[viii] **Moratorium** In certain revenue bond default situations, the defaulting municipality will be barred from entering into activities on its own, with the exception of releasing property for some industrial activity.[ix]

P. Iowa

Remedies on Default	**Mandamus** In certain situations, bondholders or their trustee may bring a court action to compel the local governing body to perform a ministerial action that it has refused to undertake, such as collecting taxes or fees where the underlying bond authorization requires such a collection.[x]
Other Bondholder Protections	**Special Revenue Bonds** As provided by Section 922(d) of the Bankruptcy Code, payments to bondholders holding special revenue bonds would not be stayed on the filing of a municipal bankruptcy petition, and payments to holders could continue. Whether an issuance would qualify as a special revenue bond depends on the provisions of the authorizing statute with respect to the bonds at issue.[xi] **Statutory Liens** Were a municipal entity to file a petition under Chapter 9 of the Bankruptcy Code, bondholders holding bonds to which statutory liens have attached would continue to receive payment on those bonds. For a statutory lien to apply, the authorizing law of the bond issue must contain such a lien. Category SL-1 or SL-2.[xii]

i IOWA CODE § 76.16 prohibits a city, county or other political subdivision from being a debtor under Chapter 9 unless as specifically provided in that chapter. In accordance with IOWA CODE § 76.16A, a city, county or other political subdivision may become a debtor under Chapter 9 if it is rendered insolvent as a result of involuntary debt. Debt is defined as obligations to pay money other than pursuant to a valid and binding collective bargaining agreement or previously authorized bond issue. To file, the city, county or political subdivision must make specific findings that (1) all or a portion of such obligation will not be paid from available insurance proceeds and must be paid from a general tax levy increase; (2) the general tax levy increase will result in a severe, adverse impact on its ability to exercise powers granted under applicable law, including without limitation providing necessary services and promoting economic development; (3) as a result of such obligation, it is unable to pay its debts as they become due; and (4) the debt is not an obligation to pay money to another city or county other organized entity or political subdivision. These provisions were intended to address situations in which a municipality has incurred a large judgment against it or a similar liability, such as damages caused by natural disasters, and cannot provide necessary services without levying a tax that would result in a severe, adverse effect on the municipality.

ii IOWA CONST. art III, § 38A (municipal corporations) and § 39A (counties).

iii *See Hawkeye Foodservice Distribution, Inc. v. Iowa Educators Corp.*, 812 N.W.2d 600, 610-11 (Iowa 2012) ("The only powers of a school district are those expressly granted or necessarily implied in governing statutes").

iv IOWA CONST. art III, § 38A (municipal home rule) and § 39A (county home rule).

v IOWA CODE § 331.423 (maximum basic levy for counties) and IOWA CODE § 384.1 (maximum basic levy for cities); *see also* IOWA CODE § 384.12 (identifying exceptions to city tax limitations). For general county services the maximum basic levy is $3.50 per $1,000 of assessed value of all taxable property in the county and, for rural county services, $3.95 per $1,000 in assessed value of taxable property. The Iowa Code also includes taxing limitations for cities for their general funds to not exceed $8.10 per $1,000 of taxable value, but it does contain exceptions. In addition, pursuant to Section 24.48 of the Iowa Code, counties and cities may appeal to the state to suspend the statutory property tax levy limitations in certain situations.

vi IOWA CONST. art. XI, § 3. As background, an Iowa court found that a park district was not a municipality distinct from the city in which the park district was located, but rather the district was an instrumentality of the city government. Thus, any bonds issued by the park district's board were a debt of the city and fell within the city's debt limit. *Orvis v. Bd. of Park Comm'r of City of Des Moines*, 56 N.W. 294 (Iowa 1893).

In *Fults v. City of Coralville*, 666 N.W.2d 548 (Iowa 2003), the Iowa Supreme Court considered a challenge by property owners in a tax increment financing ("TIF") district where the property owners contended that the TIF district's issuance of bonds would cause the city to exceed its constitutional debt limits. Because the provisions establishing the TIF district did not contain a legally enforceable obligation for the city to continue bond repayment in the future, the court found that the debt was not considered constitutional debt. 666 N.W.2d at 556-57.

The *Fults* court relied on existing Iowa case law for the proposition that "a city's debt is not considered constitutional debt where 'none of its resources or property can be taken for, or subjected to, the payment of any bond.'" *Id.* (citing *Interstate Power Co. v. Town of McGregor*, 296 N.W. 770, 777 (1941)).

vii An example of a refunding bond provision in Iowa is IOWA CODE § 419.6 (applies to project bonds issued by counties and incorporated cities). Further, when refunding bonds are issued to pay on improvement bonds, the power to create liens on the property is preserved. IOWA CODE § 384.68.

viii *See, e.g.*, IOWA CODE § 384.88 (applies to revenue bonds issued by "municipalities," including a city utility, city enterprise or combined city enterprise); IOWA CODE § 28J.23 (port authority revenue bond). The state code may be more expansive and the statutory authority for each bond issuance should be reviewed before assessing whether such a remedy is applicable.

ix *See, e.g.*, IOWA CODE § 419.4 (applies to project bonds issued by counties and incorporated cities) and IOWA CODE § 419.10 (payment of any revenue bond).

x *See, e.g.*, IOWA CODE § 384.88 (applies to revenue bonds issued by "municipalities," including a city utility, city enterprise or combined city enterprise); IOWA CODE § 28J.23 (port authority revenue bonds); IOWA CODE § 313A.20 (interstate bridges under the Department of Transportation) and IOWA CODE 419.4 (county or incorporated city project bonds). It is possible that an aggrieved bondholder could pursue a writ of mandamus even absent authorizing statutory law.

For example, in 1902, bondholders sued Sioux City, Iowa, with respect to district improvement bonds the city issued from 1886-1891 for the paving, curbing and grading of roads. The bonds were meant to be repaid with assessments on certain properties. The court found that the special assessment bonds should be deemed the direct obligations of the city, because the city had not exercised due care in managing the funds. A.M. Hillhouse, 111 MUNICIPAL BONDS: A CENTURY OF EXPERIENCE (New York: Prentice-Hall 1936).

Further, in 1975, the Supreme Court of Iowa upheld the constitutionality of IOWA CODE § 384.88 in *Sampson v. City of Cedar Falls*, 231 N.W.2d 609 (1975).

xi *See, e.g.*, IOWA CODE § 313A.16 (bonds payable by pledge of tolls from bridges). This is an example of a special revenue bond. The state code may be more expansive, and an attorney should be consulted to examine any specific situation involving a default.

xii Category SL-1 or SL-2: *See, e.g.*, IOWA CODE § 12.84; IOWA CODE § 12.90; IOWA CODE § 12.91 and IOWA CODE § 12A.8. These provisions appear to support the existence of a statutory lien even though issues could be raised as to the sufficiency of the wording, raising the question of whether further clarification is needed; hence, the SL-1 or SL-2 designation. The state code may be more expansive, and an attorney should be consulted to examine any specific situation involving a default.

Q. Kansas

Municipal Bankruptcy Authority	Kansas does not specifically authorize its municipal entities to file petitions under Chapter 9 of the Bankruptcy Code. Between 1980 and July 31, 2016, no municipal entity in Kansas has filed a municipal bankruptcy petition.
Home Rule and Taxing Power of Municipalities	**Municipalities' Ability to Self-Govern** Kansas is a Dillon's Rule state, but its state constitution provides cities with the powers of home rule and empowers cities to determine their local affairs and government, including levying taxes, unless the tax exceeds a state law of general application. In addition, the Kansas state code includes provisions authorizing home-rule powers for counties, setting forth the powers and legislative prohibitions of county governments.[i] **Taxing Limitations** Kansas state law includes tax levy limitations for counties, cities and townships.[ii]
Debt Default Prevention	**Debt Limitation** Kansas state law limits the amount of debt that a county may issue to 3 percent of the assessed value of all tangible taxable property in the county, except that the counties of Wyandotte, North and Franklin may not exceed 30 percent of their assessed value. Generally, cities may not issue debt exceeding 30 percent of the assessed valuation of the city, with the exception of a narrow provision regarding Junction City.[iii] **Refunding Bonds** In certain situations, a municipal entity may issue refunding bonds to refund and refinance outstanding debt.[iv]
Mechanisms for Resolution after Default	**Receivership** In most revenue bond default situations, a receiver may be appointed to take possession of and operate the project for which the bonds were issued.[v]
Remedies on Default	**Accounting** In certain default situations, bondholders may bring a proceeding to require the authority in question to account as if it were a trustee of an express trust.[vi] **Foreclosure** In certain default situations, bondholders may foreclosure on a mortgage and seize and sell the underlying asset.[vii]

Q. Kansas

Remedies on Default *continued*	**Mandamus** In certain situations, bondholders or their trustee may bring a court action to compel the local governing body to perform a ministerial action that it has refused to undertake, such as collecting taxes or fees where the underlying bond authorization requires such a collection.[viii]
Other Bondholder Protections	**Special Revenue Bonds** As provided by Section 922(d) of the Bankruptcy Code, payments to bondholders holding special revenue bonds would not be stayed on the filing of a municipal bankruptcy petition, and payments to holders could continue. Whether an issuance would qualify as a special revenue bond depends on the provisions of the authorizing statute with respect to the bonds at issue.[ix] **Statutory Liens** Were a municipal entity to file a petition under Chapter 9 of the Bankruptcy Code, bondholders holding bonds to which statutory liens have attached would continue to receive payment on those bonds. For a statutory lien to apply, the authorizing law of the bond issue must contain such a lien. No statutes covered by the categories were identified.

i KAN. CONST. art XII, § 5 (home-rule authority for cities); KAN. STAT. ANN. § 19-101a (home-rule authority for counties). With respect to counties, the Kansas Supreme Court has noted that "[w]e are to liberally construe home rule powers to give counties the largest measure of self government." *Gen. Bldg. Contractors, L.L.C. v. Bd. of Shawnee Cnty.*, 275 Kan. 525, 536 (2003).

ii *See* KAN. STAT. ANN. §§ 79-1945 to 79-1970.

iii KAN. STAT. ANN. § 10-306 (counties) and KAN. STAT. ANN. § 10-308 (cities). With respect to cities, bonds issued to acquire, enlarge, extend or improve any storm or sanitary sewer system; bonds issued to acquire, enlarge, extend or improve a municipal utility; or bonds issued to pay for street or all improvements immediately in front of city or school district property are not included in the bonded indebtedness calculation. KAN. STAT. ANN. § 10-309. Certain bonds are excluded from the county debt limit. KAN. STAT. ANN. § 10-307. Revenue bonds also are not included in the calculation. KAN. STAT. ANN. § 10-311.

iv An example of a refunding bond provision in Kansas law is KAN. STAT. ANN. § 12-874 (city or natural gas authority related to refunding bonds to retire interest-bearing revenue bonds). Under Kansas law, the maturity may not be longer than 40 years, and under KAN. STAT. ANN. § 10-1009 the rate of interest may not exceed the daily yield for 10-year treasury bonds, plus 3 percent, if interest is deductible from gross income for federal income taxation purposes, or 4 percent, if interest is not deductible. *See also* KAN. STAT. ANN. § 12-6a36 (general municipal general obligation bonds).

v *See, e.g.*, KAN. STAT. ANN. § 12-8,103 (Municipal Energy Agency) and KAN. STAT. ANN. § 17-2355 (allowing for municipality to designate in housing project's trust indenture the appointment of a receiver as a remedy). The state code may be more expansive than the example cited here and the statutory authority for each individual bond issuance should be reviewed before assessing whether a receiver may be appointed.

vi *See, e.g.*, KAN. STAT. ANN. § 17-2355 (allowing for municipality to designate in housing project's trust indenture an accounting as a remedy). The state code may be more expansive and the statutory authority for each bond issuance should be reviewed before assessing whether an accounting may be sought.

vii KAN. STAT. ANN. § 17-2355 (allowing for municipality to designate in housing project's trust indenture the surrender of a project as a remedy). The state code may be more expansive and the statutory authority for each bond issuance should be reviewed before assessing whether foreclosure is an option for bondholders.

viii *See* A.M. Hillhouse, 100 MUNICIPAL BONDS: A CENTURY OF EXPERIENCE (New York: Prentice-Hall 1936) (discussing application of writ of mandamus to require bondholder payment). In one case, the town of Atchison, Kansas, in 1913 had proposed an exchange offer to its bondholders on past-due 4 percent bonds. The town offered, instead, new 4 percent, 20-year bonds and bondholders declined. The bondholders then brought suit. The Kansas Supreme Court issued a writ of mandamus to compel the town to repay the bonds and also required the town to include provisions for bond repayment and repayment of the bondholders' expenses in any tax levy. It is possible that an aggrieved bondholder could pursue a writ of mandamus even absent authorizing statutory law. *See also* KAN. STAT. ANN. § 12-3715 (allowing action in equity or by suit, action, mandamus or other action with respect to sewage disposal facilities and improvements); KAN. STAT. ANN. § 68-2080 (allowing action in equity or by suit, action, mandamus or other action with respect to toll roads and turnpikes) and KAN. STAT. ANN. § 68-2308 (allowing action in equity, by suit, action, mandamus, or other action with respect to highways and freeways).

ix *See, e.g.*, KAN. STAT. ANN. § 10-1205 (utility revenue bonds); KAN. STAT. ANN. § 12-2709 (revenue bonds for operation of common water supply and waterworks systems); KAN. STAT. ANN. § 13-1255 (utility revenue bonds) and KAN. STAT. ANN. § 13-1398 (revenue bonds for swimming pools and golf courses). These are examples of special revenue bonds. The state code may be more expansive, and an attorney should be consulted to examine any specific situation.

R. Kentucky

Municipal Bankruptcy Authority	Any taxing agency or instrumentality in Kentucky may file a petition under Chapter 9 of the Bankruptcy Code. A county may not file, however, unless its proposed plan of adjustment is first approved by the state local debt officer and the state local finance officer. "Taxing agency" means any municipality or other political subdivision, including (but not limited to) any county, city, borough, village, parish, town or township; unincorporated tax or special assessment district; and any school, drainage, irrigation, reclamation, levee, sewer or paving, sanitary, port, improvement or other district. Unless an entity is specifically identified above, it is not authorized to file a municipal bankruptcy petition. Between 1980 and July 31, 2016, five municipal entities in Kentucky have filed such a petition.[i]
Home Rule and Taxing Power of Municipalities	**Municipalities' Ability to Self-Govern** Kentucky is a Dillon's Rule state. The Kentucky Constitution allows the state legislature to provide cities with the power to perform any function within their boundaries that furthers a public purpose and does not conflict with state law.[ii] In addition, on all issuances of debt by a city, town, county, taxing district or other municipality, the local government unit must provide for the collection of an annual tax sufficient to pay the debt.[iii] **Tax Limitations** The Kentucky state constitution includes certain tax rate limits for cities, counties and taxing districts for other than school purposes. In addition, Kentucky state law includes limitations on the amount that a city or urban-county government may raise property taxes in any given year.[iv]
Debt Default Prevention	**Debt Limitation** The Kentucky Constitution contains debt limitations for cities, towns, counties and taxing districts. A city with a population of 15,000 or more may not issue debt exceeding 10 percent of the taxable property in the city; cities with fewer than 15,000 but more than 3,000 people may not issue debt exceeding 5 percent of the taxable property in the city; cities with a population less than 3,000 may not issue debt exceeding 3 percent of the taxable property in the city; and counties and taxing districts may not issue debt exceeding 2 percent of the taxable property in the county or taxing district. The constitutional provision applies unless in the case of emergency, public health or safety.[v] **Refunding Bonds** In certain situations, a municipal entity may issue refunding bonds to refund and refinance outstanding debt.[vi]

R. Kentucky

Mechanisms for Resolution after Default	**Appointment of Trustee** In certain situations, the holders of 20 percent of any class of bonds may move for the appointment of a trustee where a default exceeding 30 days in payment of interest or principal exists and the district in question has failed to comply with specified law or has breached its contract with bondholders.[vii] **County Restructuring** Any county, on petition of its fiscal court, may receive the assistance of the state local debt officer to restructure and reorganize its debt. Further, if the county is in or near a default situation, the local debt officer may investigate the debt situation and credit standing of the county and negotiate with officials and creditors to formulate a plan for issuing or reissuing bonds.[viii] **Receivership** In certain situations, a receiver may be appointed to take possession of and operate the project.[ix]
Remedies on Default	**Accounting** In certain situations on default, bondholders may bring a proceeding in any court of competent jurisdiction to require the authority in question to account as if it were a trustee of an express trust.[x] **Injunctive Relief** Certain provisions of Kentucky law allow for bondholders to bring an action in equity to enjoin any unlawful act or those acts that are a violation of the rights of bondholders.[xi] **Mandamus** In certain situations, bondholders or their trustee may bring a court action to compel the local governing body to perform a ministerial action that it has refused to undertake, such as collecting taxes or fees where the underlying bond authorization requires such a collection.[xii]
Other Bondholder Protections	**Special Revenue Bonds** As provided by Section 922(d) of the Bankruptcy Code, payments to bondholders holding special revenue bonds would not be stayed on the filing of a municipal bankruptcy petition, and payments to holders could continue. Whether an issuance would qualify as a special revenue bond depends on the provisions of the authorizing statute with respect to the bonds at issue.[xiii]

R. Kentucky

Other Bondholder Protections *continued*	**Statutory Liens** Were a municipal entity to file a petition under Chapter 9 of the Bankruptcy Code, bondholders holding bonds to which statutory liens have attached would continue to receive payment on those bonds. For a statutory lien to apply, the authorizing law of the bond issue must contain such a lien. Categories SL-1 and SL-2.[xiv]

---

i KY. REV. STAT. ANN. § 66.400. Under Section 66.400, it appears that the Kentucky legislature meant to grant the authority to file bankruptcy to any taxing agency or instrumentality that Congress authorized under the 1937 Bankruptcy Act, as well as to any taxing agency or instrumentality that Congress might name in subsequent amendments. Section 66.400 was amended in 1994 by the Kentucky legislature but retained references to the Bankruptcy Act, which act was replaced with the Bankruptcy Code in 1978. Under the Bankruptcy Act, a "taxing agency or instrumentality" included only municipal entities that had the power to tax. *See In re Las Vegas Monorail*, 429 B.R. 770, 778 (Bankr. D. Nev. 2010). However, references to "taxing" were subsequently removed from the Bankruptcy Act in or about 1946. *See id.* The modern Bankruptcy Code instead utilizes the term "municipality." As such, it is unclear if Section 66.400 would be interpreted such that an entity must still possess the power to tax to be authorized to file for Chapter 9 under Kentucky law.

ii KY. CONST. § 156b.

iii KY. CONST. § 159.

iv A city with a population of 15,000 or more may not exceed a tax of $1.50 on $100 of taxable property therein; cities with less than 15,000 but more than 10,000 people may not exceed $1 on $100 of taxable property therein; for all cities with a population less than 10,000, the tax may not exceed 75 cents on $100 of taxable property therein; and for counties and taxing districts, the tax rate may not exceed 50 cents on $100 of taxable property. KY. CONST. § 157. With respect to limitations on increasing property taxes, *see* KY. REV. STAT. ANN. § 132.027.

v KY. CONST. § 158.

vi An example of a refunding bond under Kentucky law is KY. REV. STAT. ANN. § 66.161 (any issuer). Maturity may not exceed 40 years unless it meets one of the statutory exceptions. KY. REV. STAT. § 66.091.

See also 2010 KY. ACTS 1 (allowing any university that has issued or caused to be issued debt obligations through a municipality or county government for which the rental or use payments of the university substantially meet the debt service requirements of those debt obligations to refinance those debt obligations if the principal amount is not increased and the rental payments of the university are not increased).

vii *See, e.g.*, KY. REV. STAT. ANN. § 76.261 (metropolitan sewer district bonds) and KY. REV. STAT. ANN. § 76.160 (sewer and drainage system bonds).

viii KY. REV. STAT. ANN. § 66.320. Any county, on petition of its fiscal court, is entitled to the assistance of the state local debt officer in formulating a plan for reorganizing its debt structure. When any county is in default on the principal or interest of any indebtedness, gives evidence of becoming unable to meet principal or interest maturities on any funded indebtedness within a reasonable time or has an indebtedness which might, with advantage to the county, be funded or refunded, the state local debt officer may investigate the debt situation and credit standing of the county and negotiate with officials and creditors of the county for the purpose of formulating a plan for issuing or reissuing bonds.

For instance, in the mid-1900s, Magoffin County used this provision when it wanted to issue more bonds in place of outstanding ones and cause Lincoln National Bank to buy back the outstanding bonds at a price below par. The commission and the state local debt officer disapproved the county's plan. *See Lincoln Nat'l Bank, Inc. v. County Debt Com.*, 294 Ky. 642 (Ky. Ct. App. 1943); *see also* Allen E. Ragan, *State Supervision of County Finance in Kentucky*, 55 KY. L.J. 132 (1966).

ix *See, e.g.*, KY. REV. STAT. ANN. § 216.150 (municipal hospitals); KY. REV. STAT. ANN. § 183.670 (airport facilities); KY. REV. STAT. ANN. § 97.190 (city and county recreational facilities); KY. REV. STAT. ANN. § 220.430 (sanitation districts); KY. REV. STAT. ANN. § 162.220 (school property); KY. REV. STAT. ANN. § 67.515 (county building commission); KY. REV. STAT. ANN. § 103.250 (industrial buildings and pollution control); KY. REV. STAT. ANN. § 58.060 (public projects revenue bonds); KY. REV. STAT. ANN. § 106.100 (waterworks for water district or city); and KY. REV. STAT. ANN. § 76.261 (metropolitan sewer district bonds). In one case, a Kentucky court held that the appointment of a receiver to collect delinquent municipal assessments was not authorized without establishing that the municipal authorities declined to act when directed by the court. *See City of Paducah v. White*, 244 Ky. 733 (Ky. Ct. App. 1932). *See also* KY. REV. STAT. ANN. § 96.184 (allowing utility revenue bondholders on petition of 25 percent of outstanding bonds to appoint a receiver). The state code may be more expansive and the statutory authority for each bond issuance should be reviewed before assessing whether a receiver could be appointed.

x *See, e.g.*, KY. REV. STAT. ANN. § 76.261 (metropolitan sewer district bonds). The state code may be more expansive and the statutory authority for each individual bond issuance should be reviewed before assessing whether to seek an accounting.

xi *See, e.g.*, KY. REV. STAT. ANN. § 96.184(5)(b) and KY. REV. STAT. ANN. § 76.261 (metropolitan sewer district bonds). The state code may be more expansive and the statutory authority for each individual bond issuance should be reviewed before assessing whether a bond issuance provision specifically allows for injunctive relief.

xii *See City of Paducah v. White*, 244 Ky. 733 (Ky. Ct. App. 1932) (finding receiver inappropriate because municipal authorities did not decline to act when directed by court). *See also* KY. REV. STAT. ANN. § 96.184 (allowing for any bondholder to bring an action to enforce his rights to require governing body to carry out its duties) and KY. REV. STAT. ANN. § 76.261 (metropolitan sewer district bonds). It is possible that an aggrieved bondholder could pursue a writ of mandamus even absent authorizing statutory law.

xiii *See, e.g.*, KY. REV. STAT. ANN. § 96.184 (city may issue revenue bonds to finance utility improvements). This is an example of a special revenue bond. The state code may be more expansive, and an attorney should be consulted to examine any specific default situation.

xiv Category SL-1 and SL-2: *See, e.g.*, KY. REV. STAT. ANN. § 91A.280 (amount of any outstanding assessment or installments on any property constitutes a lien securing payment); KY. REV. STAT. ANN. § 96.410 (waterworks are subject to statutory lien); and KY. REV. STAT. ANN. § 216.140 (statutory mortgage lien is specifically stated in the statute on municipal hospital and appurtenances). These are examples of purported statutory liens. The language in these statutes may appear to create a statutory lien and, in the case of §§ 216.140 and 96.410 relating to hospital and waterworks, the language specifically states it is a statutory lien. However, as to § 91A.280, it does not have specific reference to a statutory lien being created, and further legislative clarification or opinion of counsel would be helpful. The state code may be more expansive, and an attorney should be consulted to examine any specific default.

S. Louisiana

Municipal Bankruptcy Authority	Any parish, municipality, political subdivision, public board or public corporation, taxing district or other agency of the state may file a petition under Chapter 9 of the Bankruptcy Code. The State Bond Commission must provide written consent for a parish, municipality, public board, political or public corporation, subdivision, taxing district, road or subroad district, school district, sewerage district, drainage or subdrainage district, levee district, waterworks and subwaterworks district, irrigation district, road lighting district, harbor and terminal district or any other political subdivision, taxing district, political or public corporation to file a Chapter 9 bankruptcy petition. The governor and attorney general also must provide written approval for the petition and plan. Unless an entity is specifically identified above, it is not authorized to file such a petition. Between 1980 and July 31, 2016, only one municipal entity in Louisiana — a hospital district — has filed a Chapter 9 petition.[i]
Home Rule and Taxing Power of Municipalities	**Municipalities' Ability to Self-Govern** Dillon's Rule applies in the state for all pre-1974 charter municipalities. The state constitution provides that a home-rule charter shall "provide the structure and organization, powers, and functions of the government of the local governmental subdivision, which may include the exercise of any power and performance of any function necessary, requisite, or proper for the management of its affairs, not denied by general law or inconsistent with this constitution."[ii] In addition, local governments may not issue bonds or levy taxes without the consent and approval of the State Bond Commission.[iii] **Tax Limitations** Louisiana state law includes provisions depending on the type of parish or municipality limiting the amount that may be levied with respect to ad valorem taxes. Municipalities and parishes, however, may exceed this limitation by a majority vote of electors. As a further matter, Louisiana state law includes provisions requiring governing authorities issuing bonds to collect a tax annually and in excess of other taxes, sufficient to pay amounts due on bonds.[iv]

S. Louisiana

Debt Default Prevention	**Debt Limitation** The Louisiana Constitution gives the legislature the power to fix a limit on bonded debt payable solely from ad valorem taxes. The state's statutes provide that a municipality shall not issue general obligation bonds or incur debt, with certain exceptions, in the aggregate that is 10 percent or more of the assessed value of the taxable property in the subdivision. For certain other purposes, a municipality may not issue bonds exceeding either 25 percent or 35 percent of the assessed value of the taxable property therein, depending on the type of municipality.[v] **Refunding Bonds** In certain situations, a municipal entity may issue refunding bonds to refund and refinance outstanding debt.[vi]
Mechanisms for Resolution after Default	**Appointment of Fiscal Administrator** If the legislative auditor, the attorney general and the state treasurer unanimously determine that a political subdivision is reasonably certain to not have sufficient revenue to pay current expenditures, or to fail to make a debt service payment, the attorney general must initiate a proceeding in state district court to appoint a fiscal administrator for the political subdivision. If appointed, a fiscal administrator has the authority to direct all fiscal operations of the political subdivision and to take whatever action he or she deems necessary to return the political subdivision to financial stability in accordance with all applicable laws, rules, regulations and policies with which the political subdivision must comply.[vii] **Receivership** In certain situations, a receiver may be appointed to take possession of and operate the project.[viii]
Remedies on Default	**Foreclosure** In certain default situations, bondholders may foreclosure on a mortgage and seize and sell the underlying asset.[ix] **Mandamus** In certain situations, bondholders may bring an action to compel the local governing body to perform a ministerial action that it has refused to undertake where the underlying bond authorization requires such an action.[x] **Bondholder Action** In certain situations, bondholders may bring an action to force a local government to impose and collect sufficient taxes for payment of interest and principal on bonded debt.[xi]

S. Louisiana

Remedies on Default *continued*	**State Taxing Authority** If a political subdivision fails to impose and collect taxes adequate for payment of principal and interest on bonded indebtedness, state tax collectors may impose and collect the required tax.[xii]
Other Bondholder Protections	**Special Revenue Bonds** As provided by Section 922(d) of the Bankruptcy Code, payments to bondholders holding special revenue bonds would not be stayed on the filing of a municipal bankruptcy petition, and payments to holders could continue. Whether an issuance would qualify as a special revenue bond depends on the provisions of the authorizing statute with respect to the bonds at issue.[xiii] **Statutory Liens** Were a municipal entity to file a petition under Chapter 9 of the Bankruptcy Code, bondholders holding bonds to which statutory liens have attached would continue to receive payment on those bonds. For a statutory lien to apply, the authorizing law of the bond issue must contain such a lien. Category SL-2.[xiv]

---

i LA. REV. STAT. ANN. §§ 13:4741 and 39:619-620.

ii LA. CONST. art VI, § 5. The current Louisiana constitution was adopted in 1974. *See also City of New Orleans v. Bd. of Comm'rs of Orleans Levee Dist.*, 640 So. 2d 237, 242-43 (1994) (discussing evolution of Dillon's Rule and home rule in Louisiana).

iii LA. REV. STAT. ANN. § 39:1410.60. This provision provides: "No parish, municipality, public board, political or public corporation, subdivision, or taxing district, and no road or subroad district, school district, sewerage district, drainage or subdrainage district, levee district, waterworks or subwaterworks district, irrigation district, road lighting district, harbor and terminal district, or any other political subdivision, taxing district, political or public corporation, created under or by the constitution and laws of the state shall have authority to borrow money, incur debt, or to issue bonds, or other evidences of debt, or to levy taxes, or to pledge uncollected taxes or revenues for the payment thereof, where they are authorized by the constitution or laws of the state so to do, without the consent and approval of the State Bond Commission."

iv LA. CONST. art VI, §§ 26-27; *see also* LA. REV. STAT. ANN. § 33:2801 (tax limitations for municipal corporations); LA. REV. STAT. ANN. § 33:2803 (tax limitations for parishes). A parish may not levy an ad valorem tax exceeding 4 mills on the dollar, with the exception of Orleans parish (7 mills limit) and Jackson parish (5 mills limit). Municipalities in Louisiana may not levy an ad valorem tax in excess of 7 mills on the dollar of assessed valuation, and in some instances 10 mills on the dollar. *See also* LA. REV. STAT. ANN. § 39:569 (required taxes for bond payments).

v LA. CONST. art. VI, § 34; LA. REV. STAT. ANN. § 39:562. Section 39:562 contains higher debt limits for certain school districts and a recreation district. As discussed, for certain other purposes, a municipality may issue debt not to exceed 25 percent or 35 percent, as outlined in the statute. Specifically, municipal corporations, including cities, towns and villages, may issue bonds for opening, constructing, paving and improving streets, sidewalks, roads and alleys;

constructing bridges; purchasing or constructing waterworks; sewers and sewerage disposal works; drains, drainage canals and pumping plants; waste disposal facilities; facilities for pollution control and abatement; light and power plants; gas plants; artificial ice and refrigerating plants; halls; courthouses; jails; public markets and abattoirs; fire department stations and equipment; hospitals; auditoriums; public parks; natatoriums; libraries; schoolhouses; teachers' homes; and other public buildings; docks, wharves, and river terminals; acquiring and/or improving lands for industrial parks, within or without the corporate limits of the municipality; and other works of public improvement as the legislature may expressly authorize. LA. REV. STAT. ANN. § 39:553.

vi Examples of refunding bond provisions in Louisiana law include LA. REV. STAT. ANN. § 33:4308 (gas utility districts); LA. REV. STAT. ANN. § 33:4331 (revenue bonds issued by municipal corporations with populations between 75,000 and 200,000); LA. REV. STAT. ANN. § 39:691 (authorizing refunding bonds for municipal corporations, parishes, and school, road, subroad, drainage and subdrainage districts, irrigation districts, and parish school boards); and LA. REV. STAT. ANN. § 33:3051 (municipalities, parishes, and parish school boards).

vii LA. REV. STAT. ANN. §§ 39:1351-57.

viii *See, e.g.,* LA. REV. STAT. ANN. § 33:4253 (utilities); LA. REV. STAT. ANN. § 51:1159 (municipal/parish industrial development); and LA. REV. STAT. ANN. § 33:4284 (receiver shall have the rights and privileges enjoyed by the municipality in operating a utility). The state code may be more expansive than the example cited here and the statutory authority for each individual bond issuance should be reviewed before assessing whether a receiver may be appointed.

ix *See, e.g.,* LA. REV. STAT. ANN. § 33:4335 (municipalities with populations between 75,000 and 200,000); LA. REV. STAT. §51:1159 (municipal/parish industrial development). The state code may be more expansive than the example cited here and the statutory authority for each individual bond issuance should be reviewed before assessing whether foreclosure is an available alternative for bondholders on default.

x *See, e.g.,* LA. REV. STAT. ANN. § 33:4335 (municipalities between 75,000 and 200,000 people); LA. REV. STAT. ANN. § 51:1159 (municipal/parish industrial development); and LA. REV. STAT. ANN. § 33:4284 (utilities) § 39:569 (allowing "preferred cause" if municipal subdivision fails to collect sufficient taxes to pay bonded indebtedness). It is possible that an aggrieved bondholder could pursue a writ of mandamus even absent authorizing statutory law.

xi LA. REV. STAT. ANN. § 39:569 (applicable to municipal corporations, parishes, school districts, road, subroad, sewer, waterworks and subwaterworks, gravity drainage and subdrainage districts with certain exceptions, irrigation districts, hospital service districts, fire protection districts and gas utility districts). In addition, this provision requires certain local governments to impose a tax to cure any default, should one occur.

xii LA. REV. STAT. ANN. § 39:569.

xiii *See, e.g.,* LA. REV. STAT. ANN. § 33:4284 (revenue bonds for public utilities) and LA. REV. STAT. ANN. § 33:130.54 (revenue bonds for industrial parks). These are examples of special revenue bonds. The state code may be more expansive, and an attorney should be consulted to examine any specific situation involving a default.

xiv Category SL-2: *See* LA. REV. STAT. ANN. § 39:1430.1 (dealing with security interest by public entity relating to a pledge or lien created in connection with an issuance of securities issued by a public entity with a pledge of revenue or other property is valid and binding, perfected from the time the pledge is made and immediately subject to the lien without further action against all other parties). This language appears to create a statutory lien although further clarification by additional language may be helpful as to reaffirming the legislative interest to create a statutory lien rather than evidence effectiveness and perfection of the lien. *See also, e.g.,* LA. REV. STAT. ANN. § 33:4284 (lien on revenues with respect to bonds issued by public utilities). *See also, e.g.,* LA. REV. STAT. ANN. § 33.130.54 (all revenue bonds must be secured by a pledge, charge and liens on revenues without delivery or further act). Again, these statutory provisions may need further clarification before it is clear that a statutory lien is intended to arise from the force and effect of the statute. The state code may be more expansive, and an attorney should be consulted to examine any specific situation involving a default.

T. Maine

Municipal Bankruptcy Authority	Maine does not specifically authorize its municipalities to file a municipal bankruptcy petition. Between 1980 and July 31, 2016, no Maine municipal entity has filed such a petition.
Home Rule and Taxing Power of Municipalities	**Municipalities' Ability to Self-Govern** Maine is a Dillon's Rule state, but the Maine Constitution grants broad home-rule powers to municipalities. The constitution provides, "[t]he inhabitants of any municipality shall have the power to alter and amend their charters on all matters, not prohibited by the Constitution or general law, which are local and municipal in character." The Maine legislature, however, has the power to prescribe the procedure as to how a municipality may amend its charter.[i] In addition, counties, cities and towns have been given the power to tax.[ii] **Tax Limitations** Maine state law includes no ad valorem taxation limits but does include provisions limiting the growth of property taxes in any given year.[iii]
Debt Default Prevention	**Board of Emergency Municipal Finance** The purpose of this board is to enable municipalities that have fallen into financial difficulties to receive state assistance to reestablish a sound financial basis. If a municipality falls one year and six months behind in payment of its taxes to the state, defaults on any bond issuance or payment of interest on a bond issuance, or neglects to pay certain salaries and has received funds from the state in support of its poor, the board may audit or investigate the municipality. After an audit, if the board decides to do so by a majority vote, it may take over and regulate the administration of the government of the municipality and the management of the municipality's financial affairs through commissioners. The board may remain in charge of the local government until its taxes due the state or expenses and obligations incurred by the commissioners appointed by the board have been paid, and the appointed commissioners or the board determine the municipality's local affairs may be resumed under local control.[iv] **Debt Limitation** Maine law limits the debt that a municipality may incur for other than school, storm or sanitary sewer, energy facilities or municipal airport purposes to no more than 7.5 percent of the municipality's last full valuation. For school purposes, a municipality may not incur debt exceeding 10 percent of its valuation; for storm and sanitary sewer purposes, the municipality may not issue debt exceeding 7.5 percent of its valuation; and for municipal airport and special districts, the debt may not exceed 3 percent of the municipality's valuation. For all types of debt, the municipality may not exceed 15 percent of its last valuation.[v]

T. Maine

Debt Default Prevention *continued*	**Earmarking** In at least one situation, the state legislature has passed legislation authorizing the city to put its 1980 tax collections into an escrow account earmarked for repaying the tax anticipation notes.[vi] **Refunding Bonds** In certain situations, a municipal entity may issue refunding bonds to refund and refinance outstanding debt.[vii]
Mechanisms for Resolution after Default	**Accounting** In certain situations, bondholders may appoint a trustee, and the trustee may bring an action requiring the agency in question to account as if it were a trustee for an express trust.[viii] **Receivership** In certain default situations, Maine law allows for the appointment of a receiver with respect to revenue bonds.[ix]
Remedies on Default	**Attachment** In at least one situation, a Maine court has allowed the attachment to a city's bank accounts.[x] **Foreclosure** In certain revenue bond situations, a trust agreement may mortgage the project in question and, in the event of default, the trustee or mortgagee may take possession, hold, manage and operate the property or, without taking possession, sell or lease the property.[xi] **Mandamus** In certain situations, bondholders or their trustee may bring a court action to compel the local governing body to perform a ministerial action that it has refused to undertake, such as collecting taxes or fees where the underlying bond authorization requires such a collection.[xii] **Any Action Necessary** Certain provisions allow bondholders, by any suitable form of legal proceedings, to protect and enforce any rights granted by the state or bond resolution, trust or other agreement.[xiii] **Appointment of Trustee** In certain situations, where a bond default has occurred and continues for 30 days, holders of 25 percent in aggregate principal amount of bonds or notes may appoint a trustee to represent holders.[xiv]

T. Maine

Other Bondholder Protections	**Special Revenue Bonds** As provided by Section 922(d) of the Bankruptcy Code, payments to bondholders holding special revenue bonds would not be stayed on the filing of a municipal bankruptcy petition, and payments to holders could continue. Whether an issuance would qualify as a special revenue bond depends on the provisions of the authorizing statute with respect to the bonds at issue.[xv] **Statutory Liens** Were a municipal entity to file a petition under Chapter 9 of the Bankruptcy Code, bondholders holding bonds to which statutory liens have attached would continue to receive payment on those bonds. For a statutory lien to apply, the authorizing law of the bond issue must contain such a lien. Category SL-3.[xvi]

---

i ME. CONST. art. VIII, pt. 2, § 1.; ME. REV. STAT. tit. 30-A, §§ 2101-09 (legislative implementation of home-rule powers).

ii ME. REV. STAT. tit. 30-A, § 701 (sets forth amounts counties must tax in a tax year) and ME. REV. STAT. tit. 36, § 502 (allowing towns and cities to collect property tax).

iii ME. REV. STAT. tit. 30-A, § 5721-A (taxation growth limits for municipalities) and ME. REV. STAT. tit. 30-A, § 706-A (taxation growth limits for counties).

iv ME. REV. STAT. tit. 30-A, §§ 6101-6113. Municipality is defined as a city or town, except as provided in chapter 225. ME. REV. STAT. tit. 30-A, § 2001. Chapter 225 defines "municipality" as a city, town, special district, county, plantation or municipal village corporation, including any corporation owned entirely by an entity previously listed and providing water, sewer or electric service or performing any other essential governmental function. ME. REV. STAT. tit. 30-A, § 5903.

v ME. REV. STAT. tit. 30-A, § 5702. Certain types of debt do not apply to these limits. *See* ME. REV. STAT. tit. 30-A, § 5703 (excluding, among other debt, tax anticipation and revenue anticipation notes).

vi *See* Advisory Commission on Intergovernmental Relations, *Bankruptcies, Defaults, and Other Local Government Financial Emergencies* 25 (March 1985). The City of Saco, Maine, in 1979 defaulted on a $2.1 million tax anticipation note. The city's budget problems were caused by (i) mismanagement and (ii) a property tax limitation approved by voters. On the city's default, noteholders obtained a court order attaching the city's $1.6 million bank account, leaving no money to meet payroll or other obligations. On January 23, 1980, the state legislature approved legislation authorizing the city to put its 1980 tax collections into an escrow account earmarked for repaying the tax anticipation note. Local banks then loaned the city $2.2 million in tax anticipation notes and $540,000 in bond anticipation notes. Proceeds from these loans provided cash to repay the 1979 tax anticipation note and meet 1980 operating obligations.

vii Examples of refunding bond provisions in Maine include ME. REV. STAT. tit. 30-A, § 5403 (a municipality may issue refunding bonds with regard to revenue-producing municipal facilities); ME. REV. STAT. tit. 30-A, § 5772 (any municipality may issue general obligation securities for refunding all or part of its debt, for any purpose for which it may raise money); and ME. REV. STAT. tit. 6, § 179 (airport authority may issue refunding bonds).

viii *See* ME. REV. STAT. tit. 35-A, § 4156 (Maine Municipal and Rural Electrification Cooperative Agency bonds).

ix *See, e.g.*, ME. REV. STAT. tit. 10, § 1065(2) (revenue bonds for building and development); ME. REV. STAT. tit. 10, § 1067 (Municipal Securities Approval Program); and ME. REV. STAT. tit. 6, § 179 (airport authority). The state code may be more expansive and the statutory authority for each bond issuance should be reviewed before assessing whether a receiver may be appointed.

x *See* Advisory Commission on Intergovernmental Relations, *Bankruptcies, Defaults, and Other Local Government Financial Emergencies*, 25 (March 1985) (noting that holders of tax anticipation notes obtained a court order attaching the city's $1.6 million bank account).

xi *See, e.g.*, ME. REV. STAT. tit. 10, § 1065(2) (revenue bonds for building and development). The state code may be more expansive than the example cited here and the statutory authority for each individual bond issuance should be reviewed before assessing whether foreclosure is available to bondholders if a default were to occur.

xii *See, e.g.*, ME. REV. STAT. tit. 10, § 1067 (Municipal Securities Approval Program) and ME. REV. STAT. tit. 6, § 179 (airport authority). It is possible that an aggrieved bondholder could pursue a writ of mandamus even absent authorizing statutory law.

xiii *See, e.g.*, ME. REV. STAT. tit. 20-A, § 11425 (Maine Educational Loan Authority); ME. REV. STAT. tit. 35-A, § 4156 (Maine Municipal and Rural Electrification Cooperative Agency bonds); ME. REV. STAT. tit. 30-A, § 5408 (Revenue Producing Municipal Facilities Act).

xiv *See* ME. REV. STAT. tit. 35-A, § 4156 (Maine Municipal and Rural Electrification Cooperative Agency bonds). The trustee may enforce the rights of bondholders and bring certain actions, such as an accounting or other suit against the agency. Before declaring the principal on the bonds due and payable, the trustee must give 30 days' written notice to the governor, agency and attorney general.

xv *See, e.g.*, ME. REV. STAT. tit. 10, § 1064 (revenue bonds for building and construction paid for solely by revenues of the project). This is an example of a special revenue bond. The state code may be more expansive, and an attorney should be consulted to examine any specific situation involving a default.

xvi Category SL-3: Review of the language of certain statutes indicates a clarification would be appropriate to determine whether what was intended was a statutory lien rather than just recognition of perfection of the lien. *See, e.g.*, ME. REV. STAT. tit. 10, § 1065 (all revenues pledged and later received by a municipality are immediately subject to the lien of pledges without physical delivery) and ME. REV. STAT. tit. 20-A, § 11423 (Maine Educational Loan Authority bonds subject to lien of pledge without physical delivery). These are examples of statutory liens. The state code may be more expansive, and an attorney should be consulted to examine any specific situation involving a default.

U. Maryland

Municipal Bankruptcy Authority	Maryland does not specifically authorize its municipal entities to file a petition under Chapter 9 of the Bankruptcy Code. Between 1980 and July 31, 2016, no Maryland municipal entity has filed such a petition.
Home Rule and Taxing Power of Municipalities	**Municipalities' Ability to Self-Govern** Maryland is a Dillon's Rule state, but the state constitution grants the City and County of Baltimore, counties and municipal corporations the ability to adopt a home-rule charter, which shall become the law of the local government, subject only to the state's constitution, general laws and any public local laws inconsistent with the charter. Although code counties have the ability to levy taxes, such a tax may not be levied unless the tax was authorized when the county became a code county or the state legislature specifically authorized the tax. In addition, municipal corporations are granted the power to tax.[i] **Tax Limitations** Maryland state law includes no ad valorem taxing limitations.[ii]
Debt Default Prevention	**Debt Limitation** The aggregate amount of bonds and other indebtedness outstanding at one time in Maryland chartered counties may not exceed 6 percent of the assessable basis of real property of the county and 15 percent of the county's assessable basis of personal property and operating property.[iii] **Refunding Bonds** In certain situations, a municipal entity may issue refunding bonds to refund and refinance outstanding debt.[iv]
Mechanisms for Resolution after Default	**Receivership** In certain default situations with respect to revenue bonds, Maryland law allows for the appointment of a receiver.[v]
Remedies on Default	**Mandamus** In certain situations, bondholders or their trustee may bring a court action to compel the local governing body to perform a ministerial action that it has refused to undertake, such as collecting taxes or fees where the underlying bond authorization requires such a collection.[vi]

U. Maryland

Other Bondholder Protections	**Special Revenue Bonds** As provided by Section 922(d) of the Bankruptcy Code, payments to bondholders holding special revenue bonds would not be stayed on the filing of a municipal bankruptcy petition, and payments to holders could continue. Whether an issuance would qualify as a special revenue bond depends on the provisions of the authorizing statute with respect to the bonds at issue.[vii] **Statutory Liens** Were a municipal entity to file a petition under Chapter 9 of the Bankruptcy Code, bondholders holding bonds to which statutory liens have attached would continue to receive payment on those bonds. For a statutory lien to apply, the authorizing law of the bond issue must contain such a lien. Category SL-3.[viii]

---

i MD. CONST. art. XI-A, § 1 (charter provisions for Baltimore and counties); MD. CONST. art. XI-E, § 3 (charter provisions for municipal corporations); MD. CONST. art. XI-F, § 9 (taxing provisions for code counties) and art. XI-E, § 5 (taxing provisions for municipal corporations). *See also City of New Carrollton v. Belsinger Signs, Inc.*, 266 Md. 229, 237 (Md. 1972) (noting that "a municipal corporation has only limited powers").

ii MD. CONST. art. XI-F, § 8 provides that the general assembly has the exclusive power to limit property taxes. The Maryland Code includes provisions providing that, at least for code counties, it is the intent of the general assembly that it will not exercise this authority unless the possibility exists that a code county will impose "an excessive rate of property taxation or is incurring indebtedness in an excessive amount." MD. LOCAL GOV'T CODE § 11-103.

iii MD. LOCAL GOV'T CODE § 10-203.

iv An example of a refunding bond provision in Maryland law is MD. LOCAL GOV'T CODE § 19-207 (refunding bonds). This provision applies to any municipal corporation, county, Baltimore City, sanitary commission or district. These entities have the power to borrow money by issuing general obligation bonds, revenue bonds or any other obligation and may issue refunding bonds for the purpose of redeeming outstanding bonds, including redemption. The refunding bonds may be issued for the purposes of (a) realizing savings to the issuer in the aggregate of debt service on either a direct comparison or present value basis; or (b) debt restructuring that (1) in the aggregate reduces the amount of debt service or (2) is determined by the governing body to be in the best interest of the issuer, consistent with the issuer's long-term financial plan, and to realize a financial objective of the issuer, including improving the relationship of debt service to a source of payment such as taxes, assessments or other charges.

v *See, e.g.*, MD. CODE ANN., ENVIR. § 9-807 (sewage facilities in which receiver can enter and take possession of the sewage facility to operate and maintain the facility; set sewage facility rates, fees or charges; and collect, receive and apply all revenue of the facility). The state code may be more expansive than the example cited here and the statutory authority for each individual bond issuance should be reviewed before assessing whether a receiver may be appointed.

vi *See, e.g.*, MD. CODE ANN., ECON. DEV. § 10-124 (Maryland Economic Development Code); MD. CODE ANN., ENVIR. § 5-301 (Susquehanna River Basin Compact); MD. CODE ANN., ENVIR. § 9-1612 (water, ice and sanitary facilities); MD. CODE ANN., NAT. RES. § 3-913 (Northeast Maryland Waste Disposal Authority); MD. CODE ANN., TRANSP. § 4-316 (financing of transportation projects). It is possible that an aggrieved bondholder could pursue a writ of mandamus even absent authorizing statutory law.

---

vii *See, e.g.*, MD. CODE ANN., ECON. DEV. § 12-111 (allowing for bonds to be paid by pledge or assignment of revenues received from project) and MD. CODE ANN., ENVIR. § 5-301 (bonds funded through pledge on rates, rents, tolls, fees, charges and revenues of facility). These are examples of special revenue bonds. The state code may be more expansive, and an attorney should be consulted to examine any specific situation involving a default.

viii Category SL-2: *See, e.g.*, MD. CODE, TRANSP. § 10-303 (tolls or other revenues or other moneys so pledged are subject to lien without physical delivery or further act). The language of this statute generally provides for pledges and liens arising out of the issuance of bonds pursuant to the statute without the use of a specific statement that it is a statutory lien and arises without any further action. It appears further clarification would be helpful as to whether the pledge and lien are intended to be a statutory lien or merely a perfection of lien. The state code may be more expansive, and an attorney should be consulted to examine any specific situation involving a default.

V. Massachusetts

Municipal Bankruptcy Authority	Massachusetts does not specifically authorize its municipal entities to file petitions under Chapter 9 of the Bankruptcy Code. Between 1980 and July 31, 2016, no Massachusetts municipal entity has filed such a petition.
Home Rule and Taxing Power of Municipalities	**Municipalities' Ability to Self-Govern** Massachusetts is not a Dillon's Rule state and its state constitution provides as a part of the state's Home Rule Amendment that: "It is the intention of this article to reaffirm the customary and traditional liberties of the people with respect to the conduct of their local government, and to grant and confirm to the people of every city and town the right of self-government in local matters, subject to the provisions of this article and to such standards and requirements as the general court may establish by law in accordance with the provisions of this article."[i] Certain municipal authorities not subject to the Massachusetts Home Rule Amendment, such as fire districts, are subject to Dillon's Rule, however.[ii] **Tax Limitations** At the local level, Massachusetts law limits ad valorem taxes to 2.5 percent of the full and fair cash valuation of the property, but upon voter approval, a municipality may exceed this limit for paying principal and interest on bonds.[iii]
Debt Default Prevention	**Debt Limitation** No city or town may authorize indebtedness exceeding 5 percent of the equalized valuation of the city or town. This amount may be increased to 10 percent on approval of a municipal finance oversight board.[iv] **Refunding Bonds** In certain situations, a municipal entity may issue refunding bonds to refund and refinance outstanding debt.[v] **State Bond Payment Intervention** The treasurer of a city, town or district, including a regional school district, if he or she finds the municipal entity is likely to be unable to pay in whole or in part the principal and interest on its bonds when due, must notify the governing board of the municipal entity. If the municipal entity investigates and finds this to be true, the fact must be certified to the commissioner of revenue, who must also conduct an investigation. If the commissioner of revenue finds an inability to pay, he or she shall report this to the state treasurer, who should then pay the sum to the paying agent.[vi]

V. Massachusetts

Mechanisms for Resolution after Default	***Ad Hoc* State Intervention** Massachusetts has typically employed a system of implementing legislation on an *ad hoc* basis to create financial control boards or overseers to turn around a municipality in severe financial distress.[vii] **Receivership** In certain default situations, Massachusetts law allows for the appointment of a receiver with respect to revenue bonds.[viii]
Remedies on Default	**Mandamus** In certain situations, bondholders or their trustee may bring a court action to compel the local governing body to perform a ministerial action that it has refused to undertake, such as collecting taxes or fees where the underlying bond authorization requires such a collection.[ix]
Other Bondholder Protections	**Special Revenue Bonds** As provided by Section 922(d) of the Bankruptcy Code, payments to bondholders holding special revenue bonds would not be stayed on the filing of a municipal bankruptcy petition, and payments to holders could continue. Whether an issuance would qualify as a special revenue bond depends on the provisions of the authorizing statute with respect to the bonds at issue.[x] **Statutory Liens** Were a municipal entity to file a petition under Chapter 9 of the Bankruptcy Code, bondholders holding bonds to which statutory liens have attached would continue to receive payment on those bonds. For a statutory lien to apply, the authorizing law of the bond issue must contain such a lien. Category SL-3.[xi]

---

i MASS. CONST. amend. art. II, §§ 1-9 (Massachusetts Home Rule Amendment).

ii *See Cohen v. Bd. of Water Comm'rs Fire Dist. No. 1, South Hadley*, 411 Mass. 744, 750 (Mass. 1992).

iii MASS. GEN. LAWS ANN. ch. 59, § 21C.

iv MASS. GEN. LAWS ch. 44, § 10. The Massachusetts General Laws may contain exceptions as to which municipalities are authorized to incur debt outside of the debt limit.

v MASS. GEN. LAWS ch. 40D, § 17 (municipalities acting by and through an industrial development financing authority may issue refunding bonds) and MASS. GEN. LAWS ch. 44, § 21A (allowing cities, towns, regional school districts and districts to issue refunding bonds).

vi MASS. GEN. LAWS ch. 44, § 19A.

vii For instance, in the 1990s the city of Chelsea was placed into a state receivership. The state legislature had passed an act authorizing a receiver for the city. The receiver cut city payroll by 25 percent and cut non-pecuniary employment benefits. In one year, the receiver was able to cut city expenses by 10 percent of the city's budget ($5 million). *See* Omer Kimhi, *Reviving Cities: The Legal Remedies to Municipal Insolvency* (N.Y.U. School of Law 2007) at 131, 205.

In March 2010 the governor signed into law provisions allowing the city of Lawrence to borrow $35 million from the market and establishing a fiscal overseer for the municipality. See 2010 Mass. Acts ch. 58. The appointment of a fiscal overseer has helped stabilize the city's finances, resulting in Moody's Investors Service upgrading the City's financial outlook in August 2012 from negative to stable. *Stable Outlook for City of Lawrence* (Aug. 17, 2012), http://www.cityoflawrence.com/stable-outlook-for-city-of-lawrence.aspx); *see also Moody's affirms the City of Lawrence's (MA) Baa1 underlying General Obligation rating and assigns MIG 1 to $6 million State Qualified G.O. BANs; Outlook revised to Stable* (Aug. 16, 2012), https://www.moodys.com/research/Moodys-affirms-the-City-of-Lawrences-MA-Baa1-underlying-General--PR_253366. The fiscal overseer remains active in Lawrence, Massachusetts. The Springfield Financial Control Board was dissolved on June 30, 2009.

Similarly, in 2004 Massachusetts extended the city of Springfield a $52 million state loan and established a financial control board to oversee the city. See chapter 169 of Acts of 2004. The Springfield Financial Control Board ended after five years of direct management on June 30, 2009. *Control Board*, CITY OF SPRINGFIELD, MASSACHUSETTS (Jun 3, 2013), http://www3.springfield-ma.gov/cos/control_board.0.html.

viii *See, e.g.*, MASS. GEN. LAWS ch. 40, § 39K (Drinking Water Protection Commission). The state code may be more expansive and the statutory authority for each bond issuance should be reviewed before assessing whether a receiver may be appointed.

ix *See, e.g.*, MASS. GEN. LAWS ch. 40, § 39K (Drinking Water Protection Commission). It is possible that an aggrieved bondholder could pursue a writ of mandamus even absent authorizing statutory law.

x *See, e.g.*, MASS. GEN. LAWS ch. 40Q, § 4 (pledge of revenues for facility bonds); MASS. GEN. LAWS ch. 40, § 39K (water protection district revenue bonds); MASS. GEN. LAWS ch. 40D, § 14 (industrial development revenue bonds); MASS. GEN. LAWS ch. 40N, § 12 (water and sewer bonds); and MASS. GEN. LAWS ch. 44, § 28C (solid waste revenue bonds). These are examples of special revenue bonds. The state code may be more expansive, and an attorney should be consulted to examine any specific situation involving a default.

xi Category SL-3: This language of the statute does not appear to impose a statutory lien but rather a lien at the discretion of the elected official involved in issuing the bonds. Further legislation clarification would be helpful as to whether there is a statutory lien or special revenue. *See, e.g.*, MASS. GEN. LAWS ch. 40Q, § 4 (project revenue accounts and general intangibles subject to lien of pledge without delivery or segregating). The state code may be more expansive, and an attorney should be consulted to examine any specific situation involving a default.

W. Michigan

Municipal Bankruptcy Authority	In certain circumstances under Michigan's Local and Financial Stability and Choice Act, with written approval of the governor, a local government may file a Chapter 9 petition if the local government adopts a resolution, by majority vote, declaring a financial emergency. The resolution must include a statement that the local government's financial condition jeopardizes the health, safety and welfare of its residents and that the local government is or will be unable to pay its obligations within 60 days following the adoption of the resolution. If the governor approves a local government to proceed with a municipal bankruptcy petition, the governor must inform the local government in writing and may place contingencies on the filing. Between 1980 and July 31, 2016, three municipal entities in Michigan have filed petitions under Chapter 9 of the Bankruptcy Code, including the city of Detroit on July 18, 2013, the largest municipal bankruptcy filing in U.S. history; a hospital in 1992; and the village of Merrill in 1987.[i]
Home Rule and Taxing Power of Municipalities	**Municipalities' Ability to Self-Govern** Michigan is a Dillon's Rule state, meaning that a local government may not take any action, unless specifically allowed for in the state's constitution or statutes. The Michigan Constitution allows cities, villages and counties to levy taxes for public purposes that are not otherwise limited by the constitution. Unless a tax was in existence prior to January 1, 1964, however, local governments are prohibited from collecting taxes other than ad valorem property taxes. As a further matter, Michigan law includes provisions allowing for cities and counties to adopt home-rule charters.[ii] **Tax Limitations** The Michigan Constitution limits general ad valorem taxes imposed on real and tangible personal property for all purposes in any one year to not exceed 15 mills on each dollar of assessed value of the property, but these amounts may be increased depending on the situation. These provisions do not apply to taxes imposed for the payment of principal and interest on bonds approved by voters.[iii]
Debt Default Prevention	**Annual Audit Reporting** Each municipality must file an annual audit report. The report must meet certain criteria for the municipality to issue municipal securities without further approval of the state. If the municipality does not meet the requirements to issue bonds without state supervision, it must obtain, for each municipal security, the prior written approval of the state.[iv]

W. Michigan

Debt Default Prevention *continued*	**Debt Limitation** The Michigan Constitution contains debt limits for cities, villages and counties. A county may not issue debt totaling more than 10 percent of its assessed valuation. The Michigan legislature may limit debt issued by cities and villages.[v] **Local Financial Stability and Choice Act[vi]** The Local Financial Stability and Choice Act, which replaced a similar act that Michigan voters had rejected in a 2012 referendum, contains 19 different possibilities that would allow for the state financial authority to conduct a preliminary review of a local government's finances to determine the existence of probable stress. The state financing board is then required to complete a final report and submit that report to the local emergency financial assistance loan board to determine if probable financial stress exists for the local government. If probable stress is found, the governor is then required to appoint a review team for that local government; the review team, after investigating the circumstances and meeting with the local government, must submit a written report to the governor within 60 days following its appointment, although it may be granted one extension of 30 days to conduct its analysis. In its report, the review team must conclude either that a financial emergency exists or that one does not exist. Within 10 days of receiving the report, the governor must also make a determination as to the existence or not of a financial emergency. The decision is appealable to the Michigan Court of Claims within 10 business days by a resolution approved by two-thirds of the members of the local government's governing body. Should a financial emergency be found, the local government must (1) enter into a consent decree with the state, (2) agree to the appointment of an emergency manager, (3) enter into a neutral evaluation process or (4) file a Chapter 9 bankruptcy petition if so approved by the governor. If it does not choose on of those four options, the local government must proceed under a neutral evaluation process. *Consent Decree Option*[vii] Under the first option, the local government may work with the state to develop a plan implementing remedial measures considered necessary to address the financial emergency and to provide for the local government's financial stability. The consent agreement may include a continuing operations agreement developed by the local government or a recovery plan developed and imposed by the state. Unless the state determines otherwise, the local government is exempt from collective bargaining requirements.

W. Michigan

Debt Default Prevention *continued*	*Emergency Manager Option*[viii] If the second option is chosen by the municipality, the governor may appoint an emergency manager to address the local government's financial emergency. The emergency manager acts in the place and stead of the governing body and its chief administrative officer and has broad powers in receivership to rectify the financial emergency and to assure the fiscal accountability of the local government. The emergency manager shall continue in its capacity until removed by the legislature in certain instances, the financial emergency is rectified or the local government, after the emergency manager has served 18 months, votes by a two-thirds vote to remove the emergency manager. A local government may be removed from receivership when its financial conditions are corrected in a sustainable manner. The local government may also seek to remove the manager before the end of the 18-month period by petitioning the governor. Among its other duties, should the emergency manager determine that no reasonable alternative exists, he or she may recommend to the governor that the local government be authorized to file a Chapter 9 petition. This is what occurred with respect to the city of Detroit. Once the financial emergency is rectified, the governor may appoint a receivership transition advisory board to monitor the affairs of the local government.[ix] *Neutral Evaluation Process*[x] Under the third option, a local government provides notice of a request for a neutral evaluation process to all interested parties. The local government and all interested parties may, through a mutually agreed-upon process, select a neutral evaluator to oversee and facilitate discussions to resolve their disputes. The process may not last for more than 60 days from the date the neutral evaluator is selected, unless the parties agree to one additional 30-day extension of the process. The process ends when the parties reach a settlement agreement; a plan of readjustment that requires the approval of a bankruptcy judge has been proposed; no agreement is reached; or the fiscal condition of the local government has deteriorated to the point that a Chapter 9 petition is necessary. If the neutral evaluation process does not result in a resolution, the governing body of the local government must adopt a resolution recommending that it proceed under Chapter 9 and submit that resolution to the governor and state treasurer.

W. Michigan

Debt Default Prevention *continued*	**Financial Recovery Bonds** If a financial emergency exists under the Local Financial Stability and Choice Act, a city is permitted to issue financial recovery bonds in amounts greater than its debt limits under Michigan law and the city's charter, but the indebtedness of the city may not exceed certain limits as set forth in the financial recovery bond provisions.[xi] **Detroit Public Schools/New and Old Districts** Legislation was enacted in 2016 to avoid a bankruptcy for the Detroit Public Schools. A new school district was created for the purpose of ongoing educational efforts and of holding educational assets. The old school district retained the past liabilities, including bond debt. Both are separate legal entities. Along with additional revenues, including from tobacco settlement funds, the *ad valorem* tax levy for the operation of the schools were available to the old district to assist in the payment of the old debt.[xii] **Refunding Bonds** In certain situations, a municipal entity may issue refunding bonds to refund and refinance outstanding debt.[xiii]
Mechanisms for Resolution after Default	**Receivership** In certain default situations, Michigan law allows for the appointment of a receiver with respect to revenue bonds.[xiv]
Remedies on Default	**Mandamus** In certain situations, bondholders or their trustee may bring a court action to compel the local governing body to perform a ministerial action that it has refused to undertake, such as collecting taxes or fees where the underlying bond authorization requires such a collection.[xv]
Other Bondholder Protections	**Special Revenue Bonds** As provided by Section 922(d) of the Bankruptcy Code, payments to bondholders holding special revenue bonds would not be stayed on the filing of a municipal bankruptcy petition, and payments to holders could continue. Whether an issuance would qualify as a special revenue bond depends on the provisions of the authorizing statute with respect to the bonds at issue.[xvi]

W. Michigan

Other Bondholder Protections *continued*	**Statutory Liens** Were a municipal entity to file a petition under Chapter 9 of the Bankruptcy Code, bondholders holding bonds to which statutory liens have attached would continue to receive payment on those bonds. For a statutory lien to apply, the authorizing law of the bond issue must contain such a lien. Category SL-1 or SL-2.[xvii]

i MICH. COMP. LAWS § 141.1566. A "local government" includes a school district; a city; a village; a township; a charter township; a county; a department of county government if the county has an elected county executive under 1966 PA 293, MCL 45.501 to 45.521; an authority established by law; or a public utility owned by a city, village, township or county. MICH. COMP. LAWS § 141.1542. On July 18, 2013, the city of Detroit became the largest Chapter 9 filing in the history of the U.S. Bankruptcy Code. The city filed after the governor granted permission to the city's emergency manager to file such a petition. In November 2010, Michigan rejected a request for permission to file a municipal bankruptcy petition by the municipality of Hamtramck. Mike Shedlock, *Michigan Forbids City of Hamtramck to Seek Bankruptcy*, UNIONWATCH (Nov. 30, 2010), http://unionwatch.org/michigan-forbids-city-of-hamtramck-to-seek-bankruptcy/.

ii MICH. CONST. art. VII, § 2 (powers of counties, noting that each charter county has the power to levy other taxes for county purposes subject to the prohibitions set forth in the constitution or law); § 21 (powers of local governments); § 22 (power of local governments to adopt charters); MICH. COMP. LAWS § 141.91; and MICH. COMP. LAWS §§ 117.1-117.38 (Home Rule City Act).

iii MICH. CONST. art. IX, § 6. Counties, townships and school districts, with voter approval, may increase this rate to not exceed 18 mills on each dollar of assessed value. The limitation may be increased to an aggregate not to exceed 50 mills per each dollar of valuation for a period not to exceed 20 years, if approved by a majority of voters voting.

iv MICH. COMP. LAWS § 141.2303 (2011). To qualify to issue municipal securities without further approval of the state, a municipality must (a) not be operating under the provisions of the Local Financial Stability and Choice Act; (b) have not issued securities in the immediately preceding five fiscal years or current fiscal year that were authorized under the Emergency Municipal Loan Act, other than certain loans authorized under that act; (c) have not been required by the terms of a court order or judgment to levy a tax in the previous fiscal year, unless it is determined that the court order did not have an adverse impact on the municipality; (d) have filed its audit report within six months from the end of its fiscal year; (e) have certified the debt retirement fund balance for any municipal security that is funded from an unlimited tax levy does not exceed 150 percent of the amount required for principal and interest payments due for the security in the next fiscal year; (f) not be exceeding its statutory or constitutional debt limits; (g) have no outstanding security not authorized by statute; (h) not be in violation of any provisions in the covenants for an outstanding security either currently or in the preceding fiscal year; (i) not have been delinquent more than one time in the preceding year in transferring employment taxes or pension, retirement or benefit plan contributions; (j) certify that its delinquent property taxes do not exceed 18 percent of the amount levied; (k) not have submitted a qualifying statement or application for any other municipal securities that was materially false or incorrect; (l) certify that it is not in default on the payment of any debt, with the exception of industrial development revenue bonds; (m) not have ended the immediately preceding fiscal year with a deficit in any fund, unless it has a plan to correct the deficit condition; (n) not have been found by a court to be in violation of any finance or tax-related state or federal statutes; (o) not have been in violation of its audit reporting requirements; and (p) have not issued a refunding security in the preceding fiscal year to avoid a potential default on an outstanding security.

If the state does not grant the municipality a "qualified status" based on its audit, the municipality must obtain, for each municipal security, the prior written approval of the state to issue a municipal security.

v MICH. CONST. art. VII, § 11 (counties); MICH. CONST. art. VII, § 21 (cities and villages). Pursuant to MICH. COMP. LAWS § 78.26, a village governed by the Home Rule Village Act may not incur indebtedness exceeding 10 percent of the assessed valuation of the real and personal property within the village subject to taxation.

vi MICH. COMP. LAWS §§ 141.1541 to 141.1575.

vii MICH. COMP. LAWS 141.1548. The following municipalities in Michigan have entered into consent decrees: Inkster, River Rouge, Royal Oak Township, Benton Harbor Area Schools and Pontiac Public Schools. *See* http://www.michigan.gov/treasury/0,1607,7-121-1751_51556-201116--,00.html (last visited Mar. 17, 2015).

viii MICH. COMP. LAWS § 141.1549. Under the new law, an emergency manager appointed under the previous version of the act is considered an emergency manager under the act and will continue in that capacity.

Under a similar previous law in Michigan, the state had taken over certain municipalities suffering severe financial emergencies. In *Flint City Council v. State of Michigan*, 655 N.W.2d 604 (Mich. Ct. App. 2002), the state treasurer reported to the governor that the city of Flint had a serious financial problem. The governor appointed a financial review team to assess Flint's financial situation and found a substantial general fund deficit. The review team also determined that Flint city officials demonstrated an inability "to accurately monitor revenues and expenditures throughout a given fiscal year and to amend city budgets accordingly." As such, the review team recommended that the governor appoint an emergency financial manager. The city appealed and the court found the governor's decision was supported.

As of June 22, 2015, emergency managers have been appointed over the municipalities or school districts of Allen Park, Benton Harbor, Detroit, Ecorse, Flint, Hamtramck, Lincoln Park, Pontiac, Detroit Public Schools, and the Muskegon Heights School District. Emergency Manager Information, Michigan Department of Treasury, http://www.michigan.gov/treasury/0,1607,7-121-1751_51556-201116--,00.html (last visited Mar. 17, 2015).

ix MICH. COMP. LAWS § 141.1563. A receivership transition advisory board has been appointed for the municipalities of Allen Park, Benton Harbor, Ecorse, Flint, Hamtamck and Pontiac. *See* http://www.michigan.gov/treasury/ 0,1607,7-121-1751_51556-201116--,00.html (last visited Mar. 17, 2015).

x MICH. COMP. LAWS § 141.1565. The city of Highland Park has initiated this process. *See* http://www.michigan.gov/treasury/0,4679,7-121-1751_51556_64472-314176--,00.html (last visited June 22, 2015).

xi MICH. COMP. LAWS §117.36a.

xii 2016 Mich. Pub. Acts 192, 193, 194, 195, 196 and 197.

xiii Examples of refunding bonds in Michigan law include MICH. COMP. LAWS § 141.2603(1) (allowing any outstanding security that has been assumed in part by another municipality to be refunded by the municipalities as to their respective liabilities); MICH. COMP. LAWS § 141.2609 (allowing refunding securities under the Drain Code of 1956); and MICH. COMP. LAWS § 141.120 (revenue refunding bonds). Municipalities may issue refunding bonds to refund all or any portion of funded indebtedness, but their issuance is subject to statutory provisions and must be necessary such as to avoid a default. MICH. CIVIL JUR., *Municipal and Public Bonds* § 51 (2010).

xiv *See, e.g.*, MICH. COMP. LAWS § 141.110 (allowing for appointment of receiver with respect to revenue bonds). Under § 141.110, a receiver may be appointed to administer and operate any public improvement as long as its revenues are pledged to pay the principal and interest on the bonds at issue. The receiver may fix and charge rates and collect revenues sufficient for the payment of any bonds or obligations outstanding but must act under the direction of the court.

For instance, in *Farmington Twp. v. Warrenville State Bank*, 185 F.2d 260 (6th Cir. 1950), bondholders asked the court to appoint a receiver. The court appointed a receiver and found that the receiver was allowed to continue to charge a specified amount each year for water hydrant rentals to help the township repay its debt.

xv *See, e.g.*, MICH. COMP. LAWS § 41.347 (providing that bondholders representing in aggregate not less than 20 percent of entire outstanding bond issue by township water supply and sewage disposal services and facilities may protect and enforce the statutory lien and compel performance of duties by officials of borrower) and MICH. COMP. LAWS § 331.8e(2) (providing that bondholders representing in aggregate not less than 20 percent of entire outstanding bond issue by hospital authority may protect and enforce the statutory lien and compel performance of duties by officials of borrower, including fixing sufficient rates to pay bonds). It is possible that an aggrieved bondholder could pursue a writ of mandamus even absent authorizing statutory law.

xvi *See, e.g.*, MICH. COMP. LAWS § 41.343 (revenue bonds for water supply and sewage disposal projects); MICH. COMP. LAWS §§ 125.667(5) and 125.709(2) (revenue bonds for housing facilities); MICH. COMP. LAWS § 141.107(4) (Revenue Bond Act); and MICH. COMP. LAWS § 120.114 (revenue bonds for port facilities). These are examples of special revenue bonds. The state code may be more expansive, and an attorney should be consulted to examine any specific situation involving a default.

xvii Category SL-1 or SL-2. While the legislation states the pledge of revenues under these statutes are a statutory lien, to the degree they are at the discretion of the local governmental body or created by resolution and not legislation, there is a question of whether further clarification is needed. MICH. COMP. LAWS § 41.346 (establishing statutory lien on net revenues of water supply and sewage disposal project); MICH. COMP. LAWS §§ 125.667(5) and 125.709(2) (statutory liens for bonds issued by housing facilities); MICH. COMP. LAWS § 141.108 (establishing statutory lien on net revenues under Revenue Bond Act); and MICH. COMP. LAWS § 331.8e (establishing statutory lien on all net revenues on bonds issued by hospital authorities). These are examples of statutory liens. Additionally, Detroit legislation in connection with its exit from bankruptcy financing required a statutory lien to obtain market acceptance. See Public Act 17 of 2015. The state code may be more expansive, and an attorney should be consulted to examine any specific situation involving a default. Also in 2014, legislation was introduced into the Michigan legislature to clarify for unlimited tax general obligations bonds ("UTGOs") that they are covered by a statutory lien. (HB4495.) The legislation passed the house and senate Finance Committee but has been held up in the senate due to opposition purportedly by the Department of Treasury for the State of Michigan and the governor in 2016. *See also* MICH. CONST. art. IX, §§ 6 and 25.

X. Minnesota

Municipal Bankruptcy Authority	Any municipality, as defined under the Bankruptcy Code, but limited to a county, statutory or home-rule charter city, or town; or a housing and redevelopment authority, economic development authority or rural development financing authority established under Chapter 469 of the Minnesota Statutes, a home-rule charter, or special law, may file a petition under Chapter 9 of the Bankruptcy Code. Unless an entity is specifically identified above, it is not authorized to file a municipal bankruptcy petition. Between 1980 and July 31, 2016, no Minnesota municipal entity has filed such a petition.[i]
Home Rule and Taxing Power of Municipalities	**Municipalities' Ability to Self-Govern** Minnesota is a Dillon's Rule state and no county, city, town or other taxing authority may increase a present tax or impose a new tax on sales or income. However, the state constitution includes provisions allowing local governments to adopt home rule charters, which may provide taxing powers to counties.[ii] **Taxation Limitations** Minnesota state law imposes detailed tax levy limitations.[iii]
Debt Default Prevention	**Back-up Payment Procedures for Municipalities** If a municipality believes it may be unable to make a principal or interest payment on an outstanding debt obligation, it must report the deficiency amount to the auditor, who will grant a loan to the issuer in an amount to satisfy the bond issuance. This is a pre-default precautionary measure.[iv] **Back-up Payment Procedures for School Districts** If a school district or intermediate school district believes it may be unable to make a principal or interest payment on an outstanding debt obligation and provides proper notification to the commissioner, the commissioner of management and budget must issue a warrant and authorize the commissioner of education to pay the paying agent for the debt obligation. This is a pre-default precautionary measure.[v]

X. Minnesota

Debt Default Prevention *continued*	**Debt Limitation** No municipality, except a school district or city of the first class, shall incur or be subject to a net debt exceeding 3 percent of the market value of taxable property in the municipality. With respect to cities of the first class, unless a city's charter permits a greater amount, it may not incur debt in excess of 2 percent of the market value. A city of the first class's charter may not allow for debt exceeding 3-2/3 percent of the market value of taxable property. School districts may not incur debt in excess of 15 percent of the actual market value of taxable property in the district.[vi] **Refunding Bonds** In certain situations, a municipal entity may issue refunding bonds to refund and refinance outstanding debt.[vii] **School District Expenditure Limitations** A school district must limit its expenditures so that its net unreserved general fund does not constitute a statutory operating debt. If it fails to do so, the commissioner may notify the state legislature. Further, if the negative unreserved general fund balance, as of June 30 each year, is more than 2.5 percent of the year's expenditure amount, the school district must submit a special operating plan to reduce its deficit expenditures to the commissioner for approval.[viii]
Remedies on Default	**Mandamus** In certain situations, bondholders may bring an action to compel the local governing body to perform a ministerial action that it has refused to undertake, such as collecting taxes or fees where the underlying bond authorization requires such a collection.[ix] **Other Appropriate Remedies** On default, bondholders may bring an action against the defaulting municipality to enforce their rights in any appropriate proceeding, including suits at law, in equity or by other proceedings.[x]
Other Bondholder Protections	**Special Revenue Bonds** As provided by Section 922(d) of the Bankruptcy Code, payments to bondholders holding special revenue bonds would not be stayed on the filing of a municipal bankruptcy petition, and payments to holders could continue. Whether an issuance would qualify as a special revenue bond depends on the provisions of the authorizing statute with respect to the bonds at issue.[xi]

X. Minnesota

Other Bondholder Protections *continued*	**Statutory Liens** Were a municipal entity to file a petition under Chapter 9 of the Bankruptcy Code, bondholders holding bonds to which statutory liens have attached would continue to receive payment on those bonds. For a statutory lien to apply, the authorizing law of the bond issue must contain such a lien. Category SL-2. [xii]

---

i MINN. STAT. § 471.831.

ii MINN. CONST. art. XII, § 4 (local government charters) and MINN. STAT. § 477A.016 (taxing authority limitation); *see also Breza v. City of Minnetrista*, 725 N.W.2d 106, 110 (Minn. 2006) (local governments "possess only those powers that are conferred by statute or implied as necessary to carry out legislatively conferred powers").

iii *See, e.g.*, MINN. STAT. §§ 275.70-275.75 (counties and cities).

iv MINN. STAT. § 475A.04. The municipal treasurer or paying agent must so report if the funds sufficient to pay the principal and interest due are not in their hands at least 15 days before the due date.

v MINN. STAT. § 126C.55. The school district must notify the commissioner as soon as possible of its inability to pay, but not less than 15 working days before the payment date.

vi MINN. STAT. § 475.53.

vii Examples of refunding bond provisions in the State of Minnesota include MINN. STAT. § 37.31 (State Agriculture Society may issue refunding bonds for state fair bonds); MINN. STAT. § 41B.08 (Rural Finance Authority may issue refunding bonds); MINN. STAT. § 41C.07 (Agriculture Development Authority may issue refunding bonds); MINN. STAT. § 136A.34 (higher education authorities may issue revenue bonds for the purpose of refunding outstanding revenue bonds); MINN. STAT. § 447.50 (a county, city or hospital district may issue refunding bonds under hospital district provisions); MINN. STAT. § 473.325 (metropolitan council may issue general obligation refunding bonds to refund outstanding obligations); and MINN. STAT. § 475.67 (bonds may be refunded if and when and to the extent that for any reason the taxes or special assessments, revenues or other funds appropriated for their payment are not sufficient to pay all principal and interest due or about to become due).

viii MINN. STAT. § 123B.83. "Statutory operating debt" is defined as debt more than 2.5 percent of the most recent fiscal year's expenditure amount for funds considered operating debt. MINN. STAT. § 123B.81. A district submitting a special operating plan to the commissioner that is disapproved may not receive certain amounts of aid until a special operating plan is approved. MINN. STAT. § 123B.83

ix *See, e.g.*, MINN. STAT. § 475.61(6) (holders of temporary bonds may have and enforce by mandamus or other appropriate proceedings all rights respecting the levy and collection of taxes, except the right to require levies to be collected prior to maturity of bonds); MINN. STAT. §§ 136A.37 and 136A.178 (allowing for suit at law or in equity or by suit, action, mandamus or other proceedings to protect and enforce rights under revenue bonds issued for higher education); and MINN. STAT. § 441.55 (holders of bonds issued for bridges may bring suit to compel performance, including the fixing, maintaining and collecting of rates of tolls or charges). It is possible that an aggrieved bondholder could pursue a writ of mandamus even absent authorizing statutory law.

x *See, e.g.*, MINN. STAT. § 136A.37 (allowing for suit at law or in equity or by suit, action, mandamus or other proceedings to protect and enforce rights under revenue bonds issued for higher education); and MINN. STAT. § 441.55 (holders of bonds issued for bridges may bring suit to compel performance, including the fixing, maintaining and collecting of rates of tolls or charges). The state code may be more expansive, and an attorney should be consulted to examine any specific situation involving a default.

xi *See, e.g.*, MINN. STAT. § 469.184 (bonds or obligations not payable from nor charged on any fund other than the revenues and properties pledged or mortgaged for their payment). This is an example of a special revenue bond. The state code may be more expansive, and an attorney should be consulted to examine any specific situation involving a default.

xii Category SL-2: *See, e.g.*, MINN. STAT. § 475.78, which deals with perfection of security interest by a pledge of revenues or funds for the payment of bonds. This appears to provide for perfection and effectiveness and not necessarily creation of a statutory lien. *See also* MINN. STAT. § 475.61, which deals with tax levies of ad valorem taxes for payment of bond obligations. The resolution and levy are to be irrevocable. While this language appears to support creation of a statutory lien, further clarification would be helpful to assure the legislative intent. *See additionally, e.g.*, MINN. STAT. § 469.184, noted above, as to municipal commercial rehabilitation loan program and the pledge and mortgage provided thereby. It is difficult to ascertain whether in addition to special revenues there is also intended a statutory lien so that it is clear the pledged revenues are not subject to any "necessary operating expenses" but rather by statute are dedicated to payment of the debt service on the bonds (see treatment in *Sierra Kings Health Care District, supra* at 144-145) or whether the language merely suggests that the pledge is complete and no further action of perfection of the lien is necessary. Further legislative clarification in this and other situations would be helpful. *See also, e.g.*, MINN. STAT. § 475.61 (dealing with tax levies to pay bonds that are to be irrevocable). Again, further clarification as to any intent to create a statutory lien or its equivalent would be helpful. The state code may be more expansive, and an attorney should be consulted to examine any specific situation involving default.

Y. Mississippi

Municipal Bankruptcy Authority	Mississippi does not specifically authorize its municipal entities to file a petition under Chapter 9 of the Bankruptcy Code. Nevertheless, four such entities have filed five separate petitions between 1980 and July 31, 2016, four of which were filed after Congress in 1994 required specific state authorization for an entity to file a petition. Of these four, one case was dismissed, one case was closed without the filing of a plan and two plans were confirmed. Despite lack of authorization, the plans likely were confirmed because no party objected to the municipality's bankruptcy filing.[i]
Home Rule and Taxing Power of Municipalities	**Municipalities' Ability to Self-Govern** Mississippi is a Dillon's Rule state, and county and municipal governments must receive taxing authority from the state legislature.[ii] **Taxation Limits** Mississippi law does not contain any form of ad valorem taxing limitations but does include provisions with respect to tax levy increases.[iii]
Debt Default Prevention	**Debt Limitation** A municipality may not incur debt above either (a) 15 percent of the assessed value of the taxable property within such municipality, or (b) 10 percent of the assessment on which taxes were levied for the fiscal year ending September 30, 1984, whichever is greater. No county may incur general obligation debt above either (a) 15 percent of the assessed value of taxable property in the county, or (b) 15 percent of the assessment on which taxes were levied for the fiscal year ending September 1, 1984, whichever is greater.[iv] **Refunding Bonds** In certain situations, a municipal entity may issue refunding bonds to refund and refinance outstanding debt.[v]
Mechanisms for Resolution after Default	**Accounting** In certain situations on default, bondholders may bring a proceeding in any court of competent jurisdiction to require the authority in question to account as if it were a trustee of an express trust.[vi] **Injunctive Relief** In certain situations, an interested person may bring an action against a board to enjoin or mandate the board to act.[vii]

Y. Mississippi

Mechanisms for Resolution after Default *continued*	**Receivership** In certain situations, Mississippi law allows for the appointment of a receiver where a default situation occurs with respect to a revenue bond issued by a public body.[viii]
Remedies on Default	**Foreclosure** In certain default situations, bondholders may foreclose on a project for which they hold a mortgage.[ix] **Mandamus** In certain situations, bondholders or their trustee may bring a court action to compel the local governing body to perform a ministerial action that it has refused to undertake, such as collecting taxes or fees where the underlying bond authorization requires such a collection.[x] **Other Appropriate Remedies** On default, bondholders may bring an action against the defaulting municipality to enforce their rights in any appropriate proceeding, including suits at law or in equity or by action or other proceedings.[xi]
Other Bondholder Protections	**Special Revenue Bonds** As provided by Section 922(d) of the Bankruptcy Code, payments to bondholders holding special revenue bonds would not be stayed on the filing of a municipal bankruptcy petition, and payments to holders could continue. Whether an issuance would qualify as a special revenue bond depends on the provisions of the authorizing statute with respect to the bonds at issue.[xii] **Statutory Liens** Were a municipal entity to file a petition under Chapter 9 of the Bankruptcy Code, bondholders holding bonds to which statutory liens have attached would continue to receive payment on those bonds. For a statutory lien to apply, the authorizing law of the bond issue must contain such a lien. Category SL-2.[xiii]

---

i *See In re Town of Winstonville*, Case No. 97-91794 (Bankr. N.D. Miss.) (case closed Feb. 10, 1998); *In re Town of Marion*, Case No. 07-50141 (Bankr. S.D. Miss.) (case dismissed June 12, 2007); *In re Natchez Regional Med. Ctr.*, Case No. 09-00477 (Bankr. S.D. Miss.) (plan confirmed Dec. 17, 2009); *In re Natchez Regional Med. Ctr.*, Case No. 14-01048 (Bankr. S.D. Miss.) (plan confirmed Sept. 30, 2014).

ii MISS. CONST. art. 4, § 80 ("Provision shall be made by general laws to prevent the abuse by cities, towns, and other municipal corporations of their powers of assessment, taxation, borrowing money, and contracting debts."). *See also* MISS. CODE ANN. § 21-17-5 and § 19-3-40 (the governing body of a municipality or county may not levy a tax or issue a bond unless it has state approval).

iii MISS. CODE ANN. § 27-39-320 (local property tax levies); *see also* MISS. CODE ANN. § 27-39-305 (setting tax levy parameters for countywide levy for construction of roads and bridges); MISS. CODE ANN. § 27-39-321 (limitation on increases of property taxes).

iv MISS. CODE ANN. § 21-33-303 (municipalities) and MISS. CODE ANN. § 19-9-5 (counties).

v Examples of refunding bonds include MISS. CODE ANN. §§ 31-27-1 to 31-27-25 (Mississippi Bond Refinancing Act, allowing for issuance of refunding bonds) and MISS. CODE ANN. §§ 31-15-1 to 31-15-27 (General Refunding Law of 1934, allowing for general obligation refunding bonds). *See also Bank of Morton v. State Bond Comm'n*, 199 So. 507 (Miss. 1941) (upholding constitutionality of law authorizing issuance of refunding bonds).

vi *See, e.g.*, MISS. CODE ANN. § 77-5-163 (power district projects). The state code may be more expansive and the statutory authority for each bond issuance should be reviewed before assessing whether an accounting may be sought.

vii *See, e.g.*, MISS. CODE ANN. § 77-5-163 (power district projects). The state code may be more expansive and the statutory authority for each bond issuance should be reviewed before assessing whether an injunction may be sought.

viii *See, e.g.*, MISS. CODE ANN. § 19-5-187 (after any default on payment of principal or interest on a bond issuance, a court of competent jurisdiction may appoint a receiver to administer the district and/or system with the power to charge and collect sufficient rates to pay bonds). *See also* MISS. CODE ANN. § 17-5-9 (bonds issued for jails, waterworks and other improvements); MISS. CODE ANN. § 21-27-53 (allowing receiver for municipal-owned utilities); MISS. CODE ANN. § 57-41-7 (allowing for receiver with respect to industrial enterprise projects); MISS. CODE ANN. § 77-5-163 (power district projects); and MISS. CODE ANN. § 57-3-21 (agriculture and industry program bonds). The state code may be more expansive and the statutory authority for each bond issuance should be reviewed before assessing whether a receiver may be appointed.

A federal court in Mississippi in 1881 ruled that a receiver and, also, mandamus may be utilized to collect unpaid obligations. A.M. Hillhouse, 307 MUNICIPAL BONDS: A CENTURY OF EXPERIENCE (New York: Prentice-Hall 1936) (discussing *Stansell v. Levee Board*, 13 Fed. 846 (1881)).

ix *See, e.g.*, MISS. CODE ANN. § 57-41-7 (allowing for foreclosure with respect to industrial enterprise projects); MISS. CODE ANN. § 57-3-21 (agriculture and industry program bonds). The state code may be more expansive and the statutory authority for each bond issuance should be reviewed before assessing what rights and remedies may be available to bondholders.

x *See, e.g.*, MISS. CODE ANN. § 31-19-33 (indicating that mandamus may be appropriate remedy against municipality as long as payment on bond commenced within 20 years after maturity date of bond); MISS. CODE ANN. § 19-5-187 (holdings of water, sewer, garbage disposal and fire protection district bonds may bring suit at law or in equity or by suit, action, mandamus or other proceedings to protect and enforce statutory liens and compel performance); MISS. CODE ANN. § 17-5-9 (bonds issued for jails, waterworks and other improvements); MISS. CODE ANN. § 21-27-53 (allowing mandamus to enforce bonds issued for municipal-owned utilities); MISS. CODE ANN. § 31-29-13 (allowing holders to enforce Institute for Technology Development bonds either at law or in equity or by suit, action, mandamus or other proceeding); MISS. CODE ANN. § 57-3-21 (agriculture and industry program bonds); MISS. CODE ANN. § 77-5-163 (power district projects); and MISS. CODE ANN. § 57-41-7 (allowing for mandamus with respect to industrial enterprise projects). Mandamus, however, may not be issued against a municipality to compel the levy of a tax beyond the statutory limit. *See Town of Jonestown v. Ganong*, 52 So. 579 (Miss. 1910); MISS. CODE ANN. § 21-17-5. It is possible that an aggrieved bondholder could pursue a writ of mandamus even absent authorizing statutory law.

xi *See, e.g.*, MISS. CODE ANN. § 19-5-187 (holdings of water, sewer, garbage disposal and fire protection district bonds may bring suit at law or in equity or by suit, action, mandamus or other proceedings to protect and enforce statutory liens and compel performance). The state code may be more expansive and the statutory authority for each bond issuance should be reviewed before assessing what rights and remedies may be available to bondholders.

xii *See, e.g.*, MISS. CODE ANN. § 19-5-187 (revenue bonds regarding water, sewer, garbage disposal and fire protection districts) and MISS. CODE ANN. § 51-8-35 (joint water management districts revenue bonds). These are examples of special revenue bonds. The state code may be more expansive, and an attorney should be consulted to examine any specific situation involving a default.

xiii Category SL-2: The following statute appears to create a statutory lien in the revenue or property related to the financing, but further legislature or opinion of counsel clarification would be helpful in reaffirming or creating a statutory lien. *See, e.g.*, MISS. CODE ANN. § 19-5-187 (creating statutory lien in nature of mortgage lien on systems created for water, sewer, garbage disposal and fire protection units); MISS. CODE ANN. § 51-8-41 (statutory lien for bonds issued by joint water management districts); and MISS. CODE. ANN. § 51-41-25 (statutory lien for bonds issued by public water authority). These are examples of statutory liens. The state code may be more expansive, and an attorney should be consulted to examine any specific situation involving a default.

Z. Missouri

Municipal Bankruptcy Authority	Any municipality or political subdivision organized under Missouri law may file a petition under Chapter 9 of the Bankruptcy Code. "Political subdivision" includes any agency or unit of the state authorized to levy taxes or empowered to cause taxes to be levied. Unless an entity is specifically identified above, it is not authorized to file a municipal bankruptcy petition. Between 1980 and July 31, 2016, 12 municipal entities in Missouri have filed petitions under Chapter 9 of the Bankruptcy Code, the most recent being the Lakeside 370 Levee District, which filed a petition on August 1, 2014.[i]
Home Rule and Taxing Power of Municipalities	**Municipalities' Ability to Self-Govern** Missouri is a Dillon's Rule state.[ii] The state does not allow municipalities and local governments to have independent tax powers. The taxing power may be exercised by counties and other political subdivisions only under power granted to them by the general assembly for county, municipal and other corporate purposes. The county shall only impose such taxes as it is authorized to impose by the constitution or by law.[iii] **Tax Limitations** Municipalities and counties in Missouri may not impose a property tax exceeding certain amounts of assessed value, depending on the type of municipality.[iv]
Debt Default Prevention	**Debt Limitation** No county, city, incorporated town or village, school district or other political corporation or subdivision may become indebted in an amount exceeding in any year the income and revenue provided for that year, plus any unencumbered balances from previous years, unless otherwise provided by the state constitution, without popular vote. With voter approval, an aforementioned municipality, county or city may become indebted in an amount not exceeding 5 percent of the value of the taxable property in the municipality, except that a school district's debt may not exceed 15 percent.[v] **Refunding Bonds** In certain situations, a municipal entity may issue refunding bonds to refund and refinance outstanding debt.[vi]
Mechanisms for Resolution after Default	**Receivership** In certain situations, Missouri law allows for the appointment of a receiver with respect to revenue bonds where a default has occurred.[vii]

Z. Missouri

Remedies on Default	**Accounting** In certain situations of default, bondholders may bring a proceeding in any court of competent jurisdiction to require the authority in question to account as if it were a trustee of an express trust.[viii] **Foreclosure** With respect to certain municipal utilities, if a default continues for more than six months, the defaulting city or special charter city may convey to bondholders or a designated trustee the municipal utility for a period of 30 years. Bondholders may also bring a foreclosure petition in a court of equity as if a mortgage or deed of trust was given to secure the same.[ix] **Mandamus** In certain situations, bondholders or their trustee may bring a court action to compel the local governing body to perform a ministerial action that it has refused to undertake, such as collecting taxes or fees where the underlying bond authorization requires such a collection.[x] **Other Appropriate Remedies** On default, bondholders may bring an action against the defaulting municipality to enforce their rights in any appropriate proceeding, including suits at law or in equity or by action or other proceedings.[xi]
Other Bondholder Protections	**Special Revenue Bonds** As provided by Section 922(d) of the Bankruptcy Code, payments to bondholders holding special revenue bonds would not be stayed on the filing of a municipal bankruptcy petition, and payments to holders could continue. Whether an issuance would qualify as a special revenue bond depends on the provisions of the authorizing statute with respect to the bonds at issue.[xii] **Statutory Liens** Were a municipal entity to file a petition under Chapter 9 of the Bankruptcy Code, bondholders holding bonds to which statutory liens have attached would continue to receive payment on those bonds. For a statutory lien to apply, the authorizing law of the bond issue must contain such a lien. No statutes covered by the categories were identified.

---

i MO. ANN. STAT. § 427.100; *In re Lakeside 370 Levee District*, Case No. 14-46094 (Bankr. E.D. Missouri). Of the municipal entities that have filed Chapter 9 proceedings in Missouri, six were cities, three were hospital districts, one was a school district and two were special municipal districts. *See also* MO. ANN. STAT. § 70.120 (definition of political subdivision).

ii *Premium Standard Farms, Inc. v. Lincoln Twp. of Putnam Cnty.*, 946 S.W.2d 234, 238 (Mo. 1997) (noting that Dillon's Rule applies to counties and townships in the state).

iii Mo. Const. art. X, § 1; Mo. Const. art. VI, § 18(d) (providing counties may only impose such taxes as they are authorized to impose by the constitution or by law).

iv Mo. Const. art. X, § 11(b) (taxing limits) and Mo. Const. art. X, § 11(c) (tax increases above constitutional limits). The Missouri taxing limitations include: (1) for municipalities, one dollar on one hundred dollars of assessed valuation; (2) for counties, 35 cents on $100 assessed valuation in counties having $300 million assessed valuation and having attained first-class classification, and 50 cents on $100 valuation in all other counties; (3) for school districts formed in cities and towns, $2.75 on $100 assessed valuation; and (4) for all other school districts, 65 cents on $100 assessed valuation. In certain instances, voters may vote to increase the taxes above constitutional limits, and counties or other political subdivisions may increase taxes above constitutional limits for library, hospital, public health, recreation grounds and museum purposes.

v Mo. Const. art. VI, § 26(a) (limitation where vote has not occurred); Mo. Const. art. VI, § 26(b) (limitation where vote has occurred for municipalities); and Mo. Const. art. VI, § 26(c) (limitation for counties and cities where vote has occurred). Further, a city, after a vote, may incur indebtedness not exceeding 10 percent of the taxable property therein to acquire right-of-way; to construct, extend or improve sanitary or storm sewer systems; or for purchasing or constructing waterworks, electric or other light plants, provided the total general obligation indebtedness of the city shall not exceed 20 percent of the assessed valuation. Mo. Const. art. VI, §§ 26(d) and 26(e).

vi Examples of refunding bonds in Missouri law include Mo. Ann. Stat. § 164.301 (allowing for refunding of revenue bonds, but that no refunding bond shall be payable more than 20 years from date thereof, and such refunding bond may not bear an interest rate above 6 percent); Mo. Ann. Stat. § 108.160 (allowing for a county itself, or on behalf of a township or other political subdivision for which the county issued a general obligation or revenue bond, and the several cities, school districts or other political corporations or subdivisions to refund, extend or unify their general obligation indebtedness); Mo. Ann. Stat. § 108.400 (allowing refunding bonds for counties of the first class having a charter form of government and containing the greater part of a city with a population of more than 450,000); and Mo. Ann. Stat. § 253.280 (state park and historic preservation refunding bonds).

vii *See, e.g.*, Mo. Ann. Stat. § 91.730. Under this provision, if a municipality defaults on a bond issuance and the default continues for more than 30 days, any holders of the bonds, or a trustee, may petition a court to appoint a receiver. The court may appoint and, if the application is made by the holders of 25 percent in principal amount of bonds outstanding or by a trustee, shall appoint a receiver. The receiver shall enter and take possession of the enterprise and shall exercise all the rights and powers of the municipality with respect to the enterprise. Such receiver shall maintain, restore, insure and keep insured the enterprise and from time to time shall make all such necessary or proper repairs that to such receiver may seem expedient; shall establish, levy, maintain and collect such fees, tolls, rentals and other charges in connection with the enterprise that such receiver may deem necessary or proper and reasonable; shall collect and receive all revenues; and shall deposit the same in a separate account and apply such revenues so collected and received in such manner as the court shall direct. *See also* Mo. Ann. Stat. § 99.190 (allowing for receiver with respect to default on housing project bonds should the bond resolution so provide); Mo. Ann. Stat. § 173.405 (higher education bonds); and Mo. Ann. Stat. § 67.789 (recreational lake authority).

The definition of "municipality" includes any county, school district, city, town, village, township, road district, public water supply district or drainage district located in whole or in part within a defense area, except any county now or hereafter having a population of not less than 200,000 nor more than 400,000 inhabitants and also except any school district, city, town, village, township, road district, public water supply district or drainage district or other political subdivision or public corporation located within any such county. Mo. Ann. Stat. § 91.630.

The state code may be more expansive and an attorney should be consulted to examine any situation that could allow for the appointment of a receiver.

viii See, e.g., MO. ANN. STAT. § 99.190 (housing projects). The state code may be more expansive than the example cited here and the statutory authority for each individual bond issuance should be reviewed before assessing whether an accounting may be sought.

ix See, e.g., MO. ANN. STAT. § 91.220; MO. ANN. STAT. § 99.190 (housing projects); and MO. ANN. STAT. § 67.789 (recreational lake authority). The state code may be more expansive than the example cited here and the statutory authority for each individual bond issuance should be reviewed before assessing whether foreclosure is an available action.

x See, e.g., MO. ANN. STAT. § 91.740 (allowing bondholders to enforce rights by mandamus or other suit, action or proceeding against the municipality to compel municipality to perform); MO. ANN. STAT. § 173.405 (higher education bonds); MO. ANN. STAT. § 99.912 (Municipal Housing - Urban Homesteading Program); and MO. ANN. STAT. § 67.789 (recreational lake authority). An aggrieved bondholder likely could pursue a writ of mandamus even absent authorizing statutory law.

xi See, e.g., MO. ANN. STAT. § 91.740 (allowing bondholders to enforce rights by mandamus or other suit, action or proceeding against the municipality to compel municipality to perform) and MO. ANN. STAT. § 67.789 (recreational lake authority). The state code may be more expansive and the statutory authority for each bond issuance should be reviewed before assessing what rights and remedies may be available to bondholders.

xii See, e.g., MO. ANN. STAT. § 71.804(2) (cities, towns and villages and special business district revenue bonds payable solely from revenues derived from subject facility) and MO. ANN. STAT. § 99.903(3) (Urban Homesteading Program revenue bonds payable solely from revenues derived from mortgages or loans). These are examples of special revenue bonds. The state code may be more expansive, and an attorney should be consulted to examine any specific situation involving a default.

AA. Montana

Municipal Bankruptcy Authority	Under Montana law, a "local entity," which is defined as a "district created under Title 7, chapter 12, a city, or a town," may file a petition under Chapter 9 of the Bankruptcy Code, along with any irrigation district. Districts created under Title 7, chapter 12 include business improvement districts; rural improvement districts; districts for lighting; districts for sanitary and storm sewers; special improvement districts; special improvement lighting districts; street maintenance districts; street parking districts and fire hydrant maintenance districts. Counties are specifically excluded from the definition of "local entity." Unless an entity is specifically identified above, it is not authorized to file a municipal bankruptcy petition. Between 1980 and July 31, 2016, four entities in Montana have filed petitions under Chapter 9 of the Bankruptcy Code, including three special municipal districts and one utility (irrigation) district.[i]
Home Rule and Taxing Power of Municipalities	**Municipalities' Ability to Self-Govern** Montana is not a Dillon's Rule state.[ii] The Montana Constitution authorizes local governments to exercise any power not prohibited by the Montana Constitution or other law and provides for the adoption of self-government charters.[iii] In addition, the Montana Code authorizes counties, cities and towns to levy and collect a property tax.[iv] **Tax Limitations** Property tax levies in Montana may not exceed the amount levied for tax year 1996, subject to procedures in Montana law for calculating tax levies. In addition, Montana law includes certain limitations on special assessments.[v]
Debt Default Prevention	**Debt Limitation** A city-county consolidated local government, county, city or town may not issue bonds for any purpose if its outstanding indebtedness exceeds 2.5 percent of the total assessed value of taxable property in the local government. A city-county consolidated government may exceed this limit by an additional 10 percent and a city or town may exceed this limit by 55 percent to construct a sewer or procure or construct a water system.[vi] **Refunding Bonds** In certain situations, a municipal entity may issue refunding bonds to refund and refinance outstanding debt.[vii]

AA. Montana

Mechanisms for Resolution after Default	**Receivership** In certain situations, Montana law allows for the appointment of a receiver with respect to revenue bonds where a default has occurred.[viii]
Remedies on Default	**Interest Penalty** With respect to municipal general obligation bonds, if a municipality fails to promptly pay an installment of interest or principal on a bond issuance, the party not promptly paid shall draw interest at 6 percent per annum from the date due until actually paid, irrespective of the bonds' actual interest rate.[ix] **Limited Remedy** Holders of municipal revenue bonds shall not have the right to compel any exercise of taxing power of the municipality to pay the bonds or the interest thereon.[x] **Mandamus** In certain situations, bondholders or their trustee may bring a court action to compel the local governing body to perform a ministerial action that it has refused to undertake, such as collecting taxes or fees where the underlying bond authorization requires such a collection. In these situations, mandamus is a possible remedy to compel performance by municipal officials.[xi] **Suit in Equity** In certain situations, bondholders or their trustee may bring a suit in equity to protect their rights.[xii]
Other Bondholder Protections	**Special Revenue Bonds** As provided by Section 922(d) of the Bankruptcy Code, payments to bondholders holding special revenue bonds would not be stayed on the filing of a municipal bankruptcy petition, and payments to holders could continue. Whether an issuance would qualify as a special revenue bond depends on the provisions of the authorizing statute with respect to the bonds at issue.[xiii] **Statutory Liens** Were a municipal entity to file a petition under Chapter 9 of the Bankruptcy Code, bondholders holding bonds to which statutory liens have attached would continue to receive payment on those bonds. For a statutory lien to apply, the authorizing law of the bond issue must contain such a lien. No statutes covered by the categories were identified.

i MONT. CODE ANN. §§ 7-7-132 and 85-7-2041. The local entity's legislative body must pass an ordinance or resolution declaring that (1) it is insolvent or unable to meet its debts as they mature; (2) it is to effect a plan of adjustment under Chapter 9; and (3) it will proceed with such an adjustment.

ii *See Granite Cnty. v. Komberec*, 245 Mont. 252, 257 (Mont. 1990) (noting that the 1972 Montana constitution modified Dillon's Rule) (overruled on other grounds).

iii *See* MONT. CONST. art. XI, § 4 (noting that "[a]n incorporated city or town has the powers of a municipal corporation and legislative, administrative, and other powers provided or implied by law" and that these powers "shall be liberally construed"); MONT. CONST. art. XI, § 5 (self-government charters) and § 6 (allowing exercise of all powers not prohibited).

iv MONT. CODE ANN. § 7-6-2501 (counties); MONT. CODE ANN. § 7-6-4401 (cities and towns).

v MONT. CODE ANN. § 15-10-402 (limitation); MONT. CODE ANN. §15-10-420 (procedure for calculating levy); MONT. CODE ANN. § 17-5-103 (special assessment limitations).

vi MONT. CODE ANN. § 7-7-107 (city-county consolidated units); MONT. CODE ANN. § 7-7-2101 (counties); MONT. CODE ANN. § 7-7-4201 (cities or towns); MONT. CODE ANN. § 7-7-108 (increasing limit for water or sewer for city-county consolidated units); and MONT. CODE ANN. § 7-7-4202 (increasing limit for water and sewage for cities and towns).

vii Examples of refunding bonds in Montana law include MONT. CODE ANN. § 7-7-4275 (subject to approval of board of investments, the council of any city or town is authorized to issue amortization bonds to refund any outstanding bond); MONT. CODE ANN. § 7-7-4503 (authorizing refunding revenue bonds and allowing that bonds to be refunded be exchanged at par plus accrued interest for all or part of such bonds or that they may be sold at a private negotiated sale or a public sale at a price not less than par plus accrued interest); MONT. CODE ANN. § 7-7-4627 (any city or town may exchange refunding bonds privately and in payment and discharge of any outstanding bonds); and MONT. CODE ANN. § 7-7-4605 (any city or town may refinance and improve any enterprise and may issue refunding bonds from time to time).

viii *See, e.g.*, MONT. CODE ANN. §§ 7-7-4630 to 7-7-4632 (allowing for appointment of receiver for holders of refunding bond in event municipality defaults in payment of principal or interest, which default continues for 30 days; if the governing body fails or refuses to comply with provisions or defaults on an agreement; or if 25 percent of holders of principal amount of bonds petition). The state code may be more expansive and the statutory authority for each bond issuance should be reviewed before assessing whether a receiver may be appointed.

ix MONT. CODE ANN. § 7-7-4263.

x MONT. CODE ANN. § 7-7-4423.

xi *See, e.g.*, MONT. CODE ANN. § 7-7-4266 (if council of a city or town fails, neglects or refuses to levy sufficient funds to pay interest and principal on bonds, the holder of a bond or any taxpayer may apply to the district court for a writ of mandate to compel the collection of proper and sufficient funds); MONT. CODE ANN. § 7-7-4429 (allowing for enforcement of notes by writ of mandamus or other appropriate action); and MONT. CODE ANN. § 7-7-4633 (allowing for holders of refunding bonds to bring mandamus action, action in equity to require an accounting as if they were the trustee of an express trust, any suit in equity or suit on the refunding bonds). It is possible that an aggrieved bondholder could pursue a writ of mandamus even absent authorizing statutory law.

xii *See, e.g.*, MONT. CODE ANN. § 7-7-4633 (allowing for holders of refunding bonds to bring mandamus action, action in equity to require an accounting as if they were the trustee of an express trust, any suit in equity or suit on the refunding bonds). The state code may be more expansive and the statutory authority for each bond issuance should be reviewed before determining what actions a bondholder may bring.

xiii *See, e.g.*, MONT. CODE ANN. § 7-7-4423 (municipal revenue bonds payable only out of revenues pledged). This provision is an example of a special revenue bond. The state code may be more expansive, and an attorney should be consulted to examine any specific situation involving a default.

BB. Nebraska

Municipal Bankruptcy Authority	Under Nebraska law, any county, city, village, school district, agency of the state government, drainage district, sanitary and improvement district or other political subdivision of the state may file a petition under Chapter 9 of the Bankruptcy Code. Unless an entity is specifically identified above, it is not authorized to file a municipal bankruptcy petition. Between 1980 and July 31, 2016, 63 Nebraska entities, all sanitary and improvement districts, have filed petitions under Chapter 9 of the Bankruptcy Code.[i]
Home Rule and Taxing Power of Municipalities	**Municipalities' Ability to Self-Govern** Nebraska is a Dillon's Rule state. Cities with a population exceeding 5,000 may adopt a home-rule charter, however.[ii] In addition, the Nebraska Constitution authorizes governmental subdivisions to levy taxes in a manner directed by the state legislature.[iii] **Tax Limitations** Nebraska state law includes tax assessment limitations for counties, cities of the first and second class and villages. With respect to cities of the first and second class, and villages, the limits do not apply to funds necessary to pay bonded indebtedness.[iv]
Debt Default Prevention Mechanisms	**Debt Limitation** Various Nebraska Code provisions contain limitations on the issuance of certain bonds. For instance, a precinct, township, city of the second class or village is authorized to issue bonds for internal improvements, but the amount of the bonds may not exceed seven-tenths of 1 percent of the taxable valuation of the taxable property therein. Counties may not issue bonds equaling more than 3.5 percent of the taxable valuation of the county.[v] **Refunding Bonds** In certain situations, a municipal entity may issue refunding bonds to refund and refinance outstanding debt.[vi]
Mechanisms for Resolution after Default	**Compromise of Debt** If a municipal entity is unable to pay its full indebtedness and one-third of the resident freeholders in the municipal entity petition, the municipal entity is required to enter into negotiations with the owners or holders of the indebtedness for scaling, discounting or compromising the same.[vii] **Receivership** Nebraska law allows for the appointment of a receiver with respect to revenue bonds in situations in which a default has occurred.[viii]

BB. Nebraska

Remedies on Default	**Foreclosure** In certain default situations, bondholders may foreclose on a project for which they hold a mortgage.[ix] **Mandamus** In certain situations, bondholders or their trustee may bring a court action to compel the local governing body to perform a ministerial action that it has refused to undertake, such as collecting taxes or fees where the underlying bond authorization requires such a collection.[x]
Other Bondholder Protections	**Special Revenue Bonds** As provided by Section 922(d) of the Bankruptcy Code, payments to bondholders holding special revenue bonds would not be stayed on the filing of a municipal bankruptcy petition, and payments to holders could continue. Whether an issuance would qualify as a special revenue bond depends on the provisions of the authorizing statute with respect to the bonds at issue.[xi] **Statutory Liens** Were a municipal entity to file a petition under Chapter 9 of the Bankruptcy Code, bondholders holding bonds to which statutory liens have attached would continue to receive payment on those bonds. For a statutory lien to apply, the authorizing law of the bond issue must contain such a lien. No enacted statutes covered by the categories were identified.[xii]

---

i NEB. REV. STAT. § 13-402. Nebraska municipal entities alone account for around 21 percent of the municipal bankruptcy petitions that have been filed between 1980 and July 31, 2016, in the United States. These filings generally were made as a means to dissolve by sanitary and improvement districts that have outlived their usefulness.

In addition, NEB. REV. STAT. § 13-2524 provides that a joint public agency may file a Chapter 9 petition and may incur and pay the expenses incident to the consummation of a plan of adjustment. "Public agency" means any political subdivision, including any municipality, county, school district, or agency or department of the state. NEB. REV. STAT. § 13-1502.

ii NEB. CONST. art. XI, § 2 (charter procedures for cities exceeding 5,000 people) and § 5 (charter procedures for cities with population exceeding 100,000). *See also Home Builders Ass'n of Lincoln v. City of Lincoln*, 271 Neb. 353, 359 (Neb. 2006) (noting that Dillon's Rule is applicable unless a city has adopted a home-rule charter).

iii NEB. CONST. art. VIII, § 1.

iv NEB. CONST. art. VIII, § 5 (counties) and NEB. REV. STAT. § 19-1309 (maximum limits for cities of the first and second class and villages). Counties may not assess taxes exceeding in the aggregate 50 cents per $100 of taxable value as determined by the assessment rolls, unless authorized by county voters. In addition, the Nebraska Code includes a limit on any all-purpose levy for cities of the first and second class and villages, but these limits do not apply to funds necessary to pay bonded indebtedness.

v NEB. REV. STAT. § 10-409 (precincts, townships, cities of the second class and villages). Section 10-409 establishes the framework for issuing bonds for internal improvements, such as voting requirements. Under § 10-409,, bonds issued for the construction of a city building, such as a city hall or fire station, may not exceed 1.4 percent of taxable valuation of the city. *See also* NEB. REV. STAT. § 10-501 (counties). The Nebraska Code also provides that bonds issued to help destitute and needy sufferers from cyclones, tornadoes or destructive windstorms may not exceed 1.8 percent of the taxable valuation of the county and may not exceed $1 million. NEB. REV. STAT. § 10-801. Bonds issued by a county or city to construct a railroad or other work of internal improvement may not exceed 3.5 percent of the taxable valuation of the county or city. NEB. REV. STAT. § 10-401. The Nebraska Code may be more expansive, and an attorney should be consulted to examine any specific situation involving limitations on the issuance of indebtedness.

All cities, towns and villages with a population greater than 800 and not more than 5,000 are classified as cities of the second class. NEB. REV. STAT. § 17-101.

vi Examples of refunding bond provisions in Nebraska law include NEB. REV. STAT. § 10-142 (allowing any county, city, village, municipal county, school district, drainage district, irrigation district, metropolitan utilities district, rural water district, airport authority, hospital authority, the Board of Regents of the University of Nebraska, the Board of Trustees of the Nebraska State Colleges, the governing board of any community college, or any other municipal or public corporation, governmental subdivision or body politic or corporate created under Nebraska law to issue refunding bonds) and NEB. REV. STAT. § 58-253 (refunding bonds for Nebraska Investment Finance Authority).

vii NEB. REV. STAT § 10-302.

viii NEB. REV. STAT. § 10-1106 (a trustee upon default has the right to have a receiver appointed for the collection of any revenue or property in which a security interest is granted). Pursuant to § 10-1106, if the revenue is from a revenue producing undertaking, a receiver may also be appointed to operate and manage the project for bondholders. *See also* NEB. REV. STAT. § 13-1104 (municipal manufacturing or industrial enterprise bonds); NEB. REV. STAT. § 70-648 (public power, public irrigation, or public power and irrigation districts); and NEB. REV. STAT. § 14-1715 (parking authority bonds). The state code may be more expansive and the statutory authority for each bond issuance should be reviewed before assessing whether a receiver may be appointed.

ix *See, e.g.,* NEB. REV. STAT. § 13-1104 (municipal manufacturing or industrial enterprise bonds). The state code may be more expansive than the example cited here and the statutory authority for each individual bond issuance should be reviewed before assessing whether a foreclosure could be pursued.

x *See, e.g.,* NEB. REV. STAT. § 13-1104 (municipal manufacturing or industrial enterprise bonds); NEB. REV. STAT. § 14-1739 (parking facility bonds); NEB. REV. STAT. § 16-809 (parking facility bonds); NEB. REV. STAT. § 10-806 (bonds to aid victims of tornadoes, cyclones and windstorms); NEB. REV. STAT. § 17-171 (off-street parking facility bonds for second-class cities); and NEB. REV. STAT. § 18-504(4) (sewage bonds). It is possible that an aggrieved bondholder could pursue a writ of mandamus even absent authorizing statutory law.

In one Nebraska case, the court found that in the absence of a constitutional inhibition, where the maximum amount of taxes authorized by the provision in question for general corporate purposes had already been imposed, the court could impose a levy of taxes to pay a judgment against the municipality. *Benner v. Cnty. Bd. of Douglas Cnty.,* 238 N.W. 735 (Neb. 1931).

xi *See, e.g.,* NEB. REV. STAT. § 16-6,101 (revenue bond lien only on revenue and earnings of waterworks plant, water system, or gas plant or gas systems); NEB. REV. STAT. § 16-803 (revenue bonds for construction of parking facilities only lien on revenues and earnings of facility); NEB. REV. STAT. § 18-412 (revenue bonds issued for power lines secured by lien on revenue and earnings of electric light and power plant); NEB. REV. STAT. § 18-502 (bonds for sewage disposal plant or sewerage system secured by revenue on utility); NEB. REV. STAT. § 39-856 (county revenue bonds to construct bridges connecting State of Nebraska with an adjoining state); and NEB. REV. STAT. § 14-1733 (revenue bonds for parking facilities). These are examples of special revenue bonds. The state code may be more expansive, and an attorney should be consulted to examine any specific situation involving a default.

xii In 2014 and 2015, the 103d Nebraska legislature, second session had introduced a proposed amended statute to create a statutory lien on any bond, including general obligation bonds. Legislative Bill 67 and 788 would amend NEB. REV. STAT. §§ 10-1101, 10-1102, 10-1103, 10-1104, 10-1105, 10-1106 and 10-1813, but of yet, this legislation has not been enacted.

CC. Nevada

Municipal Bankruptcy Authority	Nevada does not specifically authorize its municipal entities to file a petition under Chapter 9 of the Bankruptcy Code. Between 1980 and July 31, 2016, no Nevada municipal entity has filed such a petition. In the 2015 Nevada legislature, there was an attempt to pass a law specifically permitting Chapter 9 filing after the severe financial emergency process described below which is expected to last longer than three years, and the governor approved such a filing. That provision was deleted from the final version of the Assembly Bill 54 enacted in the 2015 Nevada legislative session as discussed below.
Home Rule and Taxing Power of Municipalities	**Municipalities' Ability to Self-Govern** Nevada is a Dillon's Rule state. The state legislature may provide for the organization of cities and towns and restrict their power to tax, assess, borrow money, contract debts and loan their credit.[i] The Nevada legislature has granted counties and cities the power to levy property taxes.[ii] **Tax Limitations** The Nevada Constitution and Nevada state statutes limit the total tax levy for all public purposes within the state or any subdivision. The statutory limitations are inapplicable to levies for the payment of interest and principal on bonded indebtedness.[iii]
Debt Default Prevention	**Audit Enforcement** Each local government must annually audit its financial statements and submit the audit to the Department of Taxation and identify any violations of Nevada law in the audit. The local government must take steps to prevent recurrence of the violation within 60 days after delivery of the audit. If the Department of Taxation deems the plan inadequate, it must propose an alternative plan. If the taxation director determines that the plan is not being complied with, he or she, through the attorney general, must seek a writ from a court to compel performance.[iv] **Debt Limitation** The Nevada statutes set debt limits based on the type of entities issuing the debt. For instance, the total bonded indebtedness of a county school district may not exceed 15 percent of the last assessed value of taxable property therein, excluding motor vehicles. With respect to irrigation districts, the district may not incur indebtedness exceeding $1,000,000. County hospitals and hospital districts may not incur debt exceeding 10 percent of the total of the last assessed valuation of taxable property, excluding motor vehicles in the district.[v]

CC. Nevada

Debt Default Prevention *continued*	**Refunding Bonds** In certain situations, a municipal entity may issue refunding bonds to refund and refinance outstanding debt.[vi] **Third-Party Agreements** In certain situations, a governing body of a city or town may enter into an agreement to assure payment of principal and interest, and premiums, if any, due in connection with a bond issuance.[vii]
Mechanisms for Resolution after Default	**Local Government Financial Assistance** Nevada law contains provisions for the treatment of delinquent documents, payments, technical financial assistance and financial emergency. If a governing body determines that a local government is in need of technical assistance, it may request an appearance before the Nevada tax commission to request technical financial assistance. There are 27 triggering events. If the tax commission agrees that financial assistance is warranted, it shall order the department to provide assistance. If the tax commission finds a severe financial emergency exists, it is required to take over the management of the local government as soon as possible.[viii] Legislation passed in 2015 provided some additional phases to better assist distressed local governments. These improvements for better assistance included adding a "Fiscal Watch" status where the state monitors and provides assistance prior to moving to the severe financial emergency and taking over management of the government. This is an interactive stage where the local government can request assistance in the area of most need. Further, additional powers for the state were added to the severe financial emergency phase, namely: 1. The power to renegotiate existing collective bargaining agreements as well as new ones was expanded. 2. Negotiations with creditors as to any debt liquidation plan must be done in "good faith," attempting a constructive and creative solution that avoids a litigation meltdown and delays that limit if not impair market credibility and access to the capital markets. 3. If other revenue-enhancing methods fail, the state has the power to increase property taxes for the local government in the next quarter without abatement or limits previously an issue. [ix] **Receivership** In certain situations, Nevada law allows for a receiver with respect to revenue bonds where a default situation has occurred.[x]

CC. Nevada

Remedies on Default	**Accounting** In certain default situations, bondholders may bring a proceeding to require the authority in question to account as if it were a trustee of an express trust.[xi] **Foreclosure** In certain default Situations, bondholders may foreclose on a project for which they hold a mortgage.[xii] **Injunctive Relief** At least one provision of the Nevada Code allows for injunctive relief to enjoin any act or things that may be unlawful or the violation of any right of a bondholder.[xiii] **Mandamus** In certain situations, bondholders or their trustee may bring a court action to compel the local governing body to perform a ministerial action that it has refused to undertake, such as collecting taxes or fees where the underlying bond authorization requires such a collection.[xiv]
Other Bondholder Protections	**Special Revenue Bonds** As provided by Section 922(d) of the Bankruptcy Code, payments to bondholders holding special revenue bonds would not be stayed on the filing of a municipal bankruptcy petition, and payments to holders could continue. Whether an issuance would qualify as a special revenue bond depends on the provisions of the authorizing statute with respect to the bonds at issue.[xv] **Statutory Liens** Were a municipal entity to file a petition under Chapter 9 of the Bankruptcy Code, bondholders holding bonds to which statutory liens have attached would continue to receive payment on those bonds. For a statutory lien to apply, the authorizing law of the bond issue must contain such a lien. Category SL-2.[xvi]

---

i *Douglas Cnty. Contractors Ass'n v. Douglas Cnty.*, 112 Nev. 1452, 1461 (Nev. 1996) ("This court has held that while the state can delegate its police power and power to tax to its political subdivisions, '[s]uch power is granted only where the grant plainly appears from the delegating statute" (quoting *Clark Cnty. v. Los Angeles City*, 70 Nev. 219, 221 (Nev. 1954))); NEV. CONST. art. VIII, § 8; NEV. REV. STAT. § 266.010 (granting the right of home rule and self-government to incorporated cities).

ii NEV. REV. STAT. § 244.150 (counties) and § 266.605 (cities).

iii NEV. CONST. art. X, § 2 (limiting all taxes to 5 cents on the dollar) and NEV. REV. STAT. § 361.453 (limiting ad valorem tax rate to $3.64 per $100 assessed valuation). In addition, city councils may not levy property taxes exceeding 3 percent of assessed valuation of all real estate and personal property within the city. NEV. REV. STAT. § 266.605. *See also* NEV. REV. STAT. § 350.592 (requiring annual levy sufficient to pay principal and interest on bonds).

iv NEV. REV. STAT. §§ 354.6015 and 387.303 (similar provisions for school districts).

v NEV. REV. STAT. § 387.400 (county school districts); NEV. REV. STAT. § 539.480 (irrigation districts); NEV. REV. STAT. § 450.665 (county hospitals).

vi An example of a refunding bond provision in Nevada law is NEV. REV. STAT. § 271.488 (allowing improvement districts to issue refunding bonds).

vii *See, e.g.,* NEV. REV. STAT. § 271.489 (obligation of the municipality to reimburse the third party may be provided for in the bond agreement or evidenced in another instrument).

viii NEV. REV. STAT. §§ 354.665 to 354.725. For the definition of "local government," *see* NEV. REV. STAT. § 354.474. Triggering events include situations where the local government has: not filed required financial reports or is consistently late; filed an audit report reflecting unlawful expenditure of money in excess of appropriations or funds with deficit balances; incurred debt beyond its ability to repay; not corrected violations or has serious internal control problems noted in the audit report which have not been corrected; a record of being late in its payments for services and supplies or has had insufficient cash to meet required payroll payments in a timely manner; borrowed money or entered into long-term lease arrangements without following required laws and regulations; failed to correct problems after it has been notified of such problems by the department; not separately accounted for its individual funds; improperly invested its money in financial instruments in violation of Nevada law; violated a debt covenant; not made bond and lease payments in accordance with the approved payment schedule; failed to control its assets such that large defalcations have occurred which have impaired its financial condition; recognized sizable losses through imprudent investments; allowed its accounting system and recording of transactions to deteriorate to such an extent that it is not possible to measure accurately the results of operations or to ascertain the financial position of the local government without a reconstruction of transactions; consistently issued checks not covered by adequate deposits; loaned and borrowed money between funds without following the proper procedures; expended money in violation of the provisions governing the expenditure of that money or used money restricted for a specific purpose in violation of its terms; improperly withheld money; if a school district, received a loan from the State Permanent School Fund pursuant to NEV. REV. STAT. § 387.526; had an employer in the county that accounts for more than 15 percent of the employment in the county close or significantly reduce operations; experienced a cumulative decline of 10 percent in population or assessed valuation for the past two years; experienced a decline in the ending balance in the general fund for the past two years; failed to pay, in a timely manner, contributions to the Public Employees' Retirement System, workers' compensation or payroll taxes or failed to pay, at any time, a payment required pursuant to the Federal Insurance Contributions Act. NEV. REV. STAT. § 354.685. *See* Nevada Assembly Bill 54 ("AB 54") enacted in 2015 legislative session signed by the governor on May 25, 2015, http://www.leg.state.nv.us/Session/78th2015/Bills/AB/AB54.pdf.

ix NEV. REV. STAT. § 354.105.

x *See, e.g.,* NEV. REV. STAT. § 268.546 (allowing appointment of receiver where city's resolution authorizing bonds or any indenture or mortgage securing bonds may provide that on default, a receiver with power to charge, collect and apply revenues from project may be appointed); NEV. REV. STAT. § 268.546 (City Economic Development Revenue Bond Law); NEV. REV. STAT. § 271.630 (local improvement bonds); NEV. REV. STAT. §§ 350.664, 350.666 (allowing for appointment of receiver with respect to revenue bonds issued under Local Government Securities Law). The state code may be more expansive and the statutory authority for each bond issuance should be reviewed before assessing whether such a remedy is applicable.

xi *See, e.g.,* NEV. REV. STAT. § 350.664 (Local Government Securities Law). The state code may be more expansive and the statutory authority for each bond issuance should be reviewed before assessing whether an accounting may be sought.

xii *See, e.g.*, NEV. REV. STAT. § 268.546 (City Economic Development Revenue Bond Law); NEV. REV. STAT. § 271.630 (local improvement bonds). The state code may be more expansive and the statutory authority for each bond issuance should be reviewed before assessing whether, after a default, a foreclosure action may be pursued.

xiii *See, e.g.*, NEV. REV. STAT. § 350.664 (Local Government Securities Law). The state code may be more expansive and the statutory authority for each bond issuance should be reviewed before assessing the availability of injunctive relief.

xiv *State ex rel. Walsh v. Buckingham*, 80 P.2d 910 (Nev. 1938) (court issued a writ of mandamus, finding Board of Commissioners of Mineral County, Nevada, had to pay realtor sum due on bonds). *See also* NEV. REV. STAT. § 268.546 (City Economic Development Revenue Bond Law); NEV. REV. STAT. § 350.664 (Local Government Securities Law). It is possible that an aggrieved bondholder could pursue a writ of mandamus even absent authorizing statutory law.

xv *See, e.g.*, NEV. REV. STAT. § 268.536 (principal and interest secured by a pledge of revenue on project constitutes a lien on revenues); NEV. REV. STAT. § 350.582 (special obligation municipal securities are secured by a pledge of and constitute a lien on pledged revenues if expressly so provided in any act). These are examples of special revenue bonds. The state code may be more expansive, and an attorney should be consulted to examine any specific situation involving a default.

xvi Category SL-2: *See, e.g.*, NEV. REV. STAT. § 350.662 (Local Government Securities Law). This legislation provides that pledged revenues for local government securities shall have the lien attached immediately, without any further action; the lien has a priority over all others except as to what may be provided therein subject to any prior pledges and liens previously created and shall be valid and binding against all persons and any and all claims. However, further clarification by the legislature or opinion of counsel may be needed before this can be definitively determined to be a statutory lien as opposed to a statement of perfection of a lien. The state code may be more expansive, and an attorney should be consulted to examine any specific situation involving a default.

DD. New Hampshire

Municipal Bankruptcy Authority	New Hampshire does not specifically authorize its municipal entities to file a municipal bankruptcy petition. Between 1980 and July 31, 2016, only one New Hampshire municipal entity has filed such a petition. This case was filed before Congress in 1994 greatly limited the ability of municipalities to file Chapter 9 petitions by requiring specific state authorization.[i]
Home Rule and Taxing Power of Municipalities	**Municipalities' Ability to Self-Govern** New Hampshire is a Dillon's Rule state. The authority of a local government or a municipality must be derived from the state legislature. In addition, the state legislature may authorize cities and towns to adopt and amend charters, and local governments may assess property taxes.[ii] **Tax Limitations** New Hampshire does not include any form of ad valorem tax limitations.
Debt Default Prevention	**Debt Limitation** A New Hampshire county may not incur debt exceeding 2 percent of its last assessed valuation of taxable property. A city may not incur debt, except for school purposes, exceeding 3 percent of valuation; for school purposes, debt may not exceed 7 percent of valuation of taxable property. A town may not incur debt exceeding 3 percent of valuation of taxable property; a school district may not incur debt exceeding 7 percent of taxable property; and a village district may not incur debt exceeding 1 percent of its valuation of taxable property. In addition, if several municipalities cover or extend over the same territory, the aggregate net indebtedness may not exceed 9.75 percent of valuation.[iii] **Refunding Bonds** In certain situations, a municipal entity may issue refunding bonds to refund and refinance outstanding debt.[iv]
Mechanisms for Resolution after Default	**Emergency Financial Assistance** Any town, city or county that is unable to finance its needs or meet outstanding obligations and cannot obtain financing any other way may apply to the state government for financial assistance.[v] **Receivership** In certain situations, New Hampshire law allows for the appointment of a receiver with respect to revenue bonds where a default has occurred.[vi]

DD. New Hampshire

Remedies on Default	**Contractual Remedies** In certain situations, a bond issuance may define defaults and provide for remedies, including the acceleration of maturities.[vii] **Mandamus** In certain situations, bondholders may bring an action to compel the local governing body to perform a ministerial action that it has refused to undertake, such as collecting taxes or fees where the underlying bond authorization requires such a collection.[viii]
Other Bondholder Protections	**Special Revenue Bonds** As provided by Section 922(d) of the Bankruptcy Code, payments to bondholders holding special revenue bonds would not be stayed on the filing of a municipal bankruptcy petition. Whether an issuance qualifies as a special revenue bond depends on the authorizing statute with respect to the bonds at issue.[ix] **Statutory Liens** Were a municipal entity to file a petition under Chapter 9 of the Bankruptcy Code, bondholders holding bonds to which statutory liens have attached would continue to receive payment on those bonds. For a statutory lien to apply, the authorizing law of the bond issue must contain such a lien. No statutes covered by the categories were identified.

i The single municipal bankruptcy case, *In re Sullivan County Regional Refuse Disposal District*, was filed in 1993 and closed in November 1996. No plan of adjustment was filed.

ii N.H. CONST. Part I, art. 12; *see* N.H. CONST. Part I, art. 28 ("No subsidy, charge, tax, impost, or duty, shall be established, fixed, laid, or levied, under any pretext whatsoever, without the consent of the people, or their representatives in the legislature, or authority derived from that body."); N.H. CONST. Part 1, art. 39 (charter authorization). *See also* N.H. REV. STAT. ANN. § 76:5 (establishing what taxes shall be assessed by selectmen).

iii N.H. REV. STAT. ANN. § 33:4 (counties); N.H. REV. STAT. ANN. § 33:4-a (municipalities). *See* N.H. REV. STAT. ANN. § 33:4-b for information related to valuation and aggregation of debt limits. Valuation is based on the last locally assessed valuation of the property in the municipality. Certain exclusions, as outlined by chapter 33 of the New Hampshire Statutes, may apply.

iv Examples of provisions in New Hampshire law authorizing the issuance of refunding bonds include N.H. REV. STAT. ANN. § 33:3-d (any town, school district, village district or county may authorize issuance of refunding bonds) and N.H. REV. STAT. ANN. § 33-B:8 (allowing municipality, when authorized, to issue refunding bonds).

v N.H. REV. STAT. ANN. §§ 13:1 to 13:7. If the governor and council determine an emergency exists, they may issue a certificate declaring the existence of such an emergency and authorize the municipality to issue emergency notes or bonds. N.H. REV. STAT. ANN. § 13:2. The state may guaranty the bonds.

vi See, e.g., N.H. REV. STAT. ANN. § 204-C:32 (receiver for housing finance authority). The state code may be more expansive and the statutory authority for each individual bond issuance should be reviewed before assessing whether a receiver may be appointed.

vii See, e.g., N.H. REV. STAT. ANN. § 374-B:4 (municipal electric revenue bonds). The state code may be more expansive and the statutory authority for each individual bond issuance should be reviewed to determine what contractual remedies may be available.

viii See, e.g., N.H. REV. STAT. ANN. § 33-B:7 (municipal revenue bonds); N.H. REV. STAT. ANN. § 374-B:8 (municipal electric bonds). It is possible that an aggrieved bondholder could pursue a writ of mandamus even absent authorizing statutory law.

ix See, e.g., N.H. REV. STAT. ANN. § 33-B:6 (creating continuously perfected lien for municipal revenue bonds); N.H. REV. STAT. ANN. § 33-B:2 (revenue bonds). These are examples of special revenue bonds. The state code may be more expansive, and an attorney should be consulted to examine any specific situation involving a default.

EE. New Jersey

Municipal Bankruptcy Authority	In New Jersey, only with prior approval of the municipal finance commission may any county, municipality, school district or other political subdivision of the state file a petition under Chapter 9 of the Bankruptcy Code. Unless an entity is specifically identified above, it is not authorized to file a municipal bankruptcy petition. Between 1980 and July 31, 2016, two New Jersey entities have filed Chapter 9 petitions, including Camden in 1999, although the case was later dismissed, and a medical center, which filed in 1983 and had a plan of adjustment confirmed in 1987.[i]
Home Rule and Taxing Power of Municipalities	**Municipalities' Ability to Self-Govern** New Jersey is not a Dillon's Rule state. The New Jersey Constitution provides that any laws concerning municipal corporations formed by local governments shall be construed in their favor and further that the powers of counties and such municipal corporations shall include not only the express terms of the state's laws, but also those necessary for "fair implication, or incident to the powers expressly conferred, or essential thereto, and not inconsistent with or prohibited." Likewise, the New Jersey municipal law expressly provides that municipalities are to be provided "the fullest and most complete power possible over the internal affairs of … municipalities for local self-government."[ii] Further, municipalities are granted taxing authority by the state's statutes.[iii] **Tax Limitations** New Jersey state law includes provisions limiting the amount that municipalities and counties may increase their tax levy in any given year.[iv]
Debt Default Prevention	**Debt Limitation** A municipality may not incur debt exceeding 3.5 percent of the municipality's state equalized valuation averaged over three years. Counties may not incur debt exceeding 2 percent of the same.[v] **Special Municipal Aid Act** Municipal entities in New Jersey may be eligible under the Special Municipal Aid Act, which facilitates loans and grants to certain municipalities experiencing budgetary difficulties in generating adequate local revenues to assist them in meeting their immediate budgetary needs and regaining financial stability. To be eligible, a municipality need either be under the supervision of a Local Finance Board under the Local Government Supervision Act or be identified by the director as facing serious fiscal distress.[vi]

EE. New Jersey

Debt Default Prevention *continued*	**Casino Tax Property Stabilization Act** This act provides a property tax exemption to participating casinos in Atlantic City, New Jersey for a ten-year period in exchange for participating casinos paying an annual payment in lieu of taxes. The participating casinos would also be required to make certain payments to the State of New Jersey, to be distributed to Atlantic City by the New Jersey Local Finance Board when Atlantic City devises an acceptable restructuring plan.[vii] This legislation is intended to provide increased revenue to Atlantic City and to the state to stabilize the tax revenue available to Atlantic City and avoid the uncertainty and volatility of tax litigation by the casinos. **Refunding Bonds** In certain situations, a municipal entity may issue refunding bonds to refund and refinance outstanding debt.[viii]
Mechanisms for Resolution after Default	**Local Government Supervision Act** If the Local Finance Board of the State Department of Community Affairs determines that a triggering event has occurred, the municipality is placed under the board's supervision. The municipality's financial affairs are monitored and the board may take actions such as limiting the municipality's debts and other financial obligations.[ix] **Municipal Finance Commission** Bondholders may bring an action against a municipality if the municipality has defaulted for over 60 days in payment of principal or interest on its outstanding bonds. If a court finds that a default has occurred, the municipal finance commission may then step in to help reestablish the financial stability of the municipality.[x] **Municipal Rehabilitation and Economic Recovery Act of 2002** This provision applies to any municipality that has been the subject of supervision under the Special Municipal Aid Act for at least one year; has been subject to supervision of the Local Finance Board under the Local Government Supervision Act for at least one year; and, based on the municipality's most recent budget, is dependent on state aid and other state revenue for not less than 55 percent of their budget. The governor may appoint a chief operating officer to manage the municipality along with the elected mayor. If the two disagree, a special arbitrator is appointed to resolve the dispute.[xi]

EE. New Jersey

Mechanisms for Resolution after Default *continued*	**Receivership** In certain situations, New Jersey law allows for the appointment of a receiver with respect to revenue bonds where a default has occurred.[xii] **School District Fiscal Monitor** The Commissioner of Education may appoint a fiscal monitor over a school district if the school district receives an adverse opinion or disclaimer of opinion by its independent auditor in an annual audit or if certain other circumstances exist. Among other things, the monitor shall oversee the operation and fiscal management of the school district and devise a plan to address the circumstances placing the school district under a fiscal monitor's control.[xiii]
Remedies on Default	**Accounting** In certain default situations, bondholders may bring a proceeding to require the authority in question to account as if it were a trustee of an express trust.[xiv] **Foreclosure** In certain default situations, bondholders may seek possession of a project for which they hold a mortgage.[xv] **Mandamus** In certain situations, bondholders or their trustee may bring a court action to compel the local governing body to perform a ministerial action that it has refused to undertake, such as collecting taxes or fees where the underlying bond authorization requires such a collection.[xvi]
Other Bondholder Protections	**Special Revenue Bonds** As provided by Section 922(d) of the Bankruptcy Code, payments to bondholders holding special revenue bonds would not be stayed on the filing of a municipal bankruptcy petition, and payments to holders could continue. Whether an issuance would qualify as a special revenue bond depends on the provisions of the authorizing statute with respect to the bonds at issue.[xvii] **Statutory Liens** Were a municipal entity to file a petition under Chapter 9 of the Bankruptcy Code, bondholders holding bonds to which statutory liens have attached would continue to receive payment on those bonds. For a statutory lien to apply, the authorizing law of the bond issue must contain such a lien. Category SL-1.[xviii]

i N.J. STAT. ANN. § 52:27-40. Under New Jersey law, the municipal finance commission appears to be the Local Finance Board of the Division of Local Government Services in the Department of Community Affairs. *See* N.J. STAT. ANN. §§ 52:27-1, 18A-46.

ii N.J. CONST. art IV, § VII, ¶ 11.

iii N.J. Stat Ann. § 40:42-4 (home rule provisions); N.J. Stat Ann. §40:48C-1 (taxing provisions).

iv N.J. STAT ANN. §§ 40A:4-45.3 (municipal tax levy increase limits) and § 40A:4-45.4 (county tax levy increase limits).

v N.J. STAT. ANN. § 40A:2-6. Certain exceptions apply as provided in N.J. STAT. ANN. § 40A:2-7.

vi N.J. STAT. ANN. § 52:27D-118.24 (Special Municipal Aid Act). This provision has been utilized by the city of Camden.

vii S.B. 1715, 216th Leg (N.J. 2014), signed into law May 27, 2016. This measure aims to establish a baseline revenue to help Atlantic City, New Jersey restructure.

viii Examples of refunding bond provisions in New Jersey law include N.J. STAT. ANN. §§ 40A:2-1 (Local Bond Law) and 40A:2-51 (issuance of refunding bonds). A governing body, meaning any board of freeholders of a county, or the commission, council, board or body having control of the finances of a municipality may issue refunding bonds.

ix N.J. STAT. ANN. §§ 52:27BB-1 to 52:27BB-100 (Local Government Supervision Act). Under these provisions, the Local Finance Board of the State Department of Community Affairs has the authority to determine if one or more triggering events have occurred. Triggering events (§ 52:27BB-55) include a default on bonds or notes; payments to the state, county school district or special district are unpaid for the previous year and the preceding year; an appropriation for "cash deficit of preceding year" in an amount in excess of 4 percent of the total amount of levied taxes on real and personal property is required to be included in the next budget and was required to be included in the budget for the year just closed; less than 70 percent of total taxes levied on real and personal property in the year just closed and previous year were collected; the appropriation required to be included in the next regular budget for the liquidation of all bond obligations exceeds 25 percent of the total appropriations for operating purposes for the year just ended; or a court made a determination of gross failure to comply with the Local Bond Law.

x N.J. STAT. ANN. §§ 52:27-1 to 52:27-66. New Jersey law also provides that, when a municipality seeks relief from the New Jersey Superior Court due to the municipality's inability to meet its obligations, upon entry of judgment, the municipal finance commission is authorized to function in the municipality. N.J. STAT. ANN. §§ 52:27-3.

xi N.J. STAT. ANN. §§ 52:27BBB-1 to 52:27BBB-79 (Municipal Rehabilitation and Economic Recovery Act of 2002). Under this provision, all outstanding debts or obligations incurred by the municipality or the New Jersey Housing and Mortgage Finance Agency and secured by a right of first refusal on municipally owned property as of 10 days following the determination of the commissioner, with any subsidiary of that agency with jurisdiction in a qualified municipality, other than those debts or obligations represented by bonds or other negotiable instruments, are forgiven. This provision was enacted to restructure the city of Camden. In January 2010, the New Jersey governor signed the "Camden Freedom Act," releasing Camden from the provisions of the Recovery Act.

xii *See, e.g.,* N.J. STAT. ANN. §§ 40:62-133.8 and 40:62-133.9 (public water utility); N.J. STAT. ANN. § 40:68A-49 (port authorities); N.J. STAT. ANN. § 40:66A-15 (solid waste management); N.J. STAT. ANN. § 40:14A-18 (sewer authority); N.J. STAT. ANN. § 40:37A-65 (county improvement authority); N.J. STAT. ANN. § 40:11A-14 (parking authorities); N.J. STAT. ANN. § 40A:12A-33 (local redevelopment and housing authority). The state code may be more expansive and the statutory authority for each bond issuance should be reviewed before assessing whether a receiver may be appointed.

xiii N.J. STAT. ANN. § 18A:7A-55. To be placed in control of a fiscal monitor, a school district must either receive an adverse or disclaimer of opinion by an independent auditor or meet two of the following circumstances: (1) end the fiscal year with a deficit balance; (2) receive a qualified opinion by its independent auditor; (3) receive an adverse, disclaimer or qualified opinion by its independent auditor under a certain audit section; (4) receive any audit findings identified as material weaknesses in internal controls; (5) fail to develop an acceptable plan to address a potential or actual deficit balance in the general fund, special revenue fund or capital projects fund, with the exception of a capital projects fund deficit caused by the issuance of bond anticipation notes; (6) fail to implement a plan to cure any adverse findings by an independent auditor; (7) be required to return federal funds where it is found that the school district is not in compliance with grant requirements; or (8) submit an annual audit after the required submission date.

xiv *See, e.g.,* N.J. STAT. ANN. § 40:11A-14 (parking authorities). The state code may be more expansive and the statutory authority for each bond issuance should be reviewed before assessing whether an accounting may be sought.

xv *See, e.g.,* N.J. STAT. ANN. § 40:11A-14 (parking authorities). The state code may be more expansive and the statutory authority for each bond issuance should be reviewed before assessing whether a bondholder may seek possession of a project.

xvi For instance, in 1935 a federal court in a case involving Asbury Park, New Jersey issued a writ requiring a levy be spread over a 10-year period beginning in 1935, together with the usual marshal fees for collection. The city had applied to the New Jersey Supreme Court when a municipal finance commission had been directed to function for the city, requiring under the state law at the time that all mandamus proceedings were stayed. The Third Circuit found that the lower court's decision with respect to the levy was suspended under the state's Municipal Finance Act and the U.S. Supreme Court chose not to review the decision by denying a writ of certiorari that had been brought by bondholders. A.M. Hillhouse, 281-83 MUNICIPAL BONDS: A CENTURY OF EXPERIENCE (New York: Prentice-Hall 1936) (discussing *City of Asbury Park, N.J. v. Christmas,* 78 F.2d 1003 (3d Cir. 1935)). An aggrieved bondholder likely could pursue a writ of mandamus even absent authorizing statutory law.

xvii *See, e.g.,* N.J. STAT. ANN. § 18A:74-28 (revenue bonds for education authority). This is an example of a special revenue bond. The state code may be more expansive and an attorney should be consulted to examine any specific situation involving a default.

xviii Category SL-1: *See, e.g.,* In August 2015 Governor Christie signed legislation that provided a statutory lien for municipalities that issue bonds under Municipalities Qualified Bond Act ("MQBA"). The statutory lien is on appropriated state aid pledged to the payment of the MQBA bonds. The statutory lien for the MQBA bonds is to assure full payment in case of a filing of Chapter 9 by the municipal issuer. In order to be able to issue MQBA bonds, the municipality must receive permission from the local finance board that deals with financially distressed municipalities. Municipal issuers of MQBA bonds include Atlantic City, Irvington, Newark, Paterson and Trenton. *See* S.B. 2454; 216th Leg. (N.J. 2015); N.J. STAT. ANN. § 40A:3-1 *et seq.* The legislation in part provides that the amount of debt service for MQBA bonds shall be withheld by the state treasurer from the state sharing and aid from the issuer and forwarded to the respective paying agent for the bonds by the state treasurer and the funds are subject to a statutory lien and trust superior to all other liens and interests of any kind in favor of the holders of the respective qualified bonds for the sole purpose of paying debt service on the qualified bonds. N.J. STAT. ANN. 40A:3-3 and 37 as amended. The state code may be more expansive, and an attorney should be consulted to examine any specific situation involving a default.

FF. New Mexico

Municipal Bankruptcy Authority	New Mexico does not specifically authorize its municipal entities to file a petition under Chapter 9 of the Bankruptcy Code. Between 1980 and July 31, 2016, one entity in New Mexico has filed a municipal bankruptcy petition. In the case, *In re Timberon Water and Sanitation District*, Case No. 07-12142, the court found that the municipal entity had no specific authorization under state law to file.
Home Rule and Taxing Power of Municipalities	**Municipalities' Ability to Self-Govern** New Mexico is not a Dillon's Rule state and the New Mexico state constitution includes provisions for establishing municipal home rule.[i] Partially, municipalities are prohibited from imposing income, property and excise taxes unless provided by law. However, municipalities can impose excise taxes of sales, gross receipts or any other types of products or services not expressly prohibited.[ii] **Tax Limitations** The New Mexico state constitution allows local governments to issue debt, but on voter approval, and it limits any tax levy related to the issuance of debt to 12 mills on the dollar on all taxable property. In addition, the New Mexico Constitution includes a tax levy limit for all purposes (with exceptions) of 20 mills on each dollar of assessed valuation, but this limitation does not apply to necessary levies for public debt.[iii]
Debt Default Prevention	**Audit Act** Any political subdivision of the state that receives or expends public money, including counties; county institutions, boards, bureaus or commissions; municipalities; drainage, conservancy, irrigation or other special districts; and school districts must be examined and audited by the state auditor.[iv] **Debt Limitation** No county, city, town or village shall become indebted in an amount in the aggregate exceeding 4 percent of the value of the taxable property within the municipal entity's area, as shown by the last preceding assessment for state and county taxes.[v] **Emergency Loans** In certain pre-default circumstances, the state board of finance may provide emergency loans to municipal corporations or political subdivisions. Emergency is defined as an "unforeseen occurrence or circumstance severely affecting the quality of government services and requiring the immediate expenditure of money."[vi]

FF. New Mexico

Debt Default Prevention *continued*	**Refunding Bonds** In certain situations, a municipal entity may issue refunding bonds to refund and refinance outstanding debt.[vii]
Mechanisms for Resolution after Default	**Receivership** In certain default situations, New Mexico law allows for the appointment of a receiver with respect to revenue bonds.[viii]
Remedies on Default	**Mandamus** In certain situations, bondholders or their trustee may bring a court action to compel the local governing body to perform a ministerial action that it has refused to undertake, such as collecting taxes or fees where the underlying bond authorization requires such a collection.[ix]
Other Bondholder Protections	**Special Revenue Bonds** As provided by Section 922(d) of the Bankruptcy Code, payments to bondholders holding special revenue bonds would not be stayed on the filing of a municipal bankruptcy petition, and payments to holders could continue. Whether an issuance would qualify as a special revenue bond depends on the provisions of the authorizing statute with respect to the bonds at issue.[x] **Statutory Liens** Were a municipal entity to file a petition under Chapter 9 of the Bankruptcy Code, bondholders holding bonds to which statutory liens have attached would continue to receive payment on those bonds. For a statutory lien to apply, the authorizing law of the bond issue must contain such a lien. No statutes covered by the categories were identified.

i N.M. CONST. art. X, § 6.

ii N.M. STAT. ANN. § 3-18-2.

iii N.M. CONST. art. IX, § 12 (tax levy for local government bonds); N.M. STAT. ANN. § 7-37-7 (tax limitations for counties, school districts and municipalities).

iv N.M. STAT. ANN. §§ 12-6-1 to 12-6-14. Relatedly, under Section 10-5-2, the state secretary of finance and administration may suspend an official of any public body if an audit reveals an embezzlement, fiscal management resulting in a violation of law or willful violation of the state's fiscal regulations, or a willful failure to perform a legal duty.

v N.M. CONST. art. IX, § 13. Excepted from this provision are bonds issued to construct or purchase a water or sewer system for a city, town or village.

vi N.M. STAT. ANN. §§ 6-1-1 to 6-1-13.

vii An example of a refunding bond provision in New Mexico law is N.M. STAT. ANN. § 3-31-8 (allowing municipality to refund revenue bonds, but municipality may not (a) pledge gross tax revenues to pay bonds refunding utility bonds, joint utility bonds or gasoline tax revenue bonds or the pledge of gasoline tax revenues to pay bonds that refund utility bonds, joint utility bonds or gross receipts tax revenue bonds or (b) pledge any revenues of any utility or joint utility to pay bonds refunding gross receipts tax revenue bonds or gasoline tax revenue bonds).

viii *See, e.g.,* N.M. STAT. ANN. § 3-23-7 (allowing for appointment of receiver on failure of a municipal utility to comply with specified requirements) and N.M. STAT. ANN. § 73-13-38 (allowing for receiver if municipal irrigation district becomes insolvent). The state code may be more expansive and the statutory authority for each bond issuance should be reviewed before assessing whether a receiver may be appointed.

As background, a 1931 New Mexico law allowed for a receiver to be appointed and authorized the receiver to levy and collect taxes. No default was necessary. A creditor, however, could not bring suit unless the municipal entity was insolvent, allowing for the board of directors of the district to file an application for a receiver. A.M. Hillhouse, 310-11 MUNICIPAL BONDS: A CENTURY OF EXPERIENCE (New York: Prentice-Hall 1936).

Today, the New Mexico State Fair Commission may vest in a trustee or bondholders holding a certain percentage of bonds the right to apply to a court for the appointment of a receiver, who may have and be granted powers and duties as the court may order or decree for the protection of bondholders. N.M. STAT. ANN. § 16-6-17.

ix *See, e.g.,* N.M. STAT. ANN. § 3-31-6 (allowing bondholder to apply to district court for a mandatory order requiring governing body to establish rates or enter into leases and agreements that will provide adequate revenues for a utility, joint-utility or revenue-producing project); N.M. STAT. ANN. § 4-49-21 (allowing bondholders the right of mandamus to compel the levy and collection of taxes for bonds for courthouses, jails, bridges, hospitals and libraries); and N.M. STAT. ANN. § 4-62-6 (mandamus for non-utility revenue-producing projects if governing body fails or refuses to establish rates or enter into applicable leases or agreements to provide adequate revenues). It is possible that an aggrieved bondholder could pursue a writ of mandamus even absent authorizing statutory law.

x *See, e.g.,* N.M. STAT. ANN. § 4-62-1 (permitting counties to pledge revenue bond proceeds); N.M. STAT. ANN. § 3-31-1 (permitting municipalities to pledge revenue bond proceeds); N.M. STAT. ANN. § 6-17-14 (authorizing state educational institutions to pledge bond proceeds); and N.M. STAT. ANN. § 5-7-3 (allowing fire districts to pledge revenues). These are examples of special revenue bonds. The state code may be more expansive, and an attorney should be consulted to examine any specific situation involving a default.

GG. New York

Municipal Bankruptcy Authority	A municipality or its emergency financial control board, the city of New York or the New York state financial control board may file a petition under Chapter 9 of the Bankruptcy Code. "Municipality" is defined as "a county, city, town or village." Municipalities with local ARRA bonds purchased by the New York Municipal Bond Bank Agency and secured by its pledge on tax revenues pursuant to certain provisions of New York law may not file a petition as long as those bonds are outstanding. In addition, certain public authorities in New York are allowed by their authorizing law to file a municipal bankruptcy petition. New York law, additionally, includes provisions specifically disallowing certain municipalities, such as the Metropolitan Transportation Authority, from filing a municipal bankruptcy petition. Three entities between 1980 and July 31, 2016, have filed municipal bankruptcy petitions in New York, all off-track betting facilities, including one off-track betting facility that filed two separate petitions.[i]
Home Rule and Taxing Power of Municipalities	**Municipalities' Ability to Self-Govern** New York is a Dillon's Rule state. Local governments, however, may adopt home-rule charters through the Municipal Home Rule Law. Every local government in the state is authorized to levy local taxes.[ii] **Tax Limitations** The New York Constitution includes limitations on property tax levies depending on the type of municipality, but these limitations do not apply to taxes levied to provide for the interest on and the principal of all indebtedness.[iii]
Debt Default Prevention	**Debt Limitation** The New York Constitution contains certain limitations on local indebtedness based on the average full valuation of the taxable real estate of the municipal entity.[iv] **Fiscal Stress Monitoring System** The New York State Office of the State Comptroller has implemented a Fiscal Stress Monitoring System in which it compiles a list of counties, cities, towns and villages that are under financial stress based on annual financial reports submitted by the local governments to the state comptroller each year.[v]

GG. New York

Debt Default Prevention *continued*	**Municipal Assistance Corporation** The Municipal Assistance Corporation was created by the New York legislature in 1975 to aid New York City in paying its debt. The corporation will cease to exist one year after New York City pays off its liabilities and the debt has been discharged. Specifically, the corporation is an independent corporation authorized to sell bonds to meet New York City's borrowing needs.[vi] **New York Financial Control Board** The New York State Financial Control Board was created in September 1975 to give control powers to the board with responsibilities to review and oversee the financial management of New York City and certain related public authorities.[vii] **Refunding Bonds** In certain situations, a municipal entity may issue refunding bonds to refund and refinance outstanding debt.[viii]
Mechanisms for Resolution after Default	**Appointment of Trustee** In certain situations, if the holders of 25 percent in aggregate principal amount of bonds then outstanding so declare a default, they may appoint a trustee to protect their interests.[ix] **Emergency Financial Control Boards and Fiscal Stability Authorities** The New York legislature may create for any municipality outside of New York City an emergency financial control board or a fiscal stability authority.[x] **Receivership** In certain default situations, New York law allows for the appointment of a receiver with respect to revenue bonds.[xi]
Remedies on Default	**Accounting** In certain default situations, bondholders may bring a proceeding to require the authority in question to account as if it were a trustee of an express trust.[xii] **Foreclosure** In certain default situations, bondholders have foreclosed on projects within the State of New York.[xiii]

GG. New York

Remedies on Default *continued*	**Mandamus** In certain situations, bondholders or their trustee may bring a court action to compel the local governing body to perform a ministerial action that it has refused to undertake, such as collecting taxes or fees where the underlying bond authorization requires such a collection.[xiv]
Other Bondholder Protections	**Special Revenue Bonds** As provided by Section 922(d) of the Bankruptcy Code, payments to bondholders holding special revenue bonds would not be stayed on the filing of a municipal bankruptcy petition, and payments to holders could continue. Whether an issuance would qualify as a special revenue bond depends on the provisions of the authorizing statute with respect to the bonds at issue.[xv] **Statutory Liens** Were a municipal entity to file a petition under Chapter 9 of the Bankruptcy Code, bondholders holding bonds to which statutory liens have attached would continue to receive payment on those bonds. For a statutory lien to apply, the authorizing law of the bond issue must contain such a lien. Category SL-1.[xvi]

---

i N.Y. LOC. FIN. LAW § 85.80. Municipality is defined as "a county, city, town or village." As mentioned, only two entities (for a total of three filings between 1980 and July 31, 2016) in New York have filed a municipal bankruptcy petition. With respect to one of the two entities filing a municipal bankruptcy petition, the New York Off-Track Betting Corporation, the governor of New York had signed an executive order authorizing it to file such a petition. The bankruptcy court found that the governor had the power to issue such an order because the particular entity had been placed under the state's control by the state legislature. *In re New York City Off-Track Betting Corp.*, 427 B.R. 256 (Bankr. S.D.N.Y. 2010).

Under New York law, however, no municipality may file a petition for so long as its local ARRA (American Recovery and Reinvestment Act of 2009) bonds purchased by the State of New York Municipal Bond Bank Agency and secured by its pledge of tax revenues remain outstanding. N.Y. LOC. FIN. § 85.80. As it stands, the New York Municipal Bond Bank Agency provided financing to 16 local governments before the ARRA program expired. In 2009, local ARRA bonds were purchased from the counties of Saratoga, Warren, Wayne and Montgomery and the cities of Brookhaven and Rochester. In 2010, local ARRA bonds were purchased from the counties of Allegany, Madison, Oneida, Sullivan, Broome, Putnam, Cattaraugus, Owego, Tioga and Wyoming. *See Recovery Act Bond Program*, N.Y. ST. HOMES & COMMUNITY RENEWAL, http://www.nyhomes.org/Aboutus/MBBA/RecoveryActBondProgram.htm (last visited Mar. 18, 2015).

In addition, provisions of New York law may permit particular instrumentalities of the state to file a Chapter 9 petition. For instance, New York law permits the Long Island Power Authority to file a Chapter 9 petition. N.Y. PUB. AUTH. LAW § 1020-f(q) (authorizing Long Island Power Authority to file Chapter 9 petition). The state code may be more expansive and the authority governing each state instrumentality should be reviewed before assessing whether the instrumentality has the authority to file a municipal bankruptcy petition. Conversely, New York law includes provisions disallowing some entities, such as the Metropolitan Transportation Authority, from filing a Chapter 9 petition. N.Y. PUB. AUTH. LAW § 1269(9). New York law specifically disallows the Tobacco Settlement Financing Corporation from filing a Chapter 9 petition prior to a date that is one year and one day after it no longer has any bonds outstanding. *See* Part D3, ch. 62, § 10(2) of the Laws of the State of New York (2003).

ii *See generally* the Municipal Home Rule chapter of the Laws of the State of New York. *See also* N.Y. MUN. HOME RULE LAW § 10(1)(ii)(a)(8) (taxing authority). *See also* N.Y. CONST. art. IX, § 2(c)(8) (granting local governments the power to levy and collect local taxes authorized by the legislature).

iii N.Y. CONST. art. VIII, § 10. Counties may levy a tax no greater than 1.5 percent of average full valuation of taxable property, but the legislature may increase the limitation not to exceed 2 percent. Cities and villages may levy a tax no greater than 2 percent of average full valuation of taxable property. New York City and the counties that comprise it may levy a combined tax not to exceed 2.5 percent of average full valuation of taxable property.

iv N.Y. CONST. art. VIII, § 4. The percentage limits include: Nassau County, 10 percent; all other counties, 7 percent; New York City, 10 percent; any other city with a population more than 125,000, 9 percent; cities with less than 125,000 in population, excluding education purposes, 7 percent; towns, 7 percent; villages, 7 percent; and school districts in cities with populations less than 125,000, for education purposes, 5 percent (but the city's voters may vote to increase this amount with the consent of the state).

v For a listing of municipalities, *see* N.Y. STATE OFFICE OF THE COMPTROLLER, MUNICIPALITIES IN STRESS FISCAL YEARS ENDING 2012 (2013), http://www.osc.state.ny.us/localgov/fiscalmonitoring/pdf/stress_list.pdf (last visited Mar. 18, 2015).

vi *See,* N.Y. PUB. AUTH. LAW §§ 3030-3041.

vii N.Y. UNCONSOL. LAWS ch. 22, § 5. According to the New York State Financial Control Board, "[t]he New York State Financial Control Board was created by the State legislature in September, 1975 pursuant to the New York State Financial Emergency Act of The City of New York (the 'Act'). The Act gives the Control Board powers and responsibilities of review and oversight with respect to the financial management of the New York City government and certain related public authorities. Among other things the Act requires the City to prepare and submit a 'rolling' four-year financial plan to the Control Board prior to the beginning of each City fiscal year and, to modify the plan as necessary from time to time to conform with standards set forth in the Act." *Mission Statement*, NEW YORK STATE FINANCIAL CONTROL BOARD, http://www.fcb.state.ny.us/ (last visited Mar. 18, 2015). The board assumes control over the city's finances and management during a "control period," which is declared when the city fails to meet its obligations. During a non-control period, the control board reviews "the four-year financial plan at least quarterly, and must notify the City if a plan or modification to the financial plan does not conform to the Act's standards. In addition, the Control Board must make a determination annually whether a new control period, under which the suspended powers are reimposed, should be declared." *Id.*

A "control period" occurs if the City of New York fails to pay debt service on any of its obligations when due or payable; incurs an operating deficit of more than $100 million in a fiscal year; issues notes in violation of the Act; or violates any provision of the Act, substantially impairing its ability to repay its notes or bonds or its ability to adopt or adhere to a balanced budget. *Mission Statement*, NEW YORK STATE FINANCIAL CONTROL BOARD, http://www.fcb.state.ny.us/ (last visited Mar. 18, 2015). The Act terminates when all bonds issued pursuant to it are refunded, redeemed, discharged or otherwise defeased.

In the case of *Ropico, Inc. v. New York*, 425 F. Supp. 970 (S.D.N.Y. 1976), the court discussed the creation of the New York City Emergency Financial Control Board and permitted a temporary extension of debt payments for the purpose of facilitating the city's recovery.

viii An example of a refunding bond provision in New York law is N.Y. LOC. FIN. LAW tit. 7, which applies to a municipality (any county, city, town or village), school district or district corporation and allows for refunding bonds. Under Title 7 the refunding bonds must be for less than the present value of the principal and interest amount on the bonds to be refunded after deducting costs and expenses.

ix N.Y. PUB. AUTH. LAW § 368 (New York State Thruway Authority; if the holders of 25 percent in aggregate principal amount of bonds then outstanding so declare a default and appoint a trustee to protect their interests); N.Y. PUB. AUTH. LAW § 1390 (Ogdensburg Port Authority; if the holders of 25 percent in aggregate principal amount of bonds then outstanding so declare a default and appoint a trustee to protect their interests); N.Y. PUB. AUTH. LAW § 1983 (Battery Park City Authority; if the holders of 25 percent in aggregate principal amount of bonds then outstanding so declare a default and appoint a trustee to protect their interests); N.Y. ARTS & CULT. AFF. LAW § 59.21 (American Museum of Natural History Planetarium Authority; if the holders of 25 percent in aggregate principal amount of bonds then outstanding so declare a default and appoint a trustee to protect their interests); N.Y. PUB. AUTH. LAW § 1040 (Albany Light, Heat and Power Authority; if the holders of 25 percent in aggregate principal amount of bonds then outstanding so declare a default and appoint a trustee to protect their interests); and N.Y. PUB. AUTH. LAW § 1192 (Buffalo Sewer Authority; if the holders of 25 percent in aggregate principal amount of bonds then outstanding so declare a default and appoint a trustee to protect their interests). The previously listed provisions are a representative example.

x *See* N.Y. LOCAL FIN. LAW §§ 85.00 to 85.90. Under these provisions, the New York legislature may create an emergency financial control board for a municipality. Action may not be taken unless the municipality is due or overdue on a payment of a debt or obligation, demand for payment has been made and 30 days have passed since service was demanded. If the municipality is unable to pay its bills as they mature, its emergency financial control board may petition a court for a temporary stay of claims for 90 days. Should the court grant such a petition, the municipality must also establish a repayment plan for its debts, providing for the eventual satisfaction of all debts and obligations. The stay will be extended for the period of time it takes the municipality to carry out the plan.

In November 1975, an emergency financial control board was put in place for the city of Yonkers. The control board terminated on December 31, 1978. In July 2003, the Buffalo Fiscal Stability Authority was established to oversee the finances of the city. N.Y. PUB. AUTH. LAW §§ 3850-3873. Likewise, in July 2005, the Erie County Fiscal Stability Authority was created. N.Y. PUB. AUTH. LAW §§ 3950-3973. Similarly, the Nassau County Interim Finance Authority was created in June 2000 and has the powers to monitor and oversee the county's finances. N.Y. PUB. AUTH. LAW §§ 3650-3672. In January 2011, the State Oversight Board took control of Nassau County's finances because it had failed to balance its $2.7 billion budget. David M. Halbfinger, *New York State Seizes Finances of Nassau County*, N.Y. TIMES, Jan. 27, 2011, http://www.nytimes.com/2011/01/27/nyregion/27nassau.html?_r=1&scp=1&sq=nassau+county+%242.7+billion&st=nyt (last visited Mar. 19, 2015).

xi *See, e.g.*, N.Y. PUB. AUTH. LAW § 368 (New York State Thruway Authority; if the holders of 25 percent in aggregate principal amount of bonds then outstanding so declare a default and appoint a trustee to protect their interests); N.Y. PUB. AUTH. LAW § 1390 (Ogdensburg Port Authority; if the holders of 25 percent in aggregate principal amount of bonds then outstanding so declare a default and appoint a trustee to protect their interests); N.Y. PUB. AUTH. LAW § 1983 (Battery Park City Authority; if the holders of 25 percent in aggregate principal amount of bonds then outstanding so declare a default and appoint a trustee to protect their interests); and N.Y. PUB. AUTH. LAW § 1192 (Buffalo Sewer Authority; if the holders of 25 percent in aggregate principal amount of bonds then outstanding so declare a default and appoint a trustee to protect their interests). The previously listed provisions are a representative example. The state code may be more expansive and the statutory authority for each bond issuance should be reviewed before assessing whether a receiver may be appointed.

xii *See, e.g.*, N.Y. PUB. AUTH. LAW § 1192 (Buffalo Sewer Authority). The state code may be more expansive than the example cited here and the statutory authority for each individual bond issuance should be reviewed before assessing whether an accounting may be sought.

xiii Moody's Investors Service, *U.S. Municipal Bond Defaults and Recoveries, 1970-2012* at 41 (2012). In November, 2003 the Cicero Land Development Corporation defaulted on approximately $15.3 million in debt. A foreclosure sale was held on the mortgages securing the obligations, generating $2 million. Bondholders recovered approximately 10.3 percent according to Moody's. *See also* N.Y. PUB. HOUS. LAW § 50 (allowing for receivership and/or foreclosure with respect to public housing authority). The state code may be more expansive than the example cited here, and the statutory authority for each individual bond issuance should be reviewed before assessing whether foreclosure is an alternative.

xiv *See, e.g.*, N.Y. RAPID TRANS. LAW § 34 (allowing mandamus for rapid transit bonds issued by cities); N.Y. PUB. AUTH. LAW § 1192 (Buffalo Sewer Authority); N.Y. PUB. AUTH. LAW § 1040 (Albany Light, Heat and Power Authority). It is possible that an aggrieved bondholder could pursue a writ of mandamus even absent authorizing statutory law.

xv *See, e.g.*, N.Y. GEN. MUN. LAW § 407 (granting liens for revenue-producing undertakings); N.Y. PUB. HOUS. LAW § 47 (municipal housing authorities bonds immediately subject to lien on revenue pledge). These are examples of special revenue bonds. The state code may be more expansive, and an attorney should be consulted to examine any specific situation involving a default.

xvi Category SL-1: *See, e.g.*, N.Y. PUB. AUTH. LAW §§ 3011-3012 (bonds issued by Municipal Assistance Corporation immediately subject to lien). In the language of a statute enacted in connection with Municipal Assistance Corporation and dealing with financially distressed city (New York in 1975), there is an intent to permit financing that will be acceptable to the market under the distressed circumstances. Accordingly, there appears to be the intent to create a statutory lien. Some may suggest an additional opinion of counsel or further legislation to clarify and reaffirm the creation of a statutory lien. However, constitutional provisions for general obligation debt of local governments mandate the priority payment and levying of taxes to pay such debt. This should be sufficient clarification if not a clear mandate, which, under §§ 903 and 904 of the Bankruptcy Code and the *Ashton* and *Bekins* decisions of the U.S. Supreme Court, should require a payment even in a Chapter 9. *See* the discussion *supra* at 144. It should be noted that the general obligation debt of local governments has constitutional and statutory mandates for payment. As noted above, New York courts have recognized for local government general obligation debt the good faith pledge of payment includes the requirement of a priority to use tax dollars collected to pay any unpaid general obligation debt. *See* N.Y. CONST. Art. VIII, §2 and *see also Flushing National Bank v. Municipal Assistance Corporation, supra* at 42. Also state court has ruled that local governments are constitutionally required to raise real estate taxes if necessary to pay such general obligation bond debt. *See* N.Y. CONST. Art. VIII, §12. *See also Quirk v. Municipal Assistance Corp. for the City of New* York, 41 N.Y. 644 (1977). The state code may be more expansive and an attorney should be consulted to examine any specific situation involving a default.

HH. North Carolina

Municipal Bankruptcy Authority	On approval of the Local Government Commission, any taxing district, local improvement district, school district, county, city, town or village may file a petition under Chapter 9 of the Bankruptcy Code. Unless an entity is specifically identified above, it is not authorized to file a municipal bankruptcy petition. Only one entity — a sewer authority — has filed a municipal bankruptcy petition in North Carolina between 1980 and July 31, 2016.[i]
Home Rule and Taxing Power of Municipalities	**Municipalities' Ability to Self-Govern** North Carolina is a Dillon's Rule state and does not provide its municipalities with home-rule authority.[ii] The North Carolina legislature, however, has eased the impact of Dillon's Rule on its municipalities through various legislative provisions.[iii] Municipalities may levy property taxes.[iv] **Tax Limitations** Property taxes levied by North Carolina municipalities and counties are limited to $1.50 on the $100 appraised value of property subject to taxation, but this limit does not apply to property taxes levied upon voter approval. This limit also does not apply to debt service.[v]
Debt Default Prevention	**Debt Limitation** No unit of local government shall issue bonds if the local unit's net debt exceeds 8 percent of the assessed value of the property subject to taxation in the issuing unit. The limitation does not apply to refunding bonds; water, gas or electric power bonds; sanitary sewer system, sewage disposal or sewage purification plant bonds; bonds issued for erosion control purposes; and bonds issued for erecting jetties or protection from the ocean, sounds or other bodies of water.[vi] **Local Government Debt Monitoring** Before issuing debt, a municipality must first receive the approval of the state's Local Government Commission. The commission will determine the locality's needs and ability to repay the debt. The commission will approve an issuance only if it determines that the municipality will be able to fully pay back the debt. The commission also sells the debt on the municipality's behalf.[vii] **Refunding Bonds** In certain situations, a municipal entity may issue refunding bonds to refund and refinance outstanding debt.[viii]

HH. North Carolina

Mechanisms for Resolution after Default	**Local Government Fiscal Management** If a unit of local government or municipality remains in default on bonds for 90 days, the Local Government Commission may take action it deems advisable to investigate the municipality's financial affairs, consult with its governing board and negotiate with creditors to assist the entity in refinancing, adjusting or compromising debt. The commission may also assume full control of all financial affairs of a unit of local government or public authority if the local entity defaults on any debt service payment or likely will default or willfully or negligently fails to comply with the Local Government Act.[ix] **Receivership** In certain situations involving special revenue bonds, North Carolina law allows for the appointment of a receiver with respect to revenue bonds.[x]
Remedies on Default	**Mandamus** In certain situations, bondholders or their trustee may bring a court action to compel the local governing body to perform a ministerial action that it has refused to undertake, such as collecting taxes or fees where the underlying bond authorization requires such a collection.[xi] **Foreclosure** In some default situations, bondholders may foreclose on a mortgage or deed of trust related to the project for which bonds were issued.[xii]
Other Bondholder Protections	**Special Revenue Bonds** As provided by Section 922(d) of the Bankruptcy Code, payments to bondholders holding special revenue bonds would not be stayed on the filing of a municipal bankruptcy petition, and payments to holders could continue. Whether an issuance would qualify as a special revenue bond depends on the provisions of the authorizing statute with respect to the bonds at issue.[xiii] **Statutory Liens** Were a municipal entity to file a petition under Chapter 9 of the Bankruptcy Code, bondholders holding bonds to which statutory liens have attached would continue to receive payment on those bonds. For a statutory lien to apply, the authorizing law of the bond issue must contain such a lien. Category SL-3. [xiv]

i N.C. GEN. STAT. § 23-48. The plan of adjustment in *In re South Brunswick Water and Sewer Authority*, No. 04-09053-8-JRL (Bankr. E.D.N.C. 2005), was confirmed in October 2006.

ii *See Five C's, Inc. v. Cnty. of Pasquotank*, 195 N.C. App. 410, 413 (N.C. Ct. App. 2009) ("'Counties are creatures of the General Assembly and have no inherent legislative powers. They are instrumentalities of state government and possess only those powers the General Assembly has conferred upon them.'") (quoting *Craig v. County of Chatham*, 356 N.C. 40, 44 (2002)). *See also Bowers v. City of High Point*, 339 N.C. 413, 417 (N.C. 1994), in which the North Carolina Supreme Court notes that "[i]t is a well-established principle that municipalities, as creatures of the State, can exercise only that power which the legislature has conferred upon them."

iii In 1973 the North Carolina legislature approved a provision stating, "[i]t is the policy of the General Assembly that the counties of this State should have adequate authority to exercise the powers, rights, duties, functions, privileges, and immunities conferred upon them by law. To this end, the provisions of this Chapter and of local acts shall be broadly construed and grants of power shall be construed to include any powers that are reasonably expedient to the exercise of the power." N.C. GEN. STAT. § 153A-4. The legislature has approved an almost identical provision applicable to cities. N.C. Gen. Stat. § 160A-4. The North Carolina Supreme Court in Bowers v. High Point noted with respect to § 160A-4, however, that the statute, "while reflecting our legislature's desire that cities should have the authority to exercise the powers conferred upon them, nevertheless clearly reiterates the principle that municipalities have only that power which the legislature has given them." 339 N.C. 413, 417 (N.C. 1994).

iv N.C. Gen. Stat. § 159-13.

v N.C. Gen. Stat. § 160A-209 (municipalities); N.C. Gen. Stat. § 153A-149 (counties).

vi N.C. Gen. Stat. § 159-55. "Unit of local government" includes cities, towns, incorporated villages, consolidated city-counties, sanitary districts, mosquito control districts, hospital districts, merged school administrative units, metropolitan sewerage districts, metropolitan water and sewer districts, regional public transportation authorities and special airport districts. N.C. GEN. STAT. § 159-44 (definitions).

vii N.C. GEN. STAT. §§ 159-1 to 159-210 (Local Government Finance Act).

viii An example of a refunding bond provision under North Carolina law is N.C. GEN. STAT. §§ 159-43 to 159-79 (Local Government Bond Act). A unit of local government may issue refunding bonds, but the bonds must be issued at any time prior to the final maturity of the debt or obligations to be refunded.

ix N.C. GEN. STAT. §§ 159-1 to 159-210 (Local Government Finance Act). For purposes of N.C. GEN. STAT. § 159-176 (granting commission power to investigate the municipality's financial affairs, consult with its governing board and negotiate with creditors to assist the entity in refinancing, adjusting or compromising debt), "units of local government" include counties, cities, towns and incorporated villages, consolidated city-counties, sanitary districts, mosquito control districts, hospital districts, merged school administrative units, metropolitan sewage districts, metropolitan water districts, metropolitan water and sewer districts, county water and sewer districts, regional public transportation authorities, special airport districts and municipal corporations. N.C. GEN. STAT. §§ 159-44, 102, 176. "Municipality" includes any county, town, incorporated village, sanitary district, metropolitan sewerage district, metropolitan water district, metropolitan water and sewer district, county water and sewer district, hospital authority, hospital district, parking authority, special airport district, other special districts, regional public transportation authority, regional transportation authority, regional natural gas district, regional sports authority, airport authority, certain joint agencies and the North Carolina Turnpike Authority. N.C. GEN. STAT. §§ 159-81, 176. For purposes of N.C. GEN STAT. § 159-181 (providing commission control of financial affairs), "units of local government" means municipal corporations that are not subject to the State Budget Act (Chapter 143C of the General Statutes) and that have the power to levy taxes, including a consolidated city-county as defined in N.C. GEN. STAT. § 160B-2(1) and all boards, agencies, commissions, authorities and institutions thereof that are not municipal corporations. N.C. GEN. STAT. §§ 159-7, 181. "Public authorities" include (A) municipal corporations (other than a unit of local government) that are not subject to the State Budget Act (Chapter 143C of the General Statutes) or (B) local governmental authorities, boards, commissions, councils or agencies that (i) are not municipal corporations, (ii) are not subject to the State

Budget Act and (iii) operate on an area, regional or multi-unit basis, and the budgeting and accounting systems which are not fully a part of the budgeting and accounting systems of a unit of local government. N.C. GEN. STAT. §§ 159-7, 181.

Under N.C. GEN. STAT. § 159-176, if a unit of local government or municipality remains in default for 90 days, the Local Government Commission may take such action as it deems advisable to investigate the unit's or municipality's fiscal affairs, consult with its governing board and negotiate with its creditors to assist the unit or municipality in working out a plan for refinancing, adjusting or compromising the debt. N.C. GEN. STAT. § 159-181 provides that the Local Government Commission also has the authority to assume full control of all financial affairs of a local government unit when the unit or authority defaults on any debt service payment or, in the opinion of the commission, will default on a future debt service payment if the financial policies and practices of the unit or authority are not improved, or when the unit or authority persists, after notice and warning from the commission, in willfully or negligently failing or refusing to comply with the provisions of the Local Government Finance Act.

Further, N.C. GEN. STAT. § 159-73 gives authority to local government units to adjust or refinance debt. If a local government or public authority fails or refuses to levy taxes or allocate other revenues in an amount sufficient to meet all installments of principal and interest falling due on its debt during the budget year, or to adequately maintain its sinking funds, the Local Government Commission must enter an order directing and commanding the local government or public authority to enact a budget ordinance levying the necessary taxes or raising the necessary revenue by whatever means are legally available. N.C. GEN. STAT. § 159-36.

N.C. GEN. STAT. § 159-37 provides that any local government unit maintaining a sinking fund must submit status reports regarding the fund to the Local Government Commission secretary. If the secretary determines that the sinking fund is not being properly maintained, he or she shall order the unit to take action to properly maintain the fund.

The Local Government Commission was first established by North Carolina in 1931 to deal with the debt difficulties and defaults by Asheville and other municipalities. The Local Government Act that was created in 1931 had two approaches to receivership. The first provided that on default a temporary receiver could be appointed, but if the default lasted longer than one year, on petition of 51 percent of bondholders, the director of local government could be directed by a court to appoint an administrator of finance. A.M. Hillhouse, 339 MUNICIPAL BONDS: A CENTURY OF EXPERIENCE (New York: Prentice-Hall 1936).

Examples of cities taken over by the Local Government Commission include Princeville during the beginning of the 1990s. *See* Omer Kimhi, *Reviving Cities: The Legal Remedies to Municipal Insolvency* (N.Y.U. School of Law 2007) at 294.

x *See, e.g.*, N.C. GEN. STAT. § 63A-14 (North Carolina Global TransPark Authority) and N.C. GEN. STAT. § 159D-12 (North Carolina Capital Facilities Financing Act). The state code may be more expansive and the statutory authority for each bond issuance should be reviewed before assessing whether such a remedy is applicable.

xi *See, e.g.*, N.C. GEN. STAT. § 63A-14 (North Carolina Global TransPark Authority); N.C. GEN. STAT. § 131A-15 (Health Care Facilities Finance Act); N.C. GEN. STAT. § 116D-27 (Higher Education Bonds); N.C. GEN. STAT. § 162A-12 (Water and Sewer Systems); N.C. GEN. STAT. § 160A-480.9 (Cities and Towns Facility Authority Act); N.C. GEN. STAT. § 159I-18 (Solid Waste Management Loan Program and Local Government Special Obligation Bond Act); N.C. GEN. STAT. § 159D-49 (North Carolina Capital Facilities Financing Act) and N.C. GEN. STAT. § 159B-19 (Joint Municipal Electric Power and Energy Act). It is possible that an aggrieved bondholder could pursue a writ of mandamus even absent authorizing statutory law.

xii *See, e.g.*, N.C. GEN. STAT. § 63A-14 (North Carolina Global TransPark Authority) and N.C. GEN. STAT. § 159D-12 (North Carolina Capital Facilities Financing Act). The state code may be more expansive and the statutory authority for each bond issuance should be reviewed before assessing whether bondholders could bring a foreclosure action.

xiii See, e.g., N.C. GEN. STAT. § 159-80 *et seq.* (North Carolina Revenue Bond Act). Note that this is an example of a special revenue bond. The state code may be more expansive, and an attorney should be consulted to examine any specific situation involving a default.

xiv Category SL-3: *See, e.g.* N.C. GEN. STAT. § 159.91 and 92, providing for revenue bonds, a valid and binding pledge on revenues, securities and moneys so pledged and received by the state or municipality. The lien of the pledge is immediate, without any further act or physical delivery and is thereby perfected, valid and binding against all parties with or without notice. Further clarification or reaffirmation that this is intended to be a statutory lien and not an exemption from Uniform Commercial Code filing for special revenues would be helpful. The state code may be more expansive, and an attorney should be consulted to examine any specific situation involving a default.

II. North Dakota

Municipal Bankruptcy Authority	North Dakota does not specifically authorize its municipal entities to file a petition under Chapter 9 of the Bankruptcy Code. Between 1980 and July 31, 2016, no municipal entity in North Dakota has filed such a petition.
Home Rule and Taxing Power of Municipalities	**Municipalities' Ability to Self-Govern** North Dakota is a Dillon's Rule state. The state constitution provides that the legislative assembly shall provide the laws for establishing and governing legislative subdivisions and may provide for the establishment of home rule in counties and cities. In addition, counties, cities, townships, villages and districts may assess a property tax.[i] **Tax Limitations** North Dakota law includes taxing limitations for counties and cities. Local governments, however, must levy an annual tax sufficient to pay interest and principal on bonds due in that year.[ii]
Debt Default Prevention	**Debt Limitation** No county, township, city, town, school district or other political subdivision may issue debt exceeding 5 percent of the assessed value of its taxable property. By two-thirds vote, an incorporated city may increase its debt limit by 3 percent and a school district, by majority vote, may increase its debt limit by 5 percent. For the purposes of constructing or purchasing a waterworks or sewer system, a city may become indebted in an amount not exceeding 4 percent of the assessed value of the property in the city without regard to its existing indebtedness.[iii] **Refunding Bonds** In certain situations, a municipal entity may issue refunding bonds to refund and refinance outstanding debt.[iv] **Receivership** In certain situations involving revenue bonds, North Dakota law allows for the appointment of a receiver.[v]
Remedies on Default	**Accounting** In certain default situations, bondholders may bring a proceeding to require the authority in question to account as if it were a trustee of an express trust.[vi] **Mandamus** In certain situations, bondholders or their trustee may bring a court action to compel the local governing body to perform a ministerial action that it has refused to undertake, such as collecting taxes or fees where the underlying bond authorization requires such a collection.[vii]

II. North Dakota

Other Bondholder Protections	**Special Revenue Bonds** As provided by Section 922(d) of the Bankruptcy Code, payments to bondholders holding special revenue bonds would not be stayed on the filing of a municipal bankruptcy petition, and payments to holders could continue. Whether an issuance would qualify as a special revenue bond depends on the provisions of the authorizing statute with respect to the bonds at issue.[viii] **Statutory Liens** Were a municipal entity to file a petition under Chapter 9 of the Bankruptcy Code, bondholders holding bonds to which statutory liens have attached would continue to receive payment on those bonds. For a statutory lien to apply, the authorizing law of the bond issue must contain such a lien. Category SL-3.[ix]

i N.D. CONST. art. VII, §§ 2, 6 (giving state legislature authority to establish local laws); N.D. CONST. art. X, § 4 (authorizing property tax assessed in counties, cities, townships, villages or districts).

ii N.D. CENT. CODE § 21-03-15 (bond payments for local governments); N.D. CENT. CODE § 57-15-05 (bond payments for counties); N.D. CENT. CODE § 57-15-07 (bond payments of cities). Counties in North Dakota may not levy any taxes for general or special purposes exceeding the amount produced by a levy of 23 mills on the dollar of the taxable property in the county. N.D. CENT. CODE § 57-15-06 (county limitations). *But see* N.D. CENT. CODE §§ 57-15-06.3 to 10 (additional county tax levy provisions). These provisions, however, do not apply to any statute that expressly states that it is not subject to mill levy limitations. N.D. CENT. CODE § 57-15-06.7. Cities in North Dakota may levy any tax for general city purposes not to exceed 38 mills on the dollar of the taxable property in the city, but these amounts may be increased depending on the population of the city up to 40 mills on the dollar. In addition, the city's voters may vote to increase the maximum rate by not more than 10 mills. N.D. CENT. CODE § 57-15-08. *But see* N.D. CENT. CODE § 57-15-10 (additional city tax levy provisions). Additional tax levy limitations exist in North Dakota law depending on they type of municipality. *See* N.D. CENT. CODE § 57-15-01 *et seq.* (tax levies and limitations).

iii N.D. CONST. art. X, § 15.

iv An example of a refunding bond provision in North Dakota law is N.D. CENT. CODE § 21-03-06. This provision applies to any county, city, township, public school district, park district, recreation service district or rural fire protection district empowered to borrow money and issue written obligations to repay the same out of public funds or revenues. Municipalities may issue refunding bonds on bonds not yet due or to become due or subject to redemption and prepayment within six months, if the municipality determines the refunding bonds to be in its best interest. *See also* N.D. CENT. CODE § 40-33.2-05 (Municipal Power Authority); N.D. CENT. CODE § 40-36-03 (Revenue Bond Refinancing Act, applicable to any municipality).

v *See, e.g.*, N.D. CENT. CODE § 40-33.1-14 (municipal steam heating authorities); N.D. CENT. CODE § 40-33.2-05 (municipal power agency); N.D. CENT. CODE § 40-35-15 (revenue bondholders have right to receiver if default lasts longer than 30 days); N.D. CENT. CODE § 40-61-16 (municipal parking authorities); N.D. CENT. CODE § 40-34-09 (sewage and garbage disposal bonds). The state code may be more expansive and the statutory authority for each bond issuance should be reviewed before assessing whether a receiver may be appointed.

vi *See, e.g.*, N.D. CENT. CODE § 40-61-16 (municipal parking authorities). The state code may be more expansive and the statutory authority for each bond issuance should be reviewed before assessing whether to seek an accounting.

vii *See, e.g.*, N.D. CENT. CODE § 40-33.1-14 (municipal steam heating authorities); N.D. CENT. CODE § 40-33.2-05 (municipal power agency); N.D. CENT. CODE § 40-35-16 (revenue bondholders); and N.D. CENT. CODE § 40-61-16 (municipal parking authorities). It is possible that an aggrieved bondholder could pursue a writ of mandamus even absent authorizing statutory law.

viii *See, e.g.*, N.D. CENT. CODE § 40-33.3 (municipal pipeline authorities). Note that this is an example of a special revenue bond. The state code may be more expansive, and an attorney should be consulted to examine any specific situation involving a default.

ix Category SL-3: *See, e.g.*, N.D. CENT. CODE § 40:11A-14(3) (moneys pledged for bond payment are immediately subject to lien in relation to parking authority) and N.D. CENT. CODE § 40-33.1 (moneys pledged for bond payment are immediately subject to a lien in relation to municipal steam heating authorities). While the languages of these statutes may appear to create a statutory lien, further clarification and additional language would help reaffirm that a statutory lien was the legislature's intent. Again, clarification or reaffirmation would be helpful to determine if language is limited to special revenues and the pledge to pay special revenues and no further action is required to perfect that pledge, or if language is intended to create a statutory lien so the pledged revenues are not subject to "necessary operating costs" under § 928(b) similar to the *Sierra Kings Health Care District* ruling, *supra* at 144-145. Note that this is an example of a statutory lien. The state code may be more expansive, and an attorney should be consulted to examine any specific situation involving a default.

JJ. Ohio

Municipal Bankruptcy Authority	On approval of the tax commissioner, a taxing authority of a county, municipal corporation, school district, regional water and sewer district, joint township hospital district, joint ambulance district, joint recreation district, detention facility district, township police district, township, joint fire district, county library district, joint solid waste management district, joint emergency medical services district, fire and ambulance district, fire district, joint police district, lake facilities authority, regional transportation improvement project or other political subdivision or taxing district or other local public body or agency authorized to issue certain securities may file a petition under Chapter 9 of the Bankruptcy Code. Unless an entity is specifically identified above, it is not authorized to file a municipal bankruptcy petition. Between 1980 and July 31, 2016, no entity in Ohio has filed a municipal bankruptcy petition.[i]
Home Rule and Taxing Power of Municipalities	**Municipalities' Ability to Self-Govern** Ohio is not a Dillon's Rule state. The Ohio Constitution provides that municipalities in the state may exercise all powers of local self-government and adopt and enforce laws pertaining to police, sanitary and similar regulations that do not conflict with the state's general laws. The Ohio Constitution, however, allows for the state legislature to pass laws limiting the powers of municipalities to levy taxes.[ii] **Tax Limitations** The Ohio Constitution prohibits property taxes in excess of 1 percent of a property's true value in money for all state and local purposes. Laws, however, may authorize additional taxes outside of this limitation, if either approved by a majority of voters in the taxing district voting or when provided by a municipal corporation's charter. The Ohio Code contains a so-called "ten-mill limitation" on taxes by subdivisions and taxing units.[iii]
Debt Default Prevention	**Debt Limitation** A municipal corporation may not incur debt exceeding 10.5 percent of its tax valuation or incur the debt without a vote if the debt will exceed 5.5 percent of the municipal corporation's tax valuation. A school district may not incur debt exceeding one-tenth of 1 percent of its tax valuation, but in certain instances a school district's debt may not exceed 9 percent of its tax valuation. A county with a tax valuation exceeding $100 million may not incur debt exceeding 3 percent of its tax valuation; a county with a valuation exceeding $100 million but not exceeding $300 million may not incur debt exceeding $3 million plus 1.5 percent of the tax valuation in excess of $100 million; and for a county with a tax valuation exceeding $300 million, debt may not exceed $6 million plus 2.5 percent of the tax valuation in excess of $300 million.

JJ. Ohio

Debt Default Prevention *continued*	With respect to townships, unless a township has adopted a limited home-rule government, it shall not incur net indebtedness exceeding 5 percent of its tax valuation. With respect to townships adopting a limited home rule government, the township may not issue debt exceeding 10.5 percent of its tax valuation or incur without a vote indebtedness exceeding 5.5 percent of the tax valuation.[iv] **Fiscal Caution** The state auditor may develop guidelines to identify municipal practices and budgetary conditions that could result in a future declaration of a fiscal watch or fiscal warning, as discussed below. Based on the conditions analyzed by the state auditor, it can place the municipality on a fiscal caution. The municipality, if placed on a fiscal caution, must devise a plan to alter its fiscal practices and budgetary conditions that triggered the caution.[v] **Fiscal Watch** A municipality may be placed on fiscal watch, requiring that the state auditor pay closer attention to the municipality's finances. The state auditor may provide technical and support services to the municipality as the auditor deems appropriate. A fiscal watch review may be initiated by a written request to the state auditor by the municipality's mayor, presiding officer, county board or executive, by a township board, or by the state auditor. The following conditions constitute grounds for a fiscal watch: unpaid accounts from the general fund at the end of the preceding fiscal year remaining unpaid for more than 30 days or to which a penalty has been added, less the year-end balance in the general fund, exceed one-twelfth of the general fund budget for that year; all unpaid accounts at the end of the preceding fiscal year remaining unpaid for more than 30 days or to which a penalty has been added, less the year-end balance in all accounts, exceed one-twelfth of the general fund budget for that year; total deficit amounts of all deficit funds at the end of the preceding year, less the total balance in the general fund and any special fund transferred to meet the deficit, exceed one-twelfth of the total general fund for that year and the receipts to those deficit funds during that year other than transfers to the general fund; at the preceding fiscal year's end, moneys and marketable investments in or held for the unsegregated treasury, minus outstanding checks and warrants, were less than the aggregate of the positive balances of the general fund and those special funds, the purposes of which the unsegregated treasury is held to meet, and deficiency exceeded one-twelfth of the total amount received into the unsegregated treasury during the preceding fiscal year; and the auditor of state certifies that the general fund deficit at the end of the current fiscal year will exceed one-twelfth of the general fund revenue from the preceding fiscal year.[vi]

JJ. Ohio

Debt Default Prevention *continued*	**Refunding Bonds** In certain situations, a municipal entity may issue refunding bonds to refund and refinance outstanding debt.[vii]
Mechanisms for Resolution after Default	**Fiscal Emergencies and Financial Planning and Supervision Commission** The existence of a fiscal emergency condition constitutes a fiscal emergency and is determined by the state auditor. A fiscal emergency review may be initiated by a written request to the state auditor by the governor; the county's budget commission; municipality's mayor, presiding officer, county board or executive; township board; or the state auditor. On the occurrence of such a local fiscal emergency, a financial planning and supervision commission is created to intervene in the municipality's affairs. Financial conditions constituting a fiscal emergency include: payment default lasting more than 30 days; a failure for lack of cash to make payroll to municipal employees lasting for more than 30 days, or beyond a period of extension, or beyond 90 days from the original payment date; an increase by the county budget commission in the minimum levy of the municipality resulting in a reduction of minimum levies for one or more other subdivisions or taxing districts; unpaid accounts from the general fund at the end of the preceding fiscal year remaining unpaid for more than 30 days or to which a penalty has been added, less the year-end balance in the general fund, exceed one-sixth of the general fund budget for that year; all unpaid accounts at the end of the preceding fiscal year remaining unpaid for more than 30 days or to which a penalty has been added, less the year-end balance in all accounts, exceed one-sixth of the general fund budget for that year; total deficit amounts of all deficit funds at the end of the preceding year, less the total balance in the general fund and any special fund transferred to meet the deficit, exceed one-sixth of the total general fund budget for that year and the receipts to those deficit funds during that year other than transfers to the general fund; at the preceding fiscal year's end, moneys and marketable investments in or held for the unsegregated treasury, minus outstanding checks and warrants, were less than the aggregate of the positive balances of the general fund and those special funds, the purposes of which the unsegregated treasury is held to meet, and deficiency exceed one-sixth of the total amount received into the unsegregated treasury during the preceding fiscal year.

JJ. Ohio

Mechanisms for Resolution after Default *continued*	The municipality must create a financial rehabilitation plan for the commission's approval. If the municipality fails to submit an acceptable plan, expenditures by the municipality may not exceed 85 percent of expenditures from the general fund for the same month in the preceding year, unless the commission provides otherwise. If the plan is approved, the municipality may not make any expenditure contrary to the plan.[viii] **Receivership** In certain situations involving revenue bonds, Ohio law allows for the appointment of a receiver.[ix]
Remedies on Default	**Accounting** In certain situations of default, bondholders may bring a proceeding to require the authority in question to account as if it were a trustee of an express trust.[x] **Foreclosure** In certain default situations, bondholders may take possession of a project on which a default has occurred.[xi] **General Remedy Provisions** If a payment default lasts longer than 30 days, the subdivision fails or refuses to comply with Ohio law or it defaults on any contract with bondholders, the holders of not less than 25 percent in principal amount of securities then outstanding may appoint a trustee to bring action for payment, bring a motion for writ of mandamus, bring action on the securities or for accounting as if it were a trustee of a trust, request injunctive relief or declare bonds not payable from property tax immediately due and payable.[xii] **Mandamus** In certain situations, bondholders or their trustee likely can bring a court action to compel the local governing body to perform a ministerial action that it has refused to undertake, such as collecting taxes or fees where the underlying bond authorization requires such a collection.[xiii]
Other Bondholder Protections	**Special Revenue Bonds** As provided by Section 922(d) of the Bankruptcy Code, payments to bondholders holding special revenue bonds would not be stayed on the filing of a municipal bankruptcy petition, and payments to holders could continue. Whether an issuance would qualify as a special revenue bond depends on the provisions of the authorizing statute with respect to the bonds at issue.[xiv]

JJ. Ohio

Other Bondholder Protections *continued*	**Statutory Liens** Were a municipal entity to file a municipal bankruptcy petition, bondholders holding bonds to which statutory liens have attached would continue to receive payment on those bonds. The authorizing law of the bond issue must contain such a lien. No statutes covered by the categories were identified.

---

i OHIO REV. CODE ANN. § 133.36; *see also* OHIO REV. CODE ANN. § 133.01 (identification of "subdivisions" allowed to file Chapter 9 petition). An ambiguity by misreference exists in the definitions of the Ohio Code, which could call into question whether political subdivisions, taxing districts or other local public bodies or agencies authorized to issue certain securities are permitted to file a municipal bankruptcy petition.

ii *See* OHIO CONST. art. XVIII, § 3 (powers of municipalities), § 7 (home rule provisions) § 13 (allowance of taxing limit legislature).

iii OHIO CONST. art. XII, § 2. In addition, the Ohio Code includes a "ten-mill limitation" that is applicable to all subdivisions and all taxing units, except for taxes specifically authorized to be levied in excess thereof. OHIO REV. CODE ANN. § 5705.02. Taxes levied to pay and to retire bonds are specifically subject to this limitation. OHIO REV. CODE ANN. § 5705.03.

iv OHIO REV. CODE ANN. § 133.05 (net indebtedness of municipal corporations). As a part of the net indebtedness calculation, certain bond issuances are excluded as outlined by § 133.05, including self-supporting bonds and bonds issued for water or sanitary systems in certain instances. OHIO REV. CODE ANN. § 133.06 (net indebtedness of school districts). With respect to school districts, certain exclusions apply. Further, as provided in § 133.061, in certain situations with respect to facilities and site acquisition, the district may issue debt not to exceed 125 percent of its 9 percent debt limit (counties). With respect to counties, certain exceptions to the net indebtedness provisions apply as outlined in § 133.07. OHIO REV. CODE ANN. § 133.05 (townships; but certain bonds may not count against the debt limit).

v OHIO REV. CODE ANN. § 118.025 (setting guidelines for declaration of fiscal caution). As an example, on October 2, 2014, the village of Smithfield was placed in fiscal caution, and Rush Township was placed in fiscal caution on July 22, 2014. *See* https://ohioauditor.gov/news/category/Fiscal%20Caution,%20Watch,%20and%20Emergency (last visited June 22, 2015).

vi OHIO REV. CODE ANN. §§ 118.01–.023 (fiscal watch provisions of the Local Fiscal Emergencies Act). A list of municipalities and school districts that have been on the fiscal watch list includes city of Lorain (10/17/02), city of Norwood (10/07/04), city of Portsmouth (4/19/13), Coventry Local School District (05/15/97), Niles City School District (03/10/03), Mansfield City School District (12/08/06) and East Knox Local School District (09/30/2014).

vii An example of a refunding bond provision under Ohio law is OHIO REV. CODE ANN. § 133.34. Under this provision, on determination of the taxing authority that issuing refunding bonds is in the best interest of the subdivision, the subdivision may issue general obligation securities to fund or refund any outstanding revenue or mortgage revenue, sales-tax supported or other special obligation securities previously issued by the subdivision for permanent improvements. The subdivision may also issue revenue or mortgage revenue bonds to fund or refund general obligation bonds.

A subdivision includes any county, municipal corporation, school district, regional water and sewer district, joint township hospital district, joint ambulance district, joint recreation district, detention facility, township police district, township, joint fire district, county library district or regional library district, joint solid waste management district, joint emergency medical services district, fire and ambulance district, fire district or any other political subdivision or taxing district. OHIO REV. CODE ANN. § 133.01(MM).

viii OHIO REV. CODE ANN. §§ 118.01–.99 (Local Fiscal Emergencies Act). The intent of the act is to enact procedures, provide powers and impose restrictions to assure fiscal integrity of municipal corporations, counties and townships. OHIO REV. CODE ANN. § 118.02.

Local financial planning and supervision commissions have been involved with the Local and East Liverpool School Districts. With regard to the Trimble Local School District, a former teacher brought a reinstatement action after the commission had suspended her contract. The court ordered the school district to reinstate the teacher and pay her back pay. *See State ex rel. Couch v. Trimble Local Sch. Dist. Bd. of Educ.*, 120 Ohio St. 3d 75, 82 (Ohio 2008). There have been at least three unsuccessful constitutional challenges to the Local Fiscal Emergencies Act, including one involving the East Liverpool School District (*E. Liverpool Educ. Assoc. v. E. Liverpool City Sch. Dist. Bd. of Educ.*, 177 Ohio App. 3d 87 (Ohio 2008)); the Barnesville School District (*Barnesville Educ. Assoc. OEA/NEA v. Barnesville Exempted Vill. Sch. Dist. Bd. of Educ.*, 2007 WL 745095 (Ohio Mar. 6, 2007)); and the Shelby City School District (*Shelby Ass'n of Support Staff v. Shelby City Sch. Dist. Bd. of Educ.*, 2008 WL 787042 (Ohio Ct. App. Mar. 21, 2008)).

Further, in 1979 the Cleveland School District was placed under state supervision. Recent examples of municipalities and school districts that have been placed in a fiscal emergency include the village of Trimble (5/13/2014), St. Clair Township (5/15/2014), city of Niles (10/7/2014), East Knox Local School District (2/5/2015), village of Maple Heights (2/13/2015), village of Smithfield (2/19/2015) and village of Green Camp (6/16/15).

It should also be noted that on December 15, 1978, Cleveland became the first major city to default on its debt since the Depression. *See* W. Dennis Keating *et al.*, 145 CLEVELAND A METROPOLITAN READER (1995).

ix *See, e.g.*, OHIO REV. CODE ANN. § 3735.49 (housing authorities). The state code may be more expansive and the statutory authority for each bond issuance should be reviewed before assessing whether a receiver may be appointed.

x *See, e.g.*, OHIO REV. CODE ANN. § 3735.49 (housing authorities). The state code may be more expansive and the statutory authority for each individual bond issuance should be reviewed before assessing whether an accounting is an available option.

xi *See, e.g.*, OHIO REV. CODE ANN. § 3735.49 (housing authorities). The state code may be more expansive and the statutory authority for each bond issuance should be reviewed before assessing whether a foreclosure action may be brought.

xii *See, e.g.*, OHIO REV. CODE ANN. § 133.25(B)(4) (levying property tax to debt charges on securities payable from property taxes). Pursuant to § 133.25(C)(1) the holders of not less than 10 percent in principal amount of a particular security outstanding may bring an action for mandamus or other injunction, writ, process or decree to enforce all contractual or other rights of bondholders, including to require the subdivision to assess, levy, charge, collect and apply the pledged receipts to carry out the duties of any agreement.

xiii *See, e.g.*, OHIO REV. CODE ANN. § 133.25(B)(4) and § 3735.49 (housing authorities). It is possible that an aggrieved bondholder could pursue a writ of mandamus even absent authorizing statutory law.

xiv *See, e.g.*, OHIO REV. CODE ANN. § 6115.52 (revenue bonds for sanitary districts); OHIO REV. CODE ANN. § 3349.05 (university facilities bonds); OHIO REV. CODE ANN. § 307.695 (convention center or arena bonds financed through pledge of additional lodging tax); OHIO REV. CODE ANN. § 308.08 (revenue bonds for airport authorities secured by pledge and lien on revenues of regional airport authority, including from rentals, fees, charges or other revenues from facility). These are examples of special revenue bonds. The state code may be more expansive and an attorney should be consulted to examine any specific situation involving a default.

KK. Oklahoma

Municipal Bankruptcy Authority	Any debtor municipal corporation, political subdivision, county, municipality or local improvement district organized or created for the purpose of grading, paving or otherwise improving public streets, alleys or roads; paving, drainage or reclamation district; or agency or instrumentality may file a petition under Chapter 9 of the Bankruptcy Code. Unless an entity is specifically identified above, it is not authorized to file a municipal bankruptcy petition. In Oklahoma, 14 municipal bankruptcy petitions have been filed between 1980 and July 31, 2016.[i]
Home Rule and Taxing Power of Municipalities	**Municipalities' Ability to Self-Govern** Oklahoma is a Dillon's Rule state, but any county with a population of less than 550,000, containing a metropolitan area with a population of 250,000 or more, may adopt or amend a county home rule charter for county government specifying those powers that are appropriate for said government and are not inconsistent with the laws of the state.[ii] In addition, the Oklahoma Constitution includes provisions granting the legislature authority to establish provisions allowing local governments the power to tax.[iii] **Tax Limitations** Total taxes for all purposes may not exceed 15 mills on the dollar.[iv]
Debt Default Prevention	**Debt Limitation** Unless a county, city, town, township, school district or other political corporation or subdivision of the state receives the assent of three-fifths of its voters, its debt may not exceed, in any year, the income and revenue of that year. On a vote, no county, city, township, school district or other political corporation or subdivision may become indebted in an aggregate amount exceeding 5 percent of its real property valuation. A school district, however, may become indebted in an aggregate amount exceeding 5 percent but not more than 10 percent of the assessed property value therein, for the purpose of improving or acquiring school sites, constructing, repairing, remodeling or equipping buildings or acquiring furniture, fixtures or equipment. A city or town, further, may issue debt exceeding 5 percent but not more than 10 percent of assessed property values on a showing of absolute need.[v] **Refunding Bonds** In certain situations, a municipal entity may issue refunding bonds to refund and refinance outstanding debt.[vi]

KK. Oklahoma

Mechanisms for Resolution after Default	**Receivership** In certain situations involving revenue bonds, Oklahoma law allows for the appointment of a receiver.[vii] **Settlement of Debt** In certain situations, a municipality may compromise and settle the amount due under certain bonds and warrants charged against property. In these situations, holders of matured and unpaid street improvement bonds or district sanitary sewer, storm sewer or sidewalk warrants issued by any municipal corporation, whether such bond or warrant be unpaid in part or in whole, together may negotiate to compromise and settle the amount due on the bonds.[viii]
Remedies on Default	**Accounting** In certain situations of default, bondholders may bring a proceeding in any court of competent jurisdiction to require the authority in question to account as if it were a trustee of an express trust.[ix] **Mandamus** In certain situations, bondholders or their trustee may bring a court action to compel the local governing body to perform a ministerial action that it has refused to undertake, such as collecting taxes or fees where the underlying bond authorization requires such a collection.[x]
Other Bondholder Protections	**Special Revenue Bonds** As provided by Section 922(d) of the Bankruptcy Code, payments to bondholders holding special revenue bonds would not be stayed on the filing of a municipal bankruptcy petition, and payments to holders could continue. Whether an issuance would qualify as a special revenue bond depends on the provisions of the authorizing statute with respect to the bonds at issue.[xi] **Statutory Liens** Were a municipal entity to file a petition under Chapter 9 of the Bankruptcy Code, bondholders holding bonds to which statutory liens have attached would continue to receive payment on those bonds. For a statutory lien to apply, the authorizing law of the bond issue must contain such a lien. No statutes covered by the categories were identified.

i OKLA. STAT. tit. 62, §§ 281, 282, 283, 286. The following entities may file: (i) debtor municipal corporations or political subdivisions (a debtor municipal corporation is a municipal corporation or other political subdivision of the state which is insolvent or unable to meet its debts as they mature); (ii) any county; municipality; local improvement district organized or created for the purpose of grading, paving or otherwise improving public streets, alleys or roads or other similar district; also any paving district of the state; and any drainage or reclamation district; or (iii) any other agency or instrumentality formed or existing under state law which is an agency or instrumentality having the power to incur indebtedness, either through action of its governing body or through the action of the governing body of any county, municipality, district, agency or instrumentality in which such county, municipality, district, agency or instrumentality lies.

Of the 13 municipal bankruptcies in Oklahoma, two were by municipal utilities, five were by towns or cities, two were by a hospital district, and four were made by special municipal districts. Of these filings, one was by the town of Moffett in 2007. The town filed its petition two months after the Oklahoma Attorney General and Department of Public Safety declared the town, which has a population of 178, an illegal speed trap and stripped the town of its authority to issue speeding tickets. *See Moffett Files Bankruptcy*, SEQUOYAH COUNTY TIMES, Feb. 3, 2007, http://www.thenewspaper.com/news/15/1584.asp (last visited Sept. 23, 2013). The most recent filing was by the Craig County Hospital Authority, which filed a Chapter 9 petition on March 2, 2015.

ii 19 OKLA. STAT. § 8.2.

iii *See* OKLA. CONST. art. 10, § 20 (legislature authorized to grant counties, cities, towns and other municipal corporations the power to assess and collect taxes).

iv *See* OKLA. CONST. art. 10, § 9.

v OKLA. CONST. art. 10, § 26.

vi An example of a refunding bond provision under Oklahoma law is OKLA. STAT. tit. 62, § 357 (refunding bonds issued by county, city, town, township, board of education or school district may not bear a greater interest rate than the indebtedness funded or refunded).

vii *See, e.g.*, OKLA. STAT. tit. 62, § 659 (appointment of receiver for default on bond issued under Local Industrial Development Act); OKLA. STAT. tit. 11, § 24-108 (Municipal Power Authority); OKLA. STAT. tit. 74, § 2260 (Oklahoma Tourism and Recreation Commission); and OKLA. STAT. tit. 70, § 821.4 (independent school districts). The state code may be more expansive and the statutory authority for each bond issuance should be reviewed before assessing whether a receiver may be appointed.

viii OKLA. STAT. tit. 62, § 306 (compromise and settlement of amount due under certain bonds and warrants and charged against property). When a city council approves the compromise, the county's district court must then approve the settlement and discharge the property in question.

ix *See, e.g.*, OKLA. STAT. tit. 82, § 870 (Grand River Dam Authority) and OKLA. STAT. tit. 74, § 2260 (Oklahoma Tourism and Recreation Commission). The state code may be more expansive and the statutory authority for each individual bond issuance should be reviewed before assessing whether an accounting is an available option.

x *See, e.g.*, OKLA. STAT. tit. 82, § 870 (Grand River Dam Authority); OKLA. STAT. tit. 74, § 5226 (Oklahoma Space Development Authority); OKLA. STAT. tit. 74, § 1226.9 (Native American Cultural and Educational Authority); OKLA. STAT. tit. 74, § 2260 (Oklahoma Tourism and Recreation Commission); OKLA. STAT. tit. 70, § 821.4 (independent school districts); OKLA. STAT. tit. 19, § 1257 (road improvement bonds); OKLA. STAT. tit. 70, § 23-115 (Oklahoma Educational Television Authority); OKLA. STAT. tit. 69, § 1713 (Oklahoma Turnpike Authority); and OKLA. STAT. tit. 11, § 36-303 (street improvement bonds). It is possible that an aggrieved bondholder could pursue a writ of mandamus even absent authorizing statutory law.

xi *See, e.g.*, OKLA. STAT. tit. 11, § 24-108 (Municipal Power Authority may pledge revenues and grant liens); OKLA. STAT. tit. 11, § 22-153 (municipality may create lien on utility); OKLA. STAT. tit. 11, § 22-154 (municipality may dedicate sales tax or other taxes for payment of utility revenue bonds); and OKLA. STAT. tit. 82, § 1284 (regional water districts may pledge income or revenues from district from any source). These are examples of special revenue bonds. The state code may be more expansive, and an attorney should be consulted to examine any specific situation involving a default.

LL. Oregon

Municipal Bankruptcy Authority	In Oregon, only an irrigation or drainage district may file a petition under Chapter 9 of the Bankruptcy Code. Unless an entity is specifically identified above, it is not authorized to file a municipal bankruptcy petition. Between 1980 and July 31, 2016, no entity in Oregon has filed a municipal bankruptcy petition.[i]
Home Rule and Taxing Power of Municipalities	**Municipalities' Ability to Self-Govern** Oregon is not a Dillon's Rule state.[ii] The Oregon Constitution provides that any act of the legislature incorporating towns and cities shall restrict their powers of taxation, borrowing, contracting debt and loaning credit. The constitution also permits the legislature to provide laws establishing a method for counties to adopt county charters allowing a county to exercise authority over matters of county concern.[iii] **Taxing Limitations** Oregon state law includes limitations on the amount that a particular property may be assessed each year for the purposes of property taxes.[iv] Further Oregon state law includes provisions requiring that local governments levy sufficient ad valorem taxes to pay off amounts due on principal and interest on outstanding general obligation bonds.[v]
Debt Default Prevention	**Debt Limitation** No county shall create debt or liabilities exceeding the sum of $5,000, provided, however, that a county may issue bonded indebtedness above this limit, as fixed by statute.[vi] **Municipal Debt Advisory Commission** Although not tasked with authority to restructure debt, the commission provides assistance to public bodies in planning, preparing, marketing and selling new bonds, among other things.[vii] **Refunding Bonds** In certain situations, a municipal entity may issue refunding bonds to refund and refinance outstanding debt.[viii] **Refunding Bond Cram-Down** Applicable only to irrigation and drainage districts, this provision allows these districts to refinance existing debt with refunding bonds in less than the amount of the existing bonds held by creditors. Under this provision, 80 percent of the existing holders must consent. If 80 percent of bondholders consent, the provision sets forth procedures for constructive consent of remaining unknown or non-consenting bondholders.[ix]

LL. Oregon

Debt Default Prevention *continued*	**State Guarantee** The Oregon Constitution includes provisions allowing the state to guarantee the bonded indebtedness of qualified school districts, education service districts and community college districts.[x]
Mechanisms for Resolution after Default	**Technical Assistance Program** To assist counties in fiscal distress, Oregon law includes provisions establishing a service delivery technical assistance program to (a) award public bodies and administer grants for service delivery innovation, (b) enter into agreements with public and private entities to provide technical assistance to public bodies, and (c) convene task forces and working groups to advance the technical assistance program.[xi] **Receivership** In certain situations involving revenue bonds, Oregon law allows for the appointment of a receiver.[xii]
Remedies on Default	**Foreclosure** In certain default situations generally involving revenue bonds, bondholders may foreclose on any mortgage or deed of trust related to the project.[xiii] **Mandamus** In certain situations, bondholders or their trustee may bring a court action to compel the local governing body to perform a ministerial action that it has refused to undertake, such as collecting taxes or fees where the underlying bond authorization requires such a collection.[xiv]
Other Bondholder Protections	**Special Revenue Bonds** As provided by Section 922(d) of the Bankruptcy Code, payments to bondholders holding special revenue bonds would not be stayed on the filing of a municipal bankruptcy petition, and payments to holders could continue. Whether an issuance would qualify as a special revenue bond depends on the provisions of the authorizing statute with respect to the bonds at issue.[xv] **Statutory Liens** Were a municipal entity to file a petition under Chapter 9 of the Bankruptcy Code, bondholders holding bonds to which statutory liens have attached would continue to receive payment on those bonds. For a statutory lien to apply, the authorizing law of the bond issue must contain such a lien. Category SL-3.[xvi]

---

i OR. REV. STAT. § 548.705. The statute provides that any irrigation or drainage district may file a petition under the federal bankruptcy laws at any time subsequent to a default in the payment of principal or interest upon its bonded or warrant indebtedness. No entities other than irrigation or drainage districts are specifically authorized to file a petition under the federal bankruptcy laws.

ii *See Burt v. Blumenauer*, 299 Or. 55, 61-62 (Or. 1982) (noting in relation to case involving government speech that "[i]n recent times, the judicial demand for explicit expressions of authority and a recognition of only attendant authorities 'necessarily implied' by those expressed has given way to an interpretation that local governments have broad powers subject only to constitutional or preemptive statutory prohibitions").

iii OR. CONST. art. XI, § 5 (acts restricting town and city powers) and OR. CONST. art. VI, § 10 (county charters).

iv OR. CONST. art. XI, § 11; OR. CONST. art. XI, § 11b. Pursuant to section 11b, for school purposes, the maximum allowable rate is $5 for each $1,000 of the property's real market value and, for purposes other than schools, the maximum rate is $10 per $1,000 of the property's real market value. These maximum rates do not apply to taxes imposed to pay the principal and interest on bonded indebtedness.

v OR. REV. STAT. § 287A.140.

vi OR. CONST. art. XI, § 10. For instance, a county may not issue general obligation bonds exceeding 2 percent of the real market value of the taxable property in the county (OR. REV. STAT. § 287A.100) and may not issue revenue bonds exceeding 1 percent of the real market value of all taxable property in the county (OR. REV. STAT. § 287A.105).

vii OR. REV. STAT. § 287A.630.

viii Examples of refunding bond provisions in Oregon law include OR. REV. STAT. § 287A.360–A.380 (a public body may issue current refunding bonds to refund its outstanding bonds) and OR. REV. STAT. § 287A.365 (allowing public bodies to issue advanced refunding bonds or enter into forward current refundings in accordance with statutes and rules adopted by the state treasurer).

ix OR. REV. STAT. §§ 548.715, 545.651, 545.655, 545.659, 545.663.

x OR. CONST. art. XI-K, § 1.

xi OR. REV. STAT. § 203.105.

xii OR. REV. STAT. § 468.268 (allowing for appointment of a receiver with power to charge and collect rents and to apply revenues from facilities in accordance with such proceedings in relation to county pollution control facilities) and OR. REV. STAT. § 456.210 (housing projects). The state code may be more expansive and the statutory authority for each bond issuance should be reviewed before assessing whether a receiver may be appointed.

xiii *See, e.g.*, OR. REV. STAT. § 468.268 (allowing for foreclosure in relation to county pollution control facility bonds) and OR. REV. STAT. § 456.165 (housing projects). The state code may be more expansive and the statutory authority for each bond issuance should be reviewed before assessing whether a foreclosure action may be brought.

xiv *See, e.g.*, OR. REV. STAT. § 468.268 (allowing for writ of mandamus in relation to county pollution control facility bonds). It is possible that an aggrieved bondholder could pursue a writ of mandamus even absent authorizing statutory law.

xv *See, e.g.*, OR. REV. STAT. § 287A.150 (general revenue bond provisions). Note that this is an example of a special revenue bond provision. The state code may be more expansive, and an attorney should be consulted to examine any specific situation involving a default.

xvi Category SL-3: *See, e.g.*, OR. REV. STAT. § 287A.310, which has language that provides the lien created by pledge of revenues or property to pay bonds is valid, binding and superior to and has priority over all other claims and that the Uniform Commercial Code does not apply to creation, perfection, priority or enforcement of a lien of such pledge. This language appears to be a provision for effectiveness and perfection of the lien as opposed to being a statutory lien even though it could be read as an attempt to create a statutory lien. Further clarification of the intent to create a statutory lien as opposed to exempting the perfection from the Uniform Commercial Code would be helpful.

MM. Pennsylvania

Municipal Bankruptcy Authority	Any municipality, which includes counties, cities, boroughs, incorporated towns, townships and home-rule municipalities, may file a Chapter 9 petition if it meets one of three conditions contained in so-called "Act 47" of Pennsylvania law and has sought and received the permission of the State Department of Community and Economic Development to file such a petition. In the event a court-appointed receiver has been placed in control of a municipality, that receiver may file a Chapter 9 petition on behalf of the municipality, so long as the State Department of Community and Economic Development has granted the receiver permission to do so. In addition, certain "public subdivisions" that are not eligible for Act 47 protection are entitled to file a Chapter 9 petition so long as the State Department of Community and Economic Development has approved the filing. Further, neither a city of the first class (such as Philadelphia) nor a city of the second class (such as Pittsburgh) may file a municipal bankruptcy petition unless the petition has been submitted to and approved by the governor of Pennsylvania. Pennsylvania law specifically prohibits Chapter 9 filings by all school districts, except for school districts of the first class. Unless a municipality is specifically identified, it is not authorized to file a petition. Between 1980 and July 31, 2016, five municipal entities in Pennsylvania have filed municipal bankruptcy petitions.[i]
Home Rule and Taxing Power of Municipalities	**Municipalities' Ability to Self-Govern** Pennsylvania is a Dillon's Rule state.[ii] The Pennsylvania constitution grants municipalities the right to adopt home-rule charters. A home rule municipality may exercise any power or perform any function as long as the state constitution, the state legislature or its own charter does not deny it. The Pennsylvania Consolidated Statutes contain limitations of measures municipalities may not take but grant home-rule municipalities the power and authority to enact and enforce local tax ordinances.[iii] **Taxing Limitations** Pennsylvania law includes taxing limitations based on government type.[iv]
Debt Default Prevention	**Debt Limitation** The general assembly has the authority to prescribe debt limits. Philadelphia's debt may not exceed 13.5 percent of the average annual assessed value of taxable property therein during the 10 years immediately preceding the year of the increase.[v]

MM. Pennsylvania

Debt Default Prevention *continued*	**Rehabilitation of Distressed Municipalities** *Financially Distressed Municipalities Act* (Act 47). If the State Department of Community and Economic Development determines a municipality is financially distressed, the department may appoint a coordinator to help the municipality prepare a plan to put its finances in order. The coordinator may hold public meetings and negotiate with creditors and other parties in preparing the plan. If the creditors reject the plan, a triggering event occurs, allowing the municipality to file a municipal bankruptcy petition.[vi] **Fiscal Emergencies in Municipalities** The governor may declare a fiscal emergency in a distressed municipality if certain conditions are present, requiring the Department of Community and Economic Development, within 10 days of the declaration, to create an emergency action plan for the distressed municipality during the state of fiscal emergency.[vii] **Municipal Receivership** Following a declaration by the Pennsylvania governor of a fiscal emergency, the governor may direct the Secretary of the Department of Community and Economic Development to file a petition in state court seeking the appointment of a receiver over the distressed municipality. The receiver is required to devise a recovery plan within 30 days of his or her appointment to present to the court. Among other things, with the written authorization of the Secretary of the Department of Community and Economic Development, the receiver may file a Chapter 9 petition on behalf of the municipality.[viii] **Philadelphia Rehabilitation and Oversight** *Intergovernmental Cooperation Authority Act.* This act was created to enable capital market access by cities of the first class (Philadelphia) for deficit elimination and seasonal borrowings to avoid default on existing obligations and chronic cash shortages. The authority may issue bonds and other obligations, but only at the request of the city being assisted. Further, the city assisted and the authority must develop, implement and periodically revise a five-year financial recovery plan. The authority also has the power over the city budget.[ix] **Refunding Bonds** In certain situations, a municipal entity may issue refunding bonds to refund and refinance outstanding debt.[x]

MM. Pennsylvania

Mechanisms for Resolution after Default	**Receivership** In certain default situations, Pennsylvania law allows for the appointment of a receiver with respect to revenue bonds.[xi] **Trustee Appointment** If a local unit of government defaults on the payment of principal or interest on a bond issuance and the default continues for 30 days, or if the local government unit fails to comply with any provision in a bond or note; or if allowed by the authorizing resolution, and holders of 25 percent in aggregate principal amount of bonds outstanding so choose, a trustee may be appointed to represent bondholders.[xii]
Remedies on Default	**Accounting** In certain default situations, bondholders may bring a proceeding to require the authority in question to account as if it were a trustee of an express trust.[xiii] **Mandamus** In certain situations, bondholders or their trustee may bring a court action to compel the local governing body to perform a ministerial action that it has refused to undertake, such as collecting taxes or fees where the underlying bond authorization requires such a collection.[xiv]
Other Bondholder Protections	**Special Revenue Bonds** As provided by Section 922(d) of the Bankruptcy Code, payments to bondholders holding special revenue bonds would not be stayed on the filing of a municipal bankruptcy petition, and payments to holders could continue. Whether an issuance would qualify as a special revenue bond depends on the provisions of the authorizing statute with respect to the bonds at issue.[xv] **Statutory Liens** Were a municipal entity to file a petition under Chapter 9 of the Bankruptcy Code, bondholders holding bonds to which statutory liens have attached would continue to receive payment on those bonds. For a statutory lien to apply, the authorizing law of the bond issue must contain such a lien. Category SL-1. [xvi]

---

i 53 PA. STAT. ANN. §§ 5510.11, 5571, 11701.261, 11701.103 (definition of municipalities), 12720.211, 28211; 74 PA. CONS. STAT. ANN. § 1773; 24 PA. STAT. § 6-692-A (school districts); 24 PA. STAT. § 6-602-A (definition of school districts). Pursuant to PA. STAT. ANN. § 5510.11, a parking authority in a city of the first class is not authorized to file a federal bankruptcy petition if such authority has outstanding any bonds issued pursuant to the chapter. Pursuant to PA. STAT. ANN. § 5571, a political subdivision may file a federal bankruptcy petition only after its petition has been submitted to and approved by the State Department of Internal Affairs. However, § 5571 case law indicates that § 5571 may only apply to entities such as school districts, vocational school districts and county institution districts. *See In re Carroll Tp. Authority*, 119 B.R. 61, 64 (Bankr. W.D. Pa. 1990); *but see* 24 PA. STAT. § 6-692-A (expressly prohibiting school districts except of the cities of the first class from filing a municipal bankruptcy petition). Pursuant to § 11701.261, a municipality, following a vote by a majority of the municipality's governing body, may apply to the Department of Community and Economic Development to file a petition pursuant to the federal bankruptcy laws if one of the following conditions is present: (i) imminent jeopardy of an action by a creditor, claimant or supplier that is likely to substantially interrupt or restrict the continued ability of the municipality to provide health and safety services to its citizens; (ii) one or more creditors of the municipality have rejected a proposed or adopted plan, and efforts to negotiate a resolution with those creditors is unsuccessful for a ten-day period; and (iii) a condition substantially affecting the municipality's financial distress is potentially solvable only by filing a Chapter 9 petition. Pursuant to § 12720.211, a city of the first class is not authorized to file a federal bankruptcy petition unless (a) it has no outstanding bonds issued pursuant to the Pennsylvania Intergovernmental Cooperation Authority Act for Cities of the First Class and (b) it has received approval from the governor for the filing of a federal bankruptcy petition. Pursuant to § 28211, a city of the second class is not authorized to file a federal bankruptcy petition unless (a) it has no bonds outstanding under the Pennsylvania Intergovernmental Cooperation Authority for Cities of the Second Class and (b) it has received approval from the governor for the filing of a federal bankruptcy petition. Pursuant to 74 PA. CONS. STAT. ANN. § 1773, a public transportation authority is not authorized to file a federal bankruptcy petition if such authority has outstanding any bonds issued pursuant to the chapter. *See also* 53 PA. STAT. ANN. § 101 (classification of cities).

In 2011, due to the financial situation of the city of Harrisburg, the Pennsylvania legislature passed at least two prohibitions on cities of the third class (such as Harrisburg) from filing municipal bankruptcy petitions. One such prohibition expired on July 1, 2012 (*see* PA. ACT no. 26 (printer's no. 1452, signed into law by governor on June 30, 2011)), but was extended to November 30, 2012. The moratorium has expired. Despite this prohibition, on October 11, 2011, the city of Harrisburg filed such a petition, which subsequently was dismissed by the court.

Of the five entities filing municipal bankruptcy petitions, three were cities or towns (specifically Harrisburg, a borough and a township) and two were special municipal districts.

ii *Trigona v. Lender*, 2006 Pa. Dist. & Cnty. Dec. LEXIS 371, *17-18 (Pa. C.P. Westmoreland Cy. Sept. 20, 2006) (noting that Dillon's Rule applies in Pennsylvania). The *Trigona* court citied a 1933 Pennsylvania case in which the Pennsylvania Supreme Court held: "Nothing is better settled than that a municipal corporation does not possess and cannot exercise any other than the following powers: (1) those granted in express words; (2) those necessarily or fairly implied in or incident to the powers expressly granted; (3) those essential to the declared objects and purposes of the corporation, not simply convenient, but indispensable. Any fair, reasonable doubt as to the existence of power is resolved by the courts against its existence in the corporation, and therefore denied." *In re Valley Deposit & Trust Co.*, 311 Pa. 495, 498 (1933). *See also Guthrie v. Wilkinsburg*, 508 Pa. 590, 599-600 (Pa. 1985) ("A political subdivision has only those powers expressly given it by the legislature.").

iii PA. CONST. art. IX, § 2 (home-rule charters); 53 PA. CONS. STAT. § 2962 (limiting statutes and taxation provisions).

iv 16 PA. STAT. ANN. § 1770 (counties); 53 PA. STAT. ANN. § 6924.320 (political subdivision taxing limitations). The Pennsylvania state law provisions are more expansive and these provisions are cited only to show a sample of tax limitations contained in the state's laws.

v PA. CONST. art. IX, § 10; PA. CONST. art. IX, § 12 (Philadelphia debt).

vi 53 PA. STAT. ANN. §§ 11701.101 to 11701.501. These provisions apply to any county, borough, incorporated town, township and home-rule municipality. Triggering events include the municipality maintaining a deficit over a three-year period, with a deficit of 1 percent or more in each of the previous fiscal years; expenditures exceeding revenues over a three-year period; defaulting on bond payments; missing payroll for 30 days; missing required payments to judgment creditors; failing to forward employee withholding taxes; accumulating a deficit in two successive years of 5 percent or more of its revenues; failing to make certain budgeted payments; attempting to negotiate and adjust a claim in excess of 30 percent against a fund or budget and failing in the negotiation; filing a municipal bankruptcy petition; or experiencing a decrease in a quantified level of municipal service from the preceding fiscal year, resulting in its reaching its legal limit in levying real estate taxes for general purposes. *See* 53 PA. STAT. ANN. §§ 11701.201.

There have been 29 filings under these provisions since 1987 and only ten rescissions of such filing as of November 2015. Examples of municipalities that were determined to be financially distressed include Pittsburgh in 2003 and the borough of Wilkinsburg in 1988, rescinded 1998. *See borough of Wilkinsburg v. Department of Community and Economic Development*, 728 A.2d 389 (Pa. Commw. Ct. 1999). Other cities include Farrell (1987); Aliquippa (1987); Clairton (1988); borough of Braddock (1988); borough of Franklin (1988); borough of Shenandoh (1988, rescinded 1993); borough of Rankin (1989); borough of Ambridge (1990, rescinded 1993); Duquesne (1991); Scranton (1992); Johnstown (1992); borough of East Pittsburgh (1992, rescinded 1999); borough of Millbourne (1993, rescinded 2014); borough of Homestead (1993, rescinded 2007); Chester (1995); borough of Greenville (1995); borough of North Braddock (1995, rescinded 2003); borough of West Hazleton (2003, rescinded 2014); Reading (2009); Harrisburg (2010); Altoona (2012); city of Shamokin (2014); and borough of Colwyn (2015). Distress determinations have been rescinded for certain cities, including Wilkinsburg, Shenandoah, Ambridge, East Pittsburgh, North Braddock, Homestead, borough of Milbourne, Westfall Township, borough of West Hazleton and Nanticoke. Pennsylvania Department of Community and Economic Affairs Distress Determinations, http://www.newpa.com/local-government/services-we-provide-local-governments/request-assistance/list-act-47-distress-determinations (last visited Nov. 24, 2015).

Several cases have explored the interplay between Act 47 and collective bargaining agreements; *see, e.g., Wilkinsburg Police Officers Ass'n v. Commonwealth*, 564 A.2d 1015 (Pa. Commw. Ct. 1989) (rejecting union argument that Act 47, by limiting prospective bargaining agreements, violates the constitution's requirement that municipalities engage in collective bargaining); *City of Farrell v. Fraternal Order of Police Lodge No. 34*, 645 A.2d 1294 (Pa. 1994) (upholding arbitrator's decision to increase union salaries despite challenge from the city, noting that the approved plan did not freeze or place limits on increases of police salaries, though it did prohibit increases in the cost of fringe benefits); *Pittsburgh Fire Fighters, Local No. 1 v. Yablonsky*, 867 A.2d 666 (Pa. Commw. Ct. 2005) (holding that § 252 of Act 47 applies to both arbitration settlements and arbitration determinations); *City of Scranton v. Fire Fighters Local Union No. 60*, 29 A.3d 773 (Pa. 2011) (finding that Act 47 does not impinge on arbitration awards under Pennsylvania's Policemen and Firemen Collective Bargaining Act with respect to employee bonuses, salary increases and health benefits).

At least one commentator has noted that an issue in applying Act 47 (the financially distressed municipalities provisions) is how to deal with collective bargaining after a financial distress declaration has been made. As it stands, the provisions prohibit financially distressed municipalities from entering into collective bargaining agreements conflicting with the plan. Unions argue that this is an impermissible restraint. *See* A.C. Schroeder, *The Interplay Between the Municipalities Financial Recovery Act and the Policemen and Firemen Collective Bargaining Act: an Analysis of City of Scranton v. Fire Fighters Local Union No. 60*, 19 WIDENER L.J. 541 (2010).

On September 23, 2013, a Pennsylvania court approved a recovery plan for the city of Harrisburg submitted by the receiver that was appointed over Harrisburg pursuant to Act 47. *Walker, as Secretary for the Department of Community and Economic Development v. City of Harrisburg*, Case No. 569 M.D. 2011 (Pa. Commw. Ct. Sept. 23, 2013) (Order).

In October 2014 Pennsylvania enacted HB1773, which was intended to provide enhancements to the law based on the experience of the past 28 municipalities that have been declared financially distressed under Act 47. The modifications to Act 47 included:

1. ***Time Limit:*** A five-year time limit for municipalities to exit Act 47. There is a one-time petition process to ask for a three-year extension from the local court of common pleas. The intent is to help more municipalities through the recovery plan development and enactment at a faster pace.

2. *Encourage Early Intervention:* The commonwealth will provide technical assistance through an early intervention program to provide resources to distressed municipalities sooner with financial support to develop plans for fiscal sustainability and balanced budgets.

3. *Expanded Use of a "Receiver":* Following the Harrisburg experience and the use of a receiver, the Secretary of Department of Community and Economic Affairs may request the governor act for the municipality that is unable to continue vital and necessary services or that has failed to approve the coordinator's plan or an alternate plan of recovery approved by the secretary. The governor may act for elected officials after declaring fiscal distress with all of the municipal power to collect funds, obtain emergency aid, enter into contracts. The elected officials cannot act contrary to the governor's actions. The secretary can adopt an emergency action plan. If the municipality fails to negotiate a consent agreement with creditors to adopt one negotiated, the governor may appoint a receiver to develop a recovery plan. Philadelphia, a first-class city, is exempt from disincorporation.

4. *Revenue Enhancement:* The increase in earned income tax is conditional on imposition on commuters as well as residents. This allows a municipality to triple the normal $52 maximum local service fee. Unfortunately, this increase abruptly ends once the Act 47 distressed municipality status is rescinded upon exit from Act 47. Also, Pittsburgh was exempt from this increase.

5. *Disincorporation:* If the municipality is nonviable due to long-term loss of tax base and there is a lack of interest in municipal consolidation in whole or in part for municipal services within any adjoining communities, the new amendment provides for disincorporation for the municipality too poor to exit Act 47 or develop a recovery plan. The municipality would by court order be disincorporated and become an administrative service district with the administrator power to sell or convey its assets to repay debt. The assets or proceeds would inure to the commonwealth to the extent not necessary to pay creditors.

vii 53 PA. STAT. ANN. §§ 11701.602-610. Conditions warranting a determination of fiscal emergency exist if the distressed municipality (a) is insolvent or projected to be insolvent in 180 days or less; (b) is unable to provide vital and necessary services; or (c) has failed to implement certain plans and/or directives contained in the municipal fiscal distress provisions of the commonwealth's laws. *Id.* At § 11701.602.

viii 53 PA. STAT. ANN. §§ 11701.701-712.

ix 53 PA. STAT. ANN. § 12720.101 *et seq.* These provisions were created in 1991 to deal with issues faced by the city of Philadelphia. Philadelphia continues to be under the guidance of the Pennsylvania Intergovernmental Cooperation Authority. *See supra* Section V at 79.

x An example of a refunding bond provision under Pennsylvania law is 53 PA. STAT. ANN. §§ 8241-8251 (municipal refunding bonds generally).

xi *See, e.g.,* 53 PA. STAT. ANN. § 15733 (revenue bonds issued by cities of the first class to construct sewer systems) and 53 PA. STAT. ANN. § 8264 (receiver for revenue projects). The state code may be more expansive and the statutory authority for each individual bond issuance should be reviewed before assessing whether such a receiver may be appointed.

xii 53 PA. STAT. ANN. § 8263. On written request by bondholders holding 25 percent or more in principal amount of bonds outstanding and on being furnished with indemnity, a trustee may: bring a writ of mandamus or other proceeding in equity to enforce the rights of bondholders to impose and collect rents, rates, tolls and charges adequate to carry out the agreement or carry out any other agreement with the bondholders; bring suit on the bonds; require an accounting from the local government; in the case of general obligation bonds and guaranteed revenue bonds, petition the court to levy, after a hearing and notice to real estate owners, the amount due before or after the exercise of any right to accelerate the bonds or notes, plus the estimated cost of collection; to seek an injunction; or after 30 days' prior written notice to the local government, and subject to the bond ordinance or relevant indenture, declare the unpaid principal and interest immediately due and payable.

xiii *See, e.g.*, 53 PA. STAT. ANN. § 12720.305 (Pennsylvania Intergovernmental Cooperation Authority for Cities of the First Class) and 53 PA. STAT. ANN. § 25687 (waterworks bonds). The state code may be more expansive and the statutory authority for each individual bond issuance should be reviewed before assessing whether a bondholder may bring an action for an accounting.

xiv *See, e.g.*, 53 PA. STAT. ANN. § 15733 (revenue bonds issued by cities of the first class to construct sewer systems); 53 PA. STAT. ANN. § 15920 (revenue bonds issued by cities of the first class); 53 PA. STAT. ANN. § 12720.305 (Pennsylvania Intergovernmental Cooperation Authority for Cities of the First Class); and 53 PA. STAT. ANN. § 25687 (waterworks bonds). It is possible that an aggrieved bondholder could pursue a writ of mandamus even absent authorizing statutory law.

xv *See, e.g.*, 53 PA. STAT. ANN. § 15907 (revenue bonds issued by cities of the first class shall contain a pledge and grant of security interest in project revenues). This is an example of a special revenue bond. The state code may be more expansive, and an attorney should be consulted to examine any specific situation involving a default.

xvi Category SL-1: *See, e.g.*, Pennsylvania Intergovernmental Cooperation Authority (PICA) 53 PA. STAT. §§ 12720.304 and 12710.306 (the lien created by pledge of revenues of the authority immediately valid and binding as of the time revenues pledged are received by local government without further action against all parties having a claim of any kind against such revenues or funds). This is an example of legislation providing a pledge in connection with a financially distressed city (Philadelphia), which is intended to be for improved market acceptance of any financing. The state code may be more expansive, and an attorney should be consulted to examine any specific situation involving a default.

NN. Puerto Rico

Municipal Bankruptcy Authority	Puerto Rico is not authorized to file a petition under Chapter 9 of the Bankruptcy Code, but new PROMESA legislation provides for a court proceeding to adjust the debts of the commonwealth if instituted by the Financial Oversight and Management Board.[i]
Home Rule and Taxing Power of Municipalities	**Municipalities' Ability to Self-Govern** The Puerto Rican Constitution provides the legislature with the power to determine the organization and function of municipalities and to authorize them to develop programs for the general welfare of the people.[ii] **Tax Limitations** Puerto Rican laws allow municipalities to levy a real property tax of up to 6 percent of the appraised value of the real property and a personal property tax of up to 4 percent of the appraised value of the personal property.[iii]
Debt Default Prevention	**Debt Limitation** Under the Puerto Rican Constitution, the Puerto Rican legislature may fix municipal debt limitations, but the debt limitation shall not be less than 5 percent or more than 10 percent of the aggregate tax valuation of the property within the municipality. The Puerto Rican legislature has limited municipal general obligation bonds or notes to a total principal sum that, together with the principal to be paid for all other general obligations of the municipality, may not exceed 10 percent of the total appraised value of the property within the municipality. In addition, the municipality may not incur debt from notes in advance of municipal general obligation bonds exceeding 10 percent of the total appraised value of the property in the municipality and may not issue special obligation bonds exceeding 10 percent of the average recurrent operating income of the municipality in the two fiscal years immediately preceding the current fiscal year. Further, no municipality may issue notes or instruments in advance of taxes and revenues exceeding 10 percent of the average recurrent operating income of the municipality in the two fiscal years immediately preceding the current fiscal year.[iv] **Refunding Bonds** In certain situations, a municipal entity may issue refunding bonds to refund and refinance outstanding debt.[v]

NN. Puerto Rico

Mechanisms for Resolution after Default	**First-Lien Provisions** In Puerto Rico, the Municipal Revenues Collection Center collects proceeds of a special surtax and any other property tax. The center then deposits the special surtax in the municipality's account in the Redemption Fund. If the Government Bank determines the deposits in the municipality's account are not sufficient to cover the principal and interest payments on any existing general obligation bonds, the Government Bank must notify the center, and the center must deposit into the municipality's account an amount sufficient to cover the bond payments from other income subject to the first lien created by this provision. Although this provision has never been used, on its face it would require the deposit of an amount sufficient to cover bond payments pre-default.[vi] PROMESA does not invalidate or impair any pre-existing lien securing a bond obligation, and any fiscal plan must respect lawful liens and priorities.[vii] **Receivership** In certain default situations, Puerto Rican law allows for the appointment of a receiver with respect to revenue bonds.[viii]
Remedies on Default	**Accounting** In certain default situations, bondholders may bring a proceeding to require the authority in question to account as if it were a trustee of an express trust.[ix] **Mandamus** In certain situations, bondholders or their trustee may bring a court action to compel the local governing body to perform a ministerial action that it has refused to undertake, such as collecting taxes or fees where the underlying bond authorization requires such a collection.[x]
Other Bondholder Protections	Municipalities in Puerto Rico are not authorized to file a petition under Chapter 9 of the Bankruptcy Code. Despite a lack of authorization, Puerto Rico does recognize certain special revenue bonds. **Special Revenue Bonds** As provided by Section 922(d) of the Bankruptcy Code, payments to bondholders holding special revenue bonds would not be stayed on the filing of a municipal bankruptcy petition, and payments to holders could continue. Whether an issuance would qualify as a special revenue bond depends on the provisions of the authorizing statute with respect to the bonds at issue.[xi]

NN. Puerto Rico

Other Bondholder Protections *continued*	**Statutory Liens** Were a municipal entity to file a petition under Chapter 9 of the Bankruptcy Code, bondholders holding bonds to which statutory liens have attached would continue to receive payment on those bonds. For a statutory lien to apply, the authorizing law of the bond issue must contain such a lien. Category SL-1.[xii]

---

i The term "State" is defined in the Bankruptcy Code as including "Puerto Rico, except for the purpose of defining who may be a debtor under Chapter 9 of this title." 11 U.S.C. § 101(52). However, the 2016 Puerto Rico Oversight, Management and Economic Stability Act, PROMESA, provides for a court proceeding to adjust the debt of Puerto Rico and incorporates a number of provisions from Chapter 9. Public Law 114-187, 114th Cong., 2d Sess. (June 30, 2016) ("PROMESA").

ii P.R. CONST. art. VI, § 1.

iii P.R. LAWS ANN. tit. 21, § 5001.

iv P.R. CONST. art. VI, § 2; P.R. LAWS ANN. tit. 21, § 6015.

v Examples of refunding bond provisions under Puerto Rican law include P.R. LAWS ANN. tit. 12, § 1265 (refunding bonds of Puerto Rico Industrial, Tourist, Educational, Medical, and Environmental Control Facilities Financing Authority); P.R. LAWS ANN. tit. 23, § 6445 (authorizing refunding bonds for Puerto Rico Convention Center District Authority); and P.R. LAWS ANN. tit. 3, § 1908 (authorizing refunding bonds for Puerto Rico Infrastructure Financing Authority).

vi P.R. LAWS ANN. tit. 21, § 6016. According to the Government Development Bank for Puerto Rico, this provision has never been used. *See* "Puerto Rico Municipal Finance Agency (MFA)," http://www.gdb-pur.com/affiliates/municipal-finance-agency.html (last visited Mar. 20, 2015).

vii *See, e.g.*, PROMESA, §§ 201(b)(1)(N) and 405(k).

viii *See, e.g.*, P.R. LAWS ANN. tit. 22, § 153 (allowing for appointment of receiver if a default continues for more than 30 days and 25 percent or more of bondholders make such a request in relation to the Aqueduct and Sewer Authority) and P.R. LAWS ANN. tit. 22, § 206 (Puerto Rico Electric Power Authority, should a default last more than 30 days and 25 percent or more of bondholders make such a request). Puerto Rico's code may be more expansive than the examples cited here, and the statutory authority for each individual bond issuance should be reviewed before assessing whether a receiver may be appointed.

ix *See, e.g.*, P.R. LAWS ANN. tit. 22, § 154 (Aqueduct and Sewer Authority, allowing bondholders to bring an action for accounting); P.R. LAWS ANN. tit. 22, § 208 (same for Puerto Rico Electric Power Authority). Puerto Rico's code may be more expansive and the statutory authority for each bond issuance should be reviewed before assessing whether an accounting action may be brought.

x *See, e.g.*, P.R. LAWS ANN. tit. 22, § 154 (Aqueduct and Sewer Authority, allowing bondholders to enforce rights by mandamus); P.R. LAWS ANN. tit. 22, § 208 (same for Puerto Rico Electric Power Authority). It is possible that an aggrieved bondholder could pursue a writ of mandamus even absent authorizing statutory law.

xi *See, e.g.*, P.R. LAWS ANN. tit. 18, § 824 (pledge for revenue bonds for University of Puerto Rico) and P.R. LAWS ANN. tit. 23, §§ 530, 560 (allowing revenue bonds for port commissions). These are examples of special revenue bonds. Puerto

Rico's code may be more expansive, and an attorney should be consulted to examine any specific situation involving a default. PROMESA incorporates the Chapter 9 provisions regarding special revenues (11 U.S.C. § 928).

xii Category SL-1: *See, e.g.,* COFINA Act 91 as amended by Act No. 18 (2009) (the amended statute has explicit language effectively reconfirming the existence of a statutory lien ab initio, providing that all income and revenue received by COFINA are immediately subject to a lien, without the need of physical delivery or any other act, and the lien is valid and binding and shall prevail against any third party with a claim of any kind against COFINA). This is an example of a statutory lien. Puerto Rico's code may be more expansive, and an attorney should be consulted to examine any specific situation involving a default.

OO. Rhode Island

Municipal Bankruptcy Authority	Rhode Island law includes provisions that allow a budget commission to appoint a receiver to restore fiscal stability in a city, town or fire district. Among other powers, the receiver may file a petition in the name of the city, town or fire district under Chapter 9 of the Bankruptcy Code. Outside of this situation, a municipal entity in Rhode Island may not file a municipal bankruptcy petition. Between 1980 and July 31, 2016, two municipal entities in Rhode Island have filed such a petition.[i]
Home Rule and Taxing Power of Municipalities	**Municipalities' Ability to Self-Govern** Rhode Island is a Dillon's Rule state.[ii] Although the state constitution includes an article granting the people of every city and town the right to home rule, the state legislature maintains power over those entities. The state constitution provides that cities and towns may not levy, assess and collect taxes or borrow money without authorization by the state legislature. The Rhode Island General Laws authorize certain local taxes.[iii] **Tax Limitations** Rhode Island law provides the maximum levy that a city or town may make in a year but allows the city or town to levy taxes above the maximum rate in certain situations.[iv] Rhode Island law, however, provides that the power and obligation of cities and towns in the state to pay general obligation debt are unlimited and that cities and towns must levy sufficient ad valorem taxes to pay general obligation debt.[v]
Debt Default Prevention[vi]	**Bond Issuance Requirements** To issue bonds, a city or town must (1) have a long-standing "A" credit rating; (2) represent that the proposed bonds will finance a capital asset and that the average useful life of the asset will be greater than or equal to the average maturity of the proposed borrowing; (3) be in compliance with statutory financial reporting requirements and not subject to enforcement proceedings or remedies; and (4) approve the issuance by local referendum or financial town meeting. Cities and towns must receive ministerial approval from the auditor general, who will approve only if these standards are met.[vii] **Debt Limitation** Cities and towns may not incur debt exceeding 3 percent of the full assessed value of taxable property within the city. This measure is net of (i) borrowing in anticipation of tax proceedings and (ii) the amount in any sinking fund. The state director of revenue, however, may allow a city to borrow above this limit.[viii]

OO. Rhode Island

Debt Default Prevention *continued*	**Fiscal Overseer** The director of the state department of revenue may appoint a fiscal overseer for any town or city where the elected chief executive officer and city council so request or the city or town has suffered at least two of five events, including a projected deficit in the current and upcoming fiscal years, failing to file its required audits in the past two years, being downgraded by a nationally recognized rating organization, otherwise being unable to obtain access to reasonable credit or not having promptly responded to requests from the state to assess its financial condition. The fiscal overseer shall recommend to the city sound fiscal policies, supervise all finance services and activities, advise assessors and financial personnel of the city, provide assistance in all matters related to municipal financial affairs, assist in preparing the city's budget and spending plans, review all proposed contracts and obligations, monitor expenditures, approve annual municipal budgets, and report monthly to the state on the city or town's progress. Within 120 days of being appointed, the fiscal overseer shall develop a three-year plan to achieve fiscal stability in the city or town.[ix] **Budget Commission** If the fiscal overseer concludes that the city, town or fire district is unable to balance its budget, faces a fiscal crisis that poses an imminent danger to the safety of the city, town or fire district or will not achieve fiscal stability without a budget commission's assistance, or that the tax levy of the fiscal year should not be approved, it may request that a budget commission be appointed. The budget commission has significant powers, including to approve all appropriations, borrowing authorizations, transfers and other municipal spending authorizations; to increase or decrease municipal fees; to restructure the city, town or fire district's government and departments; and to issue general obligation bonds of the city, town or fire district. If the budget commission concludes that its powers are not sufficient to restore fiscal stability, a municipal receiver could be appointed.[x] **Refunding Bonds** In certain situations, a municipal entity may issue refunding bonds to refund and refinance outstanding debt.[xi]

OO. Rhode Island

Mechanisms for Resolution after Default	**Bond Payment Guarantee** If a city or town is unable to make a payment of principal or interest on a bond, and the state certifies, the state treasurer shall pay the bond paying agent the amount of the due or overdue debt to the extent of the sum that would otherwise be then payable to the city or town and sums estimated to become payable during the remainder of the fiscal year. The amount paid will be in trust and charged against the amount that would otherwise be payable by the treasury to the city.[xii] **Municipal Receiver** If the budget commission concludes that it has insufficient power to restore fiscal responsibility to the city, town or fire district, the director of revenue shall appoint a receiver with the powers of the financial overseer and budget commission and additional powers to exercise governmental functions. The receiver's power is superior to that of the elected official of the town or city. Further, if the director of revenue determines that a fiscal emergency exists, he shall appoint a receiver without having first appointed a fiscal overseer or a budget commission.[xiii] **Receivership** In certain default situations, Rhode Island law allows for the appointment of a receiver with respect to revenue bonds.[xiv]
Remedies on Default	**Accounting** In certain default situations, bondholders may bring a proceeding to require the authority in question to account as if it were a trustee of an express trust.[xv] **Foreclosure** In certain situations, bondholders may take possession of a project in the event of default.[xvi] **Mandamus** In certain situations, bondholders or their trustee may bring a court action to compel the local governing body to perform a ministerial action that it has refused to undertake, such as collecting taxes or fees where the underlying bond authorization requires such a collection.[xvii]

OO. Rhode Island

Other Bondholder Protections	**Special Revenue Bonds** As provided by Section 922(d) of the Bankruptcy Code, payments to bondholders holding special revenue bonds would not be stayed on the filing of a municipal bankruptcy petition, and payments to holders could continue. Whether an issuance would qualify as a special revenue bond depends on the provisions of the authorizing statute with respect to the bonds at issue.[xviii] **Statutory Liens** Were a municipal entity to file a petition under Chapter 9 of the Bankruptcy Code, bondholders holding bonds to which statutory liens have attached would continue to receive payment on those bonds. For a statutory lien to apply, the authorizing law of the bond issue must contain such a lien. Category SL-1. [xix] Rhode Island law also includes strong provisions requiring that payment of bond debt will have first priority of ad valorem and property tax revenues of a municipality over all other debt.

i R.I. GEN. LAWS § 45-9-7. The Rhode Island Depositors Economic Protection Corporation is specifically *not* authorized to become a debtor under Chapter 9. R.I. GEN. LAWS § 42-116-5(a)(6). Further, the Tobacco Settlement Financing Corporation is specifically not authorized to file a Chapter 9 petition until one year and one day after the date the corporation no longer has bonds outstanding. See endnote xix for a discussion of the strong measures that Rhode Island has provided to protect bondholders in the event of a Chapter 9 filing by one of its municipalities, such as the 2011 filing by the city of Central Falls. Because of these protections, the city's general obligation bondholders were not impaired by the Central Falls bankruptcy.

ii *See, e.g., Early Estates v. Housing Bd. of Review*, 174 A.2d 117, 119 (R.I. 1961) (finding city ordinance requiring property owner to provide hot water facilities exceeded the jurisdiction of the city because state's enabling statute had no express grant of such power).

iii R.I. CONST., art. XIII (Home Rule for Cities and Towns); R.I. GEN. LAWS § 44-5-1 (authorizing certain cities and towns to levy property taxes).

iv R.I. GEN. LAWS § 44-5-2.

v R.I. GEN. LAWS § 45-12-1.

vi The Rhode Island fiscal overseer, budget commission and municipal receiver debt default resolution mechanisms are similar to those provisions that have been adopted by the Commonwealth of Massachusetts on an ad hoc basis. Rhode Island, however, has chosen to codify such provisions rather than adopt them on an as-needed basis.

vii R.I. GEN. LAWS § 45-12-2.1.

viii R.I. GEN. LAWS § 45-12-2. Section 45-12-11 allows the state director of revenue, on petition by the local governing body, to authorize it to incur indebtedness above this ceiling.

ix R.I. GEN. LAWS § 45-9-3.

x R.I. GEN. LAWS §§ 45-9-5 to 45-9-6. The Rhode Island Director of Revenue has established a budget commission for the cities of Woonsocket and East Providence. *See* City of East Providence Budget Commission, http://eastprovidenceri.net/content/619/6362.aspx (last visited Sept. 23, 2013) *and* City of Woonsocket Budget Commission, http://www.ci.woonsocket.ri.us/budget.htm (last visited Sept. 23, 2013).

xi R.I. GEN. LAWS § 45-12-5.2 (allowing any political subdivision to issue refunding bonds); *see also* R.I. GEN. LAWS § 45-50-22 (allowing municipal public buildings authority to issue refunding bonds).

xii R.I. GEN. LAWS § 45-12-32.

xiii R.I. GEN. LAWS §§ 45-9-7 to 45-9-8. In July, 2010 a receiver was appointed to oversee the city of Central Falls. On the first day on the job, the receiver fired the city's mayor. *See Rhode Island City Overseer Starts by Firing Mayor,* http://www.reuters.com/article/idUSTRE66I58520100719 (last visited Sept. 23, 2013). On November 8, 2010, the state-appointed receiver fired the five members of the Central Falls council and replaced the council with a three-member advisory council. In the statement explaining the firing of the council, the receiver noted he fired the council because "several members of the City Council have chosen to continually obstruct our efforts to return fiscal stability to the city." Romy Varghese, *Receiver Replaces Elected Council of Rhode Island City,* Dow Jones News, http://www.advfn.com/news_Receiver-Replaces-Elected-Council-Of-Rhode-Island_45198246.html (last visited Mar. 20, 2015). Additionally, a receiver has been appointed over the Central Coventry Fire District.

R.I. GEN. LAWS § 45-9-13 provides that a city or town may not be the subject of a judicial receivership proceeding.

xiv *See, e.g.,* R.I. GEN. LAWS § 45-48.1-12 (allowing receiver on default of West Greenwich Water District bonds); R.I. GEN. LAWS § 45-33-13 (redevelopment bonds); and R.I. GEN. LAWS § 46-15.1-15 (water supply facilities bonds). The state code may be more expansive than the examples cited here and the statutory authority for each individual bond issuance should be reviewed before assessing whether a receiver may be appointed.

xv *See, e.g.,* R.I. GEN. LAWS § 45-33-13 (redevelopment bonds). The state code may be more expansive than the example cited here and the statutory authority for each individual bond issuance should be reviewed before assessing whether an action for accounting may be brought.

xvi *See, e.g.,* R.I. GEN. LAWS § 45-33-13 (redevelopment bonds). The state code may be more expansive than the example cited here and the statutory authority for each individual bond issuance should be reviewed before assessing whether bondholders may take possession of a project.

xvii *See, e.g.,* R.I. GEN. LAWS § 45-50-18 (revenue bonds for municipal public building authorities under which bondholders can enforce rights through any civil action, mandamus or other proceeding) and R.I. GEN. LAWS § 46-15.1-15 (water supply facilities bonds). It is possible that an aggrieved bondholder could pursue a writ of mandamus even absent authorizing statutory law.

xviii *See, e.g.,* R.I. GEN. LAWS § 45-50-18 (revenue bonds for municipal public building authorities). This is an example of a special revenue bond. The state code may be more expansive, and an attorney should be consulted to examine any specific situation involving a default.

xix Category SL-1: R.I. GEN. LAWS §§ 45-12-1 and 45-12-22.4. (The statute specifically states it is a statutory lien, a first lien and valid and binding against all other parties and was drafted with the intention that it would be a statutory lien with all the protection as to payment in bankruptcy that statutory liens have. See *supra* at 50.) This provision has been successfully applied in the bankruptcy proceeding of Central Falls, Rhode Island and general obligation bondholders received payment above other creditors. Indeed, the Central Falls plan of adjustment left unimpaired the city's general obligation bond issuances, meaning that general obligation bondholders will continue to receive full payment on their respective general obligation bonds. *See Fourth Amended Plan for the Adjustment of Debts of the City of Central Falls, Rhode Island, In re City of Central Falls, Rhode Island,* Case No. 11-13105 (Bankr. D. R.I. July 27, 2012).

PP. South Carolina

Municipal Bankruptcy Authority	Any county, municipal corporation, township, school district, drainage district or other taxing or governmental unit organized under the laws of the state may file a petition under Chapter 9 of the Bankruptcy Code. Unless an entity is specifically identified above, it is not authorized to file a municipal bankruptcy petition. Between 1980 and July 31, 2016, five entities have filed petitions in South Carolina, including a hospital district in 2014, on hospitals in June and one hospital in October 2011, a tollway in June 2010 and a regional transportation authority in 1988.[i]
Home Rule and Taxing Power of Municipalities	**Municipalities' Ability to Self-Govern** South Carolina is not a Dillon's Rule state.[ii] South Carolina law includes the Home Rule Act, which provides broad powers for home-rule municipalities. Pursuant to the South Carolina constitution, however, municipalities may not set aside general state laws addressing, among other things, the freedoms guaranteed to every person and bonded indebtedness of governmental units. In addition, municipalities and counties are granted the power to levy property taxes.[iii] **Tax Limitations** The South Carolina Constitution provides for the assessment value for the state and its subdivisions.[iv]
Debt Default Prevention	**Debt Limitation** Political subdivisions and school districts may not issue general obligation debt exceeding 8 percent of the assessed value of all taxable property therein.[v] **Refunding Bonds** In certain situations, a municipal entity may issue bonds to refund and refinance outstanding debt.[vi]
Mechanisms for Resolution after Default	**Receivership** In certain default situations, South Carolina law allows for the appointment of a receiver with respect to revenue bonds.[vii] **Treasury Withholding** If a political subdivision in South Carolina fails to make timely payment of the principal or interest due on any of its general obligation debt, the state Treasurer shall withhold from the political subdivision sufficient funds from any state appropriation to which the subdivision may be entitled and apply so much as shall be necessary to the payment of the political subdivision's bonded debt then due.[viii]

PP. South Carolina

Remedies on Default	**Accounting** In certain default situations, bondholders may bring a proceeding to require the authority in question to account as if it were a trustee of an express trust.[ix] **Foreclosure** In certain default situations generally involving special revenue bonds, bondholders may foreclose on any mortgage or deed of trust related to the project.[x] **Mandamus** In certain situations, bondholders or their trustee may bring a court action to compel the local governing body to perform a ministerial action that it has refused to undertake, such as collecting taxes or fees where the underlying bond authorization requires such a collection.[xi] **Any Appropriate Action** In certain situations, South Carolina law allows bondholders to enforce their rights by any proceeding in law or equity.[xii]
Other Bondholder Protections	**Special Revenue Bonds** As provided by Section 922(d) of the Bankruptcy Code, payments to bondholders holding special revenue bonds would not be stayed on the filing of a municipal bankruptcy petition, and payments to holders could continue. Whether an issuance would qualify as a special revenue bond depends on the provisions of the authorizing statute with respect to the bonds at issue.[xiii] **Statutory Liens** Were a municipal entity to file a petition under Chapter 9 of the Bankruptcy Code, bondholders holding bonds to which statutory liens have attached would continue to receive payment on those bonds. For a statutory lien to apply, the authorizing law of the bond issue must contain such a lien. Category SL-1.[xiv]

---

i S.C. CODE ANN. § 6-1-10.

ii S.C. CONST. art. VIII, § 17 ("The provisions of this Constitution and all laws concerning local government shall be liberally construed in their favor. Powers, duties, and responsibilities granted local government subdivisions by this Constitution and by law shall include those fairly implied and not prohibited by the Constitution."); *see also Williams v. Town of Hilton Head Island*, 311 S.C. 417, 422 (1993) (recognizing that the Home Rule Act abolished Dillon's Rule).

iii *See, e.g.*, S.C. CODE § 5-7 (general structure, organization, power, duties, functions and responsibilities of all municipalities); S.C. CODE § 4-9-30 (providing counties with ability to levy ad valorem property tax); S.C. CONST. art. VIII, § 14 (addressing what laws local governments may not pass).

iv S.C. CONST. art. X, § 1. For instance, a legal residence and not more than five contiguous acres surrounding the legal residence are taxed at an assessment equaling 4 percent of the fair market value of the property.

v S.C. CONST. art. X, § 14 ("Political subdivision" includes counties, incorporated municipalities and special purpose districts) and S.C. CONST. art. X, § 15 (school districts).

vi Examples of refunding bond provisions in South Carolina law include S.C. CODE ANN. § 6-17-30 ("any municipality may refinance and issue refunding bonds from time to time"); S.C. CODE ANN. § 6-17-90; and S.C. CODE ANN. § 6-17-110.

vii *See, e.g.*, S.C. CODE ANN. §§ 6-17-200 to 6-17-240 (applies to counties, townships, cities, incorporated towns or special purpose districts and allows for holders of 25 percent in principal amount of outstanding refunding bonds issued to refinance revenue bonds the ability to apply for appointment of a receiver for the enterprise in event of default, but receiver may not sell municipal assets); S.C. CODE ANN. § 6-21-360 (allows holders of bonds issued to finance construction of public infrastructure and utilities by counties, townships, cities, incorporated towns, school districts and other political subdivisions to apply for receiver in event of default to fix and charge rates and collect revenues sufficient for payment); S.C. CODE ANN. § 4-29-40 (industrial development bonds); and S.C. CODE ANN. § 44-7-1460 (bonds issued by hospitals, tuberculosis camps and health services districts). The state code may be more expansive and the statutory authority for each bond issuance should be reviewed before assessing whether a receiver may be appointed.

viii S.C. CONST. art. X, § 14, ¶ 5.

ix *See, e.g.*, S.C. CODE ANN. § 6-17-250 (special purpose districts refunding bonds). The state code may be more expansive than the example cited here, and the statutory authority for each individual bond issuance should be reviewed before assessing whether an action for accounting may be brought.

x *See, e.g.*, S.C. CODE ANN. § 4-29-40 (industrial development bonds). The state code may be more expansive than the example cited here, and the statutory authority for each individual bond issuance should be reviewed before assessing whether a foreclosure proceeding may be commenced.

xi S.C. CODE ANN. § 6-21-350 (applies to systems or projects financed by revenue bonds or utilities and allows for fixing of sufficient rates, the collection of revenues, proper segregation of revenues and the proper application of revenues); S.C. CODE ANN. § 49-19-2190 (holders of construction bonds issued by drainage districts may enforce by mandamus the obligation of the district to levy and collect an annual tax to pay bonds); S.C. CODE ANN. § 4-29-40 (revenue bonds issued by counties or other incorporated municipalities for industrial development projects); S.C. CODE ANN. § 5-21-490 (holders of bonds issued by cities and incorporated townships may bring mandamus action to require levying of taxes); S.C. CODE ANN. § 6-17-250 (special purpose districts refunding bonds); S.C. CODE ANN. § 59-119-580 (allowing mandamus to enforce revenue bonds issued by Clemson University); S.C. CODE ANN. § 59-125-420(17) (Winthrop University bonds); S.C. CODE ANN. § 59-125-640(18) (Winthrop University athletic facilities bonds); S.C. CODE ANN. § 5-21-490 (allowing mandamus related to general obligation bonds issued by municipal corporations); S.C. CODE ANN. § 5-21-800 (allowing mandamus for paving bonds); S.C. CODE ANN. § 6-21-350 (revenue bonds for utilities); and S.C. CODE ANN. § 59-117-320(17) (University of South Carolina bonds). It is possible that an aggrieved bondholder could pursue a writ of mandamus even absent authorizing statutory law.

xii *See, e.g.*, S.C. CODE ANN. § 6-23-180 (joint electrical power and energy agency bonds); S.C. CODE ANN. § 6-24-160 (joint agencies) and S.C. CODE ANN. § 6-25-127 (joint authority water and sewer). The state code may be more expansive and the statutory authority for each bond issuance should be reviewed before assessing whether such a remedy is applicable.

xiii *See, e.g.*, S.C. CODE ANN. §§ 6-25-113 and 6-25-125 (special obligation bonds for joint authority water sewer systems) and S.C. CODE ANN. § 49-19-2190 (construction bonds issued by drainage districts). These are examples of special revenue bonds. The state code may be more expansive, and an attorney should be consulted to examine any specific situation involving a default.

xiv Category SL-1: *See, e.g.*, S.C. CODE ANN. § 6-21-330 (statutory lien on systems or projects financed by revenue bonds for utilities); S.C. CODE ANN. § 59-125-420(17) (Winthrop University bonds statutory lien); and S.C. CODE ANN. § 59-125-640(18) (Winthrop University athletic facilities bonds statutory lien). The language appears to create a statutory lien, so further clarification or reaffirmation of the statutory lien status should not be needed. The language could be interpreted as reaffirming the special revenue status of the revenue bonds and providing an effective pledge without further action. However, the language could also be interpreted as attempting to create a statutory lien in addition to special revenue protection to avoid any charges against the pledged revenues with regard to "necessary operating expense" under Section 928(b) of the Bankruptcy Code given statutory lien status similar to *Sierra Kings Health Care* District case, *supra* at 144-145. The state code may be more expansive, and an attorney should be consulted to examine any specific situation involving a default.

QQ. South Dakota

Municipal Bankruptcy Authority	South Dakota does not specifically authorize its municipal entities to file a petition under Chapter 9 of the Bankruptcy Code. Between 1980 and July 31, 2016, no municipal entity in South Dakota has filed such a petition.[i]
Home Rule and Taxing Power of Municipalities	**Municipalities' Ability to Self-Govern** South Dakota courts perceive the state as a Dillon's Rule state.[ii] The South Dakota Constitution, however, authorizes the state legislature to vest with cities, towns and municipal corporations with corporate authority over their own affairs, including the ability to collect taxes. South Dakota statute provides municipalities with the fiscal authority, among other things, to levy property taxes.[iii] **Tax Limitations** Municipalities in South Dakota may levy a tax not exceeding $27 per $1,000 of taxable valuation. Counties in the state may levy a tax no more than $12 per $1,000 of taxable valuation of a property and townships may not exceed a levy of $3 per $1,000 of taxable valuation.[iv]
Debt Default Prevention	**Debt Limitation** A county, city, town or civil township shall never issue debt exceeding 5 percent of the assessed valuation of the taxable property therein for the year preceding that in which said indebtedness is incurred. A county, municipal corporation, civil township, district or other subdivision may incur additional indebtedness, not to exceed 10 percent of the assessed valuation of the taxable property, for purposes of providing water, irrigation, domestic uses, sewerage and other purposes. In addition, a city with a population of 8,000 or more may incur indebtedness not exceeding 8 percent of the assessed valuation of taxable property for constructing street railways, electric lights or other lighting plants.[v] **Refunding Bonds** In certain situations, a municipal entity may issue bonds to refund and refinance outstanding debt.[vi]
Mechanisms for Resolution after Default	**Receivership** In certain default situations, South Dakota law allows for the appointment of a receiver with respect to revenue bonds.[vii]
Remedies on Default	**Mandamus** In certain situations, bondholders may bring an action to compel the local governing body to perform a ministerial action that it has refused to undertake, such as collecting taxes or fees where the underlying bond authorization requires such a collection.[viii]

QQ. South Dakota

Other Bondholder Protections	**Special Revenue Bonds** As provided by Section 922(d) of the Bankruptcy Code, payments to bondholders holding special revenue bonds would not be stayed on the filing of a municipal bankruptcy petition, and payments to holders could continue. Whether an issuance would qualify as a special revenue bond depends on the provisions of the authorizing statute with respect to the bonds at issue.[ix] **Statutory Liens** Were a municipal entity to file a petition under Chapter 9 of the Bankruptcy Code, bondholders holding bonds to which statutory liens have attached would continue to receive payment on those bonds. For a statutory lien to apply, the authorizing law of the bond issue must contain such a lien. Category SL-2.[x]

---

i The South Dakota Code provides that the following are *not* subject to the jurisdiction of the bankruptcy courts: the Health and Educational Facilities Authority; all school districts; and other public bodies and all officers or departments of the state dealing with the state or the authority pursuant to §§ 1-16A-19, 1-16A-74 to 1-16A-76, inclusive, and 13-19-1.2. S.D. CODIFIED LAWS 1-16A-76.

ii *Olesen v. Town of Hurley*, 691 N.W.2d 324, 328-29 (S.D. 2004) (noting application of Dillon's Rule and that: "Historically, South Dakota cases which have considered the scope of a City's implied powers have applied a reasonably strict standard.").

iii S.D. CONST. art. XI, § 10; S.D. CODIFIED LAWS § 9-12-2.

iv S.D. CODIFIED LAWS § 10-12-32 (municipalities); S.D. CODIFIED LAWS § 10-12-21 (counties); S.D. CODIFIED LAWS § 10-12-28 (townships).

v S.D. CONST. art. XIII, § 4.

vi Examples of refunding bond provisions in South Dakota law include S.D. CODIFIED LAWS § 6-8B-30 (any public body, including a county, municipality, township, school district, hospital district, sanitary district, irrigation district, drainage district, water user district or improvement district may issue refunding bonds); and S.D. CODIFIED LAWS § 8-11-4 (civil townships may issue refunding bonds). With respect to bonds issued by civil townships, if a judgment has been recovered against a defaulted bond issued by the township, the township governing body may issue a refunding bond to the judgment creditor in exchange for release of the judgment.

vii *See, e.g.*, S.D. CODIFIED LAWS § 9-40-33 (allowing for appointment of a receiver on default of a utility where default lasts longer than three months); S.D. CODIFIED LAWS § 9-52-27 (allowing for appointment of a receiver on default of a municipal auditorium where default lasts longer than three months); S.D. CODIFIED LAWS § 49-39-10 (allowing for appointment of a receiver on default of bonds issued by consumer power districts); and S.D. CODIFIED LAWS § 50-8-13 (allowing for appointment of a receiver on default of an airport where default lasts longer than three months). The state code may be more expansive and the statutory authority for each bond issuance should be reviewed before assessing whether a receiver may be appointed.

viii *See Minnehaha Nat'l Bank v. Toohey*, 39 S.D. 551 (S.D. 1917) (issuing writ of mandamus to compel ex officio treasurer of independent school district to honor and pay warrant in payment for certain federal bonds). It is possible that an aggrieved bondholder could pursue a writ of mandamus even absent authorizing statutory law.

ix *See, e.g.*, S.D. CODIFIED LAWS § 9-38-64 (swimming pool revenue bonds payable solely from gross revenues). Note that this is an example of a special revenue bond. The state code may be more expansive, and an attorney should be consulted to examine any specific default situation.

x Category SL-2: *See, e.g.*, S.D. CODIFIED LAWS § 9-52-15 (statutory mortgage lien for mortgage auditorium) and S.D. CODIFIED LAWS §§ 9-40-25 and 9-40-26 (utilities, sewage, drainage, waterworks and flood control system statutory mortgage liens). These are examples of statutory liens. While the language of the statute may appear to create a statutory lien, further clarification or reaffirmation would be helpful to assure that a statutory lien was intended by the legislation or an opinion of counsel to that effect as opposed to being interpreted as reaffirming special revenue status of the revenue bonds and providing an effective pledge without further acts. However, the language could also be interpreted as attempting to create a statutory lien in addition to the special revenue protection to avoid any charges against the pledged revenues with regard to "necessary operating expenses" under Section 928(b) of the Bankruptcy Code given the statutory lien status similar to the *Sierra Kings Health Care* District case, *supra* at 144-145. The state code may be more expansive, and an attorney should be consulted to examine any specific situation involving a default.

RR. Tennessee

Municipal Bankruptcy Authority	Tennessee does not specifically authorize its municipal entities to file a petition under Chapter 9 of the Bankruptcy Code. Despite this lack of authorization, between 1980 and July 31, 2016, six municipal entities have filed Chapter 9 petitions in Tennessee. Four of the petitions were filed before Congress in 1994 amended the municipal bankruptcy laws to require specific state authorization as a prerequisite to a municipal bankruptcy petition. One petition was filed in 1994 and dismissed in 1995; another petition was filed in 1997, and the municipality's plan of adjustment was confirmed in 1998. This plan likely was confirmed because no party objected to the filing of the municipality's petition.[i]
Home Rule and Taxing Power of Municipalities	**Municipalities' Ability to Self-Govern** Dillon's Rule only applies to non-home-rule municipalities in Tennessee.[ii] Specifically, the Tennessee Constitution includes provisions allowing municipalities to adopt home-rule charters and, if a municipality adopts such a charter, the state constitution provides that the state legislature may only act with respect to the home-rule municipality by laws that are of general term and effect.[iii] The state constitution also provides the state legislature with the authority to grant counties and incorporated towns in the state the right to tax.[iv] **Tax Limitation** Tennessee law includes no taxing authority limitations.
Debt Default Prevention	**Debt Limitation** Tennessee law does not impose any debt limitation on its units of local government.[v] **Emergency Financial Aid to Local Governments** To provide emergency technical and financial assistance to a local government, the state funding board may guaranty payment of a loan by another lender if (1) a majority of the local government's legislative body has requested a guarantee; (2) the local government agrees to accept emergency technical assistance and to be bound by the decision of the comptroller of the treasury; (3) the state funding board has determined the local government's revenues are insufficient to pay annual debt service and costs of operation; and (4) the local government submits a plan for the efficient operations of government services.[vi] **Financially Distressed Municipality Procedures** The state comptroller is tasked with developing and recommending procedures to identify, restructure and remedy financially distressed municipalities.[vii]

RR. Tennessee

Debt Default Prevention *continued*	**Refunding Bonds** In certain situations, a municipal entity may issue bonds to refund and refinance outstanding debt.[viii] **State Budget Supervision** If a local government issues bond anticipation notes, capital outlay notes, grant anticipation notes or tax anticipation notes, it must submit its annual budget to the state comptroller for approval.[ix]
Mechanisms for Resolution after Default	**Receivership** In certain default situations, Tennessee law allows for the appointment of a receiver with respect to revenue bonds.[x]
Remedies on Default	**Accounting** In certain default situations, bondholders may bring a proceeding to require the authority in question to account as if it were a trustee of an express trust.[xi] **Mandamus** In certain situations, bondholders or their trustee may bring an action to compel the local governing body to perform a ministerial act that it has refused to undertake, such as collecting taxes or fees where the underlying bond authorization requires.[xii]
Other Bondholder Protections	**Special Revenue Bonds** As provided by Section 922(d) of the Bankruptcy Code, payments to bondholders holding special revenue bonds would not be stayed on the filing of a municipal bankruptcy petition, and payments to holders could continue. Whether an issuance would qualify as a special revenue bond depends on the provisions of the authorizing statute with respect to the bonds at issue.[xiii] **Statutory Liens** Were a municipal entity to file a petition under Chapter 9 of the Bankruptcy Code, bondholders holding bonds to which statutory liens have attached would continue to receive payment on those bonds. For a statutory lien to apply, the authorizing law of the bond issue must contain such a lien. Category SL-2 or SL-3. [xiv]

i *See In re Mercer Utility District of Madison County*, Case No. 97-11261 (Bankr. W.D. Tenn.) (plan confirmed Feb. 23, 1998).

ii *Allmand v. Pavletic*, 292 S.W.3d 618, 625 (Tenn. 2009) ("Fundamental in [Tennessee] law is that municipalities may exercise only those express or necessarily implied powers delegated to them by the Legislature in their charters or under statutes.").

iii TENN. CONST. art. XI, § 9.

iv TENN. CONST. art. II, § 29.

v *See* TENN. CODE ANN. § 9-21-103.

vi TENN. CODE ANN. §§ 9-13-201 to 9-13-212. "Local government" is defined as any incorporated city or town, metropolitan government or county, including enterprise funds of such government entity, or utility district. TENN. CODE ANN. § 9-13-203(4).

vii TENN. CODE ANN. § 9-13-302 (the Financially Distressed Municipalities, Counties, Utility Districts, and Education Agencies Act of 1993).

viii An example of a refunding bond provision in Tennessee law is TENN. CODE ANN. §§ 9-21-901 to 9-21-908 (any local government may issue general obligation refunding bonds, but a plan for refunding must first be submitted to the state director of local finance).

ix TENN. CODE ANN. §§ 9-21-401, 9-21-403.

x *See, e.g.,* TENN. CODE ANN. §§ 9-21-311 to 9-21-315 (any county, municipality or metropolitan government). Sections 9-21-311 through 9-21-315 provide that where a payment default has continued for 30 days or more, if 25 percent or more of bondholders so petition, a receiver must be appointed to act under the supervision of the court. The receiver may enter and take possession of the public works project; operate, manage and control the project in the name of the government; exercise all powers of the local government with respect to the project; maintain, restore and keep the project insured; establish, levy and collect fees on the project, subject to court control; and deposit the revenues in a separate account. *See also* TENN. CODE §§ 69-5-929 to 69-5-930 (drainage and levy districts; allowing for a receiver if a bond is past due for two years and payment has been demanded). The state code may be more expansive and the statutory authority for each bond issuance should be reviewed before assessing whether a receiver may be appointed.

xi *See, e.g.,* TENN. CODE ANN. § 9-21-310 (allowing revenue bondholders to bring an action requiring local government to account as if it were a trustee). The state code may be more expansive than the example cited here, and the statutory authority for each individual bond issuance should be reviewed before assessing whether an action for an accounting may be brought.

xii *See, e.g.,* TENN. CODE ANN. § 5-1-107 (the performance of any duty made incumbent by law on a county may be enforced by mandamus); TENN. CODE ANN. § 9-21-216 (allowing general obligation bondholders to enforce obligations by mandamus, including compelling local government to levy and collect taxes); TENN. CODE ANN. § 9-21-916 (allowing general obligation refunding bondholders to enforce obligations by mandamus, including compelling local government to levy and collect taxes); TENN. CODE ANN. § 9-21-310 (allowing revenue bondholders to enforce their rights against local governments by mandamus); and TENN. CODE ANN. §§ 9-21-40, 216 (holders of notes issued by local government may enforce their rights by mandamus). It is possible that an aggrieved bondholder could pursue a writ of mandamus even absent authorizing statutory law.

xiii *See, e.g.,* TENN. CODE ANN. § 5-1-107 (the performance of any duty made incumbent by law on a county may be enforced by mandamus); TENN. CODE ANN. § 9-21-214 (allowing general obligation bondholders to enforce obligations by mandamus, including compelling local government to levy and collect taxes); TENN. CODE ANN. § 9-21-916 (allowing general obligation refunding bondholders to enforce obligations by mandamus, including compelling local government to levy and collect taxes); TENN. CODE ANN. § 9-21-310 (allowing revenue bondholders to enforce their rights against local governments by mandamus); and TENN. CODE ANN. § 9-21-407 (holders of notes issued by local government may enforce their rights by mandamus). It is possible that an aggrieved bondholder could pursue a writ of mandamus even absent authorizing statutory law.

xiv Category SL-2 or SL-3: *See, e.g.,* TENN. CODE ANN. § 9-22-104 (establishing pledge or lien on collateral by an issuer) and TENN. CODE ANN. § 9-21-125 (establishing immediate lien on revenues, fees, rents, tolls or other charges received by local government to secure payment on bonds). *See also* TENN. CODE ANN. § 9-22-104 (a pledge of or lien created by an issuer of bonds shall be valid and binding from the time of the pledge and inure to the benefit of the holders of the public obligation and no further action, notice or filing is necessary to preserve and protect the validity and priority of such pledge). TENN. CODE ANN. § 9-22-104 (contains a definition of issuer and collateral). The language of these statutes may appear to create a statutory lien, but further clarification or opinion of counsel would be helpful to reaffirm the intent to create a statutory lien. The state code may be more expansive, and an attorney should be consulted to examine any specific situation involving a default.

SS. Texas

Municipal Bankruptcy Authority	In Texas, the following entities may file a petition under Chapter 9 of the Bankruptcy Code: (i) a municipality if it has the power to incur indebtedness through the action of its governing body and (ii) a taxing district or other political subdivision if it has the power to incur indebtedness through the action of either its governing body or the county or municipality in which it is located. Unless an entity is specifically identified above, it is not authorized to file a municipal bankruptcy petition. Texas law, further, specifically prevents general law water districts from filing a petition until authorized by a commission. Between 1980 and July 31, 2016, 38 municipal bankruptcy petitions have been filed in Texas. Of those entities, 20 were utility districts; seven were towns or cities; six were hospital districts; two were special municipal districts; and three were transportation districts.[i]
Home Rule and Taxing Power of Municipalities	**Municipalities' Ability to Self-Govern** Texas is a Dillon's Rule state. The Texas Constitution includes provisions for cities of more than 5,000 to adopt home-rule charters.[ii] **Tax Limitations** A city with a home-rule charter may levy, assess and collect taxes, but the tax may not be higher than 2.5 percent of the taxable property in the city. Cities and towns with populations of 5,000 or less may not assess a tax exceeding 1.5 percent of the taxable property in the city or town and may be subject to additional limits depending on the use of collected taxes. Counties are also permitted to collect ad valorem property taxes, but subject to certain limits.[iii]
Debt Default Prevention	**Debt Limitation** A city with a population over 5,000 may not incur debt unless, at the same time, the city makes provisions to collect a sufficient sum yearly to pay the interest on the debt.[iv] **Refunding Bonds** In certain situations, a municipal entity may issue refunding bonds to refund and refinance outstanding debt.[v]
Mechanisms for Resolution after Default	**Municipal Receivership** In certain situations, a type-A general-law municipality may apply to a court to have a receiver appointed over its affairs. A type-A general-law municipality is a municipality with more than 600 inhabitants that has been incorporated as a type-A general-law municipality.[vi]

SS. Texas

Mechanisms for Resolution after Default *continued*	**Receivership** In certain default situations, Texas law allows for the appointment of a receiver with respect to revenue bonds.[vii]
Remedies on Default	**Foreclosure** In certain default situations, Texas law allows for foreclosure with respect to a municipal entity's property.[viii] **Mandamus** In certain situations, bondholders or their trustee may bring a court action to compel the local governing body to perform a ministerial action that it has refused to undertake, such as collecting taxes or fees where the underlying bond authorization requires such a collection.[ix]
Other Bondholder Protections	**Special Revenue Bonds** As provided by Section 922(d) of the Bankruptcy Code, payments to bondholders holding special revenue bonds would not be stayed on the filing of a municipal bankruptcy petition, and payments to holders could continue. Whether an issuance would qualify as a special revenue bond depends on the provisions of the authorizing statute with respect to the bonds at issue.[x] **Statutory Liens** Were a municipal entity to file a petition under Chapter 9 of the Bankruptcy Code, bondholders holding bonds to which statutory liens have attached would continue to receive payment on those bonds. For a statutory lien to apply, the authorizing law of the bond issue must contain such a lien. Category SL-3.[xi]

---

i TEX. LOC. GOV'T CODE § 140.001. Although Texas law does not provide specific examples of the types of municipal entities eligible to file a Chapter 9 petition, bankruptcy courts in Texas have entertained petitions from utility districts (*Roman Forest Public Utility District No. 4*, 00-30662 (Bankr. S.D. Tex.)); hospitals (*Chambers County Hospital*, 00-80240 (Bankr. S.D. Tex.)); cities and towns (*City of Rio Bravo*, 02-50287 (Bankr. S.D. Tex.)); flood control districts (*Northwest Dallas County, Flood Control District*, 92-31469 (Bankr. N.D. Tex.)); road districts (*Southwest Williamson County Road District No. 1*, 92-12274 (Bankr. W.D. Tex.)); and development corporations (*Retama Dev'p Corp.*, 96-51115 (Bankr. W.D. Tex.)). The most recent municipal bankruptcy filing in Texas was by the Hardeman County Hospital District on March 21, 2013.

See also TEX. WATER CODE § 49.456 (addressing general law water districts). Under this provision, a general-law water district may not file a petition unless a commission determines that the district cannot, through the full exercise of its rights and powers, reasonably expect to meet its debts and other obligations as they mature. In 2008, for instance, the Engelman Irrigation District sought authorization to file a bankruptcy petition and was denied by the Texas Commission on Environmental Quality. The irrigation district sued the commission to gain a reversal of its decision, but the district court affirmed its decision. The appellate court gave significant deference to the commission's findings and upheld the district court. *Engelman Irrigation Dist. v. Tex. Comm.*, 251 S.W.3d 184 (Tex. App. 2008).

ii *See Texas River Barges v. City of San Antonio,* 21 S.W.3d 347, 352 (Tex. App. 2000) ("A home rule city has all the powers of the state not inconsistent with the Texas Constitution, the general laws or the city's charter.").

iii TEX. CONST. art. XI, § 5 (home-rule cities); TEX. CONST. art. XI, § 4 (cities and towns with fewer than 5,000 people); TEX. CONST. art. VIII, § 9 (additional maximum levy of 80 cents on the $100 valuation in any one year for counties, cities and towns for general fund, permanent road improvement fund, road and bridge fund and jury fund purposes); TEX. CONST. art. VIII, § 1-a (counties not to exceed 30 cents on each $100 valuation, and the revenues must be used for the construction and maintenance of certain roads and flood control).

iv TEX. CONST. art. XI, § 5.

v *See San Antonio Union Junior College Dist. v. Daniel,* 206 S.W.2d 995 (Tex. 1947) ("[T]he Legislature has several times bestowed upon municipal corporations the power to issue refunding bonds."). An example of a refunding bond provision in Texas law is TEX. LOC. GOV'T CODE §§ 1207.001-1207.084 (refunding bonds).

vi *See, e.g.,* TEX. LOC. GOV'T CODE § 101.006. If a municipality is unable to compromise its debts or pending a compromise negotiation, the municipality may apply to the district court in the county in which it is located to have a receiver appointed. The court may only appoint a receiver on voluntary application of the municipality. The court will then decide questions of priorities between claimants and provide for ratable and equitable distribution of funds among all of the municipality's creditors entitled to the funds. *See also* TEX. LOC. GOV'T CODE § 6.001 (definition of type-A general-law municipality).

In 1885 the town of Lampasas requested a voluntary receivership with respect to failed discussions on waterworks bonds the town issued. The court appointed a receiver and authorized him to collect a 25-cent tax, as allowed by the state constitution. A.M. Hillhouse, 98 MUNICIPAL BONDS: A CENTURY OF EXPERIENCE (New York: Prentice-Hall 1936).

vii *See, e.g.,* TEX. LOC. GOV'T CODE § 601.034 (municipal parking authorities). The state code may be more expansive and the statutory authority for each individual bond issuance should be reviewed before assessing whether a receiver may be appointed.

viii In the 1885 situation involving Lampasas, the bondholders also brought a suit in equity to foreclose a lien on public buildings in the town. A.M. Hillhouse, 98 MUNICIPAL BONDS: A CENTURY OF EXPERIENCE (New York: Prentice-Hall 1936).

ix *See, e.g.,* TEX. LOC. GOV'T CODE § 601.034 (municipal parking authorities); TEX. AGR. CODE § 58.036 (Texas Agricultural Finance Authority); TEX. WATER CODE § 54.518 (municipal utility districts); and TEX. TRANSP. CODE § 441.177 (road utility districts). It is possible that an aggrieved bondholder could pursue a writ of mandamus even absent authorizing statutory law.

x *See, e.g.,* TEX. AGRIC. CODE § 58.033 (revenue bonds issued by agricultural finance authority secured by lien on property, revenues, income or other resources of the authority). Note that this is an example of a special revenue bond. The state code may be more expansive, and an attorney should be consulted to examine any specific situation involving a default.

xi Category SL-3: *See, e.g.,* TEX. LOC. GOV'T CODE §§ 1202.006 (Validity and Incontestability of Pledges) and 1208.002 (Pledged Security), which appear to deal with the effectiveness of a pledge as opposed to creation of a statutory lien, even though some of the language could be read to create a lien pursuant to statute. Clarification would be helpful as to whether language requires further perfection or an intent to create a statutory lien. *See, e.g.,* TEX. LOC. GOV'T CODE § 552.049 (income of a drainage utility system must be segregated and cannot be transferred to municipal general fund). No statutory lien appears to have been created. Further legislation or opinion of counsel clarification would be helpful. *See also,* TEX. EDUC. CODE § 45.001 *et seq.* (providing for voter-approved tax revenues to be levied so a county or municipality can issue bonds payable from ad valorem taxes). Again, further classification or opinion of counsel would be helpful to determine or reaffirm whether a statutory lien was intended. The state code may be more expansive, and an attorney should be consulted to examine any specific situation involving a default.

TT. Utah

Municipal Bankruptcy Authority	Utah does not specifically authorize its municipal entities to file a petition under Chapter 9 of the Bankruptcy Code. Between 1980 and July 31, 2016, only one municipal entity in Utah has filed a municipal bankruptcy petition. In the case, involving a mental health district, the court confirmed the plan of adjustment in July 1991. This was previous to Congress in 1994 amending the municipal bankruptcy laws to require specific authorization as a prerequisite to a municipal bankruptcy petition.
Home Rule and Taxing Power of Municipalities	**Municipalities' Ability to Self-Govern** Utah is not a Dillon's Rule state.[i] The Utah Constitution permits cities to adopt a home-rule charter with the authority to exercise all powers relating to municipal affairs, including the power to levy taxes and borrow money.[ii] **Tax Limitations** Ad valorem taxing limitations apply to counties, cities and towns in Utah. For cities and towns, an exception to the limit applies to taxes raised for payments on general obligation bonds.[iii]
Debt Default Prevention	**Debt Limitation** A county, city, town, school district or other political subdivision may not issue debt payable from and secured by property taxes in excess of the taxes for the current year without voter approval. On voter approval, no county may incur debt exceeding 2 percent of the value of the taxable property in the county; and no city, town, school district or other municipal corporation may become indebted exceeding 4 percent of the value of taxable property therein. A city of the first or second class, however, may incur additional debt not exceeding 4 percent, and any other city or town not exceeding 8 percent, for supplying water, artificial lights or sewers, if the works for supplying the water, light and sewers are owned and controlled by the municipality.[iv] **Refunding Bonds** In certain situations, a municipal entity may issue refunding bonds to refund and refinance outstanding debt.[v]
Mechanisms for Resolution after Default	**Receivership** In certain default situations, Utah law allows for the appointment of a receiver with respect to revenue bonds.[vi]

TT. Utah

Remedies on Default	**Contractual Remedies** In certain situations, the bond issuance may outline the rights and remedies available to bondholders on issuance.[vii] **Mandamus – Preferred Cause** If a local political subdivision neglects or fails to levy or collect sufficient taxes for prompt and punctual payment of the principal and interest on the subdivision's bonds, any person with an interest may enforce the levy and collect in any court having jurisdiction. The suit shall be a preferred cause and heard and disposed of without delay. In these situations, bondholders or their trustee may bring a court action to compel the local governing body to perform a ministerial action that it has refused to undertake.[viii]
Other Bondholder Protections	**Special Revenue Bonds** As provided by § 922(d) of the Bankruptcy Code, payments to bondholders holding special revenue bonds would not be stayed on the filing of a municipal bankruptcy petition and payments to holders could continue. Whether an issuance would qualify as a special revenue bond depends on the provisions of the authorizing statute with respect to the bonds at issue.[ix] **Statutory Liens** Were a municipal entity to file a petition under Chapter 9 of the Bankruptcy Code, bondholders holding bonds to which statutory liens have attached would continue to receive payment on those bonds. For a statutory lien to apply, the authorizing law of the bond issue must contain such a lien. Category SL-3.[x]

i *Price Dev. Co., L.P. v. Orem City*, 995 P.2d 1237, 1245 (Utah 2000) (noting that Dillon's Rule has been rejected in the state). For a lengthy discussion on the reasons the Utah Supreme Court rejected Dillon's rule, *see State v. Hutchinson*, 624 P.2d 1116 (Utah 1980).

ii UTAH CONST. art XI, § 5.

iii A county with a total taxable value exceeding $100 million may not assess more than .0032 per dollar of taxable value in ad valorem taxes each year; and a county with a total taxable value less than $100 million may not assess a tax exceeding .0036 per dollar of taxable value. UTAH CODE ANN. § 59-2-908 (county taxation limits). A city or town may not assess more than .007 per dollar for all purposes, with exception to payments on general obligation bonds. UTAH CODE ANN. § 10-6-133 (cities); UTAH CODE ANN. § 10-5-112 (towns). *See also* UTAH CODE ANN. § 10-7-14.2 (taxation for sewer system not to exceed .0008 per dollar of taxable value of taxable property in the municipality).

iv UTAH CONST. art XIV, § 3. A city of the first class is a municipality with 100,000 people or more. A city of the second class is a city with a population of 65,000 or more, but less than 100,000. UTAH CODE ANN. §§ 10-2-301.

v Examples of refunding bond provisions under Utah law include UTAH CODE ANN. §§ 11-27-1 to 11-27-10 (refunding bonds for the state or any agency, authority, instrumentality or institution of the state, or any municipal or quasi-municipal corporation, political subdivision, agency, school district, special district or other state governmental entity) and UTAH CODE ANN. § 53A-18-103 (refunding bonds for consolidated school districts). *See also* UTAH CODE ANN. § 11-14-309 (disallowing local governments from refunding bonds unless the right to call the bonds for redemption was specifically reserved and stated on the bonds, and disallowing any local political subdivision from calling outstanding bonds for redemption in order to refund those bonds).

vi *See, e.g.,* UTAH CODE ANN. § 17D-2-503 (allowing appointment of a receiver on default of Local Building Authority Act bonds with power to rent the property, charge and collect rent, and apply project revenue in accordance with bond proceedings) and UTAH CODE ANN. § 11-14-306 (allowing receiver on revenue bond projects issued by a city, county or local taxing district). The state code may be more expansive and the statutory authority for each individual bond issuance should be reviewed before assessing whether a receiver may be appointed.

vii *See, e.g.,* UTAH CODE ANN. § 11-17-5 (industrial facilities and development bonds of cities, counties and taxing units) and UTAH CODE ANN. § 11-14-306 (Local Government Bonding Act bonds issued by cities, counties and local taxing districts). The state code may be more expansive and the statutory authority for each bond issuance should be reviewed before assessing available remedies.

viii UTAH CODE ANN. § 11-14-310 (local government general obligation bonds). With respect to a general mandamus proceeding, it is possible that an aggrieved bondholder could pursue a writ of mandamus even absent authorizing statutory law.

ix *See, e.g.,* UTAH CODE ANN. § 17B-1-1104 (revenue bonds for special purpose districts). Note that this is an example of a special revenue bond. The state code may be more expansive, and an attorney should be consulted to examine any specific situation involving a default.

x Category SL-3: *See* UTAH CODE ANN. § 11-14-501, which provides for the creation and perfection of a government security interest. The language provides that a pledge of revenues or property to secure payment of its bonds is immediately subject to the lien of the pledge, no further act is required, and the lien is valid and binding with the priority of the time of creation and is effective until such bonds are paid. While the language of this statute may appear to create a statutory lien, this section appears to be drafted to provide for the effectiveness and priority of the lien as an exemption from the Uniform Commercial Code. Further legislative clarification of the intent or reaffirmation of the statutory lien would be helpful.

UU. Vermont

Municipal Bankruptcy Authority	Vermont does not specifically authorize its municipal entities to file a petition under Chapter 9 of the Bankruptcy Code. Between 1980 and July 31, 2016, no municipal entity in Vermont has filed such a petition.
Home Rule and Taxing Power of Municipalities	**Municipalities' Ability to Self-Govern** Vermont is a Dillon's Rule state.[i] Citizens of municipalities may approve home-rule charters, but the state legislature must approve the charter before it becomes effective.[ii] The Vermont Code allows counties and incorporated villages to tax.[iii] **Tax Limitations** Vermont state law does not include any taxing authority limitations.
Debt Default Prevention	**Debt Limitation** A municipal corporation may not incur indebtedness for public improvements exceeding 10 times the amount of the last grand list of the municipal corporation.[iv] **Refunding Bonds** In certain situations, a municipal entity may issue refunding bonds to refund and refinance outstanding debt.[v]
Mechanisms for Resolution after Default	**Receivership** In certain default situations, Vermont law allows for the appointment of a receiver with respect to revenue bonds.[vi]
Remedies on Default[vii]	**Foreclosure** In certain default situations, Vermont law allows for foreclosure with respect to a municipal entity's property.[viii] **Mandamus** In certain situations, bondholders or their trustee may bring a court action to compel the local governing body to perform a ministerial action that it has refused to undertake, such as collecting taxes or fees where the underlying bond authorization requires such a collection.[ix]
Other Bondholder Protections	**Special Revenue Bonds** As provided by Section 922(d) of the Bankruptcy Code, payments to bondholders holding special revenue bonds would not be stayed on the filing of a municipal bankruptcy petition, and payments to holders could continue. Whether an issuance would qualify as a special revenue bond depends on the provisions of the authorizing statute with respect to the bonds at issue.[x]

UU. Vermont

Other Bondholder Protections *continued*	**Statutory Liens** Were a municipal entity to file a petition under Chapter 9 of the Bankruptcy Code, bondholders holding bonds to which statutory liens have attached would continue to receive payment on those bonds. For a statutory lien to apply, the authorizing law of the bond issue must contain such a lien. Category SL-3.[xi]

---

i For the application of Dillon's Rule in Vermont, *see City of Montpelier v. Barnett*, 49 A.3d 120, 123, 129 (Vt. 2012) ("Although we are sympathetic to the City's significant concern for regulating the source of its drinking water, the City's powers are limited to those conferred upon it by the State of Vermont.").

ii 17 VT. STAT. ANN. § 2645.

iii 24 VT. STAT. ANN. § 133 (counties) and § 1309 (incorporated villages).

iv VT. STAT. ANN. tit. 24, § 1762. "Municipal corporation" includes any city, town, village, town school district, graded school district or other incorporated, union or unified school district or any entity providing educational services; a fire district; a union municipal district; a regional mass transportation authority; a local housing authority; a consolidated water or sewer district; or the unified towns and gores of Essex County. VT. STAT. ANN. tit. 24, § 1751 (definitions).

v An example of a refunding bond provision under Vermont law is 24 VT. STAT. ANN. tit. 24, § 1771 (a municipal corporation that has outstanding and unpaid orders, notes, bonds or coupons, lawfully issued, may issue other negotiable notes or bonds to pay or retire the same). Under § 1771, a municipal corporation includes any city, town, village, town school district, graded school district or other incorporated, union or unified school district or any entity providing educational services that is eligible to receive state aid; a fire district; a union municipal district created under an intermunicipal agreement; a regional mass transportation authority; a local housing authority; or a consolidated water or sewer district. *See also* VT. STAT. ANN. tit. 24, § 3684 (sewer district refunding bonds).

vi VT. STAT. tit. 24, § 1827 (allowing for appointment of receiver of public utility system of a municipal corporation to operate the utility system and collect and receive all revenues arising therefrom); VT. STAT. ANN. tit. 24, § 1871 (allowing for appointment of receiver for parking lots and meters to operate system and collect and receive all revenues arising therefrom); and VT. STAT. ANN. tit. 24, § 4018 (allowing for appointment of a receiver for housing projects of housing authorities). The state code may be more expansive and the statutory authority for each bond issuance should be reviewed before assessing whether a receiver may be appointed.

vii Vermont traditionally has had strong protections for bondholders. In or around 1936, Vermont was one of five states allowing creditors of a defaulted municipality, after receiving judgment, to secure levy and execution against private persons or corporations within the limits of the defaulting governmental unit. A.M. Hillhouse, 277 MUNICIPAL BONDS: A CENTURY OF EXPERIENCE (New York: Prentice-Hall 1936).

viii *See, e.g.*, VT. STAT. ANN. tit. 24, § 4016 (allowing housing authority to mortgage any or all of its real or personal property). The state code may be more expansive than the example cited here, and the statutory authority for each individual bond issuance should be reviewed before assessing available rights and remedies.

ix *See, e.g.*, VT. STAT. ANN. tit. 24, § 1868 (holders of parking lot and meter bonds may have the right by extraordinary relief or other suit enforce their rights); VT. STAT. ANN. tit. 24, § 1828 (public utilities); and VT. STAT. ANN. tit. 24, § 1870 (municipal and county governments). It is possible that an aggrieved bondholder could pursue a writ of mandamus even absent authorizing statutory law.

x *See, e.g.*, VT. STAT. ANN. tit. 24, § 4016 (housing authority may pledge gross or net rents, fees or revenues and mortgage all or any of its real or personal property). Note that this is an example of a special revenue bond. The state code may be more expansive, and an attorney should be consulted to examine any specific situation involving a default.

xi Category SL-3: *See, e.g.*, VT. STAT. ANN. tit. § 1822 (a municipal utility may pledge or assign net revenues to secured bonds and the municipal corporation is immediately subject to the lien). While the language of the statute may appear to create a lien, further clarification would help to assure the legislative intent. The statute could be interpreted as providing for the effectiveness and perfection of the lien on revenue and property without the need of further action. The state code may be more expansive, and an attorney should be consulted to examine any specific situation involving a default.

VV. Virginia

Municipal Bankruptcy Authority	Virginia does not specifically authorize its municipal entities to file a petition under Chapter 9 of the Bankruptcy Code. Between 1980 and July 31, 2016, only one entity in Virginia, an economic development authority in 2001, has attempted to file such a petition. The case was dismissed on November 8, 2001.
Home Rule and Taxing Power of Municipalities	**Municipalities' Ability to Self-Govern** Virginia is a Dillon's Rule state.[i] The Virginia Constitution permits the state legislature to provide for general law optional plans of governments for counties, cities or towns and to pass provisions allowing local governments to tax.[ii] The Virginia state code allows cities and towns to levy taxes on property, persons and other subjects of taxation, such sums of money necessary to pay the debts, defray the expenses, accomplish the purposes and perform the functions of the municipal corporation, in such manner as the municipal corporation deems necessary or expedient.[iii] **Tax Limitations** Virginia state law does not include any taxing authority limitations.
Debt Default Prevention	**Debt Limitation** A city or town may not incur debt exceeding 10 percent of the assessed valuation of the property therein that is subject to taxation. A county may, on voter approval, elect to be treated as a city for the purpose of the debt limit. Should a county so elect, however, the indebtedness of any town or district in that county empowered to levy taxes on real estate shall be counted in determining the county's limitation.[iv] **Refunding Bonds** In certain situations, a municipal entity may issue refunding bonds to refund and refinance outstanding debt.[v]
Mechanisms for Resolution after Default	**Bond Payment Guarantee** If a city or town fails to make a payment of principal or interest on its general obligation bond debt, and the governor investigates and finds that a default has occurred, the governor may direct the state comptroller to withhold all state payments to the municipality until the default is cured. The governor may direct that all withheld sums be paid to bondholders to cure the default.[vi] **Receivership** In certain default situations, Virginia law allows for the appointment of a receiver with respect to revenue bonds.[vii]

VV. Virginia

Remedies on Default	**Any Contractual Remedy** Certain provisions of Virginia law allow for a trust indenture to contain provisions for protecting and enforcing rights and remedies of bondholders, including appointing a receiver.[viii] **Limitation on Remedies** Certain provisions of the Virginia Code exempt property of a special municipal district from foreclosure or execution sale and judgment lien.[ix] **Mandamus** In certain situations, bondholders or their trustee may bring a court action to compel the local governing body to perform a ministerial action that it has refused to undertake, such as collecting taxes or fees where the underlying bond authorization requires such a collection.[x]
Other Bondholder Protections	**Special Revenue Bonds** As provided by Section 922(d) of the Bankruptcy Code, payments to bondholders holding special revenue bonds would not be stayed on the filing of a municipal bankruptcy petition, and payments to holders could continue. Whether an issuance would qualify as a special revenue bond depends on the provisions of the authorizing statute with respect to the bonds at issue.[xi] **Statutory Liens** Were a municipal entity to be authorized and file a petition under Chapter 9 of the Bankruptcy Code, bondholders holding bonds to which statutory liens have attached would continue to receive payment on those bonds. For a statutory lien to apply, the authorizing law of the bond issue must contain such a lien. Category SL-3.[xii]

---

i *Sinclair v. New Cingular Wireless PCS, LLC*, 283 Va. 567, 576 (Va. 2012) (noting that "local governing bodies have only those powers that are expressly granted, those necessarily or fairly implied from expressly granted powers, and those that are essential and indispensable."). In Virginia, under Dillon's Rule, if "there is a reasonable doubt about whether legislative power exists, the doubt must be resolved against the local governing body." *Id.*

ii VA. CONST. art. VII, § 2; VA. CODE ANN. § 15.2-200–209 (setting forth procedures for local government charters).

iii VA. CODE ANN. § 15.2-1104.

iv VA. CONST. art. VII, § 10.

v Examples of refunding bond provisions in Virginia law include VA. CODE ANN. § 15.2-7006 (allowing for Richmond Metropolitan Authority to issue refunding bonds); VA. CODE ANN. § 15.2-2643 (Public Finance Act refunding bonds); VA. CODE ANN. § 15.2-4908 (Industrial Development and Revenue Bond Act refunding bonds); and VA. CODE ANN. § 15.2-5346 (hospital authority refunding bonds).

vi VA. CODE ANN. § 15.2-2659.

vii *See, e.g.,* VA. CODE ANN. § 15.2-4910 (Industrial Development and Revenue Bond Act); VA. CODE ANN. § 15.2-2609 (Public Finance Bond Act relating to cities, counties, government bodies, localities and municipalities; allowing for ordinance, trust agreement or other governing document to provide for creation of a commission or appointment of receiver to manage the bonds and fix rates, rents, fees or other charges); and VA. CODE ANN. § 15.2-5213 (hospital or health center commissions). The state code may be more expansive and the statutory authority for each bond issuance should be reviewed before assessing whether a receiver may be appointed.

viii *See, e.g.,* VA. CODE ANN. § 15.2-5327 (hospital authorities); VA. CODE ANN. § 15.2-5418 (Electric Authorities Act); VA. CODE ANN. § 15.2-5612 (Public Recreational Facilities Authorities Act); VA. CODE ANN. § 15.2-6315 (authorities for development of former federal areas); and VA. CODE ANN. § 15.2-4910 (industrial development revenue bonds). The state code may be more expansive and the statutory authority for each bond issuance should be reviewed before assessing available bondholder rights and remedies.

ix *See, e.g.,* VA. CODE ANN. § 15.2-5212 (hospital and health care commissions).

x *See, e.g.,* VA. CODE ANN. § 15.2-4910 (Industrial Development and Revenue Bond Act, allowing for writ of mandamus, suit, action or proceeding at law or in equity to compel authority to perform the terms contained in the trust indenture); VA. CODE ANN. § 15.2-5418 (Electric Authorities Act); VA. CODE ANN. §15.2-7008 (Richmond Metropolitan Authority); and VA. CODE ANN. § 15.2-5360 (hospital authorities). It is possible that an aggrieved bondholder could pursue a writ of mandamus even absent authorizing statutory law.

xi *See, e.g.,* VA. CODE ANN. § 15.2-4908 (Industrial Development and Revenue Bond Act, allowing that, unless otherwise provided in the trust indenture, all bonds shall be payable solely and exclusively from the revenues and receipts of the particular facility or loan); VA. CODE ANN. § 15.2-5125 (Virginia Water and Waste Authorities Act, providing principal and interest on the bonds payable solely from funds provided for in the act for such payment); VA. CODE ANN. § 15.2-4910 (industrial development revenue bonds secured by pledge on revenues and receipts from project); and VA. CODE ANN. § 15.2-5209 (hospital or health center bonds secured by granting a lien on any property, real or personal, of the commission). These are examples of special revenue bonds. The state code may be more expansive, and an attorney should be consulted to examine any specific situation involving a default.

xii Category SL-3: *See, e.g.,* VA. CODE ANN. § 15.2-5358 (hospital authority bonds immediately subject to lien on pledge). Note that this is an example of language that could be interpreted as a statutory lien but may have been intended to provide for the perfection, effectiveness and enforcement of the lien created as an exemption from the filing requirement of the Uniform Commercial Code. Clarification by legislative action or opinion of counsel would help determine or reaffirm whether a statutory lien was intended and created. The state code may be more expansive, and an attorney should be consulted to examine any specific situation involving a default.

WW. Washington

Municipal Bankruptcy Authority	In Washington, any taxing district may file a petition under Chapter 9 of the Bankruptcy Code. "Taxing district" includes "[a]ny municipality or other political subdivision, including (but not hereby limiting the generality of the foregoing) any county, city, borough, village, parish, town, or township, unincorporated tax or special assessment district, and any school, drainage, irrigation, reclamation, levee, sewer, or paving, sanitary, port, improvement or other district." Unless an entity is a taxing district, it is not authorized to file a municipal bankruptcy petition. Between 1980 and July 31, 2016, four entities have filed a municipal bankruptcy petition in Washington.[i]
Home Rule and Taxing Power of Municipalities	**Municipalities' Ability to Self-Govern** Washington is a Dillon's Rule state. The Washington state constitution, however, permits the formation of home-rule charters for municipalities over 10,000 people and home-rule charters for counties. Further, the Washington state constitution vests with the state legislature the authority to authorize counties, cities, towns and townships to tax.[ii] **Taxing Limitations** The Washington state constitution limits tax levies on real and personal property by the state and all taxing districts to 1 percent of the fair market value of the property. The Washington state code includes additional limitations for taxing districts.[iii]
Debt Default Prevention	**Debt Limitation** No county, city, town, school district or other municipal corporation may become indebted in an amount exceeding 1.5 percent of the taxable property in the local unit, without the assent of three-fifths of voters of the local unit, which may approve a debt ceiling of up to 5 percent of the value of the taxable property therein. A city or town may be allowed to become indebted in a larger amount, not exceeding 5 percent of the value of the taxable property for supplying water, artificial lights and sewers when owned by the city or town. Any school district may become indebted up to 5 percent for capital outlays.[iv] **Refunding Bonds** In certain situations, a municipal entity may issue refunding bonds to refund and refinance outstanding debt.[v]

WW. Washington

Mechanisms for Resolution after Default	**Designation of Trustee** Certain bond issuances allow for the designation of a trustee with the right to enforce the payment of the bonds and to take possession and use, operate and manage the project.[vi] **Receivership** In certain default situations, Washington law allows for the appointment of a receiver with respect to revenue bonds.[vii]
Remedies on Default[viii]	**Injunctive Relief** Certain provisions of the Washington Code allow for injunctive relief to enjoin any act or things that may be unlawful or the violation of any right of an obligee of the authority.[ix] **Foreclosure and/or Penalty** In certain default situations, if a city or town fails to collect local improvement assessments when due, a bondholder may sue to collect the assessment and foreclose the lien and may recover, in addition to principal and interest, 5 percent, plus costs. In other situations, a bondholder may seek to foreclose on a facility.[x] **Mandamus** In certain situations, bondholders or their trustee may bring a court action to compel the local governing body to perform a ministerial action that it has refused to undertake, such as collecting taxes or fees where the underlying bond authorization requires such a collection.[xi]
Other Bondholder Protections	**Special Revenue Bonds** As provided by Section 922(d) of the Bankruptcy Code, payments to bondholders holding special revenue bonds would not be stayed on the filing of a municipal bankruptcy petition, and payments to holders could continue. Whether an issuance would qualify as a special revenue bond depends on the provisions of the authorizing statute with respect to the bonds at issue.[xii] **Statutory Liens** Were a municipal entity to file a petition under Chapter 9 of the Bankruptcy Code, bondholders holding bonds to which statutory liens have attached would continue to receive payment on those bonds. For a statutory lien to apply, the authorizing law of the bond issue must contain such a lien. No statutes covered by the categories were identified.

---

i WASH. REV. CODE §§ 39.64.020 and 39.64.040. The municipal entities filing municipal bankruptcy petitions include two utility districts, a city and a transportation district. Before filing, the taxing district must first adopt a resolution authorizing it to file a municipal bankruptcy petition.

It is important to note that the current version of the Bankruptcy Code does not contain a definition of the term "taxing district," and this definition was included in provisions found unconstitutional by the U.S. Supreme Court in *Ashton v. Cameron County Water Imp. Dist. No. 1,* 298 U.S. 513 (1936). As one court in Idaho, whose statutes also incorporate the definition of "taxing district" into the provisions authorizing municipal bankruptcy petitions, stated: "The current Bankruptcy Code lacks a definition of 'taxing district.' Instead ... it uses the term 'municipality' to describe those entities that may seek relief under chapter 9, provided that they are authorized to do so under state law. This raises questions regarding the interpretation and effect of [the Idaho Code]. For example, does [the Idaho Code] continue to incorporate by reference the description of 'taxing district' contained in the now-repealed Bankruptcy Act of 1898, does it somehow embrace the definition of 'municipality' in the current version of the Code, or is the definition of 'taxing district' for purposes of [Idaho law] left open-ended or untethered due to the repeal of the Bankruptcy Act?" *In re Boise County, Idaho,* 465 Br. 156, 167 (Bankr. D. Id. 2011) (presenting questions, but finding court need not answer because the county was ineligible to file a Chapter 9 petition on other grounds). With respect to the Washington statute, the same questions could be presented in any challenge.

ii WASH. CONST. art XI, § 10 (home rule for first-class cities with populations over 10,000 people); WASH. CONST. art XI, § 4 (home-rule authorization for counties); WASH. CONST. art XI, § 12 (vesting authority to authorize local governments to tax). Various provisions of the Washington state code permit local governments to tax. WASH. REV. CODE § 35.22.280 (specific powers of first-class cities, including taxing power); WASH. REV. CODE § 35.23.440 (specific powers of second-class cities to issue a tax); and WASH. REV. CODE § 35.27.370 (specific power of towns to tax, among other things).

iii WASH. CONST. art VII, § 2. In certain circumstances, with voter approval, a local taxing district may legally exceed this limitation. WASH. REV. CODE § 84.52.043 includes additional limitations for junior taxing districts and senior taxing districts.

iv WASH. CONST. art. VIII, § 6. Recently, the Washington Supreme Court analyzed the application of Washington's constitutional debt limits to determine that an agreement that was "essentially a guarantee" would create debt within the meaning of the state constitution and, thus, trigger the state's constitutional debt limits. *In re Bond Issuance of Greater Wenatchee Reg'l Events Ctr. Pub. Facilities Dist.*, 175 Wash. 2d 788 (2012).

v Examples of refunding bond provisions in Washington law include WASH. REV. CODE § 35.92.110 (municipal utilities; allowing refunding bonds); WASH. REV. CODE § 35.45.170 (local improvement refunding bonds authorized, but with limitations); WASH. REV. CODE § 35.58.470 (refunding bonds for general obligation bonds of metropolitan municipal corporations); and WASH. REV. CODE § 35.89.010 (water redemption bonds).

vi *See, e.g.*, WASH. REV. CODE § 35.82.150 (housing authority bonds).

vii *See, e.g.*, WASH. REV. CODE § 39.84.160 (industrial development bonds). The state code may be more expansive and the statutory authority for each bond issuance should be reviewed before assessing whether a receiver may be appointed.

viii Until the Jefferson County, Alabama municipal sewer bond default, the largest municipal bond default in history was that of the Washington Public Power Supply System ("WPPSS"), which defaulted on over $2 billion in municipal bonds issued to construct municipal power plants. The Washington State Supreme Court ruled that the Washington state public agency that issued the bonds lacked authority, and the court rendered the bonds void along with the source of debt service payments. Approximately 40 percent of the principal and interest outstanding on the bonds was recovered in a 1998 class action lawsuit. Moody's Investors Service, *U.S. Municipal Bond Defaults and Recoveries, 1970-2012*. Specifically, the WPPSS originally defaulted on its bond payments in 1983 and the Supreme Court for the State of Washington in *Chemical Bank v. Washington Public Power Supply System* found that the bonds were not authorized, as the participation agreements involved were invalid because the municipalities did not have the authorization to enter into them. 99 Wash. 2d 772 (1983). The court's finding was despite almost $2.3 billion in bonds that had already been issued.

ix *See, e.g.*, WASH. REV. CODE § 35.82.170 (housing authority bonds). The state code may be more expansive than the example cited here, and the statutory authority for each individual bond issuance should be reviewed before assessing the availability of injunctive relief.

x *See, e.g.*, WASH. REV. CODE § 35.45.080 (local improvement bonds issued by cities and towns); WASH. REV. CODE § 39.84.160 (industrial development bonds). The state code may be more expansive than the example cited here, and the statutory authority for each individual bond issuance should be reviewed before assessing whether a foreclosure action may be pursued.

xi *See, e.g.*, WASH. REV. CODE § 35.67.180 (system of sewerage revenue bonds allowing bondholders to bring suit against the city or town to compel it to do so); WASH. REV. CODE § 35.82.170 (housing authority bonds); WASH. REV. CODE § 35.71.070 (Municipal Revenue Bond Act); WASH. REV. CODE § 35.45.030 (local improvement bondholder remedy limited to enforcement of special assessment); and WASH. REV. CODE § 39.84.160 (industrial development bonds). It is possible that an aggrieved bondholder could pursue a writ of mandamus even absent authorizing statutory law.

xii *See, e.g.*, WASH. REV. CODE § 35.58.460 (metropolitan municipal corporation revenue bonds payable out of special fund for sole purpose of paying interest and principal on bonds); WASH. REV. CODE § 35.57.090 (creating special fund from which revenue bonds shall be paid); and WASH. REV. CODE § 35.82.130 (housing authorities bonds). These are examples of special revenue bonds. The state code may be more expansive, and an attorney should be consulted to examine any specific situation involving a default.

XX. West Virginia

Municipal Bankruptcy Authority	West Virginia does not specifically authorize its municipal entities to file a petition under Chapter 9 of the Bankruptcy Code. Despite a lack of authorization, between 1980 and July 31, 2016, four such municipal bankruptcy petitions have been filed.[i]
Home Rule and Taxing Power of Municipalities	**Municipalities' Ability to Self-Govern** West Virginia is a Dillon's Rule jurisdiction. Although the state is a Dillon's Rule jurisdiction, the West Virginia Constitution includes provisions authorizing municipalities with populations exceeding 2,000 people to adopt a home-rule charter.[ii] The West Virginia Constitution permits the legislature to authorize the corporate authorities of cities, towns and villages to assess and collect taxes.[iii] **Taxing Limitations** The West Virginia Constitution limits property taxes in the state based on class of property, and the West Virginia state code includes aggregate levy limits based on the class of property.[iv]
Debt Default Prevention	**Debt Limitation** No county, city, school district or municipal corporation may incur indebtedness in the aggregate exceeding 5 percent of the value of the taxable property therein.[v] **Refunding Bonds** In certain situations, a municipal entity may issue refunding bonds to refund and refinance outstanding debt.[vi]
Mechanisms for Resolution after Default	**Receivership** In certain default situations, West Virginia law allows for the appointment of a receiver with respect to revenue bonds.[vii]
Remedies on Default	**Accounting** In certain situations of default, bondholders may bring a proceeding to require the authority in question to account as if it were a trustee of an express trust.[viii] **Foreclosure** In certain default situations, West Virginia law allows for foreclosure with respect to a municipal entity's property.[ix] **Injunctive Relief** In certain situations, a bondholder may bring suit for injunctive relief to enjoin an act that may be unlawful or to enjoin the violation of any of the rights of an obligee of the authority involved.[x]

XX. West Virginia

Remedies on Default *continued*	**Mandamus** In certain situations, bondholders may bring an action to compel the local governing body to perform a ministerial action that it has refused to undertake, such as collecting taxes or fees where the underlying bond authorization requires such a collection.[xi]
Other Bondholder Protections	**Special Revenue Bonds** As provided by Section 922(d) of the Bankruptcy Code, payments to bondholders holding special revenue bonds would not be stayed on the filing of a municipal bankruptcy petition, and payments to holders could continue. Whether an issuance would qualify as a special revenue bond depends on the provisions of the authorizing statute with respect to the bonds at issue.[xii] **Statutory Liens** Were a municipal entity to file a petition under Chapter 9 of the Bankruptcy Code, bondholders holding bonds to which statutory liens have attached would continue to receive payment on those bonds. For a statutory lien to apply, the authorizing law of the bond issue must contain such a lien. No statutes covered by the categories were identified.

---

i Two of these petitions were by utility districts and two were by special municipal districts. Of these filings three were filed before 1994 when Congress greatly limited the Bankruptcy Code provisions to municipalities in states specifically authorizing such a filing. The fourth filing was in 1995, and despite lack of authorization, the municipality's plan of adjustment was confirmed on January 27, 2000. *In re Procious Public Service District*, Case N. 95-20222 (Bankr. S.W. Va.) (plan confirmed Jan. 27, 2000). This municipal entity's plan likely was confirmed because no party objected to the service district's bankruptcy filing.

ii W.VA. CONST. art. VI, § 39a.

iii W.VA. CONST. art. X, § 10-9; W. VA. CODE § 8-13-1 (authorizing municipalities to levy taxes).

iv W. VA. CONST. art. X, § 10-1; W. VA. CODE § 11-8-6.

v W. VA. CONST. art. X, § 8. The West Virginia Supreme Court has held that statutes limiting indebtedness to less than the constitutional limit are valid. *Pfalzgraf v. Wood Cnty. Court*, 73 W. Va. 723 (W. Va. 1914).

vi Examples of refunding bonds in West Virginia include W. VA. CODE § 13-2-1 (public bonded indebtedness refunding bonds allowing any county, municipal corporation or school district to issue refunding bonds); W. VA. CODE § 8-38-19 (Municipal Economic Opportunity Development District refunding bonds); W. VA. CODE § 16-13-22c (refunding bonds for sewage works and stormwater works bonds); W. VA. CODE § 16-13A-20 (refunding revenue bonds for public service districts); W. VA. CODE § 16-29A-13 (allowing refunding bonds for West Virginia Hospital Finance Authority); W. VA. CODE § 17-16A-21 (refunding bonds for West Virginia Parkways Authority); W. VA. CODE § 17-16B-22 (refunding bonds for public port authorities); W. VA. CODE § 18-9D-4 (refunding bonds for school building authority); W. VA. CODE § 18-11B-5 (revenue refunding bonds for university facilities, buildings and structures); and W. VA. CODE § 18-11D-6 (revenue refunding bonds for West Virginia University athletic facilities).

vii See, e.g., W. VA. CODE § 19-21-23 (allowing for appointment of receiver over drainage district when bonds remain unpaid 30 days after maturity); W. VA. CODE § 8-19-16 (municipal and county waterworks and electric power systems bonds); W. VA. CODE § 8-20-15 (combined systems of municipal corporations revenue bond financing); W. VA. CODE § 10-2A-23 (athletic establishment bonds); W. VA. CODE § 7-3-8 (bonds issued for county real estate, buildings and property acquired); W. VA. CODE § 16-15-23 (housing authority bonds); W. VA. CODE § 16-13-21 (sewage works and stormwater works bonds); W. VA. CODE § 8-16-24 (municipal public work projects); W. VA. CODE § 16-13A-17 (public health and public service districts); and W. VA. CODE § 17-17-33 (toll bridge bonds). The state code may be more expansive and the statutory authority for each bond issuance should be reviewed before assessing whether a receiver may be appointed.

viii *See, e.g.*, W. VA. CODE § 16-15-23 (housing authority bonds). The state code may be more expansive and the statutory authority for each bond issuance should be reviewed before assessing whether to seek an accounting.

ix *See, e.g.*, W. VA. CODE § 10-2A-21 (statutory mortgage lien on bonds for athletic establishments) and W. VA. CODE § 16-15-23 (housing authority bonds). The state code may be more expansive and the statutory authority for each bond issuance should be reviewed before assessing whether a foreclosure action may be pursued.

x *See, e.g.*, W. VA. CODE § 16-15-22 (public health and state housing law bonds). The state code may be more expansive and the statutory authority for each individual bond issuance should be reviewed before assessing whether injunctive relief may be pursued.

xi *See, e.g.*, W. VA. CODE § 8-20-15 (combined systems of municipal corporations revenue bond financing); W. VA. CODE § 8-27-17 (municipal corporations urban mass transportation systems); W. VA. CODE § 10-2A-23 (athletic establishment bonds); W. VA. CODE § 16-13-21 (sewage works and stormwater works bonds); W.VA. CODE § 16-13A-17 (public health public service districts); W. VA. CODE § 16-15-22 (public health and state housing law bonds); W. VA. CODE § 17-16B-19 (public port authority bonds); W. VA. CODE § 18-11D-4 (revenue bonds for West Virginia University athletic facilities); W. VA. CODE § 17-17-33 (toll bridge bonds); W. VA. CODE § 22-16-7 (Solid Waste Landfill Closure Assistance Program bonds); W. VA. CODE § 19-21-21 (drainage district bonds); and W. VA. CODE § 8-19-16 (Municipal and County Waterworks and Electric Power System bonds). It is possible that an aggrieved bondholder could pursue a writ of mandamus even absent authorizing statutory law.

xii *See, e.g.*, W. VA. CODE § 22-16-8 (Solid Waste Landfill Closure Assistance Program bonds are payable solely from revenues pledged for their payment); W. VA. CODE § 20-5-10 (proceeds of park development revenue bonds deposited with treasurer of State of West Virginia, who shall deposit them in a separate account); W. VA. CODE § 8-16-12 (revenue bonds for municipal public works payable solely from net revenue of project); W. VA. CODE § 8-19-7 (municipal and county waterworks and electric power systems bonds payable solely from revenues of system); W. VA. CODE § 10-2A-10 (bonds for athletic establishments payable solely from special fund created for payment); W. VA. CODE § 16-29A-12 (pledge valid and binding from time made regarding West Virginia Hospital Finance Authority Act bonds); and W. VA. CODE § 18-11D-5 (revenue bonds for West Virginia University athletic facilities). These are examples of special revenue bonds. The state code may be more expansive, and an attorney should be consulted to examine any specific situation involving a default.

YY. Wisconsin

Municipal Bankruptcy Authority	Wisconsin does not specifically authorize its municipal entities to file a petition under Chapter 9 of the Bankruptcy Code. Between 1980 and July 31, 2016, no municipal entity in Wisconsin has filed such a petition.
Home Rule and Taxing Power of Municipalities	**Municipalities' Ability to Self-Govern** Wisconsin is a Dillon's Rule state. The Wisconsin Constitution permits cities and villages to determine their own local affairs and government, subject only to the constitution and state law. In addition, although Wisconsin is a Dillon's Rule state, the Wisconsin statutes provide that laws governing charter cities shall be "liberally construed in favor of the rights, powers and privileges of cities to promote the general welfare, peace, good order and prosperity of such cities and the inhabitants thereof."[i] **Tax Limitations** Wisconsin state law requires any county, city, town, village, school district, sewerage district or other municipal district incurring debt to provide for the collection of a direct annual tax sufficient to pay interest on the debt as it falls due and to pay and discharge the principal within 20 years from the time of contracting.[ii] In addition, Wisconsin state law includes provisions limiting the amount a political subdivision may increase its levy in any year.[iii]
Debt Default Prevention	**Debt Limitation** The Wisconsin Constitution includes debt limit provisions for counties, cities, towns, villages, school districts, sewage districts and other municipal corporations. Specifically, these entities' debt, with certain exceptions, may not exceed 5 percent of the value of taxable property located in the entity equalized for state purposes as provided by the state legislature. Bonds issued for school purposes by cities may be issued up to an additional 10 percent, and bonds issued by school districts offering grades one through twelve may be issued up to 10 percent of the taxable property.[iv] **Deficiency Protection for Public Improvement Bonds** If a local government issues public improvement bonds and if the local government determines there will be a deficiency in a bond fund for the ensuing calendar year, the municipality must make up the deficiency, up to its municipal debt limit.[v] **Refunding Bonds** In certain situations, a municipal entity may issue refunding bonds to refund and refinance outstanding debt.[vi]

YY. Wisconsin

Remedies on Default	**Foreclosure** Certain provisions of Wisconsin law allow for a mortgage lien in relation to payment on project bonds.[vii] **Mandamus** In certain situations, bondholders or their trustee may bring a court action to compel the local governing body to perform a ministerial action that it has refused to undertake, such as collecting taxes or fees where the underlying bond authorization requires such a collection.[viii]
Other Bondholder Protections	**Special Revenue Bonds** As provided by Section 922(d) of the Bankruptcy Code, payments to bondholders holding special revenue bonds would not be stayed on the filing of a municipal bankruptcy petition, and payments to holders could continue. Whether an issuance would qualify as a special revenue bond depends on the provisions of the authorizing statute with respect to the bonds at issue.[ix] **Statutory Liens** Were a municipal entity to file a petition under Chapter 9 of the Bankruptcy Code, bondholders holding bonds to which statutory liens have attached would continue to receive payment on those bonds. For a statutory lien to apply, the authorizing law of the bond issue must contain such a lien. No statutes covered by the categories were identified.

i WIS. STAT. ANN. § 62.04.

ii WIS. CONST. art. XI, § 3.

iii WIS. STAT. ANN. § 66.0602.

iv WIS. CONST. art. XI, § 3. *See also* WIS. STAT. § 67.03 (establishing general limitations on indebtedness).

v *See, e.g.*, WIS. STAT. ANN. § 66.0619(6) (public improvement bonds). Under Wisconsin law, the debt of any municipality shall not exceed 5 percent of the value of the taxable property located in the municipality. WIS. STAT. ANN. § 67.03.

Note that this provision only applies to public improvement bonds. Other issuances, such as the bond anticipation notes on which the city of Menasha, Wisconsin defaulted on September 1, 2009, were not affected by this provision. *See Am. Bank v. City of Menasha,* 627 F.3d 261 (7th Cir. Nov. 29, 2010) (describing bond issuance); *The Lafayette Life Ins. Co. v. City of Menasha,* Case No. 09-64 (N.D. Ind. Dec. 1, 2011) (Order and Final Judgment).

vi Examples of refunding bond provisions in Wisconsin law include WIS. STAT. ANN. § 66.0621 (refunding bonds for revenue bonds) and WIS. STAT. ANN. § 66.0623 (refunding village, town, sanitary and inland lake district bonds).

vii *See, e.g.*, WIS. STAT. ANN. § 66.0621 (securing payment of revenue bonds). The state code may be more expansive than the example cited here, and the statutory authority for each individual bond issuance should be reviewed before assessing whether bondholders could pursue a foreclosure action.

viii *See, e.g.*, WIS. STAT. ANN. § 182.34(9) (bondholders may bring suit at law or in equity by suit, action, mandamus or other proceeding to protect their rights with respect to turnpike project bonds). It is possible that an aggrieved bondholder could pursue a writ of mandamus even absent authorizing statutory law.

ix *See, e.g.*, WIS. STAT. ANN. § 62.185 (sewer district bonds are payable solely out of special sewer district tax) and WIS. STAT. ANN. § 67.16 (general obligation local improvement bonds; providing that all collections must be placed with the treasurer of the local governmental unit in a special debt service fund designated and identified for the issue of the bonds). These are examples of special revenue bonds. The state code may be more expansive, and an attorney should be consulted to examine any specific situation involving a default.

ZZ. Wyoming

Municipal Bankruptcy Authority	Wyoming does not specifically authorize its municipal entities to file a petition under Chapter 9 of the Bankruptcy Code. Between 1980 and July 31, 2016, no municipal entity in Wyoming has filed such a petition.
Home Rule and Taxing Power of Municipalities	**Municipalities' Ability to Self-Govern** Wyoming is a Dillon's Rule jurisdiction. The state constitution allows for cities and towns to determine their local affairs and government, subject to state law and statutes governing limits of indebtedness. Further, the state constitution vests in the legislature the authority to dictate how cities and towns should levy taxes.[i] **Tax Limitations** With respect to counties, a county may not levy an annual tax exceeding 12 mills on the dollar, except for the payment of its public debt and interest thereon. Additionally, incorporated cities and towns may not levy a tax exceeding 8 mills on the dollar in any one year, except for the payment of its public debt and the interest thereon.[ii]
Debt Default Prevention	**Debt Limitation** No county may incur debt exceeding 2 percent of the assessed value of taxable property within its boundaries. The debt limit for a city or town is 4 percent of the assessed value of taxable property in the city or town, except that an additional 4 percent is allowable for sewage disposal systems. Indebtedness for supplying water to cities or towns is excluded from the limitation. No school district may create indebtedness exceeding 10 percent of the assessed value of the taxable property in the school district for acquiring land or for erecting, enlarging and equipping school buildings.[iii] **Refunding Bonds** In certain situations, a municipal entity may issue refunding bonds to refund and refinance outstanding debt.[iv]
Mechanisms for Resolution after Default	**Receivership** In certain default situations, Wyoming law allows for the appointment of a receiver with respect to revenue bonds.[v]
Remedies on Default	**Accounting** In certain default situations, bondholders may bring a proceeding to require the authority in question to account as if it were a trustee of an express trust.[vi]

ZZ. Wyoming

Remedies on Default *continued*	**Injunction** In certain situations, an interested person may bring an action against a board to enjoin or mandate the board to act.[vii] **Foreclosure** In certain default situations, Wyoming law allows for foreclosure with respect to a municipal entity's property.[viii] **Mandamus** In certain situations, bondholders may bring an action to compel the local governing body to perform a ministerial action that it has refused to undertake, such as collecting taxes or fees where the underlying bond authorization requires such a collection.[ix]
Other Bondholder Protections	**Special Revenue Bonds** As provided by Section 922(d) of the Bankruptcy Code, payments to bondholders holding special revenue bonds would not be stayed on the filing of a municipal bankruptcy petition, and payments to holders could continue. Whether an issuance would qualify as a special revenue bond depends on the provisions of the authorizing statute with respect to the bonds at issue.[x] **Statutory Liens** Were a municipal entity to file a petition under Chapter 9 of the Bankruptcy Code, bondholders holding bonds to which statutory liens have attached would continue to receive payment on those bonds. For a statutory lien to apply, the authorizing law of the bond issue must contain such a lien. No statutes covered by the categories were identified.

i WYO. CONST. art. XIII, § 1(b).

ii WYO. CONST. art. XV, § 5 (counties); WYO. CONST. art 15, § 6 (incorporated cities and towns).

iii WYO. CONST. art. XVI, § 3 (counties); WYO. CONST. art. 16, § 5 (municipal, county and school district debt).

iv *See, e.g.*, WYO. STAT. ANN. §§ 15-8-101 (allowing for refunding bonds for sewage systems) and 15-7-504 (sewage system refunding bonds).

v An example of a refunding bond provision under Wyoming law is WYO. STAT. ANN. § 15-1-704 (allowing for appointment of a receiver, mandamus or foreclosure with respect to industrial development project bonds issued by cities and towns). "Project" includes any land, building, pollution control facility or other improvement and all necessary and appurtenant real and personal properties suitable for manufacturing, industrial, commercial or business enterprises or for health care facilities. *See also* WYO. STAT. ANN. § 41-10-139. The state code may be more expansive than the examples cited here, and the statutory authority for each individual bond issuance should be reviewed before assessing whether a receiver may be appointed.

In addition, Wyoming has provided for receiverships with respect to defaulting drainage and irrigation districts whose obligations were owned by the state. A.M. Hillhouse, 344 MUNICIPAL BONDS: A CENTURY OF EXPERIENCE (New York: Prentice-Hall 1936).

vi *See, e.g.*, WYO. STAT. ANN. § 41-10-139 (water and sewer district bonds). The state code may be more expansive, and an attorney should be consulted to examine any specific situation involving a default.

vii *See, e.g.*, WYO. STAT. ANN. § 41-10-139 (water and sewer district bonds). The state code may be more expansive, and an attorney should be consulted to examine any specific situation involving a default.

viii *See, e.g.*, WYO. STAT. ANN. § 15-1-704 (allowing for appointment of a receiver, mandamus or foreclosure with respect to industrial development project bonds issued by cities and towns). "Project" includes any land, building, pollution control facility or other improvement and all necessary and appurtenant real and personal properties suitable for manufacturing, industrial, commercial or business enterprises or for health care facilities. The state code may be more expansive than the example cited here, and the statutory authority for each individual bond issuance should be reviewed before assessing whether a foreclosure action could be pursued.

ix *See, e.g.*, WYO. STAT. ANN. § 15-1-704 (allowing for appointment of a receiver, mandamus or foreclosure with respect to industrial development project bonds issued by cities and towns). "Project" includes any land, building, pollution control facility or other improvement and all necessary and appurtenant real and personal properties suitable for manufacturing, industrial, commercial or business enterprises or for health care facilities. *See also* WYO. STAT. ANN. § 41-10-139 (water and sewer district bonds). It is possible that an aggrieved bondholder could pursue a writ of mandamus even absent authorizing statutory law.

x *See, e.g.*, WYO. STAT. ANN. §§ 15-7-506 (providing waterworks and sewerage system bonds payable solely from revenues of project) and 15-7-704 (providing industrial development project bonds secured by pledge of revenues of project). These are examples of special revenue bonds. The state code may be more expansive, and an attorney should be consulted to examine any specific situation involving a default.

IX. Conclusion to Second Edition

A. History

As described in the beginning sections of this book, the financial distress of states and local governments is not new or unique to the early twenty-first century. In fact, you can go back at least as far as the fourth and fifth centuries B.C. and find examples of financial distress in the Greek city states. What is new to the last century is the effort to develop, by treaty, statute or practice, new and better methods to address the financial distress, resolve troubled debt-financing issues and assist the state or local government in recovering both financially and operationally by improved government services and economic stimulus. The motivation for states and local governments to pay their debts varies and has evolved from devaluation of currency, trade embargos, sanctions and tariffs to denial of access to the capital markets and increased borrowing costs. For states and local governments in the United States of America, the reason to honor one's debts is linked to the need to continue to borrow funds now for the health, safety and welfare of citizens. Continued borrowing is required due to uneven and delayed tax payments and the need to fund large capital projects and to pay for needed infrastructure improvements.

The spirit of Washington and Hamilton exhorts states and local governments to timely pay their debts and to identify and dedicate a specific tax source sufficient for repayment when incurring any debts. Hamilton referred to this as the "immortality of debt." For that and other reasons discussed in prior sections, the default rate for state and local government debt in the United States has been significantly lower than for corporate debt: 1/50 to 1/100. The causes of default vary from time to time from economic downturns or large unaffordable liabilities arising from major weather disasters, epidemics, failed projects, fraud and mismanagement to, more recently, unaffordable unfunded pension obligations and personnel costs and deferred maintenance and infrastructure improvements. The selected case studies discussed in the book have identified actual living examples of these various causes for default and growing concern about deferred infrastructure improvements and unfunded pension liabilities. Generally, the reasons for default come down to the absolute inability to pay due to one of the causes, which is a problem, but it is understandable that a government can only pay to the extent it has revenues to pay. Most recently with Jefferson County and Detroit, the issue has been raised as to whether the reason is unwillingness to pay rather than absolute inability, which unwillingness causes a harsher response by the financial markets and is less understandable to investors.

B. State Debt Resolution Mechanisms

States are co-sovereign with the federal government and, for that reason, the role of the federal government and federal courts in state and local government problems is limited. Municipalities (cities, towns, villages, counties, special tax districts, municipal utilities and enterprises, etc.) are creatures of the state. The sovereignty of municipalities evolved from the state and, generally, municipalities only have those powers granted to them by the state given the nature of their creation, and municipalities have no independent source of sovereignty (Dillon's Rule). Accordingly, while debt obligations started as moral obligations, now state constitutions and statutes are the source of the ability of states and municipalities to obtain financing. Likewise, state constitutions and statutes contain provisions such as tax limitations, debt limitations and the ability to refund debt, all of which are targeted at preventing debt defaults. In addition, many states have enacted laws providing for oversight, supervision and assistance for fiscal emergencies of local governments. These laws can range from monitoring the issuance of debt to providing technical assistance, to supervision of financial matters and required state approval of the budget to ensure the budget is balanced and affordable and sustainable. Further, supervision can be more direct through use of receivers, emergency managers, control boards, refinancing authorities, etc. The structure of oversight or emergency financing may vary but the goal should remain the same: the development of a recovery plan that reinvests in the troubled municipality to assure that needed services and infrastructure at an acceptable level are provided and that there is a well-conceived economic development plan to attract new businesses and encourage businesses there to expand and grow. This type of recovery plan with services and infrastructure at an acceptable level fosters the growth of new, good jobs and businesses that attract new residents. This creates new tax revenues, which help solve financial distress and lead to recovery. Recently, there have been various efforts at constructing the best sovereign debt resolution mechanism, both for countries in the international setting and for local governments. The outline of such mechanisms is discussed in this book to encourage further dialogue and development. Regardless of what mechanism is used to address financial distress, one important rule is that the traditions and principles of government financing, as discussed herein, must be respected to result in a successful recovery plan. The failure to do so will lead to less market acceptance and higher borrowing costs.

C. Debt Holders

Bondholder rights and remedies have evolved over time, from moral obligations with no constitutional or statutory support to specific provisions mandating or requiring payment, sometimes from a specific pledged or dedicated source. Remedies in case of default have been provided by state statute. Depending on the state and its laws, as detailed in section VIII, possible remedies include, but are not limited to, acceleration of principal, mandamus, receivership, suit for judgment, declaratory judgment, accounting, injunctive relief or foreclosure or for instructions by the court to the trustee approving a settlement or other action to be taken by the bond trustee for the benefit of the bondholders. Bond trustees and bondholders pursuing remedies for a defaulted bond issue should consider what consultants may be necessary to provide guidance for appropriately resolving the matters. Sometimes, acceptance of the default by the parties, along with acknowledgment of the debt due and consent to judgment by the debtor municipality, may be all that is needed to have the matter addressed by refunding, refinancing or other corrective actions. Litigation meltdown is to be avoided as wasteful and less beneficial than reasonable compromise. The last resort is always Chapter 9 municipal bankruptcy.

D. Chapter 9

Municipal bankruptcy filings are rare because Chapter 9 filings have consequences as to future access to the market and costs of borrowing. Chapter 9 proceedings are time consuming, intense, complicated and expensive and generally do not result in what the parties originally desired. In order to file, a municipality must be specifically authorized by its state. As noted above, many states do not authorize the filing of a Chapter 9 petition by their municipalities. Only 12 states generally authorize filing and another 12 states conditionally authorize filing, requiring some further action or approval by a state agency or elected official. A federal bankruptcy court has limited jurisdiction over a municipality under (i) the U.S. Constitution (Tenth Amendment), (ii) case law (see *Ashton* and *Bekins*) and (iii) the provisions of Chapter 9 of the Federal Bankruptcy Code (see §§ 903 and 904). The Chapter 9 bankruptcy court cannot order, stay or interfere with the property, revenue, government or political affairs of the municipality unless the municipality consents. Further, the municipality cannot consent to matters that are contrary to state law (§ 904 of the Federal Bankruptcy Code). Chapter 9 does not limit or impair the power of a state to control by legislation or otherwise a municipality's exercise of political or governmental powers, such as the use or expenditure of funds (§ 903 of the Federal Bankruptcy Code). Accordingly, municipal bonds with a statutory lien or special revenue pledge are to be respected in the Chapter 9 filing and should be unimpaired and paid as originally scheduled and provided for consistent with the rulings of *Ashton* and *Bekins* and the provisions of §§ 903, 904, 922(d), 927 and 928 of the Bankruptcy Code. The priority of payment in a Chapter 9 proceeding ranges from payment to secured creditors in full or at least to the extent of the validity of their lien or pledge and the value of the respective collateral (tax pledges or revenues), to payment for unsecured claims consistent with similar claims in the same class to the extent it is fair and equitable and found by the court to be in the best interest of creditors and is feasible. Administrative expenses (expense of municipal operation postpetition) are to be paid in full before unsecured claims. A municipality in a Chapter 9 proceeding is unlike a corporation in a Chapter 11 proceeding: (1) only a municipality can initiate a Chapter 9 proceeding or file a plan of debt adjustment, (2) there is no priority for unpaid wages, vacation or benefits (including pension) unlike the statutory amount per worker in a Chapter 11, (3) labor agreements can be rejected at the request of the municipality if the agreement burdens the municipality and the equities are in favor of rejection without the elaborate exchange of information, negotiation and hearing required by Section 1113 of the Bankruptcy Code for corporations, (4) there is no limit on damages for a real estate lease, (5) the payments to defease bonds or pay current principal or interest due within 90 days of filing of the Chapter 9 proceeding are not capable of being vacated or deemed a preference, and (6) the plan of debt adjustment cannot be a liquidation *per se*.

At the confirmation hearings, the municipal debtor must demonstrate to the court *inter alia* that: (a) the plan of debt adjustment is fair and equitable and does not unfairly discriminate in treatment of a creditor claim as compared to similar claims unless the creditor consents; (b) the plan conforms with the requirement of Chapter 9 and state law (the court cannot confirm a plan that requires the municipality to take action contrary to state law), (c) the plan is in the best interest of creditors (which means it does not under- or overpromise and reinvests in the municipality's services and infrastructure so recovery is possible and future payment can be made) and (d) the plan is feasible (it is capable of being implemented and performed).

Bankruptcy courts in the Detroit, Stockton and Central Falls cases have held that pension underfunding liabilities can be impaired in a Chapter 9 proceeding. As discussed herein, Detroit and Bridgeport, Connecticut have demonstrated that a financially distressed city that raises taxes and lowers services in an attempt to balance its budget loses corporate and individual taxpayers and collects less revenue than before. Repeating this year after year can lead to a death spiral, resulting in less funds to pay workers, retirees and creditors. Reinvestment in the municipality, as discussed herein, is an important step to recovery.

Chapter 9 is not a one-size-fits-all solution, but rather should be designed to address the specific problems of the municipality in the most effective manner. Historically, Chapter 9 has not been an effective and preferred resort for school districts. Education is vital to a local government since the necessary training of the future workforce and the quality and effectiveness of public education have a direct effect on the ability to attract new, good businesses and to help the municipality to grow and thrive. For those reasons, Chapter 9 is not the best method of dealing with a school district's financial, operational or educational problems. State and local monitoring, supervision and, if necessary, formal use of an oversight board or receiver with the ability to adjust operations, salaries and benefits seem to be the preferred mechanism and, if all else fails, replacing the superintendent and management or consolidating school districts (ideally merging the weak with the strong) is a last resort.

E. To Be Continued

The purpose of this presentation of a 50-State Survey is to begin to bring clarity to the various ways in which state and local governments have attempted in the past to address the issues and the various alternatives, remedies and vehicles of assistance that they have created in order to help municipalities find a resolution to financial distress before the situation goes too far. This survey is meant to aid state and local governments and their legislators, investors and others in appreciating the efforts that have been made to provide oversight, protection and assurances to those who invest in state and local debt obligations. The survey includes on a state-by-state basis an analysis of the rights and remedies available to bondholders, along with a review of the provisions that states have adopted to monitor and rehabilitate municipalities at the first sign of financial distress. The survey provides an overview of what limitations exist with regard to taxes and revenue as well as the availability of various alternatives, including whether Chapter 9 is really specifically authorized and available. Likewise, the survey provides a general overview of the uniqueness of each state, the District of Columbia and Puerto Rico in addressing these matters. Given the fluidity of legislation and state laws, the survey cannot be said to be exhaustive but rather is an overview. It should not be viewed as the end of the dialogue but rather the beginning. Any compilation is meant to provide an indication of the direction that has been taken. Obviously, specific situations, based upon specific facts and documents, require specific analysis and specific advice. This material is to provide the general review in hopes of showing to: (i) state and local legislators what has been done by others and what might be helpful to them, (ii) the investors a view of what is presently there and what has been done on a state-by-state basis and (iii) the general market an indication of the intention, dedication and focus of state and local governments to make sure that they live up to their obligations so that they can continue, as they have in the past, to make those vital decisions as to what essential governmental services and infrastructure improvements can be made and financed on a local basis.

It is the desire that this presentation will help clarify the real difference between the myth and reality of state and local government debt and what results can be expected in an economic downturn. All of this will hopefully help state and local governmental officials, investors in state and local government debt and the market generally make a better informed decision when examining specific situations or seeking to determine what trends or outcomes may occur.

The review of the evolution of how to deal with financially distressed state and local governments and the analysis of current state law and constitutional provisions dealing with distressed local governments can encourage further dialogue and creativity. This should lead to developing new mechanisms and approaches to dealing with the financial distress of municipalities, even more effective and efficient than those set forth herein. Only time will tell, as will be reported in the next edition.

Appendix A – Economic Downturn and Recovery Charts

In Economic Downturns, Increased Issuance of State and Local Bonds Is Followed by Increases in Employment and GDP Growth

U.S. Economic Trends, 1949-2009:
State/Local Bond Issuance, Real GDP, Employment
(year-on-year % change)

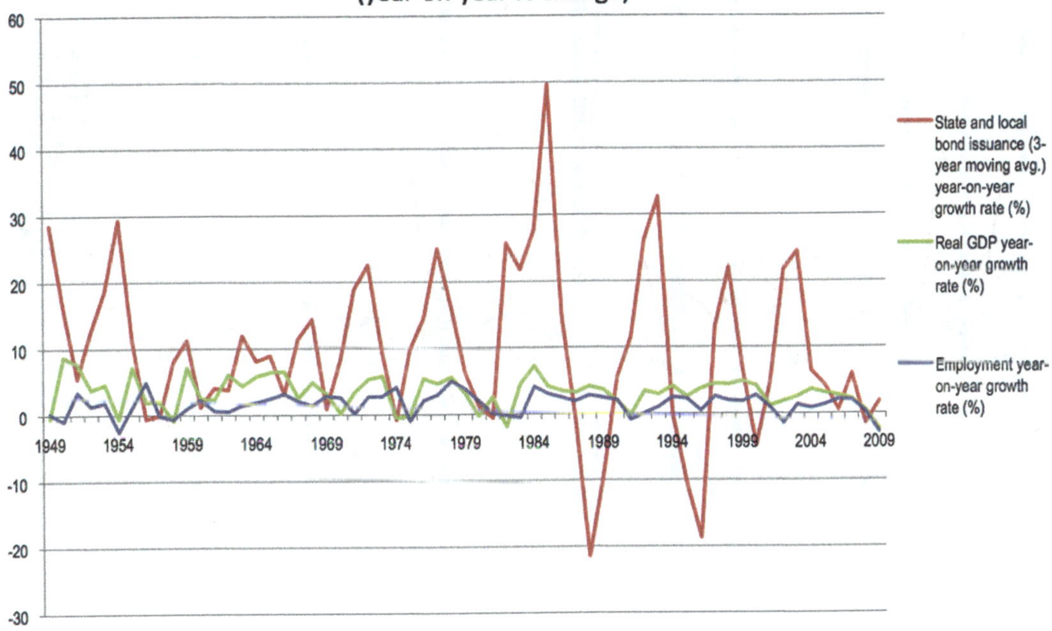

In Economic Downturns, Increased Issuance of State and Local Bonds Is Followed by Increases in Employment and GDP Growth

U.S. Economic Trends, 1949-2009 (year-on-year % change):

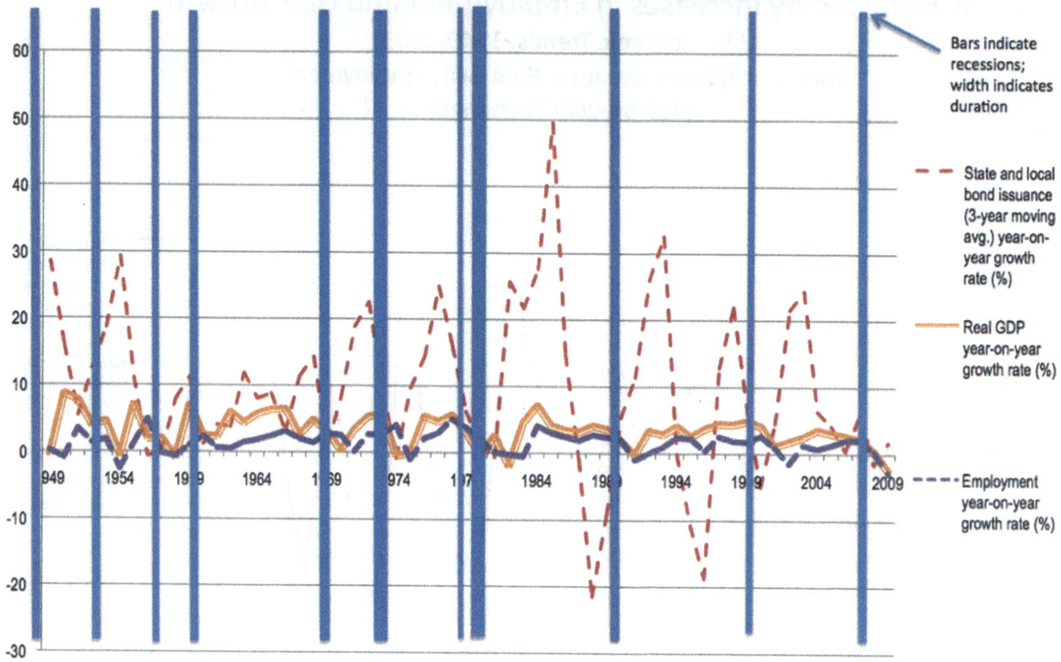

Appendix B – Analysis of 50-State Survey of Rights and Remedies Provided by States to Investors in Municipal Bond Debt State Oversight and Supervision of Financial Emergencies and Authorization to File Chapter 9 Bankruptcy

General Overview of Municipal Insolvency Provisions															
State	Municipal Bankruptcy Authorization	Debt Limitation	Municipal Restructuring Mechanism	Receiver	Refunding Bonds	Other Default Resolution Remedies	Accounting	Foreclosure	Injunction	Mandamus	Other Remedies	Special Revenue Bonds	Statutory Lien SL-1*	Statutory Lien SL-2**	Statutory Lien SL-3***
ALABAMA	Y (bonds only)	X		X	X			X	X	X		X	X		
ALASKA	N				X	X (taxing limits; appointment of trustee)		X		X		X		X	
ARIZONA	Y	X	X (School District Receivership)	X	X	X (any action necessary for holders)		X		X	X (any action necessary)	X			
ARKANSAS	Y	X		X	X	X (taxing limits; appointment of an assessor)				X		X		X	
CALIFORNIA	Conditional (use of a neutral evaluator or declaration of fiscal emergency)	X	X (California Debt and Investment Advisory Commission)	X	X	X (negotiations; school district budget requirements)	X	X	X	X	X (bondholder action and any other action and special tax bonds)	X	X		
COLORADO	Limited	X		X	X		X		X	X	X (bondholder action)	X	X		
CONNECTICUT	Conditional	X	X (ad hoc state intervention)	X	X	X (appointment of a trustee; revenue set-aside)			X	X	X (bondholder action and contractual remedies)	X		X	
DELAWARE	N	X			X					X		X			
DISTRICT OF COLUMBIA	N	X	X (District of Columbia Financial Responsibility and Management Assistance Authority)		X		X		X	X	X (declare all bonds due and payable)	X			
FLORIDA	Conditional		X (Bond Financial Emergencies Act and Division of Bond Finance and Local Government Financial Technical Assistance Program)	X	X		X		X	X		X	X		
GEORGIA	N (specifically prohibited)	X	X (Georgia Local Government Financial Monitoring)	X	X	X (debt compromise)				X	X (court action to enforce collection)	X			
HAWAII	N	X		X	X		X	X		X	X (bondholder action)	X			
IDAHO	Y	X	X (debt readjustment plans for certain districts)	X	X	X (Bond Guaranty Act)	X	X		X		X	X		
ILLINOIS	Limited	X	X (Financially Distressed City Law and Financial Planning and Supervision)	X	X			X	X	X	X (appropriate relief)	X	X	X	
INDIANA	N	X	X (Distressed Political Subdivision and Township Protections)	X	X	X (redemption bonds)	X	X	X	X		X	X	X	
IOWA	N, with exception	X		X	X	X (moratorium)				X		X	X	X	
KANSAS	N	X		X	X		X	X		X		X			
KENTUCKY	Conditional	X	X (county restructuring)	X	X	X (taxing limits; appointment of trustee)	X		X	X		X	X	X	
LOUISIANA	Conditional	X	X (appointment of Fiscal Administrator)	X	X	X (state taxing authority)		X		X		X		X	
MAINE	N	X	X (Board of Emergency Municipal Finance)	X	X	X (earmarking)		X		X	X (attachment and any action necessary)	X			X
MARYLAND	N	X		X	X					X		X		X	
MASSACHUSETTS	N	X	X (ad hoc state intervention)	X	X	X (state bond payment intervention)				X		X			X
MICHIGAN	Conditional	X	X (Emergency Financial Management and Local Government and School District Fiscal Accountability Act)	X	X					X		X	X	X	

* The language of the statute appears to strongly support a determination that it is a statutory lien.

** While the language of the statute may appear to create a statutory lien, further clarification would be helpful to reaffirm the intent to create a statutory lien.

*** While the language of the statute may appear to create a statutory lien it is insufficient and additional language is required to clarify the intent and to create a statutory lien. The language could be read as just providing for perfection of a pledge or lien without the intent and effect to create a statutory lien.

General Overview of Municipal Insolvency Provisions															
State	Municipal Bankruptcy Authorization	Debt Limitation	Municipal Restructuring Mechanism	Receiver	Refunding Bonds	Other Default Resolution Remedies	Accounting	Foreclosure	Injunction	Mandamus	Other Remedies	Special Revenue Bonds	Statutory Lien SL-1*	Statutory Lien SL-2**	Statutory Lien SL-3***
MINNESOTA	Y	X	X (Back-Up Payment Procedures for Municipalities and School Districts)		X	X (school district expenditure limitations)				X	X (appropriate remedies to enforce bondholder rights)	X		X	
MISSISSIPPI	N	X		X	X	X (municipal borrowing)	X	X	X	X	X (other appropriate remedies)	X		X	
MISSOURI	Y	X		X	X		X	X		X	X (other appropriate remedies)	X			
MONTANA	Y, but not counties	X		X	X					X	X (limited remedy and interest penalty; suits in equity)	X			
NEBRASKA	Y	X		X	X	X (debt compromise)		X		X		X			
NEVADA	N	X	X (Local government Financial Assistance and Audit Enforcement Act)	X	X	X (third-party agreements)	X	X	X	X		X		X	
NEW HAMPSHIRE	N	X	X (Emergency Financial Assistance)	X	X					X	X (contractual remedies)	X			
NEW JERSEY	Conditional	X	X (Local Government Supervision Act; Municipal Rehabilitation and Economic Recovery Act of 2002 and Special Municipal Aid Act)	X	X	X (school district fiscal monitor and Casino Tax Property Stabilization Act)	X	X		X		X	X		
NEW MEXICO	N	X	X (financial auditing and emergency loans)	X	X	X (emergency loans from state)				X		X			
NEW YORK	Conditional	X	X (Emergency Financial Control Board, Municipal Assistance Corporation; New York Financial Control Board)	X	X	X (appointment of a trustee)	X	X		X		X	X		
NORTH CAROLINA	Conditional	X	X (local government debt monitoring; local government fiscal management)	X	X	X (local government commission)		X		X		X			X
NORTH DAKOTA	N	X		X	X		X			X		X			X
OHIO	Conditional	X	X (state auditor's fiscal caution and fiscal watch; fiscal emergencies; financial planning and supervision commission)	X	X		X	X	X	X	X (general remedies provision, including appointment of trustee and action to declare bonds not paid from property taxes immediately payable)	X			
OKLAHOMA	Y	X		X	X	X (settlement of debt)	X			X		X			
OREGON	Limited	X	X (County Public Safety Emergency and Fiscal Control Board; Municipal Debt Advisory Commission)	X	X	X (refunding bond cram-down)		X		X		X			X
PENNSYLVANIA	Conditional	X	X (Financially Distressed Municipalities Act; Intergovernmental Cooperation Act)	X	X	X (appointment of a trustee)	X			X		X	X		
PUERTO RICO	N	X	X (Puerto Rico Oversight, Management and Economic Stability Act)	X	X	X (first lien provisions)	X			X		X	X		
RHODE ISLAND	Conditional	X	X (fiscal overseer; municipal receiver; budget commission)	X	X	X (bond issuance requirements; bond payment guarantee)	X	X		X		X	X		
SOUTH CAROLINA	Y	X		X	X	X (state treasurer withhold of state appropriation)	X	X		X	X (any appropriate action)	X	X		
SOUTH DAKOTA	N	X		X	X					X		X		X	
TENNESSEE	N		X (financially distressed municipalities procedures)	X	X	X (emergency financial aid to local governments)	X			X		X		X	X
TEXAS	Y	X	X (municipal receivership)	X	X			X		X		X			X
UTAH	N	X		X	X					X	X (contractual remedies)	X			X
VERMONT	N	X		X	X			X		X		X			X
VIRGINIA	N	X	X (bond payment guarantee provisions)	X	X					X	X (any contractual remedy)	X			X
WASHINGTON	Y	X		X	X	X (designation of trustee)		X	X	X		X			
WEST VIRGINIA	N	X		X	X		X	X	X	X		X			
WISCONSIN	N	X	X (Deficiency Protection for Public Improvement Bonds)		X			X		X		X			
WYOMING	N	X		X	X		X	X	X	X		X			
Total****		49	30	47	52	29	24	28	15	52	18	52	16	15	10

**** These numbers include both the District of Columbia and Puerto Rico where applicable and totals may differ from other materials that only review 50 states.